The Pope's Soldiers

The Pope's Soldiers

A Military History of
the Modern Vatican

David Alvarez

University Press of Kansas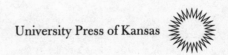

Published by the University Press of Kansas (Lawrence, Kansas 66045), which was organized by the Kansas Board of Regents and is operated and funded by Emporia State University, Fort Hays State University, Kansas State University, Pittsburg State University, the University of Kansas, and Wichita State University

Library of Congress Cataloging-in-Publication Data
Alvarez, David J.
  The pope's soldiers : a military history of the modern Vatican / David Alvarez.
    p. cm. — (Modern war studies)
  Includes bibliographical references and index.
  ISBN 978-0-7006-1770-8 (cloth : alk. paper) 1. Vatican City. Guardia svizzera pontificia—History—20th century. I. Title.
UA749.5.A48   2011
355.009456'34—dc22

                                              2010054019

British Library Cataloguing-in-Publication Data is available.

Printed in Canada

10 9 8 7 6 5 4 3 2 1

In memory of Robert A. Graham, S.J.
(1912–1997)

Contents

A photo section follows page 192

"The pope! How many divisions has he got?"
—Stalin's response to a suggestion by Pierre Laval,
the French foreign minister, in May 1935 that the Russian leader
stop persecuting Catholicism in order to curry favor with the pope

Does the modern papacy even have a military history? Students of history are aware, if only dimly, that in the distant past, popes occasionally had recourse to armed force to defend their political and economic interests in that broad swath of central Italy that was known as the Papal States. Most assume, however, that the age of warlord popes ended with the Renaissance. As a cultural icon, the white-robed, prayerful, and pacific Holy Father has replaced the belligerent, armor-clad Supreme Pontiff. The armies and navies that once fought and conquered under the papal banner have been reduced to the colorful and unthreatening Swiss Guard, which contributes a decorative element to the global tourist attraction known as the Vatican.

Even among professional historians and the historically attuned public, few people are aware that the military history of the papacy did not end with the bellicose Pope Julius II (1503–1513) or with the victory of Catholic powers at the Battle of Lepanto (1571). Few know that well into the modern period popes were, by choice or necessity, frequently involved with wars and military affairs. Most people would be surprised to learn that between 1796 and 1870, the papacy participated in six wars or military campaigns; that the political unification of Italy in the nineteenth century required the military subjugation of the papacy; that in 1870 the Papal States had, per capita, one of the largest armies in Europe; that as late as 1878 there was still a warship flying the papal flag; that the papal army was one of the first armies in Europe to adopt the machine gun; that between 1820 and 1913 there were three mutinies in the Swiss Guard, one so serious that the guardsmen had to be disarmed and the pope dissuaded from abolishing his famous corps of guards; and that during World War II the Vatican fielded an army of more than two thousand soldiers, who actually came under fire. These facts suggest that the military aspects of modern papal history may well be richer, more interesting, and more important than historians have previously imagined.

There are many excellent books, several in English, that consider the political history of the modern papacy. There are also biographies of the various popes who have sat on the Throne of Saint Peter since the French Revolution, although most of these biographies, particularly those of the pontiffs of the eighteenth and nineteenth centuries, are in French, German, or Italian. Most of these histories and biographies make no reference at all to military affairs, and the few that do address such affairs do so only in passing, often devoting only a few sentences to the subject.

A handful of Italian and French historians have studied aspects of the military side of the modern papacy. The large majority of these studies appeared before 1950; indeed, most appeared in the nineteenth century. What these memoirs, books, and articles have in common is a narrow focus on particular units or campaigns. Each examines one piece of papal military history (e.g., eighteenth-century administrative reforms, the Battle of Mentana, the Swiss Guard), but none assembles the pieces into a complete mosaic. Several French historians, for example, have been attracted to the experience of the regiment of pontifical Zouaves in part because that colorful regiment recruited large numbers of Frenchmen and in part because after the final collapse of the Papal States in September 1870, many members of the now defunct unit went on to serve with distinction in the last battles of the Franco-Prussian War. None of these French studies have been translated into English, and most are out of print.

Although the history of the unification of Italy is in large part a history of the military conquest of the Papal States by the House of Savoy, the story of that conquest has been largely neglected by Italian historians who have, like their American, French, and German counterparts, preferred to focus on the diplomatic, political, social, and cultural aspects of unification. A few Italian specialists have studied particular aspects of the wars against the Papal States. Some of the results, notably monographs on the War of 1860 and the capture of Rome in 1870 prepared in the 1920s by the history office of the Italian army, are serious studies, but even the best forsake a comprehensive survey in favor of an episodic approach that focuses on particular battles or campaigns. None of these Italian works has been translated into English. Like their French counterparts, most are long out of print; indeed, some are considered rare books that attract high prices among antiquarian book dealers.

American and British historians have been no more attracted to the military history of the modern papacy than their colleagues in France and Italy. Only four English-language books address aspects of that history, but with one exception they are as narrow in scope as their French and Italian counterparts. One is a 1929 monograph on the short-lived (three months) Irish Battalion of the papal army of 1860. Another is a popular history of the pope's Swiss Guard published in 2006 to coincide with the five hundredth anniversary of that corps. The third is a rather hagiographic history of the papal regiment of Zouaves. Only one, D. S. Chambers's *Popes, Cardinals and War: The*

Military Church in Renaissance and Early Modern Europe, has attempted a more general history by describing the way in which the papacy has been influenced by direct experience with war and military force, but Chambers is interested primarily in an earlier period, devoting only ten pages (out of 234) to the period after 1796.

My intention is to present a general military history of the papacy from the French Revolution to the present in the hope of illuminating a shadowy and little-visited corner of the vast edifice of papal history. Since the emphasis will be on the military—generals and their soldiers, campaigns and their battles—it is important to be clear about what this book is not. Although military developments are placed in the larger context of political events in Rome, Italy, and Europe, this book is neither a political nor a diplomatic history of the modern papacy. Those seeking extended accounts of particular popes will be disappointed. Less about popes than their soldiers, this book considers particular pontiffs only to the extent that their attitudes and actions impinged on the preparation and deployment of the papal armed forces. Since modern pontiffs rarely spent much time in consideration of their armed forces, popes, some of whom played major parts on the stages of diplomatic and ecclesiastical history, appear in distinctly secondary roles in this production. Similarly, the book does not attempt a comprehensive examination of the Risorgimento and the struggle between the papacy and the House of Savoy, preferring to focus exclusively on the military elements of that conflict. For the interested reader there are many excellent papal biographies and political, diplomatic, and ecclesiastical histories of the modern papacy. There is, however, no general history of the papal armed forces. This book is an attempt to remedy that deficiency.

Several individuals facilitated the research for this book. Colonel Daniel Anrig, the commandant of the Pontifical Swiss Guard, kindly authorized the use of photographs from the guard archive. Stefan Meier and Christian Richard, both former noncommissioned officers in the Pontifical Swiss Guard, patiently answered questions about the history of the guard and their own experiences in that venerable corps. Domenico Giani, director-general of the Vatican Gendarmeria, found time in his busy schedule to discuss the work of his service, and Fabio Vagnoni, another gendarmeria officer, proved a delightful and informative chaperone during visits to his service's offices. At the Vatican Secret Archive, Simone Venturini provided advice concerning the records of the pontifical armed forces. Rosanna di Pinto opened the photographic collection of the Vatican Museums, and Debora Virgili did the same at the Instituto Centrale per il Catalogo e la Documentazione. Marcella Scialino of the venerable Roman establishment Fotografia Felici, at one time official photographers for the Vatican, generously granted permission to use images from the firm's historical collections. John Pollard shared his extensive knowledge of the papal court and its finances. Roger Cook of the Ordinance Society explained the early history of automatic weapons in European armies. Massimo Coltrinari, the foremost student of the Battle of Castelfidardo, kindly answered questions concerning that important event, and Virgilio Ilari provided copies of his pathbreaking publications on the eighteenth-century pontifical army and navy. Emily Banwell assisted with several German-language texts. Darin Jensen provided cartographic advice, and Kaitlin Jaffe drew the maps. Frank Coppa read the entire manuscript and pointed out where it could be improved. Brian Sullivan went over the manuscript with as much care as if it were his own work. His suggestions concerning style and content were invariably helpful. No author could hope for a more sympathetic and constructive critic.

The Faculty Development Fund at Saint Mary's College of California provided support for my research. Alle Porter in the college's library tracked down obscure books and negotiated with distant libraries that were reluctant to lend rare or fragile volumes. Her patience and experience were invaluable.

Major (ret.) Peter Hasler of the Pontifical Swiss Guard kindly welcomed me to the Swiss Guard barracks inside Vatican City. When, as a serving officer, he answered an e-mail from an American historian inquiring about historical photographs of the guard, he had no idea that two years later, now retired after more than forty-three years in the military service of the papacy, he would still be answering questions about his corps, its personalities, and its practices. Custodian of the guard archive, probably the smallest but certainly the best organized archive in Italy, Major Hasler patiently responded to every request to confirm a date or a name; located old photographs; and generously provided photocopies of documents from the archive. With characteristically self-deprecating humor he shared his experiences in the guard from his first days as a young halberdier to the time when, by then a senior officer providing close-in protection for the Holy Father during a public appearance in St. Peter's Square, he broke an ankle wrestling to the ground a disturbed man who attempted to reach the pope. His discretion, loyalty, and professionalism exemplify the very best traditions of the Swiss Guard.

The Marchese Giulio Patrizi di Ripocandida recalled his twenty-five years of service in the Noble Guard, particularly during World War II, and shared his album of photographs of the guard. The Noble Guard has yet to attract its own historian, but the Palatine Guard has been more fortunate. Antonio Martini, a noncommissioned officer in the Palatine before its abolition in 1970, has assiduously collected material on the history of his unit and generously shared his research and his memories of the corps in which he proudly served. The Vatican has been fortunate to have such men in its service.

An author usually identifies a lengthy list of individuals without whose assistance his or her book allegedly could not have been written. This polite and quite harmless convention might well lead a literal-minded reader to conclude that the appearance of the book in question was the merest accident of fortune because the absence or inadequacies of any one of the listed collaborators would presumably have guaranteed the failure of the entire enterprise. In the case of this book the claim is literally true of one individual. Elisabeth Giansiracusa, my colleague and associate in Rome and a professional researcher of remarkable talents, made an indispensable contribution to this book. Time and again her imagination, initiative, and persistence identified research leads that might otherwise have remained unnoticed, and her ability to explain and promote the project to current and former Vatican officials, as well as the custodians of documentary and photographic collections, opened doors that seemed tightly closed. In every way this book is as much hers as mine.

My family survived yet another book project but has unanimously requested a respite from further enthusiasms.

Territory of the Papal States

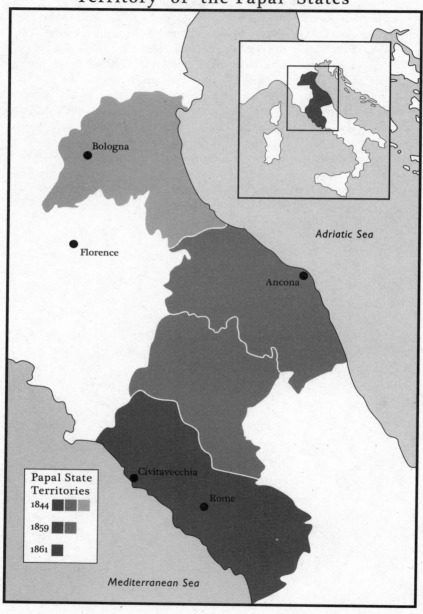

Adriatic Sea

Bologna

Florence

Ancona

Papal State
Territories
1844
1859
1861

Civitavecchia

Rome

Mediterranean Sea

CHAPTER 1

The Worst Army in Europe

In 1796 Pope Pius VI may have had the worst army in Europe. He wasn't particularly distressed by that deficiency, but many of his predecessors would have been scandalized by his neglect of martial affairs. The papacy had once been a significant military power in Europe. In addition to their spiritual authority over the Catholic faithful, popes, beginning with the demise of the Roman Empire, had gradually accumulated secular power over territories and populations. As secular lords they often acted as military leaders, constructing great fortifications, establishing arsenals, levying war taxes, raising armies, launching war galleys, and occasionally leading those armies and galleys into battle to defend the church and the territories that the church had accumulated over the centuries against religious and secular foes. At the end of the sixth century Pope Gregory I raised and provisioned troops and made dispositions for the defense of Rome in the face of a threat from the Lombards. In the ninth century Leo IV led an armed force of Romans to the mouth of the Tiber River to repel Muslim pirates; he also fortified with walls and bastions the area adjacent to Saint Peter's Basilica. Fifty years later John VIII contributed additional fortifications to the Eternal City and assumed personal command of a galley in a campaign against pirates who were ravaging the southern coasts of the Italian peninsula. In 915 John X led an expeditionary force to battle corsairs on the Garigliano River, later boasting to the archbishop of Cologne that he had twice entered the fray.[1]

By the Middle Ages pontiffs were less inclined to lead men personally into battle, but they did not hesitate to send other churchmen—cardinals and archbishops—to command in their place. In 1247, for example, Cardinal Gregory of Montelungo defeated the army of Emperor Frederick II near Parma and captured imperial fortresses and supply camps. Enraged and embarrassed by the military presumption of this prelate and the pope he represented, Frederick complained, "These priests of ours wear cuirasses instead of liturgical vestments [and] bear lances instead of a pastoral staff."[2] In a throwback to earlier times, Pope Julius II considered war a matter too important to delegate; between 1506 and 1511 he campaigned at the head of his troops in defense of the papacy up and down the Italian peninsula. By this time a political entity known as the States of the Church or the Papal States had emerged in central Italy, and like any other political entity, this state had political, economic, and security interests that had to be defended.

Julius was the last of the warlord pontiffs, and his pontificate represented the apogee of the militaristic papacy. Although his immediate successors kept the papacy at the forefront of military affairs and innovation (the first example of what would be called the *trace italienne*, the "modern" fortification that replaced the high walls and towers of the medieval castle, appeared at the papal port of Civitavecchia in 1519, and the papal army of the late sixteenth century was second only to Venice in moving to adopt a common uniform for its soldiers), there was a gradual lessening in the bellicosity of popes. The Papal States might be drawn unwittingly into the wars of larger powers, such as Spain and France, which used the Italian peninsula as a battleground for their ambitions, and sometimes the consequences of these conflicts, such as the sack of Rome by the imperial army of Charles V in 1527, were calamitous, but by the seventeenth century popes rarely sought out trouble. In coalition with other European powers they occasionally participated in joint expeditions against the Muslims. In 1571 Pius V contributed 12 war galleys and 1,600 naval infantry to the Christian fleet that broke the Turkish navy at the Battle of Lepanto. Between 1645 and 1669 Innocent X, Alexander VII, and Clement IX sent funds and naval vessels during each campaigning season to support Venice's efforts to keep the island of Crete from Muslim hands. Innocent XI was the last pope to participate in such a venture when, in 1684, he contributed several warships to the fleet of Venetian admiral Francesco Morosini, which swept Turkish vessels from the central Mediterranean in the First Morea War.[3] Even less frequently there was conflict with other Italian states, such as the war against the Duchy of Parma in 1642–1644. The waning of Muslim power after the failure of the Turkish siege of Vienna in 1683 and the emergence in the early eighteenth century of a relatively stable political order in central Italy (based on several small kingdoms and duchies that had few ambitions for territorial or political aggrandizement at the expense of the Papal States) greatly reduced the immediate threat for eighteenth-century popes and lessened the need for an active military posture and a significant military organization. Great powers, such as France, Spain, or Austria, might still use the Italian peninsula as a battlefield or a military highway, and their military adventures occasionally spilled over into the Papal States, but such powers no longer had much interest in deposing popes or annexing papal territory. Even if they did, it was apparent by the late seventeenth century that the papacy lacked the human, financial, and material resources to mobilize a serious military response against a major power. In short, powers the papacy could match militarily, such as the duchies of Modena and Tuscany, posed little threat, whereas countries that were potentially a serious threat, such as France and Austria, were so beyond the military capabilities of the papacy that there was little sense in even trying to prepare and maintain a military response. Moreover, the issues that complicated Rome's relations with other governments in the eighteenth century—such as the suppression of the Jesuits and the independence of national churches—were not the sort usually settled by recourse to arms. Diplomacy and the spiritual authority of the Holy Father, not regiments and warships, were now the principal instruments of papal policy, and popes no longer resorted to war. Soldiers were kept to lend color and display to ceremonies and to maintain order and security in the towns and provinces of the Papal States, but no one expected them to face battle. Pius VI, therefore, did not care that his army might be the worst in Europe because he never expected to use it. Of course, he did not anticipate the French Revolution. And no one could have anticipated Napoléon Bonaparte.

Asserting the primacy of reason over faith; change over tradition; the people over established elites; and the popular will over legitimacy, custom, and revelation, the French Revolution probably could not have avoided a collision with the papacy, which by contrast cherished such values as faith, tradition, and legitimacy. Beginning in August 1789 the Constituent Assembly in Paris embarked upon a sustained program of ecclesiastical reform that eventually included the elimination of tithes and annates, the nationalization of church property, the termination of ecclesiastical immunities from taxation, the abolition of most religious orders, and the refusal to recognize Catholicism as the state religion. By threatening the wealth, status, and authority of the church, such acts would have caught the full attention of any pope, but the assembly assured the enmity of Pius VI when it passed the Civil Constitution of the Clergy, which unilaterally reduced the number of dioceses and parishes in France; made bishops and priests employees of the state; required the election of bishops and priests by the people they served, including non-Catholics; and affirmed the dissolution of religious orders except for those engaged in education. The Constituent Assembly further decreed that all clergy would have to swear an oath to accept and support the Civil Constitution of the Clergy and that those who refused would be removed from their positions. Despite the explicit threat of sanctions, less than one-third of the priests in France and only 7 of the 160 bishops took the oath. The oath takers were known as the Constitutional Church and openly collaborated with the republican regime. Many of the dissenters sought refuge in other countries, and those who stayed formed what was effectively an underground church.[4]

As early as March 1790 Pius began to denounce what he considered the French assembly's illegal and unwarranted interference in ecclesiastical affairs. His protests culminated in April 1791 when he issued an encyclical, titled *Caritas quae*, in which he condemned the Civil Constitution of the Clergy as sacrilegious and schismatic, denounced the Constitutional Church, and suspended all clergy who had sworn the constitutional oath unless they retracted in forty days.[5] *Caritas quae* had no impact on the revolutionary leaders in Paris except to accelerate what was becoming an outright persecution of clergy outside the Constitutional Church. In the years immediately following the encyclical, relations between Paris and Rome continued to deteriorate, with each side hardening its position. In the French capital the papacy was increasingly seen as one of the traditionalist regimes that were, by definition, the natural enemies of the revolution. This perception sharpened in June 1792 when Pius sent an émigré French archbishop, Jean-Sifrein Maury, who had fled to Rome to escape the wrath of the revolution, to represent him at the Diet of Frankfort, a conference of several European powers to discuss measures to restrain if not chastise France. In Frankfort Maury, perhaps exceeding his authority, encouraged representatives of the other powers to believe that the Holy Father was prepared to enlist in an anti-French alliance. In fact, when invited in the fall of 1792 to join the so-called First Coalition, a grouping that would eventually include Austria, Britain, the Netherlands, Prussia, Sardinia, and Spain, in a war against France, Pius declined on the grounds that he had neither troops nor money to contribute to the effort. However, his refusal did little to assuage suspicions in Paris.[6]

For his part, Pius had little reason to adjust his opinion of the revolutionary regime. Political and religious refugees, including relatives of King Louis XVI (executed in January 1793) and hundreds of bishops and priests who had refused the oath of allegiance, poured into the Papal States with hair-raising tales of political fanaticism and anticlerical excesses in France. The antics of the revolution's few partisans in the Eternal City only contributed to the growing hostility. French students in Rome, particularly those affiliated with the French Academy, eagerly embraced the revolution and delighted in the ostentatious display of tricolored cockades, vocal proclamation of republican sentiments, and public manifestations of solidarity with their countrymen in France. These activities offended many Romans who tended to hold rather traditional attitudes concerning politics, religion, and social order. The arrival in Rome of Nicholas Hugo de Basseville, sometime journalist and full-time propagandist, who then held the nominal position of secretary in the French embassy to the Kingdom of Naples, exacerbated the offense. Basseville's pretensions, arrogance, and self-promotion irritated other diplomats in the Eternal City and practically everyone else he met. Papal authorities were particularly annoyed by his demands for the release of several French students who had been arrested for disorderly conduct and by his insistence on the immediate replacement of monarchical symbols on the French embassy with symbols of the new republic. Both of these demands were refused. The lack of official permission did not deter the representative of the revolution. In January 1793 Basseville hosted a banquet at which he announced that the hated symbols should be replaced forthwith. Republican enthusiasts from the French Academy accepted the charge; overnight they cobbled together a revolutionary coat of arms and set it up at the embassy. The next morning a Roman crowd tore down and destroyed the display. Exhibiting the imprudence that made his name a byword in Rome for arrogance and buffoonery, Basseville decided to demonstrate his disdain for the opinions of the people of Rome. Joined by his wife and by Charles de la Flotte, a visiting French naval officer, the impetuous young diplomat decorated his carriage with revolutionary cockades and insignia and drove down the Corso, the main street of the city. When their appearance was met by a hail of stones and curses, Basseville ordered his driver to seek shelter in a nearby courtyard. Unfortunately, the crowd followed and assaulted the coach. In the tumult Basseville received a mortal knife wound, and la Flotte barely escaped through a nearby house. Madame de Basseville was not physically harmed.

The murder of Basseville enraged authorities in Paris and further enflamed French-papal relations. The French government demanded a formal apology, the arrest and punishment of the killer, the immediate placement of republican symbols on the French embassy, the expulsion of all French émigrés from Rome, and the payment of an indemnity. The pope refused to consider these demands. Distracted by more pressing matters, such as a war of national survival against the armies of the First Coalition, authorities in Paris did not pursue the protest, but they considered the Basseville affair an affront to France that confirmed the papacy as an enemy of the revolution and the republic. They would bide their time, and when conditions were more opportune and the appropriate means available they would deal with that enemy. Three years later both the opportunity and the means were at hand.

Despite some early successes, the First Coalition had foundered in its effort against France. Calling the nation to arms to protect the revolution, the National Convention (successor to the Constituent Assembly) had expelled the invaders from France and then carried the war into other nations' territories. By the spring of 1796 only Austria, Britain, and the Kingdom of Sardinia-Piedmont were still fighting. The first of these allies controlled large parts of northern Italy, particularly the region of Lombardy. To open a southern front and force the diversion of Austrian troops from the central front along the Rhine, the convention sent a young general, Napoléon Bonaparte, to command the republic's Army of Italy, a neglected and rather ragtag force that had been covering the French-Piedmontese border. Within four weeks of entering Italy, Bonaparte had defeated Austrian and Sardinian armies, forced Sardinia from the war with the Armistice of Cherasco, captured Milan, and pushed the Austrians back into the fortress city of Mantua. With the Austrians and Sardinians neutralized, the northern provinces of the Papal States, the so-called Legations centered in the region of the Romagna, were exposed and threatened. Although the papacy was not at war with France, the convention saw an opportunity to strike at an ideological enemy, revenge the death of Nicholas Hugo de Basseville, and refresh the finances of the Army of Italy and the republic by plundering the wealth of the papacy. As early as February 1796 the Directory (which had superseded the convention as the executive arm of the French government) had suggested to the commander of the Army of Italy that he should march on Rome. From his headquarters in Milan, General Bonaparte, on May 21, 1796, issued a proclamation that revealed that he was looking south after vanquishing the Austrians and Piedmontese. "We are friends of all the people," he announced, "especially the descendants of Brutus and the Scipios. We want to renew the Campidoglio . . . and liberate the Roman people from their long servitude."[7] These words were not intended to reassure the pope and his government. Perhaps the general's words were nothing but revolutionary rhetoric, but if they were more than mere bluster, then for the first time in the memory of any pontifical official the Papal States faced the prospect of war—a prospect for which the papacy was entirely unprepared.

In the spring of 1796 the pontifical army was struggling to emerge from decades of neglect by embracing, albeit rather fitfully, reforms intended to rationalize its organization and improve its capabilities. Since the late seventeenth century the force levels of the regular army had hovered around 5,000 men, although occasionally the numbers would fall as low as 3,000.[8] Supporting this small force was a citizen militia that, in theory, could mobilize 80,000–90,000 men in an emergency. For reasons lost in the mists of time and the dusty shelves of archival cabinets, control over the regular army was divided among three authorities, each of which jealously protected its prerogatives. The Commissioner of Arms always commanded the bulk of the officers and men, but depending on the historical period as much as a quarter of the total force, particularly garrisons beyond Rome and the Guardie di Finanza (customs guards), was under the authority of the Treasurer General, and the Secretary of the Consulta always controlled a few hundred personnel. A fourth authority, the master of the Apostolic Palace, directed the pope's palace guard, which was not considered part of the army. These household troops included the famous Guardia Svizzera (Swiss Guard), which in this period numbered between 100 and 130 men, and two mounted units, the Lance Spezzate (approximately 20 men) and the Corpi dei Cavalleggeri (approximately 80 men).[9] This division of authority reflected a division of functions. By the late eighteenth century the papal army was performing a variety of roles, including ceremonial honor guard, fortress garrison, border patrol, customs police, coastal surveillance, and urban and rural law enforcement. Administrative responsibility for these tasks was divided among different offices in the papal bureaucracy.

The regular troops were scattered across the Papal States in small garrisons and detachments. In 1792 the largest concentration of soldiers, 930 men, was at Civitavecchia, the main port on the west coast of the country, but most of the posts had fewer than 500 soldiers, and many had fewer than 100. The garrisons of the 34 fortified towers constructed in the sixteenth and seventeenth centuries to protect the coastlines from North African corsairs rarely numbered more than a half-dozen men, and even major fortresses, such as the citadels at Perugia, San Leo, and Pesaro, mustered fewer than 30 soldiers.[10] Whatever their post, the troops were inexperienced, ill-trained, and ill-equipped. With the exception of a handful of officers recruited from foreign armies, the army had no experience of warfare. The last time papal soldiers had marched to battle was 1739, when the cardinal legate (governor) of the Romagna region mobilized a force of 500 militiamen and attacked the tiny republic of San Marino in a brief dispute over legal immunities and privileges. Regular soldiers received little training, rarely practicing with their muskets and never operating in units larger than a battalion. Most units performed few military functions beyond guard duty at barracks, public buildings, and city gates; ceremonial service at public and religious celebrations; and support for police and customs authorities. Except for elements of the Reggimento delle Guardie di Nostro Signore (Guards Regiment of Our Lord) that every summer embarked on papal naval vessels for antipiracy patrols, few units went into the field often enough to be considered operational. Fortifications were antiquated and ill-maintained, and many, particularly the coastal towers, were useless against any threat more serious than that posed by bandits or marauders. There was no field artillery, and the obsolete cannons in the fortresses were the responsibility not of specialist gunners but of *bombardieri*, a militialike guild of artisans and shopkeepers long dominated by particular families who ran the papal artillery like a family fief. The bombardieri opposed innovation and reform as threats to their many legal and economic privileges, such as exemption from certain taxes and the right to free two imprisoned criminals on certain holidays. Not surprisingly, the militia, intended to reinforce the standing army in an emergency, was in worse shape than the regulars.[11] In short, the pope had an army incapable of offensive operations, ill-prepared for defensive measures, and at best adequate for ceremonial and internal security purposes. It attracted little respect even among the citizens of the Papal States, who made the pope's soldiers the butt of countless stories, ditties, and pasquinades. One student of the eighteenth-century papacy observed, "For at least a century Rome's army had been a running joke. It was small, ineffectual, top-heavy with superannuated officers, and existed primarily for parades and to provide guards for theaters and troops for policing the carnival."[12]

In 1796 the pope's navy was in somewhat better condition than his army, but barely so. The once proud papal fleet that had contributed a dozen warships to the Christian line at the Battle of Lepanto in 1571 had disappeared into history, its place taken by a handful of antiquated vessels manned by a motley force of convicts, Muslim prisoners, and land infantry. Along with the Knights of Malta, the pontifical navy was the last European navy to employ galleys: long, narrow vessels propelled primarily by rowers laboring on benches inside the hull of the ship. Most European fleets had fully embraced sail in the seventeenth century, and even the Maltese had begun commissioning sailing vessels in the early 1700s. However, the papacy waited until 1755 to introduce its first sailing ship, and it did not exactly rush to transform its fleet. In 1796 three galleys were still in commission, along with two coastal corvettes and several light vessels. It was the smallest navy in Europe, deploying significantly fewer ships and crews than even the other minor powers on the Italian peninsula.[13]

The capabilities of the pontifical navy were as modest as its size. Most units put to sea only in the months between May and October, spending the winter laid up in the port of Civitavecchia on the west coast of the Papal States. The personnel were not professionals. Many officers and all crewmen (except convicts) were engaged for a single cruising season with no promise of further service, and most had little experience beyond sailing small merchant or fishing vessels along the Mediterranean coasts. The handful of full-time officers secured their posts through nepotism. Not surprisingly, skill levels were not high. When the pontifical navy acquired its first sailing vessel in 1755 it had to entrust its command to officers hired from the French navy because no papal officers knew how to handle a warship under sail. Even the most basic skills could not be taken for granted. An internal report of 1795 admitted that with the exception of one individual, none of the officers of the navy possessed even a minimal understanding of navigation.[14] The crews were no better. A majority of the oarsmen were convicts sentenced by papal courts to the galleys for various crimes or prisoners captured in the course of engagements with North African pirates. A small number of rowers (about 10 percent of the total) were unskilled free men who, for lack of any other employment opportunity, had volunteered for the galleys out of economic desperation. The volunteers received a meager wage and more and better food than did the prisoners. The fighting crew consisted of soldiers from the pontifical army who would be detailed to the galleys during the cruising season.[15]

The principal mission of the pontifical navy at the end of the eighteenth century was the suppression of piracy by Muslim vessels sailing from North African ports. These "Barbary pirates" captured vessels at sea and raided coastal towns and villages. Although dozens of fortified towers had been constructed to defend the pope's coasts, by the late 1700s these towers and their cannons were in disrepair, and their garrisons rarely consisted of more than a handful of soldiers, ill-trained and poorly motivated, so the burden of defending the maritime borders of the Papal States fell primarily upon the pope's navy. Since the Adriatic coast was considered sufficiently protected by the large fleet of the Republic of Venice, the pontifical navy's operations were limited to the Tyrrhenian Sea. Each cruising season papal galleys would deploy on coastal patrols from their base in Civitavecchia. The warships served primarily as a deterrent, but occasionally they encountered and engaged pirate craft. Between 1722 and 1757 there were eight naval actions between papal warships and North African corsairs, some of which ended in victories for the pope's sailors. As late as 1795 two papal warships chased and captured a pirate vessel off the western shores of the Papal States. Despite these occasional successes, the operational capabilities of the pontifical fleet were so modest that it is surprising that these ships caught any pirates at all. They were lightly armed and were no match for even the smaller men-of-war of other Mediterranean navies. Vessels were so poorly maintained that at any given time only some of the ships were available for patrols—no small problem for a fleet in which the total number of commissioned vessels could be counted on two hands. Galley officers constantly feared an uprising by the convict oarsmen, who invariably outnumbered the crew and soldiers, and this concern discouraged lengthy patrols. The problem became more severe in the 1790s as oarsmen began to organize protests and circulate petitions against their poor living conditions. There were several disturbances, the most serious occurring in August 1793 when the oarsmen on the galley *San Pietro* mutinied, seized the officers, and forced the ship ashore so that they could flee into the countryside.[16] Clearly, this was not a navy prepared for war.

Papal authorities were well aware of these military deficiencies, and in 1792, as the traditional powers of Europe consulted on measures to constrain revolutionary France, these officials began to consider improvements in the pontifical armed forces. The result was a flurry of more or less efficacious activity. In the summer of 1792 the Pontifical Congregation of State adopted a series of military measures, including the recruitment of Swiss mercenaries for the army, the construction of a new galley for the navy, the renovation of several coastal towers, and the strengthening of Castel Sant'Angelo, the fortress near the Vatican, originally the tomb of the Emperor Hadrian, that dominated the Eternal City. Except for the recruitment of mercenaries, these measures were anachronisms, suitable for the sixteenth century but irrelevant to the kind of warfare the papacy was likely to face at the end of the eighteenth century. Various plans to reorganize, reform, and revitalize the papal military were proposed and investigated, although few were fully implemented. Some reforms, such as efforts by Lieutenant Colonel Francesco di Paola Colli to modernize and professionalize the pontifical artillery, improved the papacy's military capabilities, but most were blocked or compromised by financial constraints; the opposition of entrenched interests; and the routine inertia of the papal bureaucracy, which was a byword in Europe for lethargy and inefficiency. Common attitudes and conventional wisdom, however, were probably the most important impediments to military preparedness. The days when Pope Julius II believed it was his holy duty to lead papal armies in defense of the rights and interests of the papacy were long past. The image of the Pontifex Maximus (Supreme Pontiff) leading the church militant against political as well as religious enemies had given way to the softer image of the Holy Father guiding the community of the faithful and, as much as possible, engaging threats to that community with compassion, forgiveness, and goodwill. The warrior popes and the militarism they had embraced were now embarrassments best shut away in the darkest, least-visited corners of papal history.

The popes of the eighteenth century still believed they had to defend the temporal and spiritual rights of the papacy, but they were much less inclined to use armies and navies to so. This was not a posture of pacifism, since the pontiffs accepted the use of armed force under certain conditions. In the eighteenth century popes were prepared to use their army and police to suppress rebellions in the Papal States, since a revolt against the Vicar of Christ on Earth was, by definition, illegal, immoral, and irreligious. They might also use their military to defend the Papal States against aggression, but this condition was qualified by considerations of appropriate force, the likelihood of success, and the impact on civilians. In February 1774 Cardinal Francesco Zelada, Pius VI's secretary of state, captured the ambivalence of papal policy regarding the use of military force when, in response to complaints from Austria and Britain that the papacy should more actively contribute to the First Coalition alliance against France, he observed,

> The Pope, as Common Father of the faithful, must strive for the conversion, not the death of him who has become an enemy of Religion and of the Church, and for this purpose must not use arms other than those given to him by his supreme spiritual authority. . . . As sovereign of his states, he ought to try in every way to guard and defend them against invasion but not to carry the terror, desolation and horrors of war into other countries.[17]

This posture did not by itself undermine military preparedness in the name of defense or armed neutrality, but when combined with financial constraints, organizational politics, and bureaucratic inertia, it discouraged the pontifical government from an active let alone energetic interest in military affairs. It also left it helpless in the face of an "enemy of Religion and of the Church" who was not impressed by the pope's position as "Common Father of the faithful."

On June 17, 1796, Napoléon's Army of Italy invaded the Papal States. It was an occupation more than a war. The pontifical army made no effort to defend the pope's domain against the aggressors; in fact the whole affair seems to have been carried off without any casualties. Units surrendered at the first appearance of the French or simply dissolved as troops deserted upon learning of the invasion. The commandant of one papal fortress did not even wait for the enemy to appear outside his walls but hurried to the town of Modena to present the keys of the fortress to Napoléon in person. The only unit of the pontifical army to behave with even a modicum of discipline, professionalism, and sense of duty was a small mixed force of infantry and cavalry under Lieutenant Colonel Oliviero Ronca, which fell back in good order as the Army of Italy invaded the Legations and, despite desertions, maintained unit cohesion as it retreated south into the region known as the Marche. It is, however, a sad testimony to the state of the pontifical army that the one bright spot in its response to the invasion of 1796 was that at least one unit did not entirely fall apart.[18]

Within a week of their entry the French had occupied most of the Romagna, including the significant cities of Bologna and Ferrara. A functioning pontifical military no longer existed in those regions, and all papal fortresses and garrisons were under the control of the French army, which happily collected 164 cannons and some 8,000 muskets from papal magazines and depots—a significant addition to the resources of an army that largely relied on confiscations and plunder for its supplies. In an effort to prevent the invaders from moving even deeper into the Papal States, Pope Pius VI hurriedly dispatched representatives to negotiate with Napoléon, who was open to a settlement because he needed time to consolidate French control over the occupied areas and did not want to move too far south so long as the Austrians, still ensconced in the Trentino and other parts of northern Italy, remained a threat. The Armistice of Bologna, signed on June 23, 1796, confirmed the French in their possession of the Romagna, levied on the Papal States an indemnity of 21 million *scudi*, required the Vatican to transfer to Paris 100 works of art and 500 manuscripts, compelled the closure of all papal ports to the ships of France's enemies, and obliged the pope to send a representative to Paris to negotiate a final peace treaty and apologize for the murder three years earlier of Nicholas Hugo de Basseville.[19] Pius accepted these onerous terms because he had no alternative. His army was useless; he had no means with which to defend his domain, and no other country was prepared to defend it for him. The armistice, moreover, was not an unmitigated disaster. Pius remained in possession of the bulk of his territory; Roman authorities could contrive "unforeseen problems" to delay the payment of the indemnity and the shipment of paintings and sculptures; and papal diplomats in Paris could draw out negotiations to provide a breathing space during which events, such as a successful Austrian offensive into northern Italy, might change the balance of forces in Italy and improve the papacy's position.

In the short term the strategy of delay seemed to pay dividends. While the pope's representatives in Paris deliberately strung out negotiations, Cardinal Secretary of State Ignazio Busca opened secret talks in Vienna to investigate the possibility of military cooperation with Austria, which by July 1796 had renewed operations in the north to relieve the siege of Mantua and drive the French from the Lombard plain. Encouraged by these developments, the pope in August 1796 suspended the peace negotiations in Paris. In October, having paid only the first installment of the indemnity, he refused further payments. Meanwhile, abandoning their traditional indifference to martial affairs, papal authorities hurried to improve the military posture of the Papal States. Pius established a special military congregation to centralize military authority and direct the expansion, preparation, and deployment of the pontifical army. The congregation ordered improvements and repairs for the pope's remaining fortresses, promoted promising junior officers in order to invigorate the senior commands, and supervised the creation of a Civic Guard recruited and funded in part by prominent families of the papal domain. The latter initiative proved a particular success. There was no conscription in the Papal States. Traditionally, the pontifical army had filled its ranks by offering a bonus for enlistment and by rewarding with officer rank any individual who collected and presented for enrollment a large number of neighbors, relatives, or dependents—a practice not unknown in other European armies. Someone appearing before a recruiting officer with 100 men would be rewarded with a commission as a lieutenant; 1,600 able bodies were worth a colonelcy.[20] This practice populated the papal officer corps with local notables who had no particular qualification for their ranks beyond an ability to raise a body of men. Not surprisingly the nobility strongly supported the Civic Guard and considered it a matter of family pride to contribute generously. Prince Pietro Colonna, scion of an ancient Roman family, subsidized an entire infantry regiment. The small middle class also donated; the banker Acquaroni, for example, offered to pay the cost of outfitting thirty infantrymen with muskets and uniforms. There was also a public subscription to raise money from the tradesmen, shopkeepers, and workers of Rome. By January 1797 these efforts had increased the size of the pontifical army to 10,000 men. Finally, the pope's military commission approached Austria about providing military assistance and secured from Vienna a tentative promise to provide an experienced general and several thousand soldiers.[21]

Raising regiments proved easier than preparing plans to employ those regiments. The new army lacked a strategic vision or plans for systematic operations; indeed, it wasn't clear that the inexperienced and undertrained officers, many of whom had just abandoned civilian life for military service, were even capable of contriving such a vision or plans. The idea seems to have been that with Napoléon and his forces defeated or at least distracted by the Austrians in northern Italy, papal troops could reoccupy the Romagna, now stripped of French troops. Nobody seems to have given much thought to what the troops would do if the Austrians did not neutralize Napoléon and the French general again turned his attention to the pope's territories. In November 1796 Colonel Carlo Ancajani marched the Regiment of the Romagna, consisting of two infantry battalions, a squadron of cavalry, and ten pieces of artillery (2,141 men), north from Rome to establish a base in the Romagnese town of Faenza, 50 kilometers southeast of Bologna. Once settled in Faenza Colonel Ancajani initiated no operations, although it is not clear whether this passivity reflected orders from Rome or the colonel's own temperament. Early in the new year another infantry battalion and ten cannons arrived in Faenza to reinforce Ancajani's regiment, but the papal force remained passive. A second concentration of papal troops, approximately 2,000 men, was in the fortress port of Ancona, another 200 kilometers farther south on the Adriatic coast. The remainder of the pontifical army was in Rome or scattered in company-sized detachments among the fortresses and towns of the Papal States.[22] For the papacy the mobilization of an army and the deployment to forward positions of elements of that army represented a level of military activity unseen in almost a century. The result would be a military debacle on a scale also unseen for almost a century.

Even before Colonel Ancajani moved his force north to return the Romagna to papal rule, the conditions necessary for the success of that mission had disappeared. Rather than the defeat of Napoléon and the expulsion of French armies from northern Italy, the Austrian offensives of the summer and fall of 1796 had resulted, after some initial successes, in a string of serious setbacks for the Austrians that would culminate in defeat at the Battle of Rivoli on January 14, 1797, and the subsequent surrender of the fortress of Mantua and its garrison of 30,000 soldiers. The papal army, which had expected the Austrians to deal decisively with Napoléon and never anticipated having to fight the French directly, now found itself facing the prospect of actual war without the support and protection of a powerful ally. Papal authorities were about to discover that they could not just conjure an effective military force when they needed one and that brief spasms of energy and enthusiasm could not reverse decades of neglect. Despite several years of fitful reform and the efforts since the summer of 1796 to increase its size and improve its capabilities, the army remained weak and ineffective. There were now more battalions, but they were still ill-trained, ill-equipped, and ill-led. At a time when the French in general and Napoléon Bonaparte in particular were changing the meaning and conduct of warfare, the pope still had a parade-ground army, limited in its capabilities, impoverished in its resources, marginal in its status, unimaginative in its leadership, and narrow in its experience. Reviewing the impact of the pre-1798 reforms, the leading authority on the eighteenth-century pontifical armed forces sadly concluded that the pope's army amounted to little more than a constabulary: "The main function of the pontifical troops remained, even after the reforms that had sought to transform them into an organization at least modestly operational, the maintenance of public order."[23] Another student of the late-eighteenth-century papacy put it more bluntly: "The most charitable thing to say about [the papacy's] police and army is to say nothing at all."[24]

Papal authorities had expected Austrian support to compensate for the deficiencies of their army. In its secret talks with Vienna the papacy had asked for Austrian officers, troops, and matériel. Once again reliance on another country would prove an imprudent and disappointing policy, although after its setbacks in northern Italy in the summer and fall of 1796 Vienna may have been hard-pressed to provide any assistance at all. On January 12, 1797, the much-anticipated Austrian support arrived at Ancona in the form of a single ship. Instead of files of well-trained and experienced Austrian infantry, batteries of artillery, and pallets of powder and shot, two officers moved down the gangway as the ship's crew manhandled several crates of muskets onto the dock. In addition to 3,000 muskets, Vienna had sent to Rome's aid only two soldiers: General Michelangelo Alessandro Colli and his aide, General Bartolini.

A career officer from the Italian territories of the Austrian Empire, General Colli had participated in wars against Prussia and Turkey, received a wound in battle, and most recently fought with Austria's Piedmontese allies against the French in the War of the First Coalition. His mission was to evaluate the condition of the pope's army and advise the pontifical government on its deployment and operations. His first step was to conduct a quick inspection of Ancona's garrison and fortifications, both of which he found woefully inadequate, the garrison (most of whom were hastily mobilized civic guards) lacking training and the fortress lacking cannons and ammunition. Leaving General Bartolini to repair as best he could the deficiencies in Ancona's military defenses, Colli made a flying visit to Colonel Ancajani's regiment at Faenza (arriving while Napoléon was battering the Austrian army at Rivoli) before proceeding to Rome to meet the Holy Father and senior officers of the papal army. Apparently he made a good impression. On January 22, 1797, two days after his arrival in the Eternal City, Pope Pius appointed him commander-in-chief of the army of the Papal States.[25]

Having spent his career to that point in one of Europe's best armies, General Colli now found himself in command of one of the worst. Accustomed to the highest standards of discipline, professionalism, and martial spirit, the pope's new commander had to adjust to an entirely different military world. The differences extended beyond disparities in training and equipment. The pontifical army and its masters represented a fundamentally different military culture with different standards and expectations concerning the purposes and usages of the armed forces. This was an army, after all, that required its cavalry squadrons, before riding to war, to perform eight days of spiritual exercises.[26] In normal circumstances both the army and its new commander would have needed a period of time for adjustment and familiarization. But in early 1797 the circumstances were not normal, and there would be no time.

From intercepted correspondence, Napoléon had learned of the papacy's military collaboration with Vienna, but with the Austrians on the offensive in the summer and fall of 1796 the commander of the Army of Italy postponed any confrontation with the Vatican. After his decisive victory at Rivoli, Napoléon could turn his attention to the States of the Church. On February 1, 1797, he denounced the Armistice of Bologna on the grounds (largely substantiated) that the papacy had violated the armistice by conducting secret military negotiations with the Austrians and failing to honor its commitments under the agreement. That same day a column of French and Italian troops (6,000 to 10,000 men, depending on the source) under General Claude Victor-Perrin occupied the papal town of Imola and moved down the ancient Via Emilia toward Faenza, 16 kilometers farther south, where the papal force under Colonel Ancajani was encamped.[27] On the late afternoon of February 1 Ancajani, learning that a French force was approaching, marched from Faenza toward the Senio, a minor river a few kilometers north along the road to Imola. The departure of the pope's army from Faenza seemed more a religious festival than a military operation. Cheered by citizens and accompanied by chanting priests carrying crosses and religious banners, the pope's troops, fired with enthusiasm, marched in gay and colorful formations. The officers looked as if they were going to a garden fete, stepping out with umbrellas on their shoulders, multiple rings on their fingers, large watches dangling from their belts, and elegant silver buckles on their shoes. Everyone believed they would be in Bologna the next day.[28]

Upon reaching the Senio that evening Ancajani established makeshift defensive positions along the right bank and summoned his officers for a council of war. More information concerning the approaching enemy was now available, and it was clear that the papal force would be outnumbered. The earlier braggadocio and enthusiasm collapsed in the face of this sobering intelligence. Aware that they faced a real fight, several officers advised an immediate withdrawal. Ancajani, however, decided to hold fast, arguing that a demonstration of resolve might cause the enemy, though numerically superior, to reconsider its advance and withdraw. However unlikely this scenario, the colonel remained firm and dismissed his officers with the order to prepare for battle on the morrow. In his stubbornness, the papal commander seriously underestimated the resolve of the French troops and overestimated the resolve of his own. The pontifical army of the late eighteenth century did not exactly make a fetish of obedience to superiors and loyalty to the chain of command, so news of the fresh intelligence and the disagreements among the officers quickly spread through the units, where confidence gave way to defeatism. During the night men in increasing numbers slipped away from their positions to make their way home, and officers did little to stem the desertions. Those who remained to face the dawn and the approaching enemy were probably not the steadiest soldiers the papacy had ever put into the field.[29]

Colonel Ancajani had decided that the bridge that carried the Via Emilia across the Senio was the key to his defense. He placed a battery of four cannons to cover that crossing and deployed his infantry in crude entrenchments along the riverbank immediately above and below the bridge. He positioned his cavalry—either 145 or 500 troopers, depending on the source—back from the river in reserve.[30] Apparently, it did not occur to the papal commander that the river might be fordable at nearby points or that General Victor might send elements of his force to cross not at the bridge but at these nearby fords—which was exactly what Victor did. The French general opened the battle by sending a strong infantry column toward the bridge. This force immediately came under musket and cannon fire from the pontificals on the opposite bank and halted without attempting the bridge. While the papal troops were focused on this enemy, Victor sent columns to ford the river above and below the bridge. Crossing with little opposition, these columns immediately threatened Ancajani's flanks. Without any effort to rectify his position, the papal commander promptly ordered a general retreat and directed his cavalry to move forward from its reserve position to cover the withdrawal. The troopers, however, were not up to the job; in fact, they weren't up to any job. Without moving a step closer to the enemy, the papal cavalry turned and galloped in disorder away from the battlefield. The panic immediately spread to other units, and soon the pope's soldiers, including their commander, Colonel Ancajani, were in headlong flight toward Faenza and beyond, the French close on their heels. The debacle on the Senio cost the pontifical army more than 600 men killed, wounded, or captured. French losses were 40 dead or wounded.[31]

With the rout of the principal papal field force, the way south was open to the French. They occupied Faenza without resistance and, preceded by fleeing papal soldiers, advanced on Ancona, reaching that port on February 8. Upon his arrival in the Papal States, General Colli had left his colleague, the Austrian general Bartolini, to organize Ancona's defenses. It was a daunting task. Though imposing in appearance, the city's fortifications were in poor condition, the artillery largely unserviceable, and supplies and munitions insufficient to withstand a siege. Bartolini did what he could: distributing some Austrian muskets; pulling into the city the small, isolated detachments assigned to Senigallia, Fano, and Pesaro, thereby raising the garrison of regulars to two thousand men; and mobilizing three thousand local militiamen to support these regulars. These measures did little to reverse the defeatism and demoralization that infected the city and its garrison. The city administrators appealed to Bartolini to spare the port the horrors of a siege, and the Austrian general, convinced perhaps that his task was hopeless, readily agreed. On February 8 Bartolini left Ancona by sea for an Austrian port, leaving the garrison commander, Miletto Miletti, to surrender the city when the French arrived. On the evening of February 8 the French entered the city through an open and undefended gate and disarmed the papal troops without resistance, capturing in the process more than 3,000 muskets and 120 cannons (although most of the latter were not immediately serviceable). It was another humiliating loss for the pontifical army, although it might have been worse. Before the arrival of the French, Miletti had loaded several thousand pounds of gunpowder, 2,000 muskets, and 8 cannons from the fortress magazines onto a ship and dispatched it to the safety of the Austrian port of Fiume.[32]

On February 6 General Colli was having breakfast in Rome with the cardinal secretary of state when he learned of the disaster at the River Senio. He immediately left the Eternal City for the north, reaching Loreto on February 8, the day that Ancona fell. At Loreto he encountered the dispirited survivors of the Battle of the Senio. Concluding that the remnants of Colonel Ancajani's force were in no state to defend Loreto, the Austrian general ordered the soldiers to withdraw southward. At Recanati, several kilometers south of Loreto, he established a force of four hundred men and four cannons, reinforced by several hundred local militiamen under Colonel Carlo Antici, to serve as a blocking force should the French move south from Ancona while Colli retreated into Umbria to set up a line around Foligno with whatever forces he could pick up along the way. Colonel Antici had little stomach for combat and allowed himself to be convinced by the notables of Recanati that resistance would only expose the town and its inhabitants to destruction and looting. Antici's timidity, however unseemly from a professional point of view, had little effect on the course of the "war," which was, in fact, already over. Although General Colli assured officials in Rome that he still had enough troops to establish a strong line in central Umbria and resist the attackers, the pope and his advisers had lost their nerve. The rapid French advance and the collapse of the pontifical army in the north had created panic in Rome. Papal advisers were so alarmed that for a time there was talk of the pope fleeing Rome for the safety of Naples. Before any decision could be finalized, however, Napoléon, who thought he was in a position to obtain all that he required without the trouble of actually occupying Rome, put out the word that peace negotiations were possible, a suggestion that was accepted with barely disguised relief.[33]

The Treaty of Tolentino (February 19, 1797) ended the brief war with France, but on terms even more onerous than those of the Armistice of Bologna, requiring the papacy to recognize the Directory as the legitimate government of France, cede the Romagna, reduce the size of its army, pay a larger indemnity, and transfer to Paris additional manuscripts and artworks to be selected by special French commissioners. Initially the Directory had been inclined to occupy Rome and sweep away the entire temporal power of the papacy by eliminating the Papal States, but Napoléon, who did not want to tie down troops in an occupation that served no military purpose, had counseled patience. It was unlikely, the general believed, that the Papal States could long survive the loss of its richest provinces and the imposition of a crushing indemnity. "This ancient mechanism will self destruct," he assured Paris.[34]

The debacles at the Senio and Ancona confirmed earlier impressions that the pontifical army was undisciplined, unprepared, and unreliable. Roman authorities, who had been perfectly content to send to war a ramshackle military force whose serious deficiencies were the result of decades of indifference and neglect, found it convenient to shift blame for the defeat onto the shoulders of General Colli, and he was dismissed in disgrace. There can be little doubt that the Austrian general was the designated fall guy when one considers that Colonel Carlo Ancajani, who had seriously mishandled his command at the Senio and then outraced his soldiers in a precipitous flight to the rear, not only escaped postwar censure but received a choice assignment in Rome as commander of one of the two "legions" into which the papal army was reorganized after the Treaty of Tolentino.[35] Colli's disgrace suggested that an individual, not the system, was at fault, even though that individual had assumed command of the pontifical army only ten days before Napoléon attacked the Papal States. The fault, of course, was with the system that had systematically run down the capabilities of its armed forces and then embarked on a course of action that required those enervated and deprived forces to perform at a high level. Decades of neglect could not be reversed overnight by borrowing a general and a thousand muskets from Austria. Count Monaldo Leopardi, a prominent citizen of the Papal States who observed at first hand the collapse of the pope's army, saw things more clearly than the cardinals and monsignors in Rome: "The State certainly lacked the organization, the capacity, and the imagination for war. . . . Dress, spirit, and morale do not change in a moment, and there is not time to knead the bread when it comes to the table. Time, discipline, and experience can make good soldiers of these people, but to ask the [papal army] to wage war now would be like asking a Hungarian hussar to say mass."[36]

French successes against Austria, Sardinia-Piedmont, and the Papal States were not universally condemned by the inhabitants of the Italian peninsula. Many, especially in the middle classes, welcomed the demise of old social and political structures as a precursor to reform and modernization and an opportunity to enhance their own status and influence. Even in Rome, the very heart of the traditional order, there were a few Jacobins who hoped to tear down the theocracy and set up a republic in its place. After the Treaty of Tolentino, these secret republicans welcomed the arrival of Joseph Bonaparte, Napoléon's brother, as French ambassador to the pope. The ambassador was generally prudent in his relations with the papal administration, but the same could not be said about members of his entourage. One of these, General Léonard Duphot, exhibited the same revolutionary fervor and indifference to local sensibilities that had brought Nicholas Hugo de Basseville to an untimely end. Like his predecessor, Duphot seemed to believe it was his duty to revolutionize Rome by igniting republican sentiments in the bosoms of oppressed Romans. To this end he delighted in organizing noisy (though poorly attended) demonstrations in support of liberty, equality, fraternity, and other revolutionary ideals. On December 28, 1797, a Roman crowd heckled and disrupted one such demonstration, chasing the protesters, who sought refuge in the French embassy in the Corsini Palace. Ambassador Bonaparte was hosting a dinner at the embassy but, hearing a commotion at the gate, went out to investigate. He found the two groups, demonstrators and counterdemonstrators, taunting each other, and he tried to defuse the situation. A detachment of pontifical soldiers arrived, but their presence only contributed to the turmoil, and in the pushing and yelling the soldiers fired several shots. Sources differ on what followed. One account says that the gunfire mortally wounded General Duphot in front of the embassy.[37] Other accounts maintain that after the shots Duphot, armed with a sword, and a group of republicans chased the soldiers from the embassy toward the Porta Settimiana. Their pursuit carried them to a weapons magazine of the pontifical army near the Ponte Sisto. Although it is not clear whether Duphot's group intended to seize the weapons, the small detachment of soldiers guarding this magazine had been threatened by republican enthusiasts earlier in the day, and when the approaching Duphot and his crowd refused an order to halt, the soldiers opened fire, mortally wounding the French general.[38] The various accounts, although differing in details, agree that Duphot was killed by a papal musket ball.

This incident was more serious than the Basseville affair because Duphot was killed not by a mob but by a pontifical soldier, making the death a diplomatic incident. The following day Joseph Bonaparte left Rome for Florence, where he prepared a report for Paris that placed all blame for the incident on papal authorities. The Directory, which had long nourished a wish to eliminate the Papal States and the pope's temporal power, rejected the apology of papal representatives and refused to pursue a diplomatic solution. From his headquarters in Milan, Napoléon ordered French forces, which in violation of the Treaty of Tolentino had already occupied several towns in the northern provinces of the Papal States, to advance on Rome. General Louis-Alexandre Berthier had orders to occupy the capital of the Papal States, overthrow the temporal power, and establish a republic, although during his preliminary contacts with papal officials he was to hide his ultimate intentions. Declaring pompously that "revenge is just, but it must be without dishonor," Berthier marched south, occupying various papal towns along the way and arriving outside the walls of the Eternal City on February 9, 1798. The pontifical army made no effort to block or impede his advance. The Treaty of Tolentino had required a reduction in the size of the papal military, but the pope still controlled a force of eight thousand men, including several battalions of infantry deployed as two "legions," one stationed in the north and the other in Rome. These troops were so dispirited and ineffectual that they simply surrendered or dispersed at the first sign of the advancing French.[39]

On the morning of February 10 General Berthier demanded the surrender of the Castel Sant'Angelo, the principal fortress and arsenal of Rome, which commanded the Vatican side of the Tiber River hardly more than a kilometer from Saint Peter's Basilica. Papal troops were to evacuate the fortress within twenty-four hours, leaving behind all weapons and munitions. The fortress commander immediately complied with the demand, and by early afternoon the garrison had vacated the castle under the watchful eyes of a detachment of French dragoons whom General Berthier had sent into the city to confirm compliance with his demand. Within an hour of the departure of the last papal soldier, French cavalry entered the Porta Angelica, the city gate immediately north of the Vatican, trotting under the windows of the papal palace, past Saint Peter's Square, and down the narrow streets to take possession of the fortress. The next day French infantry entered through the Porta del Popolo, occupied the principal squares and buildings of the city, and established barracks in various convents and monasteries from which the monks and nuns were evicted.[40]

Hoping to placate the French general, Pope Pius sent him a gift of a sturgeon and forty bottles of wine, but Berthier was unmoved. On February 13 he presented a list of twenty-one nonnegotiable demands, including a formal apology for the death of Duphot, transfer to French custody of officials responsible for the incident, dismissal of allegedly anti-French members of the pope's higher administration, payment within six months of a special indemnity, consignment of yet more artworks and books to Paris, transfer of three thousand horses to the French army, and the immediate reduction of the pontifical armed forces to a battalion of five hundred men and the pope's palace guards. His capital in hostile hands, enemy troops in every piazza and street, his own forces impotent to resist (even if there had been the will to resist), Pius had no choice but to accept the humiliating conditions in the hope of salvaging something of his temporal authority. Such hopes were in vain. Berthier's arrival in Rome was not about extracting horses and coin from the pope (although the French, who relied largely on plunder to maintain their army in Italy, were glad to have both) but about removing the pope and ending the temporal power of the papacy; the pontiff's concession to any number of demands would not have deflected that purpose.

The French purpose unfolded on February 15. At the very time that the Holy Father was officiating at a special ceremony in Saint Peter's to celebrate the twenty-third anniversary of his election to the Throne of Saint Peter, across town a coup was under way. A group of Roman republicans ("a multitude of people," according to the official French report; "four paid scoundrels and a handful of Jacobins," according to papal accounts) gathered in the ancient Forum to raise a Tree of Liberty, proclaim the Roman Republic, and announce that from that day forward the people would rule and the pope would exercise only religious power.[41] In the name of the Directory, General Berthier applauded the decision of the people to free themselves from theocracy and tyranny and placed the fledgling republic under the protection of the French army. Later that day a French officer went to the papal palace to inform the Holy Father that sovereignty in Rome had passed to the people and that, consequently, the pope was politically redundant. On February 16 French troops took control of the gates to the pope's two city residences, the Apostolic Palace inside the Vatican and the Quirinal Palace on the other side of the Tiber. At both sites the Swiss Guards, who were responsible for guarding the entrances, withdrew into the palaces, having received orders to offer no resistance. At the Vatican the French actually penetrated into the palace and hoisted the tricolor on a flagstaff. Several papal attendants were beaten by intruders who entered the papal apartments demanding food and drink. The next day General Berthier summoned the pope's palace guards to appear fully armed in Saint Peter's Square on the pretext of participating in a formal military review. When the guards marched into the square they were immediately surrounded by a larger French force, which confiscated their weapons and ordered them confined to their barracks. That same day the five hundred soldiers who were all that remained of the pontifical army were disarmed and dismissed from service.[42]

Pius was now effectively under house arrest in his palace. This was not enough for the French, who feared that the helpless pontiff might become the focus of popular discontent and jeopardize the flimsy legitimacy and stability of the new Roman Republic. A French commissioner, freshly arrived in the Eternal City to supervise the transfer of artworks and money to Paris, informed Pius that he would have to leave Rome within three days. When the ailing eighty-one-year-old pontiff asked to be allowed to die in Rome, the commissioner brusquely replied, "One can die anywhere."[43] Early on the morning of February 20, 1798, French officers placed Pius and several of his attendants in carriages and drove them under close escort to a convent outside Siena. The pope was a prisoner of the French. Over the following months his captors moved him (always in close custody) to Florence; Bologna; Turin; and eventually a fortress in the French town of Valence, where on August 29, 1799, he died.

Never more than a collaborationist regime without any claim to the loyalties or sympathies of the people it claimed to represent, the Roman Republic did not long survive the sovereign it had displaced. Its earnest efforts to break with the past, such as painting tricolor the statue of Saint Michael at the pinnacle of the Castel Sant'Angelo or renaming the Piazza di Spagna "The Piazza of Liberty" and the Piazza Venezia "The Piazza of Equality," were received with ridicule, and other actions, such as a non-Christian funeral for General Duphot, complete with republican speeches, inside Saint Peter's Basilica were deeply resented.[44] Within a week of Pius's kidnapping, the residents of the Trastevere district rose against the new republic and its French protectors, a revolt that required the French to have recourse to artillery and mass executions. Similar revolts were suppressed in nearby towns, including Albano and Velletri. Since the Roman Republic was maintained by French bayonets, its political status waxed and waned with French military fortunes. When, for example, Napoléon left Italy in the spring of 1798 to campaign in Egypt, Austria and the Kingdom of Naples grabbed the opportunity to challenge France's position in the peninsula, and in December a Neapolitan army briefly occupied Rome and drove out the republic before being in turn driven out by French troops who reestablished the republican government.

Despite this success against the Neapolitans, by the spring of 1799 the French and their Italian satellite regimes were increasingly hard-pressed by internal rebellions and external attack by various alliances or joint operations involving at various times Austria, Britain, Naples, Russia, and Turkey. Peasant bands, many fighting under the papal flag or wearing Catholic symbols and led by priests and friars, waged a savage guerrilla war against the French and those perceived to be their puppets.[45] Former members of the defunct pontifical armed forces occasionally played a role in the growing resistance to the Roman Republic. In February 1799, for example, when the old papal port of Civitavecchia rose against the republic, sailors from the papal navy spearheaded the rebellion. Unlike their counterparts in the old pontifical army, many of whom had accepted service in the new republican military, the pope's sailors did not embrace the new order. In 1798 the small papal fleet had been further depleted when the French drafted several of its vessels (but not all of their crews) into Napoléon's Egyptian expedition. Left behind in barracks in Civitavecchia or reassigned to coastal watchtowers when their ships sailed with Napoléon, the sailors formed a center of antirepublican sentiment that flared into armed resistance. Led by the seamen, the townspeople of Civitavecchia repulsed attacks by French and republican troops who managed to retake the port only after an extended artillery bombardment. In reprisal the French executed one hundred townspeople. To discourage future revolts and punish the sailors, the French confiscated and melted down for coinage all naval cannons and many of the (admittedly unserviceable) artillery pieces in the coastal towers, throwing in for good measure the silver ex-votos from the naval chapel in Civitavecchia. Some of the pope's sailors found refuge in Port'Ercole, a small harbor on the island-like Promontorio dell'Argentario on the coast 70 kilometers north of Civitavecchia, from which they sailed small ships to attack French merchant and fishing vessels along the west coast of Italy.[46]

At the end of September the French and their Italian allies, besieged by foreign armies and domestic insurgents, withdrew from central Italy, taking the remaining die-hard Roman republicans with them. A Neapolitan army occupied Rome, and a provisional government awaited the return of the pope. On March 14, 1800, almost eight months after the death in French captivity of Pius VI, the College of Cardinals, meeting in Venice, elected his successor. Their choice, the bishop of Imola, Cardinal Luigi Barnabà Chiaramonte, took the name Pius VII. The new pope returned to his capital on July 3, 1800, to face the daunting prospect of reestablishing ecclesiastical governance over the Papal States.

Although Pius VII arranged some minor military matters, such as reconstituting his Swiss Guard (which had been dissolved after the French coup of February 15, 1798) and establishing (in 1801) a new unit of household cavalry, the Guardia Nobile (Noble Guard), in succession to two older units of mounted guards, the Lance Spezzate and the Cavalleggieri, which had also been disbanded by the Roman Republic, the restored papal administration devoted relatively little attention to its armed forces.[47] This inattention may have reflected a preoccupation with more pressing problems, a belief that the problems of the discredited papal army were so severe as to require a major reform initiative that was best postponed until more auspicious times, or an awareness that the financial circumstances of the papal administration were so pinched that the administration would be hard-pressed to find money for *any* initiatives. There was too little money to support even the pope's modest military schemes. In the reconstituted Swiss Guard, for example, there was no money to replace the weapons lost to the French in 1798 or to pay the full salaries of the men, who received only one-third of what they were due. When, in 1803, the Swiss commandant appealed to Pius VII, noting that impoverished halberdiers were resigning to return to Switzerland or live on the streets of Rome, the Holy Father could only express a hope that financial conditions would improve in the future; until then the guard would have to suffer patiently, since every part of the papal administration was in the same condition.[48]

Another reason that Pope Pius neglected his army may have been that he had no intention of using it. France remained the only military threat on the horizon, and in the early years of the new century that threat seemed to be receding. The restoration accompanied a period of relative détente in French-papal relations. In November 1799 Napoléon had overthrown the Directory and established a new regime in France, the Consulate, with himself as first consul and effective dictator. More conservative and less reflexively antireligious than the ideologues of the Directory, Napoléon believed that religion was as necessary an element of social and political order as a police service, and he was prepared, even eager, to make peace with the Catholic Church, both at home and abroad, so long as that peace was on his terms. He expected the Church to support his regime, comfort and encourage his citizens, and afflict his enemies. These terms would eventually prove unacceptable to Pope Pius VII, but for several years the papacy would pursue accommodation with the new power in Paris. This effort, complicated by Napoléon's volatile temper and devious personality, his changing political agenda, and his seemingly endless wars against European enemies, included the negotiation of the Concordat of 1801, which regularized church-state relations by, among other things, recognizing Catholicism as "the religion of the great majority of the French," ending the schism with the Constitutional Church, abolishing the popular election of bishops and priests, providing state salaries for Catholic (as well as other) clergy, guaranteeing the property rights of those who had acquired ecclesiastical buildings and lands after the confiscations of the National Assembly, reducing the number of dioceses, and prudently obfuscating the issue of loyalty oaths.[49] The rapprochement between France and the papacy culminated in Notre Dame cathedral in December 1804 when Pius VII presided over Napoléon's coronation as emperor of France.

The détente, no matter how welcome, was shallow. Napoléon believed that the church should be the handmaiden of the state and the pope the chaplain of the empire. He had no interest in a relationship he could not dominate or a partner he could not control, and he had no intention of honoring agreements or understandings if they no longer served his purposes. Relations soon soured, particularly after Napoléon, in March 1805, accepted the crown of the Kingdom of Italy, a French-controlled territory stretching from the Veneto in the northeast to the formerly papal Romagna in the center. Facing the armies of the Third Coalition (1803–1806), Napoléon insisted that Pius declare his support for the empire, close papal ports to its enemies, and expel from papal territory all subjects of the coalition partners. The War of the Fourth Coalition (1806–1807) produced similar demands. The pope declined these demands, refusing to become an ally of the French Empire and insisting on his neutrality. Already irritated by the pontiff's refusal to annul the marriage of his brother, Jerome Bonaparte, to an American Protestant, Napoléon ignored Pius's declaration of neutrality and ordered his troops to occupy the papal ports of Ancona and Civitavecchia. By 1807 the emperor was muttering to his aides that perhaps it was time to demote the pontiff to a simple bishop of the French Empire. In November of that year Napoléon ordered his viceroy in Milan to send troops to occupy the papal provinces of Fermo, Macerata, and Urbino. On January 10, 1808, he ordered French troops into Rome.[50]

When French troops had moved into Ancona, Civitavecchia, and other papal towns, the pontifical army had offered no resistance, simply standing aside or withdrawing as the emperor's forces entered the towns. At least in the early stages of the French advance this passivity was the result less of direct orders from Rome than of the papal army's usual enervation. This was not, after all, an army in which martial qualities were determinedly cultivated, and the pope's soldiers probably (and correctly) considered themselves completely outmatched by the invaders. As the French neared Rome, Pius decided not to defend the city. When, on the cold and foggy morning of February 1, 1808, General Sextius de Miollis approached the walls of the Eternal City with a small force of French troops, he found the gates open and undefended. Treating Rome as a hostile city, the invaders moved quickly to occupy strategic points: one column racing to occupy the Castel Sant'Angelo, another setting up four cannons in the central Piazza Colonna, and a third deploying eight cannons in the Quirinal Square, right on the pope's doorstep. Once again monks and nuns were evicted from their monasteries and convents around the city to provide quarters for the occupying troops. Pius responded with a formal protest and condemnation of French aggression.[51]

Technically the pope's sovereignty remained undisturbed, but while papal officials remained at their desks and continued their normal functions, General Miollis quickly made it clear that he was in charge and that the Papal States were under French suzerainty. One of his first acts was to neutralize the papacy's capacity (modest though it was) to resist encroachments. All units of the pontifical armed forces were incorporated into the French army under French command. On March 1 Miollis had informed senior papal officers of his intentions, and the officers had immediately informed the Holy Father. Pius was disposed to frustrate French intentions at every opportunity, and he had no intention of allowing the occupiers to use his own army against him. He instructed his senior officers to gather their units secretly before Miollis could act, inform them of French plans, and allow the soldiers to leave the papal army and return to their homes rather than enter French service. Before it could be implemented this plan was betrayed to the French by a Swiss colonel in papal service, a certain de Fries (not an officer of the Swiss Guard), who hoped to curry favor with the new masters of Rome. General Miollis immediately arrested the papal army officers involved in the plan and ordered Colonel de Fries to issue an order of the day announcing the immediate amalgamation of all pontifical army units into the French army and assuring the troops that the Holy Father approved of this action. By March 5 the pontifical army had ceased to exist, and the only armed forces left to the pope were his household units, the Noble Guard and the Swiss Guard, which numbered fewer than two hundred men.[52]

The occupation of territories, the absorption of the papal army, the arrest and deportation of cardinals, and the replacement of pontifical rule by French decrees were all efforts by General Miollis to intimidate the Holy Father and compel him to bend to Napoléon's will by aligning the papacy with the French empire. Pius, however, was not easily intimidated. Though effectively under house arrest in the Quirinal Palace, with French troops patrolling the nearby streets and French cannons in the piazza beyond the palace gate, Pius refused to be intimidated. "You may tell them at Paris," he coolly informed a French representative sent to make him see reason, "that they may hack me to pieces; that they may skin me alive; but always I will say no." Returning to Paris to report the failure of his mission, the representative advised Napoléon that he should not expect to bully this pope. "You do not know this man," he cautioned the emperor.[53] Paris chose to ignore the advice and instead directed Miollis to increase the pressure. The general's first act was to neutralize the remaining armed force available to the pontiff. On April 7 an armed company of French soldiers appeared at the main gate of the Quirinal Palace and demanded that the Swiss Guards on duty at the closed and barred gate admit them. The guards refused but decided to allow one officer to enter. The French agreed. When the Swiss opened a small postern, however, the entire company rushed the door, overwhelming and disarming the guards. At gunpoint the guardsmen were compelled to lead the French to the Swiss commandant, who was curtly informed that he was now under French command and should no longer accept orders from papal authorities. The commandant, Colonel Karl Pfyffer von Altishofen, politely but firmly refused, asserting that he took his orders only from the Holy Father. The French then departed, but not before confiscating all the firearms in the guard armory. That same day French troops appeared at the quarters of the Noble Guard, confiscated weapons, and transported several of the guardsmen under arrest to the Castel Sant'Angelo.[54]

General Miollis increased the pressure in the face of a popular campaign of nonviolent resistance by papal officials and citizens. Although some of the pope's subjects collaborated with the French, the vast majority continued to recognize the pope as their sovereign, refused to acknowledge French authority, and took every occasion to frustrate Miollis's efforts to establish a new order.[55] Though incorporated into the French army and subject to French discipline, pontifical army units could not be trusted. In June 1808 former papal battalions in Perugia, Spoleto, and Todi had to be disarmed and their officers arrested for failure to accept French command and renounce their loyalty to the pope.[56] The peak of resistance came with the season of the Carnival, the long-standing event, marked by promenades along the Corso (Rome's main thoroughfare), masked merrymakers, horse races, and balls, that had been recorded in letters, diaries, and books by countless visitors to the Eternal City. It was the high point of the social season, and everyone, from the lowliest beggar to the grandest prince, participated—that is, until the Carnival of 1809. Despite Miollis's efforts to maintain the appearance of normalcy by insisting that the celebration proceed, that buildings along the Corso be decorated, and that everyone participate, the event was a humiliating failure. Pius had issued a proclamation requesting his people to avoid the celebration so long as Rome remained occupied and the papacy remained in chains. On the opening day of the Carnival no one appeared on the streets except French soldiers, shops remained closed, and members of Roman society conspicuously avoided the balls and soirees hosted by Miollis and his officers. French occupation authorities were further humiliated a few nights after the end of the Carnival when, without any apparent orders or instructions, the entire city was illuminated to celebrate the anniversary of Pius VII's election. Reporting this provocation to Paris, the French police administration in Rome frankly articulated what everyone in the Eternal City already knew: "The pope rules more here with his little finger than we do with bayonets."[57]

In the spring of 1809 General Miollis received new orders. Paris had decided to abandon the pretense that the pope remained sovereign in his capital and impose direct French rule by declaring Rome an "imperial city." On the morning of June 10 Romans woke to discover the bridges across the Tiber closed by French infantry and cannons. The news spread quickly through the city. At 9:00 that morning anxious citizens were startled by two cannon blasts from Castel Sant'Angelo, and soon thereafter those looking toward the fortress saw the papal flag fall from the flagstaff on the battlements and the standard of the French empire rise in its place, accompanied by the first shots of what would be a one-hundred-gun salute. As the last echoes of the cannonade receded, a group of French officers, preceded by a cavalry detachment in gala uniform, appeared at the Capitol, the traditional center of Roman administration overlooking the remains of the ancient Forum, to read an exhortation from the Emperor Napoléon and proclaim the end of papal sovereignty.

At the first sound of cannons, Cardinal Secretary of State Bartolomeo Pacca, who had taken up residence in the papal apartments after Pius had personally thwarted an attempt by French officers to arrest him (as they had arrested and deported his predecessor, Cardinal Giulio Gabrielli), rushed to the pope's suite. As he entered Pius turned and whispered, "It is finished." Within minutes Pacca's nephew, Tiberio Pacca, arrived with a copy of the imperial decree that the French were posting around the city. As the pope read the order stripping him of his sovereign rights, he became manifestly angry. The French coup was not entirely unexpected. Over the previous days Pacca had received information suggesting that the occupiers were about to strike, and a formal protest had been composed in anticipation of the event. The document sat now on the pope's desk, awaiting only the papal signature. After reading the French decree, Pius walked to his desk, signed several copies of the protest, and directed that they be placarded about the city that very day. He also signed copies of a decree (also prepared in advance) excommunicating from the Catholic Church anyone who cooperated with the overthrow of pontifical authority and the expropriation of the Papal States. By the afternoon of June 10 copies of this excommunication were nailed on the doors of all the major churches of Rome.[58]

Napoléon was infuriated, rightly considering the excommunication an act of defiance and an affront to his imperial power. Although the excommunication mattered nothing to him in a spiritual sense (he was not named specifically in the document and wouldn't have cared if he was), he understood that it mattered to many Catholics in the empire, and he recognized the propaganda value of the pope's action. Fuming that the Holy Father was "a dangerous madman who must be restrained," he informed his surrogates in Italy that the pope would have to be arrested if he continued to defy imperial authority.[59] The emperor would not have long to wait for new signs of defiance. As one of its first acts, the "Roman Consulta," which under the chairmanship of General Miollis nominally governed the city, established a Civic Guard, but the citizens refused to volunteer for this militia. Turning to conscription, the Consulta on June 21 directed parish priests to submit the names of all males between the ages of eighteen and sixty, who would be liable for service in this militia. The next day Pius issued a decree prohibiting parish priests from providing lists of names and requiring the priests to inform their parishioners that service in the French-sponsored Civic Guard was forbidden.[60] For the French this was the last straw.

On the evening of July 5, 1809, Cardinal Pacca learned from employees of the Quirinal Palace that French cavalry pickets had closed the streets leading to the pontifical residence. There were also rumors that French infantry had appeared on the bridges across the Tiber. Concerned that something was afoot, the cardinal delayed retiring to bed and insisted on accompanying Lieutenant Am Rhyn of the Swiss Guard as he made the rounds of the palace guard posts. Previously Pacca had directed the Swiss Guard to keep all gates and entries locked or barred at all times and never to open a gate wider than was necessary to allow a single person to squeeze past. By 3:30 on the morning of July 6, however, all remained quiet, and there was no movement in the piazza in front of the palace or in the streets visible from the palace gates and windows. Concluding that his concern had been premature, Pacca retired to his bedroom to salvage a few hours of sleep from what remained of the night. He had hardly settled into the bed when a frantic servant rushed into the room to announce that the French were inside the palace. Rushing to his window, which overlooked the interior gardens of the residence, the cardinal saw many men, armed and carrying torches, running about the grounds, searching for a door into the palace. There was no sign of the pope's guards.

Tiberio Pacca shared his uncle's rooms, and the cardinal immediately sent his half-dressed nephew to warn the Holy Father, who was sleeping on the other side of the pontifical apartments. Minutes later the secretary of state was hurrying in his dressing gown and slippers along the same corridors to the pope's side. The once quiet darkness was now broken with the yells of men and the sound of axes and sledgehammers crashing against doors. When he entered the papal suite, Pacca found Pius awake and surprisingly calm. The Holy Father dressed in his pontifical robes and walked to the room where he sometimes held audiences. The cardinal vicar of Rome, Antonio Despuig y Dameto, a few clerks from the Secretariat of State, and several servants had already assembled in the chamber. Kissing the pope's hand, Cardinal Despuig murmured, "So, here we are, Holy Father. Now is the time to ask for divine help so that you will behave well at this moment."[61] The sound of axes splintering wood had ceased, but there were voices on the other side of the door to the audience chamber. Pius walked to the center of the room, and the two cardinals took up protective positions on either side of their pontiff. In a quiet voice the pope ordered a servant to open the doors.[62]

French authorities had found the decision to seize the Holy Father easier than the choice of method. From spies inside the Quirinal Palace they were aware of the special security measures instituted by Cardinal Pacca, and they feared the political consequences of a botched raid. The few Swiss Guards inside the palace had earlier been stripped of their firearms and could not repulse a determined attack, but any resistance at all by the pope's guardians would certainly destroy the element of surprise, raise an alarm inside the residence and around the general neighborhood, and possibly buy time for the pope to escape or for enraged Romans to descend on the palace to save the Holy Father. The operation had to be quick and clean. General Miollis had consulted with General Etienne Radet, who would lead the kidnappers. Commander of the Roman gendarmeria, Radet was a curious figure who delighted in discussing theology, composed hymns to the Virgin Mary, and distributed to his police agents disquisitions on the nature and attributes of God. When not occupied in these edifying pursuits, the general chased other men's wives and secretly bought up (under various aliases) valuable ecclesiastical properties that he had confiscated in his official capacity as chief police administrator for Rome.[63] Miollis and Radet had settled on a plan that would involve an attack on the Quirinal Palace from four directions by a mixed force of French gendarmes and pro-French Romans. One group would seek to enter the long wing of the palace that extended along the road to the Porta Pia. A second party would use ladders to climb the wall adjacent to the Courtyard of the Bakery. A third group would use their ladders to enter the staff quarters. The main party, under General Radet's personal command, would gain access to the palace roof from an adjoining building and enter the papal residence through the tower on the left of the main gate.[64]

Late on the night of July 5 the raiding parties with their ladders, grappling hooks, and ropes gathered in a square a few blocks from the Quirinal Palace. To prevent citizens from rushing to the pope's defense, troops had been deployed along the streets leading to the palace. The raiders had planned to attack at 1:00 on the morning of July 6, but General Radet postponed the assault when a Swiss Guard officer was observed surveying the palace from the tower that was one of the attack objectives. By 2:30, however, the officer had departed and the assault began. The attack got off to an inauspicious start when the ladders of the main force under Radet splintered as the attackers tried to reach the roof, forcing the group to forsake its plan to scamper across the tiles and seize the palace tower. Improvising quickly, Radet abandoned any pretense of covert movements and simply ordered his men to storm the main gate. This maneuver, however, proved no more successful than the abortive rooftop escapade because the Swiss Guards had closed and barred the entrance. Alerted to danger by yells and the sounds of running feet from various parts of the palace, the guards refused to open the gate for anyone, particularly a large group of armed Frenchmen. General Radet was left standing, frustrated and impotent, in the Piazza dello Cavallo, and his annoyance was not relieved by the arrival of General Miollis, who had been monitoring the operation from a nearby building and, observing Radet's failure, had rushed to the scene to sort things out. Fortunately for the French generals, some of their other teams had better luck. The party assigned to climb the wall of the Courtyard of the Bakery had incurred casualties when a couple of its men had fallen while trying to surmount the wall. The remainder of the group, however, had made it into the courtyard, although when one man tried to climb another wall to the pope's apartments he found the windows of the pontifical suite chained from within. Focusing on the ground level, the raiders found a door, broke it down, and streamed into the palace, manhandling some servants who stood in their path. Another assault party had used ladders to reach the second-floor rooms of the pope's chamberlain and sacristan. Smashing the windows with their swords, they clambered into the rooms and then moved quickly to occupy other parts of the palace. Some of the raiders ran to the main gate, which was still being held by Swiss Guards. In accordance with their orders to refrain from active resistance, the halberdiers surrendered, and the attackers opened the gates to Radet's group, which was still standing in the piazza.[65] Radet rushed immediately to the pope's rooms. As the invaders flooded into the palace, Swiss Guards at various posts fell back on the papal apartments (one picket briefly coming under musket fire from a group of attackers), so when Radet reached the locked doors to the antechamber of the papal suite he encountered some forty guardsmen, armed with antique halberds and swords, drawn up behind their commandant, Colonel Karl Josef Leodegar Pfyffer von Altishofen. In conformity with the wishes of the Holy Father, Colonel Pfyffer von Altishofen solemnly surrendered his force without a fight, but he refused to assist the invaders in their effort to open the doors to the papal suite.[66]

When the pope's servants opened the doors, General Radet strode into the room followed by several officers. The intruders drew up in a line facing the Holy Father, but the normally voluble general now found himself at a loss for words. Pius saw no reason to help him. After a few moments of awkward silence, Radet found his voice and stated that he had a painful and disagreeable task to perform but that he was bound by oath to his duty. In the name of the Emperor Napoléon, he informed Pius that he must immediately renounce his temporal sovereignty over Rome and the Papal States; failure to do so would require the French officers to conduct the pontiff to General Miollis, who would specify a place of detention. Pius considered this ultimatum in silence and then replied calmly that since General Radet felt bound by his oath to obey the emperor's orders, he would certainly understand that the pope was similarly obligated by his oath to maintain all the rights of the papacy, secular as well as spiritual. "We have not the power to renounce that which does not belong to ourselves," Pius noted; "neither are we ourselves other than the administrators of the Roman Church and of her temporal dominion." When Radet acknowledged that the emperor owed the pope much, Pius retorted, "More than you know." The pope then asked if he was to enter custody alone, and the general replied that Cardinal Pacca could accompany him.[67]

Assuming that they would be taken to General Miollis's headquarters in the nearby Doria Palace, neither the Holy Father nor his cardinal secretary of state packed any bags. Surrounded by French gendarmes, they made their way to the principal courtyard and out the main gate to the piazza, which was full of French soldiers. Observed by a handful of palace attendants, they entered a waiting carriage and, blinds lowered and Radet perched on the coachman's bench, set off at a brisk trot, not for the Doria Palace but for the Porta Pia. Exiting Rome, they passed along the outer city walls, noticing cavalry detachments stationed along the roadway. When they stopped outside the Porta del Popolo to harness fresh horses, the passengers knew they had been tricked. The carriage, escorted by French cavalry, immediately headed north. Recognizing that they were headed into exile, Pius and Pacca reviewed the state of their finances and discovered that between them they had only a few coins. Displaying the coins in the palm of his hand, Pius laughed and said, "Look here. This is all I possess, all that remains of my principality."[68]

The French moved the pope north, first to the Certosa monastery outside Florence (where he was separated from Cardinal Pacca, who was carried off toward Bologna), then over the Alps to Grenoble; on to Valence; and back across the mountains to Savona, a town near Genoa, where, after a journey of some forty days, he was established in the bishop's residence, comfortable but under house arrest. For the next three years Pius refused to cooperate in the fiction that he was the honored guest of the emperor. He rejected the offer of a generous income, refused to go out from the residence or accept invitations from French officials, and declined to celebrate mass publicly.

Deliberately isolated from his advisers and the offices of ecclesiastical government in Rome (where the French expelled the cardinals, seized the archives, closed monasteries, and shipped to camps in Corsica and north Italy clergy who refused an oath of loyalty to the emperor while at the same time instituting any number of useful legal and social reforms, including equal rights for Jews), the pontiff had little work to perform. He passed the days of his exile in reading and prayer, living so simply that he did his own washing and mending, his only luxury prodigious quantities of snuff. Pius maintained this simplicity even after Napoléon in June 1812 forcibly relocated him to the chateau of Fontainebleau, where he steadfastly refused to use the fifteen carriages the emperor placed at his disposal.[69]

In March 1814, militarily pressed by the armies of the Sixth Coalition and angry at the betrayal of his brother-in-law, Joachim Murat, king of Naples, who had defected to the allies and sent his army to occupy Rome, Napoléon released Pius and allowed the pope to return to the Eternal City. The exiled pontiff returned to his capital on May 24, 1814, and began the process of reconstituting his domain and reasserting his temporal and spiritual powers. The restoration of the Papal States, ably negotiated at the Congress of Vienna by Cardinal Secretary of State Ercole Consalvi, involved not just the restitution of lost territories but also the return of traditional papal legal, political, and economic institutions to lands that for years had been governed (not always for the worse) by French laws and institutions. Cardinal Consalvi, a moderate reformer, hoped to maintain some of the innovations introduced by the French, particularly lay participation in administration, the rationalization of the courts, and the abolition of baronial privileges, but traditionalists and religious zealots in the restored papal administration resisted the abandonment of long-standing practices and any gesture toward modernization. Eventually the traditionalists would prevail, but for a time Consalvi used his position as trusted confidant of the pope and de facto chief minister of the papal government to embark on a program of reform. The list of things that needed to be done was vast and varied, from the rejuvenation of distressed finances to the regulation of clerical dress; from the recovery of alienated properties to the reopening of seminaries. Among the many issues demanding attention, the condition of the pontifical armed forces did not rank very high.

After the kidnapping of Pius VII and the incorporation of the Papal States into the French empire, the pontifical armed forces effectively ceased to exist as separate entities. Those units not abolished were incorporated into the French military or the militaries of French vassal states such as the Kingdom of Italy. With the restoration of papal power, the armed forces had to be reestablished. First the pope's household guards were reconstituted. Both the Noble Guard and the Swiss Guard had been disbanded by the French, but some of the discharged guardsmen had remained in Rome, and these individuals formed the basis for the new palace guard. When, on May 24, 1814, Pius VII reentered his capital in triumph, several Swiss were in uniform to meet the pontiff at the Porta del Popolo and escort him to the Quirinal Palace, but it would be two years before the number of halberdiers returned to the level necessary for the guard to perform its duties at the pontifical palaces. The Noble Guard recovered more quickly. When, in October 1814, the Holy Father visited his summer villa at Castel Gandolfo in the hills outside Rome, a full detachment of mounted Nobles escorted the papal carriage.[70] The household units proved easy to rebuild because their numbers were small and their functions limited and noncontroversial, but the pontifical army posed a bigger problem. Cardinal Consalvi did not want a return to the feebly trained, badly equipped, and poorly motivated army of the eighteenth century that was good only for ceremonial performances or static security duties. This army had been completely discredited by the events of the Napoléonic period. In its place the cardinal envisioned a larger and more mobile force, more martial in outlook, less bound to small garrisons and forts, and capable of operating in the field. By the time of his resignation as cardinal secretary upon the death of Pius VII (July 20, 1823) Consalvi had not advanced his vision of a new army very far, but he had managed to secure some important changes in the organization of the armed forces. He established a Presidenza delle Armi (Presidency of Arms) and subordinated to this office all military forces except the pope's palace guards, who reported to the master of the Apostolic Palace, and the handful of coast guard vessels that fell under the control of the treasurer general. The *presidenza* thus effectively became an embryonic armed forces ministry in the pontifical administration.

Consalvi also reformed and reorganized the pontifical police. During the eighteenth century the Papal States had been as badly policed as most other countries in Europe. A regular army unit, the Corsican Regiment (which by the late eighteenth century was Corsican only in name), had increasingly assumed responsibility for law enforcement, deploying its personnel in small detachments (five to ten men) in the countryside and somewhat larger stations (fifty to one hundred men) in the cities. Another force, the Company of Carabineers (known popularly as "the bandit chasers"), had policed the main roads across the Appenine mountain range. Both of these units had been suppressed during the Napoléonic period. Primary responsibility for policing fell to a force known popularly as *sbirri*, a slang term close in meaning to the American term "cops" but carrying a more derisive quality. Operating in long-established, guildlike "clans," the *sbirri* worked in towns and villages but were reviled by the people for their lack of discipline and routine extortions and abuses of authority. This force was further discredited when most of the agents collaborated with the French. Deciding against reconstituting any of these old services, Consalvi established a new unit, the pontifical *cara-*

binieri, with 2,280 men organized into mounted and foot companies. This paramilitary force, a significant step toward centralizing and professionalizing police services, would be responsible for public safety and internal security, and would operate in both rural and urban locales under the authority of the cardinal secretary of state, but could revert to military control during emergencies.[71]

Although useful, such modest changes had little influence on the pontifical army that emerged after the restoration. Fundamentally this army differed not at all from the discredited force that had performed so miserably during the Napoléonic period. There remained the same lack of discipline, inattention to training, and absence of martial spirit that had made its predecessor a byword for incompetence and unreliability. The absence of external military menace combined with the indifference of higher authorities to cloak temporarily the deficiencies of the pope's army, but the first appearance of armed threat would strip away that thin cloak. The outbreak of revolution provided just the occasion. After the death of Pius VII and the resignation of Consalvi, the throne of Saint Peter was occupied by a series of pious, well-intentioned men whose vision of the church and its temporal domains led them along an increasingly conservative path. During their pontificates the most traditionalist and intransigent elements of the pontifical administration, the so-called *zelanti* (zealots), were ascendant, and these reactionary elements turned their faces away from any hint of political, economic, or social modernization and reform. The *zelanti*, and the popes they served, had no intention of accommodating the modern world, and this resolve was manifested in a series of actions—ranging from the reconfinement of the Jews in the Roman Ghetto and strictures against attendance at scientific conferences to the prohibition of encores in theaters and of street games on Sundays—that sparked outrage or laughter across Europe. Their resistance to change, and the continued mismanagement, inefficiency, and inequalities that resulted from that resistance, encouraged political opposition on the part of a variety of groups that represented a range of political opinion and advocated an array of political goals but remained united by their hatred of the pontifical regime and their commitment to its demise. During the 1820s this resistance (which had its counterparts in the other principalities on the Italian peninsula) remained largely underground, although the pontifical police were aware of conspiratorial groups and took more or less effective measures to suppress the subversion. The true extent of the resistance and its popularity among the population became evident only in 1831, when most of the Papal States rose in revolt.

On February 2, 1831, the conclave of cardinals elected Bartolomeo Alberto Cappellari to succeed Pius VIII, whose pontificate had lasted only twenty months. The new pope, who took the name Gregory XVI, had hardly removed the papal tiara from his head when he faced a major crisis. On

February 3, 1831, the people of the Duchy of Modena swept away Archduke Francesco IV and established a provisional republican government. The news flashed across central Italy like a wildfire, sparking revolutionary conflagrations in the Duchy of Parma and the Papal States. On February 4, Bologna, the second city of the Papal States and the capital of the rich Romagna region, rose in revolt, and within days the rebellion spread to other towns in the papal domain. Everywhere papal authority collapsed at the first appearance of crowds in the streets. Senior authorities fled in unseemly haste, and most lower-level officials joined the rebels. The pontifical army simply disintegrated. At no point in the early days of the rebellion did any military units oppose the insurgents; indeed, many of the pope's soldiers defected to the rebels. These defectors formed the core of a "National Army" commanded by Giuseppe Sercognani, a former officer in the Napoléonic army in Italy, who marched on Rome, picking up recruits from towns along the way. By the last week in February Sercognani had reached the Tiber River valley, and his army now numbered some six thousand men, a column larger than the ragtag force of hastily mobilized civic guards and still loyal regulars who were available to defend Rome. A skirmish with papal regulars at Felice Bridge on February 27—the first time papal troops had stood and fought— inflicted only a few casualties on the insurgents but caused Sercognani to slow his advance. The rebel commander became even more cautious after his effort on March 8 to capture the provincial town of Rieti, 80 kilometers north of Rome, was foiled by Lieutenant Colonel Domenico Bentivoglia of the pontifical *carabinieri*, whose police detachment repulsed three rebel assaults.[72] In the end, however, Rome and the pope's temporal sovereignty in central Italy were saved not by the actions of a few pontifical military units but by the intervention of the Austrian army. In Vienna Prince Clemens von Metternich, the chief minister of the imperial government, who nurtured a visceral hatred of revolution, had observed the rebellions in Italy with increasing concern that the insurgencies might spread to Austrian-controlled territories in northern Italy or so destabilize the peninsula as to attract the intervention of other powers, particularly France. At the invitation of the papal government, Austrian troops invaded the rebellious territories, occupying Ferrara (March 7), Modena (March 9), Parma (March 13), and Bologna (March 21). The rebellion promptly collapsed, and the National Army dispersed without a fight.

The Austrian occupation lasted several months, during which time Vienna instigated an international conference in Rome at which the representatives of Austria, Britain, France, Prussia, and Russia proposed to Pope Gregory XVI a series of administrative and financial reforms for the Papal States that would assuage popular discontent and prevent another rebellion. In July 1832 Gregory announced his intention of implementing the suggested reforms. Concluding that the papacy could now reestablish control over its provinces, Austria withdrew its troops on July 15. Both the conclusion and the withdrawal proved premature. Rome lacked the will to attract popular support by implementing the reforms outlined in the great-power proposal (which quickly became a dead letter), and it lacked sufficient armed force to impose its authority in the absence of such support. After the defections of February 1831 the pontifical army could muster scarcely two thousand troops, and their competency and reliability were problematic. These troops were concentrated at Rimini, and they lacked the numbers to move into other towns in the rebellious Romagna. To avoid a breakdown in civil order once the Austrians departed, papal authorities in Rome were compelled to reactivate the local civic guards, most of whom had actively supported the recent rebellion and many of whom had joined the National Army. This act transferred civil power in the towns across the Romagna to antipapal elements who immediately acted as if they were free from papal authority, ignoring directives and decrees from Rome, refusing to pass tax revenues to Rome, and stripping papal insignia from uniforms and flags. The pope was sovereign in these territories only in name.[73]

Throughout the summer and fall of 1831 Cardinal Tommaso Bernetti, the pope's secretary of state, slowly recruited additional troops, and by December he had some five thousand men in Ferrara and Rimini under the overall command of Cardinal Giuseppe Albani, an elderly prelate who knew nothing of military affairs. Rome's intention was to dispatch these forces into the Romagna to disarm the civic guards and reimpose pontifical authority. To assist and advise the octogenarian cardinal, Prince Metternich had sent to Rimini Colonel Wenzeslaus Marschall, an experienced soldier-diplomat. When he arrived at Albani's Rimini camp on January 2, 1832, Marschall was shocked by the condition of the pontifical force. He found that the pope's soldiers lacked discipline and even the most rudimentary military skills and that the officers were "so incompetent, so lacking in all training, that they must be guided in everything."[74] The Austrian colonel instituted a two-week crash course in basic military skills to address the most glaring deficiencies, but the capabilities of the pontifical force remained uncertain when on January 19 it marched from Rimini toward Bologna. Its first test came outside Cesena, where it encountered a force of civic guards and, after a brief combat, sent it fleeing. Unfortunately, upon entering Cesena the victorious papal troops pillaged the town as if it were occupied enemy territory. Not even the churches were spared, and any inhabitants who protested were treated roughly. Colonel Marschall was horrified by this undisciplined behavior, but it was only with great difficulty that he got the troops out of the town and back on the road to Bologna. On January 21 the column peacefully entered Forlì, but that evening rumors circulated among the troops that the inhabitants were planning a treacherous attack on the unsuspecting soldiers. When, later that night, a patrol was fired upon, the truth of the rumors seemed confirmed.

The papal troops responded with an orgy of violence, racing through the streets and firing indiscriminately into houses. By the time officers restored order twenty citizens had been killed and many more wounded. Word of the outrage spread quickly across the region, and towns mobilized their civic guards and prepared to resist the advance of the pontifical army, fearing that opening their gates to the pope's soldiers would provide no guarantee against depredations and reprisals. Albani and Marschall quickly agreed that the army was in no condition to confront a country in arms, so the cardinal appealed for help to the Austrian commander in northern Italy. On January 24, 1832, ten thousand Austrian troops entered the Legations, peacefully occupying most of the important towns. The intervention, however, had serious political consequences for the papacy. Suspicious of Austrian intentions and concerned that Vienna was extending its influence over the Italian peninsula, France insisted on its right to participate in any occupation in order to affirm its interests in central Italy and maintain its international prestige. On February 23 a French expeditionary force landed at Ancona and occupied that papal port. The Austrians and French would maintain their respective occupations until 1838.[75]

The insurrections of 1831–1832 were a serious blow to the international reputation of the papacy. It was apparent to everyone (except the inhabitants of the pontifical palace) that disgust with papal administration was sufficiently pervasive in some regions of the pope's domain that elements of the population were prepared to revolt at the first opportunity. It was also evident that the pope was unable to maintain his authority over these regions without the intervention of other powers. As the pope's subjects found historical, legal, and religious justifications for the papacy's temporal power less compelling, that power increasingly seemed to rest on foreign bayonets, if only because the pope had no reliable bayonets of his own. The events of 1831–1832 revealed once again the complete inadequacy of the pontifical armed forces and the bankruptcy of a posture that asserted that the papacy was somehow above any need for armed force while relying on someone else's armed force to maintain temporal power. The hypocrisy was apparent to Prince Metternich, who was tired of securing the pope's throne at the cost of fueling revolution by perpetuating the abuses and mismanagement of the papal administration and irritating other powers, such as France. The Austrians pressed Pope Gregory and his advisers to reform the administration of the Papal States so as to ameliorate popular discontent and grievance, going so far as to send to Rome Giuseppe Maria Sebregondi, a senior official in the Austrian administration of Lombardy and Venetia, to advise the Holy Father on reform. Among his many efforts Sebregondi, seconded by Colonel Marschall, advocated the complete reorganization and reform of the pontifical armed forces to produce a professional and competent military capable of maintaining order and breaking the papacy's reliance upon foreign armies.

High on the list of recommendations was the employment of mercenaries, preferably Swiss because the Swiss had a long tradition of contributing soldiers to European armies, to compensate for the reluctance of any but the most dissolute and unemployable of the pope's subjects to join his army.[76]

Few of Sebregondi's reform initiatives bore fruit, and this was particularly true of his proposals for the pontifical military. Although the recent performance of the pontifical army and the fact that the pope's soldiers were on the verge of mutiny over delayed pay, threadbare uniforms, and harsh corporal punishments in disciplinary cases suggested the need for immediate attention, Cardinal Secretary of State Bernetti felt little urgency. His most important initiative was to secure from the Swiss Confederation permission to recruit in Switzerland two infantry regiments and an artillery company to stiffen the pope's indigenous troops.[77] In all other areas, Bernetti procrastinated. He appointed commissions to consider the issues, and in due course these commissions presented reports calling for superficial or cosmetic changes that did nothing to address the problems of recruitment, discipline, training, and professionalism. Colonel Marschall's reaction to one of the reports was derisory: "Music, plumes, pompoms, the braid on uniforms; these are the important subjects one will find there."[78] What the Austrian colonel failed to grasp was that Cardinal Bernetti and his colleagues in the papal administration were perfectly content with fancy braid, striking plumes, and good music. These were the attributes of a parade-ground army, adequate for display and ceremony, which was all Bernetti wanted from the army. He was actively opposed to the formation of a force sufficient in size, training, and equipment to protect the Papal States. Experience had taught him that the army was unreliable and nothing but a "useless burden" on the state because it consumed resources without providing benefits in return. A larger, better-equipped army would just be a more costly version of the old force, especially if that army relied on expensive mercenaries.[79] Bernetti preferred to ignore the army in favor of raising and arming a citizen militia from among the socially and religiously conservative peasantry. This militia, named "Centurions" by the cardinal, would be cheaper because its volunteers would wear no uniforms and receive pay only when mobilized for service, and it would be more reliable because the members would join from loyalty and attachment to the Holy Father and the conservative order. In practice the Centurions (and a sister paramilitary organization known as the Papal Volunteers) proved a greater liability than the regular army they were intended to displace. Loosely organized, responsible only to the cardinal secretary of state, and beyond supervision by local officials, these auxiliaries, little more than irregulars, all too often degenerated into armed bands that used their authority and privileged status to abuse the populace for personal profit or vendetta.[80] The Centurions and Papal Volunteers were suppressed in 1836 by Bernetti's successor as cardinal secretary of state, Luigi Lambruschini, but during their existence they distracted attention and resources from the regular armed forces and further discredited papal authority in the eyes of the population.

Though in general no less suspicious of reform than his predecessor, Cardinal Lambruschini had a more pragmatic view of the pontifical army. If the Papal States ever wanted to be rid of the Austrian and French occupation troops, it had to be able to maintain order in its territories, and if it did not want to rely on irregulars such as the Centurions to guarantee that order, it needed a reliable military force. Lambruschini understood the importance of a serious army (no small attribute in an administration indifferent to military affairs) and in his limited way tried to build such an army. In 1844 he promulgated a new regulation outlining the structure and size of the pontifical armed forces. This regulation placed the Presidency of Arms under the cardinal secretary of state, who served as the president of a council of six members, each responsible for particular aspects of military administration such as accounts, personnel, discipline, and matériel. The plan envisioned a force of 12,679 men organized into nine infantry battalions (including four Swiss battalions); a cavalry regiment; an artillery regiment; two regiments of paramilitary police; a corps of engineers; a naval service; and various service and depot units responsible for training, sanitation, the military prison, and invalids. Operational control was in the hands of a general staff of senior officers. The plan was unremarkable and in the context of the papacy's general neglect of military affairs actually had much to recommend it. It identified a force level that increased the size of the military and described a balanced force representing the various arms, including components, such as the engineer corps, that had been previously absent from the army. The plan centralized administrative authority in the cardinal secretary and operational control in a military staff.[81] These were all appropriate gestures toward change, but, as had been the case with previous efforts to improve the pontifical armed services, they were little more than gestures. Well-meaning and conscientious administrators, such as Lambruschini, readily created armies on paper but found it harder to follow through with the systematic attention and support (particularly financial support) necessary to make those armies a reality. The result, inevitably, was a gap between vision and practice. The plan of 1844, for example, projected a military force of 12,679 men but said nothing about how the pontifical army, historically hard-pressed to meet even lower force levels, would reach that projected size. The grandly named "corps of engineers" seemed impressive on paper, but it hardly improved the capabilities of the army because the corps contained only eleven men. The discrepancy between vision and practice was magnified by a tendency in the papal bureaucracy to equate military reorganization (changing the number and types of units and the administrative relationships among those units) with military reform (changing the culture and performance of units). Reorganization may contribute to reform, but by itself it does not guarantee reform. In the Napoléonic period and the decades immediately following the restoration of the Papal States, the problems of the papal military were those of quality, not quantity; application, not appearance. The superficial though earnest plans of Cardinal Lambruschini and his predecessors did not adequately address those problems. Certainly the perpetually understrength pontifical army needed additional resources (additional infantry battalions, additional cavalry squadrons, additional artillery batteries), but even more than extra soldiers, it needed better soldiers. The pontifical army of the Napoléonic and restoration periods was not the worst army in Europe because it was the smallest or the most disorganized. The papal troops who ran from the Senio River in panic and surrendered Ancona without resistance in 1797, who melted away in the face of invading French troops in 1798 and 1808, who went over to the insurgents in 1831 were not grossly outnumbered but grossly outclassed—sometimes in equipment and training, always in spirit, confidence, discipline, and purpose. The popes had armed men in uniforms, but they had no soldiers. To become soldiers these men needed something no reorganization plan could give them; something they could find only in the exhaustion of long marches, the privations of rough bivouacs, and the noise and smoke of battlefields—something like professional pride, something like a cause worth fighting for.

CHAPTER 2

A Cause Worth Fighting For

No newly elected pontiff of the nineteenth century was as well received by his people as Giovanni Maria Mastai-Ferretti. Within weeks of his election on June 16, 1846, the new pope, who took the name Pius IX, embarked on a series of initiatives that seemed to signal a deliberate break from reaction and tradition and an embrace of reform and modernity. Outgoing, friendly, and quick to laugh, Pius IX made himself more accessible than his predecessors, particularly the widely unpopular Gregory XVI. Although those predecessors had certainly cared about the well-being of their subjects, they had rarely appeared to care. Pius's early initiatives promised to make significant changes to economic, political, and social conditions in the Papal States. To set an example of frugality in an administration whose finances were always distressed, he reduced expenditures in the papal palace. He lowered the cost of salt, initiated plans for the construction of railroads and telegraph lines and the improvement of agriculture, lifted the prohibition on participation by citizens of the Papal States in foreign scientific conferences, announced a commission to reform the judicial system, and proclaimed an amnesty that allowed the release of political prisoners and the return of political exiles. Such reforms were received joyously by the citizenry, who chose to see in the new pontiff an "Apostle of Liberty" who, unlike his unpopular predecessors, sympathized with their desire for political, economic, and social transformation in the States of the Church.[1] In fact, Pius was a conservative reformer who sincerely wanted to better the lives of his subjects by introducing prudent, though modest, changes that would ameliorate the gravest injustices and abuses in society, increase the efficiency and honesty of administration, and improve economic conditions without weakening the status and authority of the papal administration or upsetting the established social structure. He certainly had no desire to compromise or dilute the traditional sovereign rights and powers of the pope by sharing those rights and powers with popular institutions.[2] He was neither a democrat nor a populist but saw himself as a conservator of papal monarchy. His people, however, saw him differently.

Pius's subjects received each reform with cheers of approval and praise and then called for more. Rather than satisfying popular expectations, the reforms merely raised them. To his growing alarm, the pope discovered that, once begun, change is often hard to control and may lead down unexpected (and undesirable) paths, but he was reluctant to disappoint his subjects—

especially when those subjects were demonstrating in the streets. By the spring of 1847 the popular pressure for change was increasingly focusing on reform of political institutions to make them open to participation by laymen and responsive to popular influence. In reaction to this pressure, in April 1847 Pius instituted a Council of State with representatives from every province of the Papal States to advise him on administrative policies. Though it had power neither to initiate nor to veto policies, it was hailed by the Roman crowd as a prototype for a legislative assembly and as a precursor to provincial and municipal councils. In June the pontiff established a Council of Ministers to discuss all important initiatives before they reached the Holy Father for decision. Then, in July, Pius reluctantly acceded to a demand from the Roman populace for the rejuvenation of the civic guard (a venerable city institution that had fallen into neglect) to supplement the pontifical army and police.[3]

These concessions did little to slow rising expectations or discourage the public meetings and demonstrations that wildly applauded the Holy Father for his latest initiative before demanding further concessions. Many senior cardinals opposed the pope's concessions from concern that they would inevitably lead to a form of republican government that would be incompatible with the papacy's temporal and spiritual authority. Prelates, moreover, were not the only critics who observed the course of events in Rome with alarm. In Austria Prince Metternich, still directing affairs of state, worried that the pope had lost control of events and that the popular agitation for republican liberties would lead to increasing instability in the Papal States. Such instability would bode ill strategically and politically for Austrian interests in northern Italy, where the conservative Habsburg monarchy exercised sovereignty over Lombardy and the Veneto. In the recent past Austria had intervened to suppress revolution in the Papal States, and Metternich, anticipating that a similar occasion was on the horizon, decided to enhance Austria's military presence in the papal domain. Under the terms of the Congress of Vienna, which had arranged the borders and regimes of post-Napoléonic Europe, Austria had the right to maintain a garrison in the fortress of the papal city of Ferrara. In August 1847 Metternich, without notifying Rome beforehand, sent a column of more than eight hundred troops across the pope's borders to reinforce that garrison. This provocation outraged Pius and inflamed public opinion in the Papal States, where people suspected that the Austrians were preparing once again to crush political reform by military intervention.[4]

The suspicions of the pope's subjects were part of an increasingly prevalent anti-Austrian sentiment, marked by protests, boycotts, and proclamations, in central and northern Italy, where the Habsburgs were despised as foreign occupiers. The sentiment itself was not new, but the determination to do something about it was. Two forces propelled this will to action. The first was a growing sense of nationalism, particularly among the political, intellectual, and social elites, who articulated a vision of an Italy not only free from foreign domination but politically united rather than fragmented into small and weak principalities. The second was a desire by one of those principalities, the Kingdom of Sardinia-Piedmont, to capitalize on this resurgent nationalism to serve its political and dynastic interests by fostering and leading a movement to expel Austria from the peninsula. The king, Carlo Alberto, would soon have an opportunity to advance both of these purposes.

In Europe 1848 would become the year of revolutions. In January a revolt in Sicily forced King Ferdinando to concede a constitution. By the second week in February the popular clamor for constitutional government had spread across the Italian peninsula. In Sardinia-Piedmont King Carlo Alberto promised a constitution, as did the Grand Duke of Tuscany. In Rome Pius, who had already promulgated more reforms than his last ten predecessors combined, was constrained by popular demand to publish in March a constitution providing for a cabinet open to laymen and councils, some of whose members would be elected, that could propose legislation. Meanwhile, in February a brief uprising in Paris overthrew King Louis Philippe and established a republic. Perhaps inspired by the French, student-led demonstrations in Vienna on March 13 compelled the Emperor Ferdinand to dismiss Prince Metternich and appoint a liberal cabinet. The unprecedented events in Vienna, the capital of conservatism, sparked protests and uprisings across the Habsburg Empire. On March 18 Milan, the capital of Austrian Lombardy, revolted, and in five days of street fighting (the famous Cinque Giornate) forced Field Marshal Josef Radetzky to withdraw with his troops from the city. The Milanese appealed to Sardinia-Piedmont for support, and on March 23 Carlo Alberto, seeing an opportunity to strike at the despised Austrians and seize the leadership of the nationalist movement, sent his army into Lombardy.

The First War of Italian Independence would throw the papacy into political and military crisis. The conflict with Austria was enormously popular (especially when the Piedmontese scored some early victories), and political leaders across the peninsula could not resist the call for all Italians, not just the Piedmontese and Lombards, to join the effort to expel foreign occupiers from Italian soil. The Eternal City did not escape the war mania, and the pope came under extreme pressure, from his cabinet ministers as well as from the Roman populace, to ally politically and militarily with King Carlo Alberto and send an army to fight alongside the Piedmontese. Pius resisted this pressure because he did not believe that, as a spiritual father and leader of all Catholics, Austrian as well as Italian, he should assume the mantle of warlord and send troops to fight any of his children. He did not, however, consistently communicate an inflexible antiwar position to his officials or his people, perhaps because his resolve was not firm (if a pope should not attack the lands and people of another country, could he fight to defend his own lands and subjects?) or because he hoped to placate public opinion with militant gestures short of war (after the Austrian reinforcement of Ferrara he had sent a military force to observe the Austrians but not to act against them, and when the Piedmontese went to war against Austria he allowed fund-raisers to collect money in Rome on behalf of the national war effort).[5]

The tension between the roles of temporal and spiritual leadership that would afflict Pius throughout the crises of 1848 was especially apparent in his attitude toward the pontifical armed forces. The several efforts at reorganization and reform since the restoration of 1815 may have marginally improved the capabilities of the army (although they had done little for the navy), but fundamentally it remained a third-rate force orientated primarily toward ceremonial service, fortress duties, and internal security and policing. In 1847 the regular army included four battalions of Swiss mercenary infantry, six battalions of "indigenous" infantry (i.e., battalions raised in the Papal States), sixteen pieces of field artillery organized into two batteries (one indigenous, the other Swiss), five squadrons of cavalry (indigenous), and two companies of engineers (indigenous). Though separate from the army, the carabinieri (the paramilitary police) were also available for combat duty. Excluding support and auxiliary units, the regular pontifical army of 1847 could theoretically put into the field a combat force of approximately 7,000 infantry, 800 cavalry, and 16 cannons. In practice, however, the army was understrength; had little experience operating in units above the battalion or squadron level; and deployed the bulk of its troops, much as in the eighteenth century, across the Papal States in small garrisons and detachments, some of only company size.[6]

The capabilities of the pope's navy remained even more modest than those of his army. Ironically, it was the navy, little esteemed even within the pontifical armed forces, that conducted the only operation to bring credit to those armed forces during the pontificate of Gregory XVI. In 1823 the venerable basilica of Saint Paul Outside the Walls had been destroyed in an accidental fire, and a massive restoration project was immediately set in hand. As a gesture of friendship to the Holy Father, the Ottoman viceroy of Egypt, Mehmet Ali, offered alabasters from historic quarries east of the Nile River to be shaped into columns to support the roof of the rebuilt basilica, but the papacy would have to arrange delivery of the massive slabs. Under the command of Alessandro Cialdi, a hydrologist of European reputation and a lieutenant colonel in the pontifical navy (which used army ranks), a squadron of three armed papal ships (whose crews included a naturalist, an artist, and three engineers) sailed from Civitavecchia on September 21, 1840, reached Alexandria on November 22, and then sailed up the Nile to Cairo. While waiting for the alabasters to arrive at Cairo, Cialdi took one of his ships upriver as far as Aswan, showing the papal flag where it had never been seen before. Unfortunately, Egypt was experiencing a plague epidemic, and four sailors of the papal navy died before the small squadron returned to the Papal States with its cargo of precious alabaster in August 1841.[7] Despite this successful mission, by 1847 the pontifical navy had practically ceased to exist as a military force. At the port of Civitavecchia the ministry of arms had two ships: the schooner *San Pietro* (the only ship from the Egyptian cruise that remained in commission), which was disarmed and laid up, and a small gunboat. The customs service of the ministry of finance controlled four old coast guard vessels and several launches divided between Civitavecchia and Ancona, but these were of little military value; indeed, the coast guard units were in such poor condition that they rarely put to sea. The finance ministry also ran several unarmed steamers on the Tiber, and these were the most modern ships under the papal flag. They had been constructed in England under the supervision of Alessandro Cialdi. Upon their completion, Cialdi had sailed the ships to Rome via the French canal system and French and Italian coastal waters. They were employed as government transports carrying passengers and matériel along the navigable portion of the Tiber between Rome and the Felici Bridge, approximately 112 kilometers upstream from the Eternal City.[8]

In early 1847, in response to petitions from several citizens' groups concerned about the poor state of the army, Pope Pius established a special military commission under the chairmanship of Monsignor Lavinio De Medici Spada, the minister of arms. Almost immediately Monsignor Spada retired, and without its designated leader the special commission never met, a failure of initiative typical of the listless papal bureaucracy. It eventually got down to work in the fall of 1847 after the appointment of one of its original members, Prince Francesco Barberini, as chairman. In January 1848 Pius accepted the commission's recommendation that the papacy contract for the services of experienced senior officers from abroad to advise on the reorganization, training, and direction of the pontifical army, an implicit admission that the papal officer corps was not up to the task. By the spring of 1848 two officers from the Piedmontese army, Lieutenant Colonel Isidoro Rovero (infantry) and Major Carlo Otto Wagner (cavalry), were attached as advisers to the pontifical army with the rank of colonels.

As for specific reforms, prospects for significant change were dim owing to the perpetually troubled state of papal finances, but the special commission did not hesitate to add another entry to the long line of army reform proposals that cluttered the shelves of the archives. In February 1848, as the prospect of a national war against Austria loomed large on the horizon, the special military commission submitted its final recommendations. Judging correctly that any army divided into dozens of small detachments and scattered across the countryside could not be an effective military force, the commission proposed to concentrate the army by rejoining detached companies to their battalions and combining battalions into regiments. These larger units would be stationed in a small number of strategic locations. The commission also recommended the closure of all the antiquated coastal towers (some now three hundred years old), which had long lost any military utility they may have once possessed and now served only to divert soldiers from more useful assignments. To meet the demands of modern warfare the commission called for the creation of a military academy to prepare junior officers and the expansion and improvement of the field artillery and the army engineers. Finally, it proposed to triple the size of the army, to twenty-five thousand men, and recommended the institution of conscription for men between the ages of eighteen and twenty-five if voluntary enlistments were insufficient to raise the force to that level. The army, which was not completely blind to its deficiencies, embraced the reform plan enthusiastically, so much so that on March 14, 1848, a delegation of officers representing all branches of the service called on Prince Pietro Odescalchi, successor to Prince Barberini as chairman of the commission, to express their pleasure at the proposals. The military commission circulated copies of the plan among the members of the Council of State, which would vote on the proposals, and the commissioners were encouraged when the councilors expressed no explicit doubt or opposition. Surprise and disappointment were, therefore, all the greater when on March 18 the Council of State rejected without explanation the entire reform plan. If the papacy did indeed go to war, it would have to do so with the army it already had.[9]

Pope Pius may have had reservations concerning the propriety of a pontiff going to war, but he was prepared to countenance the military mobilization and deployment of his army to the edges of a war zone. On March 23, 1848, the day that King Carlo Alberto's troops marched into Austrian Lombardy, the pope's minister of arms appointed General Giovanni Durando, a sometime officer in the army of Sardinia-Piedmont who had also been in Portuguese and Spanish military service, commander of a "Corps of Observation" that would be deployed to the northern borders of the Papal States. The next day the first elements of this new command, two battalions of regular infantry and two squadrons of cavalry, departed Rome for Bologna. Separately, General Durando rushed ahead, picking up detachments of regulars at towns along the line of march. To reinforce the small regular army, the ministry of arms on March 27 ordered the mobilization of the civic guard and the formation of a "Legion of Volunteers." There had already been demonstrations calling on the papal government to mobilize the population behind the national cause by arming the citizens, so the response to the appeal for volunteers was overwhelming. Inspired by nationalist zeal, resentment of the Austrians, and above all certainty that their great reforming pontiff, Pio Nono (Pius IX), would bless and support a cause that would liberate and unify Italians across the peninsula, men of all social classes rushed to enlist under the yellow-and-white papal flag. No one could remain safely home, close to hearth and family, when Italy and the Holy Father called their sons to duty. Years later one such son, Demetrio Diamilla-Muller, a student of mathematics and physics whose father was a functionary in the pontifical palace, recalled how he and his friends, "driven by fanaticism and enthusiasm for Pius IX [and] moved by feelings of patriotism born and nurtured in young hearts without discussion" thought only of fighting for pope and country.[10] These eager volunteers joined the civic guards to form the "Roman Legion" under the command of General Giuseppe Ferrari.

The pope's ambivalence about the use of force was reflected in uncertainty about what the regulars and volunteers were supposed to do once they reached the northern provinces. Although Cardinal Giacomo Antonelli, chief of the pope's council of ministers, told the cardinal legates (governors) of Bologna and Ferrara in late March that the troops would not cross the River Po, he seemed to have delayed transmitting actual orders to that effect to General Durando. Aside from a vague injunction to ensure "the security and tranquility of the State," the pope's military commanders received no military orders or plans from Rome.[11] Were they merely to defend the borders (which were not threatened by anyone), or were they to join the war against the Austrians? Were they intended to be a symbolic token of the papacy's implicit support for the national cause, or were they to make an operational contribution to that cause? Would they act alone or in conjunction with the Piedmontese? In the absence of firm direction from Rome, General Durando seized the initiative. As a result of decisions at the Congress of Vienna, Austrian troops maintained garrisons in two papal cities: Ferrara and Comacchio. Durando decided to neutralize these garrisons. He ordered the garrison of the papal city of Ravenna to dispatch a force to secure the Austrian troops stationed in Comacchio. Two companies of Swiss infantry, supported by a detachment of pontifical dragoons, marched from Ravenna and reached Comacchio, 28 kilometers to the north, on the evening of March 29. The next day the Austrian garrison of 140 men surrendered without firing a shot. The prisoners were placed on board the papal revenue cutter *Annibale* and repatriated to the Austrian port of Trieste. In the meantime, Durando had dispatched a detachment of Swiss infantry and a half battery of field artillery supported by a battalion of Bolognese civic guards to secure the surrender of the Austrian garrison at Ferrara. These Austrians, unlike their compatriots at Comacchio, were not inclined to surrender, but papal authorities avoided hostilities by obtaining from the Austrian commandant a commitment to keep his troops inside the fortress and to refrain from any movements or operations beyond the citadel's walls in return for a promise from local authorities to provision the garrison.[12]

These operations, particularly the forced capitulation of the garrison at Comacchio, could be interpreted as acts of war, and they indicated that, in the absence of explicit orders to the contrary from Rome, papal commanders were inclined to adopt a belligerent and aggressive policy. General Durando did not hide his intentions from Rome. On April 3 he informed the ministry of arms (formerly the *presidenza delle armi*) that the Piedmontese army was preparing to move against the Austrians and that he was considering pushing his troops across the Po and into the Veneto, a region that was part of Austrian-controlled Italy.[13] He asked Rome to send him shallow draft vessels suitable for river movements, and he specifically requested the services of Alessandro Cialdi to command such vessels. General Durando's intentions were manifest in an order of the day that he issued to all troops on April 5. The pope's commander told his troops that their task was to liberate their compatriots from Austrian rule and called on them to go into battle wearing a cross on their uniform coats. In a further echo of the medieval crusades, he ended his proclamation with the words "Our battle cry will be 'God wills it!'" The impact of this provocative proclamation on the army and the civilian population was electric, in part because many assumed that it was a call to war and that the general was speaking on behalf of the pope. On all sides there were calls to march against the Austrians, and in Ferrara the governor had to take precautions to ensure the safety of the Austrian garrison interned in the fortress. The impact on papal authorities in Rome was no less immediate. The ministry of war had had indications that its commander in the north intended to adopt a more aggressive posture (why else would he request river-crossing craft?), but these indications seem not to have reached the Holy Father, who was surprised by Durando's order of the day. Papal authorities were constrained to distance Pius, who was furious at the general for implying that the pope had blessed the war against Austria, from the militant words of the proclamation. The *Gazzetta di Roma,* the newspaper that served as the mouthpiece of the pontifical administration, published a disclaimer that noted, "When the Pope wishes to declare his sentiments he will speak for himself and not use the voice of subordinates."[14]

Suitably chastised, Durando hastened to genuflect before the pope's authority, but the rhetorical slap on the wrist did little to dampen his belligerency. In the first weeks of April he continued to increase his force, adding regulars from various garrisons in the northern Papal States, shifting units from Bologna toward Ferrara, 46 kilometers farther north and near the River Po, and collecting supplies, including a shipment of French rifles transported from Civitavecchia to Ancona by the Tiber steamship *Roma.* The *Roma* had been diverted to military service under the command of Alessandro Cialdi, who, though most recently employed as director of navigation on the Tiber, retained his rank as lieutenant colonel in the pontifical navy. The general could only have assumed that Rome quietly approved his plans for a more aggressive posture when, in response to his earlier request for ships to transport his regulars across the Po, the ministry of arms (after consultations with the ministry of finance) placed at his disposal Cialdi and a flotilla of small craft, including the *Roma*, the revenue cutters *Annibale* and *Cesare*, and several customs launches.[15] In a clear sign that he anticipated military operations beyond the papal frontier, he sent a liaison officer to consult on common measures with authorities in Venice, which had revolted against Austrian occupation and declared its independence as the reborn Venetian Republic. The Venetians responded by sending to Durando's headquarters one of their own officers along with 150 Congreve rockets and three experts to instruct the papal troops in their use.[16]

Meanwhile, General Ferrari had marched his Roman Legion, including a young aide-de-camp, Captain Demetrio Diamilla-Muller, north from Rome, picking up civic guards and volunteers from towns along the way. It was a triumphal progress. "There was joy on the face of every volunteer," Captain Diamilla-Muller recalled. "They went to war as if to a carnival."[17] At every stop the pope's citizen-soldiers were feted by the townspeople, who refused to accept payment for food, drink, and lodging, while local notables hosted dinner parties and soirees for officers. So many new volunteers enlisted as the force moved north that officers had to form a second and then a third Roman Legion. Never had military service been so popular among the pope's citizens. On April 10 the force, now known as the Volunteer Division, reached Ancona, where it stopped for a few days to reorganize, rest, and refit. From the start, deficiencies in equipment and discipline bedeviled Ferrari's command as it tried to shape enthusiastic but ill-prepared civilians into a military force. There were not enough uniforms or guns (well into April many volunteers still wore their civilian clothes, and some were armed only with pikes), and training was dispensed along the line of march by veterans of the Napoléonic Wars. Many who rushed to the colors in the first wave of patriotic fervor were ill-suited for military life and resistant to command and discipline. Before moving from Ancona to Bologna on April 14, Ferrari found it necessary to place in custody and transport to the prison in Spoleto some two hundred unruly men.[18] Now that the first rush of youthful enthusiasm had passed, the more thoughtful of the pope's volunteers began to feel anxious about the future. Captain Diamilla-Muller was one who was increasingly concerned. "We were entering into the campaign carelessly and without a prepared plan, against a major military power," he noted. "Will our army be able to win?"[19]

Still without orders from Rome, General Durando decided to send two of his staff officers to the headquarters of King Carlo Alberto on the Mincio River near Mantua to discover Piedmont's plans and consider the possibility of joint operations. Although Marshal Radetzky had fallen back in the face of the insurrections in Lombardy and the Veneto and the military intervention of Piedmont, by early April his army had recovered its footing and was preparing to take the offensive. From the Friuli region in the northeast General Laval Nugent de Westenrath advanced his army into the Veneto, brushing

aside resistance from local volunteer units and moving to link up with the
army of Radetzky, which was holding within the fortresses of the Quadrilateral, the system of fortifications bounded by Verona, Legnago, Mantua, and
Peschiera. The combined Austrian force would pose a serious threat to the
Piedmontese army, which had remained surprisingly inactive after its initial advance. General Nugent's offensive alarmed the newly proclaimed and
militarily exposed Venetian Republic and discomfited Piedmontese headquarters, which feared a conjunction of two Austrian armies. To support the
hard-pressed Venetians and block Nugent's movement, it was advisable to
push troops into the Veneto, but the Piedmontese were reluctant to advance
any of their units for that purpose, particularly because Radetzky stood in the
way. The pontifical army, however, was closer to the theater. When, therefore, Durando's staff officers returned from Piedmontese headquarters they
carried a request from Carlo Alberto that the papal general cross the Po and
advance to Ostiglia some 50 kilometers northwest of Ferrara on the Austrian
side of the river in anticipation of action in support of the Piedmontese army.
On April 19 Durando began to move his units to the right (papal) bank of the
Po. On April 22 the general and his staff embarked for Ostiglia on the *Roma*,
which had steamed upriver from the Gulf of Venice; the following day the
ship repeated the voyage to Ostiglia with the first papal regulars, two Swiss
infantry battalions. Other elements of Lieutenant Colonel Cialdi's river flotilla moved additional papal regulars across the river at Polesella downstream
from Ferrara. On April 26, again in response to directives from the Piedmontese high command, which seems to have been considering an offensive toward Verona with the pontifical army operating on the right flank, Durando
began to advance his forces toward Padua.[20] The pontifical army was now
acting offensively on Austrian territory in conjunction with the Piedmontese,
but it wasn't clear that it was acting in conjunction with Rome.

The papal administration remained ambivalent over the papacy's appropriate role in a war that was evolving into a national struggle against Austria.
Pius continued to believe that his spiritual office did not allow him to join
the war, while his more bellicose ministers argued that his responsibilities as
a temporal ruler required immediate belligerency. Efforts to find a formula
that would overcome the pope's scruples, such as a proposal that he evade direct responsibility by allowing his council of ministers to declare war without
requiring him personally to endorse the action, went nowhere. On April 25,
by which time pontifical regulars were already across the Po, the council of
ministers formally concluded that national circumstances and public opinion
required entry into the war. At a meeting with his cardinals on April 29 the
pope announced that although he could not prevent his subjects from joining
the military effort against Austria, he could not as a spiritual father declare
war against any of his spiritual children, an argument he repeated on May 11
in an open letter to the people of Rome. The pope's position caused a politi-

cal crisis in Rome as his ministry promptly resigned and his people agitated in the streets.[21] Surprisingly, the declaration of April 29 did not change the behavior of the pontifical army, perhaps because the confusion and vacillation in policy in Rome was reflected in mixed signals to its military units in the north, or perhaps because the pope had lost control of his own soldiers. Pius would not wage war, but he would not or could not stop his subjects, including his ministry of war and his army, from doing so. Two weeks before Pius reaffirmed for his cardinals his refusal to declare war, a papal representative (dispatched, perhaps, by the pope's chief minister, Cardinal Giacomo Antonelli, who was searching for a middle ground between the Holy Father and his militant ministers) was at Piedmontese headquarters arranging to place the papal army at the disposal of King Carlo Alberto. By April 17 the ministry of war in Rome had informed General Durando that he was henceforth under the operational control of the Piedmontese.[22] Whatever the feelings of the Holy Father, the commander-in-chief of the pontifical army was marching into battle.

To block General Nugent, who was advancing southward, and to respond to Venetian appeals for support against the Austrians, the Piedmontese high command ordered Durando deeper into the Veneto. From Padua the papal general advanced to Treviso, where he established his headquarters. On May 4, after receiving reports that General Nugent was advancing on Bassano, he moved to block the Austrians by marching his force northwest from Treviso toward Montebelluna and then beyond to Quero before falling back several kilometers to Pederobba. Meanwhile, he had ordered General Ferrari and his Volunteer Division to hurry forward in support. By the end of April Ferrari had moved most of his volunteers from Bologna to Ferrara, but his division continued to suffer from problems of discipline and morale. Before leaving Bologna the commanders of some of the volunteer units had presented their general with a petition (to be forwarded to Rome) demanding a clear expression of the pope's attitudes and intentions regarding the national war against Austria and affirming the importance of a papal blessing on the effort to liberate Italy from foreign occupation. The ministry of arms answered curtly that volunteers had the right neither to petition the government nor to presume to direct the actions of their sovereign, a reply that was not likely to raise the spirits of the pope's citizen-soldiers.[23] The departure from Bologna had been further delayed when the 1st and 2nd Battalions of the so-called Roman Legion refused to march until they had received promised uniforms and equipment. Once in Ferrara the troops exhibited further signs of discontent and indiscipline, and the Roman Legion remained the center of unrest. The officers of the legion, joined by their counterparts in the University Battalion formed from Roman students, ignored the chain of command and sent another petition directly to the ministry of arms in Rome, this one appealing for a formal declaration of war against Austria. The petitioners were motivated not only by militant nationalism but also by a concern that without such a declaration the Austrians might execute captured papal volunteers as *francs tireurs*. It is not clear that Rome, distracted by the political controversy surrounding the pope's antiwar statement of April 29, even bothered to reply.[24]

By May 7 Durando had intelligence that the Austrians had occupied Belluno and Feltre and that Nugent's advance parties were operating around Quero on the upper Piave River, only a few kilometers from the papal general's main force of regulars at Pederobba. Durando believed that the Austrian general had two choices: He could continue south beyond Quero along the Piave in an attempt to break into the Venetian plain and the lower river below Cornuda, capture Treviso, and then wheel west to capture Vicenza and link up with Marshal Radetzky around Verona, or he could move southwest from Feltre to take Bassano before turning west across the Alpine foothills to fall upon Vicenza from the north. Durando suspected that Austrian movements toward Quero were a feint to distract the pontifical army from the main advance, which would be toward Bassano. In anticipation of such a move, the papal general decided to shift his regular division to Bassano, 26 kilometers west of Pederobba, from which position it could move south to meet any Austrian deployment from Quero toward Montebelluna and Treviso or north to meet a more likely Austrian march on Bassano from Feltre. To provide early warning of the latter maneuver, Durando sent an advance detachment of troops under Colonel Alessandro Casanova to Primolano, 28 kilometers north of Bassano, on the main road west out of Feltre. To create a blocking force in the event that the Austrians tried to break out into the plains and advance on Treviso, the papal commander-in-chief ordered General Ferrari, who by this time had marched his volunteers farther north, first to Padua and then to Treviso, to take steps to ensure the security of the lower Piave while positioning his forces to block any Austrian advance down the Piave by relocating his command to Montebelluna and pushing troops up the road toward Quero, 19 kilometers farther north. Along with his orders, Durando sent a squadron of regular dragoons (about one hundred troopers) and a half battery of artillery (two guns) to bolster Ferrari's volunteers.[25]

On the morning of May 8 General Durando, who was outside Bassano, learned that local civic guards had clashed with a detachment of Austrians probing west from Feltre. This intelligence confirmed the general's conviction that General Nugent's main movement would be toward Bassano and that any Austrian maneuvers around Quero would be nothing but feints to draw papal troops away from the main line of attack.[26] At Montebelluna, where he had just established his headquarters, General Ferrari knew that the Austrians were in the area, but he had no indications of their movements or intentions. It was a surprise, therefore, when, just as the general's staff was sitting down to a late lunch, a messenger galloped into headquarters with news that papal outposts north of Cornuda had been attacked and were falling back on that village, 8 kilometers north of Montebelluna. The attack caught the pontifical army dispersed across a discontinuous front of some 49 kilometers. The bulk of the army, Durando's Regular Division, was at Bassano. A majority of Ferrari's volunteers, approximately 3,800 men, were 27 kilometers away around Montebelluna, while the remaining 2,500 volunteers were deployed at various locations south of Montebelluna (some as far as 22 kilometers away) to cover the lower Piave in accordance with Durando's instructions. From Montebelluna, Ferrari responded to news of the Austrian attack by sending forward to support the embattled outposts two battalions of Roman civic guards, a battalion of Bolognese civic guards, the university battalion, and a detachment of the regular dragoons and the half battery of artillery contributed earlier by Durando. The reinforcements reached Cornuda as darkness fell and established a line just north of the village. The papal volunteers managed to hold that line and halt the Austrian advance. In the face of this resistance the Austrians, around 9:00 P.M., abandoned the attack and fell back some distance from the village.[27]

At 9:45 P.M. Ferrari sent a message to Durando announcing that the Austrians had been temporarily checked and that he intended to hold his position at Cornuda. The pontifical volunteers, who had performed remarkably well for half-trained men who had never before experienced fire, settled down for an uneasy night. In the village Captain Diamilla-Muller, who had galloped north from Montebelluna with General Ferrari's suite, lay down fully clothed on a pile of straw, his saddled horse only a few feet away. Nearby, Colonel Patrizi, commander of the 2nd Roman Legion, tossed and turned on another pile of hay. Unable to sleep, the two spent the night talking quietly in the dark. At one point the colonel whispered to himself, "What will become of us tomorrow?" and Diamilla-Muller thought, "We'll just have to win." At 3:00 A.M. on May 9 General Ferrari woke those few officers who were still asleep and ordered the troops readied for the attack that everyone knew was coming. An inspection of the lines revealed a disturbing situation. The previous evening, in the course of throwing back the Austrian attack, the volunteers had occupied several low hills north of Cornuda. During the night, however, the inexperienced volunteers had abandoned these advantageous positions and retired into the relative security and comfort of the village. At dawn Ferrari discovered that the Austrians had quietly returned under shelter of darkness to occupy this high ground, from which they could fire down on the papal positions. This bad news was offset when, at 4:00 A.M., a messenger arrived from Bassano with word that Durando was marching with his regulars to join Ferrari and that he was pushing a battalion of light infantry forward as an advance force. Three hours later the general seems to have repeated his intentions in another message, adding that he might not reach the battlefield until the evening of May 9.[28]

These messages brought welcome encouragement to Ferrari. The night had been quiet, but with the first light the Austrians, now reinforced, renewed the attack. For the first few hours the papal troops held their positions, ably supported by a half battery of artillery under the command of Lieutenant Federico Torre, which demolished several farm buildings from which the Austrians were firing.[29] By midmorning, however, the pontifical troops were increasingly hard-pressed, and Ferrari sent off another message to Durando requesting immediate support. Around 11:00 the papal general learned that Austrian cavalry had been observed moving forward. To preempt the Austrian attack and buy time for his now wavering volunteers to recover, Ferrari ordered the only papal cavalry on the scene, a half squadron of regular dragoons (the other half of the squadron was at Montebelluna), to counterattack. It was a measure born of desperation because the fifty cavalrymen would be advancing on a numerically far superior enemy force with no particular tactical plan or goal beyond distracting the enemy as long as possible. Charging against heavy fire, the dragoons broke through the Austrian front ranks and for several minutes sowed mayhem and confusion behind the lines. Some troopers penetrated more than a kilometer into the Austrian rear before wheeling about and cutting their way back through the lines to the relative safety of Cornuda. In terms of daring, initiative, execution, and courage, it was the most spectacular action by a unit of the pontifical army since the sixteenth century, but it was a costly achievement. Of the fifty dragoons who spurred their mounts toward the Austrian lines outside Cornuda around noon on May 9, 1848, only ten returned. Captain Diamilla-Muller observed one of the survivors, a noncommissioned officer, stumbling wounded back to the papal lines, his horse dead on the battlefield, his broken and bloody sword still in his hand.[30]

The attack by the papal dragoons temporarily disrupted the Austrians, but Ferrari was unable to capitalize on its success by following up with an infantry attack. The volunteers were exhausted by hours of combat, and their morale was slipping. Around noon Ferrari received Durando's reply to his earlier request for help: "I'm coming quickly." To rally his failing troops, Ferrari spread the word that the regulars would soon arrive, and he may have (sources differ) ordered the troops to lessen their fire in order to conserve ammunition. By early afternoon, however, the situation was becoming desperate. Additional Austrian units had entered the battle, and some of these units turned the papal right flank by marching through the cultivated fields that bordered the Piave 2 kilometers from the battlefield. To anchor his other flank while he dealt with the developing crisis on his right, Ferrari decided to send two companies of the 2nd Legion, which had been waiting in reserve, to reinforce the extreme left of the line. As he looked around for an officer to carry the necessary orders, his eyes fell upon Captain Diamilla-Muller. In the mid-nineteenth century, junior officers attached to a commander's staff during a battle were still largely employed as messengers carrying orders and requests for information between the commander and his units, so Diamilla-Muller had spent the morning of May 8 either riding in the suite of the general or galloping around the battlefield accompanied only by his batman, Cacciani, an enlisted man detailed from the mounted carabinieri. This was the young captain's first combat, and he cursed himself for reflexively ducking his head every time an enemy musket ball hummed past his head (like "the mewing of a cat" he would later recall). His chagrin had been all the greater when earlier that morning General Ferrari had noticed him hunching down over his horse's neck. "You there," the general had shouted in his gruff voice, "what are you doing, ducking at the sound of bullets? Don't you know that bullets are like letters in the mail? If they have your address, they will always reach you."[31] Now, as the general looked around for an officer to carry his orders to the reserve companies of the 2nd Legion, Diamilla-Muller was again embarrassed as his commander's glance fell on him at the very moment that he was slurping down a raw egg, his only nourishment since the previous afternoon, when the staff's lunch had been interrupted by news of the Austrian attack. The commander chose to ignore the snack as he ordered Diamilla-Muller to race to the reserve companies and lead them to the left flank. The captain hastened to fulfill his mission, but when he reached the companies he found them in turmoil. Several packets of ammunition (supplied by the arsenal in Venice) had been found to contain cartridges too big for the rifles carried by the soldiers. Some in the 2nd Legion began to talk of treachery, suggesting openly that the issue of useless cartridges could only be part of a deliberate plot by Austrian sympathizers to sabotage the volunteers. Precious time was lost as Diamilla-Muller, pointing out that only a few packets were affected and that there was plenty of functional ammunition, calmed the excitement and recalled the men to their duties. Having guided the companies to their positions in the line, the captain, accompanied as always by his batman, Cacciani, was galloping back under fire to General Ferrari's headquarters when his horse collapsed and he was thrown to the ground. The horse was dead from a musket ball that had entered its head and exited from its lower neck, slightly penetrating Diamilla-Muller's lower leg. The wound was bloody but not serious, although the young officer was rendered semiconscious by his fall and could not speak. Cacciani, who had been riding at his side, stopped and, with the help of some soldiers who ran to the scene, lifted Diamilla-Muller over his saddle and made it safely to the papal lines. As he passed through the lines, still stunned, the young captain heard someone say, "Poor Diamilla has been killed," and he thought this was what it was like to be dead, to be a detached observer of events. By the time Cacciani got him into the medical station that had been improvised in the only café in Cornuda, Diamilla-Muller had recovered enough to realize he wasn't dead after all and could limp into the station. The leg wound was so minor that the surgeon was able to pop out the enemy musket ball with the pressure of his hand, but he put the captain on an ambulance for Montebelluna.[32]

By midafternoon the volunteers, weary from hours of combat and discouraged by the failure of General Durando's reinforcements to arrive, gave up the fight and began to fall back, a movement that quickly turned into a disorderly flight from the battlefield. Unable to stem the rout, Ferrari and the few units still responsive to his command retreated, first to Montebelluna and then to Treviso, the Austrians on their heels. As the dispirited volunteers straggled into the latter town, their anger and frustration turned against General Durando. The volunteers had fought the Austrians for almost twenty-four hours, but where were the regulars? Why had the promised support never arrived? Whispers of betrayal and treason were heard, even in the conversations of senior officers. Although Ferrari's direction of the action at Cornuda had been marked by missteps (his failure to order forward reinforcements from Treviso until well into the battle on May 9 is inexplicable), most in the volunteer division, including their general, blamed Durando for their defeat. In fact, the commander of the Regular Division had become a victim of his own preconceptions. He had always suspected that any Austrian attack down the Quero-Cornuda-Montebelluna road would be a feint to divert his attention from the real attack, which would be launched farther west from Feltre toward Bassano. When, early on the morning of May 9, Durando began to advance his regulars from Bassano toward Cornuda in response to Ferrari's appeals for support, he did so slowly while always looking over his shoulder, fearful that he was being tricked. His plan seems to have been to approach the Piave near Pederobba before dropping down on the rear of the Austrians facing Cornuda. He was a few kilometers short of Pederobba and could actually hear the sounds of cannons from the battlefield when his fears were confirmed. An officer, whipping his horse to exhaustion, overtook the papal column with important news from Colonel Casanova, the commander of a small force that Durando had earlier sent to Primolano, a village north of Bassano, to watch the Feltre-Bassano road. Casanova reported that several thousand Austrians accompanied by artillery were advancing from Feltre toward Bassano. It was exactly what Durando had anticipated! The action around Cornuda was a feint by a smaller force to draw the pontifical regulars away from Bassano, while General Nugent with his main force broke out farther west. Only a few kilometers short of Ferrari's battlefield at Cornuda, the pope's commander turned his column around to face what he considered the main threat. Quick-marching back to Bassano, the column met another horseman riding hard to catch Durando. This time the messenger was Colonel Casanova himself. The colonel reported that the Austrian unit that had advanced from Feltre had marched only several kilometers from town before turning around and marching back. Bassano was not in danger. Durando had been tricked. The probe from Feltre, perfectly timed by Nugent, was the real feint, meant to draw the papal regulars away from Cornuda, where the Austrians were intent on destroying Ferrari's force before marching on Montebelluna and Treviso. By the time Durando discovered that Cornuda was the real battle, it was too late to save Ferrari and his volunteers.[33]

For the pontifical army Cornuda was not particularly costly in terms of casualties (acknowledging that his figures were unreliable, Ferrari reported 30 dead and 56 wounded, certainly an underestimate since the pontifical dragoons alone suffered 40 dead or missing), but it broke the spirit of the volunteer division.[34] Desertions became a serious problem. Many volunteers simply left for their homes, and others made their way to Venice, where they passed their days forlornly in cafes, selling their weapons and other equipment to sustain themselves. Those who remained in Treviso no longer trusted their officers and performed their duties sullenly. To repair the spirit of his troops, General Ferrari decided on May 11 to lead a reconnaissance force to probe the Austrian positions north of Treviso, but the papal column was badly mauled during its first encounter with the enemy and had to return precipitously to town. Morale plummeted further. Recognizing the need to refresh and reorganize what was left of the volunteer division, General Durando instructed Ferrari to fall back 18 kilometers to Mestre, leaving the defense of Treviso in the hands of the local civic guard, which soon had its hands full as the Austrians appeared on the outskirts of the town on May 12. Now convinced that General Nugent's intention was not to march west to join Marshal Radetzky but rather to capture Treviso, Durando moved his regulars to link up with Ferrari's force at Mestre as a preliminary to a joint operation against the Austrians around Treviso. Prospects were not bright. At their meeting in Mestre, Durando and Ferrari spent most of their time exchanging recriminations over the defeat at Cornuda. Durando was further discomfited to discover the volunteer division much reduced in size due to desertions and Ferrari's decision to dissolve his less reliable units. Prospects for the relief of Treviso, where the civic guards had gamely held off the Austrians for several days, were not good, but the papal commanders were spared potential embarrassment when on May 18 General Nugent received orders from Radetzky to break away from Treviso and move immediately toward Verona, the way west having been cleared of blocking papal troops now that Durando, believing Nugent's goal was Treviso, had shifted his force south to Mestre.[35]

Upon learning that the Austrians had abandoned their siege of Treviso and were moving west, Durando correctly guessed that Vicenza would be their next objective. With General Ferrari absent on a special mission to Bologna to liaise with a recently arrived Neapolitan corps (an absence contrived, in part, to end the jealousies and recriminations that poisoned relations between the pope's two principal generals), Durando ordered several volunteer units (the 3rd Legion and the University Battalion) to move by train to reinforce the local volunteers and civic guards that made up the Vicenza garrison while he followed behind with elements of the Regular Division fleshed out by some volunteer units. The volunteers reached Vicenza on May 20, just in time to help the garrison under Colonel Domenico Belluzzi, a veteran of the Napoléonic Wars, repel the first Austrian assaults. Most of the fighting was in the suburb of Santa Lucia, where the defenders erected street barricades and converted houses and shops into makeshift strong points. After several hours of combat, during which each side suffered around one hundred casualties, General Thurn, who had replaced General Nugent when the latter fell ill, broke off the attack and, deciding that Vicenza was not worth the time and casualties, resumed his advance toward Verona. As Thurn marched his army around the northern fringes of the city to rejoin the Verona road to the west, the Vicenza garrison, emboldened by its successful repulse of the Austrian attack, sent out a reconnaissance in force, which harassed the Austrian rear guard until night fell and the Italians returned to their city.[36]

General Durando and his column of papal regulars—the two Swiss infantry regiments, an indigenous infantry regiment, a squadron of dragoons, the battery of Swiss artillery, and two regiments of civic guards from Padua—entered Vicenza on May 21, too late to impede Thurn's move toward Verona but in time to defend the city against a second assault.[37] Thurn's decision to bypass Vicenza did not please his superior, Marshal Radetzky, who peremptorily ordered him to turn around and take the city. The second assault came on the night of May 23 in the midst of a pelting rain. Initially the Austrian infantry, supported by an artillery battery, advanced through the suburb of San Felice toward the Castello gate. The Austrians forced back the civic guards who from behind street barricades defended the approaches to the gate, but the attackers were, in turn, forced to retreat by a counterattack by a battalion of the pope's Swiss infantry. As the Swiss advanced, however, they came under close-range fire from the Austrian battery and were compelled to retire back to the city. The attackers immediately pushed forward more artillery and opened a bombardment against the Castello gate. Meanwhile, the Austrians had opened a second front by attacking the nearby Santa Croce gate, where over the course of the night the defenders, a battalion of volunteers stiffened by several companies of Swiss regulars, repulsed three assaults before throwing back the Austrians with a bold counterattack, an action in which a junior officer in the Swiss regiment, Lieutenant Hermann Kanzler, particularly distinguished himself.[38]

By the morning of May 24 the Austrians controlled the San Felice neighborhood, but at no point had they entered Vicenza, and everywhere they remained under heavy fire from the city's defenders, including a well-served battery of Swiss artillery that had boldly established itself on the heights of the Berici hills on the outskirts of the city. Fired by patriotism, the population of Vicenza had rushed to the city's defense. During the night of Austrian attacks the streets had been illuminated as if for a festival, and the tolling bells of the churches had provided a counterpoint to the sounds of muskets and cannons. As troops rushed to reinforce the gates they were encouraged by the cheers of women and children. The defense was determined, and from the Austrian lines the prospects for a quick capitulation seemed dim. They seemed even dimmer after early-morning assaults against the Castello and Santa Croce gates were repulsed and the bloodied attackers pushed back at bayonet point by counterattacking papal regulars who took many prisoners. Deciding that without substantial reinforcements further attacks would prove equally futile, Thurn decided once again to abandon his attack and march toward Verona.[39]

With the departure of the Austrians, General Durando issued an order of the day praising the conduct of the pontifical units, regular and volunteer, during the battle for Vicenza. The praise was well earned. In conjunction with local civic guards, the pope's soldiers had twice driven off some of the best troops in Europe, and in so doing the pontifical army scored its first significant military victories since 1739, when a small force of papal militia had earned little glory by bullying the lilliputian Republic of San Marino. At Vicenza the regulars, notably the Swiss infantry and artillery, had fought well, but the volunteers surprised everyone by their aggressiveness, discipline, and steadfastness under fire. These were not the patriotic innocents, playing at soldiers, who had marched north from Rome in the spring. Most of those sunshine soldiers had melted away in the face of discipline, hardship, and battle. Only the truly committed remained, and these had been tempered by the hard experiences of long route marches, rough bivouacs, and fierce battle. Their resilience, however, was soon to be tested again.

Marshal Radetzky wanted Vicenza, and General Thurn had twice failed to give his superior what he wanted. The third time Radetzky would do it himself, and do it right. Marching east from his positions in the Quadrilateral in early June with 30,000 troops and 124 cannons, he invested the city, which was defended by 36 cannons and 11,000 troops, half of whom were pontifical regulars.[40] The Austrian commander wanted to seize Vicenza, but he also intended to capture Durando's army, so he encircled the city so as to prevent any retreat. His plan was to direct secondary attacks through the eastern suburbs while his primary attack captured the Berici heights, which dominated the city from the south. Anticipating Radetzky's maneuvers, General Durando entrusted the defense of the eastern suburbs and city walls to the volunteers and civic guards, stiffened by some companies of Swiss infantry, while he deployed the bulk of the regulars and the pick of the volunteers along the road that followed the crest of the Berici hills before dropping down to the city. To deny the heights to the enemy, the regulars established strongpoints at the Madonna del Monte, a large church positioned just where the road dropped steeply down to the city, and at Bella Vista and the Villa

Guiccioli, vantage points on the heights where the narrow crest widened out to form topographical platforms. At the foot of the vine-terraced hillsides, papal troops occupied the Palladian Villa Rotonda and the nearby Villa Valmarana (home to priceless frescoes by the eighteenth-century painter Giambattista Tiepolo).[41]

Marshal Radetzky opened the assault against Vicenza at dawn on June 10. By 9:00 A.M. Austrian troops on the east had pushed in Durando's outposts and established artillery positions in the suburbs outside the city gates. By 11:00 the defenders had repulsed several infantry assaults, particularly at the Porta Santa Lucia and the Porta Padova, where Colonel Natale Del Grande, commander of the 1st Roman Legion, was killed in the defense of the gate. Meanwhile, the main Austrian attack began in the Berici hills that overlooked the city on the south. By 7:00 A.M. the Austrians had overrun the Bella Vista strongpoint, which the defenders had abandoned in flames. After a pause to receive reinforcements and to allow the assaults on the other fronts to develop, the Austrians renewed their advance along the Berici crest, overcoming one papal position after another against strong resistance. The University Battalion, forced to abandon the Villa Rotonda, retreated to the nearby Villa Valmarana, where it made a stand until it was overrun by superior numbers. The Swiss regulars counterattacked in a gallant attempt to retake Bella Vista but were repulsed with heavy losses and fell back on the Villa Guiccioli, the Austrians so close on their heels that the papal artillery emplaced on the grounds of the villa could not fire for fear of hitting the Swiss. After a hard fight the pontifical troops were forced from the villa. By midafternoon the only position on the Berici heights still in papal hands was the church of the Madonna della Monte, which became the focus of intense combat. Durando rushed to the scene to rally his troops, and at one point the fighting moved into the church itself, with riflemen firing from chapels and sheltering behind columns and monks from the attached monastery entering the fray to defend their sanctuary against the Austrians. Inevitably the outnumbered defenders were forced to retreat into the city, leaving the Madonna della Monte and the strategic Berici hills in enemy hands.[42]

The Austrians quickly established artillery on the heights, and these guns began to bombard the city in support of renewed infantry assaults against the eastern and southern gates. By late afternoon resistance was waning, although the fighting around the Padova and Monte gates continued even as it lessened at other points around the city. With their artillery batteries out of action, the surviving pontifical units fell back to the city's main square, where General Durando decided to capitulate. The decision was greeted with disbelief and indignation by many in the population who refused to surrender their city to the despised Austrians. When Durando ordered a white flag to be raised over the main square, many of the local volunteers yelled their objections, and some fired their muskets at the flag. Resistance continued in areas of the city throughout the night, but by early morning even the diehards acknowledged that the cause was lost. The cost had been high; 293 of the defenders of Vicenza had died, and another 693 were wounded. The highest casualties, 148 dead and 388 wounded, had been incurred by the two Swiss regiments of the pontifical army. Under the terms of surrender, the pontifical troops were allowed to march from Vicenza with full military honors in recognition of their steadfast defense of the city, but each of the pope's soldiers had to swear an oath that he would not serve in any capacity against Austria for the next three months. An Austrian column then proceeded to Treviso, where, after a brief bombardment, the papal garrison capitulated under the same terms, including the three-month parole.[43]

From Vicenza and Treviso the pontifical troops, now effectively neutralized for three months by the terms of their surrender, retreated to Ferrara and Bologna. The only sizable papal forces still in the field were several all-volunteer regiments encamped in Padua. After the loss of Vicenza, these regiments, deciding they could not resist an attack by the Austrians, received permission from Rome to withdraw to Venice, where they supported the forces of the recently proclaimed Venetian Republic by garrisoning defensive positions in the Venetian lagoon and participating in several minor actions against Austrian forces seeking to suppress the republic. They were joined by elements of the pontifical navy. After transporting General Durando's army across the River Po in April, the flotilla of small craft, including the steamer *Roma* and a handful of coast guard cutters and customs launches, had moved to Venice to join the combined Sardinian-Neapolitan fleet that was shielding Venice from the Austrian navy and operating against Austrian targets in the north Adriatic. After refitting and arming in the Venetian naval arsenal, the *Roma* participated in the bombardment of Austrian forts at Santa Margherita and Caorle on June 1, the last offensive combat operation of the pontifical navy. To enhance the capabilities of the pontifical navy in the north Adriatic, the ministry of arms in Rome considered refurbishing and rearming the *San Pietro*, the largest ship in the navy, which was still laid up at Civitavecchia, but after inspecting the vessel, Lieutenant Colonel Cialdi judged the project unfeasible, and the ministry abandoned it.[44]

Although the army units from Vicenza and Treviso were encamped in Ferrara and Bologna, their military effectiveness was seriously compromised not only by the terms of their parole (in the nineteenth century soldiers took such things seriously) but by the dissolution of many of the volunteer units and the return of their personnel to civilian life. Feeling defenseless, the population of the Romagna rightly feared an Austrian invasion because, despite the antiwar posture of Pope Pius, the pontifical army had fought Austrian armies in five battles—Cornuda, Treviso, and Vizenza (thrice)—and in the eyes of most governments, this qualified the papacy as a belligerent. Whatever Pope Pius wanted to believe, the papacy was at war, and it was not alarmist to expect that Austria would carry the war to papal territory—which was exactly what it did. On July 13 an Austrian column of 6,000 infantry and 220 cavalry under General von Lichtenstein crossed the Po and advanced on Ferrara. Three days later the ministry of arms ordered the commander of the Bologna garrison, Colonel Zuccari, to move his troops north to resist the invasion. Since the Bologna garrison had not participated in the defense of either Vicenza or Treviso, it was not subject to the prohibition against fighting Austria. The authorities in Ferrara, however, were not inclined to risk a battle for their city, especially since, under the terms of the agreement worked out at the end of March, an Austrian garrison still occupied the city's fortress. The city's governor, Count Francesco Lovatelli, sent emissaries to General von Lichtenstein to determine his intentions. The general was brief and blunt. He demanded that the pontifical government guarantee provisions for the Austrian garrison for two months and fully provision his own mobile column for two days. Furthermore, he insisted on a revision of the March agreement to end restrictions on the movement of the garrison and allow the Austrian soldiers the freedom of the city. If these demands were not immediately accepted, the general would attack Ferrara. Lovatelli, who had only 1,327 papal troops in the city, 897 of whom were bound by their parole not to fight Austria, acceded to the demands. His purposes served, General von Lichtenstein returned to the Veneto, leaving behind an infantry brigade that established itself at strategic points around the papal city.[45]

Austrian boldness toward the Papal States reflected a more general shift in the fortunes of war. After some initial victories, the Piedmontese had been unable to dislodge the Austrians from their positions around Mantua and Verona. Once reinforcements had arrived from Austria and King Carlo Alberto's papal and Venetian allies had been neutralized, Marshal Radetzky launched an offensive against Sardinia-Piedmont. An extended battle at Custozza (July 22–25) resulted in a decisive defeat for the Piedmontese, who retreated toward Milan. By the end of July Carlo Alberto and his generals had concluded that their army could not carry on the struggle. A temporary armistice provided for the suspension of hostilities, including the abandonment of Milan by the Piedmontese and their withdrawal from Lombardy to positions on the Piedmontese side of the Ticino River. On August 9 Sardinia-Piedmont and Austria signed the Armistice of Salasco, which suspended hostilities for a further six weeks and compelled the Piedmontese to evacuate Lombardy, the Veneto, Parma, and Modena. Even before the armistice Vienna had decided that it was time to sort out the lesser Italian states. One papal city, Ferrara, was already effectively under Austrian occupation. On the morning of August 3 the commandant of the Austrian garrison in that city sent a message to Governor Lovatelli, asking whether the governor was a friend or an enemy of Austria. If the governor were a friend, he would prove it by moving papal troops from the city. If he were an enemy, then the fortress would begin bombarding the city before noon. Lovatelli acceded to the ultimatum and before noon ordered the troops to depart. By the next day Austrian troops had crossed into the Romagna at several points and were on the roads to the south, disarming any pontifical military units they encountered along the way. By August 6 the Austrians were in possession of Bologna, after Rome the second city of the Papal States.[46]

In Rome the papal administration was helpless in the face of defeat and occupation. After Pius's refusal in his allocution of April 29 to declare war on Austria, a position publicly reaffirmed in his statement to the Roman people on May 11, the pope's citizens increasingly turned against their sovereign. In protest, the Council of Ministers, including the pope's chief minister, Cardinal Antonelli, resigned. Pius appointed a new ministry under a layman, the philosopher and writer Terenzio Mamiani, who had been a political leader in the antipapal revolution of 1831. His new ministers, however, reflecting the militant mood of the streets, moved beyond the simple prowar position of their predecessors by calling for the secularization of the papal administration and the restriction of the pope's prerogatives to the purely spiritual realm. Spurred by populist rabble-rousers such as Angelo Brunetti, known to the crowd as Ciceruacchio (Big Boy), the population of Rome became more radicalized and pushed the ministers to demand more change, while the civic guard increasingly saw itself as the instrument of self-appointed popular leaders rather than an element of the pontifical armed forces. There was frequent disorder in the streets, and the loyalty of the civic guard and the papal police became uncertain. Failure to resolve the war question and control the streets led the Mamiani ministry to resign at the end of July. Its successor, under the leadership of Count Eduardo Fabbri, lasted hardly two months before succumbing to the same political pressures. The pope's next chief minister, Pellegrino Rossi, proved more resistant to the demands of the street. The new minister hoped to resolve the war question by creating an Italian Confederation (of which the Papal States would be a member) that would declare and wage war on its own authority, thereby relieving the Holy Father of the decision. Rossi alienated public opinion by defending the pope's refusal to declare war unilaterally. Despised by the more radical elements in Rome, Rossi was murdered on November 15, 1848, by an assassin who thrust a dagger into his throat as he entered the Palace of the Chancellery.[47]

The assassination of the pope's chief minister, which was hailed rather than condemned by leaders of the popular faction, cowed papal authorities, most of whom quickly made themselves scarce. The murder also emboldened the agitators, who, convinced that they were on the verge of power, saw no reason to moderate their demands. The papal authorities who remained at their posts concluded that the republican movement had become irretrievably radicalized and that further violence against the personnel and institutions of the papal regime could be expected. The authorities, however, were not sure that they could defend the regime. The popular faction controlled the streets, elements of the army and the police had been infected by republican sentiments so that their loyalty could no longer be taken for granted, and the civic guard was completely under the influence of the crowd. At the Quirinal Palace, the papal residence, there was mounting concern for the pope's safety. On the evening of November 15 the recently appointed commandant of the Swiss Guard, Colonel Franz Xavier Leopold Meyer von Schauensee, discussed the security situation with Pius and Cardinal Antonelli, who had assumed the post of master of the Apostolic Palace. The commandant, a former officer in the pontifical army who had distinguished himself in the defense of Vicenza and had transferred to the Swiss Guard only two months before, expected serious trouble. After his discussions in the papal apartments, he immediately reinforced the Swiss posts at the gates and placed his men on alert. At this time the Swiss Guard mustered around 120 men, but 50 of these men were on duty at the Vatican, the papal palace adjacent to Saint Peter's Basilica on the other side of the Tiber, so the commandant had to defend the Quirinal Palace with a reduced force. Normally the Swiss mounted guard with their signature halberds and swords, but the guard armory contained muskets, and the commandant set the armorer to cleaning and testing the guns for possible action. The muskets had seen little use, and some required repairs, but after the armorer had worked through the night and into the next morning, a sufficient number of firearms were serviceable for the commandant to issue a musket and three rounds of ammunition to each of the guards at the gates.[48]

On the morning of November 16 there was a large political demonstration in the Piazza del Popolo during which representatives of the pontifical army, the police, and the civic guard proclaimed their allegiance to the republican cause and called on the pope to form a popular government. The demonstrators then marched on the Quirinal Palace to press their demands on the pope. By early afternoon a sizable crowd had gathered in the Piazza di Monte Cavallo, the large square in front of the palace's main gate. The pope was besieged. Only two cardinals, Giacomo Antonelli and Ceroni Sogli, had joined the Holy Father in this time of danger; the rest of the princes of the church had scurried to safety. Aside from a few aides and servants and the ambassadors of those countries that maintained diplomatic relations with the papacy, the pope sat alone in the vast palace. For defense he had only the small contingent of Swiss Guards.[49] "You see," Pius said to the diplomats, "the Quirinal is deserted and almost all have abandoned me. If you were not with me, I would be alone with the swords of the brave men who will defend me."[50] At the orders of their commandant, those brave men had at the approach of the demonstrators closed and barred all the palace entrances, but at Cardinal Antonelli's direction they granted entry to a delegation from the crowd. This group met with Antonelli and pressed on him their demand that the pope form and empower a popular government. The cardinal secretary of state assured the delegates that Pope Pius would consider their position, but the Holy Father could not give in to the threat of violence. After this audience the delegates received permission to address the increasingly large and unruly crowd that was gathering outside the palace. From a balcony overlooking the Piazza di Monte Cavallo, the delegates informed the citizens of Antonelli's assurances and invited the assembly to disperse. The crowd, however, was in no mood for appeasement, and it reacted angrily. Citizens, including some soldiers and civic guards, began to press around the gates, yelling, "Death to the Swiss." Soon the mob began throwing rocks and cobblestones, and then it set the main gate on fire. What happened next is disputed. Republican partisans insist that the Swiss Guard, without provocation, opened fire on the unarmed crowd from the windows of the palace, wounding several of the protesters.[51] The standard history of the guard maintains that as the main gate of the palace was set afire by the shouting mob, several shots were fired from the crowd, although a more recent history of the unit suggests that a musket was inadvertently discharged inside the palace.[52] Whatever the origin of the first shot, the Swiss then opened fire, clearing the square save for a couple of wounded protesters. Shouting, "To arms, to arms" and "The Swiss are killing our brothers," the crowd raised the alarm. From a nearby military barracks additional weapons were distributed, and soon the papal residence was under fire from several directions, including the bell tower of the neighboring church of San Carlo, where several civic-guard snipers fired down into the palace grounds. Musket balls thudded against masonry and shattered palace windows. One struck and killed Monsignor Giovan Battista Palma, a papal aide who was standing with the pope near a window. Civic guards wheeled into the Piazza dello Cavallo an army cannon, its barrel embossed (as was the custom with papal artillery) with the name of a saint—in this case Saint Peter.[53]

Meanwhile, the delegates who had entered the palace to confer with Cardinal Antonelli were still inside the building, watching aghast as the protest degenerated into a pitched battle. Papal authorities assured the delegates that they were not prisoners and were free to leave, but the emissaries declined, protesting that they might be shot by the Swiss Guard as they exited the palace. Colonel Meyer von Schauensee might have pointed out that the delegates were in greater danger of being shot by their own people, who were now firing indiscriminately from every direction, than by the Swiss halberdiers, who at least remained under discipline and had held their fire after their initial volley. Instead he offered to ensure the safety of the emissaries by escorting them personally across the square, asking only that they give their word of honor to guarantee his safety. The delegates immediately agreed. When the palace gates opened, the firing ceased, and Meyer von Schauensee escorted his charges safely to the large fountain in the middle of the square. At that point the delegates, forgetting the promise they had made only minutes before, ran to the shelter of nearby buildings while armed civic guards rushed up to surround the pope's officer. Angrily the civic guards taunted their prisoner: "Whose side are you on, the side of the people or the side of the pope?" The colonel calmly replied, "I am on the side of duty," adding contemptuously, "Shoot, if you're brave enough, an officer who fought at Vicenza for Italian independence." The insurgents then positioned him in front of the cannon, as if to blast him to pieces with a cannonball, but the colonel retained his composure. "I know this cannon," he remarked. "It's called Saint Peter. If you fire it, history will record that on November 16 the Romans executed the officer who, with twenty-five infantrymen, at Vicenza recaptured this very same cannon after it had fallen into Austrian hands."[54] Their bluff called, the civic guards pulled the colonel from in front of the cannon but held him in close custody until his release later that evening.

Throughout the evening of November 16 the armed insurgents held their positions around the Quirinal Palace, unwilling to test the resolve of the Swiss Guards who held the palace gates. The next morning another delegation appeared to inform the Holy Father that unless he agreed to a civilian ministry proposed by "the people," the demonstrators would attack the palace in earnest. To avoid further bloodshed Pius submitted to this demand, and the new ministers were announced that very day. The delegation also demanded that the pontiff withdraw and disarm his Swiss Guard, which had aroused the anger of the Roman people by resisting the attack on the pontifical residence. Again Pius submitted to the threat of force. He summoned Colonel Meyer von Schauensee and ordered him to confine his guardsmen to their barracks. The colonel transferred the unit's muskets to the custody of the newly appointed minister of the interior on the condition that the firearms would remain in the palace, a condition the popular authorities promptly violated by loading the weapons onto a wagon and moving them to a depot in another part of the city. Responsibility for guarding the Holy Father now fell on the civic guard, which posted men at every gate of the Quirinal Palace.[55]

Pius was under no illusions about his status; the civic guards at his gates were his warders as much as his protectors. Abandoned by most of his officials, isolated behind the bayonets of armed insurgents, convinced that the new regime would challenge his temporal power, and afraid that his "protectors" would pressure him to act against his conscience and sense of duty, Pius allowed Cardinal Antonelli, who had remained at his side in his capacity of master of the Apostolic Palace, to plot the pope's escape with the cooperation of the Bavarian, French, and Spanish ambassadors. Antonelli also approached senior officers of the pope's Noble Guard, but these men declined to join the conspiracy for fear of the consequences for themselves and their families should their participation be revealed.[56] By November 24 everything was ready. That evening civic guards escorted the French ambassador, François d'Harcourt, to the papal apartment for an audience with the Holy Father. While the ambassador sat in a chair and pretended to carry on a conversation in a voice loud enough for the guards outside the main door to notice, Pius, disguised by dark glasses, a woolen muffler, and the cassock of a simple priest and accompanied only by a trusted personal servant bearing a lighted taper, moved through the dark corridors of the palace to a door that opened onto a side street where a common city carriage waited. The servant calmly greeted the guards on the street and entered the carriage with the "priest." The carriage set off in one direction, but once out of sight of the palace it doubled back and proceeded to the church of Saints Peter and Marcellinus, where the Bavarian ambassador, Count Karl Spaur, was waiting with his own carriage. Pius transferred to the ambassador's coach. At the city's San Giovanni gate Spaur showed his diplomatic passport to the guards, who allowed the coach to pass without hindrance or delay. At the village of Ariccia, 25 kilometers south of Rome, Spaur's wife was waiting with a heavier traveling carriage.[57] Traveling through the night (and stopping to rendezvous with Cardinal Antonelli, who, dressed in a three-cornered hat, bulky clothes, and a red scarf obscuring his face, had separately escaped Rome), the pope reached Gaeta, a fortress town in the Kingdom of Naples on November 25. From this refuge he immediately began planning his return. Gradually additional cardinals and officials joined him, and Antonelli used the time to sound opinion and support among the European powers. By January 1849 Pius was ready to act. That month he excommunicated those responsible for the insurrection of November and denounced the general assembly convened in Rome to consider the disposition of the Papal States in the face of their "abandonment" by the Holy Father. In March Pius hosted a conference of Catholic powers—Austria, France, Naples, and Spain—whose participants agreed to cooperate in restoring the pontiff to his throne.[58]

In Rome a provisional government moved to consolidate and legitimize its authority. The general assembly that had convened in December had assumed legislative and executive authority. On February 9, 1849, this assembly declared the papal monarchy abolished and announced the formation of the Roman Republic, with sovereignty over all the territory of the now defunct Papal States. The prospect of military intervention by Catholic powers compelled the new republic to look immediately to its defenses. That prospect became more pressing and dangerous when Piedmont, with whom the republic had formed a secret military agreement, denounced the armistice with Austria and renewed the war only to suffer a crushing defeat at Novara on March 23. This defeat forced Carlo Alberto to abdicate in favor of his son, Prince Vittorio Emanuele; removed from the military scene the Roman Republic's only ally; allowed the hostile Austrians to push troops into central Italy, from which positions they could menace the Eternal City; and encouraged the French, always concerned with counterbalancing Austrian influence in the peninsula, to intervene with their own force in support of the pope's restoration. In April a French expeditionary force landed at Civitavecchia while Neapolitan and Spanish forces entered the papal domain (territory now claimed by the republic) from the south.

Upon declaring a republic, the new regime in Rome set about creating an army. A grandiose plan had been proposed to raise, equip, and train an army of 50,000 men to defend against a possible intervention from the Kingdom of Naples to restore the pope and (even more unrealistically) to support future Piedmontese operations in north Italy should Turin denounce its armistice with Austria (as it did on March 12). This plan, however, was set aside while the regime dealt with the immediate crisis posed by the arrival of a hostile French expeditionary force at Civitavecchia. Although many volunteers rushed to defend the republic, including a force of 1,200 men that Giuseppe Garibaldi led into Rome on April 27, the core of the republican army depended on personnel and equipment from the pontifical military, specifically some 3,900 regulars, carabinieri, and customs police stationed around the Eternal City. There were also more than 2,500 men who had served with the volunteer battalions in the Veneto campaign.[59] The more radical republicans doubted the loyalty of the pope's regulars, objecting particularly to these troops wearing their old uniforms, whose buttons bore the tiara and crossed keys of the papacy. Despite such distrust, most of these soldiers served the Roman Republic well because they sympathized with the liberal regime; accepted the republic as the legitimate successor to the papal government; or simply needed the salary, food, and lodging provided by the army.[60] There was no effort to draft the pope's household guards into service, probably because doubts concerning their loyalty were more widespread. The Swiss Guard was simply disbanded and the halberdiers dismissed with one month's pay. The Swiss commandant, Colonel Meyer von Schauensee, made his way to the pope's side at Gaeta. In January 1849 Pius entrusted him with a secret mission to the Romagna, where authority was being contested among papal officials, republicans, and Austrian occupation forces. Elements of the pope's regular infantry regiments, including Swiss battalions, were still in this region after their withdrawal from the Veneto. The pope's scheme required the colonel, traveling incognito, to contact the officers of these regiments and convince them to reorganize their units and march them south, the length of the Papal States, to Neapolitan territory, where they would form the core of an army that would restore the pontiff to his lands. The mission failed when local papal officials convinced Meyer von Schauensee that the departure of the few reliable pontifical units still under arms in north Italy would embolden republican elements and destroy the remaining vestiges of papal authority.[61]

Rome's new rulers also concluded that they could not trust the Noble Guard, the pope's mounted bodyguard. They disbanded the unit, sent the guardsmen home, and confiscated whatever material they could get their hands on. The republic was only a week old when, on February 16, representatives of the new regime appeared at the stables of the Noble Guard and demanded to be shown the cavalry unit's mounts. Two days later, Prince Barberini, commander of the guard, received a letter from the republic's ministry of war announcing the requisition of horses for the republican army. Shortly thereafter, several officials arrived to inventory the mounts in the stables and the saddles, bridles, and other equipment in the tack room. The officials described each horse in a register (ignoring a scruffy donkey that lived compatibly with the grander cavalry chargers), but the inspectors found the tack room empty, the valuable equipment having been removed earlier by guardsmen who had anticipated just such a visit. On February 22 another group of republican officers appeared at the headquarters of the Noble Guard with an order to seize all firearms from the armory. When the leader asked the guard duty officer to open the armory, the officer threw the key at him and told him to open it himself. The intruders left with fifty cavalry carbines and sixty-five pistols. Eventually the republican army would take over the headquarters itself, although guardsmen managed to carry away the unit's archive, its plate, ten sabers, and two pistols before the new owners arrived. Several guardsmen made their way to Gaeta to join the pope in his temporary exile.[62]

The Roman Republic failed its first military test. In anticipation of French intervention, authorities in Rome ordered the fortified port of Civitavecchia to resist any attempt to land troops. When, however, a French fleet appeared outside the port on April 24, the city's defense committee decided to surrender without resistance. The committee members claimed there was no support for resistance among the population and that local notables had pleaded with them to avoid an action that would risk heavy losses of life and property, but in Rome there were whispers of treason. The following day the commander of the French expeditionary force, General Charles Nicolas Oudinot, announcing that he had come to liberate Rome from "the foreigners who had come from all over Italy to oppress the people of the Eternal City," sent a message to the Roman Assembly asking if it, like the people of Civitavecchia, would receive the French in a friendly manner. The Assembly replied that it would meet force with force and prepared to fight the French army. The Roman Republic would do much better in this test.[63]

General Oudinot was overconfident, assuming that the republican leaders were bluffing and that the citizens would not risk the destruction of the Eternal City in an all-out battle. He was so sure of an easy victory as he approached Rome from the west with about five thousand men that he did not bother to reconnoiter the city's defenses. Late on the morning of April 30

he opened the assault by sending an infantry column against the Porta Per-
tusa, a gate in the sixteenth-century walls just below the medieval Tower of
Saint John at the western extremity of the Vatican gardens. The French commander seems to have been unaware that this gate had been bricked up for
more than a century and provided no access to the city. Expecting a gate but
finding only a brick wall,.the French attackers came under intense fire from
republican forces, mainly regulars from the old pontifical army, positioned
along the walls and bastions. In response to this setback, Oudinot divided his
attack, sending troops to the right to attack the Porta Cavalleggeri near Saint
Peter's Square and to the left to attack the Porta Angelica on the other side
of the Vatican. These assaults failed under heavy fire from the defenders, but
the situation around the Porta Cavalleggeri soon turned critical. Before the
arrival of the French, Garibaldi, who had been entrusted with the defense of
this sector of the city, had moved troops into several villas outside the walls
below the Cavalleggeri gate, and he ordered these troops to attack the right
flank of the French struggling around the Porta Cavalleggeri. This movement resulted in heavy fighting among the suburban villas and walled gardens just outside the Roman walls. At one point the republican forces were
forced to fall back toward the city walls, but the timely appearance of several
companies of regulars from the former papal army allowed Garibaldi to push
back the French at bayonet point. As Garibaldi attacked, a strong republican
force sortied from the Porta Cavalleggeri. In the face of these determined
counterattacks, which threatened to envelop his assault column, General
Oudinot decided to extricate his force. By 5:00 P.M. the battle was over. For
the French it was an embarrassing defeat. Oudinot returned to Civitavecchia having suffered some 500 casualties and left 365 of his men behind as
prisoners in the hands of the republicans. That night Romans celebrated by
illuminating the city with bonfires, torches, and candles.[64]

After the failure of Oudinot's attack there was a tacit truce between the
two parties. The French settled in Civitavecchia and refrained from a second
assault, and the republicans made no effort to dislodge them from that port
city. The republic, however, had to face other enemies. A Neapolitan force,
operating in desultory support of the French, had entered the pope's former domains from the south and by May had reached the hills southeast of
Rome. Garibaldi led a republican force that turned back the Neapolitans after sharp actions near the towns of Palestrina (May 9) and Velletri (May 19).
Meanwhile, from the north an Austrian army advanced into the Romagna
and the Marche to restore papal authority. At both Bologna and Ancona the
Austrians had to overcome strong resistance from prorepublic infantry and
police units, including former units of the pontifical army and carabinieri,
before occupying the cities.[65]

The French, however, remained the most immediate threat to the republic, especially after the arrival of reinforcements that increased the ex-

peditionary force to thirty thousand men. On June 1 General Oudinot announced that the tacit truce was over, but he added helpfully that although the French would approach Rome, they would certainly not attack before June 4 in order to give French citizens an opportunity to leave the threatened city. Trusting Oudinot's assurances, the republicans felt little urgency in preparing their defenses; indeed, as late as June 2 some strongpoints beyond the walls received word that they need not be vigilant until June 4.[66] Of course Oudinot's assurances were merely a ruse. On the night of June 2–3 General Jean-Baptiste Vaillant, who had arrived from France to assume command of field operations, quietly moved troops into the area of suburban villas just outside the San Pancrazio gate near the Trastevere district on the right bank of the Tiber. These units surrounded several villas that had been turned into strongpoints by the republicans in order to defend the approaches to the gate, and at a signal they attacked, easily capturing or putting to flight the defenders. Surprise was complete. Throughout the day of June 3 the republican generals threw troops into the combat in a vain effort to regain the initiative and recapture the strategic villas, but the French held firm. At the end of the day the republicans had suffered almost one thousand casualties and had been forced to withdraw behind the city walls. Rome was now besieged, and the republic could expect little help from outside. In the face of declining morale, increasing casualties, and disputes over defensive tactics and measures, the defenders held out for twenty-six days. Most of the fighting occurred below the Gianicolo hill along the stretch of wall between the San Pancrazio and Portese gates. On the night of June 29 the French breached the wall, and the attackers entered the city. Early on the morning of June 30 the republic's council of war discussed the crisis. A majority favored continuing resistance in the streets, but Garibaldi advised the government and the army to abandon Rome and escape to the Appenines and continue the war from the provinces rather than pursue a glorious but futile resistance that would result only in their death or capture. When consulted, the popular assembly voted to remain in the city but authorized Garibaldi to break out with as many troops as possible. On July 1 the city authorities arranged a truce to remove the dead and wounded. The next day Garibaldi and a column of four thousand diehards left Rome on the first leg of an odyssey that over the summer would take the republican hero and his steadily diminishing band of loyalists across the length and breadth of the peninsula and end in his exile from Italy. On July 3 the French took possession of the Eternal City and ended the Roman Republic.

Pope Pius did not return to his recovered capital until April 12, 1850, but in the interim he instituted in the city a commission of three cardinals to reestablish papal authority and rule in his name. As its first order of business this commission, on August 2, 1849, annulled all decrees and laws enacted after November 16, 1848 (the date of the Roman insurrection and the attack on the Quirinal Palace), and withdrew all ranks or authorities granted by the republic. It then set up a board to review the behavior of all papal employees under the republic and determine whether such behavior warranted their continuance in office. The pontifical armed forces received special scrutiny. Few of the veterans of the old papal army who had joined the republican cause chose to follow Garibaldi into the political wilderness. During the French occupation these veterans were placed under French command to await the will of the commission of cardinals. In the eyes of the pope's loyal cardinals, the armed forces were deeply compromised. These were, after all, the troops that had eagerly participated in the war against Austria, despite the pope's expressed desire to avoid war. Furthermore, the army and police had been infected by revolutionary sympathies, as evidenced by their wholesale defection to the Roman Republic. The cardinals had no doubt that the armed forces needed to be purged and reorganized. On August 18 they issued a decree abolishing the civic guard and all volunteer units; expelling all officers who had entered military service after November 16, 1848; requiring all officers enrolled before November 16, 1848, to revert to the ranks they had held on that date, but only after a special review board had affirmed their suitability and loyalty; and recalling to the colors all officers and men who had been forcibly retired from the army by the republic—a retirement that was prima facie evidence of their loyalty to the Holy Father.[67]

The cardinals were serious about purging disloyal elements from the armed forces. Even the Swiss Guard, the only unit to actively defend the Holy Father on November 16, 1848, did not escape scrutiny. Before the guard was reconstituted, halberdiers suspected of sympathy toward the republic were examined; several were disciplined, and one was denied readmission to the corps.[68] Some units were simply abolished. The carabinieri, the paramilitary police of the Papal States, had gone over to the republic, fighting resolutely in the defense of Rome, Ancona, and Bologna. The restored papal administration dissolved this unit and created a new police service, the Veliti Pontifici, in its place. In 1851 this corps was renamed the Gendarmeria Pontificia (Pontifical Gendarmeria). The Guardia di Finanza (customs police), another armed unit that had embraced the republic, survived as an organization, but most of its personnel were purged. To replace the discredited Roman civic guard, which had become the armed instrument of revolution in 1848, papal authorities in 1850 established the Guardia Palatina (Palatine Guard). A citizens' militia recruited from among Roman artisans and shopkeepers of "unblemished moral and political character," the Palatine Guard, like the Swiss and Noble Guards, fell directly under the command of the pontifical palace, which could deploy the unit to maintain order in the city or to defend the palace and the person of the Holy Father. In 1851 the unit joined the Swiss and Noble Guards in providing honor-guard services at important papal ceremonies and the reception of important guests in the papal palace.

Established initially as a battalion of 320 men organized into four companies, the Palatine Guard soon added a second battalion.[69]

The reconstitution of the pontifical army required time. It was not until June 1852 that the pontifical minister of arms, Filippo Farina, formalized the organizational structure that would characterize the army through the remainder of the decade. In this arrangement the ministry of arms (divided into a secretariat general and directorates for administration, personnel, and matériel) was responsible for all matters concerning the organization and administration of the pope's armed forces. The minister was appointed by the Holy Father, whereas the deputy minister, the minister's personal assistant, and the heads of the directorates were selected from the senior officer corps. Operational matters were left to a general staff composed of all officers holding the rank of general assisted by several captains and majors selected on the basis of their intelligence, character, and capacity for work as revealed during their regimental service or tenure at the cadet school. There was no school or training program to prepare staff officers. A separate staff supervised the several fortresses of the Papal States.[70]

The restoration army fielded four line infantry regiments, two foreign (mainly Swiss) and two indigenous; a *cacciatore* (light infantry) battalion; and two *sedentari* battalions. The sedentari were long-service veterans or soldiers with large families who were limited to garrison duties. Each regiment had two battalions (eight companies each) and a depot company. Enlistment was voluntary and for a period of six years in the indigenous units and four years in the foreign units. Once or twice a year each foreign regiment sent recruiting sergeants to its country of origin to seek enlistments. The colonels of the foreign regiments sometimes engaged civilian recruiters who were paid a fee for every man they could enlist. Contrary to conventional wisdom (then and now), the pontifical army was not an army of foreign mercenaries. In the 1850s it is unlikely that foreign enlistments ever represented more than 25 percent of the army's force level, and at times the proportion was probably closer to 20 percent.[71] Recruits had to present evidence of their good character (testimonials from parish priests or teachers were adequate) and, for those with previous military service, discharge papers to weed out deserters. The infantry uniform followed the pattern of the French army: a blue tunic with a red (indigenous) or amaranth (foreign) collar and white buttons with the regimental number, red pants, and a shako. Until the late 1850s the standard weapon of line infantry was a percussion version of a musket from 1822, although by the end of the decade more modern weapons, such as the Belgian model 1857 rifle or (for the light infantry) the locally produced Mazzochi model 1857 carbine, were coming into service.[72]

The cavalry arm consisted of one dragoon regiment (indigenous) of five squadrons, including a depot squadron responsible for recruiting, provisioning, and training men and mounts. In the 1850s the dragoons were armed with pistols and swords. The artillery regiment (mostly indigenous) deployed a depot company; five fortress or coast defense batteries; and three mobile field batteries, each with six guns. The pontifical army's order of battle also included an array of service or support units, including an engineering company; a disciplinary company; and sanitary, veterinary, chaplaincy, and military justice sections.

Two organizations were considered elements of the pontifical armed forces even though they had their own chains of command. As a paramilitary police force, the Gendarmeria Pontificia (three mounted squadrons and fourteen foot companies) fell under the jurisdiction of the ministry of the interior, but in times of military threat the corps functioned under army command, and its foot and mounted units were available for combat operations. Normally the gendarmes, armed with carbines, pistols, and sabers and often working in small detachments, maintained law and order in towns and villages, patrolled roads, and watched the borders. Noted for their strict discipline and knowledge of the countryside, the gendarmes were something of an elite force. Recruits had to be papal subjects, literate, and without connection to political groups or the revolutionary events of 1848–1849. The pope's palace guards—the Noble, Palatine, and Swiss Guards—were organized as the Military Household of the Holy Father and were responsible to the master of the Apostolic Palace, not the ministry of arms or the general staff. Normally their duties were limited to the palace and the vicinity of the Holy Father, and they were not available for field or combat operations.[73] The Swiss Guard had no connection to the Swiss battalions that formed the foreign regiments of the pontifical army; it was recruited, maintained, and commanded separately.

Unfortunately, the untimely death in July 1857 of Filippo Farina, the energetic and capable minister of war, seriously retarded the development of the army. Upon Farina's death, Cardinal Giacomo Antonelli, the pope's secretary of state and principal minister, added the ministry of war to his many responsibilities. Distracted by other duties, uninterested in military affairs, and inclined to advance the careers of his favorites, Cardinal Antonelli paid little attention to his army; consequently, many of the deficiencies of that army, which Farina had been working to ameliorate, remained unresolved and continued to undermine the capabilities of the pope's armed forces. Recruitment and training were particular concerns. All too often advancement in the officer corps depended less upon energy and ability than patronage and nepotism (a situation not unknown in other European armies), with the result that many field and staff officers were mediocre (again, perhaps, a condition shared with other European military organizations). Although not conclusive, the comments of contemporary witnesses are suggestive. "Few of the officers are good, most achieving their ranks through favoritism," one observed, and another noted, "The ministry of arms is populated either by aged and decrepit men or disreputable men, notoriously unscrupulous."[74]

The enlisted ranks had no better reputation, and their comportment suffered from the lack of serious training. Never a strong point in the pontifical army of the early nineteenth century, training improved immediately after Pius IX's restoration as veterans of the 1848 Veneto campaign tried to impart to the purged and reorganized infantry battalions lessons learned at Cornuda and Vicenza. Unfortunately, this initiative proved short-lived, and by the end of the 1850s training had declined to a focus on parade-ground exercises, marching, and close-order drill. The preoccupation with appearance also dominated the cavalry arm, where instruction in equitation was excellent but field maneuvers received little attention. Training was the weakest in the artillery regiment, where the guns were so rarely fired that the gunners were slow and clumsy in servicing their weapons and the horses were unaccustomed to the sound of cannon fire. There were no proper schools for military instruction in the army until 1855, when the ministry of arms established a cadet school to train sublieutenants in a three-year program that included courses in tactics, fortifications, topography, mathematics, report writing, swimming, and French. There were specialized courses for cadets destined for the cavalry or artillery. The cadet school never numbered more than forty students.[75]

No one believed that the restoration army alone was competent to defend the Holy Father against foreign or domestic enemies. Throughout the 1850s the Austrians continued to maintain units in Ancona, Ferrara, and Piacenza in the north of the Papal States while French troops garrisoned Rome. The protection provided by Austrian and French garrisons encouraged papal administrators to believe that the security of the Papal States did not depend on improving papal military capabilities. As in the past, few in Rome worried about the inadequacies of the pontifical armed forces until a crisis exposed those inadequacies. By 1858 such a crisis was on the horizon. Despite its defeat in the First War of Italian Independence in 1848–1849, the Kingdom of Sardinia-Piedmont had not abandoned its dream of expelling Austria from Italy and unifying the peninsula under the leadership of the House of Savoy. No one clung to this dream more than Count Camillo Cavour, the prime minister of the royal government, who recognized that to achieve its vision Piedmont required the assistance of a powerful friend. A friend appeared in the person of Louis-Napoléon, a nephew of the great Napoléon, who had managed to get himself elected president of France in December 1848, then followed in his uncle's footsteps by staging a coup and, in December 1852, convincing the French to accept him as their emperor. Despite his imperial ambitions, Louis-Napoléon (a man of somewhat contradictory tendencies) fancied himself a republican at heart. In his impetuous youth he had marched on Rome with the insurgents during the abortive rebellion in the Papal States in 1831. Many things were dear to the emperor's heart (though not at the same time), but few more so than weakening Austria, a desire exceeded only by a need to bedazzle Europe (and his own subjects) with his successes and influence in international affairs. Encouraged by Cavour, the French emperor saw an opportunity to secure both ambitions by collaborating with Piedmont against their mutual enemy, Austria. Of course Cavour had some additional items on his agenda, such as expanding the influence and territory of the House of Savoy at the expense of the Papal States, but these were small points that could be settled between friends.

The settlement came on July 21, 1858, when the French emperor and the Piedmontese prime minister met secretly at a French spa, Plombières. By the end of the day they had agreed on a joint military campaign to expel Austria from Italy and reorganize the peninsula into four sovereign units in a manner that would significantly reduce the size of the Papal States. Under the House of Savoy, a kingdom of Upper Italy would encompass Piedmont, Lombardy, the Veneto, the Romagna, and the Legations. The latter two regions were currently parts of the Papal States. A kingdom of Central Italy would include Tuscany and two additional papal regions, Umbria and the Marche. The Papal States would be reduced to Rome and its immediate environs, and the Kingdom of Naples would remain in the south. The plan clearly revealed Cavour's desire to advance the cause of national unification under the Savoyard dynasty by striking at both Austria and the papacy, both of which goals required French cooperation because Piedmont was not strong enough alone to expel Austria, and French troops, almost ten years after the Roman Republic, still occupied Rome to guarantee the security of the Holy Father.

For Louis-Napoléon the proposed reduction of the Papal States without reference to the wishes or interests of the Holy Father was a dangerous matter because it would complicate French domestic politics and potentially destabilize his throne by alienating his Catholic subjects. To neutralize this potential problem and convince himself that he was not really acting against the pope, the emperor allowed himself to be convinced by Cavour that Piedmont had no intention of entirely dispossessing the pontiff of his temporal power, that the sovereignty of the Holy Father in Rome and the surrounding provinces would be guaranteed, and that the loss of papal provinces to the projected kingdoms of North and Central Italy was an unfortunate but necessary step to ensure the stability of the Italian peninsula. The emperor's reservations were further assuaged by the offer to transfer to France the Piedmontese territories of Nice and Savoy, the latter the homeland of the dynasty.[76]

On April 23, 1859, Vienna presented Turin with an ultimatum demanding that Piedmont cease preparations for war. Cavour, of course, had no intention of acceding to such a demand since the military preparations were meant to provoke Austria. On April 29 Austria declared war and sent its troops across the Ticino River into Piedmontese territory; almost immediately France announced that it would stand beside Piedmont. Cavour had the war he wanted.

From the start things went poorly for the Austrians. In May they experienced several small but dispiriting military setbacks, and on June 4 they suffered a major defeat at the hands of a French force at the Battle of Magenta, which compelled them to abandon Milan, the capital of Austrian Lombardy, and accelerate the withdrawal of their troops from Ancona, Ferrara, and other cities of the papal Romagna and Legations. These troops had guaranteed order in the pope's northern territories. Their recall, coupled with the surge of national enthusiasm that followed upon Piedmontese successes and the example of the populations of the duchies of Parma, Modena, and Tuscany, who drove out their sovereigns and appealed for Piedmontese protection, sparked antipapal uprisings in those territories. By mid-June the papacy had lost control of Bologna, Ferrara, Forli, and Ravenna, and the insurrection had spread south to the regions of Umbria and the Marche, where the major cities of Perugia and Ancona rose against papal authority. The pope's rebellious subjects appealed for help to the Kingdom of Sardinia-Piedmont, an appeal most welcome to Cavour. Anticipating an opportunity to absorb the pope's northern territories, Cavour diverted two thousand troops from the front lines to "maintain order" in the Romagna and sent agents into the region to advance the cause of Piedmont and undermine that of the papacy. The prospect that thrilled the Piedmontese prime minister, however, distressed the French emperor. Louis-Napoléon wanted the demise of Austrian power, not papal power, and he was increasingly concerned that, if left unchecked, Piedmontese expansion at the pope's expense would compromise France's foreign and domestic politics by upsetting French Catholics who expected the emperor to protect the Holy Father. After all, why else were French troops garrisoned in Rome?[77]

Aware of the emperor's concerns, Cavour refrained from annexing outright the pope's rebellious territories, but he ordered his agents and propagandists to continue their efforts to encourage pro-Piedmontese aspirations among the population and to prevent the return of papal authority. With the emperor peering over his shoulder, he could not capitalize on the opportunities presented by the insurrections in Umbria and the Marche. With the Piedmontese in temporary check, Cardinal Antonelli sent pontifical troops to reestablish control over Umbria and the Marche. The 2nd Foreign Regiment (Swiss) under the command of Raphael De Courten easily regained control of Ancona and Sinigaglia, but another column, consisting of the 1st Foreign Regiment (Swiss) and an artillery battery under Colonel Anton Schmidt, had to fight its way into Perugia. Under orders from the ministry of arms (some sources say the orders came directly from Cardinal Antonelli) to treat the rebellious population harshly as an example to other cities, Schmidt callously allowed his troops to loot the city and abuse the citizens. What Piedmontese and antipapal propaganda described as the "massacre" of Perugia seriously compromised the reputation of the papacy, although the citizens of this Umbrian city were not entirely the defenseless victims murdered and ravaged by ferocious papal mercenaries portrayed in the European press. The insurrectionists in Perugia fought the 1st Foreign Regiment for six hours before capitulating on June 20, and fatalities in this extended battle amounted to ten Swiss and twenty-seven Perugians, although some of the latter may have been murdered during the sack of the city.[78] Though successful in suppressing the insurrections in Umbria and the Marche, the pontifical army made no effort to reestablish papal authority in the Romagna and the Legations. After the Austrian defeat at Solferino (June 24) and the subsequent armistice of Villafranca (July 11), Rome may have decided to await events in the hope that peace negotiations would return the lost provinces to papal control, or Cardinal Antonelli may have questioned the prudence of advancing the pope's army into hostile territory significantly closer to Piedmontese troops than Perugia and Ancona. If the pope and his cardinal secretary of state expected diplomacy to secure the return of the Romagna and the Legations, they were disappointed. The final settlement of the Second War of Italian Independence treated the papacy almost as if it, not Austria, had lost the war. There would be months of negotiations and deals made and unmade, principles proclaimed and then abandoned, consciences pricked and then salved, but in the end, after Napoléon III contrived a series of face-saving (for him) expedients and for his trouble graciously accepted from King Vittorio Emanuele the gift of Nice and Savoy, Rome lost almost as much territory as Vienna. The disposition of the Romagna and the Marche was left to plebiscites, the results of which, not surprisingly, overwhelmingly supported union with the Kingdom of Sardinia-Piedmont. Too weak to prevent the loss of half of his domain and too dutiful to accept compromises that would diminish the patrimony of which he considered himself a trustee, Pope Pius could do little but issue formal protests and deploy those spiritual weapons of which he had a surfeit. On March 26, 1860, Pius formally excommunicated all those involved in the usurpation of the traditional lands of the Papal States. This solemn action recovered not a square centimeter of the lost territories.

The period between the First and Second Wars of Italian Independence (1848–1859) was a turbulent and difficult time for the Papal States. It is tempting for political and diplomatic historians to understand that period as one of accelerating political decline as external and internal groups were increasingly emboldened to challenge the pope's secular rule while the instruments of state (and religion) available to the pontiff were increasingly ineffectual in deflecting those challenges. For the military historian, however, the first fourteen years of the pontificate of Pius IX are not an era characterized entirely by diplomatic disappointments, political reversals, and territorial losses. In one area at least—albeit not an area where a historian of European or papal affairs would think to look—the position of the papacy was actually improved. In the early years of Pius's reign, almost without anyone outside the institution noticing or even caring, a new pontifical army was emerging from centuries of abject mediocrity. This new army, still only dimly visible and far from complete in 1859, was not the result of yet another reorganization plan by yet another special commission. For all its very real deficiencies in training, finance, and logistics, the fundamental problems of the pontifical army in the late eighteenth and early nineteenth centuries were not organizational or financial but motivational. The soldiers who stood resolutely and fought the Austrians at Cornuda and Vicenza in 1848 did so not because they were better organized or better funded than the soldiers who had scampered from the French at the Senio River in 1797 or defected to the rebels in 1831. They stood and fought because they were better motivated.

The pontifical army that crossed the Po in the spring of 1848 had a cause—a cause it shared with the vast majority of the pope's subjects. Never in the recent history of the Papal States had civilians and soldiers shared such common purpose; never had papal soldiers been so honored and popular. These soldiers were committed to fighting for "Pope and Patria," a commitment that carried them—many naive and ill-prepared—to the fields of Cornuda or the walls of Vicenza and kept them on the fields and on the walls long after their predecessors would have given up or run away. In the process, they learned something.

They learned to be soldiers. In fact, during the First War of Italian Independence the entire pontifical army learned something. A parade-ground army, unused to duties outside small garrisons, unpracticed in the usages of arms, inexperienced in battle, ill-considered by its political superiors, and ill-directed by officers who asked and expected little of themselves and their troops, discovered in the classrooms of Cornuda and Vicenza that it could be something else—something more. Officers and men discovered, even in defeat, qualities that had long been absent from the papal military: duty, courage, honor, and confidence. The lessons remained incomplete, and later some would be forgotten, but the examples were there—in the selfless courage of a handful of dragoons at Cornuda, in the professional steadiness of an artillery battery on the Berici heights outside Vicenza, in the initiative of an infantry counterattack at that city's Castello gate, in the fatigue and discomforts of dozens of forced marches. Thoughtful observers—particularly junior officers—caught a glimpse of what their army could be, and they would recall that vision when war came once again to the Papal States.

CHAPTER 3

A War Too Soon

Frédéric François Xavier de Mérode was not the typical ecclesiastical courtier. Few priests in the pope's entourage had been in combat, fewer had received a medal for bravery under fire, and not one had killed a man in a duel. Monsignor de Mérode could legitimately claim the first two experiences and was suspected of the third. Born in 1820 to a politically and socially prominent Belgian family (his father had been foreign minister and war minister in the national government), de Mérode attended the Jesuit College of Namur but settled early on a military career. He graduated from the Royal Military College in Brussels and accepted a commission in the Belgian Army but quickly became bored with the quiet, undemanding life of peacetime garrisons. In 1844 the young sublieutenant successfully petitioned King Leopold, a friend of the family, for permission to join the French army, then fighting in Algeria to suppress the indigenous rebellion led by Abd al-Qadir, as a temporary observer. Initially attached to the staff of the French governor and commander-in-chief in Algeria, General Ambrose Bugeaud, the young Belgian officer sought every opportunity to get into the field, where he came to know General Christophe de Lamoricière, an aggressive and innovative officer who had earned a reputation for leadership of indigenous troops. While attached to French columns, de Mérode participated in two significant engagements and several skirmishes, was mentioned in dispatches, and received the Légion d'Honneur for his conduct in the action at Aydoussa. Later in his life, when asked to tell the story behind his medal, de Mérode, who was always modest about his achievements and cynical about the value of prizes and honors, replied simply, "I did no more than the vast majority of men who were there."[1]

Despite the promise of a glittering military career, de Mérode unexpectedly resigned from the Belgian army, allegedly to avoid a scandal after killing a man in a duel. Even more unexpected was his decision to go to Rome to study for the priesthood. Ordained in the fall of 1849, he entered the chaplaincy service of the pontifical army, serving briefly in the army hospital in Rome before being transferred to the garrison at Viterbo. Once again a budding military career was cut short. In the spring of 1850 Pope Pius IX, informed of the good character and sharp intelligence of the young chaplain and no doubt alert to his social and political connections in Belgium, brought him into the papal court as a private chamberlain and granted him the honorific title of monsignor. De Mérode quickly impressed Pius with his energy and initiative, and the pontiff asked his new chamberlain to look into the conditions of Rome's prisons, about which there had been many complaints. Pursuing the task, Monsignor de Mérode found a penal institution that had hardly changed since the Middle Ages. With the determination and vigor that characterized all of his endeavors, he embarked on a program of reform, introducing improvements in sanitation and food and astounding hardened wardens by insisting that the prisoners be allowed recreation and access to instruction in literacy and useful trades so that they might make their way successfully in society upon their release. His success in reforming the Roman prisons led to invitations from the governors of other papal cities to examine and revamp their jails.[2]

In the last weeks of 1859 Pius often spoke with de Mérode about the future of the pontifical army, and he discovered that his chamberlain had decided views on the subject. De Mérode believed that it was a mistake for the pope to rely upon diplomatic agreements or French bayonets for the defense of his domain. A confirmed legitimist, he despised Louis-Napoléon as a crass usurper and serial opportunist and had no confidence in the emperor's commitment to protect the pope's temporal power. The emperor's acquiescence in the loss to the Piedmontese of the Romagna and the Legations was, for de Mérode, incontrovertible evidence of his duplicity and unreliability. The monsignor believed that the papacy had to be prepared to stand alone should Paris renege on its commitment, and to this end he advocated the creation of a modern army that could defend the Papal States. As imagined by de Mérode, this army would be a multinational force of pious and loyal believers recruited from the Catholic countries of Europe for a new crusade. Rather than a campaign against infidels, this crusade would be a call to defend the territory and independence of the papacy. This multinational army not only would protect the Holy Father but, by linking military service to religious commitment, would also turn European eyes toward Rome, revitalize piety, and counter the growing threat posed by the new "religions" of nationalism and secularism. Pope Pius found this argument appealing. The humiliating loss of the Romagna and the Legations and the hollowness of Austrian and French security guarantees had soured the pope on diplomatic methods. The pontiff was particularly incensed by the double-dealing of the Emperor Napoléon, whose assertions of fidelity to the papacy were contradicted by his calls for reform and reorganization in the Papal States and his acquiescence in Piedmont's expansion into central Italy. As far as Pius was concerned, diplomacy, though consistently touted by his secretary of state, Cardinal Giacomo Antonelli, as the only path to security, had manifestly failed to protect the territorial integrity of the Papal States, and there was no assurance that it would do better in the future. Convinced by de Mérode that the papacy could not rely on others and that it was time to consider the state of the country's defenses and the appointment of a commander-in-chief who could see to those defenses, Pius asked his favorite chamberlain to recommend a new leader for the army. Fortunately, the monsignor had someone in mind.[3]

Though the sands and mountains of North Africa were a world apart from the marble and frescoes of the Vatican, Monsignor de Mérode had not forgotten Christophe de Lamoricière, the dashing general he had met and admired in Algeria. After that campaign Lamoricière had returned to Paris and pursued a political career, running successfully for the National Assembly and serving as minister of war. Unsympathetic to the coup of December 1851 that eventually led Louis-Napoléon to the imperial throne, he had gone into exile for five years in Belgium, where he had developed contacts with the de Mérode family. In Rome de Mérode took every opportunity to extol the virtues of the exiled general: pious, conservative, and a proven leader of men with a distinguished combat record. Pius liked what he heard and in the fall of 1859 entrusted Claude de Corcelle, a devout Catholic and a former French diplomatic representative in Rome, with the mission of visiting Lamoricière at his château in Piccardy and raising the possibility of entering the pope's service as commander-in-chief of the pontifical army. Upon hearing the proposal, the general responded, "I think that is a cause for which I should be happy to die." In March 1860 Pius, encouraged by this response, sent de Mérode to Piccardy to settle the details. Lamoricière arrived in Rome on April 2, 1860, and was immediately received by the Holy Father. His appointment as commander-in-chief of the pontifical army was made public five days later.[4]

It did not take long for the new commander to realize that the task of reforming the papal army was a massive undertaking. Since the French Revolution there had been several reform initiatives, but none had achieved more than minor or ephemeral changes. Most had foundered on the shoals of complacency, mediocrity, and penury. All had suffered from the absence of a patron or advocate sufficiently respected and powerful to push the army and its affairs from the margins to the center of papal affairs. Meaningful reform would require leadership by men of vision, initiative, energy, and persistence. Even more important, it would require leaders with sufficient political influence to overcome the resistance and inertia that were any bureaucracy's natural reaction to change—none more so than the Vatican bureaucracy, which was notorious for its conservatism and lethargy. Lamoricière would need a helpmate and an ally, preferably one who knew how to navigate the corridors of power inside the Vatican and, more important, who had the pope's ear. Since the death of Filippo Farina, Cardinal Secretary of State Giacomo Antonelli had exercised the functions of minister of arms, but the office received little of his attention. The cardinal was the leader of the faction inside the Vatican that believed the security of the Papal States depended not upon a strong military force but upon the goodwill of the major

Catholic powers—Austria, France, and Spain—which could guarantee the pope's temporal power against any threat. For Antonelli, diplomacy, not military preparedness, was paramount, and he cared little about expanding or improving the pope's armed forces. He agreed that the pope required forces sufficiently strong to suppress internal insurrections, thereby maintaining domestic tranquility and avoiding a pretext for intervention by the Kingdom of Sardinia-Piedmont, but he believed that for such purposes a small, lightly equipped army was sufficient. With such an attitude, Antonelli was more likely to be an opponent than a collaborator in any program to reform the pontifical army. General Lamoricière discussed the matter with Pope Pius, and the Holy Father, who hesitated to embrace the antimilitarist position of Antonelli, agreed that the heavy burdens of the Ministry of Arms should be lifted from the shoulders of the busy secretary of state and assigned to someone else. That someone was Frédéric François Xavier de Mérode.[5]

De Mérode's military background and his distrust of foreign (especially French) security guarantees made him a perfect collaborator for Lamoricière. They agreed on the need to build a bigger and better pontifical army, and together they embarked upon the most ambitious program of military reorganization and reform that the papacy had seen in centuries. It would prove a difficult journey, with obstacles blocking their path at every step. "Introducing reforms in the Vatican," de Mérode would later complain, "is like cleaning the pyramids of Egypt with a toothbrush."[6] United in their purpose, the partners brought to their collaboration complementary qualities. The minister of arms was energetic, confident, and relentless in the pursuit of his goals but was also self-centered, sharp-tongued, impatient with lines of authority, and insensitive to the attitudes of others. He made enemies easily and didn't worry about it. No less committed to his goals, Lamoricière was more moderate in their pursuit, more accepting of the inevitable discrepancy between theory and practice, ideal and reality, and less inclined to frustration and anger when all difficulties could not be resolved immediately. He understood that change solved some problems, but not all, and often created new problems, an insight that de Mérode could never embrace. "You tell me you have not the habit of command," the general wrote affectionately to his friend and superior. "I may answer that you have given a great proof of this by being surprised that, having suddenly changed all the works of your machine, you find that everything does not act with the perfection you expected."[7] They were a good team, and they set out on their difficult journey with a clear sense of their destination and a determination to reach that objective. It is no reflection on their intelligence and fortitude that they did not get very far.

Their focus would be on the army. By 1860 the capabilities of the handful of small coastal vessels still afloat in the long-neglected pontifical navy had been so reduced that the organization had been abolished as a separate entity and its ships absorbed into the maritime section of the papal customs service, the Guardia di Finanza.[8] General Lamoricière wasted no time on that lost cause. Nor did he intend to interfere with the "Military House-hold of the Supreme Pontiff," the collection of palace guard units (Noble Guard, Palatine Guard, and Swiss Guard) that were under the authority of the cardinal secretary of state and the master of the Apostolic Palace. These units were purely household troops, with little or no operational capabilities. There were more than enough problems in the regular army without attend-ing to leaky ships and decorative guardsmen.

Lamoricière's first act as the new commander-in-chief was to meet his command. At the end of April 1860 he made a tour of the Papal States, visiting garrisons, surveying fortifications, introducing himself to local com-manders, and inspecting units.[9] The tour confirmed his suspicions about the men and matériel of his army. At best the force was a parade-ground army, suited for ceremonial occasions and the maintenance of local order but lack-ing the training, equipment, and spirit necessary for defending the Papal States against external aggression. Everything—from soup to staff, from guns to garrisons—would have to change. The first priority was personnel. The army needed more men. When he assumed command, Lamoricière found a force of 16,836 men, but once he had subtracted administrative, service, garrison, and depot personnel (many too old for active service), only slightly more than half this number was actually available for military opera-tions. Numbers were not the only issue. The new commander had not been impressed by the quality of personnel. The problem was especially evident, he believed, in the senior officer corps, many of whose members treated their posts as sinecures. In agreement with Monsignor de Mérode, the gen-eral decided to increase immediately overall force levels to 20,000, with the expectation of further growth over time to achieve a force of 28,000 troops, more than half of which would be in combat units.[10] It was unlikely that the increase could be achieved solely by recruitment among the pope's own citizens. De Mérode and Lamoricière agreed that they would have to look beyond the borders for new recruits, a decision in keeping with the minister of arms's vision of a multinational force. Foreign enlistments were nothing new—since the 1830s, for example, the pontifical army had included two "foreign" (mainly Swiss) infantry regiments—but the intention now was to recruit more broadly among the Catholic populations of Western Europe. From Rome would come a call for a new crusade, not to retake distant lands long lost to Islam but to defend the traditional rights of the Holy Father in his own domain. De Mérode and Lamoricière hoped that this appeal to loyalty and piety would touch the hearts and fire the imaginations of young Catholic men in Austria, Belgium, France, Germany, Ireland, and Spain and that the resulting enlistments would increase the size of the papal military and improve its troops' spirit and commitment.[11]

Lamoricière began with the senior officer corps. To help him reorganize and direct the pontifical army, he needed experienced commanders who shared his vision of reform and had the energy and spirit to make it a reality. There was no place for lethargic time-servers or superannuated veterans who had grown comfortable in the old service; such individuals were retired or eased aside to make room for new blood.[12] Many of the new officers came from outside the papal military, particularly from the French army. Among the first was the Marquis Georges de Pimodan, the scion of a legitimist French noble family who had withdrawn from the military academy at Saint Cyr rather than take an oath of fealty to King Louis-Philippe during the so-called July Monarchy.[13] After completing his military studies in Vienna, he entered a cavalry regiment of the Austrian army. He fought in the Italian War of 1848 and the Hungarian Revolution of 1849 and rose to the rank of colonel before retiring and returning to France in 1855. Lamoricière, who wanted Pimodan as his deputy, convinced him to return to military life. Promoted to general, Pimodan would assume command of one of the combat brigades in the pontifical army. Colonel Louis de Becdelièvre, a Saint Cyr graduate and veteran of the Crimean War, during which he had fought in the battles of Alma and Inkermann, resigned from the French army to accept command of the pope's French and Belgian volunteers. Major Théodore de Quatrebarbes, who had known Lamoricière when they were young officers in Algeria, accepted an invitation from his old friend to enter the pope's service. Another French recruit was Captain Blumensthil, a twenty-year veteran of the French army who had fought in the Crimean War and most recently had commanded the artillery detachment of the French garrison in Rome. Lamoricière, who had plans for the pope's cannons, made him a lieutenant colonel and placed him in command of the papal artillery regiment. Other officers, including a promising young French-born lieutenant named Athanase de Charette, came from the now defunct ducal armies of Parma and Modena.

To facilitate the enlistment of European Catholics, the papal Ministry of Arms established recruiting offices in Paris, Marseilles, Brussels, and Vienna. The Austrian government cooperated by facilitating the movement of Austrian and German volunteers from Austrian ports to the papal port of Ancona. In other areas local bishops and notables publicized the new crusade and organized volunteers. In France, for example, Count Gaspard de Bourbon-Chalus formed a small cavalry detachment of young Catholic noblemen who provided their own horses and equipment and, as a group, entered the pontifical army as the "Squadron of Guides." In Ireland Count Charles McDonnell, an émigré in Austrian service, visited Dublin and with the cooperation of Alexander Sullivan, editor of the leading nationalist paper the *Nation*, organized mass meetings to publicize the papal cause, raise funds, and encourage enlistments under the slogan "£80,000 and an Irish

Brigade."[14] A stream of recruits flowed through the papal ports of Civitavecchia and Ancona, and when they arrived in Rome they were organized into national units. Enough Austrians arrived to form five battalions of *bersaglieri* (light infantry). More than a thousand Irish volunteers organized the "Battalion of Saint Patrick." In addition to the mounted guides, French and Belgian volunteers, many from noble families, formed an infantry battalion. By May new enlistments had swollen the size of the pontifical army to 18,777 men; by July the number was 22,077. Despite the increased recruitment of non-Italians, the pontifical army was still not entirely the "foreign" force of mercenaries so often portrayed in antipapal propaganda. Italians retained a slight majority in Lamoricière's army, representing 57 percent of the total force in July 1860 (down from 79 percent in January 1859).[15]

As volunteers poured in, Lamoricière had to attend to the administrative and logistical structure of the pontifical army, which was ill-prepared to arm, equip, feed, and clothe the growing number of troops. Armaments and fortifications, for example, required immediate attention. The artillery force consisted of a handful of antiquated guns of different types and calibers, some of which had not been fired in years. Variety and obsolescence also characterized infantry weapons; indeed, it was not unusual for a single battalion to have several different types of musket. Munitions were so carelessly manufactured and poorly stored that ammunition issued to troops was often unusable.[16] Lamoricière moved to modernize and standardize armaments. The arsenal and foundry established by Pope Sixtus V (1585–1590) in the Belvedere wing of the Vatican Palace had fallen into disuse. Once it had cast everything from church bells to cannons and stored and maintained weapons for four thousand infantry, but production of war matériel had long since been suspended. Casts, machinery, and tools had been shoved into corners and cellars, and interior spaces had been partitioned into workshops for papal craftsmen and coach-makers. During an inspection tour de Mérode and Lamoricière were dismayed by the condition of the facilities and the state of the machinery, some of which was more than a century old. Lamoricière immediately ordered the renewal of the arsenal. The artisans were evicted, the spaces cleared and cleaned, old machinery rebuilt and new machinery purchased, and skilled armorers and workers recruited. A factory for the manufacture of cartridges and shells was established that employed 120 women, perhaps the first time in the Papal States that women were employed in anything but household or cottage industries. While the arsenal was restarting its production lines, the commander-in-chief initiated efforts to purchase modern artillery and rifles from Austria and Belgium.[17]

Another inspection tour revealed the dismal state of fortifications, some of which dated back to the Renaissance. Many of the forts, such as the old coastal towers that had protected the coastline from Barbary pirates, were

antiquated and irrelevant to modern defensive requirements. Other installa-
tions suffered from disrepair and the lack of modern facilities. Lamoricière
instituted a program to renovate and modernize these fortifications by adding an engineering and construction company to the army, repairing and
reinforcing defensive walls and outworks, preparing magazines for the storage of food and munitions, and constructing new barracks for garrisons. To
support field operations, supply depots were established at Monterotondo,
Palombara, and Corinaldo. All of these initiatives received the enthusiastic
support of the minister of arms, who proved an invaluable ally when papal
auditors blanched at the costs of the new programs. For his part, de Mérode,
who saw in the renewal of the pontifical army an opportunity to advance the
more general modernization of the Papal States and its administration, embarked on a program of public works relevant (but not exclusive) to national
defense. He opened new roads in the provinces, for example, and laid down
telegraph lines to connect Rome to provincial centers such as Civita Castellana, Perugia, Spoleto, and Viterbo. He also opened a topographical office in
the Ministry of Arms to prepare maps and town plans.[18]

While engaged with military infrastructure, de Mérode and Lamoricière
did not neglect people. The commander-in-chief was especially concerned
with the morale and spirit of his troops. The pride and confidence discovered
on the battlefields of Cornuda and Vicenza had dissipated in the years after
1848, and the pontifical army had returned to its bad habits. Lamoricière
took command of an army enervated by a culture of mediocrity that discouraged initiative, imagination, and achievement; entangled in a Byzantine
bureaucracy that required for every decision the approval of several officials,
often ecclesiastics, who jealously protected their prerogatives and authority; and emasculated by the absence of any military spirit that might instill
pride and confidence. The rot was everywhere. Troops so seldom left their
garrisons or barracks that when the new command instituted a regimen of
conditioning marches, the events attracted the notice of peasants and villagers who were unaccustomed to the passage of soldiers along the roads. On
one occasion, when the newly formed Franco-Belgian Battalion halted for
the night in a village, the district governor sent a detachment of gendarmes
to investigate reports of a large body of armed men in the neighborhood.[19]
Soon after assuming command, Lamoricière was flabbergasted by a training
directive that crossed his desk announcing that a scheduled training march
would take place only if the weather was good. He was no less scandalized
to learn that weapons and munitions stored in a particular magazine were
accessible only in the mornings because the attendant responsible for the
facility always went home after lunch. On a visit to one of his garrisons, the
commander-in-chief was pleasantly surprised to discover that, unlike their
brethren in other batteries of the artillery regiment, the gunners of the local

battery had actually fired their cannons in practice.[20] These were the attitudes and behaviors of a parade-ground army that was meant for display, not combat. Everything had to change.

Change would come, in part, through intensified training and discipline, which in turn would rely on the efforts of professional, experienced officers. Georges Pimodan, for example, came to the pontifical army with a reputation as a strict disciplinarian. To better prepare and instruct his command, Lamoricière established training camps at Foligno, Macerata, and Spoleto. Change would also come from clarifying the chain of command and the apportionment of authorities and responsibilities. To rationalize the administration of military discipline and justice, the commander-in-chief established a special commission of staff and line officers to compile a new code of military justice and regularize disciplinary sanctions so that regulations and punishments were the same across all army units. Finally, change would come through instilling confidence and unit pride in men from diverse national, linguistic, economic, and educational backgrounds. In many ways this was the roughest path toward change. It was difficult to instill pride and improve morale when troops experienced nothing but indifference and neglect from authorities. They could have no good opinion of themselves in the face of the bad opinion of others. Lamoricière and de Mérode strove to reverse this indifference and neglect, and they began with seeking improvements in the living conditions of the common soldiers: renovated barracks, new and better uniforms, improved rations and provisions, and better medical care. Lamoricière in particular was aware that small comforts contributed greatly to overall morale. He insisted, for example, that troops have as much coffee and sugar as they wanted.[21] Traditionally, private contractors supplied uniforms, provisions, and other necessities to the army, but all too often the contractors were unscrupulous businessmen who padded their profits by providing inferior products. Neither the minister of arms nor the commander-in-chief intended to perpetuate this abuse of trust, but their intentions put them on a collision course with entrenched and powerful interests who did not appreciate a threat to their comfortable incomes. On one occasion Lamoricière appeared unannounced in a troop mess and insisted on tasting the bread served at the tables. Finding it so distasteful that he could not take a second mouthful, he asked a chemist at the university in Rome to analyze it and discovered that the flour had been mixed with alum and ground pebbles by the businessman who held the contract for supplying bread to the barracks. Lamoricière ordered the contract immediately terminated, only to discover that the provider was an influential figure in the society and administration of the Papal States who successfully pressed his friends in high places to countermand the order. In the past the affair would have ended there, but the pope's new general had not accepted his command to perpetuate a discredited and rotten system. He announced that if the contract was not terminated and the corrupt contractor denied further business with the army, he would resign his command immediately. De Mérode stood by his friend. The contract was canceled, and a new source of bread for army tables was found. On another occasion the general went directly to the pope to obtain permission to arrest a prominent citizen of the town of Velletri who had made illegal profits in the provision of railway supplies.[22]

The plan developed by Monsignor de Mérode and General Lamoricière was expansive in its scope and detailed in its particulars. It aimed at nothing less than the creation of a new pontifical army: bigger, better trained, better equipped, and more motivated than the small, lethargic, unmotivated force it would replace. Above all the new army would be a fighting army prepared to defend the temporal rights and territorial sovereignty of the Holy Father. It was an ambitious plan, but by the summer of 1860 improvements were already noticeable. Looking back on the reforms from a distance of a century, a professional military critic would conclude, "This work addressed almost every aspect of military organization with notable results. The army acquired stability, mobility, and manageability. It was concerned with proper combat training, previously neglected, and had improved its armaments. Defensive capabilities were also improved."[23] Still, although some aspects of the reform program, such as increased recruitment, were well in hand, most, particularly those elements concerned with training and equipment, remained in the early stages of execution. A program as ambitious as that embarked upon by de Mérode and Lamoricière required time to complete; no one, no matter how committed or capable, can reverse centuries of neglect and poor practices in a few months. Within two years the outlines of the army envisioned by the minister of arms and the commander-in-chief would have become clear, and within five years the complete, fully operational form would have emerged. Lamoricière needed years to build a new army, but unfortunately he would be given only months.

The success of the war against Austria and the acquisition of Lombardy, the duchies, and the Romagna fueled rather than dampened Turin's ardor for uniting all the peninsula under the House of Savoy. In early 1860 only the States of the Church and the Kingdom of Naples remained outside the fold, and by the spring events offered an opportunity to remove both of these obstacles to unification. In April a rebellion broke out in Palermo, the second city of the Neapolitan realm. Giuseppe Garibaldi immediately embarked for Sicily with a force of republican fighters to aid the rebels. Camillo Cavour, the Piedmontese prime minister, provided clandestine financial and logistical support for this mission in the expectation of undermining the Neapolitan monarchy and exploiting the revolution to advance the goal of unification under the House of Savoy. Garibaldi's arrival in Sicily energized the revolt; by June the Neapolitan authorities had been kicked out of Palermo, and by August they had lost the entire island. Announcing, "I came here to fight for the cause of Italy, not of Sicily alone," Garibaldi carried the revolt to the mainland.[24] On September 7 he was in Naples, the Bourbon king, Francesco II, having abandoned his capital the previous day. Although Francesco had not abdicated and the royal army remained in the field, Garibaldi made no secret of his intention to march from Palermo into the Papal States and carry the revolution to the steps of Saint Peter's.

Long before his entry into Naples, Garibaldi's successes in Sicily and Calabria had caused consternation and dismay in Paris, Rome, and even Turin. Not surprisingly, papal authorities were alarmed by the appearance of their longtime nemesis and his revolutionary army on their southern border and were convinced that Piedmont was behind the whole thing. Aware of Garibaldi's publicly expressed enmity toward France for its role in the suppression of the Roman Republic in 1849, its "tyrannical" monarchy, and its absorption of Nice (his homeland), the Emperor Napoléon was concerned about the political and propaganda consequences of a successful republican revolution in southern Italy and feared that republican sentiments might creep northward. For his part, Cavour, who considered a republican revolution in the south a means rather than an end, worried about controlling events to ensure that they complemented the interests of Piedmont, advanced unification under the House of Savoy, and did not unduly alarm the French into affirming their defense of the papacy. In Garibaldi's bluster and success, the "Piedmontese Machiavelli" saw an opportunity to address all these concerns. Exploiting Napoléon's fear of republican revolution and Garibaldi's well-known antagonism toward the imperial government in Paris, Cavour convinced the emperor that action was necessary to block the spread of insurrection. The threat would appear more immediate and the response more politically palatable if "revolts," suitably prepared, controlled, and supported by Turin, were to break out in the Papal States, particularly in Umbria and the Marche, regions along the Piedmontese–Papal States border. In such a situation the Piedmontese army would intervene to occupy those regions in order to suppress the rebellion and "restore order." Once in control of the territory, Turin's representatives would organize plebiscites similar to those that had brought the Romagna and the duchies into the Savoyard kingdom. Such plans hinged on persuading Napoléon that the political threat from Garibaldi was more serious than the political threat from French Catholics committed to the rights of their pope. In a secret meeting at the French town of Chambery at the end of August, Generals Enrico Cialdini and Manfredo Fanti convinced Napoléon that the revolutionary threat was real and that its northward march could be blocked only by Piedmontese occupation of the Papal States. The emperor acquiesced, insisting only that the pope be allowed to retain Rome and its immediate environs. He also emphasized that the invasion and occupation had to be completed before the Vatican, by portraying itself as a victim of Piedmontese aggression, could mobilize world opinion, particularly the opinion of French Catholics, on its behalf. "Good luck, but act quickly," were his final words to Turin's emissaries.[25]

Turin moved very quickly indeed. Generals Cialdini and Fanti were hardly back from Chambery when Cavour secretly summoned to Florence various leaders of the clandestine nationalist movement in the pope's northernmost lands: the regions of Umbria and the Marche. The prime minister revealed the plan to invade the Papal States and secured the leaders' agreement to launch insurrections in their regions between September 8 and 10. These outbreaks, even if suppressed, would form the pretext for Piedmont's intervention. What mattered was the fact of insurrection, not its success or its viability. As the leaders of the underground returned to their homes in papal territory to prepare their men, Cavour set in motion the preliminaries to war. On August 31 senior army and navy commanders were informed that the government had decided irrevocably to annex the papal regions of Umbria and the Marche, that the pretext for invasion would be the outbreak of revolutionary disturbances in the pope's territory, and that the invasion would proceed even if these disturbances were promptly controlled by papal authorities. On September 7 the Council of Ministers in Turin formally authorized the invasion of the Papal States and approved an ultimatum to be delivered immediately to the Vatican.[26]

In the summer of 1860 the Kingdom of Sardinia-Piedmont possessed an army of 214,000 men. No one in the Piedmontese government, however, believed that the war against the papacy would require the mobilization and deployment of the entire force. Large-scale military movements and preparations would forewarn Rome of an attack and alarm Austria and France, which might then consider intervention in support of the Holy Father. Military and political authorities in Turin intended to deploy only a force sufficient in size to overcome quickly any papal resistance. To cloak their aggressive intentions, they would maintain the bulk of the army in its peacetime dispositions and form the invasion force from units already deployed along the papal frontier in the IV and V military departments. The preinvasion operational movements of these units would be explained as routine maneuvers or deployments to monitor the activities of revolutionary bands along the border. Speed was crucial. The invading army had to be ready to move as soon as the "insurrections" that would provide the pretext for invasion broke out, so that the pontifical army would not have time to suppress the outbreaks before the Piedmontese could intervene. The rapid occupation of Umbria and the Marche would also present the world with a fait accompli.

General Manfredo Fanti commanded the invasion force, which included IV Army Corps (4th, 7th, and 13th Divisions) under Lieutenant General Enrico Cialdini and V Army Corps (1st Division and Reserve Division) under Lieutenant General Enrico Morozzo della Rocca. The force totaled more than 38,000 men, including 2,500 cavalry and 78 cannons.[27] General Fanti decided to divide this army into two operational groups: one to operate against Umbria and the other against the Marche. This decision reflected his awareness of the political imperative to occupy the two regions as quickly as possible as well as his belief (based on intelligence reports) that the ability of the already numerically inferior pontifical army to concentrate against him was compromised by the dispersal of its units across papal territory. Such dispersal would be further accelerated by the need to rush troops here and there to suppress the many nationalist insurrections that would break out across the countryside ahead of the invasion. Fanti correctly surmised that General Lamoricière, confident that Rome and Civitavecchia were adequately secured by the presence of French soldiers who had been garrisoned in these cities since 1848, would concentrate as many of his troops as possible and march north to defend Ancona, now the second city of the Papal States and the probable port of entry for any army that Austria might dispatch to contest Piedmont's invasion. The Piedmontese commander, therefore, intended IV Corps to operate south along the Adriatic coast of the Papal States, capturing Pesaro, cutting the Macerata road toward Umbria, and then marching on Ancona in order to invest this important port and block the pontifical army from reinforcing its garrison. As it moved south, IV Corps would send the Division inland to take Urbino and Fossombrone, with the intention of advancing toward Perugia. Meanwhile, V Corps would launch from southern Tuscany into Umbria and advance, via Città di Castello and Umbertide, to capture Perugia as a base for future operations. From Perugia, V Corps would move toward Foligno, placing itself athwart the papal army's main line of communications for moving troops north toward Ancona or south toward Rome.[28]

Of course none of these plans were known in Rome. By September 1860 General Lamoricière could not even be sure from what direction to expect a threat. In the south Garibaldi was still engaged with the Neapolitan army, but the commander of the Red Shirts had not abandoned his animus toward the papacy, and there was no guarantee that operations would not spill across the papal frontier. In the north there was the threat of an attack by the large Piedmontese army. Within the Papal States nationalist insurrections, perhaps abetted by cross-border incursions by sympathizers in Tuscany or the Romagna, could jeopardize internal security and domestic order. In the worst-case scenario, all these threats could emerge at the same time. With a larger army Lamoricière might have deployed his forces to counter every threat, but his modest force was much too small to simultaneously seal the frontiers against raiders, deter or suppress revolutionary outbreaks, and remain concentrated to respond in force to an invasion. The pope's commander revealed his frustration in a letter to one of his field commanders: "I cannot develop more extensive plans because we are not yet at war with anyone, but we can be attacked from any quarter. I have been forced to deploy our forces in response to this bizarre situation."[29]

To best address this complex threat horizon, Lamoricière intended to dispose his forces roughly along the diagonal that ran from Rome through Terni, Spoleto, Macerata, and Ancona. The ends of this diagonal were secured: Rome by its French garrison (two infantry regiments plus artillery and support units) and Ancona by its fortifications. The Terni-Spoleto area provided prompt access to any front that might develop in Umbria, and Macerata did the same for operations along the Adriatic coast. Excluding service, support, and auxiliary personnel, the papal commander now had some 13,000 troops available for combat operations, including 30 cannons and approximately 500 cavalry. Most of these troops were organized into four brigades: 1st (General Anton Schmidt) at Perugia, 2nd (General de Pimodan) between Narni and Terni, 3rd (General Raphael De Courten) around Macerata, and Reserve (Colonel Cropt) at Spoleto.[30] Each brigade consisted of several infantry battalions, a couple of squadrons of cavalry or mounted gendarmes, and one or two artillery batteries (each with six guns).

The balance of forces seriously disadvantaged the papal army. The invading Piedmontese would outnumber the pontificals three to one, and Lamoricière's effective strength was further compromised by his decision to maintain small detachments of infantry and gendarmes in various towns to deter insurrections. Numbers, however, were not the pontifical army's only deficiency. For all the efforts of de Mérode and Lamoricière, the army was not yet an effective fighting force. It had been only six months since they had instituted their program of reform and reorganization, and there simply had not been enough time to absorb new personnel; train and equip them; and inculcate in them discipline, unit pride, and fighting spirit. The decision to organize recruits into national units (for example, Austrian light infantry, French cavalry, and Swiss line infantry) eased the transition from civilian to military life and cushioned the shock of a new country, culture, and language, but relations among these national units were often uneasy. Lamoricière's army had four languages of command—English, French, German, and Italian—and garrison and brigade commanders sometimes required translators to communicate with their units. Everything, including the most basic necessities, remained in short supply. Despite efforts to purchase weapons from various European powers, most battalions still did not have modern rifles. The field artillery lacked horses and had to requisition mounts whenever it took to the field, which was not often because it also lacked trained drivers.[31] Every unit faced shortages. At the beginning of September 1860 the Irish Battalion, for example, still lacked uniforms, boots, haversacks, and ammunition pouches. There weren't even enough prayer books for the weekly masses. There were too few muskets to equip the battalion, and remedies appeared so remote that the commander of the companies assigned to the garrison at Spoleto tried unsuccessfully to establish in Ireland a subscription to purchase additional weapons. Many of the recruits in the foreign battalions, who felt they had joined with the promise of fine uniforms, modern weapons and equipment, good food, and comfortable lodging, were disappointed by the realities of an army just emerging from years of neglect and decay. In many battalions morale was poor, and not a few disgruntled volunteers were sent home before their ill-feeling could poison an entire unit. Desertion was common.[32] All these problems might be solved, but the solution would require time, and time was now one of the many things the pontifical army did not have. There may never be a good moment to go to war, but there can be little doubt that from General Lamoricière's perspective, the conflict that was about to break over the pontifical army came at least two years too soon.

On September 7, 1860, Luigi Masi, a well-known poet and orator of Italian unification who had fought alongside Garibaldi in the defense of the Roman Republic in 1848 and who held a commission as colonel in the Piedmontese army, arrived at Chiusi and began organizing nationalist volunteers who had hastened from various towns in Tuscany and Umbria to participate in the overthrow of the pope's temporal power. Under Masi's leadership, a column of irregulars marched on the papal border town of Città della Pieve. Upon their arrival, the town's detachment of customs police promptly defected with their arms to the revolutionary cause, but the local gendarmeria post of ten men resisted, losing two killed and three wounded before surrendering.[33] After pausing to pick up additional supporters, the irregulars, now numbering some eight hundred men, moved to attack Orvieto, an ancient cathedral town perched high atop an isolated plateau of tufa rock and defended by a company of infantry and a detachment of pontifical gendarmes. Reaching his objective on the evening of September 10, Colonel Masi decided on an immediate attack. He sent armed parties to two of the town gates, the Porta Romana and the Porta Maggiore, both of which he expected to be opened by nationalist sympathizers inside the town. A third detachment headed for the monastery of San Bernardino, from which they planned to climb over the town walls by means of a rope ladder lowered by another sympathizer. To Masi's great frustration, none of the detachments succeeded in entering the town. The gates were not open as expected, and the group scaling the heights from the San Bernardino monastery was met by a hail of gunfire from pontifical gendarmes who had been alerted to their attack by a loyal monk. Several attackers who had begun to climb the rope ladder became casualties when the defenders cut the ladder, dropping the climbers to the rocky ground below. The gendarmes maintained such a lively fire that the irregulars were forced to fall back from the walls, and Colonel Masi decided to suspend operations until the following day. In the end there would be no need for a second assault. Although the attack had been repulsed, it had shaken the citizens of the town. The next morning the mayor, Count Tommaso Piccolomini, appealed to the papal governor, Monsignor Cerruti, to intervene to avoid further bloodshed. The governor was inclined to continue the resistance, as were the officers of the garrison, but the bishop, Monsignor Giuseppe Vespignani, counseled surrender, as did a vociferous crowd that gathered outside the governor's palace. Cerruti submitted to this pressure and directed the garrison to surrender.[34]

As Masi's group of irregulars captured Città della Pieve and moved on Orvieto, insurrectionary outbreaks, most involving men and matériel infiltrating from Piedmontese territory, broke out across the pope's northern borders. On the evening of September 7, for example, a band of two hundred irregulars in the Marche attacked Urbino, which was garrisoned by a detachment of forty gendarmes. When the irregulars appeared outside the gates, the outnumbered gendarmes established themselves around the cathedral and the town hall and for an hour fought off the attackers, who were joined by many citizens of the town, before surrendering. The next day armed antipapal bands took over the nearby town of Pergola, and on September 10 insurgents seized Fossombrone.[35] On September 11 irregulars attacked the village and fortress of San Leo, about 35 kilometers southwest of Rimini. Garrisoned by a company of the 3rd Papal Bersaglieri (mainly Austrians) under the command of Captain Gallas, the fortress served primarily as a prison for particularly important or incorrigible inmates of the pontifical prison system. "Count" Alessandro Cagliostro, the notorious swindler and forger, had died in one of its cells. Upon learning of the insurrections in the Marche, Captain Gallas had brought into the redoubt enough food to withstand a long siege, so when the irregulars appeared and demanded his surrender he did not hesitate to refuse. Styling themselves the "Cacciatori di San Leo," the irregulars (almost five hundred in number, including some papal customs police who had defected to the insurrection) blockaded the fortress and prepared to take it by assault.[36]

These scattered attacks achieved their purpose of distracting and misleading papal authorities. When he learned of the attack at Città della Pieve, General Lamoricière faced a crucial decision. If these were purely local insurrections, then he could disperse his units to suppress them, but if they were actually precursors to an invasion by Sardinia-Piedmont, then he needed to keep his units together in order to meet the greater threat with concentrated force. Papal intelligence seems to have failed the pope's commander when he needed it most, since it provided little insight into the scope and nature of the threat in the north. The information available suggested that there was no immediate threat of Piedmontese aggression. In early September Monsignor de Mérode informed General Lamoricière that Piedmont had notified France that it did not intend to invade the Papal States. As recently as

September 9 Cardinal Secretary of State Antonelli had assured the general that any military problems would be limited to local insurrections and that there was no immediate threat of intervention by the Piedmontese army.[37]

Initially, Lamoricière was not entirely convinced by such assurances. If the intelligence was wrong and the Piedmontese army attacked while papal units were dispersed across the countryside chasing irregulars, the results could be catastrophic for the papacy. He delayed deploying his forces against the irregulars until the situation became clearer. On September 9 the general asked Cardinal Antonelli for more information, expressing his concern that the Piedmontese would not remain inactive during the insurrectionary disturbances. He pressed his political superiors again on September 10, insisting that he could not correctly deploy his forces without firm information about Piedmont's intentions: "Against the bands I can disperse my forces, but against the Piedmontese I must concentrate them."[38] Lamoricière, however, could not wait indefinitely while the irregular bands spread insurrection across the northern provinces of the papal domain. He may also have been influenced by recent events. In late spring a band of insurgents had crossed from Tuscany into papal territory but had been dispersed and chased back across the border by a column of troops and gendarmes under General Pimodan. The appearance of irregulars in the spring had not been a harbinger of Piedmontese invasion, so Lamoricière may have concluded that their reappearance was not a harbinger in September. On September 10, betting on Antonelli's assurances and past experience, he ordered General Anton Schmidt to move part of his brigade from Perugia to reinforce Orvieto, which the papal commander wrongly believed would withstand any attack by irregulars. That same day he authorized two troop columns from De Courten's brigade at Macerata to deploy against the irregulars around Urbino. Lamoricière, who above all feared a Piedmontese attack that would catch his small army spread across the countryside, was beginning to disperse his troops, gambling that "France and Austria will stop Piedmont from attacking."[39]

By the evening of September 10 the threat horizon had darkened considerably. That afternoon Lamoricière received an emissary from General Manfredo Fanti. The emissary carried a communication in which the Piedmontese commander informed his papal counterpart that, by order of King Vittorio Emanuele, his troops would immediately invade and occupy the Marche and Umbria if pontifical garrisons suppressed "nationalist" demonstrations or actions in any of the cities of these regions or if papal commanders deployed troops to any city experiencing such demonstrations or actions. Effectively, the communication promised invasion should the papacy take any action to defend itself against the irregular bands. That evening Cardinal Secretary of State Antonelli received a similar letter from another emissary from Turin, Count Pes della Minerva. The notes seemed to presage a Piedmontese invasion, particularly since there was no prospect that Pope Pius, never more combative than when threatened, would meekly submit to Turin's threats. Still, General Lamoricière did not immediately recall the troops he had sent against the irregulars because the latest intelligence still seemed to counsel against such action. Informed immediately of the Piedmontese ultimatum, the French ambassador in Rome, Antoine Gramont, had assured Cardinal Antonelli that the Emperor Napoléon had warned the king of Sardinia that if Piedmontese troops, "without legitimate reason," entered the Papal States, he "would be compelled to oppose" such action.[40] Unaware of his emperor's agreement at Chambery a few weeks earlier to acquiesce in Piedmont's seizure of Umbria and the Marche, the ambassador became an unwitting accomplice in imperial duplicity. Strongly propapal, Gramont may also have left Antonelli with the impression that the emperor's "opposition" would include military force, though the message did not explicitly say so. Grasping at any straw in the increasingly threatening wind, the cardinal secretary of state and the minister of arms chose to believe that French guarantees would deter Turin. Late on the evening of September 10 Antonelli informed Lamoricière that the French emperor had threatened to respond with force against any attack by Piedmont. Separately, de Mérode sent the general the same assurances, again mentioning the prospect of French military intervention. Although he was inclined to test French resolve by requesting the French commander in Rome to move some of his troops as far north as Viterbo, Lamoricière set aside his suspicions in the face of the assurances from his political superiors. Consequently, when the Piedmontese attacked on the morning of September 11, they achieved strategic and tactical surprise.[41]

General Enrico della Rocca, commanding the Piedmontese V Corps, initiated his advance into Umbria early on the morning of September 11 by sending the 1st Division reinforced by the 16th Bersaglieri Battalion and several artillery batteries against Città di Castello, the first papal town of any size on the route from the frontier to Perugia, some 55 kilometers to the south. The town had a gendarmeria post of seventy-two men but no garrison of soldiers. When the Piedmontese arrived, they were fired upon by gendarmes at the town gates. Ridiculously outnumbered, the gendarmes fell back to the municipal building, which they barricaded and from which they continued to fight as the attackers occupied the town. Rather quickly it became evident that an extended resistance would prove both futile and foolhardy against a foe whose cannons could demolish the municipal building in minutes. The gendarmes surrendered, and the Piedmontese army had its first victory. With hardly a pause General della Rocca renewed his advance into Umbria, his eyes set on Perugia, the principal city of the region.[42]

While V Corps overwhelmed Città di Castello, General Enrico Cialdini's IV Corps, launching from Cattolica on the Adriatic coast of the Romagna, crossed into papal territory and sped toward Pesaro, throwing out the 13th Division (General Raffaele Cadorna) in the direction of Urbino. At Pesaro, Lieutenant Colonel Giovan Battista Zappi, a former officer in the Austrian cavalry who had resigned from the imperial army in 1851 to accept a commission in the pontifical dragoons, commanded a garrison consisting of two companies of the 1st (Indigenous) Infantry Regiment, two companies of the 1st Foreign Infantry Regiment, five companies of auxiliaries, 70 gendarmes, 40 customs guards, and 11 artillerymen, slightly more than 1,200 men in all, with the real fighting force, the four companies of regular infantry (indigenous and foreign), representing about 500 of the total. On September 10 Lieutenant Colonel Zappi had been planning an operation to recapture Urbino from the irregulars, having been told by army headquarters in Rome that Piedmontese intervention in support of the insurrection could be excluded from consideration. He was, therefore, rather surprised on September 11 to learn from some of his officers that rumors were racing through the town that Piedmontese troops had crossed the frontier and were approaching Pesaro. Unable to obtain news from headquarters because the telegraphic connections with Ancona to the south had been interrupted, the veteran cavalryman decided to ride north to see for himself. He didn't have to ride far. At the bridge across the Foglia, the river that emptied into the Adriatic within sight of the town's walls, Zappi observed Italian cavalry scouts probing along the main road from the north, and he knew the worst was at hand. He raced back to town to prepare his command for battle.[43]

Guessing that the papal garrison would abandon Pesaro and fall back on Ancona rather than fight a superior force, General Cialdini sent a regiment of lancers around the town to capture the town of Fano, 11 kilometers to the south, and block the road to Ancona while he deployed the remainder of his force before the walls and gates of Pesaro. The Piedmontese general wanted to avoid needless bloodshed, and he assumed his papal counterpart, recognizing that the garrison was vastly outnumbered, would want the same. About 2:00 in the afternoon Cialdini sent into the town a staff officer under a flag of truce to demand the surrender of the garrison. Zappi curtly refused. The Piedmontese commander may have been surprised by this response, but he did not hesitate to order his artillery to open fire on the town gates. After more than an hour of bombardment the wall alongside the Porta Cappuccini collapsed, and Cialdini's infantry rushed through the breach and into the town to open the gates from inside. By 4:00 P.M. two Piedmontese regiments were inside the town.

Realizing that he was greatly outnumbered, Lieutenant Colonel Zappi had decided against defending the entire town. After closing and barring the gates, he ordered his men into the Rocca, the fifteenth-century fortress that dominated the town, where he was joined by the papal governor and several officials of the pontifical government. The detachment of customs guards, whose service had been thoroughly penetrated by pro-Piedmontese sympathies, chose this moment to mutiny, rejecting the order to retire into the Rocca and refusing to defend the town. Leaving the mutineers to their own devices, Zappi pulled the rest of his force behind the high walls of the fortress. The attackers therefore encountered no resistance when they assaulted the gates and walls, but as they moved along the streets toward the fortress they came under intense rifle fire. Each of the four towers of the fortress had a cannon (two of these, unloaded only the day before from the papal naval vessel *San Paolo*, were small bore), and these guns added shot and shell to the musketry from the parapets. The attackers could make no progress against the strong position, and as darkness fell General Cialdini suspended the assault until the following morning. During the night the rattle of rifle fire would occasionally startle resting soldiers, but the night remained largely tranquil until 3:30 on the morning of September 12, when Cialdini ordered his artillery to open up against the fortress. Under sustained bombardment, the old walls began to crumble. Amid the exploding shells and collapsing masonry, Zappi remained resolute, deploying and encouraging his men in anticipation of the infantry assault he knew would follow the bombardment. His resolution, however, was not shared by all of his command. After ninety minutes under the fire of Piedmontese cannons, the men of the 1st Auxiliary Battalion, a recently raised second-line unit, had had enough and openly called on their commander to surrender. Even in the face of this insubordination, Zappi was determined to resist as long as possible, understanding that so long as the bulk of the Piedmontese force was assaulting his fortress, it would not be advancing against the strategically more important target of Ancona. Already he had bought Lamoricière almost twenty-four precious hours to prepare, and additional time might well be worth the sacrifice of the Pesaro garrison. Despite the grumbling of the auxiliaries, Zappi held his command together and kept them fighting as the bombardment intensified, casualties increased, and the enemy edged ever closer to the walls. By dawn the situation was increasingly desperate, and the pontifical governor, the pope's representative in the town, added his voice to those calling on the commander to avoid further bloodshed by accepting the inevitable. Zappi could no longer hold out against the rising chorus of surrender. At 8:00 A.M. he capitulated. Twenty-one of the pope's soldiers died in the defense of the Rocca at Pesaro, and another twenty-five were wounded. Piedmontese losses were three dead and twenty wounded.[44]

Meanwhile, Cialdini's lancers were in action to the south. As it neared Fano late on the afternoon of September 11, the cavalry regiment the IV Corps commander had sent south to block the road to Ancona detached squadrons to cover the town's four gates. As it deployed, one of these squadrons surprised a small column of pontifical troops that earlier that day had marched from Fano to deal with the insurrectionists around Fossombrone.

The sound of cannon fire from the direction of Pesaro convinced the column commander, Major Dosi (who was also the Fano garrison commander), to return to his base. Upon encountering the pontificals on the road, the quick-thinking commander of the Piedmontese squadron improvised a mounted charge, hoping to overrun the small force before it could prepare. Major Dosi, however, was no less quick-witted. He immediately deployed his small force (two companies of light infantry and a detachment of gendarmes) into the rougher, less horse-friendly, ground on either side of the road and opened fire on the enemy, who were advancing straight down the road. The first volley from the papal infantry rocked the Piedmontese squadron, breaking its charge, dropping three lancers, and forcing the remainder to withdraw hurriedly. Now cautioned, the squadron commander decided against another charge until reinforcements arrived. With the enemy keeping their distance, Major Dosi and a few soldiers entered Fano while the bulk of the column marched toward Senigallia, a town farther south and only 18 kilometers from Ancona.

The commander of the Piedmontese lancer regiment was probably already pondering the problem of horsemen storming a walled town at night, so the brief but brisk skirmish on the Fossombrone road may only have confirmed his judgment that an assault on Fano should be postponed until the arrival of infantry and artillery. He pulled back his lancers and waited for IV Corps to appear. Reinforcements arrived early on the morning of September 12 in the form of General Alberto Leotardi's 7th Division. Leotardi saw no reason to hesitate. He immediately launched the 26th Infantry Regiment, bolstered by two companies of bersaglieri and four cannons, against the Porta Maggiore while directing the 25th Infantry Regiment, reinforced by two bersaglieri companies and four cannons, against the Porta San Leonardo. At both points the artillery shattered the gates, but as the infantry moved in it encountered stiff resistance from the garrison of 250 soldiers and gendarmes. The outnumbered defenders, however, could not keep the attackers from breaking into the town, especially since the bersaglieri had bypassed the gates by using ladders to climb over the walls. With the enemy pouring into Fano from two directions and his men being pressed back toward the town square, Major Dosi abandoned resistance and surrendered the town. The road to Ancona was now open.[45]

In Rome General Lamoricière learned of the invasion at noon on September 11, several hours after General Fanti's two army corps had crossed the frontier. The news was a shock. Accepting the assurances of Antonelli and de Mérode that Piedmont would not invade, the pope's commander had dispersed his forces in order to suppress the irregular bands that had suddenly appeared. Now the Piedmontese had invaded in God knew what numbers, and his combat forces were spread across the northern provinces in small columns or garrisons. His worst nightmare had become reality. The pope's commander, however, did not despair. He expected that the garrisons near the frontier would delay the enemy and buy him time to recall his scattered forces before the enemy penetrated too deeply into the Papal States. Also, he still hoped for French intervention; indeed, as late as September 12, he informed General Georges Pimodan that he had received official assurances that a large French expeditionary force would soon arrive to support the pontifical army and that he would deploy this force to hold Umbria.[46] Orders went out to pontifical units west of the Apennines to concentrate at Foligno. Only the next day, when he reached Foligno, did Lamoricière learn of the loss of Città di Castello, Orvieto, and Pesaro, news that indicated the Piedmontese were advancing more quickly than he expected. The war was only two days old, and already the strategic situation of the pontifical army was critical. Fortunately, the safety of Rome was not an immediate concern. Although Lamoricière may now have wondered about the value of French guarantees, he was prepared to gamble that the French garrison in Rome would deter any military threat to the Eternal City. Ancona was the problem. If the port was to remain in papal hands and provide an entry point for the hoped-for Austrian intervention, it needed to be reinforced. The pope's commander might have relied upon General De Courten's brigade, which was deployed around Macerata, to retire into the city to support the garrison while he concentrated all troops west of the Apennines in central Umbria to check the advance of General della Rocca's V Corps. He chose instead to move the bulk of his force toward Ancona, perhaps believing that even with De Courten's brigade, the port's garrison would be inadequate to resist Cialdini's IV Corps and that della Rocca's corps would not advance too deeply into Umbria for fear of sparking a French response. Of course, this plan required him to reach Ancona before Cialdini and to move north before della Rocca could engage him or cut him off. Given the former consideration, Lamoricière's decision is curious because by the afternoon of September 12 elements of IV Corps were on the coastal road south of Fano, hardly 20 kilometers from Ancona, while the papal commander was at Foligno, 120 kilometers across the Apennines mountain range from the port.

The rapid Piedmontese advance seriously complicated Lamoricière's efforts to concentrate his forces. In the Marche, General Raphael De Courten, commanding the 3rd Brigade at Macerata, decided to avoid a direct engagement with General Cialdini's advancing IV Corps in favor of withdrawing into Ancona. As De Courten moved toward the port with the main body of his brigade, he sent orders to two small columns he had earlier detached to deal with irregulars around Fossombrone to rejoin immediately the brigade in Ancona. For the column commanded by Colonel Hermann Kanzler, the orders were the prelude to an ordeal by fire. While trying to work its way around Senigallia, recently occupied by the Piedmontese, Kanzler's force—the 2nd Battalion of the 1st (Indigenous) Infantry Regiment, the 1st Foreign

Bersaglieri Battalion, and a section of field artillery—ran into elements of General Leotardi's 7th Division. Seriously outnumbered, Kanzler decided to outrun his enemy, dropping back two companies of his indigenous infantry and two companies of bersaglieri as a rear guard to cover the escape of the rest of the column. Leotardi's cavalry caught up with the pontificals outside the village of Sant'Angelo, forcing Kanzler's rear guard to turn and fight. A charge by two squadrons of Piedmontese lancers broke the papal bersaglieri, mainly Austrian volunteers, who after an initial volley threw down their weapons and surrendered. The indigenous infantry, however, held, repulsing not one but two cavalry charges. Falling back in good order on the heels of their comrades retreating down the road, the pope's Italian soldiers halted to repel a third cavalry charge, this one supported by Piedmontese light infantry units that had rushed forward to reinforce the lancers. Bloodied, the Piedmontese fell back and refrained from pressing the escaping pontificals with further attacks. On September 14 Kanzler led his exhausted column through the gates of Ancona to be greeted by the cheers of a garrison that had assumed the column had been lost to the Piedmontese. It had been, however, a costly achievement; more than 150 pontifical troops were killed, wounded, or captured in the desperate action along the Sant'Angelo road.[47]

In Umbria the rapid advance of General della Rocca's V Corps combined with missteps by General Schmidt, the commander of the pontifical 1st Brigade in Perugia, to seriously compromise Lamoricière's plan to concentrate quickly his units and march north toward Ancona. On September 10, the day before the Piedmontese invasion, the pope's commander-in-chief had ordered Schmidt to march on Città della Pieve, 55 kilometers southwest of Perugia, to deal with Colonel Masi's irregulars. Upon reaching Città della Pieve on September 11, the 1st Brigade commander learned that the insurgents had already moved toward Orvieto. Schmidt might have chased the irregulars or returned to Perugia, but inexplicably he sat in Città della Pieve for three days, ostensibly to reestablish papal authority in the town and to gather intelligence before deciding on his next move. During this sojourn he was out of touch with General Lamoricière and unaware of the commander-in-chief's orders for units to concentrate immediately at Foligno. If better intelligence was his purpose, he failed miserably because on September 13, when he decided to return to Perugia, he was still unaware of the Piedmontese invasion; indeed, when his force marched into the city shortly after dawn on September 14, he did not know that General Maurizio de Sonnaz's 1st Division was only a few kilometers to the north.[48]

On September 14, unable to wait any longer for the 1st Brigade and uninformed about its movements, Lamoricière sent a message to Perugia instructing the senior officer present to inform Schmidt upon his return that it was too late to link up with the main force and that 1st Brigade should defend Perugia at all costs in order to tie down the advancing IV Corps and cover the advance of the pontifical army northward. The papal commander probably did not anticipate that the defense of Perugia would begin that very day. Upon reaching Perugia, Schmidt had drawn up his column in the Piazza Rivarola before dismissing to their barracks his exhausted and hungry troops, who had marched through the night. When, about 7:30 A.M., he learned that the Piedmontese were approaching, his troops were dispersed around the town, most in the sixteenth-century fortress (Rocca) Paolina, stowing their gear and preparing to eat and sleep. Thoroughly surprised by the appearance of Piedmontese troops outside the walls, Schmidt sent to the gates whatever soldiers were immediately at hand and dispatched messengers to the barracks to sound the call to arms. It was too late. The advance guard of the Piedmontese 1st Division had reached the eastern outskirts of Perugia just as the tail end of Schmidt's column was entering the city. Deciding on an immediate attack, General de Sonnaz sent one of his staff officers, Major Rizzardi, with a small reconnaissance party to scout the defenses around the Porta Sant'Antonio. Although the gate was barred, Rizzardi surmounted the adjacent wall by means of a ladder let down by sympathetic citizens, who had been drawn to the walls by rumors that the Piedmontese were close, and he observed that there were no papal soldiers guarding the gate. The major convinced the helpful citizens to open the Sant'Antonio gate while he rushed back to inform General de Sonnaz that the way into the town was open. While Major Rizzardi was completing his mission, the 16th Bersaglieri Battalion had cautiously approached the Sant'Antonio gate so that when the portals were thrown open by friendly townspeople, the unit immediately rushed into the town. Capitalizing on the opportunity, de Sonnaz immediately pushed through the open gate the 1st, 3rd, and 4th Battalions of the 1st Grenadier Regiment and a section of artillery. He also sent the 2nd Battalion of the Grenadier Regiment along the walls to the Santa Margherita gate, perhaps expecting that sympathizers would have opened that entry also.[49]

When General Schmidt rushed men to the gates, he did not yet know that the enemy was already in the town. The first sign of trouble was the sound of gunfire from the direction of the Porta Santa Margherita. A small number of pontifical soldiers under Lieutenant Bonifazi Alvaro reached the gate just as the Piedmontese grenadiers were approaching and immediately engaged the attackers. Hearing the sound of battle but lacking information about what was happening either at the gate or in other parts of the town, Schmidt sent orders for two companies of the 2nd Foreign Regiment to reinforce the Santa Margherita gate; gathering the few soldiers still standing about the Piazza Rivarola, he ran to the scene to see for himself. At the Porta Santa Margherita, Lieutenant Alvaro was still holding off the attacking grenadiers, but a group of Piedmontese engineers rushed the gate and, under intense fire from the gate towers and walls, used their axes to open a small breach through which three sappers squeezed. These men then opened the gate from the inside, allowing the infantry to charge into the town. As the grenadiers poured through the gates, they met the two companies of the pope's 2nd Foreign Regiment who were running to reinforce the defenders. For a time, the papal troops were able to hold the enemy just inside the gate, but eventually they were forced to fall back along the streets leading to the center of town. General Schmidt, who had rushed to the scene only to find himself in the middle of an intense firefight, barely escaped capture. The Piedmontese now were pouring into Perugia through two gates.[50]

Inside the town the attackers encountered little resistance until they approached the cathedral square, where, after an exchange of rifle fire and some hand-to-hand fighting, a pontifical group was forced back along the streets leading to the Rocca Paolina. General de Sonnaz ordered the 1st Grenadier battalions forward: the 1st Battalion advancing on the fortress along the Corso, the main street of the town; the 3rd moving up a parallel street, the Via Riaria; and the 4th hanging back in reserve. He also pushed forward an artillery section to support the grenadiers' advance by bombarding the Rocca. By now, however, the defenders were organizing a resistance, thanks largely to the initiative of Colonel Lazzarini, Schmidt's deputy, who assumed command in the absence of the general, from whom nothing had been heard since he had last been seen, running off like a glory-seeking subaltern, to defend the Porta Santa Margherita. The colonel ordered the cannons of the fortress into action, and this cannon fire soon forced the Piedmontese artillery section to withdraw from the action. Lazzarini next ordered three companies from the 2nd (Indigenous) Infantry Regiment to counterattack along the Corso. This movement checked the advance of the 1st Grenadier Battalion and threatened the flank of the 3rd on the parallel Via Riaria. While the Italians of the pope's indigenous regiment pushed back against the Piedmontese, a detachment of Irish riflemen occupied the upper story of a building on the Corso, from which height they could fire down the length of the main street. Despite the increased opposition, the Piedmontese grenadiers rallied and renewed their attack, with the lead elements simply bypassing pockets of resistance. The Irish and a detachment of indigenous infantry that had taken up positions in the town hall were left to the attentions of the 4th Battalion, which followed close behind the assault battalions.[51]

Colonel Lazzarini's counterattack had slowed but not stopped the Piedmontese advance. Additional defensive efforts were compromised by a breakdown in command and discipline in some of the pontifical units, particularly the foreign regiment, which was composed largely of Swiss volunteers. Some officers seem to have abandoned their posts, and many of the enlisted men succumbed to defeatism and indiscipline. Despite Lazzarini's efforts to organize a defense, resistance was soon reduced to isolated groups of papal soldiers who continued to fight, often against daunting odds. One such group was a detachment of twenty Irish volunteers under the com-

mand of Corporal Allman (who had interrupted his medical studies at Cork
to defend the Holy Father), which had been sent to defend the Sant'Angelo
gate. These men (along with their countrymen fighting on the Corso) were
part of the newly raised Irish Battalion, but that unit had experienced some
problems with discipline and training, and its companies had been separated
and distributed among the garrisons of Ancona, Perugia, and Spoleto. Upon
reaching their assigned post, the Irishmen found the doors to the gate towers
locked, so the men deployed on either side of the closed portals. No Piedmontese troops were visible, but soon the sound of gunfire from other parts
of the town was clearly audible. Concluding that the enemy was inside the
town, the group was considering whether to fall back on the Rocca to avoid
being cut off when a large party of armed men in strange uniforms appeared
at the top of the street leading from the gate. Almost immediately the party
opened fire on the Irish, who responded with a ragged volley of their own
before retreating down a side street, the Piedmontese in pursuit. The encounter turned into a running skirmish as the pontificals ran down one street
while their pursuers ran down parallel streets in an attempt to cut them off.
At every cross street the two sides briefly exchanged fire until at one such in-
tersection the Irish decided to rush the enemy on one flank in order to break
through their pursuers and make their way to the Rocca. Leading the charge,
Corporal Allman was almost immediately cut down with a bullet in his chest,
while Corporal William Synan was hit in the jaw and Private Power took
a bullet to his foot and collapsed in the street. The other Irishmen sought
cover in doorways and against building walls, but Private Michael Murphy
braved enemy fire to rush into the street and drag the wounded Power to the
relative safety of the buildings. At this point the group split into two groups.
Six men dashed across the street to find new cover while Corporal Synan,
bleeding heavily from his face wound, led the remainder of the detachment
down a side street. Finding no way to evade the enemy, the first group soon
surrendered, but Synan's group used their rifle butts to smash down the door
of a house where they hoped to hide until nightfall. That hope was short-
lived. The Piedmontese discovered their hideout, surrounded the house, and
then attacked. Pressed back from the doorway and ground-floor windows,
the pontificals retreated to the second floor and held the top of the stairs
against several assaults. From the lower floor, the street, and neighboring
buildings, the Piedmontese kept up a heavy fire against the stairway and
through the upper windows of the besieged house. Corporal Synan received
a second wound, and several others were hit. Command of the group fell to
Private Patrick Clooney, but the situation was increasingly desperate. There
was little chance of rescue and even less of escape. The survivors might hold
the stairs until their ammunition ran out, but at the risk of further casualties
from the bullets that were flying through the broken windows. After consulting his comrades, Private Clooney decided to surrender. As the Irish were

led from the bullet-pocked building, the first Piedmontese officer they met insisted on expressing his deep admiration of their gallant fight.[52]

By 10:00 A.M. the Piedmontese had stamped out pockets of resistance and effectively occupied the entire town except the Rocca Paolina, where the remaining defenders had taken refuge. Reluctant to assault the fortress, General de Sonnaz sent two officers under a flag of truce to discuss the situation with papal commanders. Despite their white flag, the Piedmontese emissaries were fired upon by skittish riflemen in the castle, and both fell wounded. Papal officers immediately halted the firing and calmed their men. General Schmidt had unexpectedly returned from his adventure at the Santa Margherita gate and recovered the garrison command from Colonel Lazzarini, who had held together the defense while his superior was skirmishing along the streets of the lower town. He went out from the fortress to meet General de Sonnaz and make amends for the unfortunate breach of military protocol. The papal general realized that the battle was over and that all that remained was to secure honorable terms for the surrender of the town. The two commanders had agreed on a temporary truce to allow extended discussions when General Manfredo Fanti, the commander-in-chief of the Piedmontese invasion, whose headquarters had followed closely behind the advancing V Corps, appeared and took control of the negotiations. General Schmidt had expected that capitulation terms would allow his garrison to march from the city with its flags, arms, and baggage, a routine professional courtesy that symbolically allowed a defeated force to surrender with honor. Fanti, however, cared little for the honor of the pontifical army and saw no reason for extended negotiations. The Piedmontese general told his papal counterpart that the garrison would not be allowed to depart from the fortress with its flags and weapons. The men could carry their personal baggage but nothing more. The pope's foreign troops would be immediately repatriated to their home countries, and the native-born soldiers would be allowed to return to their homes or to enlist in the Piedmontese army at their papal ranks. All papal troops would sign a pledge not to take up arms against the forces of the Kingdom of Sardinia-Piedmont for the remainder of the war.

For Schmidt, the retention of weapons was the sticking point, so he broke off negotiations and returned to the Rocca, although both parties agreed to extend the truce until 4:00 P.M. The papal commander may have assumed that neither Fanti nor de Sonnaz wanted to storm the citadel and that the prospect of continued resistance would encourage them to compromise. Schmidt, however, discovered that effective resistance was increasingly unlikely. Demoralization and disorder were spreading among the defenders inside the Rocca. Troops, including officers, were leaving their posts, and while the generals were discussing capitulation terms, some had actually left the fortress to fraternize with the Piedmontese soldiers deployed in the nearby streets. Morale was not improved by public demonstrations of antipapal sentiments by the civilian populace, many of whom (perhaps recalling General Schmidt's ruthless suppression of the nationalist insurrection only a year earlier) welcomed King Vittorio Emanuele's army as liberators.[53] Twice more Schmidt appealed to Fanti to allow the garrison to march out with its weapons, if only as far as the outskirts of town, before surrendering the guns. The Piedmontese commander was immovable, and he announced that if the citadel were not surrendered by 5:30 that afternoon, he would immediately attack. Schmidt may have thought Fanti was bluffing because when the appointed hour arrived, there was still no white flag flying over the ramparts of the citadel. True to his word, Fanti ordered his artillery (which had moved into positions around the fortress) to open fire. As the first shells exploded against the masonry, the defenders' spirit, which had been weakening for some time, broke completely, and within minutes Schmidt realized that he had lost control of his troops and that further resistance was impossible. He raised the white flag and accepted Fanti's conditions for surrender. In the defense of Perugia the pontifical army lost 37 dead and 60 wounded. Piedmontese casualties were 7 dead and 56 wounded. For General Lamoricière, hurrying his field force toward Ancona, the strategic loss was far more serious than the human. The commander-in-chief had expected Schmidt to cover his movement north by holding della Rocca's V Corps outside Perugia for several days; instead Perugia had held out only several hours, and Schmidt's 1st Brigade had been eliminated as a fighting force. The following day (September 15), V Corps moved on to capture Foligno, which the papal field force had abandoned only two days before. Now the enemy was in Lamoricière's rear.[54]

From Foligno General Fanti pushed the bulk of V Corps north toward Tolentino and Macerata, chasing after Lamoricière in the hope of pinching the pontifical commander in the center of what was now a three-pronged Piedmontese advance: Fanti's force, General Cialdini's IV Corps coming down from the north, and General Cadorna's 13th Division moving south from Urbino against no opposition. To consolidate his control of Umbria, however, Fanti had to neutralize the small papal garrison at Spoleto, 26 kilometers south of Foligno. To deal with this minor problem, the Piedmontese commander ordered General Filippo Brignone to capture Spoleto with a force composed of the 3rd Grenadier Regiment, the 9th Bersaglieri Battalion, two squadrons of cavalry, and six pieces of field artillery—a total of approximately 2,400 men. Fanti was confident that Brignone's column was sufficient to take the town in a couple of hours. The column would then consolidate Piedmont's control over Umbria by moving farther south to occupy the towns of Terni and Reiti, the latter only 80 kilometers from Rome.[55]

Built on the side of a hill at the top of which stood an imposing fourteenth-century citadel, Spoleto had never been intended by General Lamoricière to be a strong point in the defense of the Papal States. Militarily, it served the pontifical army as a training station and a depot for soldiers deemed unfit for field service because of health or disciplinary problems. Under the command of Major Myles O'Reilly, the small garrison of 670 men included two companies of the Irish Battalion; a training company for recent Swiss recruits; a detachment of pontifical gendarmes; and various Austrian, Belgian, French, and Italian personnel left behind when their units marched with Lamoricière's field force. Most of the troops were only partially trained (the Swiss recruits were hardly trained at all), and they lacked weapons, ammunition, and food.[56] Upon learning of the Piedmontese invasion, Major O'Reilly had traveled to Foligno in search of needed supplies. He managed to secure some ammunition but could find no wagons to transport the munitions to Spoleto. As he canvassed the streets of Foligno in quest of an officer or vendor who could provide transport, O'Reilly encountered General Georges de Pimodan, who was preparing his 2nd Brigade for the march north. When asked by the general where he was going, the major replied, "To try and get carts to carry ammunition." Pimodan, who by then was well aware of the deficiencies of the pontifical army and the regime it served, replied with more than a little fatalism, "And do you imagine you will get any? No, no; you will get nothing in this country in such a hurry; we can get nothing done."[57] Frustrated by the greed and lethargy of local provisioners, the Spoleto commander was no more successful in securing additional food supplies for his men.

On September 15 word of the fall of Perugia and Foligno reached Spoleto. Believing that his small garrison was now threatened by the entire Piedmontese V Corps, O'Reilly sent a message to the Ministry of Arms in Rome asking if there was any chance of reinforcement and affirming his intention to hold the town to the last. In reply, Monsignor de Mérode cabled, "If the telegraph conveyed tears, there would be some of mine on this. I can only say, do your duty. The true reward is not for the stronger." The Spoleto commander may have found this response edifying, but he did not find it very helpful. "It told me we fought without hope," he recorded in his diary, "but it did not tell me what I wanted to know—to what extremity I was to carry resistance."[58] It was apparent to Major O'Reilly that he and his men were on their own. With the enemy only 26 kilometers away, an early attack could be anticipated, but the defenses of Spoleto were woefully inadequate. Not only was the garrison small and ill-prepared, but the fortifications were obsolescent. Constructed in the fourteenth century, the imposing Rocca was well designed to repel medieval infantry but completely unsuited to withstand attack by a force armed with rifles and artillery. The citadel stood at the summit of the hill and was surrounded by a defensive wall constructed lower down on the slopes. Though thick-walled, the flat-roofed building was unsuited for modern warfare because it had few windows or firing slits and lacked a parapet that might protect defenders firing from the roof. The defense of the citadel, therefore, depended on holding the outer walls, especially the south wall and its gate on the town side, a difficult task for a few hundred men. On the east the Rocca abutted a steep ravine on the other side of which (only a few hundred meters away) rose the slopes of Monte Luco, which overlooked the citadel. Sheltered by trees and rocks, riflemen and cannons on these slopes could fire down on the fortress. The garrison possessed only three cannons, only one of which was serviceable.

On the evening of September 16, Major O'Reilly pulled in his outposts, including the guards at the town gates, and ordered all his troops inside the walls of the Rocca. Everyone anticipated an early attack, but even so the troops moving across the cathedral square just below the citadel in the gathering darkness were startled by the sudden appearance of two Piedmontese lancers who, without any warning (and as if out of thin air), galloped into the square. The intruders pulled up their horses and exchanged startled glances with the papal soldiers who stood around them before turning their mounts and galloping from the square. The episode was so brief and unexpected that many of Major O'Reilly's soldiers, frozen into inaction by their surprise, might have wondered if they had witnessed an apparition. Unfortunately for the garrison, the cavalrymen were only too real, and their abrupt appearance, though not supernatural, was no less an evil omen than the appearance of the Furies in a classical Greek drama. The Piedmontese were already in the city.

General Brignone and his column had marched from Foligno on September 16 and had advanced without incident to the village of San Giacomo, about 6 kilometers from Spoleto, when a detachment of lancers, scouting in advance of the column, had encountered a patrol of mounted pontifical gendarmes. The pontificals turned immediately and raced back toward Spoleto, with the lancers in pursuit. Five of the gendarmes were captured during the chase, but the last, perhaps because his horse was stronger, made it home, although two lancers remained hot on his heels. As soon as he passed through the gates (which were undefended after Major O'Reilly's order for the guards to withdraw into the fortress), the gendarme jumped from his exhausted mount and escaped on foot into the narrow, twisting streets of the town. Unaware that their target had eluded them but encouraged by the fact that the town appeared to be undefended, the two lancers, whose boldness (or imprudence) was extraordinary, pressed forward. Their foray carried them into the cathedral square, which seemed to be teeming with papal soldiers, who were no less surprised than they by the encounter. Wheeling about, the cavalrymen spurred their sweat-flecked horses from the square, shaken by their brush with death but eager to report that the gates and walls of Spoleto were undefended and the town open to attack.[59]

As General Brignone hurried his division forward, he sent his cavalry squadrons around the town to cover the road south to Terni and Rome and block that avenue of retreat. By early morning on September 17 the Pied-

montese were occupying positions inside the town. Two battalions of the 3rd
Grenadier Regiment, with two companies of bersaglieri and two sections
of artillery, moved close to the gate of the fortress while two companies of
bersaglieri occupied the slopes of Monte Luco, from which their rifles could
dominate the fortress below. By 6:00 A.M. the troops were deployed, and
Brignone sent his chief of staff to the citadel's gate under a flag of truce with
a request to speak to the fortress commander. Fearing that if admitted the
Piedmontese officer would notice how small the garrison was, Major O'Reilly
stepped out to meet him in front of the closed gate. The emissary demanded
the surrender of the Rocca. O'Reilly politely refused but agreed to send one
of his own staff, Captain John Coppinger, to meet General Brignone while
O'Reilly and the emissary waited outside the gate.[60] At the Piedmontese
general's makeshift headquarters, Coppinger listened as Brignone explained
that the garrison's position was hopeless and that there was no dishonor in
capitulating before superior force. The papal captain replied that surrender
was out of the question. When Coppinger returned from this brief encounter, the Piedmontese staff officer, who could not understand why the papal
commander would not accept the obvious, made a final plea. Reiterating the
futility of resistance and reminding the pontifical commander that no one
would come to his rescue, he insisted that no commander could be expected
to defend a completely untenable position. O'Reilly again demurred, noting
that as a soldier, the Piedmontese officer must surely understand that duty
required him to defend the position entrusted to him and adding that General Brignone might discover that the fortress would prove harder to subdue
than he imagined. The papal commander, however, asked if his wife, the wife
of one of his officers, and two female servants, the only women inside the fortress, might be allowed to depart the citadel before any attack. General Brignone immediately agreed to this request, and the women returned to the
Piedmontese lines with the emissary. As the small party under its flag of truce
disappeared into the town, an ominous silence fell over Spoleto. Behind the
Rocca's walls, Major O'Reilly and his men prepared for the inevitable.[61]

They didn't have long to wait. At 10:00 A.M. the Piedmontese opened
fire with cannons and rifles, and from loopholes in the Rocca's outer defensive wall the fortress garrison responded with rifle fire of their own. For
the defenders, the fusillade from Brignone's bersaglieri on Monte Luco was
especially worrisome, not just because the Piedmontese sharpshooters could
fire down on the papal positions but also because the enemy riflemen were
beyond the range of the antiquated muskets with which most of the pope's
soldiers were equipped. Still, the defenders kept up a brisk fire, and Major O'Reilly moved about from one section of the walls to another, showing
himself to his troops and shouting words of encouragement. About 11:00
the Piedmontese fire ceased, and once again a party bearing a flag of truce
approached the citadel's gate. Hoping that an hour's worth of bombardment

might have knocked some sense into the defenders, General Brignone sent forward another emissary, Spoleto's bishop, Monsignor Giovanni Arnaldi, with the task of convincing Major O'Reilly to capitulate. Once again the papal officer, accompanied by Monsignor Pericoli, the papal governor, who had moved into the fortress with the troops, stepped outside the gate, knowing full well what the messenger would say. Bishop Arnaldi advised the commander and the governor that further resistance was futile and that even the pope would not want blood shed in a hopeless cause. O'Reilly politely explained to the elderly prelate that he simply could not surrender his post so long as there was a reasonable prospect of defending it. He was duty-bound to fight. For his part, Monsignor Pericoli declared that he would leave military decisions to the military but that he was prepared to share the fate of the garrison. Bishop Arnaldi could dissuade neither the major nor the governor. Disappointed, he gave the papal officer his blessing and returned to town to report to General Brignone.

During this conversation, the defenders inside the Rocca were able to grab some food, gulp down water, and replenish their ammunition pouches, so when the Piedmontese renewed their bombardment, the troops were slightly refreshed. Surprisingly, the morale of the papal troops was high. Though they understood that they were isolated and outnumbered, the largely untrained recruits and depot personnel had endured an hour of heavy bombardment and stood resolutely at their firing positions, an experience that had enhanced their confidence and elevated their spirits. For their part, the Piedmontese seem to have been rather disconcerted by the refusal of the papal troops to see reason and surrender. When by midafternoon the renewed bombardment still had not knocked sense into the defenders, General Brignone ordered his artillery to cease fire. An affair that he had expected to take only a couple of hours had now continued for more than twice that time. Brignone decided to put an end to the business with a direct infantry assault against the citadel's gate.

The front entrance to the Rocca opened onto the large Piazza Santo Simone, whose other sides were enclosed by town buildings. Behind an unfortified outer gate, an inclined road ran to the right for about 100 meters to the main gate, which was at a right angle to the citadel's outer wall. On its left this approach road abutted this outer wall so that attackers moving toward the main gate had to run a gauntlet of fire from defenders situated along the top of the fortification. Brignone believed that if covering fire from the buildings around the piazza could force the defenders from the wall, a sudden, spirited charge could quickly traverse the killing zone beneath that wall and carry through the gate, which had been damaged during the earlier bombardment. The Piedmontese general formed an assault party of two companies of bersaglieri with a battalion of grenadiers in reserve. Another company of bersaglieri took up positions in the windows and on the roofs of nearby buildings to provide covering fire. The assault party, in ones and twos, moving from doorway to doorway and shadow to shadow and cursing every thud and rattle caused by their weapons and equipment, crept along the streets and into the piazza, hoping to move unnoticed as close to the outer gate as possible. About 3:30 in the afternoon, they were in position, and for several minutes there was neither sound nor movement in the piazza. Then the uneasy silence was broken by the call of a trumpet followed immediately by the blasts of rifles, and the empty piazza was suddenly full of yelling, charging infantry. The bersaglieri, some carrying axes, ran up to the undefended outer gate, which they smashed through quickly. They then turned right to rush up the approach road to the main gate as bullets from the covering fire of their comrades across the square whined over their heads. They ran directly into a deadly firestorm.

From the start Major O'Reilly understood that when the Piedmontese came, they would come through the main gate, so he had positioned his best soldiers, the two Irish companies under Captain Coppinger, immediately behind the gate and along the wall overlooking the approach road. He also placed his one working cannon in the embrasure of the gate. Behind the main portal was a small courtyard whose far end was closed by another gate. Against this interior gate O'Reilly moved two large wagons to be overturned and used as a barricade and a second line of defense in the event the main gate was forced. Behind these wagons the major positioned a section of Irish troops to serve as a reserve. Despite the efforts at stealth by the bersaglieri, their movement into the Piazza Santo Simone had been observed by Irish riflemen on the wall. Guessing that an assault was imminent, O'Reilly alerted the men behind the gate and sent Captain Christian de Baye, a veteran of the French army and his most trusted officer, to command the cannon in the embrasure alongside the portal. The major took up his own position in the courtyard near the wagons, where he could take personal command of the Irish reserve when, as he fully expected, the Piedmontese carried the gate.

As the attacking bersaglieri charged up the approach road, they endured withering musketry from the Irish infantry on the wall and from those shooting through loopholes at the gate. As the assault party neared its goal, it was rocked by a blast of grapeshot from Captain de Baye's cannon, but Captain Prevignano of the bersaglieri bravely rallied the party and pressed forward. The bersaglieri reached the gate and began hacking with axes at the timbers, which were already splintered and broken in places by the earlier bombardment. From their side, the Irish fired and jabbed bayonets through the gaps, and the Piedmontese responded in kind. For several minutes (which surely seemed like hours to the participants), the furious combat continued, the combatants, blinded by gun smoke and deafened by guns firing next to their heads, shooting and stabbing within inches of each other, separated only by the thickness of the gate planks. Captain Prevignano narrowly escaped death when he grabbed the muzzle of an Irish musket and turned it aside just as its owner fired, then promptly dodged a bayonet thrust to cheat death a second time. The bersaglieri wielding an ax at his side was not so lucky, falling dead from a bayonet in the chest. Suddenly the brassy call of bugles sounding "Retreat" could be heard above the tumult. General Brignone, observing the assault from a building across the square and noticing that the attack was stymied, was recalling his troops. For a second time, the bersaglieri had to brave a gauntlet of fire as they ran back down the approach road under continuous attack from the papal riflemen on the wall and from de Baye's cannon, which chased them with a final shot. The gallant Captain Prevignano was the last to reach the safety of the piazza. Behind him, along the road and around the gate, lay the bodies of eleven dead bersaglieri. Another twenty-two attackers were wounded. Among the defenders casualties were light: one dead and several wounded.[62]

For the Piedmontese, things were definitely not going as planned. Though mortified by his failure to secure Spoleto, an affair that had been supposed to be wrapped up in a couple of hours, General Brignone did not relish another costly frontal assault. He decided to pound the garrison into submission, ordering his cannons back into action and sending to General Fanti for artillery reinforcements. Throughout the remainder of the day, Major O'Reilly and his garrison endured an intense bombardment against which they were largely helpless to respond. About 8:00 P.M. O'Reilly requested a truce to retrieve the dead and wounded, and the cannonades stopped. By then the garrison had suffered only three dead and ten wounded, and all had fallen within the walls of the fortress, so retrieval of casualties was not a major issue for the pontificals, but the truce brought a welcome respite during which the papal commander called a council of his captains to consider the situation. For twelve hours and at the cost of relatively few casualties the undermanned, underequipped, and undertrained garrison had held the Rocca under intense fire from a superior force and had repelled a significant infantry assault on the fortress. Except for their Piedmontese counterparts, no one was more surprised by the course of events than the pontifical officers, who had always been well aware of the deficiencies of their command. The question was, could they—should they—prolong the resistance? There was no chance of relief. Continued resistance would enhance the honor of the garrison, but aside from tying down a relatively small number of Piedmontese units, a prolonged defense would serve little military purpose. An extended resistance might not even be possible. Although a stream and an aqueduct ran just outside the walls, the Rocca itself was inadequately supplied with water, and the defenders were feeling the effects of thirst. Ammunition was running low, as were the spirits of the troops, who, without the distractions of immediate combat, were beginning to realize that they were surrounded and abandoned. Already some of the greener troops inside the main building had panicked under the bombardment, which had caused several fires on the roof of the citadel. As the situation of the garrison worsened, it would be more difficult to secure favorable surrender terms.[63]

With the truce still in effect, Major O'Reilly sent Monsignor Pericoli, the papal governor, to General Brignone to raise the possibility of surrender and to inquire about terms. The emissary returned to the citadel with a report sufficiently promising that O'Reilly, accompanied by Captain de Baye, left immediately for Piedmontese headquarters. Brignone, who saw an opportunity to end without further blemish to his reputation a wretched operation that had now cost him fourteen dead and forty-nine wounded, received the papal officers with every courtesy and expressed his desire to offer the best terms consistent with his orders to occupy Spoleto and its fortress.[64] O'Reilly skillfully considered his few cards. Aware that Brignone remained ignorant of the deteriorating conditions inside the citadel and guessing that his opponent relished the prospect of neither a long siege nor another bloody assault, the papal commander readily acknowledged that surrender was probably inevitable but added that he was confident that the garrison could continue to hold out for some time. He indicated that the only question in his mind was whether to surrender then or later, and that he was prepared to be influenced toward the former by the offer of attractive terms. Brignone was only too happy to influence him; indeed, O'Reilly might well have held out for even better terms. In the end the two officers agreed that the garrison would capitulate, that papal officers would retain their swords (a particular point of honor in nineteenth-century armies) but agree not to take up arms again during the war, and that the papal soldiers would surrender their weapons but remain free to return to their homes. General Brignone then dictated a statement to be included in the capitulation agreement to the effect that "the officers and men will everywhere be treated with that courtesy which is due to troops that are honorable and brave as they have shown themselves to be during the fighting today." Turning to O'Reilly, the Piedmontese general added, "It is only the truth, and I feel bound to state it."[65]

While General Fanti was rapidly moving into Umbria, General Lamoricière was rapidly moving out. On September 13 the papal commander had marched his field force northeast from Foligno toward Ancona. The force moved in two columns, the lead column under Lamoricière's personal command marching a day ahead of a column led by General De Pimodan. By September 15 the lead column, pressing forward despite oppressively hot weather, had reached Macerata. Speed was critical if the force was to reach Ancona before the Piedmontese could bar the way, but Lamoricière decided to interrupt his progress in order to escort to the small harbor of Porto di Recanati a trunk of money destined for the financial relief of the garrison in Ancona. Although a detachment of gendarmes would have been sufficient to ensure the safe arrival of the shipment, the papal commander unaccountably decided to assign his entire column to the task. This untimely diversion, tenuously justified on the grounds that the money could move more safely in the hold of the small steamer *San Paolo* (one of the pope's few remaining naval units), which had been sent down from Ancona to rendezvous with the land escort, distracted Lamoricière at the very moment when he should have focused all his (and his force's) energies on pushing quickly up the road to Ancona. To resume his march toward Ancona, Lamoricière intended to re-turn inland and proceed to Loreto, a town several kilometers from the coast on a main road toward the port city. While waiting for the *San Paolo* at Porto Recanati, the general received word that the Piedmontese had occupied Loreto. This was very unwelcome news. If the intelligence was accurate, then the enemy was athwart his line of advance. He immediately dispatched a patrol of mounted gendarmes to reconnoiter. This patrol entered Loreto and found the town empty of soldiers, but townspeople confirmed that the Piedmontese were on the other side of the Musone, a river just beyond the northern limits of the town. Scouting toward the bridge that carried the road to Ancona across the river, the pontifical gendarmes came under fire from riflemen positioned on the far (left) bank. Lamoricière had encountered the Piedmontese army before he could reach Ancona, precisely the eventuality he had hoped to avoid. As he led his troops into Loreto on the evening of September 16 to await the arrival of General Pimodan's column, which was a day's march behind on the Macerata road, the papal commander knew he would have to fight.[66]

On the night of September 14–15, General Cialdini had received in-telligence that the pontifical army in two columns was marching north via Macerata toward Ancona, and he hurried to bar its way, first by establishing elements of IV Corps around Osimo, 27 kilometers north of Macerata on a main road to Ancona, and then by shifting other units southeast toward Lo-reto to block another important road to the·port city. The latter units were ensconced on the hills around the neighboring villages of Castelfidardo and Crocette, which commanded the Ancona road just north of Loreto and the Musone river. By September 17, when General Lamoricière was establish-ing his force in Loreto, the Piedmontese IV Corps was deployed along a 10-kilometer front extending from Osimo to Castelfidardo, with the outposts of its extreme left flank established on the left bank of the Musone, just below Loreto, where the hills sloped down to the seaside plain.[67] This deployment posed a considerable problem for Lamoricière. He could not allow himself to be bottled up in Loreto, but a retreat would force him to abandon Ancona and require him to face the Piedmontese V Corps hurrying up the road he had just marched. To advance up either of the two main roads to Ancona, he would have to fight his way through Cialdini's IV Corps, a numerically supe-rior force. Whatever his choice, he would have to implement it with an army tired and hungry from a long forced march.

Campaign of September 1860

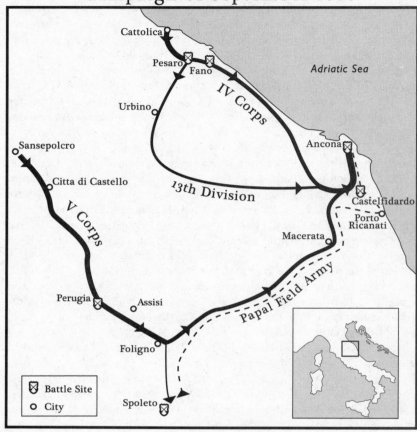

Lamoricière chose to advance, but not along the roads controlled by the enemy. Studying his maps and consulting the local inhabitants, the general determined that a secondary road ran north from the point where a small river, the Aspio, joined the Musone just below Loreto and just beyond the easternmost outposts of IV Corps's line. Passing through the coastal villages of Umana and Sirolo, this road continued north to Ancona, approximately 30 kilometers to the north. Assured by reconnaissance patrols that the Musone was not fordable below Loreto, General Cialdini had not deployed units to cover this secondary road, preferring to concentrate his forces around the main roads and bridges upriver.[68] Lamoricière, however, had been assured by locals that the river was indeed fordable at several points below the town. With this knowledge, the papal general decided on a daring plan. Divided into three columns, his force would cross the Musone at three separate points downstream from Loreto. The first (left) column, commanded by General De Pimodan, whose exhausted force had staggered into Loreto on September 17, would ford the river at a group of buildings known as the Casa Arenici on the right bank, brushing aside what was expected to be only light opposition; establish itself on the far bank at another collection of rural structures, the Casa Andreani-Catena (the Lower Farm); and then wheel left to face Cialdini's left flank. Because this was the end of the Piedmontese line, Pimodan would have a temporary advantage of numbers. He would roll up the enemy's flank, advancing uphill a couple of hundred meters to another agricultural complex, the Casa Serenella del Mirà (the Upper Farm), and then on to the summit of the hill (Montoro, the first hill rising from the coastal plain), which was crowned by yet a third set of buildings (the Casino Sciava). At this point Pimodan would halt, establishing a blocking position to prevent the Piedmontese from moving downriver along the left bank. Meanwhile, the second (center) papal column, commanded by General Lamoricière, would ford the Musone a few hundred meters below the first column and then wheel left to establish a reserve line in support of Pimodan's force. The third (right) papal column, consisting primarily of the baggage train, reserve artillery, and a detachment of gendarmes, would cross the river a bit farther downstream and make directly for the escape road.

Although the directives for the initial phases of the operation were clear enough, Lamoricière's intentions concerning the subsequent course of the battle seem to have been poorly articulated. In its simplest form, the operation required Pimodan's column to seize the high ground and, perhaps sacrificing itself, hold the Piedmontese in order to allow the bulk of the pontifical army (the center and right columns) to escape north along the Umana road. The deployment, however, of the central column as a reserve for Pimodan's force, facing the enemy and available to move forward to support the front line, suggests that flight was not the only option in Lamoricière's mind. Was the central column meant to fight or flee? Every unit pushed forward to fight on the slopes and crest of Montoro was one less unit escaping intact along the road to Ancona. If the escape of the bulk of the army to reinforce Ancona was the point of the operation, there was little sense in committing two of the three columns (approximately three-fourths of that army and almost all of its combat units) to fighting a potentially costly holding action against a superior force while the remaining column (mainly the baggage train) made it away. Perhaps Lamoricière expected the units holding the Piedmontese to disengage after a suitable period and retreat in good fighting order in the wake of the baggage train, but an officer as experienced as the papal commander would have realized that such a maneuver was difficult to execute, and, since no one could assume that the Piedmontese would decline pursuit, an experienced officer also would have recoiled from the prospect of a fighting retreat of more than 30 kilometers to Ancona. Alternatively, Lamoricière may have been tempted by the prospect of a victorious battle despite the disparity in numbers. If Pimodan's column could quickly roll up the exposed left flank of Cialdini's line and seize the heights of Montoro, perhaps rather than establishing a blocking position to protect the escape of the other columns, it could continue to advance (supported by the ready reserve of the second column) before Cialdini could redeploy his forces from south to east. Such a bold attack might force the Piedmontese to disengage and withdraw, thereby scoring a tactical victory and ensuring the escape of the bulk of the pontifical army. Whatever his expectations, it is clear from Lamoricière's deployments that he wanted to keep his options open and be in a position to respond to opportunities as they developed on the field of battle.

The papal army moved on the morning of September 18. At dawn General Lamoricière and his senior officers attended mass in the famous Sanctuary of the Holy House, the church that contained what pious Catholics believed to be the house of the Blessed Virgin Mary, while chaplains circulated among the various units. The troops prepared, checking their equipment, making coffee, and waiting for breakfast, which was distributed so late that it was not yet cooked when the officers commanded the men to form the line of march. Thus, many of the men (including General Pimodan, who had to make do with a slice of bread) marched to battle unfed.[69] The first to move out, at 8:30 A.M., was General Pimodan's column, consisting of five battalions of infantry, two batteries (12 pieces) of artillery protected by a rifle company from the Irish Battalion, and two squadrons of cavalry—approximately 3,500 men. Before marching, Pimodan, mounted on a jet-black mare, trotted the length of the column, speaking words of encouragement to the various national battalions in their native tongues—French, German, Italian—and pausing to converse and shake hands with their officers. To one group of officers he commented, "When you are again with your families, you will secretly yearn for this day."[70] Thirty minutes later Lamoricière marched with the center column of 3,300 men, representing four infantry battalions, a detachment of cavalry, a half squadron of mounted gendarmes, and the artillery park. The baggage column departed at the same time.

The operation achieved tactical surprise. Although IV Corps controlled the left bank of the Musone and occupied the heights overlooking Loreto, the Piedmontese had poor intelligence about the intentions and movements of their opponents. Cialdini and his staff did not expect to fight on the 18th, and when the battle came they did not expect it to occur on the extremes of their left flank. Although a picket from the 26th Bersaglieri Battalion, which was established in the Lower Farm and Upper Farm as the extreme end of that flank, had waded across the Musone at Casa Arenici (at which point the river was hardly 2 feet deep) to establish an advance observation post on the right bank exactly where General Pimodan's column would cross, the Piedmontese command persisted in its belief that the river was not fordable below Loreto.[71] When firing broke out from the river below Montoro, General Cialdini's troops were cleaning up after breakfast, and IV Corps commanders initially were not sure whether this gunfire was a skirmish between patrols, a probe in force, or an outright attack.

Knowing that surprise and speed were his greatest assets, General Pimodan rushed his column across the Musone, brushing aside the Piedmontese outposts on the riverbanks. For many of the troops struggling up the far bank, reeds and mud were bigger obstacles than bersaglieri riflemen. Trying to extricate himself from the viscous mud, Alfred de la Barre de Nanteuil, a private in the Franco-Belgian Battalion, accidentally pulled his feet from his boots and was unable to recover the lost footwear in the press of cursing, pushing, shouting men. Abandoning the effort, he rejoined the charge in his socks.[72] The objective was the Lower Farm, which was occupied by the 101st Company of the 26th Bersaglieri Battalion under Captain Fessia. Though surprised by the assault, the bersaglieri units that were holding IV Corps's left flank reacted with remarkable alacrity and bravery; indeed, those light infantrymen saved Cialdini from very serious trouble. Driven in from their positions on the riverbanks, the advance pickets did not retreat to higher and safer ground but scattered among the reeds, from which cover they continued to snipe at the pontificals splashing across the waterway. When gunfire first erupted, Captain Barbavara di Gravellona, commanding the 26th Battalion at the Upper Farm, immediately dispatched three companies to reinforce the company at the Lower Farm. A company (47th) from the 12th Bersaglieri Battalion had been passing behind the Lower Farm to establish a position nearer the Aspio River, but at the sound of rifle fire, its commander, Captain Della Casa, abandoned that mission to rush his men to the threatened point. It was immediately apparent to Captain Fessia, observing from the farmhouse the men, horses, and cannons splashing across the river, that this was no probe or reconnaissance in force but an all-out attack. It required no military genius to realize that his company was in a tight spot, but he saw that his position would become especially critical as soon as the attackers left the river and deployed around his position. If, however, he could act while the mass of the attackers was still crossing or struggling up the muddy banks, he might check the advance, if only briefly, and buy time for the arrival of reinforcements, which were even then hurrying down the hill from the Upper Farm and the Casino Sciava. Fessia ordered an immediate counterattack, which engaged the lead elements of Pimodan's column (two companies of Swiss carabinieri) in fierce hand-to-hand fighting before the Piedmontese were forced back to the Lower Farm, around which additional companies of bersaglieri were deploying. One such company worked its way around the advancing pontificals and slanted down to the river, where a half battery of papal artillery was still in the water. Seeing a chance to disrupt the crossing and perhaps capture the cannons, the company commander, Captain Nullo, ordered his men into the water, but in a fierce firefight the bersaglieri were repulsed by the Irish company escorting the papal gunners. Nullo rallied his company and rushed forward again, but again the Irish, alternately firing their muskets and pushing the caissons as the gunners feverishly whipped their horses to the riverbank, threw back the attack, capturing several of the bersaglieri, including the mortally wounded Captain Nullo.[73]

The bersaglieri were bravely contesting the area between the Musone and the Lower Farm, but as more and more of Pimodan's units crossed the river, the Piedmontese (by now five companies of bersaglieri were in action) were pushed back to the farmstead. The advance of Pimodan's Swiss carabinieri on the farm buildings was temporally disrupted when they came under fire from another pontifical unit, the 2nd (Indigenous) Cacciatori Battalion, which was advancing in their rear. Although the Swiss would later complain that this "friendly fire" incident was a result of treason and betrayal by the Italian riflemen of the 2nd Cacciatori, confusion and the "fog of battle" were the more likely culprits, since once order was reestablished the Italians returned to the battle and there were no further incidents. In the midst of the fight for the Lower Farm, however, Pimodan relieved the Italian commander of the 2nd's sister battalion, the 1st Cacciatori, for "the most deplorable timidity" under fire and replaced him with his deputy, Major Achille Azzanesi.[74]

By 10:00 Pimodan had three battalions and several pieces of artillery on the left bank. By 10:30 the Swiss carabinieri, supported by the Franco-Belgian Battalion, had pushed the stubborn bersaglieri from the Lower Farm. As the Piedmontese retreated to the Upper Farm, the general halted his force among the farm buildings in order to regroup and form an assault line facing uphill. The first of his artillery to make it across the river, two cannons under Lieutenant Daudier, a former artillery captain in the French army, set up next to a large haystack in the farmyard while six guns under the battery commander, Captain Richter, established themselves farther back from the building complex. By this time the infantry battalions of the second echelon of Pimodan's column (2nd [Indigenous] Cacciatori Battalion and 2nd [Austrian] Bersaglieri Battalion) were across the river, and the general deployed them as a reserve line among the trees near the ford. His cavalry units, the French Squadron of Guides and three squadrons of Indigenous Dragoons, remained on the far right bank awaiting orders to deploy. Realizing that he had to secure the top of the hill before the Piedmontese commanders could respond with reinforcements for the hard-pressed bersaglieri, who were still holding off the papal army by themselves, Pimodan moved quickly. Private Hyacinth de Lanascol, a rifleman in the Franco-Belgian Battalion, would later recall that after fighting its way into the Lower Farm, his company had only a few minutes' rest behind the walls of the buildings before it moved forward against the Upper Farm.[75]

While Pimodan prepared to renew his attack, the Piedmontese commanders were trying to determine what was happening. Although the sounds of battle and frantic messages from the 26th Bersaglieri Battalion on Montoro indicated that something serious was happening on their left flank, the commanders still worried that the action was only a feint to distract them from the main attack against the center of the Piedmontese line. After all, there were no bridges below Loreto, so how many troops could General Lamoricière actually get across the Musone? Initially, General Bernardino di Villamarina del Campo, commander of the 4th Division and senior officer on the left flank, decided to shift only two battalions of the 10th Infantry Regiment from the village of Crocette to the Upper Farm. Soon thereafter, as he received additional alarming reports from the scene, Villamarina ordered the regiment's two remaining battalions and a section of artillery to reinforce the front. At corps headquarters in Castelfidardo, General Cialdini could get no definite intelligence about what was happening downriver and for the first hour of the battle was effectively isolated from events.[76]

At the Upper Farm the bersaglieri of the 26th Regiment needed all the help they could get. Pimodan had launched his force up a rough country lane that connected the Lower and Upper Farms. The Swiss carabinieri, supported by the Irish company, which had ably defended the artillery at the crossing, were on the left; the Italians of the 1st (Indigenous) Cacciatori Battalion were on the lane in the center; and the Franco-Belgian Battalion was on the right. Only a few hundred meters separated the two farms, but the pope's soldiers, supported by Daudier's and Richter's cannons, had to advance uphill across largely open ground under heavy rifle fire from an enemy ensconced behind the walls of the Upper Farm. The attackers charged forward, the path of their advance marked by dead and wounded comrades. During the assault, Private Lanascol (who had just noticed a fellow Breton in the Franco-Belgian Battalion fall with a wound to his chest) had stopped to reload in a "shower of balls" when a bullet clipped his left calf. Ignoring the wound, he fired his own musket, reloaded, and then advanced. He had taken only a few steps when another ball struck the same leg. Somehow still standing, he pressed on, although this second wound "slackened my pace a little"; almost immediately, a third bullet pierced the same leg. Private Lanascol went down, marveling that the Piedmontese "were so determined on having this leg."[77] Pressing forward under intense enemy fire, the pontifical forces, with General Pimodan at their head, reached the Upper Farm and forced the Piedmontese from their position after fierce hand-to-hand combat, during which Captain Athanase de Charette, a young company commander in the Franco-Belgian Battalion, demonstrated particular courage and leadership. As the surviving bersaglieri retreated to the top of the hill, Pimodan, who was bleeding from a wound to the face, rallied his troops for an assault on the crest. With a shout, the pope's Belgian, French, Irish, Italian, and Swiss volunteers, who in the space of an hour had forded a river under fire and taken two defended positions, always advancing uphill, charged the summit. They were within meters of their goal when a wave of Piedmontese infantry swept over the crest.[78]

The two battalions of the 10th Regiment dispatched by General Villamarina to reinforce the bersaglieri had reached the crest of Montoro without being noticed by the combatants below, and they immediately entered the fray. Their counterattack stopped the advancing pontificals in their tracks and threatened to push them downhill toward the Upper Farm, but General Pimodan, who by this time had received a second wound, a bullet to his foot, rallied his men, and the papal line held. When the hard-pressed papal troops saw their commander, who was always in the thick of the action, they shouted, "Hurray for Pimodan! Hurray for our general!" Pimodan shouted back, "Don't cheer boys; charge."[79] As the Piedmontese counterattack broke against the bayonets of the pope's soldiers (the Italians of the 1st [Indigenous] Cacciatori Battalion particularly distinguishing themselves), Pimodan regained the initiative by ordering his line forward. Once again the pontificals approached the crest of Montoro, pushing the enemy before them, and once more they were only meters from their goal when the Piedmontese (reinforced by the remaining battalions of the 10th Infantry Regiment and additional field artillery) counterattacked. This time the papal line could not hold, despite the support of an artillery piece that Lieutenant Daudier had, under heavy fire, pushed forward to the Upper Farm. The counterattack forced the pontificals, who for the first time had lost the advantage of numbers, back to the Upper Farm, which once again became the scene of furious hand-to-hand combat. Soon the main house was on fire, and the columns of smoke billowing from the ruined farmstead combined with the smoke of muskets and Daudier's cannon, which was now blasting away at point-blank range, to shroud the upper slope of Montoro literally in the fog of war.[80]

From the plain below, General Lamoricière could not make out what was happening on the hill. While Pimodan's column was pushing the Piedmontese up the slopes of Montoro, the battalions of the central column had crossed the Musone unhindered, but rather than hurrying these units along the open road to Ancona while General Pimodan distracted the enemy, Lamoricière had held them on the left bank, the battalions in battle lines facing Montoro. The third (baggage) column was still on the right bank of the river. Although the point of the operation had been to effect an escape down the Musone-Umana-Sirolo-Ancona road, not a single papal soldier was yet moving down that road. The operation had gone exactly as planned; Pimodan was blocking the Piedmontese, and the route to Ancona was open, but inexplicably, Lamoricière failed to capitalize on this success. The papal commander seems to have been distracted from his original purpose by the combat on Montoro. With a handful of aides, he galloped forward to get a better sense of the battle, a reconnaissance that took him as far as the Lower Farm. He arrived in time to see several soldiers carrying Pimodan, barely conscious, into the main farmhouse. While trying to rally his troops around the Upper Farm, the general had been hit again, this time fatally in the right side. When Captain Filippo Carpegna, his aide, helped him from his horse and said he would rush to find a surgeon, Pimodan replied, "Don't bother. I'll soon be dead," and pleaded that the troops who had rushed forward to carry him to the rear allow him the honor of dying on the battlefield rather than in some aid station.[81] Whether from the sight of his deputy bleeding out his life; a reluctance to abandon comrades fighting only meters away; the refusal of a professional officer, a veteran of dozens of engagements, to run away from a battle; or a belief that a battlefield victory was still within his grasp, Lamoricière seems to have abandoned all thought of escape. He decided to embrace the very fight that he had originally intended to avoid, and in so doing he lost everything.

Concluding that the troops fighting around the Upper Farm could not possibly hold without reinforcements, Lamoricière ordered forward the second echelon of Pimodan's column, the 2nd (Indigenous) Cacciatori Battalion and the 2nd (Austrian) Bersaglieri Battalion, which had been waiting in reserve behind the Lower Farm while the first echelon engaged the Piedmontese on the slopes of Montoro. He also ordered Pimodan's cavalry, still holding on the right bank, to cross the river and deploy on the papal right flank, a rather curious order because it required the horsemen to traverse the battlefield from left to right. To replace the advancing Italians and Austrians, the papal commander ordered the entire center column to advance toward the Lower Farm to form a new reserve line. These troops—1st and 2nd Battalions, 1st Foreign Infantry Regiment; 2nd Battalion, 2nd Foreign Infantry Regiment; 2nd Battalion, 2nd (Indigenous) Infantry Regiment; and a squadron of cavalry—should have been on the road to Ancona, but now they were being drawn into the battle. Indeed, with this decision, Lamoricière had committed all of his combat units to the fight, a decision that would result in calamity. As the troops of Lamoricière's central column moved forward, the fall of enemy cannon shot nearby threw the 1st Foreign Infantry Regiment into disarray. Confusion quickly turned to panic, and the foreign infantry, who had yet to take a casualty and were still several hundred meters from the fighting line, threw down their guns and ran. The panic immediately spread to the other units of the central column (infantry and cavalry), who joined the flight for safety. Within minutes and without firing a shot, the central column collapsed as an effective fighting force. The panic also spread forward to infect the second echelon of Pimodan's column, which had been ordered into the fight on the slopes of Montoro. The Papal (Austrian) Bersaglieri Battalion moved resolutely forward, but the 2nd (Indigenous) Cacciatori Battalion (the sister battalion of which was fighting bravely around the Upper Farm), observing the furious combat before them and the confused tumult to their rear, broke and ran, as did the cavalry squadrons, with the exception of the French Squadron of Guides.[82] Desperately, Lamoricière and senior officers tried to stem the panic and rally the troops. The *abbé* Caillaud, chaplain of the guides, rode in front of the pope's frightened Italian dragoons and pleaded with them to recall their duty. Trooper Anselme, the personal servant to Captain Gontaut of the guides, took more direct measures, raining blows and kicks on the fleeing horsemen.[83]

The collapse of part of their reserve and the entire center column left Pimodan's first echelon alone on Montoro. Their position was increasingly desperate. All four battalions of the Piedmontese 10th Regiment were now in action, joining the surviving companies of the 26th Bersaglieri Battalion, and another battery of Piedmontese field artillery joined the battle. General Cialdini and his commanders were rushing more infantry and field artillery to the battlefield, but the exhausted remnants of Pimodan's battalions could expect no succor from their side because the bulk of Lamoricière's army was scattering across the countryside. Hard-pressed, the pontificals abandoned the Upper Farm and fell back under heavy fire toward the Lower Farm. Lieutenant Daudier and his gunners, who had, under constant fire, manhandled a cannon up the hill during the advance, refused to abandon their gun to the enemy and now, again under heavy fire, manhandled their cannon downhill. Private de Nanteuil, who had been fighting for more than two hours in his stocking feet since leaving his boots in the mud of the Musone, stopped to strip the boots from the body of a dead Piedmontese bersagliere. He had fought his way to the top of Montoro in his stocking feet, but he was not going to fight his way back down similarly inconvenienced, even if he had to stop in the middle of a furious battle to reequip himself. Now well shod, he picked up his gun to rejoin the fight but had taken only a few steps in his new boots when a musket ball to the head dropped him dead.[84] His comrades tried to establish a line at the Lower Farm, and once again the battered buildings were the scene of ferocious hand-to-hand fighting, during which Captain de Charette of the Franco-Belgian Battalion received his second wound. Joining the battle (when so many others were running away), the Austrians of the papal bersaglieri battalion, all that remained of Pimodan's reserve, rushed up in support. Their arrival briefly checked the Piedmontese attack, but one battalion, no matter how resolute, could not save the day for the pontificals.

Lamoricière apparently thought he could still salvage something from the debacle if he could collect the scattered elements of his command, reestablish some order, and send the troops up the Umana road toward Ancona before the Piedmontese closed that route. Leaving Colonel Enrico Goudenhoven in command of the battle, the papal commander precipitously departed from the battlefield to search for his troops.[85] Left to deal with the Piedmontese,

Colonel Goudenhoven quickly decided that a handful of battered battalions could do little against the gathering strength of Cialdini's IV Corps. He ordered the remnants of Pimodan's column, most still fighting around the Lower Farm, to retreat to Loreto. The bulk of these troops now broke off contact and, covered by the Austrian bersaglieri and Count Bourbon-Chalus's French guides (the only papal cavalry unit that did not break and run), recrossed the Musone. Exhausted infantrymen dragged themselves and their wounded comrades across the river as Piedmontese musket balls splashed into the water around them. Count Bourbon-Chalus saw his friend Colonel Becdelièvre, the commander of the Franco-Belgian Battalion, reach the river with about fifty of his men. "Look! This is all that I have left," the colonel shouted to his friend. "Let's retreat together. Under fire, the French always find each other."[86] Becdelièvre, who had fought bravely at the front of his battalion, did not know that he had left some of his men behind. During the retreat across the Musone, two dozen survivors of the Franco-Belgian Battalion continued to defend the main building of the Lower Farm, which sheltered many wounded papal soldiers, including General Pimodan. Barricading the door and windows with sacks of corn, they withstood cannon fire (which collapsed the chimney and part of the roof) and repulsed three infantry assaults on their position, holding out for more than an hour after all other elements of the pontifical army had abandoned the battlefield. When, at about 2:00 in the afternoon, the pontificals finally surrendered the house, the Piedmontese found Pimodan on a bloody pallet. Despite his weakened state, the papal general managed to ask a Piedmontese officer how many troops had opposed his advance up Montoro. When told there had been only about 1,500 infantry and maybe 400 bersaglieri in the battle, Pimodan whispered, "They were very good."[87] With the surrender of the French and Belgian holdouts in the Lower Farm, the battle ended. The pontifical army had lost 88 men killed (including General Pimodan who died that night in a Piedmontese aid station) and more than 400 wounded. Piedmontese losses were 62 dead and 140 wounded.[88]

The broken battalions of Pimodan's column had retreated into Loreto, where papal officers frantically tried to establish defensive positions. Surgeons, assisted by nuns from a nearby convent, established a hospital behind the Renaissance bronze doors of the Sanctuary of the Holy House; for many mortally wounded soldiers, the fifteenth-century frescoes in the dome of the church would be the last thing they saw. A detachment of French guides rode downstream along the right bank of the Musone in search of General Lamoricière but returned after an hour to report that the commander was nowhere to be found.[89] Although General Cialdini had not yet sent his units across the Musone, it was clear that the position of the papal troops in Loreto was untenable. In the evening Colonel Goudenhoven convened a meeting of senior officers to determine a course of action. Gaspard de Bourbon-Chalus, commander of the French guides, argued for a breakout from Loreto toward the Apennines, but this proposal received no support from officers who considered their exhausted and demoralized troops incapable of further combat. The council recommended capitulation. That evening Goudenhoven sent two staff officers to General Cialdini under a flag of truce to propose a meeting the next morning to discuss terms. When the commanders met, they quickly settled the terms of capitulation. The pontifical forces under Goudenhoven's command surrendered Loreto but were allowed to march from the town under arms and with the "honors of war." With bands playing and rifles on their shoulders, the pope's troops marched out of Loreto and down the road to Recanati, where they deposited their weapons (officers kept their swords). After two days under loose Piedmontese supervision, during which royal officers hosted a dinner for their papal counterparts, the pope's Italian personnel were demobilized and released to return to their homes; foreign volunteers were transferred to Livorno for repatriation to their home countries.[90]

Having left Colonel Goudenhoven to deal with the battle and its aftermath, General Lamoricière had ridden downstream in search of his dispersed troops. Few were still lingering on the outskirts of the battlefield, although the country roads and trails leading south were busy with soldiers fleeing, singly or in small groups, toward Recanati. Any semblance of military organization was lost in the general rout. Most battalions simply dissolved, although a few units maintained discipline and coherence. Lieutenant Uhde of the artillery regiment, for example, managed not only to keep the men of his section together but also to extricate from the battlefield the section's two cannons, and he was marching his guns toward the sea in the hope of finding a boat to take them to Ancona. The Marquis de Chérisey, a sublieutenant in the Franco-Belgian Battalion, became separated from his unit during the withdrawal across the Musone when he stopped to help some gunners who were trying to free their cannon from a ditch. He joined a group of Swiss and Austrian soldiers and marched them south, evading Piedmontese patrols and obtaining food from sympathetic villagers. On October 3 he marched them into Rome.[91]

Near the confluence of the Aspio and Musone, Lamoricière managed to find several remnants of his dispersed units, principally elements of the 1st and 2nd Foreign Infantry Regiments and a detachment of cavalry under Captain Zichy (approximately 400 infantry and 45 cavalry). Sending Zichy and several troopers to determine whether the road to Umana was still open, the papal commander hurriedly organized his survivors into the semblance of a fighting column. When Zichy returned to report that the way was open, Lamoricière decided to waste no time in collecting additional troops; he immediately set his small force on the road. He knew he was in a race. If he could reach Umana before the Piedmontese closed the road, he could probably make it to Ancona, but if the enemy got in front of him, escape was unlikely. He was within sight of Umana, the race almost won, when musket fire broke out on his left. The Piedmontese had caught him.

It took General Cialdini and his commanders a while to discover that they had won a major battle. By midday Piedmontese commanders knew they had halted the papal attack and were pushing back their opponents, but the full scope of the papal collapse was for a time obscured by the heavy smoke that lay over the battlefield and the foliage that lined the banks of the Musone. When it became apparent that the pontifical army had been broken, they rushed to block escape routes toward Recanati and, most important, Ancona. The 9th Infantry Regiment hurried north to block the road to Umana. Just south of this town, the regiment's advance companies caught up with Lamoricière's small force and immediately engaged it. The Swiss and Austrians of the foreign infantry regiments regained some of the honor they had lost on the field at Castelfidardo by holding off the Piedmontese while Lamoricière, with a small number of aides and cavalry troopers, galloped north. Passing through Umana and Sirola, stopping only for a few minutes' rest and refreshment in a monastery near Camerano, the papal party reached Ancona late on the evening of September 18. A week earlier the pope's commander-in-chief had set off to reinforce Ancona with an army of more than six thousand soldiers; when he entered the city, his command had been reduced to a few dozen exhausted and dispirited men. When Colonel Théodore de Quatrebarbes, the military governor of the city and an old friend from North African days, congratulated him on his safe arrival, Lamoricière turned away with the words "I no longer have an army."[92]

The general was not the last papal officer to make it into Ancona before the Piedmontese besieged the city. Lieutenant Uhde, who had extricated his artillery section from the battle and marched the two guns and their crews to the sea, had managed to convince a fisherman to take them to Ancona on his large boat. After wrestling the cannons aboard, the gunners had a tense voyage as they passed through a line of Piedmontese naval vessels established south of Ancona to prevent just such a passage. Their safe arrival on the dawn of September 20 surprised the garrison, as did the appearance later that day of another group of refugees from Castelfidardo. In the fight at Castelfidardo, Lieutenant Roger de Terves of the French Squadron of Guides had served as an aide to General Lamoricière. When the pontifical second column had broken and run, the general had dispatched several of his aides, including the young Frenchman, in a futile attempt to stem the flight and rally the panic-stricken troops. When his horse was wounded, Terves returned on foot to the now largely abandoned battlefield but could not locate his commander. He met two Swiss soldiers from the foreign infantry regiment, and the trio remained under cover until nightfall, when they tried to cross the Musone in the hope of finding papal units around Loreto. The presence of Piedmontese troops along the riverbanks forced them to abandon that plan in favor of striking east toward the sea. Reaching the water, they asked a fisherman to sail them to Ancona. When the man refused, Terves told him he had to make a choice. "I showed him my pistol and my money," the lieutenant later recalled. "He wisely chose the money."[93] The arrival of Uhde, Terves, and their handful of comrades provided a much-needed boost to the garrison's morale. Furthermore, General Lamoricière needed every man he could get if he expected to defend the city.

The second city of the Papal States and, after Venice, the most important Italian port on the Adriatic Sea, Ancona rises on steep hills that form a crescent around a harbor that is protected by two long moles. Built on the inward side of a curve of land jutting into the Adriatic, the core of the city looks west rather than east. Upon assuming command of the pontifical army, General Lamoricière had made the improvement of the city's fortifications a priority. By the summer of 1860 two hundred masons and almost eight hundred laborers were employed in the repair of walls, the construction of magazines and barracks, and the preparation of redoubts. Financial constraints, however, retarded progress, so when the Piedmontese invaded the Marche the improvements remained incomplete.[94] The main defensive position was the Citadel, a large but antiquated brick fortress on the highest point of the city. The landward defenses included a large fortification, the "Entrenched Camp," just below the citadel and several redoubts and strongpoints, some more than a thousand meters beyond the walls. The harbor was defended by two forts. At the end of the northern mole was the Lanterna, a fortified lighthouse, and near the base of the southern mole and just below the Citadel was the Lazzaretto, a polygonal redoubt connected to shore by a short wooden bridge. When news of the Piedmontese invasion reached the city, Colonel de Quatrebarbes ordered the garrison to stretch a heavy chain across the narrow mouth of the harbor between the two moles. The garrison of approximately 7,500 men included seven battalions of infantry (some understrength and one, the 5th Papal Bersaglieri Battalion, still in formation and training); a company of gendarmes; a detachment of cavalry; and various gunners, administrative staff, and depot personnel.[95]

Ancona was ill-prepared to withstand a serious attack. Although improved, the fortifications remained inadequate to repulse a large modern army. The city's artillery, some 129 smooth-bore guns of various calibers, was largely obsolete and lacked the range and accuracy of the modern rifled artillery of the Piedmontese.[96] The cannons of the Citadel, for example, did not have the range to support several of the redoubts beyond the walls. When in 1859 the Austrians had withdrawn their protective garrison from the port, they had offered to sell sixty pieces of modern artillery to the pontifical government, but Cardinal Antonelli, who put his trust in diplomacy rather than armaments, had declined the offer. The guns, which would have contributed immeasurably to the city's defenses, had departed with the Austrian troops. Aware that the defenders would be seriously outgunned by an attacking Piedmontese force, Lamoricière lamented to Colonel de Quatrebarbes, "I'm in the position of a man with a pistol facing an adversary with a rifle."[97] Artillery, however, was not the general's only concern. Modern guns were useless without trained crews to serve them, and trained personnel were in short supply in Ancona. In the event of sustained attacks at several points from land and sea, the papal commander simply had too few riflemen and gunners to hold the walls and redoubts and work the cannons. Moreover, the resolve of the troops was problematic. Lamoricière was well aware that the morale of the garrison was low. The destruction of the pontifical army at Castelfidardo had been a severe blow to the spirit and confidence of the troops inside Ancona, who realized that there could now be no reinforcements. As the Piedmontese army and navy gathered around Ancona, it was obvious to everyone that the garrison was seriously outnumbered and outgunned. Many, including officers, doubted that the city could be held, and some openly asserted that any resistance would be futile. In an effort to stem the spreading defeatism and rally his command, Lamoricière convened a meeting of all officers. Aware that the situation required a demonstration of control and confidence, the general first assured his subordinates that they were in a strong and well-supplied fortress and had the advantage of defending ground from prepared positions. Then, realizing that the defensive capabilities of the garrison were a source of more concern than assurance, the general quickly moved to matters of professional conduct. Military honor, he argued, would not allow the abject surrender of a fortress without a fight so long as the defensive capabilities of the garrison remained intact. Capitulation without a fight would stain not only the reputation of the pontifical army but also the personal reputations of every officer in the command, from the lowliest sublieutenant to brigade generals. It was dishonorable to speak of surrender before a single shot had been fired or to consider giving Ancona to the enemy before their ability to take the city had been tested. When and if the enemy breached the walls and entered the city, it would be time to discuss surrender—but not before. Lamoricière's passionate call to duty rallied the officers, who returned to their units to stiffen their men. When the Piedmontese came, they would face a fight.[98]

The battle for Ancona began on September 18 when a squadron of seven Piedmontese warships under the command of Admiral Carlo Pellion di Persano appeared off the port and opened a bombardment of the fortifications that would continue intermittently during daylight hours (and occasionally at night) over the course of the siege. After the surrender of Loreto, General Cialdini had turned IV Corps toward Ancona, and by September 22 this force had been joined by General Fanti and V Corps, which had been following General Lamoricière's army north from Umbria, and General Cadorna's 13th

Division, which at the start of the invasion had been detached to neutralize Urbino. With the exception of General Brignone's small column in southern Umbria, the entire invasion force was gathered at Ancona. Piedmontese commanders could concentrate their forces on the papal port because military operations in other parts of the Papal States had effectively ended and no pontifical military units were operational threats. Brignone's column and Colonel Masi's irregulars, who were operating independently, had advanced deeper into Umbria, taking Civita Castellana, Narni, Terni, Viterbo, and Montefiascone. They had met with no opposition except at Montefiascone, where a detachment of papal gendarmes resisted, killing four irregulars and wounding another four before surrendering. By September 24 Brignone was poised to move into Latium, the province immediately surrounding Rome. The only pontifical force actively fighting beyond Ancona was the small garrison at San Leo, which after eleven days of siege and intermittent attacks was still holding out against a force of irregulars, even though General Cialdini had sent some artillery to support the attackers.

The land attack began on September 24 (the day that San Leo finally capitulated) with infantry and artillery assaults on pontifical outposts, most of which were lightly defended and easily captured. The most important success came on the Piedmontese left, where papal defenders, after scant resistance, abandoned Monte Scrima, a fortified hill some 2,000 meters south of the city walls. The attackers immediately emplaced artillery on the crest of the hill, which was within range of the Citadel and the Entrenched Camp. Feeble efforts that evening by papal troops to recapture Monte Scrima were easily repulsed. The following day witnessed further Piedmontese infantry probes on the eastern side of the city. These attacks cleared papal outposts from several outlying hills (upon which the Piedmontese established artillery batteries), but the advance stalled when the attackers were unable to dislodge the defenders from their positions on Monte Pelago.[99]

Fighting intensified on September 26. The day opened with a pontifical attack that had more to do with regimental honor than with tactical opportunities. Pietro della Croce was a hamlet about 500 meters in front of the papal positions on Monte Pelago on the eastern side of the city. The previous day the Piedmontese had entered the village but had been unable to push out the defenders, a company of the 3rd Papal Bersaglieri Battalion (mainly Austrians), who continued to hold one end of the village while the Piedmontese Bologna Brigade established itself at the other end. That night, Captain Simon de Castella of the 1st Foreign Infantry Regiment had appeared at Lamoricière's headquarters to request permission to lead a force to expel the enemy from Pietro della Croce. The general had earlier made some comments about the performance of the 1st Foreign Regiment (two battalions of the regiment had broken and run at Castelfidardo, and personnel of the regiment had not distinguished themselves during the lackluster defense of

Monte Scrima on September 24) that Castella interpreted as impugning the honor of the regiment, and he pleaded for an opportunity to demonstrate the resolve and bravery of the unit by recapturing the contested hamlet. Lamoricière did not consider the village crucial to the defense of Ancona, and he had authorized the Austrians to retire on Monte Pelago in the event of an attack by a larger force, but he gave in to Castella's plea. Before dawn the intrepid captain gathered two companies of the 1st Mixed Battalion (an ad hoc battalion formed from depot personnel and surviving companies of the 1st Foreign Regiment) at the papal end of Pietra della Croce and immediately led them in a headlong rush along the central road. The alert Piedmontese responded with rifle fire from houses on either side of the road. The heavy fusillade halted the attackers, who knelt in the road or sought cover in doorways or against walls and returned fire. What had begun as a charge turned into a fierce firefight, but after only a few minutes Castella's companies gave way and retreated in some disorder, leaving three of their number dead in the road. Although not pressed by the Piedmontese, who held their positions, Castella's companies retreated from Pietra della Croce, picking up the Austrian bersaglieri on their way out of the village. The escaping pontifical soldiers reached the shelter of the redoubt on Monte Pelago, where the local papal commander, Hermann Kanzler, recently promoted to general, integrated the Austrians into his defenses but ordered Captain Castella's shattered companies to retire into the city, another humiliation for the ill-starred 1st Foreign Regiment.[100]

General Fanti, the Piedmontese commander-in-chief, had his eyes on Monte Pelago, not only because its capture would neutralize the most important papal outwork on the land side of Ancona but also because Piedmontese artillery positioned on that hill would bring a heavy fire down on the Citadel and the Entrenched Camp. Before assaulting the papal redoubt, however, Piedmontese commanders needed to ensure their control of Pietra della Croce. Though the pontificals had been expelled from the village, the houses and streets remained under intermittent rifle fire from Austrian bersaglieri sent by Kanzler to skirmish on the outskirts of the hamlet. The plans of generals and colonels, however, were preempted by the actions of captains. About 9:00 A.M., company commanders of the Bologna Brigade in Pietra della Croce were alarmed by signs of an impending papal attack. General Kanzler was an aggressive commander who preferred an active defense and had no intention of waiting passively for the Piedmontese to assault Monte Pelago. He wanted to surprise and unbalance the enemy with counterattacks, and pushing the Austrian bersaglieri forward was a preliminary to such an operation. Harassed by the Austrian fire and concerned that an attack was imminent, captains on the Piedmontese front line took the initiative to order their companies forward to disrupt the gathering papal attack. Their initiative surprised and unsettled the Austrians, who promptly fell back on the

Monte Pelago redoubt. Maintaining their momentum, the Piedmontese advanced on the heels of the retreating Austrians, chasing the pontificals up the hill and into the fort, establishing a tenuous foothold on the parapet of the redoubt, and speeding messengers back to Pietra della Croce to summon reinforcements. Surprised by the unauthorized advance of his companies but recognizing an opportunity to win Monte Pelago, the commander of the Bologna Brigade immediately ordered his units forward. By 9:45 several Piedmontese battalions were swarming up Monte Pelago. The assault found the papal defenders without their commander. General Kanzler had gone to the Citadel to secure permission from General Lamoricière for limited offensive operations, leaving his command in the hands of less resolute subordinates. Outnumbered, the pope's soldiers abandoned Monte Pelago and retreated into the city. Their withdrawal marked the loss of not one but two important papal positions. Watching Piedmontese troops overrun the fortifications on Monte Pelago, papal troops holding the redoubt on nearby Monte Pulito also abandoned their position and withdrew into Ancona.[101]

Energized by their capture of Monte Pelago and Monte Pulito and fixed on exploiting these unexpected successes while the pontificals were off balance, the Piedmontese immediately turned to attack the Santo Stefano redoubt, the last major fortification beyond the city walls. The element of surprise, however, had been lost, and the defenders of Santo Stefano, a company of Austrian bersaglieri and a company of the Irish Battalion, not only repulsed the assault but sortied from their position to press the Piedmontese infantry as they fell back on Monte Pelago.[102] The small success at Santo Stefano, however, could not obscure the disaster at Pelago and Pulito. The loss of these important forts meant that the Piedmontese controlled almost all the outworks of the Ancona garrison and were now at the city's walls. Artillery emplaced on the captured hills now added their shot and shell to the bombardment from the sea, which each day caused twenty to twenty-five casualties inside the city.[103] The effect on the morale of the defenders was so serious that General Lamoricière felt compelled on the evening of September 26 to summon his officers for another pep talk. Although each day the general asked the local commander of the Pontifical Gendarmeria (whose service still ran informants into the countryside) if there was word of an advancing French column and every morning sent an officer with a powerful telescope to sweep the seaward horizon for signs of an Austrian fleet, few in his command retained any hope of foreign intervention. A certain fatalism was also creeping into Lamoricière's words and actions. Before meeting his officers, the general ordered Colonel de Quatrebarbes to transfer quietly the garrison's treasury to the custody of the Austrian consulate, where the laws of diplomatic immunity would protect it against seizure by the Piedmontese. When he addressed the assembled officers, his words suggested resignation more than confidence. "The sovereigns of Europe may have abandoned An-

cona," Lamoricière observed, "but all the Catholic world is watching Ancona's defenders, and these defenders cannot without dishonor refuse to
continue the fight so long as the ramparts and fortifications are intact."[104]

Fortunately for the garrison, which needed time to regain its equilibrium
after the unsettling losses, September 27 was relatively quiet. The weather
was inclement, and General Fanti avoided combat operations, limiting his
activity to establishing artillery batteries on Monte Pelago and nearby positions, while the blockading warships interrupted their bombardment after
only a few hours. The next day, however, brought Lamoricière more bad
news. About 1:00 A.M., a small boat containing a half company of Piedmontese bersaglieri and a team of sappers stealthily approached the Lazzaretto,
the large harbor fort at the southern end of the port. Unnoticed by sentries,
the boat pulled alongside the stone walls of the redoubt, and the attackers
entered the structure through an open casemate. The papal garrison was
taken completely by surprise. There were a few musket shots, but almost
immediately the fort's defenders broke and ran, most fleeing along the short
causeway that connected the fort to the shore, some jumping into the water and swimming for land, and a few simply dropping their weapons and
surrendering on the spot. For the Ancona garrison, it was an irretrievable
disaster. Capable of sheltering more than a thousand people (although only a
hundred or so papal soldiers seem to have been in the structure at the time
of the attack) and equipped with several cannons. the Lazzaretto was only a
few hundred meters from the Citadel and only a pistol shot from the docks
and streets of the port. This fort anchored the city's southern defenses, and
its capture exposed the city's southern district around the Borgo Pio.

The loss of this vital installation shook papal commanders even more
than the loss of Monte Pelago. Although the redoubt's garrison was seriously
understrength, there were undoubted lapses in preparedness and nighttime
surveillance, and the abject collapse of the defense after the most superficial resistance struck senior officers as disgraceful. Colonel de Quatrebarbes
wanted to execute the Lazzaretto's commanding officer for cowardice and
dereliction of duty in the face of the enemy, but General Lamoricière preferred to avoid such drastic measures. The general realized, however, that
the loss of the harbor fort, following so closely on the loss of Monte Pelago
and Monte Pulito, would have a devastating impact on garrison morale. To
salvage the situation, he ordered Captain Castella of the 1st Foreign Regiment to recapture the fort. Castella had been kicking around headquarters
since the failure of his attack at Pietra della Croce and was probably thrilled
to have an opportunity to expunge the embarrassment of that ill-advised operation. He gathered a force of two hundred men and prepared to embark
on the papal steamer *San Paolo* in order to approach the Lazzaretto from the
water under covering fire from cannons in the Citadel and the Lanterna. The
venture was problematic at best, and Captain Castella was probably spared

further professional embarrassment by a decision to cancel the operation when it was discovered that the Piedmontese had moved an entire battalion of infantry into the captured redoubt. Rather than recapture the position, the papal garrison would try to isolate it by artillery bombardment.[105]

The fall of the Lazzaretto on the morning of September 28 was a serious blow to the garrison, but the afternoon would bring the crisis. About 2:00 P.M. three Piedmontese warships moved toward shore and opened fire on the port's artillery defenses, particularly the fortified lighthouse, the Lanterna. After an hour of bombardment, one of the ships, the *Carlo Alberto*, moved to within 200 meters of the lighthouse and focused all its fire on that position. Serving a dozen old cannons, the Lanterna's small garrison sought to drive off its attacker, but the pontificals were significantly outgunned. "In the face of the incessant bombardment by the Italian warships," the Italian official history would report, "the pontificals acted bravely. The artillery batteries of the Lanterna, commanded by Lieutenant Wesminsthal and Sublieutenant Delle Piane, maintained a tenacious and resolute defense, even after the rampart of their batteries, reduced to rubble, offered only weak and limited cover."[106] Around 5:00 in the afternoon, a second warship, the *Vittorio Emanuele*, approached the now heavily damaged lighthouse and, from a range of 40 meters, loosed a broadside that demolished the upper structure and dismounted many of the papal cannons. Refusing to abandon or surrender his post, Lieutenant Wesminsthal ordered into the lower casemate of the fort the handful of men who were still alive. From this final refuge, the defenders could still serve three cannons, and, with their commander yelling encouragement and lending a hand amid the explosions and collapsing walls, the papal gunners fought the enemy warships, which were now pouring shells into the remains of the Lanterna from point-blank range. Sublieutenant Delle Piane and a few riflemen under Lieutenant Verbeck tried to secure the embrasures and casemate openings against the expected assault by naval landing parties. It was, of course, hopeless. Within minutes the last of the garrison's cannons was knocked out, and Wesminsthal lay mortally wounded. At 5:30 the survivors (25 out of the garrison of 150) raised a white flag, and when the Piedmontese guns fell silent, they began to make their way out of the ruins of their fort. The ordeal of the Lanterna, however, was not over.

From the Citadel, papal officers had watched the dramatic battle for the lighthouse. When the white flag appeared, Captain Castella, who may not have been the most level-headed of the pope's officers but stood second to none when it came to courage, volunteered to replace that symbol of surrender with the white-and-yellow flag of the papacy. The intrepid captain ran the few hundred meters to the docks and out along the narrow causeway that connected the lighthouse with the shore. He reached the battered entrance to the fort just as Lieutenant Verbeck and a few shaken survivors were emerging. "They resembled demons more than soldiers," Castella would later recall. "Their hair and their clothes were burned, their faces blackened and covered with blood and plaster." Stupefied, the captain asked Verbeck what had happened. "See for yourself," the lieutenant replied and led him into the ruined casemate, which was now on fire. Castella thought he had entered hell. "No human pen can describe the horror of the scene," he reported. "Smoke and blood was everywhere. There were large gaps in the walls. The wounded cried out." Noticing amid the fallen masonry a prone and still figure with an officer's sword by his side, Castella asked, "Who is that officer?" Tears streaming down his dirty face, Verbeck replied, "The commander of the battery, Lieutenant Wesminsthal." Pushing the young officer toward the doorway with the assurance that there was nothing further he could do, Castella turned to climb the stone staircase that originally led to the top of the lighthouse tower, from which the white flag hung in the wind. Now the tower was mostly destroyed, and the stairs crumbled under his feet as he climbed through the dust and smoke, but Castella reached the top. With his sword, he cut the lines holding the white flag and contemptuously threw it at the Piedmontese warships, now anchored hardly a hundred meters away. Noticing a box of signal flags amidst the rubble, Castella searched through its contents until he found a flag that was yellow and white. It wasn't an official papal flag, but it would have to serve. He fixed it to what remained of the parapet and then quickly made his way out of the ruins and back to shore.[107] With the disappearance of the white flag, Admiral di Persano's ships reopened fire. Almost immediately a shell penetrated the powder magazine, and the remains of the Lanterna disintegrated in a huge explosion, which threw a large cloud of smoke and dust into the sky, sent masonry flying across the harbor and raining down on portside buildings, and snapped the heavy chain that closed the mouth of the harbor. Complete silence followed this blast. Guns ceased firing on every front as all eyes turned toward the harbor and the Citadel. It was as if everyone knew the battle had ended.

General Lamoricière realized that with the capture of his outer redoubts on the inland side of the city, the Piedmontese were poised for a direct attack on Ancona's gates and walls. The loss of the Lazzaretto and the Lanterna meant that the enemy could sail into the port and land troops inside the city itself. No one believed that the garrison had the spirit or the resources to defend the city to the last bullet, and no one wanted to see Ancona destroyed by close bombardment or house-to-house fighting. At 6:00 P.M. on September 28, Lamoricière sent an adjutant, Major Mauri, aboard the *Carlo Alberto*, Admiral di Persano's flagship, to request a truce in order to discuss surrender terms. The admiral received the papal envoy with courtesy but insisted that he did not have the authority to grant a truce. He suggested that Mauri call on General Fanti and offered to accompany the major to the Piedmontese commander's headquarters, but Mauri declined the offer and returned to the Citadel without securing a truce. Learning of this episode, General Fanti concluded that Lamoricière was simply stalling for time in order to rest and revitalize his garrison and repair damage to his positions. The Piedmontese commander decided to reopen hostilities, and by 9:30 P.M. his artillery batteries were back in action. Papal guns did not respond to the renewed bombardment; the garrison had effectively ceased resistance. Around 11:00 P.M. there was the sound of trumpets from the pontifical lines, and Major Mauri appeared outside the eastern walls of the city with a request to be escorted to General Fanti. Upon meeting the Piedmontese commander, Mauri requested an armistice of forty-eight hours. Fanti dismissed the request out of hand, adding that he was interested only in arranging the immediate capitulation of the garrison. When the papal major suggested that his commander was disposed to negotiate terms but that he (the major) had no authority to discuss terms, he was curtly dismissed and returned to the city.[108]

Fanti saw no reason to ease the pressure on his opponents by allowing them a de facto truce. He ordered the reopening of hostilities, and by midnight on September 28–29 Piedmontese artillery was again bombarding papal positions. Facing the prospect of continuous bombardment and an imminent attack against the gates and walls of the city, Lamoricière realized there was no point in delaying the inevitable. At 7:00 A.M. on September 29 he sent a message to General Fanti that he was prepared to surrender the city. At 9:00 Major Mauri, accompanied by Captain Lepri, appeared at Piedmontese headquarters to arrange the details. Fanti was not inclined to grant the garrison any particular rights or honors; he insisted that the garrison troops deposit their weapons in Piedmontese custody immediately upon exiting their fortifications and accept prisoner-of-war status and internment in Piedmont pending the final resolution of the war. Mauri replied that he was not authorized to accept such terms, but the Piedmontese general (who probably wondered why this papal officer kept calling at his headquarters if he had no intention of concluding a surrender) allowed Captain Lepri to return to the city to consult with his commander. By noon he had returned with word that Lamoricière had granted his representatives full powers to negotiate a surrender. By early afternoon all issues were settled. In the end General Fanti accepted more lenient terms than those he had originally proposed. The Ancona garrison was allowed to march from the city with arms and proceed to the village of Torreta, where the troops received the salute and honors of war from Piedmontese troops drawn up on the road for that purpose. The soldiers then stacked their weapons and marched to an internment camp. Officers, including Lamoricière, boarded a Piedmontese warship and sailed to Genoa, where they were released on parole. Details concerning papal casualties during the defense of Ancona are lacking, but credible observers report several hundred dead or wounded, while Piedmontese losses were 27 dead and 188 wounded.[109]

The War of 1860 had lasted a mere nineteen days and had been a military and political disaster for the papacy. The pontifical army had been effectively destroyed by an unbroken series of defeats, which left the Kingdom of Sardinia-Piedmont in possession of the Marche and Umbria, the richest and most populous regions of the Papal States. To explain the humiliating debacle, papal apologists emphasize the great disparity in the strengths of the contending armies.[110] Certainly this disparity was no small factor. The Piedmontese put 38,000 men into the field, whereas the papacy could send only 13,000 soldiers against them, an imbalance of almost three to one in favor of the attackers. Even if the papal army had performed optimally, it is difficult to see how it could have prevailed against such a superior force. Numbers alone, however, do not entirely explain the outcome of the war. The lack of accurate political and military intelligence in August and September of 1870, particularly concerning the intentions of Piedmontese forces on the frontier and the degree to which France would oppose Piedmont's invasion, encouraged complacency in Rome and severely compromised General Lamoricière's ability to prepare his units and deploy them effectively. Better intelligence, however, would not have improved the combat capabilities of the pontifical military. The pope's army was not just outnumbered by its opponent; it was also outclassed. Monsignor de Mérode and General Lamoricière had embarked on an ambitious program to reform and modernize the army, but this program was incomplete upon the outbreak of the war so that the units that marched against General Fanti's divisions remained undertrained and underequipped. More important, perhaps, they remained undermotivated. On several occasions—the action at Sant'Angelo, the defense of Spoleto, the combat around the Lower and Upper Farms at Castelfidardo, the battle for the Lanterna—the pope's soldiers fought with remarkable courage and resolution, but all too often troops displayed a distressing lack of confidence, energy, and military spirit. The humiliating flight of Lamoricière's second column at Castelfidardo was the most dramatic manifestation of this problem, but it was also evident in other encounters, such as the loss of the Lazzaretto at Ancona, where papal troops simply surrendered or fled after offering little or no resistance.

The papal cause was also undermined by unwise strategic and tactical decisions. The defense of permeable papal borders against a significantly larger and better-equipped enemy was a problem whose solution probably would have taxed the skills of a military genius. General Lamoricière was a gifted and experienced officer, but he was not a genius, and in retrospect it is apparent that he made some poor choices. His strategy of marching the bulk of his field force to reinforce Ancona reflected the questionable assumptions that Austria would quickly intervene to protect the Papal States and that such intervention would require a major port on the Adriatic. Even if Austria was inclined to intervene, the success of the strategy required the papal army to defend Ancona until the Austrians arrived, and the success of that defense depended on reinforcing the Ancona garrison. If that port was the key to the military salvation of the Papal States, then Lamoricière needed to get as many troops as possible into the city. On his own terms, therefore, his decision at Castelfidardo to advance the second column to reinforce Pimodan's embattled first column on the slopes of Montoro was a serious mistake. By trying to win the battle of Castelfidardo instead of sacrificing the first column and escaping with the bulk of his force to Ancona, the papal commander ensured that he would neither win the battle nor sufficiently reinforce the port city. Of course, even if Lamoricière had managed to get most of his troops to Ancona instead of losing them on the field at Castelfidardo, it is still unlikely that, in the absence of Austrian or French intervention, he would have been able to hold the port for long. Ancona was a trap for the pontifical army no matter how many soldiers defended it.

The decision to march the pontifical army to Ancona represented an expectation of Austrian support, but it also reflected a belief that with the intervention of Austria and/or France to chastise Piedmont, the papacy could emerge from the war without a significant loss of territory. The decision to reinforce Ancona, therefore, represented a decision to defend everything, and when neither Austria nor France intervened, the pontifical army was left isolated and surrounded by land and sea in a distant city from which it could neither attack nor retreat, while the remainder of the Papal States was defenseless. The result was the loss of both the Marche and Umbria. If Lamoricière had decided from the start to abandon the Marche and ordered the northern garrisons, including Ancona, to march south to reinforce the main army in Umbria, he would certainly have lost one rich and populous region of the papal domain, but he would have improved his chances of holding another. With a reinforced field force fighting along interior lines in Umbria, the papal commander might well have enjoyed local superiority, checked if not defeated General della Rocca's V Corps, held Perugia and Spoleto for the papacy, provided his green troops with an experience of success rather than failure, perhaps forced General Fanti and his superiors in Turin to reassess their goals, and still bought time for possible French or Austrian intervention. This strategy of withdrawal and concentration would not have ensured victory in the war, but it was less likely to end in abject defeat and humiliation. There is no evidence, however, that Lamoricière considered, let alone proposed, such a defensive strategy, which, while militarily attractive, would have been politically abhorrent in Rome. Although the pope and his cardinals were inclined to leave military plans to their military commanders, they probably would have considered a plan that accepted the willing abandonment of any papal provinces as a dangerous precedent that would, by compromising the papacy's absolutist claims to traditional territories and temporal authorities, jeopardize claims to other territory in the future. No one in Rome, particularly Pius IX, wanted to create the impression that the pope would abandon his provinces to expediency.

The War of 1860 revealed in stark detail the dilemma faced by a papal administration insistent on defending the temporal power. Diplomacy had manifestly failed to deter Sardinia-Piedmont, avoid war, and prevent the loss of the Marche and Umbria, but so had military defense. To be successful, diplomacy required a degree of political imagination, compromise, and accommodation that was in short supply in mid-nineteenth-century Rome (and Turin). On the other hand, successful military defense required a commitment of resources, energy, and will that was also beyond the reach of Rome (but not Turin). The war demonstrated that Sardinia-Piedmont was politically willing and militarily prepared to fight to annex the Papal States and that the papacy was politically willing but not militarily prepared to fight to retain its territorial patrimony. These circumstances boded ill for the future of the Papal States and seriously complicated the labors of the young general who would replace Lamoricière as commander-in-chief of the pontifical army.

CHAPTER 4

Red Shirts and Brigands

There would be no formal peace conference to conclude the War of 1860, but the surrender of Ancona and the capture of its garrison effectively ended the conflict and left the Kingdom of Sardinia-Piedmont in de facto possession of the Marche and Umbria. Pope Pius IX found his lands reduced to Rome and the immediately surrounding districts, a territory barely one-third the extent of the prewar Papal States, with a population of some 700,000 inhabitants, less than a quarter of its prewar size. The war also left the pontifical army in tatters. After the succession of defeats at Spoleto, Perugia, Castelfidardo, and Ancona, the majority of officers and men were in Piedmontese custody, and most of their artillery and equipment had been captured or destroyed. Few units remained operational. There were fears that after their victory at Ancona, the Piedmontese would renew their offensive and march south on Rome, and these fears multiplied when word reached Rome that on October 1, 1860, Garibaldian irregulars had defeated a Neapolitan army at the Volturno River. This victory not only affirmed republican control over the Kingdom of Naples but also raised the prospect of Garibaldi's army invading the Papal States from the south and linking up with the Piedmontese V Corps, whose Cacciatori del Tevere (antipapal irregulars) had advanced as far south as Civita Castellana, barely 53 kilometers from the Eternal City. The intervention of Piedmontese troops into the former Bourbon domain as a precursor to its incorporation into the Kingdom of Piedmont (soon to be renamed, by the acclamation of the parliament in Turin in March 1861, the Kingdom of Italy) merely replaced one threat with another. The military forces remaining to the papacy (hardly more than some depot and garrison troops, a few detachments of gendarmes, and the pope's palace guards) were completely inadequate to deflect either a Piedmontese or a Garibaldian invasion, and the intentions of the French troops still bivouacked in Rome, ostensibly to protect the Holy Father, were impossible to predict with any confidence. A determined enemy could have been within sight of the Eternal City in a few days.

The immediate military threat to Rome and what remained of the Papal States dissipated as the Piedmontese government under Prime Minister Camillo Cavour refrained from overplaying its hand. Cavour recognized that while Napoléon III was prepared to acquiesce in Piedmont's absorption of most of the Papal States, the French emperor was not yet prepared to countenance the complete overthrow of the pope's temporal power and the occupation of Rome by Piedmontese troops. Even before the surrender of Ancona, elements of the French garrison in Rome had moved north, forcing the Cacciatori del Tevere to withdraw from positions south of Civita Castellana. By the first week of October, French troops (followed by small detachments of the pope's soldiers) were spreading out from Rome to ensure papal authority in the districts immediately around the Eternal City.[1] Rather than risk encounters between Piedmontese and French troops, Cavour, willing (for the time) to settle for Umbria and the Marche, ordered royal units and their irregular auxiliaries to fall back into Umbria. In addition, the prime minister believed that the triumphs of the Garibaldian invasion of Sicily and Naples required immediate attention to ensure that those successes served the interests of the House of Savoy rather than advancing the cause of revolutionary republicans who, with their democratic sentiments, were potentially as much a threat to the Savoyard dynasty as to the papacy. Cavour therefore found it politically expedient to consolidate the successes in Umbria and the Marche and sound out the possibility of an accommodation with the papacy, knowing that a diplomatic démarche would appeal to Napoléon, who desperately hoped that the differences between Turin and Rome could be negotiated away. This moderate policy was continued by Bettino Ricasoli, who succeeded Cavour as prime minister upon the latter's death in June 1861. Beyond vague references to "a free Church in a free State," the precise nature of such an accommodation remained obscure, but it is doubtful that any settlement satisfactory to both Turin and Rome was possible because on neither side was there any inclination to compromise over the fundamental issues that divided them. These were issues of sovereignty and territory. The partisans of a united Italy would not abandon their vision of a single country under a single, secular sovereign, with Rome as its capital, whereas the partisans of the papacy would not abandon their commitment to the maintenance of an ecclesiastical state under a pope-king, with Rome as its capital. There was no way to negotiate these differences; indeed, after the loss of much of his dominion in the War of 1860, Pope Pius IX was even more firm in his resolve not to give up another inch of his territory.[2]

Although the immediate prospect of Italian cannons on Monte Mario and Italian infantry at the Porta del Popolo had passed, few in the pontifical government believed that the House of Savoy had abandoned its ambition to unify all of Italy under its banner, or that the long-term political and military threat to the temporal power had dissipated. No one remained more acutely aware of this threat than Monsignor Frédéric François Xavier de Mérode, the pope's minister of arms. Undeterred by the recent defeats and the destruction of the army he had worked so hard to reform, the energetic monsignor set about reconstituting the pontifical armed forces. This time, however, he labored without the advice and support of his friend and ally,

General Christophe de Lamoricière. Upon his release by the Piedmontese, the commander of the pontifical army had returned to Rome to report to the Holy Father and prepare a written account of the disastrous campaign. Pius received his commander with kindness and affection, thanking him for his efforts to protect the Papal States, asking him to remain in his employ, and offering him a title of nobility in recognition of his services. The general, however, deeply mortified by his defeat, declined every honor and, while retaining the title of commander-in-chief of the pontifical army, departed for his home in France on indefinite leave. When the French government awarded him a magnificent ceremonial sword in recognition of his military services, he politely refused this honor too, explaining, "A sword of honor is given to a general for a great victory. . . . Now, as is too well known, I have done nothing of the sort. The provinces I was defending have been invaded; the towns taken; our war material is lost; and the whole army has been carried into captivity. . . . I cannot forget that a general who has done nothing but save the honor of his flag does not deserve and cannot receive any reward."[3]

As officers and enlisted men straggled into Rome from the battlefields or gained parole or release from Piedmontese custody, Monsignor de Mérode began to rebuild units. At first the emphasis was on consolidation of broken regiments and battalions and a reduction in the overall size of the army. The two Swiss regiments of the line were abolished, as was the Irish Battalion. The Squadron of Guides, the cavalry detachment of French volunteers who had bravely covered the retreat across the Musone River at Castelfidardo, was also disbanded, and the remaining indigenous cavalry elements (who had performed poorly at Castelfidardo) were reorganized into two squadrons. The remnants of the two indigenous (Italian) line regiments were merged with those of the two cacciatore battalions to form two infantry battalions. The survivors of the five bersaglieri battalions with which the pontifical army had begun the war were consolidated into a single battalion, and the Franco-Belgian Battalion was reconstituted as a battalion of Zouaves.[4] The reorganized army would be smaller than its prewar predecessor, but it still required material support. As always, de Mérode was as concerned with the infrastructure and resources of his small army as he was with its personnel. He began to replenish stocks of arms and equipment; established a military hospital in Rome; and built a new military encampment, complete with barracks and exercise grounds, on the outskirts of the Eternal City.[5]

Throughout this period of consolidations and reconstruction, Monsignor de Mérode behaved as if the recent war were merely a temporary, though unfortunate, interruption in his long-term program to build a strong pontifical army to sustain the temporal power of the papacy. Any other personality—less self-confident, less self-righteous—would never have been able to pull it off. Defeat made de Mérode no less bellicose or ambitious, and it certainly did not cause him to reconsider his belief that military strength was the best guarantee of papal political interests. At times his perception of the military realities confronting the Papal States bordered on fanciful. In January 1861, for example, he decided that, by means of a bold military stroke, the pontifical government might well recover some of the territory it had lost in the recent war. He dispatched a force of infantry, dragoons, and gendarmes to attack the Piedmontese outpost at Passo Corese, a small village on the new frontier separating the Papal States from the Kingdom of Piedmont-Sardinia in the region known as Sabina. On the night of January 24–25 the pontifical force captured the village, killing one Piedmontese soldier, capturing fifty, and sending dragoon patrols to show the papal flag in nearby towns and villages. The initial euphoria in the pontifical Ministry of Arms, however, gave way to frustration when the commander of the French force that still occupied (and protected) Rome protested and warned that the operation jeopardized the future of his mission. Since the presence of French troops in Rome was more important than the presence of papal troops in Passo Corese, Monsignor de Mérode canceled the operation and withdrew his force. For their part, the Piedmontese chose to ignore the provocation.[6]

The minister of arms did not realize that the political and financial conditions necessary for the development of a strong military force and the adoption of a forward military policy were no longer present. Defeat may not have changed de Mérode, but it had changed much else. Many in the papal administration now believed that the recent military debacle demonstrated conclusively the irrelevance of the military option. The papacy, so the argument went, could never create a military force sufficiently large, well equipped, and motivated to deter, let alone defeat, the army of the newly proclaimed Kingdom of Italy, so why pretend otherwise? Moneys diverted to military preparedness would only be wasted at a time when the papal administration was scrambling for funds to meet its many obligations. The loss of the rich regions of Umbria and the Marche represented a serious economic loss to the pontifical government, whose income by 1863 was less than half of its expenditures.[7] Though the reorganization of "Peter's Pence," the collection of monetary donations from Catholics around the world for the maintenance of the papacy, would provide a much-needed influx of money into papal coffers, there was no appetite within the Apostolic Palace for expensive programs, and an army (at least the kind of army de Mérode had in mind) was a very expensive program. In the years immediately following the defeat of 1860, military expenditures steadily declined so that by1864 the army was spending only half of what it was in 1859.[8]

The appetite for military experiments and expenditures was especially curtailed in Cardinal Giacomo Antonelli. The recent military debacle only confirmed the pope's secretary of state in his conviction that there could never be an effective military response to the threat against the pope's temporal power. On the day after Castelfidardo, the cardinal had told the French ambassador in Rome, "For their defense against aggression, small states must rely entirely upon international law, and their armies can have no purpose other than maintaining internal order."[9] Although his reliance on diplomacy and the cultivation of French support had proved no stronger a reed to lean on in September 1860 than de Mérode's reliance on the pontifical army, the cardinal secretary of state was no more inclined to abandon his approach than the minister of arms was prepared to forsake his. In the aftermath of the War of 1860, Antonelli continued to assert the primacy of diplomacy and denigrate the efficacy of military preparedness, and he labored diligently to remind Napoléon III, as emperor of a nation of Catholics, of the moral and political imperative of supporting the pope's temporal power. This policy was not only different from de Mérode's, it was incompatible with the approach advocated by the minister of arms, who despised Napoléon III and repudiated the very idea of basing the security of the Papal States on an unreliable French connection. The monsignor's caustic comments about the emperor and the reliability of French assurances were not helpful to a cardinal secretary of state who was trying to nurture good relations with Paris and secure a French guarantee of the pope's temporal power. The disagreements between the pope's two most important ministers turned into a fierce and often public competition for the ear of Pius and control over papal policy. From this competition Cardinal Antonelli emerged the victor.

For all his loyalty and energy, attributes freely acknowledged even by his critics, Monsignor de Mérode made many enemies. He could neither control his venomous tongue nor conceal his relentless ambition. In pursuit of reform, reorganization, and modernization, he constantly interfered in the affairs of other departments of the papal administration and trampled on the authority and prerogatives of his ministerial colleagues without caring (or perhaps even realizing) that his behavior gave offense. He believed that positive results would compensate for hurt feelings, but he was wrong. He was easy to admire but hard to like, in contrast to Cardinal Antonelli, who could ingratiate himself with others despite a somewhat tarnished personal reputation. By the summer of 1865, when he fell ill with malaria, the minister of arms had few allies inside the papal palace and many enemies who constantly whispered in the pope's ear. Pius had ignored previous suggestions that he dismiss his controversial minister, on one occasion commenting, "He has his enemies, but who has not. He does not flatter, but he serves me faithfully. . . . I know he has defects of manner, but they are only the excesses of his devotion and honesty. I cannot think of separating myself from de Mérode."[10] Enemies, however, were too numerous and too influential, and gradually they brought the pope around to their position. Hints were dropped that a resignation would be welcome, but the minister remained unmoved. By the time de Mérode returned to work from his sickbed, irritable and enervated because of his refusal to accept a restful convalescence, his position had been irreparably undermined. In October Pius sent one of his chamberlains to inform de Mérode that his resignation was required. De Mérode replied that if the pope wanted to be rid of him, His Holiness had only to announce his resignation. Pius accepted the invitation. On October 20, 1865, the minister of arms received a brief letter curtly informing him that in view of his precarious health, the Holy Father had relieved him of his duties. The usually brash and combative monsignor went quietly, declining all face-saving honors, retiring from public life, and withdrawing to a small apartment in the Vatican. Eventually, at the pope's urging, he accepted the position of papal almoner, the official responsible for dispensing the pope's charitable gifts. He devoted the remainder of his life and most of his personal fortune to organizing and supporting schools for orphans and children of the poor.[11]

Cardinal Antonelli probably assumed that the dismissal of de Mérode represented the end of the policy of military preparedness, for which the fallen minister had been the principal advocate. Confident that the issue had been settled, he made no effort to control the direction of military affairs by adding the armed forces portfolio to his many responsibilities, and he offered no protest when Pope Pius selected General Hermann Kanzler as the new minister of arms. For the army, it would prove an excellent choice. Born in the Grand Duchy of Baden (Germany) on March 28, 1822, Hermann Kanzler attended the military college of Karlsrühe before entering the army of Baden in 1840. After four years he resigned from the grand ducal army to enter the armed forces of the Papal States as a lieutenant in the 1st Foreign (Swiss) Infantry Regiment. In the Italian-Austrian War of 1848 he was wounded during the defense of Vicenza (May 24–25 and June 9–10) and was mentioned in dispatches. During the brief Roman Republic, when many of his colleagues in the pontifical army joined the republican army, Kanzler remained loyal to Pope Pius IX and joined the pontiff at Gaeta after the Holy Father fled from Rome. During his temporary exile, Pius entrusted the young lieutenant with several secret missions into the Papal States. After the pope's restoration to Rome, Kanzler rose through the ranks of the reconstituted pontifical army, serving primarily in the 1st Indigenous (Italian) Infantry Regiment, a unit he eventually came to command. In the early days of the War of 1860, Colonel Kanzler distinguished himself by leading a small column of papal infantry that fought its way through the Piedmontese 7th Infantry Division to reach the safety of Ancona, and during the siege of that port city, he commanded the crucial Monte Pelago sector. Taken captive when Ancona fell, he was detained at Genoa until the end of the war, when, by then a general, he returned to Rome to assume the post of inspector-general of papal troops. His selection as minister was a surprise because, with one exception, no serving line officer had ever held the portfolio. He was known and trusted by the Holy Father, however, and respected and liked within the army, especially among the pope's Italian soldiers.[12]

If Cardinal Antonelli expected de Mérode's removal to push military affairs to the margins of papal policy, he was disappointed. The new minister of arms (who kept his military rank and assumed the second office of commander-in-chief of the pontifical army, General de Lamoricière having died in September 1865) proved no place-filler content to allow the pope's military to revert to the modest parade-ground army it had been before Monsignor de Mérode and General de Lamoricière had begun to lift it from its complacency and mediocrity. As much as his predecessor, General Kanzler believed in the efficacy of a small but well-trained, well-equipped, and well-motivated professional army that could guarantee the internal security and tranquillity of the Papal States against domestic insurrection and external attacks by Garibaldian bands (thereby avoiding any excuse for Italian intervention to restore order or suppress revolution) and buy time in the event of outright invasion by the Kingdom of Italy for diplomacy to mobilize international support for the papacy. Unlike his predecessor, however, Kanzler considered military force a complement of, not a replacement for, diplomacy, and he was politically astute enough to realize that his program of military preparedness would be facilitated by keeping a low profile, minding his own affairs, controlling his tongue, and above all avoiding conflicts with the powerful cardinal secretary of state. He would embrace de Mérode's goals but not his methods.

During his tenure as inspector-general of pontifical troops, Kanzler had had the opportunity to observe the various units and components of the papal army, assess their preparation and performance, and note their deficiencies. He understood his army, its strengths and its weaknesses, and knew what had to be done. Within three weeks of entering office, the new minister had completed a plan for the reorganization of the army. This plan proposed an all-volunteer force that could put in the field 10,787 men in combat units (including the gendarmeria, which was always considered a military force) supported by an array of garrison, service, and auxiliary units. Specifically, Kanzler envisioned an army consisting of one regiment (three battalions) of line infantry, three independent battalions of light infantry, two squadrons of dragoons, five batteries of field artillery (six guns each), twelve companies of gendarmes, a company of engineers, one battalion of older veterans (sedentari) for garrison duties, and various service and support units (medical, veterinary, chaplaincy, etc.). This force would be organized into two brigades, each headquartered in Rome. The 1st Brigade, under General Raphael De Courten, was responsible for the provinces, which were divided into four military zones: Viterbo (1st Zone, Colonel Achille Azzanesi), Civitavecchia (2nd Zone, Lieutenant Colonel Giuseppe Serra), Tivoli (3rd Zone, Lieutenant Colonel Athanase de Charette), and Velletri (4th Zone, Lieutenant Colonel Giorgi). The 1st Brigade contained the bulk of the combat units. The 2nd

Brigade, commanded by General Giovanni Battista Zappi, would be responsible for Rome and its immediate environs.[13]

General Kanzler's army would be only half the size of the force envisioned by Monsignor de Mérode and General de Lamoricière in their reorganization of 1860, but the new minister of arms was a pragmatist, not a visionary. He may have preferred a larger army, but he understood better than his predecessor that, given the political and economic realities, an ambitious program would find little support. A moderate approach was less likely to alarm the antimilitarists in the papal administration, and once adopted it would serve as the basis for incremental but steady growth. Also, Kanzler intended to emphasize quality over quantity in the formation of his army, believing that ten well-trained, well-equipped, and well-disciplined men were always preferable to a hundred ill-motivated, undisciplined, and poorly trained ones. Finally, a small army would allow the papacy to reduce its dependence on foreign enlistments, a dependence that had allowed the enemies of the church to belittle the pontifical army as little more than a foreign occupation force and its soldiers as nothing more than cruel mercenaries. As an officer who had commanded Italians for most of his career, Kanzler had a high regard for the fighting qualities of the pope's subjects, and he expected to increase significantly their presence in the papal army. In the proposed military program only two battalions of light infantry, the carabinieri and Zouaves, would enroll non-Italians, and foreigners would represent less than a quarter of the combat troops available to the pope.

On November 20, 1865, the pope's council of ministers (including Cardinal Antonelli) endorsed General Kanzler's proposal for a new army, and on December 16 the pope approved the plan. If Monsignor de Mérode were following events from his retirement in the Vatican, he might well have wondered at this sudden concern for military preparedness only weeks after his dismissal for (in part) persistently advocating such a policy. Of course Kanzler's early success may have reflected his less confrontational and abrasive manner as well as relief inside the papal palace that his plan was not nearly as expansive (and expensive) as his predecessor's vision. Also, Kanzler's proposal coincided with one of those rare occasions when papal authorities actually were concerned about the state of their military defenses. The previous year, on September 15, 1864, France and Italy had signed an agreement (the "September Convention") concerning the security of the Papal States and the status of the French troops garrisoned in Rome and Civitavecchia. Supposedly, these troops were a guarantee of the pope's independence and a deterrent to any attempt to evict the pontiff from his throne. They signaled to any power intent upon such eviction (the Kingdom of Italy was really the only power exhibiting such an intention) that it might have to fight France to achieve its goal. Of course the French troops had not proven much of a deterrent in 1860, but that unwelcome fact did not dissuade Cardinal Antonelli from believing that only the presence of a French garrison in Rome kept the Italian army away from the walls of the Eternal City, a belief that made the cultivation of French goodwill the centerpiece of papal diplomacy. Emperor Napoléon III remained conflicted about his commitment to defend the pope. He sympathized (at least at times) with the national aspirations of the House of Savoy and its vision of a united Italy, but he could not embrace the prospect of the pope being forcibly displaced from his throne, especially in the face of long-standing French guarantees of that throne. For Napoléon, French honor was at stake, as was the political future of his own throne, which was not so stable that he could afford to alienate conservative French Catholics for whom the temporal and spiritual sovereignty of the pope was an article of faith. The emperor needed the political support of French Catholics, and the defense of the Holy Father seemed to be the price for that support.[14]

Under the terms of the September Convention, France agreed to a phased withdrawal of all of its troops from the Papal States within two years in return for a pledge from Italy to respect and protect the independence and security of the Papal States. To mollify Paris and signal its commitment to respecting the territorial integrity of the papal domain, the Italian government seemingly repudiated its intention of making Rome the capital of a united Italy by agreeing to move the capital from Turin to Florence. The Italians also withdrew their opposition to the recruitment of foreign troops into the pontifical army.[15] When, therefore, Pope Pius and his cardinal secretary of state received Kanzler's plan to reorganize the pontifical army, they understood that within a year the protective shield of the French army—a shield that had in the past considerably reduced the need for a serious papal military force—would be withdrawn in favor of a promise from King Vittorio Emanuele to respect the territorial integrity of the Papal States and abandon his designs on Rome—a promise that no one inside the Vatican expected the king to keep. With the French on their way out the papacy was well advised to look to its defenses.

The minister of arms needed no encouragement. He began immediately to implement the new army program. The first priority was money to finance the projected increase in personnel, the acquisition of new equipment, and the modernization of services and facilities. Revealing a political acumen unexpected in a career army officer, Kanzler convinced parsimonious papal finance officers to accept a level of army expenditures for 1866 that was more than 30 percent higher than the spending levels of the preceding year. Next the minister of arms moved to personnel. After the recent war, enlistments had dropped off considerably, in part because reductions in the size of the army eliminated the need for aggressive recruitment efforts. Foreign enlistments were particularly sparse. In 1860, for example, 177 Belgians had volunteered for the pontifical army, but in 1861 the number of Belgian enlistments fell to 74. In 1862 the number further declined to 21, although it increased to 48 the following year. After Kanzler's appointment, the Ministry of Arms sought to reenergize recruitment both in the pope's own provinces and in Austria, France, Belgium, and Holland, countries that had proven important sources of manpower in 1860. In these countries "Committees for Pontifical Activities" established recruitment offices and disseminated appeals to young Catholic men, especially those from "good" families. The result was an influx of recruits for the Zouaves and carabinieri regiments, the units of the pontifical army designated as "foreign." From Holland alone came 1,500 volunteers in 1866 and 1867. European recruitment was so successful that the Zouaves, assigned a force level of 1,206 men in Kanzler's reorganization plan of November 1865, grew to 2,237 men by October 1867, and the commander-in-chief had to revise upward his plans concerning the number of foreigners in the army. The program to expand the pontifical army received an unexpected boost in June 1866 when the Emperor Napoléon authorized the formation of a battalion composed solely of veterans or serving personnel of the French army. This battalion was absorbed as a unit into the pontifical army. A volunteer to the Légion d'Antibes (named for the town in southern France where the recruits assembled) enlisted for four years, but these years were added (for purposes of seniority and pension rights) to the volunteer's French army record. French army officers who enlisted in the legion retained their ranks in their national army. In September 1866 the unit was renamed the Legione Romana (Roman Legion).[16]

It was not enough to attract more men; the men had to be equipped and trained. As soon as his reorganization plan received the pope's blessing, Kanzler began the long (and expensive) process of providing the material support (weapons, munitions, uniforms, boots, horses, wagons, rations, medicines) necessary for an operational military force. As much as possible, he wanted to free the pontifical army from dependence on foreign suppliers. For example, the standard infantry weapon in the pontifical army was the Belgian model 1857 percussion rifle, and he pushed the papal arsenal inside the Belvedere wing of the Vatican Palace to develop the capability to manufacture this rifle in quantities sufficient to meet the needs of the army. To ensure the provision of supplies and support to troops operating in the field, Kanzler established magazines and depots in every military zone to store munitions, food, and forage and also assigned to each zone a team of medical personnel with ambulances.[17] Training, however, was the highest priority. Kanzler was not interested in commanding a parade-ground army that made a brilliant impression at ceremonies but collapsed at the first volley of rifles. He expected his soldiers to be fighters, man for man the equal of any group of soldiers in Europe. To enhance discipline and improve military skills, the general ordered that every battalion establish a training platoon in which recruits could learn the basics of soldiering from veterans before being assigned to a line company. For recruits, the day was full of inspections, drill, weapons instruction, guard duty, and the care and cleaning of barracks and equipment. Marksmanship was emphasized, as was physical conditioning. Once assigned to a line company, the new soldiers would develop and maintain their skills in a systematic training regimen of shooting, marching, and drilling.[18] Units regularly gathered for large-scale maneuvers, which, on at least one occasion, included repulsing a landing from the sea in the form of "enemy" forces put ashore from the papal steam corvette *Immacolata Concezione*. Of course there was nothing better for sharpening skills than actual combat, and Kanzler soon had an opportunity to school his new army in that tough classroom.

Brigandage had long been a problem in the Papal States, and gendarmeria detachments spent much of their time clearing robber bands from roads and villages. Encounters between brigands and police were invariably violent, and their frequent counterbrigand operations made the gendarmeria the most field-savvy and combat-experienced element of the pontifical armed forces in the period 1815–1860. Such operations might extend over several weeks as police detachments pursued a band across the countryside. In 1819, for example, gendarmeria sergeant Carlo Canori was promoted to lieutenant for his initiative and bravery in leading a patrol against a band led by Rufillo Monti, a bandit chieftain notorious for his cruel predations around Forli. The operation began on January 7, 1819, when Sergeant Canori (who had previously attracted favorable notice in his corps by single-handedly engaging two armed bandits during a skirmish and capturing both after wounding one with his saber) identified and arrested two armed members of Monti's group outside Forli. This encounter put the sergeant on the trail of the larger band, which he relentlessly tracked over the following three weeks. On January 27 he learned that Monti, his equally notorious deputy, Luigi Sant'Andrea, and another member of the band named Lombardi were hiding in a farmhouse. At the time Canori had only three gendarmes with him, but, without waiting for reinforcements, he led his small detachment in an assault on the house. In a sharp engagement, the police shot their way into the building, killing Monti and Sant'Andrea and taking Lombardi prisoner.[19]

By 1860 bandit activity was increasingly restricted to the southern districts of the papal domain, but the events of that year would significantly alter the nature of the problem and the gendarmeria's response. The fall to Garibaldi's fighters of the Bourbon Kingdom of the Two Sicilies (also known as the Kingdom of Naples), the subsequent incorporation of that realm into the Kingdom of Italy, and the flight of King Francesco II and his court into exile in Rome now added a political element to what had been a purely criminal enterprise. Francesco and his supporters, lacking an organized army, saw an opportunity to continue the war against the "usurpers" in Naples by mobilizing legitimist sentiment among the peasantry of the old kingdom. Directed by regular officers from the old Bourbon army (and volunteers from other countries, particularly Spain), civilians and former soldiers formed guerrilla bands to raid the northern districts of the old kingdom, occupying towns and villages, killing officials of the new Savoyard regime, and attacking Italian army and police outposts. Many of the recruits to these bands were legitimists fighting for the old dynasty, but more than a few were young men seeking to evade arrest (and possible execution) for failing to respond to an Italian government decree of December 1860 drafting young men into the Italian army.[20] The Italian army inadvertently facilitated the work of the Bourbon recruiting committees by its heavy-handed efforts to suppress the guerrillas. In August 1861, for example, Pontelandolfo, a town 64 kilometers northeast of Naples, was occupied by a "brigand" band of about forty men who stayed but a night but in that time managed to ransack the offices of the town government, deface images of King Vittorio Emanuele and Giuseppe Garibaldi, rip the crest of the House of Savoy from the national flags, destroy birth registers in the town hall (used by authorities to determine who was eligible for conscription), despoil the homes of notables associated with the new regime, release inmates from the jail, and murder the local tax collector. The citizenry welcomed the irregulars and seemed to be energized by their brief visit. When an Italian army detachment, sent out to investigate rumors that brigands were in Pontelandolfo, neared the town, it was attacked by peasants who drove off the unit, killing forty-one soldiers. Authorities immediately dispatched a larger force to occupy the town and make an example of it. The troops had orders to kill everyone but women and children, and when the "action" was complete, more than four hundred inhabitants of Pontelandolfo were dead, dozens of women had been raped, and the town had been burned to the ground.[21] Intended to intimidate the peasants, such brutal measures were as likely to inflame them, and from their refuge in Rome the Bourbons effectively used such atrocities to mobilize opinion and recruit fighters against the new rulers in Naples.

Initially, the pontifical government facilitated the guerrilla war against the Italians in the south. Sheltering the exiled Bourbon court in Rome was certainly a gesture of moral support, but collaboration extended to operational assistance for the legitimist bands raiding into Italian territory. Commanders of such bands regularly and without fear of molestation visited Rome to acquire men, money, and instructions for future raids. Papal authorities allowed the Bourbons to recruit fighters openly on pontifical territory. In Rome there were recruiting offices in the Piazza Farnese and Piazza Montanara, while provincial recruiting centers were established in the southern papal towns of Agnani and Velletri. Along the southern frontier, legitimist bands found refuge on the papal side of the border when they were hard-pressed by Italian troops, and border posts of the Pontifical Gendarmeria regularly provided food, shelter, and guides to guerrilla groups raiding into Italian territory. At first the Bourbon cause—punishing and weakening the Kingdom of Italy—seemed to be the pope's cause, but by the autumn of 1864, the papacy was reassessing its attitude toward this guerrilla war.[22]

After the September Convention removed the protective umbrella provided by French troops, Cardinal Antonelli feared that continued collaboration with the Bourbons would provide a pretext for the Kingdom of Italy to send its forces across the border to "restore order." In addition, the bands had become a serious law enforcement problem for papal authorities. As the energy of Bourbon reaction waned and the Italian government consolidated its control over the unruly southern provinces by pouring troops into the region to suppress the reaction (in 1864 Italy had 100,000 soldiers—more than half its army—deployed to the area), the bands lost their political aspect and evolved into purely criminal organizations. Their targets were no longer Italian military units and symbols of Italian authority but travelers who could be robbed or kidnapped for ransom and towns whose shops and municipal treasuries could be looted. Since such economic targets were as plentiful on the papal side of the frontier as on the Italian, the armed bands saw no reason to limit their activities to the latter region. As early as 1862 some bands, abandoning all but the pretense of political and military direction by the Bourbon exile government in Rome, had already turned to outright banditry on both sides of the border, and by late 1864 brigandage had become a serious threat to the security of the pope's southern provinces.[23]

Initially, the burden of suppressing the bandits fell upon the Pontifical Gendarmeria, but by 1866 regular army units were routinely deployed to the region to support the gendarmes. As commander of the 1st Brigade, which was responsible for the provinces, General Raphael De Courten was in overall control of the joint army-police effort, but a gendarmeria major, Count Leopoldo Lauri, directed daily operations. The brigands benefited from their knowledge of local conditions and terrain, their ability to strike and then disappear into the hills and rough countryside, and their capacity to purchase or extort intelligence and supplies from the inhabitants of their territory. Major Lauri developed a strategy that aimed at isolating the brigands from their sources of support, tracking them relentlessly to their places of refuge, and destroying them with overwhelming force. To prevent bandits from entering villages and towns to secure supplies, the areas around such locales were patrolled day and night. To prevent individuals from carrying supplies from the villages to the brigands in the countryside, farmers, woodcutters, herders, or anyone else whose business took them into the hills were prohibited from carrying anything but minimal provisions, and in some places they were forbidden to carry any provisions at all, having to return to their village when they needed to eat. Locals (some reformed or amnestied brigands) familiar with the springs, caves, ravines, and woods of the area were recruited as *squadrigliere*, auxiliaries to guard villages, guide papal patrols, question peasants, and identify suspects. Mobile columns and roving patrols of gendarmes and soldiers scoured the countryside, collecting information from peasants and travelers, checking potential hiding places, and scanning hillsides and valleys for the smoke of campfires or the dust of a band of men on the move. When discovered, bands were chased until they could be brought to battle. Recognizing that brigandage was a problem that afflicted both Italy and the Papal States, Major Lauri negotiated an agreement with his Italian counterpart, General Lodovico Fontana, providing for mutual cooperation and support. Named after the town that hosted the negotiations, the "Cassino Convention" of February 24, 1867, a rare example of formal cooperation between the two countries, provided for the exchange of intelligence and captured brigands and allowed police services to cross the frontier while in "hot pursuit" of fleeing bandits.[24]

The campaign against the brigands (1864–1868) was a war of skirmishes and running firefights. These small-unit actions rarely involved more than forty or fifty men on each side, but they were as violent as any wartime battle. The tempo of operations is suggested by the fact that between November 1866 and June 1868 in the province of Frosinone alone there were thirty engagements. In January 1867, for example, a large band of bandits tried to enter the commune of Sonnino but was driven off by a detachment of pontifical gendarmes. In April of that year a column of regular infantry encountered a band near Roccasecca and, after a sharp engagement, put the bandits to flight, capturing two. The next month a detachment of gendarmes, alerted by informants, ambushed a group of brigands, who promptly fled, leaving behind two dead. In July a patrol of gendarmes and squadrigliere attacked a bandit group near Sezze, killing three and driving off the rest. Sometime the engagements extended over several days. In June 1868 a band led by the notorious chieftain Panici engaged a gendarmeria patrol, killing two policemen before escaping into the hills. A mixed column of gendarmes and soldiers gave chase, tracking the fleeing brigands for several days before bringing them to bay in a sharp encounter that left three of the bandits dead. The rest of the band fled, the papal column close on their heels. Seeking refuge in a forest, the band was overtaken again and in the resulting firefight lost two more dead while wounding two papal soldiers. The surviving bandits, including Panici, scattered and managed to evade capture.[25]

It was a war without pity or mercy. Between 1865 and 1870 papal forces hunted down and killed 701 brigands.[26] To deter or punish bandits and their supporters, papal authorities adopted severe punitive measures. Families (including children and the aged) of known brigands were incarcerated, with their release dependent on the surrender, capture, or death of the bandits. Bandits who turned themselves in could expect leniency, but those captured, particularly leaders, received harsh penalties, including execution, by special tribunals established solely to suppress banditry. The brigands were no less ruthless and implacable, showing no mercy toward their enemies, especially the feared gendarmeria and squadrigliere. Bandit chieftains placed bounties on the heads of gendarmeria officers and rewarded anyone who captured a police agent and turned him over to the brigands. Prisoners could expect no leniency. Often captured gendarmes were tortured; on one occasion a captured noncommissioned officer was dismembered. In this war noncombatants were not safe from attack. Families, particularly those of squadrigliere, were often the targets of violent reprisals.[27]

Gradually, the brigands lost ground, and by 1867 the once serious threat had been reduced to a nuisance. In addition to securing the countryside against criminal depredations, the successful campaign against the brigands complemented General Kanzler's plan to build a skilled and professional army by providing an opportunity for his soldiers to gain valuable field and combat experience. By 1866 regular army units were increasingly deployed into the southern provinces to support the gendarmeria and squadrigliere, and by 1867 most units of the pontifical army (particularly the line infantry, Zouaves, cacciatore, carabinieri, and dragoons) had rotated battalions or companies through the "bandit zone." The tempo and nature of operations provided a tough school for the pope's soldiers. Marching (often at the quickstep) cross-country with full field packs in all weathers, bivouacking on rough ground, living on field rations for days at a time, watching for ambushes, deploying and advancing in the face of the enemy, and seeing comrades fall (and sometimes die) under hostile fire were exercises and experiences that could not be duplicated on barracks squares or rifle ranges. "The brigandage required of the troops serious sacrifices and claimed not a few lives," General Kanzler would later recall, "but it was an excellent school, accustoming them to long marches, even at night, frequent combat, and the danger of surprise."[28] By the summer of 1867 many of the pope's soldiers had graduated from this dangerous school, but some would soon discover that the "bandit zone" was not the only dangerous place in the Papal States.

In the summers the more privileged classes fled the heat of Rome for the Castelli Romani, a string of small towns and villages scattered across the Alban Hills southeast of the city. Cool in the summer, these locales were also thought to be less susceptible to the malarial fevers that often afflicted Rome and the lower reaches of the Tiber. Albano, a charming hillside town only 29 kilometers from Rome, was especially favored by the Eternal City's more prosperous citizens, lay and ecclesiastic, both for its picturesque setting and its historical connections to imperial Rome (the town rose over the ruins of structures associated with Pompey and the Emperor Domitian). Unfortunately, a reputation as a pleasant and healthful summer retreat would prove no charm against an enemy that cared nothing for local charm and natural beauty.

In the spring of 1867 a cholera epidemic that had been moving across Europe reached Italy, where it would eventually claim more than 100,000 lives. Rome registered its first cholera death on May 4. In June 145 Romans succumbed to the disease, and in July the number increased to 608. By late summer the epidemic had spread to the Castelli Romani, and Albano was especially hard-hit. There was no cure for the disease, which in its extreme form was so fast-acting that a victim might die within twenty-four hours of exhibiting the first symptoms. Typically, the citizenry's response to its arrival differed little from the response of their forebears to the appearance of the Black Death. The uninfected fled, and the infected stayed and (mostly) died. Upon the first sign of the outbreak, the mayor and other town officials immediately decamped, as did most of the wealthy summer visitors. The desperate situation was redeemed not by politicians and notables but by priests and nuns. In stark contrast to the craven behavior of lay authorities, the ecclesiastical leaders understood their duty. The bishop of Albano, Cardinal Ludovico Altieri, was in Rome when the epidemic struck, but he hurriedly returned to his town despite the warnings of friends that he was rushing to his death. Upon arriving in Albano, the cardinal established himself in the local hospital run by the Sisters of Charity (who remained resolutely at their posts throughout the crisis), where he worked around the clock, hearing the confessions of the dying, consoling the sick, and praying with the survivors. A few days after his arrival, he too succumbed to the disease.[29]

Upon learning of the disaster at Albano, Pius IX immediately ordered two companies of the pontifical Zouaves to the town on a mission of humanitarian relief. When the Zouaves arrived they viewed a scene that might have served as an illustration for the story of the Four Horsemen of the Apocalypse. The dead filled the houses, and bodies lay in the streets, contributing to the already fetid atmosphere. There were no municipal authorities to organize the burials, the care of the sick, or the safety of the uninfected. The only functioning group in the devastated community was the handful of surviving Sisters of Charity who kept the hospital running. The first task was to bury the dead. Lieutenant Zénon de Résimont of the 2nd Company of the 1st Zouave Battalion led by example. When his men, shocked by the horror before them and mindful of the danger of the infection, hesitated at the edge of town, de Résimont strode up to a body that was lying in the street, lifted the corpse over his shoulders, and began walking toward the town cemetery. Encouraged by this example of discipline and courage, the Zouaves turned to the unpleasant task of clearing the town of cadavers. While some collected the dead, others dug graves (ninety on the first day alone) in a new cemetery or assisted the nuns in the hospital. The work continued around the clock, although the physical and emotional burden on the Zouaves eased a bit when a detachment of pontifical gendarmes arrived to reinforce the effort.

As occasionally happens, the deadly disease ran its course and disappeared as quickly as it had appeared. The survivors tried to recover their lives, while the returning political and social notables tried to recover their reputations. The Zouaves returned to Rome, leaving behind two of their comrades in the cemetery they had built but attracting praise from all who heard of their unselfish labors in Albano. General Kanzler warmly praised the Zouaves for their courage and selflessness, adding that he was proud to command such a unit. For his leadership and courage, Lieutenant de Résimont was decorated with the Cross of Pius IX, and all the enlisted men who had participated in the relief of Albano received a special gold medal struck to commemorate their service.[30]

While the pope's soldiers were fighting bandits and disease, a more serious threat was gathering along the borders. In June 1866 Austria and Prussia had gone to war over the latter's ambitions for hegemony over the South German states. Italy joined Prussia in this war. Although the Austrians were prepared to cede Venice and the surrounding province of Veneto in return for Italy's neutrality, the Italian government wanted more. Vittorio Emanuele II sought the prestige of a glorious military victory over the Austrian army. His ministers hoped to acquire from Austria additional territory, particularly Friuli to the east of Venice and Trentino to the northwest. Although neither its army nor navy distinguished themselves in the campaign, Italy secured its territorial ambitions in the wake of Prussian military victories, which compelled Austria in late July to agree to peace terms, including the cession of the Veneto to Italy. In Florence this "victory" was tempered by anger that Berlin had not consulted its Italian partner before agreeing to peace; chagrin over Italy's pitiful military performance; and humiliation at acquiring Venice not through a glorious national effort but through the good offices of Napoléon III, who had mediated the Austrian-Prussian peace negotiations. Also, the incorporation of the Veneto into the Kingdom of Italy reemphasized the problem of Rome, since the small papal domain now remained the major part of the peninsula not under the rule of the House of Savoy. When informed of the results of the plebiscite in the Veneto that overwhelmingly endorsed the area's incorporation into the Kingdom of Italy, King Vittorio Emanuele acknowledged that it was a great achievement but noted that although Italy was now mostly united, it remained incomplete. He was thinking of Rome, and when Vittorio Emanuele began thinking of the Eternal City, trouble usually resulted.[31]

In April 1867 Urbano Rattazzi became prime minister of Italy, succeeding Bettino Ricasoli, who had resigned in part because of his inability to resolve tensions with the papacy through negotiations and moral suasion. Rattazzi was a favorite of the Action Party, the movement of republican nationalists who favored direct and immediate action against the papacy to demolish its temporal power and complete Italian unification. Giuseppe Garibaldi, his military reputation burnished by his successful command of a unit of volunteers during the war with Austria, provided the heart and soul of the Action Party. In the spring of 1867 the charismatic hero began to agitate for military action against the Papal States. Garibaldi and the Action Party (along with their supporters inside the royal government) believed that an insurrection in Rome would spark an uprising by the pope's subjects that would in turn provide a pretext for intervention by the Italian army to "restore order." The time seemed opportune because the withdrawal of the last French troops from Rome in December 1866 left the pope with only his own soldiers to defend his throne, and no one believed they would be equal to the challenge. To be sure, the September Convention required Italy to respect the sovereignty of the Holy Father, but Paris, increasingly preoccupied by the growing power of Prussia, was embroiled with Berlin in a diplomatic fight over territorial adjustments along the Rhine. Thus, it was easy for the Action Party and its sympathizers to conclude that France would be too distracted to support Rome.[32]

The Rattazzi government initially did not silence Garibaldi's calls for an attack on the Papal States; indeed, it provided moral and material support for the general's effort to organize volunteer units to invade papal territory, and it began clandestinely channeling money to a revolutionary committee inside Rome. Rattazzi had, however, underestimated France's continued interest in papal affairs. After Napoléon registered his disapproval regarding reports of imminent military action against the pope, the prime minister increasingly had to distance his government from Garibaldi's invasion plans. This course adjustment was further encouraged by disagreements within the Italian cabinet. Certain powerful ministers, particularly the minister of war, General Genova di Revel, balked at offending the emperor by violating the spirit if not the letter of the September Convention. To keep his critics at bay, Rattazzi on September 23, 1867, reluctantly ordered the arrest of Garibaldi, who had been visiting towns in Tuscany and Umbria to preach his latest crusade against the papacy. The republican general was transferred under custody to his home on the island of Caprera. Hopeful that this public detention of the most vocal advocate of war against the pope would pacify its critics, the Italian government secretly continued to encourage the volunteer bands that were preparing for just such a war.[33]

On the evening of September 28, 1867, just five days after the arrest of their leader, an armed band of forty Garibaldians slipped across the Tiber River, the frontier between the Kingdom of Italy and the Papal States, and made their way undetected to Grotte San Stefano, a small town north of Viterbo. With surprise on their side, the Red Shirts easily captured the town's small gendarmeria post and its four policemen. The attackers confiscated the local treasury, effaced the papal insignia from public buildings, raised the Italian flag over the main square, and harangued the townspeople before releasing the disarmed gendarmes and departing to repeat their efforts at nearby villages.[34] Over the next two days, other bands of Garibaldi's followers (some numbering in the hundreds) crossed the northern frontier and fell upon Acquapendente, Bagnorea (modern-day Bagnoregio), Canino, and Caprarolo, sweeping aside the gendarmeria posts that represented the only local defenses.

With multiple attacks, the Garibaldians probably hoped to dissipate the defensive response by forcing papal commanders to disperse rather than concentrate their troops. The smaller bands raided from village to village, but the larger groups intended to capture and hold towns that would serve as recruitment and resupply centers for the insurrections the incursions were expected to set off among the population. Bagnorea, a town of three thousand 4 kilometers from the frontier, fell without resistance to a band of five hundred Red Shirts on October 1, 1867. Acquapendente, a larger center with several thousand inhabitants, proved harder to capture. The town lacked an army garrison but had a gendarmeria post of twenty-seven men under the command of Lieutenant Settimi. Upon learning that a strong Garibaldian band commanded by a certain "Count Pagliacci" (perhaps a nom de guerre) had crossed into pontifical territory and was operating near Acquapendente, Settimi alerted the Ministry of Arms in Rome and requested reinforcements. He also sent out scouts to fix the location of the invaders and provide warning should they advance on the town. The scouts, however, failed to detect the enemy who, three hundred strong, appeared without warning at the gates on the late morning of September 30. Aware that his gendarmes were too few to defend the gates and walls of the town against a superior force but determined not to surrender without a fight, Settimi ordered his men into the police post, where they barricaded the doors and windows and prepared to make a stand. Count Pagliacci, loathe to risk an unnecessary battle and confident that the vastly outnumbered pontificals would act reasonably and capitulate if given the chance, sent an emissary to offer the gendarmes their liberty if they peacefully surrendered and abandoned their weapons. Playing for time in the expectation that help was on its way, Lieutenant Settimi boldly asked for twenty-four hours to consider the proposal. The Red Shirts refused his request and promptly opened fire on the police post from the shelter of nearby buildings. For three hours the gendarmes withstood the fire, bravely defending their position and repulsing a direct assault against the main door of the building. It was only when the attackers gained access to the roof from a neighboring structure and set it on fire that Settimi, concluding that further resistance was futile, decided to surrender. The Red Shirts, concerned more about possession of the town than possession of prisoners, set the gendarmes free after they signed an agreement not to take up arms again for three months. Leaving a small force to occupy Acquapendente, Pagliacci led the rest of his band south to seize the nearby town of San Lorenzo.[35]

The attacks did not take the pontifical Ministry of Arms entirely by surprise. By late September the ministry had received intelligence indicating that incursions by armed supporters of Garibaldi were imminent, but General Kanzler, aside from alerting his commanders, took no special defensive measures. So long as the invaders were only irregulars, he was confident that his soldiers and gendarmes could deal with the threat. It had been only two years since he, the newly appointed minister of arms, had embarked on the reorganization of the pontifical army, but his plans had already borne fruit. In October 1867 Kanzler commanded an army of 12,981 men. This number included 10,520 men in fighting units (only 267 below the goal identified in the reorganization plan of 1865). Appraising their capabilities from a distance of more than half a century, a professional observer, himself a general, judged them "mercenary troops, mostly foreign and of diverse nationalities, but disciplined and animated by strong religious sentiment and devotion to the pope; trained in the French manner; and well-conditioned and toughened by the rigors of the difficult war against the brigands in the southern provinces of the state."[36] In fact, the pope's soldiers were neither mostly foreign nor professional mercenaries. The foreign personnel had enlisted specifically to serve the Holy Father and (with the possible exception of the French veterans in the Legione Romana) would not have sought military employment in any other army. They were, however, experienced, disciplined, motivated, and well trained.[37] The pope's commander-in-chief was not inclined to scatter this relatively small force in what promised to be a futile attempt to seal the borders of the Papal States, preferring instead to hold troops in readiness in the principal towns until they could be dispatched to deal with specific incidents. Once Kanzler identified a point of attack, he would rush units to the location to deal with the threat. This approach placed the burden of defending the Papal States on the commanders of the four military zones, whose ability to locate the marauders and then quickly deploy sufficient troops to repulse or destroy them would make or break Kanzler's strategy of mobile reaction.

Along the northern frontier, the focus of the first incursions, responsibility for locating and destroying the irregular bands fell to Colonel Achille Azzanesi, a twenty-eight-year veteran of the pontifical army and the commander of the 1st Military Zone, centered on Viterbo. To confront the invaders, the colonel had at his disposal two companies of the Pontifical Gendarmeria, the 2nd Battalion of the Regiment of the Line, two companies of the Regiment of Zouaves, a detachment of dragoons, and a section of artillery.[38] Colonel Azzanesi responded with alacrity to the first reports of armed bands. When he received news of the attack at Grotte San Stefano, he immediately sent to the scene a company of line infantry, which caught and dispersed the San Stefano band near the village of Ronciglione, capturing ten of the invaders. Upon learning of the assault on Acquapendente, he personally led a mixed column of line infantry, Zouaves, and gendarmes to expel the attackers. On the way he intercepted and dispersed Pagliacci's band outside San Lorenzo, taking twenty-one prisoners, and then moved on to retake Acquapendente.[39] To deal with the occupation of Bagnorea by three hundred Red Shirts, he dispatched a mixed force of fewer than one hundred line infantry, Zouaves, and gendarmes. Given the size of the enemy band, the papal detachment was rather small, but Colonel Azzanesi may have been misinformed about the strength of the enemy because many reports from gendarmeria posts reported groups of only forty or fifty armed men moving across the countryside. More likely, he may have hesitated to commit too many troops to a single venture when attacks might break out elsewhere in his military zone.[40] Whatever his intention, he did not anticipate the bellicosity of the detachment's commander, Captain Paolo Gentili of the 2nd Battalion, Regiment of the Line. Upon reaching the outskirts of Bagnorea, Gentili rashly ordered an immediate attack. His men drove in the Garibaldian outposts but faltered before the heavy rifle fire of the defenders ensconced behind the walls and windows of the town buildings. Seizing the initiative, the numerically superior Garibaldians counterattacked, rushing from the town to drive off their attackers. When the gun smoke cleared, the Red Shirts still held the town. Captain Gentili retreated toward Bolsena, leaving behind three of his men dead and twenty-four as prisoners of the invaders. The irregulars suffered fifteen casualties.[41]

In Rome, General Kanzler was not pleased by this setback at Bagnorea. Only 4 kilometers from the border with Italy, the town was well placed to serve as a support base should Garibaldi or the Italian government (which Kanzler believed was behind the attacks) decide to commit additional forces to the invasion. Also, continued possession of the town by the Red Shirts served as a propaganda victory for Garibaldi and a reproach to the pontifical army. Bagnorea had to be retaken, and half measures would not do. Kanzler ordered Azzanesi to retake the town immediately, adding that this time the colonel should employ a "suitable force" for the effort, a not-so-subtle criticism of the colonel's previous decision to send a small detachment to do the job.[42] Aware that the commander-in-chief had taken a personal interest in the operation, the colonel assumed personal command of a force consisting of slightly more than three hundred men organized into two columns: one consisting of the 3rd and 4th Companies of the 1st Zouave Battalion and the second including the 1st, 4th, and 5th Companies of the 2nd Battalion of the Line, two pieces of artillery, and a detachment of dragoons and mounted gendarmes. The movement across the countryside of so many soldiers, horses, and cannons could not escape observation, and the occupiers of Bagnorea, who had been reinforced by survivors of the bands that had been chased from San Stefano, Acquapendente, and San Lorenzo, were alerted to the approach of the pontifical force. Upon the advice of officers from the regular Italian army who had been secretly detached to support the irregulars, the Red Shirts had constructed barricades across the approach roads and had fortified the outlying Convent of San Francesco, an ecclesiastical building set amid grapevines and fruit trees. Azzanesi would have to battle his way into Bagnorea.[43]

The column of papal Zouaves reached Bagnorea on the morning of October 5, having fought a short but sharp action to clear a Garibaldian outpost from the ruins of an old castle 1.5 kilometers from the town. Without waiting for the second column, the Zouaves attacked, driving the Garibaldian outposts back into the Convent of San Francesco. At this point Azzanesi's second column came hurrying forward. Together the two columns assaulted the convent, which was stoutly defended by the Red Shirts, who maintained a heavy, if inaccurate, fire from the building. In a letter to his family after the battle, a Zouave recalled that "the rifle fire from the bell tower and windows was so heavy that the bullets dug up the dirt at our feet and made the leaves from the grapevines rain down on our head."[44] A party of Zouaves led by Sublieutenant the Baron Victor de Vigier de Mirabal rushed the main door and, wielding axes and rifle butts, forced an entry into the building. More Zouaves poured through the shattered door, driving the defenders at bayonet point back into the central cloister of the convent. The Red Shirts were quickly overcome, some dying under papal bayonets, most throwing down their weapons in surrender, but a few escaping through windows and back doors. As the Zouaves neutralized the convent, other pontifical troops moved against the town's main gate, overrunning two outlying barricades before halting in the face of heavy fire from defenders behind the gate and walls. Seeing his troops falter, Colonel Azzanesi ordered up his two cannons, which blasted the wooden gate off its hinges. The town was now open to the attackers, but as the pontificals rushed into the town, the remaining Red Shirts rushed out through another gate, scattering across the countryside. Azzanesi promptly telegraphed his success to General Kanzler. It was a lopsided victory. Bagnorea had been retaken at the cost of 1 papal soldier killed and 5 wounded. The Red Shirts suffered 90 killed or wounded and 178 captured.[45]

Although the first Garibaldian incursions had occurred in the north, the attacks soon spread to other parts of the papal domain. In the 3rd Military Zone, northeast of Rome, irregular bands briefly occupied the towns of Montemaggiore, Moricone, and Nerola before being driven off by pontifical gendarmes, who took several prisoners.[46] These raids were preliminaries to a significant thrust by a well-armed force of six hundred Red Shirts under the command of Garibaldi's eldest son, Menotti, who crossed into the Papal States without any interference from Italian border authorities. On October 6 elements of this force withdrew after an encounter with pontifical forces at Casal Falconieri. Two days later a papal column under the command of Lieutenant Colonel the Baron Athanase de Charette, commander of the 3rd Military Zone, attacked the main body of Menotti's force, but the Red Shirt commander again withdrew, choosing to postpone a fight until he had received reinforcements. Some of the Garibaldians sought temporary refuge across the border. De Charette, however, did not pursue the Red Shirts into their sanctuary, preferring to stay well away from the frontier to avoid an incident with Italian troops.[47]

In the first week of October the Garibaldians also opened a front south of Rome in the pontifical army's 4th Military Zone. Most of the attacks proved minor. At Vallecorsa, a small town southeast of Frosinone, the gendarmeria post drove off a force of Red Shirts, killing several of the attackers. On October 11 a group of thirty to fifty irregulars under the command of the Milanese count Emilio Blenio, a regular officer in the Italian army who had resigned his commission to join Garibaldi, attacked Subiaco. This town, 70 kilometers south of Rome, was garrisoned by a company of Zouaves under Lieutenant Desclée, but that unit had taken the field to run down rumors that a band of Red Shirts was operating in the neighborhood. When the rumors were confirmed by the appearance of the band at the municipal gates, the only defenders were a handful of pontifical gendarmes, who immediately barricaded themselves in their barracks and prepared to make a stand. Reluctant to risk his men in a direct assault on the post, Count Blenio asked the local bishop, whom he had taken hostage, to appeal to the police to surrender. The prelate refused. While the Red Shirt commander considered his options, a storm broke over the town, drenching the attackers and making an assault on the police post even less attractive. Blenio's tactical situation was not improved by the unexpected return of the papal Zouaves.

While patrolling with his company, Lieutenant Desclée had asked an elderly peasant woman if she knew of a party of armed men moving across the countryside. When the woman replied that she had seen such a group and that she believed it had entered Subiaco, the lieutenant wheeled his company around and marched at the double back through the heavy rain to town. Once in sight of the gates, Desclée split his force into two sections, one to circle the town and block a possible escape by the enemy and the other to attack under his personal command. Disdaining a lengthy exchange of rifle fire, the Zouaves fixed bayonets and charged, their lieutenant at the front. There was a brief but sharp melee, during which Desclée received three saber cuts before shooting Count Blenio dead with his revolver. Seeing their commander fall, the Red Shirts surrendered. In addition to Blenio, two other Garibaldians lay dead. Papal casualties were two wounded. For his bravery, Lieutenant Desclée received a decoration and a promotion to captain.[48]

After the elimination of Blenio's force, the Garibaldians made one more effort in the south. A large band under Giovanni Nicotera, a veteran Red Shirt who had fought alongside Garibaldi in many battles, seized the village of Salvaterra, where Nicotera confiscated public funds, abused the local priests and papal functionaries, and proclaimed a provisional government.

His rule was short-lived because the rapid approach of papal troops caused him to abandon the town. He withdrew into a rough area known as the "Wilderness of Posi," but the lack of readily available provisions in the area compelled him to send out foraging parties. Despite instructions to avoid contact with papal forces, one party exchanged fire with a patrol of pontifical gendarmes that it encountered. The irregulars were no match for the experienced gendarmes who had fought dozens of similar engagements against brigands in that very area. The gendarmes held the enemy in place while a messenger summoned reinforcements. With the arrival of additional men, the papal police attacked and easily scattered the Red Shirts, who left several of their number dead, wounded, or prisoner. Nicotera promptly moved the remainder of his band to the safety of the Italian border.[49]

By the second week of October General Kanzler could feel some satisfaction with the course of events. From the start of the crisis, he had made it clear that he was no mere political minister but a seasoned professional soldier who intended to command the pontifical army in the field. Though he normally wore civilian clothes in the ministry, he now wore full uniform and signed all his orders "Commander-in-Chief of the Pontifical Army" rather than "Minister of Arms." With his units in frequent contact with the enemy, Kanzler rarely left the ministry on the Piazza Pilotta, preferring to remain close to the telegraph that connected him with his garrisons and zone commanders.[50] The calm and purposeful demeanor of the pope's commander-in-chief and his staff in the Ministry of Arms in the first weeks of the fighting was notably different from the near panic that seized many papal officials, including Cardinal Antonelli. The cardinal secretary of state considered the Red Shirts a mortal and uncontainable threat to the Papal States, the survival of which now depended entirely upon the immediate intervention of the French. France's commitment to defend the pope, however, now seemed alarmingly uncertain. Some in the Vatican openly suggested that the pope should abandon Rome for a more secure refuge.[51] In contrast, Kanzler, who rarely communicated with Cardinal Antonelli during the crisis, always remained confident that his troops could deal with the irregulars. Indeed, he believed that any one of his better-trained, better-equipped, and better-disciplined soldiers was easily the equal of five of Garibaldi's irregulars.[52] The tactic of rapid reaction, developed and tested in the campaign against the brigands, appeared to be working. The Red Shirts had not succeeded in occupying any town for more than a couple of days, and wherever Garibaldi's irregulars appeared, they were chased and easily crushed by papal forces. Aside from Captain Gentili's embarrassment at Bagnorea in the early days of the campaign, no field force of the pontifical army had been defeated. Papal casualties had been few. Army morale remained high, and there was no sign of subversion or disloyalty. In short, although the situation was serious, there was no cause for alarm.[53]

There were, however, clouds on the military horizon. For the pope's soldiers, the tactic of rapid reaction was unfolding as a succession of marches and countermarches, interrupted only by pitched battles and brief intervals of rest. Many of the units, particularly the gendarmeria and line infantry, had practiced such operations in the campaign against the brigands, but even veterans of that difficult campaign found the effort against the Red Shirts exhausting. In a large army units could be rotated into the field, allowing the withdrawn troops a period of recuperation, but in the small pontifical army there were few reserves to relieve the frontline units. The operational tempo placed a heavy physical burden on men, horses, and equipment. So long as the enemy operated in many small bands, the pope's commanders might well run up a string of tactical successes but exhaust their troops while strategic victory eluded them. The situation would change from serious to critical should the Kingdom of Italy militarily intervene in support of the Garibaldians. Although Kanzler was confident that his troops were more than a match for much larger numbers of Red Shirts, he was under no illusion that they could handle an invasion by the numerically and materially superior Italian army. Throughout October the question of Italy's intentions would preoccupy the papal Ministry of Arms, but there could be no military solution to the problem. If the Italian army came, it would do so in large numbers—army corps and divisions, not battalions and companies. Kanzler saw no sense in sacrificing his outnumbered units to such a juggernaut. He certainly was not prepared to risk another Castelfidardo, a strategic defeat from which neither his reputation nor his army nor the Papal States would emerge intact. If the Italians crossed the frontiers, the pope's commander-in-chief planned to abandon the provinces and concentrate his forces on Rome and the port city of Civitavecchia, He would defend those cities as long as possible in an effort to buy time for French intercession on behalf of the papacy.

In early October the threatening clouds of force exhaustion and Italian intervention darkened only the distant horizon. A more immediate problem was the failure to fix and engage the large (and growing) band of more than six hundred irregulars operating under Menotti Garibaldi in the Sabine Hills north of Rome. With groups of volunteers crossing the frontiers to reinforce the original band, Garibaldi *fils* was becoming a serious threat. Pontifical troops under Lieutenant Colonel de Charette had been scouring the area for the elusive enemy when, on October 13, a local farmer brought word that Menotti was moving to attack the town of Montelibretti. In an attempt to preempt the enemy, the papal commander promptly ordered Lieutenant Arthur Guillemin to quick-march his company of Zouaves to occupy the town. If the Garibaldians were already there, the lieutenant was to act as he deemed appropriate. He could attack the enemy or wait for the arrival of two other detachments (one composed of Zouaves and the other of companies of the Legione Romana) that de Charette was ordering forward.[54]

Lieutenant Guillemin, who had fought as a private in the War of 1860 and had received a serious bayonet wound to the chest at Castelfidardo, was famous in the regiment of Zouaves for his attention to the well-being of his men, who affectionately referred to the popular officer as their "guardian angel." He reached Montelibretti on the evening of October 13 to discover that Menotti Garibaldi had beaten him to the prize. The first sign the Zouaves had that they were too late was a volley of rifle fire from Garibaldian outposts, which then withdrew to the safety of the walls. Observing the enemy scuttling through the town gate, Guillemin chose boldness over prudence. Deciding not to wait for reinforcements, he divided his small force into two sections, one under his command and the other under the command of Sublieutenant Urbain de Quelen, and ordered the attack. With drawn saber and the cry "Forward for Pius IX!" Guillemin, more brave than wise, led his men in a furious charge up the road to the main gate of Montelibretti and into the annals of the pontifical Zouaves.

The Zouaves ran through a storm of bullets as the well-prepared defenders opened a withering fire on the attackers. Almost immediately Guillemin staggered with a bullet in his shoulder, but he recovered his footing and pressed on, always in the lead, urging his men forward. He had just reached the town gate when a bullet struck him in the head. As Zouaves tried to pull their mortally wounded guardian angel to safety, a fierce combat broke out in the area in front of the gate as Red Shirts rushed forward to repulse the attackers. Sublieutenant de Quelen fell dead, struck by several bullets. With the officers down, Sergeant Major Alois Bach assumed command as the Zouaves fought their way into the town. Beyond the gate the papal troops found themselves in a warren of narrow streets and courtyards, with the enemy firing from the upper stories of buildings and counterattacking from side streets. The battle became a fierce and desperate combat of bayonets, rifle butts, and fists as the outnumbered Zouaves fought to extricate themselves from the swarm of Red Shirts that fell upon them. Surrender seems not to have been an option for the pope's foreign volunteers. Forced into an angle between two walls by six attackers, Corporal Collenridge, an Englishman, fought off two of them before being shot down by the rest. A pair of Belgians, Privates Rebry and Mijthenaiere, fought back to back, shouting encouragement to each other in their native Flemish and thrusting their bayonets at the enemy that pressed upon them. In a desperate attempt to break through to their comrades who were falling back to the gate, the two friends charged side by side into the mass of Garibaldians, only to disappear under a hail of slashing sabers, stabbing bayonets, and clubbing rifles. Corporal Pieter Jong, an athletic Dutchman known throughout the regiment for his size, was last seen standing alone, blood pouring from several wounds and swinging his rifle like a club, in a circle of Red Shirts, several of whom lay dead or wounded at his feet.[55]

The Zouaves were being massacred. In the confusion of close combat, Sergeant Major Bach had disappeared. The last surviving noncommissioned officer, Sergeant Paul Bégassière, standing in an inferno of screaming men, clashing steel, and whining bullets, concluded that to continue the battle in the narrow streets meant death. He chose life. The sergeant shouted the order to retreat. Fighting every step of the way, the surviving Zouaves fell back through the gate and into the relative safety of the open countryside, leaving seventeen of their comrades dead in the streets of Montelibretti. The Garibaldians, who were no less battered by the ferocious street combat, did not pursue the escaping pontificals, allowing Bégassière to regroup the remaining Zouaves outside the town and lead them to safety in Montemaggiore, the nearest papal garrison. The Red Shirts may also have declined pursuit because the battle for Montelibretti was not entirely over. Unbeknownst to Sergeant Bégassière and the other survivors of Guillemin's command who were making their way to safety, several of their comrades were still alive and fighting inside the town. Sergeant Major Bach, as it turned out, was neither dead nor missing in action. During the melee in the town streets, the sergeant major, along with several other Zouaves, had become separated from the main body of his unit. To escape the Red Shirts who threatened to overwhelm them, the group had broken into a house and barricaded the windows and doors with furniture, mattresses, and whatever else could block an entrance or provide shelter from bullets. Incredibly, the handful of Zouaves, surrounded and grossly outnumbered, refused to surrender and defended their makeshift strongpoint for several hours into the night before chancing an escape through a breach in the back wall of the building. Their escape was facilitated by the fact that the Garibaldians also wanted to get out of town; indeed, Menotti Garibaldi had decided to abandon Montelibretti that very night. The ferocious street battle had exacted a heavy toll not only on the Zouaves. Seventy Red Shirts were dead or wounded, and their commander anticipated that the next day would bring an attack on his depleted and exhausted band by a much larger force of pontificals. By the early morning of October 14 he was leading his men to the nearby town of Nerola.[56]

Nerola would prove a false refuge. Lieutenant Colonel de Charette was hurrying troops to the area. Learning that pontifical forces were approaching, Menotti Garibaldi departed with the bulk of his force for Montorio Romano, leaving a few hundred irregulars under the command of Major Valentini to defend Nerola "to the last cartridge." Shortly after Garibaldi's departure, de Charette appeared outside the town with a force of Zouaves, gendarmes, and Roman legionnaires. The pontifical troops easily drove in Valentini's outposts and assaulted the town's turreted castle, where the Red Shirts had taken refuge. The infantrymen of the Legione Romana, facing their baptism of fire under the pontifical flag, bore the brunt of the attack. The Garibaldians, well positioned behind the thick walls of the castle, put up a stiff resistance.

From turrets and embrasures the irregulars kept up a heavy fire, shooting de Charette's horse from under him and forcing the papal infantry to stay under cover. Initially, the pontificals could find no weakness in the defense, but the course of the battle shifted when de Charette ordered up his artillery, which began blasting shells into the strong walls of the castle. Despite the bombardment, Major Valentini, true to his commander's order to fight to the end, wanted to prolong the resistance, but eventually he gave in to the appeals of his men to avoid useless slaughter. A white flag appeared over the castle, and firing ceased. Casualties were relatively light: four pontifical soldiers were dead and several wounded, while the Garibaldians had one dead and ten wounded. One hundred and thirty-four Red Shirts were taken prisoner.[57]

Menotti Garibaldi and his force were still at large, but in the third week of October more dangerous threats began to loom on the horizon. In Florence, King Vittorio Emanuele II and the war party had been disappointed by the poor showing of the Red Shirts and frustrated by the failure of the incursions to spark popular uprisings in the Papal States that would justify intervention by the Italian army. To improve the situation, the government began to increase its clandestine support of the irregulars by encouraging volunteers to join the bands, providing free travel for volunteers on trains organized by the government, facilitating their transit across the Italian–Papal States frontier, and supplying weapons and munitions from royal arsenals.[58] In Rome, the Ministry of Arms was aware of at least some of this activity. In the first week in October, for example, it received reports from pontifical units near the northern frontier that Italian army personnel were colluding in the movement of Red Shirts across the border. By October 19, however, the intelligence reports had assumed a more alarming aspect. From Civitavecchia, the commander of the 1st Military Zone, Colonel Giuseppe Serra, forwarded to Rome several intelligence reports indicating that the regular army of the Kingdom of Italy was preparing to invade the Papal States in support of the irregulars. Italian troop trains were allegedly moving south, and the Spanish consul in Livorna had reportedly been overheard saying that a second Castelfidardo was imminent.[59] General Kanzler may not have had complete confidence in Colonel Serra's judgment (he ordered to Civitavecchia General Zappi, commander of the 2nd Brigade in Rome, to determine the true state of affairs and assume command of the 1st Military Zone in the event of an attack from Italy), but the intelligence could not be ignored. Upon learning on October 20 of the resignation of Prime Minister Urbano Rattazzi the previous day, the pope's commander-in-chief feared a political crisis in Florence that would enhance the voice of the war party and encourage Vittorio Emanuele to launch an invasion to buttress his throne. As additional reports of Italian troop movements reached Rome, Kanzler warned his zone commanders at Civitavecchia, Frosinone, and Viterbo that an Italian attack was likely and ordered them to prepare to demolish bridges and railway lines connecting the Papal States with the Kingdom of Italy. The commanders were further directed to fall back to Rome should the Italian army cross the frontier. The general also rushed to mine the bridges over the Tiber and Teverone rivers, although his plans were somewhat constrained when the Holy Father, in one of his few directives to his military commander, made it clear that he did not want any of the city's spans prepared for demolition. Under the supervision of military engineers, the Rome garrison began constructing earthworks and fortifications outside the main gates of the city and sealing secondary gates with dirt and masonry.[60]

While worrying about the threat along the frontiers, Kanzler could not ignore a menace closer to home. Garibaldi and his supporters in the Italian government expected that the invasion of Red Shirt bands would be the signal for a popular insurrection in Rome that would spread through the pope's provinces. In turn, this rebellion would provide a pretext for the Italian army to intervene to restore order. The Italian government secretly channeled funds to Rome to encourage and support such an insurrection by subsidizing revolutionary propaganda and bribing officers in the pontifical army and police. Francesco Cucchi, a deputy in the Italian parliament, traveled clandestinely to the Eternal City to organize the uprising. In Florence, government ministers spoke openly of the anticipated "spontaneous" insurrection against the pontifical government.[61] To their great discomfiture, the expected revolt never occurred, due in part to disorganization and disagreements within the clandestine revolutionary movement inside Rome and the passivity of the majority of Roman citizens, many of whom may have wished for change but were not prepared to lift a finger to achieve it. The most important impediments to revolt, however, were the continued loyalty of the pontifical armed forces and the strong countermeasures adopted by papal authorities.

Papal army and security officers were well aware of the presence of revolutionary cells in Rome and the provinces; indeed, the Pontifical Gendarmeria had penetrated many of these cells, identified their members, and monitored their activities. As soon as the Red Shirt bands appeared on papal territory, the Pontifical Gendarmeria began arresting known and suspected subversives. By the end of October, almost five hundred individuals had been taken into custody.[62] General Kanzler also put as many police and soldiers from the Rome garrison as possible on the city streets in a show of force intended to discourage potential revolutionaries. Infantry detachments reinforced gendarmes at the city gates, riflemen and cavalrymen bivouacked in the main squares, and joint police-army teams patrolled the streets. Special measures were taken to ensure the security of the Vatican. Colonel Alfred von Sonnenberg, the commandant of the Swiss Guard, placed his men on alert, and Swiss Guards carrying rifles instead of halberds patrolled the walls and gardens of the pontifical palace. The Palatine Guard, the pope's citizen militia, was mobilized, and each night thirty guardsmen were on duty inside the Vatican. Other Palatines reinforced gendarmes on patrol in the city.[63]

In the weeks following the first Red Shirt incursions, there were a few isolated and uncoordinated acts of revolutionary violence in Rome: Shots were fired at patrols, uniformed soldiers walking alone at night were assaulted, and bombs were thrown at the Zouave Club and a gendarmeria barracks.[64] On October 20 word began to spread throughout the city that the revolutionary cells were about to strike, and some rumors insisted that the uprising would occur on the night of October 22. Few citizens of the Eternal City were prepared to dismiss the stories. Shopkeepers closed and shuttered their stores; lawyers, physicians, and notaries forsook their offices for the safety of their homes; and cabs and carriages disappeared from the streets. An unnatural silence fell over the city, and few people, aside from gendarmes and soldiers, appeared on the streets. The rumors proved accurate. The revolutionary committee planned an uprising for the night of October 22. A bomb in the Piazza Colonna would be the signal for attacks on the Capitol, the Ministry of Arms, the San Michele prison, and various barracks and military posts. Authorities seem to have received intelligence of the insurrection (no revolt was ever better advertised) because on October 22 they closed all city gates to prevent the infiltration of Red Shirts from the countryside and rendered two of the bridges across the Tiber temporarily impassable by taking up the planks of their roadbeds. That evening pontifical gendarmes raided a villa just outside the walls, seizing two hundred rifles, several cases of ammunition, and forty suspected Garibaldians, one of whom was mortally wounded when he resisted.[65] Troops and police were on high alert when, at 7:00 P.M., an explosion ripped through the Piazza Colonna and gunfire broke out at several points across the city. At the Campidoglio, overlooking the Roman Forum and since the time of the ancient republic the center of Rome's municipal government, a group of armed men rushed up the long flight of stairs designed by Michelangelo. Passing between the monumental antique sculptures of Castor and Pollux that flanked the head of the stairs, the attackers brushed aside the municipal guards on duty, ran to the second-century bronze statue of the emperor Marcus Aurelius that stood at the center of the piazza in front of the municipal buildings, and draped a revolutionary flag over that symbol of autocracy. It was the proclamation of a new Roman Republic. It was a short-lived regime. Within minutes detachments of soldiers and gendarmes rushed up the same stairs and scattered the revolutionaries in a hail of bullets.[66] Other threats proved equally ephemeral. A plan to seize the gasworks was exposed by a police informant, and the guards were able to drive off the attackers. Another plot, this time to explode a gunpowder store in the Castel Sant'Angelo with the assistance of a couple of noncommissioned officers of the pontifical artillery regiment who supported the revolution, failed when the plotters were discovered before they could blow up the fortress (and the several hundred Red Shirt prisoners who were held there). A group of armed men attacked the guard post at the Porta San Paolo, but the eight gendarmes on duty held the attackers at bay until reinforcements arrived to capture most of them and disperse the rest. Another detachment of gendarmes drove off revolutionaries who attacked the Ponte dei Quattro Capi, the bridge connecting the Tiber Island with the left bank of the river. The most serious incident occurred at 7:45 P.M., when revolutionaries detonated a bomb placed in the cellars of the Palazzo Serristori, the barracks of the pontifical Zouaves, killing twenty-five people, the majority of whom were members of the regimental band.[67]

Within hours of breaking out, the rebellion collapsed. General Kanzler telegraphed his senior officers in the provinces, "Ridiculous attempt at insurrection in Rome. Suppressed immediately."[68] The revolutionaries certainly had failed in their attempt to take over the city, but claims of their complete demise were premature. Rome remained tense. Bombs were still exploding around the city on October 23 as gendarmes hunted down suspects and collected rifles and pistols discarded in the street by fleeing insurgents, and for several days there were isolated bombings and attacks on police and soldiers. Learning that revolutionaries had acquired some army and police uniforms, the Ministry of Arms ordered small changes in the uniforms of the pontifical Zouaves and gendarmes in order to foil any attempt by insurgents to infiltrate buildings or guard posts in disguise.[69] On October 25 heavy gunfire echoed across the city when gendarmes and Zouaves, acting on intelligence from a police informant, raided a house in Trastevere belonging to Giulio Ajani. According to the informant, the house was a center for revolutionary activity and contained a weapons cache and a bomb factory. It is not clear from the records that the police knew that at the time of the raid some forty revolutionaries were meeting in the house. When the raiders hammered on the door with rifle butts and shouted for entry, someone threw a bomb down from an exterior balcony, and others opened fire from inside the building. The commander of the papal force sent to the closest army barracks for assistance, and soon a detachment of Zouaves arrived. Now reinforced, the commander ordered an assault. Smashing down the door, the raiders poured into the house, ruthlessly shooting or bayoneting anyone in front of them. The Ministry of Arms recorded sixteen Garibaldians dead (including at least one woman), twenty-five captured, and a large cache of weapons and explosives confiscated. The papal force lost one dead and four wounded.[70]

Outside Rome the Garibaldians had formulated a vague plan to assist the uprising in the city by floating men and weapons down the Tiber on ships that would disembark their loads at the Porto di Ripetta, the quay on the left bank near the Mausoleum of Augustus (and the present-day Ponte Cavour) that served as a port of entry for small boats moving cargo in and out of the city. On October 20 seventy-eight Red Shirts under the command of Enrico

Cairoli departed from Terni for the border post at Corese. On October 21 they boarded three boats (without any interference from Italian authorities) and sailed down the Tiber. The force was delayed when they stopped to capture a papal customs launch and its two crewmen, and they did not reach the Ponte Molle (the ancient Ponte Milvio) about 3 kilometers north of the city until the early afternoon of October 23. They missed a planned meeting near the bridge with representatives of the Roman insurrectionary committee. They also missed the insurrection. Since the revolutionary leaders who were not already dead or in the hands of the pontifical police were in hiding on October 23, there was no one to meet the tardy Red Shirts to discuss their deployment.

Enrico Cairoli decided to move his men to Monte Parioli, a low hill just beyond the northern walls of Rome, where they established themselves in an unoccupied country house, the Villa Glori. The group, perhaps expecting to be supported by local revolutionary committees, had carried few provisions, so Cairoli sent one of the men into the city to purchase food. This individual was taken into custody at the Porto del Popolo when the false papers he was carrying aroused the suspicion of gendarmes. The band seems also to have made contact with Francesco Cucchi, the leader of the revolutionary underground in the city.[71] In the meantime, a detachment of papal cavalry, patrolling beyond the northern walls, learned that a large group of men had suddenly appeared at a country house that was supposedly unoccupied. At any time such news would have aroused suspicion, but given the events of the preceding twenty-four hours, the information was certain to prompt an immediate response from authorities. The cavalrymen, while keeping a distant eye on the Villa Glori, sent a rider into the city with the news. A detachment of fifty soldiers from the Foreign Carabinieri Battalion was dispatched under Captain Meyer to investigate. As the papal troops approached the villa, the Red Shirts opened fire, and Captain Meyer immediately sent for reinforcements. Discovering that his men could not maintain a steady fire because their ammunition had been dampened during their river journey (the whole expedition seems to have been woefully mismanaged), Cairoli ordered a bayonet charge, perhaps in the hope of breaking out into open country before more papal troops arrived. The Red Shirts, however, could not break the pontifical line, and the charge dissolved into a melee of hand-to-hand combat. Meyer and Cairoli dueled at sword point until the papal captain fell, seriously wounded. As their commander fell under Cairoli's saber cuts, nearby carabinieri shot the Red Shirt leader. Seriously wounded, Cairoli refused an order to surrender, and a carabinieri sergeant rushed forward and bayoneted him to death. By the time papal reinforcements arrived, the fight was over and the area around the Villa Glori was dotted with dead and wounded. Twenty-eight Red Shirts were dead, and many were wounded, including Giovanni Cairoli, the brother of Enrico.[72]

The engagement at the Villa Glori ended efforts by the Red Shirt bands to directly support an insurrection in the Eternal City, but it was not the last act of the abortive uprising. On October 30 a captain of the Palatine Guard detachment on duty at the Vatican was approached by a citizen who reported that supporters of Garibaldi were gathering at the Villa Cecchini, a city house near the Palazzo Serristori that had been demolished by a bomb on the evening of October 22. The Palatine officer immediately passed the intelligence to higher authorities. The Ministry of Arms dispatched Captain Adeodato du Fournel and a company of Zouaves to investigate. As the troops approached the building, they were met with a fusillade of rifle fire. Captain du Fournel fell, mortally wounded, but the Zouaves charged through the gunfire, forced the door, and poured into the building. In a scene reminiscent of the incident at the Casa Ajani, the defenders tried to barricade stairways and interior doors, but the Zouaves smashed their way from room to room and floor to floor, indiscriminately shooting and bayoneting anyone in their way. The dead and wounded apparently included several Garibaldians, but the casualties also included several innocent individuals who were simply in the building at the time of the attack.[73]

Although the revolution died in Rome, Giuseppe Garibaldi personally took to the field to keep it alive in the countryside. Aware of the lackluster performance of the Red Shirt bands and hoping to invigorate their effort by his presence, the old republican, on October 14, had slipped away from his house arrest on Caprera. Eight days later he was in Florence, openly meeting with political leaders and publicly advocating an invasion of the Papal States. His presence precipitated another governmental crisis as Italian authorities, pressured by Paris to honor the terms of the September Convention, could not decide whether to arrest him or support him.[74] Prime Minister Urbano Rattazzi, an advocate of clandestine support for the Red Shirts, resigned. While political and military leaders argued, Garibaldi acted, crossing into papal territory on October 24 and joining (along with his fourth son, Ricciotti) the Red Shirt column commanded by his eldest son, Mennotti. Reinforced by new volunteers, the band now numbered several thousand irregulars. Undeterred by the collapse of the Roman insurrection (on October 23 he may not have been aware of how total that failure was), Garibaldi seems to have imagined ("planned" may be too strong a word to describe operations that were poorly coordinated and only vaguely conceived) an advance on the Eternal City by three columns of irregulars: his column moving down the left bank of the Tiber, via Monterotondo; a column under Giovanni Acerbi moving, via Viterbo, down the right bank; and a force under Giovanni Nicotera advancing from the southeast.[75] Garibaldi's command moved on Monterotondo, a small town of three thousand inhabitants 26 kilometers north of Rome on the main railway line from Umbria and Tuscany. On the night of October 23 a company of Red Shirts had occupied the train station about 2 kilometers from the town, capturing several papal soldiers and gendarmes on guard there. One soldier escaped to carry the alarm to Monterotondo. If Garibaldi had prosecuted his attack immediately, he might well have carried the town by surprise, but he waited almost thirty-six hours, perhaps to collect additional men, although the Red Shirts already grossly outnumbered the papal garrison.[76] The delay allowed the defenders to prepare.

Monterotondo was defended by two companies of the Legione Romana, one company of carabinieri, a unit of gendarmes, a detachment of dragoons, and a section of artillery with two guns, 323 men in all under the overall command of Captain Robert Costes of the Legione Romana. Costes had orders from General Kanzler to defend the town against any Garibaldian force. When the survivor of the action at the train station brought news of the attack, stating that there were two hundred Red Shirts involved, the captain immediately climbed into the tower of the old castle (a property of the princely Piombino family) that dominated the town to survey the countryside. The darkness and intermittent rain made observation difficult. Even if there were only two hundred irregulars at the station, the captain suspected that many more Red Shirts were close by and that Monterotondo was their target. Whatever the odds, Costes had his orders and was determined to hold out as long as possible. A message was dispatched to Rome with news of the attack.[77] Early on the morning of October 24 a reconnaissance party of papal dragoons sortied from the town to determine the size of the enemy force. They returned to report that at least four thousand Red Shirts were preparing to attack Monterotondo. This meant that the garrison would be outnumbered by more than ten to one. This unwelcome news did not alter Captain Costes's determination to fight. He sent out three gendarmes in civilian clothes to linger along the approaches to the town and give warning of an enemy advance. Next he set about deploying his small force. The defense was compromised not only by the small size of the garrison but by the fact that less than half of the town's perimeter was enclosed by a defensive wall, the rest consisting of the outer walls of buildings and houses with many doors and windows opening to the countryside. Captain Costes had to spread his few soldiers very thinly to protect this perimeter and the town's three unfortified gates. During the night of October 24–25, the papal soldiers slept at their posts in their uniforms, with their rifles and ammunition pouches at their sides.[78]

About 5:30 on the morning of October 25 the gendarme scouts who had been watching the roads hurried into town to announce that the enemy was approaching, and by 6:00 any citizens still abed were wakened by the rattle of musketry and the crash of cannons. The Red Shirts opened the assault by storming the three principal gates, Porta San Rocco (also known as the Porta Romana), Porta Ducale, and Porta Canonica, each defended by a section of Roman legionnaires. For three hours the irregulars threw themselves against the gates but were repulsed with heavy casualties by the defenders, who were assisted by two cannons brought into action by Lieutenant Bernard de Quatrebarbes, a twenty-seven-year-old artillery officer whose uncle had been the military governor of Ancona during the Piedmontese siege of that port city in the war of 1860. At one point de Quatrebarbes actually pushed one of his guns in front of one of the gates in order to open a better field of fire, although he could not maintain such an exposed position for long. At 9:00 the Garibaldians requested a truce to remove the dead and wounded. By noon the battle had been renewed, with two more futile assaults by the Red Shirts, who were now pressing the attack at various points around the town, particularly those points not protected by the town walls. The attackers simply could make no headway against the heavy rifle fire of the defenders, although they occupied several buildings just beyond the walls.[79] Always in the middle of the action, moving his cannons from one threatened spot to another, Lieutenant de Quatrebarbes was twice hit by enemy bullets and fell seriously wounded (he would eventually die from his wounds four weeks after the battle). Since his second in command had been mortally wounded earlier in the battle, command of the artillery section, now down to one gun, the second piece having become jammed and inoperable, fell to the surviving noncommissioned officer, the twenty-two-year-old Count Carlo Maria Antamoro, who ably fought his small command under intense fire.[80]

By the late afternoon of October 25, the Red Shirts, despite further assaults and heavy fighting, were no further along than they had been in the early morning, and all they had to show for their efforts were exhausted men, depleted ammunition, and a lengthening casualty list. This was not what Garibaldi had expected, and the general seems to have considered the possibility that he would have to abandon the attack and withdraw.[81] About 7:00 P.M. Garibaldi, who reproved some of his senior officers for the attack's lack of success, decided to make a final effort against the Porta Romana. This time the attackers loaded a farm cart with bundles of wood, sulfur, and oil. Under heavy rifle fire from the walls, they pushed this cart up to the gate and ignited it. The conflagration soon spread to the wooden gate, and the defenders could not bring up enough water to control the conflagration. As the gate burned, the Red Shirts wheeled up two small cannons, which opened fire against the weakened wood. By late evening the gates had collapsed, and the Garibaldians rushed into the town, overrunning a makeshift barricade of bricks the defenders had erected on the town side of the gateway.[82] Captain Costes ordered his men to fall back to the castle—really a large but unfortified villa—and most of the papal soldiers, fighting street by street, made it to that refuge, although the dragoons, perhaps because they misunderstood the order, retreated to their barracks, where they surrendered. From the castle the remaining defenders resisted through the night, but their position was increasingly precarious. By midmorning of the next day, the Red Shirts had fought their way into the first floor of the building, where fires were soon burning, and the papal troops, their ammunition nearly exhausted, were hard-pressed to hold the stairways to the upper floors. From the castle tower Captain Costes anxiously scanned the roads to the south for signs of a relief column advancing from Rome, but rescue was not on the horizon.[83] Concerned that the attackers might introduce explosives into the ground floor and blow up the castle and its defenders, and convinced that reinforcements would not arrive in time, the papal commander raised a white flag. Garibaldi sent his two sons to receive the surrender, and upon meeting Captain Costes, they complimented him on his heroic defense of the town.[84] For the attackers, it had been a costly battle. Garibaldian sources acknowledge 40 irregulars dead and more than 150 wounded, although in Rome General Kanzler believed that about 400 Red Shirts had been killed or wounded, a figure accepted by most historians. The defenders of Monterotondo recorded only 1 dead and 15 wounded, although some of the wounded died after reaching a hospital. More significantly for the Red Shirt cause, the unexpectedly fierce resistance of the pope's soldiers had shaken the irregulars, and concerns about morale forced Garibaldi to rest and regroup his force for two days before resuming his advance toward Rome.[85]

Garibaldi's success at Monterotondo was counterbalanced by a reverse at Viterbo, where a column of more than a thousand irregulars under a veteran Red Shirt commander, Giovanni Acerbi, failed in an effort to seize that provincial capital. Acerbi had been haunting the northern districts of the Papal States in anticipation of an advance down the right bank of the Tiber toward Rome in cooperation with a move south along the left bank by Garibaldi. Such a movement would require the neutralization of the papal garrison at Viterbo. On October 24 Acerbi led his men into Celleno, a village 19 kilometers from the town. While resting his men, the Garibaldian commander received an unexpected visit from several inhabitants of Viterbo, who assured him that republican sympathizers inside the town were prepared, upon receiving an order, to rise up and seize the pontifical barracks, disarm the troops, occupy the municipal buildings, and open the Porta Fiorentina to the Red Shirts. This news energized Acerbi, who was not enthusiastic at the prospect of a bloody assault or extended siege. Here was an opportunity to capture the provincial capital and its garrison with little risk to his force. The commander and his Viterbese visitors made plans to act that very night.[86]

Colonel Achille Azzanesi, commanding the pope's northern military zone from Viterbo, was aware that Acerbi was operating in his area, and upon learning that the Red Shirts were at nearby Celleno, he anticipated an early attack. His expectations were confirmed when a police informant revealed the plans for a republican insurrection inside the town. The colonel, who had joined the pontifical army as a simple rifleman in 1839 and risen through the ranks, distinguishing himself at the battles of Cornuda and Vicenza (1848) and Castelfidardo (1860), was not one to lose his head in a crisis. Immediate police action quashed any prospect of an internal revolt, and with equal celerity, Azzanesi moved to prepare for external attack. To defend Viterbo, the colonel had five companies from the regiment of the line, an understrength company of Zouaves, small detachments of dragoons and gendarmes, and an artillery section of two guns, a total of approximately six hundred men. Azzanesi immediately sent out a picket of sixteen dragoons under Lieutenant Fabiani to cover the road from Celleno and raise the alarm at the first sign of the enemy. He also deployed a company of the line under Captain De Simone to defend the junction where the roads from Celleno and Quercia met just outside the walls of Viterbo. Captain De Simone's orders were to delay the approaching Red Shirts as long as possible and then fall back into the town.[87]

Advancing confidently down the Celleno-Viterbo road in the early evening of October 24, the Red Shirts were surprised to encounter Lieutenant Fabiani's patrol about 2.5 kilometers from Viterbo. The papal dragoons opened fire on the irregulars, and in the resulting skirmish Fabiani was wounded and one of his troopers killed. Heavily outnumbered, the injured lieutenant ordered his men to fall back, and the detachment galloped back to the safety of the town, passing through Captain De Simone's infantry company at the crossroads. Having brushed aside the papal cavalrymen, the Red Shirts resumed their advance. As they approached the road junction, they received a volley from De Simone's infantry company, which, though also outnumbered, continued to exchange fire with its enemies for several minutes before falling back in good order into the town. If these brisk skirmishes did not convince Acerbi that his plan to walk into Viterbo to the acclaim of the citizens might require revision, what followed could have left him in no doubt. As they neared the Porta Fiorentina, which they expected to be in the friendly hands of the town's republicans, the Red Shirts were surprised to be met by gunfire rather than cheers. The situation was now perfectly clear: If Acerbi wanted Viterbo, he was going to have to fight for it.

Lacking any particular plan of attack, Acerbi simply ordered a frontal assault against the Porta Fiorentina. When after almost an hour of combat the attackers had failed to carry that portal, the Red Shirt commander ordered simultaneous assaults against the town's other gates. At the Porta Verità an attempt to set afire the wooden gates succeeded, but the Red Shirts could not advance against the heavy fire of the defenders, who had constructed a barricade just behind the burning portals. The battle for Viterbo continued into the night. The Garibaldians had failed to cut the telegraph wires, so the defenders were able to provide a running commentary on the battle for General Kanzler and his anxious staff in the Ministry of Arms in Rome. The short messages, often only minutes apart, captured the intensity of the combat: "We are being attacked at all six gates of the city." "Heavy gunfire. The Garibaldians are outside the Porta Fiorentina." "The Porta della Verità is in flames." "Garibaldians are attacking at six points [around] Viterbo. They are repulsed."[88] Throughout the night Azzanesi seemed to be everywhere in the town, galloping from one threatened point to another, dispatching reinforcements here and there, and directing and encouraging the defenders. After four hours of fighting, Acerbi called off the attack. His men had expended almost all of their ammunition, and papal reinforcements could be expected at any moment. The Red Shirts retreated into the countryside, leaving behind 5 dead and 15 wounded. Another 33 Garibaldians were captured uninjured by Azzanesi's troops. Papal losses were remarkably few: Only 2 soldiers were wounded defending the town gates. The successful defense of Viterbo thrilled the pontifical army, and Azzanesi's fellow officers were quick to cable their congratulations. Pope Pius was especially pleased to learn of the victory and sent his personal benediction to the garrison.[89]

The success at Viterbo thrilled papal commanders, who would not learn of the surrender of Monterotondo until October 26, but Hermann Kanzler was enough of a professional to realize that even without the loss of Monterotondo, things were no longer going well for the pontifical cause. By the third week in October the demands of the campaign against the Red Shirts were clearly taking a toll on the papal army. Casualties had been relatively light, but the constant marching and countermarching in response to the seemingly random appearance of irregular bands had exhausted the troops. There simply were not enough soldiers to cover the threats, which seemed to be proliferating in every province.[90] The bigger problem, however, was Italy. By October 26 intelligence reaching Rome had convinced the Ministry of Arms that military intervention by Italy was imminent. For the pontifical army, an invasion by the Italian army while Red Shirt bands were raiding across the countryside was the worst-case scenario. A signal that the worst was happening came at midday on October 27, when Lieutenant Colonel Charette telegraphed from Tivoli, "[Italian] regular troops invaded at Grillo." General Kanzler knew that if the lieutenant colonel was right about Italian troops invading east of Tivoli, the crisis was at hand. He cabled back to Tivoli, "Are the Piedmontese really at Grillo? You are taking a grave responsibility on yourself by giving me this news." Charette, always more the rough soldier than the polished diplomat, promptly replied with barely concealed temper, "I report intelligence according to my knowledge and my duty. The word here is that regular troops have entered at Arsoli and Grillo."[91]

In fact, although Italian troops were certainly on the border, there had been no invasion. Informants had observed an unusually well-turned-out party of mounted Red Shirts on the papal side of the border and assumed they were Italian cavalry. The mistake would become known only later; for the moment Kanzler had to assume that within hours Vittorio Emanuele's army would be pouring across the frontier. He sent out messages to his zone commanders ordering all units to fall back without delay on Civitavecchia and Rome. Most commanders executed this order immediately, and by the evening of October 27 troops were on the roads.[92] Some commanders, understanding that the order from Rome would strip the provinces of their protection and open them to the Red Shirts, expressed shock at the prospect of abandoning territory that they had been fighting to hold. From Viterbo Colonel Azzanesi, who for almost four weeks had been fighting and defeating the Garibaldians, asked, "Should I just abandon the province?" while the commander at Civita Castellana simply refused to credit the directive from Rome, cabling back, "The zonal commander has ordered the withdrawal of all troops to Rome. I suspect treachery. I request immediate confirmation."[93] Kanzler maintained his resolve. He was under no illusion as to what would happen in the provinces once the troops were withdrawn, but he was prepared to sacrifice territory to preserve his army and to buy time.[94] As everyone foresaw, Red Shirt bands promptly filled the military vacuum created by the withdrawal of papal troops, and by October 29 Garibaldian flags were flying over several towns, including Viterbo and Tivoli. By that time, however, a different flag was to be seen at another papal city, the port of Civitavecchia.

Italy's tacit support of the Red Shirts had undermined its relations with France. This support and its implicit repudiation of the September Convention embarrassed the Emperor Napoléon, who could not compromise his political standing among French Catholics or his personal (if variable) sense of honor by remaining passive while the pope was under attack. The emperor had recently suffered several political embarrassments, particularly the decision in 1866 to withdraw French troops from Mexico, where they had been unsuccessful in propping up the throne of the French-sponsored Emperor Maximilian. Acquiescence in Italy's disregard for the September Convention would be another humiliation, another sovereign betrayed, and the emperor may have wondered how many humiliations his throne could survive. By October 21 enough French troops and ships to form an expeditionary force (and a warning to Florence) had gathered at the port of Toulon in southern France, but every time the emperor inched toward a decision to intervene, Italian assurances or political qualms would push him back from the edge. To reassure the Vatican (and perhaps signal Florence not to push too far), Napoléon authorized modest gestures of support for the papacy. As early as October 19 a French warship in Civitavecchia harbor had landed one hundred gunners to reinforce the harbor defenses. Four days later a French general of engineers arrived to advise the papal Ministry of Arms on strengthening the defenses of Rome, and a French admiral surveyed Civitavecchia's port facilities in anticipation of the arrival of French convoys. On October 26, finally convinced that the Italian government would respond not to words but only to actions, Napoléon ordered French troops to the Papal States. The next day King Vittorio Emanuele, perhaps in a last-ditch effort to forestall a French landing, announced the appointment of General Luigi Menabrea as prime minister of Italy. Menabrea, recognizing that Italy's tacit support of the Red Shirts had seriously alienated France, immediately decided to distance his government from the activities of the irregulars. A proclamation signed by the king explicitly affirmed that the Red Shirts were operating without the support of the royal government and implicitly condemned their activities. The clandestine flow of volunteers, money, and weapons ended.[95] Garibaldi was now on his own.

The failure of the Red Shirt incursions to spark popular insurrections, particularly in Rome, seems to have discomfited Garibaldi, who never had a well-considered strategic plan for fighting the pontifical army, apparently believing that all he had to do was announce his presence, fire a few shots into the air, and advance toward Rome for the people to rise and the pope to fall.[96] A vague plan to have three columns of Red Shirts advance on the Eternal City from different directions was derailed when the column commanded by Giovanni Acerbi was bloodied and turned back at Viterbo. The plan was further undermined by Garibaldi's decision to divert the bulk of his force to the assault on Monterotondo. If he had simply bypassed the town or detached a couple of battalions to invest it and bottle up the small garrison, he would have avoided a costly battle and been able to march directly on Rome before General Kanzler concentrated his own forces there and before the French expeditionary force arrived to reinforce the papal army. After the battles at Monterotondo and Viterbo, the Red Shirts had in fact lost the operational initiative, but the Red Shirt commander could not yet admit it.

On October 28 Garibaldi moved his force south from Monterotondo along the left bank of the Tiber, apparently still nurturing the hope that as he neared Rome the anticipated revolution would break out. The advance was slow and listless, perhaps because along the way Garibaldi was angered and discouraged by news of the imminent arrival of French troops and the "betrayal" by the new government in Florence. A plan to cross the Teverone, a river that flows into the Tiber from the east just a few kilometers north of Rome, at the Ponte Salario, collapsed with the bridge as the papal detachment guarding the span blew it up (in accordance with standing orders from General Kanzler, who had also ordered the removal of all boats from the northern bank of the river) as soon as the Red Shirts were in sight. Adding insult to injury, the pontifical soldiers, undeterred by the size of the opposing force, opened a lively rifle fire across the river, forcing the invaders away from the bank. Garibaldi next sent troops to try the Ponte Nomentano (a little over a kilometer upriver from the Ponte Salario), which was defended by a company of the Legione Romana. Though outnumbered, the legionnaires held the bridge against Red Shirt attacks until the arrival of three companies of Zouaves discouraged further assaults. Foiled again, Garibaldi retreated to the nearby village of Casale dei Pazzi to regroup and consider his next move. He decided to return to Monterotondo.[97]

The campaign had not gone well for Garibaldi. Hopes of a Roman insurrection had been abandoned, and even in the countryside the pope's subjects had not rushed to join the Red Shirts. Rather than being welcomed as liberators, the irregulars had been forced to fight their way into most of the towns they briefly occupied. The pontifical army had not collapsed in a confusion of disloyalty, desertion, and indiscipline but had demonstrated a distressing willingness to fight it out with the Red Shirts even when seriously outnumbered by the invaders. At the end of October the Garibaldians held Monterotondo, Viterbo, and several other towns, but only because General Kanzler's decision to concentrate his forces in Rome and Civitavecchia had temporarily stripped these locales of their defenders. The precariousness of Red Shirt control was revealed on October 30 when Giovanni Nicotera's column precipitously abandoned Velletri upon the approach of a pontifical force dispatched by Kanzler, who, now that the French expeditionary force had arrived, felt able to return some of his troops to the 4th Military Zone south of Rome. The arrival of the French significantly strengthened the military position of the papacy, and the loss of Italian support was a psychological and material blow to the Garibaldian cause. If the campaign had not gone well so far, the prospects for the future were even grimmer.

The French expeditionary force disembarked at Civitavecchia, the main port of the Papal States, on October 29. The force included two divisions of infantry, a brigade of cavalry, and several batteries of artillery under the overall command of General Pierre Louis de Failly, a professional who earlier in his career had acquired a reputation for cruelty due to his role as a young officer in the suppression of disorders in Paris in 1834. More recently he had commanded a division in the Crimean War. Leaving a small force at Civitavecchia, Failly marched the bulk of his command to Rome, where the Romans turned out to cheer as the French soldiers paraded down the Corso, the principal street of the capital. On November 1 General Kanzler met with Failly to review the pontifical army's operations against the Red Shirts and to discuss plans for the next stage of the campaign. The French general, perhaps reflecting instructions from Paris, counseled moderation. He proposed to concentrate his forces on Rome, thereby acting as a deterrent to any Garibaldian advance on the city and allowing General Kanzler to free troops for operations in the field. Although prepared to support papal troops from a distance, Failly did not envision any direct deployment of French soldiers in combat against the Red Shirts; indeed, he seemed to expect the irregulars to lose heart and simply fade away now that the French had arrived. He was especially concerned with avoiding any possibility of an encounter with the Italian army. That very day intelligence had reached Rome that units of the Italian army had crossed the frontier to occupy Civita Castellana, Acquapendente, and Frosinone, towns within a few kilometers of the border, but the units were not advancing farther into papal territory.[98] The Italian units were specifically enjoined by their government to respect papal authority in the occupied towns and avoid provocations. Rather than an act of support for Garibaldi, this intervention was a face-saving gesture intended to create the impression that Italy was not cowed by the arrival of French troops. General Failly, however, could not be sure of the purposes of the government in Florence, so he was wary of any operational plan that, by bringing about an armed encounter between French and Italian troops, would throw Franco-Italian relations into crisis.[99]

General Kanzler received Failly's proposals with disbelief and dismissed them with scarcely concealed scorn. The pope's commander had no intention of adopting a safe, defensive strategy and waiting for the Red Shirts to give up and go away. This was the moment for boldness, not moderation. Kanzler believed that the Garibaldians had lost the initiative and were militarily and psychologically off balance due to the failure of the Roman insurrection, the withdrawal of Italian support, the arrival of the French, and several bloody defeats at the hands of papal troops. He saw an opportunity to strike a decisive blow against the Red Shirts by marching immediately against Garibaldi at Monterotondo before additional bands of irregulars could reinforce him. A decisive blow would annihilate the largest force of irregulars, perhaps capture their leader, dishearten the remaining bands, and remove any excuse for intervention by the Italian army. Boldness, however, was required because if Garibaldi had time to withdraw to the safety of Italian territory, he and thousands of his followers would return to fight another day, and their escape would cheer the enemies of the pope. There was no question of risk. Kanzler was supremely confident that his troops would prevail over the enemy, and he assured General Failly that the pope's soldiers would form the attacking force and that French troops were required only as a ready reserve.[100] This assurance suggests that Kanzler preferred an aggressive approach not just for strictly military reasons. The general was rightly proud of the army, which he had rebuilt from the ashes of the disastrous War of 1860, often in the face of skepticism from powerful figures such as Cardinal Antonelli. This army—*his* army—had surprised many observers (particularly among the commanders of the Red Shirts) with its discipline, loyalty, and professionalism, and Kanzler intended to personally lead it against the archfoe of the papacy, Giuseppe Garibaldi.[101] A decisive victory would be an operational success that would end the war, but such a victory would also vindicate Kanzler's vision of a professional pontifical army and silence the skeptics inside the Vatican who dismissed as ridiculous the idea of such a force. More important, a decisive victory would be a necessary and proper reward for an army whose historical record, at least until October 1867, was not distinguished by a surfeit of battlefield successes. Kanzler believed his army deserved a chance to beat the Red Shirts. He understood that for these reasons, there could be no temporizing. For the pontifical army, an immediate attack was not just an operational question; it was a question of honor.

Eventually and somewhat reluctantly, General Failly accepted Kanzler's arguments. The generals agreed to join forces and march on Monterotondo in the early morning of November 3, a launch date less than forty-eight hours away. The following hours witnessed a flurry of activity as the respective armies prepared men and equipment for the operation. Kanzler's biggest problem was the assembly of a field force. Some of the pontifical army was still scattered across the provinces, and even if time permitted (which it did not), most of these units could not be redeployed to join Kanzler's force without exposing those provinces to the predations of other Red Shirt bands that were lurking about the countryside. The papal commander decided to rely primarily on troops from the 2nd Brigade centered in Rome, reinforced by a handful of companies recalled from nearby garrisons. Within the pontifical army, enthusiasm for the expedition ran so high that many officers from units not selected for the operation begged permission to join the march in any capacity.[102]

It was still dark when, on the morning of November 3, 1867, General Kanzler mustered his force on the parade ground of the Campo Pretorio, the military encampment constructed by Monsignor de Mérode along the northeastern walls of Rome. After reading a blessing from the Holy Father and adding his own exhortation on behalf of duty and honor, the pope's commander-in-chief led his force through the Porta Pia. It was a cold, rainy Sunday, and as the men trudged northeast toward Monterotondo along the Via Nomentana (a road trodden by countless armies since the days of ancient Rome), they were probably happy that they carried on their backs kit for only two days in the field. Evidently, their commander did not expect a long campaign. The papal column, 2,913 men strong, consisted of two battalions of Zouaves, a battalion of foreign carabinieri, a battalion of the Legione Romana, a field artillery battery of six guns, a company of engineers, a detachment of gendarmes, and a squadron of dragoons scouting ahead and covering the flanks. The papal troops were followed at a distance by 2,000 French: a brigade of five infantry battalions, a cavalry troop, and four pieces of field artillery under the overall command of General Balthazar de Polhés, who had marched from Rome at 5:30 that morning. The joint forces totaled approximately 5,000 men.[103]

At the Ponte Nomentana, where the road crosses the Teverone River, General Kanzler divided his force, sending Major de Troussures and three companies of Zouaves to advance up the Via Salaria, a few kilometers west of and parallel to the Via Nomentana. Should the main column encounter Red Shirts on the road ahead, the papal commander expected Troussures to turn east and take the enemy's flank as the main column engaged its front.[104]

At Capobianco, a village about halfway between Rome and Monterotondo, Kanzler halted his column to let his troops rest and eat before the anticipated battle and allow the French to catch up. During this stop a chaplain celebrated a heavily attended mass in the village's small church. At this point the papal commander still believed that Garibaldi and his force were at Monterotondo. In fact, the Red Shirts too were on the march.

In Rome, Francesco Cucchi, Garibaldi's representative to the revolutionary committee, had somehow managed to secure information about the Franco-papal war council of November 1. On November 2 Cucchi sent a trusted shepherd north to Monterotondo to warn Garibaldi that Kanzler would take the offensive the next day with a force that included French troops. The warning accurately described the size and line of march of Kanzler's force. After receiving this intelligence, the Red Shirt leader spent most of November 2 consulting his staff and examining maps. He was uncharacteristically indecisive, in part because he did not entirely credit the intelligence from Cucchi, particularly the news that French troops were marching with Kanzler. The French might put troops into Rome to secure the city, but Garibaldi believed they would not actually take the offensive as part of a pontifical army.[105] Initially, he was inclined to avoid battle by withdrawing eastward toward the Abruzzi mountains but then spoke of taking the offensive should numbers favor his side. The size of Garibaldi's army remains uncertain. General Kanzler believed that he was marching against 10,000 irregulars, and the Red Shirt commander may well have had nearly that number in and around Monterotondo. Menotti Garibaldi, however, would later recall that at the beginning of November there were about 8,000 irregulars under his father's command, but desertions (an increasingly serious problem for the Red Shirts, as the failure to take Rome, the lack of supplies, and the pressure of the pontifical army discouraged the fainthearted) and the need to deploy detachments to secure nearby towns and villages reduced the effective field force to between 4,500 and 4,800 fighters.[106] Garibaldi could not decide whether to attack or retreat. On the morning of November 3 he ordered his force to depart Monterotondo and march toward Tivoli, a town east of Rome and in the direction of the Abruzzi that had been occupied by a thousand Red Shirts under Luigi Pianciani after the recall to Rome of the papal garrison on October 27.[107] If Garibaldi hoped to evade his enemies, this was a curious maneuver because the direction of movement actually brought him closer to the advancing pontificals. Perhaps he was keeping his options open and wanted to move toward Tivoli and a juncture with Pianciani while remaining in a position to attack should the balance of forces be in his favor. Such a plan depended on the ability to identify the size of the opposing force in time to decide whether to fight or flee. Garibaldi was, however, tactically blind. He had ordered a battalion to screen his movements by occupying the heights along the right flank of his line of march, but this unit had failed to complete its assignment, claiming that the rain and cold had impeded its movements. Although his force included a small number of mounted men (probably fewer than a hundred), he seems not to have used them effectively as a cavalry screen to reconnoiter in advance of the foot soldiers and identify the size and location of the enemy. The pontifical army suffered from no such deficiency. As Garibaldi's force reached the town of Mentana (its departure from Monterotondo had been delayed by the need to distribute shoes among the men), it was observed by papal dragoons scouting ahead of the pontifical column. When notified that papal scouts had been sighted, Garibaldi concluded that the enemy was upon him and that he had no choice now but to fight. He immediately began to deploy his men around Mentana, a small agricultural town of seven hundred inhabitants surrounded by ravines and farm-studded hills and dominated by a small medieval castle and a sixteenth-century villa belonging to the Borghese family.

At Capobianco the papal-French force had been resting for almost ninety minutes. Officers had just given orders to the troops to collect their equipment and prepare to resume the march when the cavalry scouts rushed into camp with news that the Red Shirts were just up the road at Mentana. Kanzler immediately ordered the advance with the pontifical column in the front and the French a kilometer behind. Excitement ran through the papal bivouac. Infantrymen doused cooking fires, readied their packs, and checked their weapons and ammunition; gunners harnessed horses to caissons; dragoons galloped from the camp to establish a protective screen ahead; and chaplains led the men in hurried prayers and blessed the units as they formed up on the road. Everyone expected a big battle, but spirits were high, and the pope's soldiers were confident of victory. Within the hour they were moving toward Mentana, where the Red Shirts awaited them.[108]

Inside the town, Garibaldi had hurriedly deployed his men at the gates, around the walls, and inside the large Villa Borghese. The veteran general was far too experienced, however, to believe that the walls were his first line of defense and that the battle would begin only when the enemy marched up to the gates. He planned a forward defense that would engage the pontifical force beyond the town and force it to fight and die before it even reached those gates. From the south, the road into Mentana passed between two hills that pressed closely on the highway a couple of kilometers outside the town. Garibaldi sent three battalions of his best men to occupy those heights. One of these battalions occupied the Casale Santucci, a tall stone farmhouse with a vineyard enclosed by a wall, which was situated near the crest of the hill on the right of the road, about a kilometer outside town. Transformed into a strongpoint, this farmhouse, supported by riflemen scattered among the bushes and farm buildings of the hill opposite (Monte Guarnieri), could control the road along which Kanzler's force would approach the town. Although Garibaldi's force had four cannons, including two captured at Monterotondo, the commander unaccountably chose not to deploy any of these guns to the Casale Santucci. The Red Shirt commander also established a redoubt closer to town by sending men to fortify an abandoned monastery, known as "Il Conventino," situated 200 meters from the Casale Santucci on the right of the approach road.

As the Garibaldians frantically prepared their positions, the Franco-papal force neared Mentana. Scouting forward was a troop of pontifical dragoons under Lieutenant de la Rocchette, whose orders were to locate the enemy's front line. Informed by a peasant that armed men were in the area, de la Rocchette spread out his men. Sent by the lieutenant to check a stand of trees off the main road, Trooper Arduino came upon a group of irregulars sheltering in the shade. Assuming that any armed men to his front had to be enemies, the cavalryman fired his carbine at the group; wheeled his mount; and, chased by a hail of Red Shirt bullets, galloped to find his lieutenant. Trooper Arduino had located the enemy and fired the first shot of the Battle of Mentana.[109]

General Raphael De Courten, commanding the pontifical advance guard, ordered the Zouaves forward. Two companies under Captain Alain de Charette (younger brother of Colonel Athanase de Charette) attacked directly up the road while a company under Lieutenant Jean Thomalé advanced on the Casale Santucci on the heights to the right of the road and another company, commanded by Lieutenant Numa d'Albiousse, moved up Monte Guarnieri on the left. Companies of the carabinieri esteri supported the flanks of the attacking Zouaves. Captain de Charette, who had fought as a private at Castelfidardo and served in all the enlisted ranks before his promotion into the officer corps, aggressively pushed his companies forward, and after several volleys the Garibaldians emplaced along the road withdrew up the hills to the left and right. On the right, Lieutenant Thomalé's men came into an open area spotted with culverts and thickets behind which Red Shirts sheltered and opened a lively fire that stopped the advancing Zouaves in their tracks. Noticing that the attack was faltering on the right, De Courten ordered Colonel Athanase de Charette forward with reinforcements. Ordering his men to drop their field packs, the charismatic colonel, sword drawn, turned his horse toward the front rank; shouted, "Forward, Zouaves! If you won't go, I'll go alone"; and wheeled about to charge across the field. With yells of "Hurray for Pius IX!" "Hurray for the colonel!" the Zouaves moved forward, driving the Garibaldians at bayonet point from tree to tree and thicket to thicket, the path of their advance marked by dead and wounded Red Shirts.[110]

General Kanzler and his staff had moved forward on the heels of the attacking Zouaves. Noticing that a farmhouse on a nearby hill, only just occupied by the carabinieri esteri, offered a clear view of the Casale Santucci, the pope's commander ordered an artillery piece emplaced on that height to support the Zouaves who were struggling under heavy fire to invest that fortified villa. As papal gunners under Count Bernardini, a young noncommissioned gunner, galloped forward and wheeled their cannon into position, additional Zouaves joined their comrades in the attack on the villa. Once again Colonel de Charette was in the middle of the action, cheering the men forward, seemingly indifferent to the bullets that flew past his head. Then, suddenly, the charismatic officer was down, his horse thrown violently to the ground and the colonel rolling in the dust. Alarmed Zouaves ran to their commander's side, fearing the worst, but the colonel raised himself from the dirt unharmed, although his horse lay dead with three bullets in its body. The Zouaves returned to the attack, flushing Red Shirts from the woods on either side of the Casale Santucci and pressing so close to the villa's walls that the shells from Bernardini's cannon, now in action from the neighboring hill, posed as great a danger to them as to the defenders. After a brief effort to defend the wall that surrounded the vineyard, the Garibaldians fell back into the main house, from whose windows they maintained a lively fire on the papal troops that now swarmed around the building. The Zouaves rushed the main door, smashing it down with axes and rifle butts, and poured into the house. The Red Shirts defending the entrance hallway immediately went down under Zouave bayonets, but their compatriots quickly threw down their weapons in surrender.[111]

The loss of Casale Santucci and the nearby heights proved a serious blow to the defenders of Mentana. Not only was the way to the town now open, but cannon on the hilltops would be well placed to support an infantry assault against the gates and walls. General Kanzler was quick to perceive the latter opportunity. He immediately ordered to the heights a section of pontifical field artillery and sent a staff officer galloping to the rear with a request that General de Polhés (whose troops had remained in support behind the battle lines) immediately rush forward a section of artillery to reinforce the papal gunners. The general complied with this request, and soon two French cannons were in action from the heights overlooking Mentana, the first appearance of the French on the field of battle. To support the cannon fire from the hilltops, Kanzler pushed forward along the Mentana road another of his artillery pieces, which opened fire only 500 meters from the town walls.[112]

It was now about 2:00 P.M. The Casale Santucci and the heights on the right of the approach road were in papal hands, as were the slopes around Monte Guarnieri on the left, where the Legione Romana had moved forward to support the Zouaves. Eager to maintain offensive momentum, General Kanzler, who had established his headquarters in the Casale Santucci, ordered his troops to press the attack under the covering fire of the pontifical and French cannons. From the Casale Santucci the Zouaves moved downhill and, after a brief but sharp action, forced the Red Shirts from the Conventino. The carabinieri esteri battalion had come up to reinforce the Zouaves on the right, but efforts by these units to advance against the town walls, now only a few hundred meters away, faltered under intense rifle fire from the Garibaldians installed in the castle and behind the windows, doors, and walls of town buildings. For some time the two sides exchanged fire, and the Red Shirt artillery joined the action from emplacements on the heights behind the village. Shortly after 2:00 P.M. Garibaldi, noticing that the pontifi-cal attack had stalled, decided to counterattack. He sent two columns from the town to envelop both flanks of the attackers. The counterattacks sur-prised the papal units. On the pontifical left the Legione Romana, joined by a squadron of dismounted dragoons, held and repelled the Red Shirts in a furious firefight, but on the right the carabinieri esteri bent under the attack and began to give way. The carabinieri commander, Lieutenant Colonel Cas-tella, was grievously wounded, and for a time battlefield command fell upon a simple rifleman who only moments before had been standing shoulder to shoulder with his comrades, firing and reloading in a fog of gun smoke as the attacking Garibaldians slowly pressed back the papal soldiers. Private [Count] Victor de Courten had joined the Swiss regiment of the pontifical army in 1832 and in 1848 had fought as an officer in the defense of Vicenza. Promoted through the officer ranks, he had retired from the papal army in 1861 as a lieutenant colonel. When the Red Shirts invaded the Papal States, he felt honor bound to offer his services to the Holy Father and enlisted as a private in the carabinieri battalion. Now, before the walls of Mentana, duty called again. He put down his rifle and assumed temporary command of a section of the threatened line.[113]

The threat was very real. The carabinieri were barely holding, and if the Red Shirts broke through, they could roll up the papal flank and recapture Casale Santucci. Kanzler needed to reinforce the danger point immediately, but few of his troops were available. The Zouaves, closest in line to the cara-binieri, were exhausted by three hours of continuous combat and could not provide enough support for their comrades-in-arms without denuding the center of the papal line, which was still engaging the Garibaldians in the town. From his command post in the Casale Santucci, Kanzler dispatched a message to Colonel d'Argy, commanding the Legione Romana on the left of the line, directing him to shift his unit to the right to bolster the threatened flank. D'Argy, however, was fully occupied with his own counterattacking Garibaldians to his front and could free only two companies. Fortunately, the arrival of the legionnaires helped the carabinieri stabilize their line and throw back the Red Shirts. The counterattacks repulsed, the papal troops renewed their attack with one company of legionnaires actually capturing some houses just outside the walls.[114]

With the repulse of Garibaldi's flanking attacks, Kanzler saw one crisis pass, but rather quickly another appeared. It was now about 3:30 P.M., and the Red Shirts decided to risk everything on another counterattack. Kanzler now probably regretted his decision earlier that morning to detach Major de Troussures and three companies of Zouaves to march up the Via Salaria. All available pontifical units had been committed to the battle. Some units were low on ammunition, and all were tired. Major de Troussures and his precious Zouaves were somewhere to the west, marching perhaps to the sound of guns but unlikely to appear in time to turn the battle that was unfolding below Kanzler's perch at the Casale Santucci.[115] Kanzler needed more troops now. However much the pope's commander wanted the battle with Garibaldi to be a papal victory, he now had no choice. It was time to call in the French.

Aside from the single artillery section deployed in support of the papal assault, the French column had remained to the rear, in full battle order but inactive. General de Polhés (almost certainly following orders from Paris) made no effort to join the battle, eschewing any initiative and allowing the pope's soldiers to engage the Red Shirts. Upon receiving Kanzler's request for assistance, the French general seems to have hesitated, or at least failed to respond with the alacrity and enthusiasm expected by his ally. Kanzler, suspecting that Paris preferred to keep its troops out of combat, may have muttered something about betrayal and his intention to inform the capitals of Europe about the treachery of French generals.[116] Threatened or not, de Polhés launched his troops forward, deploying a battalion reinforced by three companies and an artillery section to the right of the papal line and a battalion and one artillery piece to the left. While the pontifical units pressed the attack in the center, the French columns enveloped the town from two sides, driving in the Red Shirts. The sudden appearance of the French, many of whom carried the new breech-loading *chassepot* rifle that was far superior in range and rate of fire to the muzzle-loading percussion rifles carried by the irregulars and the pontifical infantry, certainly had a serious impact on the defenders of Mentana. The effect was mainly psychological but also tactical, ending any hope of a successful counterattack and threatening the road to Monterotondo. The Red Shirts, however, did not give up the game at the first sight of the tricolor. Some surrendered, others fled into the countryside, but most simply withdrew into the town, from which they maintained a steadfast resistance. Chassepots or no, the battle continued, with the pontifical units directly assaulting the town while the French skirmished on the flanks. At one point in the early evening Captain Daudier, a papal artillery officer who in 1860 had commanded a forward battery at Castelfidardo, raced to within 100 meters of the walls with two pieces of horse-drawn field artillery and, under intense fire, began slamming round after round into the defenses at point-blank range. The position was dangerously exposed, and within minutes two of Daudier's gunners were wounded and most of his horses were dead. The loss of the horses immobilized the cannons, and the brave but impetuous captain was in an increasingly tight spot. Red Shirt marksmen were picking off the gunners, and a sortie from the town could easily have captured the cannons. Then Count Bernardini, who earlier in the battle had pushed forward an artillery piece to support the assault on the Casale Santucci, galloped up with replacement horses. The arrival of this troop attracted the attention of more enemy riflemen, but Bernardini, bullets whizzing past his head and kicking up dirt around his horse, calmly directed his team as they hitched the horses to the guns. Within minutes the guns began to pull out, still under intense fire. As Bernardini spurred his horse to follow the cannons he had saved, he was knocked dead from his horse by bullets to his neck and chest.[117]

By the early evening Kanzler believed his opponents to be so exhausted that a grand assault could carry the town. Up the main road from Rome he launched two battalions of the French 59th Regiment, followed by a battalion of French chasseurs under the personal command of General de Polhés. The French bravely pressed the attack, but despite the vaunted chassepots their advance faltered in the face of heavy fire from a group of buildings immediately outside the town gate and from makeshift barricades thrown across the road by the Red Shirts. As the attack of the French forces waned, companies of pontifical Zouaves and Roman legionnaires rushed to their support. When the pontificals received the order to advance, Captain de Chappedelaine, who had resigned from the Zouaves before the war only to return to his regiment when the first Red Shirts crossed into papal territory, drew his sword and shouted to his men, "So, it's another mess. Fix bayonets. Forward!" At bayonet point the Zouaves fought their way into the outbuildings that the defenders had turned into strongpoints. At a barricade in front of one building, Garibaldians fired from the windows and from adjoining structures. Private Jean Moeller, a former officer who had resigned his commission after Castelfidardo only to reenlist as a common rifleman when the Garibaldians invaded, threw his kepi over the barrier, shouted to his mates, "Who has the heart to follow me?" and rushed the fortification, followed by other Zouaves. Almost immediately he was struck by an enemy bullet. "I'm wounded," he murmured to the Zouaves who rushed to pull him to safety. "What luck!" He did not survive.[118]

Unable to penetrate the town, Kanzler called off the assault. Darkness had fallen, and his troops were exhausted. With pontifical and French units ensconced on the heights and roads around the town, however, the allies held secure positions and prevented the enemy's retreat or reinforcement. The papal commander decided to refrain from further action that night and renew the assault on the morrow with troops that were rested and fed. The night passed quietly. Early on the morning of November 4 an emissary under a white flag approached the allied lines with a request to meet General Kanzler. The messenger offered the general the surrender of Mentana on the condition that the defenders could depart unmolested, with their weapons and baggage. The pope's general, who anticipated taking the town that morning and saw no reason to allow the Red Shirts to escape capture, summarily rejected the proposal. He reconsidered his decision, however, after a consultation with General de Polhés, who pointed out that the allied force already had more prisoners than it could handle and that it would be more practical to allow the surviving defenders to proceed under escort to the Italian border, leaving behind all their weapons, ammunition, and equipment. Kanzler accepted this compromise, and on the morning of November 4 allied troops entered Mentana as the disarmed Red Shirts departed and began their retreat to the frontier, accompanied by a detachment of French infantry.[119]

Hermann Kanzler had the decisive victory he so greatly desired. The papal commander reported that more than 1,000 Red Shirts had been killed or wounded during the battle for the town, and 1,398 irregulars had been captured by the allied force along with quantities of arms and munitions. Garibaldian accounts admit to 150 dead and 206 seriously wounded without mentioning those captured or suffering light wounds. Thirty pontifical soldiers lost their lives in the battle, and 103 received wounds. The French expeditionary force suffered 2 dead and 36 wounded.[120] The casualty and prisoner lists did not include Giuseppe Garibaldi. The Red Shirt commander had fled Mentana for Monterotondo sometime during the afternoon of November 3, before the allies could close the roads. Monterotondo proved only a brief stop because, as the battle wound down, a French detachment began marching toward that town. Papal territory was no longer safe, so Garibaldi crossed the frontier at Corese. Italy, however, offered no welcoming haven. Although perfectly content to use the Red Shirts for its own purposes, the royal government was not pleased that the irregulars had created an embarrassing imbroglio with France. Traveling to Florence by train, Garibaldi was arrested at a small station outside the capital and taken to the fortress at La Spezia, where he was held for three weeks before being transported to his home on Caprera.

Mentana marked not only the end of the Red Shirt campaign but also the vindication of the pontifical army. Hermann Kanzler, and Monsignor de Mérode and General de Lamoricière before him, had insisted that with attention, effort, and purpose the Papal States could create and maintain a capable army. That army would be an effective instrument for maintaining the security of papal territory and defending the temporal rights of the pope, a useful and necessary complement to papal diplomacy. Surrounded by skeptics, Kanzler had set out to create such a force, and the units that suppressed brigands in the Comarca, assisted disaster victims in the Alban Hills, hounded Red Shirts across the length and breadth of the papal domain, and marched on Mentana were a testimony to his commitment and effort. The pontifical army, at least in the nineteenth century, was never entirely the incompetent and lackadaisical force portrayed by critics of the papacy and its temporal power, but its consistent record of defeat before 1867 (no matter how tempered by sacrifice and bravery) encouraged little respect and less confidence among even the most loyal supporters of the papacy. Kanzler changed that. He created an army worthy of respect. More important, he created an army that respected itself.

Few historians, even among students of the Risorgimento, have considered the campaign of 1867 worth much attention; indeed, those who do not ignore the campaign entirely usually treat it cursorily. A recent history of Italy since the French Revolution devotes only one paragraph out of 653 pages to the campaign and does not mention the papal army once in that paragraph.[121] Except for extreme papal partisans, the few historians who have considered the military aspects of the crisis of October–November 1867 have usually denigrated the role of the pontifical army. The standard military history of the Risorgimento dates the onset of the campaign of 1867 from the day Giuseppe Garibaldi entered the Papal States, not from the day, three weeks earlier, when the Red Shirt bands first attacked papal territory and engaged pontifical military units. It considers the campaign entirely from the Garibaldian perspective, so privileging the Red Shirt narrative at the expense of the pontifical that a reader would conclude that the Red Shirts did not lose a battle before Mentana.[122] Another history of the campaign baldly asserts that when the first Red Shirt bands appeared on papal territory, the pontifical army refused combat and simply retreated to Rome to await rescue by the French.[123] Supporting this perspective, a more recent account concludes, "In 1867, General Kanzler and his men preferred, in the face of Garibaldi's attack, to shelter behind the walls of Rome rather than prepare plans for a counterattack. Only after the arrival of French troops did the papalists find the courage to confront the enemy on the battlefield."[124] A leading authority on modern Italy states that the Red Shirts at Mentana were defeated by a French army and seems ignorant of the fact that a pontifical army was even present at the battle, let alone that it carried the principal burden of the fighting.[125] More generously, one of Garibaldi's most recent biographers is prepared to acknowledge that papal troops were present with the French at Mentana, although merely in a supportive role.[126] Even well-informed students of modern papal history are inclined to attribute the success over the Red Shirts to the allegedly greater size of the Franco-papal forces at Mentana and the efficacy of the famous French chassepots while ignoring the operations of the pontifical army that preceded that final battle.[127] By neglecting the military aspects of the crisis of 1867, such accounts seriously underestimate—when they do not actually denigrate—the performance of the pope's soldiers and distort the history of that crisis.

The pontifical army—Hermann Kanzler's army—fought and won the campaign of 1867. Over a period of more than a month (September 30–November 2) that army, *on its own*, suppressed an insurrection in Rome, fought more than a dozen small-unit actions in the field, defended several provincial towns against Red Shirt invaders, and inflicted hundreds of casualties on the Garibaldians. Under the direction of an intelligent and capable commander-in-chief, its response to the invasion by Red Shirt bands was immediate and determined. It relentlessly pursued the invaders and seized every opportunity to engage them. Field commanders exhibited initiative and aggressiveness, and soldiers were consistently steadfast and disciplined. Even when isolated and significantly outnumbered, papal units stood and fought. There was no repetition of the humiliating scenes at Castelfidardo during which entire units had thrown down their weapons and fled from battle. In particular, the behavior of the units composed entirely of Italian personnel—the artillery, cavalry, gendarmeria, and line infantry regiments—was exemplary, surprising those who anticipated that such units would prove unreliable in the face of an antipapal/nationalist army. Even at Mentana, the only battle at which French troops were present, the papal units carried the main burden of combat, clearing the approach road of enemy riflemen, capturing the high ground, subduing the strongpoints at Casale Santucci and the Conventino, bringing the fight to the walls of the town, and repelling Red Shirt counterattacks on both flanks. They did all this *before* the French infantry entered the fray. Mentana was not a French victory but a joint success in which the pontifical army played a dominant, not a subordinate, role. In the end Kanzler's army simply outfought its enemy. Explaining the failure of the Red Shirts, an Italian historian accurately noted, "In this campaign Garibaldi faced an opponent who was resolute and animated by a strong will to combat. Not one pontifical unit collapsed, and there were no cases of desertion. In addition, Garibaldi had as an antagonist a commander [Kanzler] greatly superior in skill and character to the Bourbon [Neapolitan] generals."[128] It was a just and accurate appraisal, but Giuseppe Garibaldi and his Red Shirts, although dangerous, were not the most serious threat to the independence of the Papal States. For Hermann Kanzler and the pontifical army, a bigger test lay in the future.

General Hermann Kanzler (seated center) with officers of the pontifical army, 1862. (Collection Instituto Centrale per il Catalogo e la Documentazione, Rome)

Pontifical army units on field maneuvers, 1862. Zouaves in tents; dragoons in the background. (Archive of the Pontifical Swiss Guard, Vatican City)

Officer of the special mounted detachment of the Pontifical Gendarmeria, circa 1860. The tall bearskin hat was worn by the special detachment, which performed ceremonial and guard functions in Rome and the papal palace. (Courtesy of Professor Piero Crociani)

The breach in the Roman wall at Porta Pia, September 21, 1870. (Archive of the Pontifical Swiss Guard, Vatican City)

Uniforms of the Swiss Guard, circa 1900. (Archive of the Pontifical Swiss Guard, Vatican City)

Swiss Guard, circa 1870. (Archive of the Pontifical Swiss Guard, Vatican City)

Noncommissioned officers of the Swiss Guard with the newly acquired Mauser model 98 rifle, 1912. (Archive of the Pontifical Swiss Guard, Vatican City)

Colonel Jules Repond (second from left) with a Vatican official and two officers of the Swiss Guard: Major Adolf Glanzmann (far left) and Captain Johann Vogelsang (far right), 1913. (Archive of the Pontifical Swiss Guard, Vatican City)

Swiss Guards at bayonet practice, circa 1920. (Archive of the Pontifical Swiss Guard, Vatican City)

German paratroopers at the Saint Peter's Square border of Vatican City, September 1943. (Courtesy of Antonio Martini)

A Swiss Guard detachment deploys to the Vatican Gardens to protect Pope Pius XII during his daily walk, October 1943. (Archive of the Pontifical Swiss Guard, Vatican City)

Commandant Heinrich Pfyffer von Altishofen addresses the Swiss Guard after the German occupation of Rome, September 1943. Sergeant Major Joseph Imesch stands at the right. (Archive of the Pontifical Swiss Guard, Vatican City)

Officers of the pontifical armed forces consider the defenses of Vatican City, October 1943. Swiss Guard commandant Colonel Heinrich Pfyffer von Altishofen (far left) speaks with the commandant of the Noble Guard, Brigadier General Prince Francesco Chigi della Rovere. Commissioner Soleti of the Vatican police is in civilian clothes. (Archive of the Pontifical Swiss Guard, Vatican City)

New recruits to the Palatine Guard follow an officer inside the Vatican, November 1943. (Courtesy of Antonio Martini)

Palatine Guards on patrol, November 1943. (Courtesy of Antonio Martini)

Refugees find shelter in the papal villa at Castel Gandolfo, February 1944. (Courtesy of Antonio Martini)

Palatine Guards search for survivors after Allied bombs hit the papal villa at Castel Gandolfo, February 1944. (Courtesy of Antonio Martini)

Noble Guard on duty in the Apostolic Palace, Vatican City, 1946. (Courtesy of
Giulio Patrizi di Ripacandida)

Pope John XXIII with his Noble Guards, circa 1960. (Courtesy of Giulio Patrizi di Ripacandida)

Swiss Guard recruits learn how to handle the halberd. (Courtesy of Stefan Meier)

Swiss Guard recruits at rifle practice. (Courtesy of Stefan Meier)

Swiss Guards practice unarmed combat. (Courtesy of Stefan Meier)

CHAPTER 5

The Last Stand of the Papal Army

The view had always been magnificent, but the prospect was especially grand that early evening on September 19, 1870. From the crest of the Gianiculum, the long ridge that extends south along the right bank of the Tiber from the Vatican to the San Pancrazio gate, General Hermann Kanzler, minister of arms to His Holiness and commander-in-chief of the pontifical army, and his chief of staff, Major Fortunato Rivalta, could see all of Rome. The officers had interrupted their tour of the city's walls and spurred their horses up the slope to catch the magnificent sunset. At their feet, the arms of Bernini's famed colonnade reached out to embrace Saint Peter's Square. Before them loomed the awe-inspiring basilica, the largest and most famous church in Christendom, with Michelangelo's majestic dome seeming to float above Carlo Maderno's stately facade. Beyond it loomed the complex of apartments, loggias, chapels, museums, and gardens that composed the Vatican Palace. In the background the stones and stucco of the churches, palaces, squares, and antiquities of the Eternal City glowed in the light of the setting sun. It offered a breathtaking scene recorded in countless paintings, drawings, prints, and literary accounts. When the papal general and his chief of staff turned away to look out across the western and southern approaches to the city, they witnessed a scene less common but no less arresting: the tents and fires of a large Italian army besieging Rome and preparing to take the city by assault.

When, after their victory against Garibaldi and his army at Mentana in 1867, General Kanzler had marched his proud soldiers in triumph through the gates of Rome, he could not have anticipated that three years later he would be deploying the same soldiers to defend the same gates against the army of King Vittorio Emanuele II, a foe far more dangerous than the Garibaldians. It was a daunting prospect: a small force behind weak fortifications standing against an enemy far superior in size and matériel. When, on September 12, Italian troops had invaded the Papal States, many in Rome, including the pope's principal adviser, Cardinal Secretary of State Giacomo Antonelli, were convinced that any military response to the aggression would be futile. To some minds, a defense of Rome would be not only pointless but possibly blasphemous. The pope himself had serious reservations about the propriety of an active defense. Could the Holy Father—the Vicar of Christ, the Prince of Peace—spill innocent blood and submit Rome, the holiest city in Christendom, to bombardment simply to defend his throne? Were the city and the pope's temporal power worth combat along bullet-pocked streets and amid the rubble of destroyed churches and monuments?

It is unlikely that General Kanzler bothered himself much with such questions. They were the responsibility of ecclesiastical lawyers and theologians who were paid to argue ethics, morality, and law. Armies, in contrast, were paid to fight, and *his* responsibility, affirmed by solemn oath, as the commander of the pontifical army, was to lead that force against any enemy that threatened the temporal or spiritual domain of his sovereign, Pope Pius IX. Of course, as a professional soldier who had spent a lifetime in uniform, Kanzler instinctively recoiled from the thought of surrender without a fight, but his revulsion reflected more than an exaggerated sense of military honor. Rome was not just any city. It was the capital not only of the Papal States but of the universal church, and as such its "citizens" included all Catholics, not just those who inhabited the banks of the Tiber River. Rome was a symbol of enormous emotive power, and for Kanzler, that power was inextricably connected to the popes. The evidence lay everywhere, not only in the streets, squares, churches, and palaces of the city but in the imaginations of people across the globe. The papacy was Rome, and Rome was the papacy; so it had been for more than a millennium. Did this not count for something, even in the calculations of lawyers and theologians? Gazing out over the city, his chief of staff at his side and his dragoon escorts waiting patiently at a distance, Kanzler felt the weight of history and duty on his shoulders. "Can it be," he whispered, almost to himself, "that a church that gave birth to such splendors will end with a whimper?" The general knew what his answer had to be. Others might counsel surrender, but the commander-in-chief of the pope's army was determined to fight for Rome.[1]

The defeat of the Garibaldian invasion of the Papal States in the fall of 1867 had thrilled the Catholic world and rekindled enthusiasm for the defense of the pope's temporal power against allegedly godless enemies who, at least in the eyes of papal loyalists, defamed the Holy Father, blasphemed against the true religion, and desecrated its churches and shrines. The papal army was a special beneficiary of the renewed fervor. Across Europe, but particularly from the more conservative Catholic regions of Belgium, France, Germany, Holland, and Switzerland, zealous young Catholic men rushed to show their loyalty to Pius IX by joining the army of Il Papa Re (the Pope King). In Rome, the Ministry of Arms was hard-pressed to absorb the new recruits. Many units, such as the Legione Romana (formerly the Légion d'Antibes of French volunteers), doubled in size. Within a year of Mentana, the papal Zouaves, the most glamorous and well-known unit in the pontifical army, had expanded from one battalion to five, an increase that required the ministry to elevate the unit to regimental status and put in place the necessary command and logistical structure.[2]

Religious zeal produced more than recruits. Many Catholics who could not pick up rifles picked up their wallets. Bishops and lay leaders, more accustomed to establishing charities for orphans and widows or endowments for the restoration of churches, now set up committees to raise money to purchase armaments and other military supplies for the defense of the Papal States. In France, for example, the bishop of Poitiers organized a "Committee for Pontifical Artillery" that raised 55,600 francs to purchase cannons. When French manufacturers declined to accept an order for pontifical artillery, the good Catholics of Poitiers simply took their business elsewhere and discovered that the Belgian national arsenal at Liège was more than happy to produce six artillery pieces. A delegation from the diocese proudly accompanied their new weapons to Rome, where, in March 1868, they were accepted personally by the Holy Father. There were similar contributions from elsewhere in Europe. The French diocese of Nantes raised funds to purchase two cannons and one ambulance for the pope's army. In Belgium, fund-raising committees underwrote the manufacture by the Liège arsenal of 5,000 breech-loading Remington rifles and two million cartridges. By 1870 Belgian, French, and German Catholics had underwritten the production of 13,500 Remingtons for the pontifical army.[3]

The triumph against the Garibaldian bands also had a direct impact on the spirit of the pontifical army. That success had boosted the morale and confidence of officers and men who believed, with justification, that they had outmaneuvered and outfought a dangerous enemy. Of course professional military observers might have judged the underequipped and undertrained irregulars of Garibaldi as something less than a first-class foe, but an army unused to victory embraced the success with pride and enthusiasm.

The experience of 1867 also seemed to confirm the efficacy of the reforms instituted by General Kanzler when he had assumed command of the pope's armed forces in 1865. After the rout of the Garibaldian bands, the pope's commander-in-chief was more convinced than ever that in time he could produce a disciplined, trained, and spirited force that, except in size, would compare favorably to any European army. To this end, Kanzler accelerated his efforts to expand and improve the papal armed forces. No element of the military establishment was too small or obscure to escape attention. In one month alone (February 1868) the energetic commander established a sanitary board to monitor and improve troop hygiene, reorganized the equipment train of transport wagons that supplied troops in the field, and ordered the expansion of the medical service.[4] His relentless pursuit of additional funding resulted in an increase in the annual military appropriation from 11 million lire in 1865 to 20 million lire in 1869. Between 1867 and 1869 the army spent more than in the previous six years combined.[5] In 1869 Kanzler launched an initiative to create a reserve force to enhance the strength of the regular army and support the professionals by taking responsibility during military emergencies for local operations and security. Training and conditioning remained a priority. One day a week the infantry units held live-fire rifle practice, and three days a week there were field exercises to rehearse small-unit tactics. Frequently, units engaged in sham battles to practice deploying in the field and maneuvering against opponents, and to build endurance there were long-route marches (in good and bad weather), with each soldier carrying full campaign gear: rifle, bayonet, sixty rounds of ammunition, knapsack, blanket, overcoat, and tent and tent pegs. Each year the entire army encamped in the Alban Hills outside Rome for several weeks of training, including night and day exercises.[6]

Kanzler was especially concerned with modernizing the armaments of the pontifical army. As the standard weapon for the papal infantry he adopted the breech-loading Remington model 1868 rifle, a weapon at the forefront of contemporary technology. To increase the firepower of his soldiers, he purchased a Claxton gun, a precursor to the modern machine gun, making the papal army the third in Europe (behind the British and French armies) to deploy rapid-fire weapons.[7] He sent a promising young artillery officer, Captain Giulio Marini, to study the machinery and methods employed by the arsenals and armaments factories of Britain, France, and Belgium. Upon his return to Rome, Captain Marini reorganized the small arsenal then located inside the Vatican in the Belvedere wing of the papal palace, and soon this shop was capable of producing two thousand Remington rifles a year. When the artillery corps warned that it did not have enough trained gunners to man the new cannons arriving from Belgium and France, Kanzler ordered that designated personnel in infantry units receive basic instruction in handling cannons so that they could be attached to artillery batteries in emergencies.[8]

The cumulative effect of these reforms was the emergence of a well-trained and highly motivated, though small, military force. Five infantry units, recruited from both the indigenous population of the Papal States and other countries, were available for field operations and formed the fighting core of the army: one regiment of the line (indigenous), one regiment of Zouaves (indigenous and foreign), one regiment of carabinieri (foreign), one battalion of cacciatore (indigenous), and the Legione Romana (foreign). The cavalry arm was represented by a regiment of dragoons (indigenous), and the field artillery (indigenous) deployed five batteries, each of six guns. Veterans approaching the limits of military age formed a sedentari battalion (indigenous), which provided detachments for fortress and depot duty. Support units (all indigenous) included an engineering company, a transport company, and various service elements (medical, sanitary, veterinary, and chaplaincy). The twelve companies and one mounted squadron of the paramilitary Pontifical Gendarmeria (indigenous) performed routine police and border-control duties, but they were considered an integral part of the army and were available for military operations. In contrast, the household units (Noble Guard, Swiss Guard, and Palatine Guard) that mounted guard inside the papal palaces were not combat units and were unavailable for field operations. These protective units, organized as the Military Department of His Holiness, were under the direct authority of the pope and his cardinal secretary of state and were not considered part of the pontifical army.[9]

The caliber of personnel was high. The officer corps was probably the equal of any in Europe, with the possible exception of Prussia. All the senior officers and most of the junior had recent combat experience. Looking back on the events of 1870, the official historian of the Italian army acknowledged, "The quality of the officers was excellent in terms of intelligence, loyalty to the flag, and devotion to His Holiness. Militarily they were also good due to experience acquired during the suppression of brigandage from 1867 to 1869 and the campaigns of 1860 and 1867."[10] The same professional observer concluded that excellent leadership contributed significantly to the morale, preparation, and performance of the troops: "In fact, because of the ability of the officers, recruitment, the assignment of individuals to units, the deployment of various units, and the administration of services functioned splendidly. . . . Theoretical and practical instruction proceeded methodically. The pontifical soldier excelled due to the constant training under the guidance of experienced officers and noncommissioned officers."[11]

This pontifical army was nothing like the ill-trained, ill-equipped, and ill-led formations that had marched off to war in 1798 or 1848 and was far removed from the undisciplined, predatory foreign mercenaries so often described as the scourge of the Papal States and the shame of the papacy by anti-Catholic commentators or propagandists. Although foreign enlistments accounted for a significant percentage of the army's strength (though still less than half), these foreigners were not "mercenaries" in the sense of soldiers who enlisted solely for pay without any attachment to the people and place they ostensibly defended. The Austrian, Belgian, Canadian, Dutch, French, German, Irish, Spanish, and Swiss citizens who rallied to the papal standard were not the impoverished dregs of European society but pious, largely middle-class (and often upper-class) Catholics who enlisted out of affection for Pope Pius IX and loyalty to the Catholic Church. They fought not for money but to defend the Holy Father against his enemies. For them, service in the pope's army was a noble gesture in comparison with which concerns for personal advancement and financial reward were insignificant. This attitude of sacrifice and service was especially apparent among the many men, young and old, from noble families who, in a practice unheard of in other armies, abjured officer rank to enlist as common soldiers. The Marchese Aldobrandino Rangoni Santacroce, for example, was the scion of one of the richest and oldest noble families in Italy, but he served as a private in the regiment of Zouaves. Duke Ladislao de Dabrowa Garwanowicz, a Polish nobleman, was a rifleman in the same regiment. In Joseph Powell's Zouave company, one of the corporals was a German baron, and Private Powell would stroll in the countryside with another Zouave rifleman who happened to be a Spanish count. Indeed, the Zouaves seem to have made a fetish of mixing social classes. "In our army everyone enters the ranks no matter what his station in life may be," Powell would recall, "so that we number a prince and men of noble blood amongst the privates." Previous military experience did not necessarily privilege anyone. Count Victor de Courten had first entered the papal army in 1832 and by the time of his retirement in 1861 had risen to the rank of lieutenant colonel. During the Garibaldian invasion of 1867 he returned to the colors, this time as a fifty-seven-year-old private in the carabinieri battalion, and fought in the front ranks at the Battle of Mentana. Count Sormani Calcaghi resigned his commission as a major in the Austrian army to enlist in the papal infantry as a common rifleman.[12]

Discipline was excellent, in part because all of the soldiers were volunteers (unlike many European armies, which relied on conscription) but also because recruiters made an effort to establish the background and moral character of the men who appeared at their offices. To be accepted, an applicant usually had to present a testimonial from a parish priest or a respected figure in the community. Once enlisted, the recruit was incorporated into a military community characterized by explicit religious values and practices (daily mass, prayers, and each year an annual spiritual retreat) and a belief, actively cultivated by General Kanzler and senior officers, that the military life was a noble calling. The sense of a military brotherhood was further encouraged by the expectation that all soldiers would treat each other with respect regardless of rank and social background. There was an easy camaraderie among officers and enlisted men. In the elite regiment of Zouaves, for example, the deputy commander, Lieutenant Colonel Athanase de Charette, each night invited a cross-section of his unit to his dinner table. Community was also nurtured by the practice of recruiting officers from the ranks of veteran and able sergeants. Many of the captains and lieutenants who led papal troops at Bagnorea, Montelibretti, Monterotondo, and Mentana during the campaign of 1867 had fought as privates, corporals, and sergeants at Ancona, Castelfidardo, and Perugia during the War of 1860.[13]

By 1870 the papal army was beginning to attract notice from foreign military commentators. No observers were more impressed than officers in the army of the kingdom of Italy, the force most likely to face Kanzler's troops in the field. Such officers were often sent into the Papal States on clandestine intelligence missions to gauge political opinion and assess papal military capabilities, and they invariably returned with favorable impressions of the pope's soldiers. A report on the pontifical Zouaves prepared in August 1870 by an

Italian intelligence officer recently returned from papal territory was probably typical: "The Zouaves, most of whom are French, are in general very fine
men and well equipped, and include individuals from every region and class.
Officers and men treat each other with the greatest familiarity, and at the café
you will see soldiers of all ranks at the same table. It is evident that there are
among these Zouaves many individuals of distinction and education."[14]

Although pleased with the development of his army, General Kanzler
realized that it was one thing to create an efficient fighting force but quite another to use it effectively. Everything depended on the nature of the threat.
In preparing his war plans and deploying his troops, the pope's commander-
in-chief had to consider four possible scenarios: domestic insurrections by
revolutionaries intent on overthrowing the papal regime; cross-border incursions or outright invasions by irregular forces, such as those directed by
Garibaldi in 1867, operating with or without the support of the Italian government; an outright invasion by the regular Italian army in the manner of
the war of 1860 but this time from positions on the northern, eastern, and
southern borders of the Papal States; or (the worst case) a combination of
all three. Since the pontifical army had actually faced all of these scenarios
within the past ten years, Kanzler could not dismiss one as less likely than
another. He had to prepare for all eventualities. This threat horizon would
have strained the resources of even a large army; for a small army, it posed
almost insurmountable problems.

General Kanzler conceived an operational plan that included both offensive and defensive elements. The general concentrated the bulk of his
forces in Rome. To deal with local insurrections, he stationed detachments
of troops in various towns across the papal dominion. In cooperation with
the gendarmeria, who were deployed even more deeply into the countryside, these detachments would deter political unrest and respond promptly
to suppress any disturbances in their areas. In the event of cross-border incursions by bands of irregulars, local commanders would concentrate their
forces and, reinforced if necessary by troops from Rome, take the offensive
by attacking the irregulars as soon as they left the border area. The pope's
commander was confident that his soldiers could deal with rebels and irregulars. The army of the Kingdom of Italy posed a far more serious danger.
Greatly superior to the pontifical army in numbers and equipment, deployed
in positions that surrounded the papal domain on three sides (with the Italian navy controlling the Mediterranean coast on the west), the Italian army
posed a mortal threat to the Papal States.

The pope's general realized that he could not defeat a full-fledged invasion by Italian regulars. In such an eventuality he intended to assume a primarily defensive posture. The small detachments across the country would
maintain their positions as long as possible in order to deter local insurrections in support of the invaders, report the movements of the Italian forces,

and compel the Italians to advance cautiously. To preserve their manpower and operational integrity, these detachments were to avoid engaging superior forces and gradually fall back to Rome. Only the garrisons at Civitavecchia and Civita Castellana were authorized to put up a fight, mainly to gauge the degree to which the Italians were prepared to apply military force. With most of his troops inside Rome, Kanzler expected to conduct an active and prolonged defense that would include counterattacks and sorties as tactical opportunities presented themselves. The defense would have two goals. First, it would force the Italians, in full view of the world, to assault the Eternal City, an international symbol of history, culture, and religion. Second, it would buy time for the Vatican to secure diplomatic intervention by other powers that would impose a settlement that would, presumably, maintain the political rights and territorial possessions of the papacy.[15]

To implement his plans, General Kanzler required additional resources: material and laborers to strengthen the ancient walls of Rome; fortress artillery to arm the city's bastions; explosives to mine the bridges across the Tiber; additional field artillery; and, as always, more soldiers, uniforms, rifles, munitions, horses, and wagons. When the general first broached his plans to papal authorities at the end of 1868, the responses ranged from incredulity to vociferous opposition. Some of the pope's officials dismissed Kanzler's plans as fanciful, believing that King Vittorio Emanuele would never have the temerity to attack the Eternal City, and even if he did, other powers, such as Austria, Spain, and France (which still maintained troops in Rome and Civitavecchia), would immediately intervene, with force if necessary, to stop such an outrage. Other officials, concerned with the distressed financial position of the Papal States and aware that the army had already benefited from increased appropriations after Mentana, balked at the cost of implementing additional military programs.[16]

The powerful cardinal secretary of state, Giacomo Antonelli, proved Kanzler's strongest critic. The cardinal's office combined the functions of prime minister and foreign minister. Antonelli had long believed it was madness for the pope to rely on military means to maintain his temporal power, if only because the Papal States could not hope to maintain an army of sufficient size to deter or repel an Italian invasion. He preferred to rely on diplomacy to secure the sympathy and support of the continental powers and hoped that those powers would guarantee an international settlement that would maintain the pope's temporal power. The cardinal had been the strongest opponent of Monsignor Frédéric François Xavier de Mérode when the latter, as minister of arms in the years 1860–1865, had pursued a policy of building up the papacy's military forces, and he had successfully connived to secure de Mérode's dismissal in 1865. At the time, Antonelli had felt that a military posture had been explicitly repudiated, explaining to the British diplomatic representative in Rome, "The Pope was not a military prince . . . and the Pope was therefore resolved not to add a soldier to his present army."[17] Five years later he saw no reason to change his mind, and his abhorrence of armed force was shared by significant elements of the clergy in Rome.[18]

The refusal of Vatican officials to acknowledge that the papacy faced a military threat that required a response in kind—if only to purchase time for diplomacy to work—compelled General Kanzler to set aside his more ambitious plans for the defense of the Papal States. The situation changed, however, in the summer of 1870 when events forced even the most wishful thinkers to confront reality. The outbreak of war between France and Prussia on July 18 dealt a serious blow to those in the curia, such as Cardinal Antonelli, who saw France as a guarantor of the pope's temporal power. The cardinal secretary of state, who had tried to mediate a peaceful resolution of Franco-Prussian differences, realized that the war was as much a threat to the Papal States as it was to France. Paris would now consider the Roman Question a distraction and, requiring every available soldier to defend the homeland, would inevitably recall from Rome and Civitavecchia the French garrisons that symbolized France's commitment to defending the pope's temporal rights. Antonelli's pessimism was justified when, on August 5, the remnants of the French expeditionary force that had reinforced the papal army during Garibaldi's incursions in 1867 left papal territory. He also rightly placed little faith in assurances from Paris (echoed in Florence) that the Italian government would not take advantage of France's plight to challenge the pope's possession of Rome.[19] In fact, as a series of defeats in the field made France's military position increasingly precarious, Emperor Napoléon sent a secret emissary to Florence to secure Italian assistance in the form of an expeditionary force of seventy thousand men. In return, the emissary told Italian diplomats, King Vittorio Emanuele could ask what he liked. Implicit in this offer was the assurance that France would not protest an Italian move against the Papal States.[20]

With France fighting for its life and Austria anxious to curry Italian favor as a support against further Prussian expansionism, the government of Vittorio Emanuele did not need French permission, implicit or otherwise, to resolve the Roman Question on its own terms. Neither the bellicose king, who equated war with glory and conquest, nor his government had abandoned their ambition to absorb the Papal States and finally unify all of Italy under the House of Savoy. Domestic political considerations also counseled action. The popularity of the regime had been undermined by parliamentary scandals and the imposition of new taxes on consumption and the grinding of grain. The taxes sparked popular disturbances in 1869 that were violently suppressed by the army at the cost of hundreds of civilian deaths. Nationalist sentiments were also fanned by left-wing and anticlerical elements in the press and parliament who vociferously reminded the royal ministers of their national duty to make Rome the capital of a unified Italy.[21]

Vittorio Emanuele's government, therefore, saw in France's discomfiture an opportunity to secure dynastic goals and deflect attacks from the political left by moving against the Papal States. Quietly and methodically, the Italian government began its preparations. As a rationale that would provide a fig leaf to hide naked aggression, the royal ministry decided to claim that intervention was necessary to reestablish security and prevent revolutionary excesses in a land torn by disorder. In August the Ministry of War began recalling young men to the colors and formed an army "Corps of Observation" under the command of General Raffaele Cadorna. This force was deployed toward the border with the Papal States. On August 16 Parliament was called into session to approve extraordinary military credits. The diplomatic ground was prepared later that month when the Foreign Ministry sent notes to the European powers suggesting Florence's intention to intervene in the Papal States, an initiative that generated no protests.[22]

The Italian government could not hide its preparations. Hermann Kanzler understood that good intelligence was an important resource for a small army facing a larger opponent. During his tenure as minister of arms, the general had worked to improve military intelligence, such that "the intelligence service of the pontifical army . . . [was] a small thing; but in 1870 it was among the best organized."[23] Responsibility for espionage fell primarily upon the Pontifical Gendarmeria, whose border-patrol and internal-security functions led them to recruit informants on both sides of the frontier with Italy. Seeking details concerning rumored Italian troop concentrations in Umbria, Kanzler in early August ordered the gendarmes to increase their surveillance of the Italian side of the border. In frontier districts, police commanders were authorized to spend whatever sums were necessary to employ informants, and they were ordered to report any items of information, no matter how small, that might suggest Italian intentions. In the districts immediately surrounding Rome, police authorities were directed to intensify surveillance to detect insurrectionary activity. To ensure the timely communication of crucial intelligence, Kanzler ordered that telegraphers be on duty day and night throughout the countryside. In rural locales beyond the telegraph lines, mounted couriers were always to be available to hurry dispatches to the closest telegraph office.[24]

The first sign of trouble came on August 11 when Athanase de Charette, the colonel of Zouaves then commanding the military district of Viterbo on the northern frontier, reported that, according to informants, Italian army officers in Umbria had been overheard talking about an invasion of the Papal States and boasting that they would be in Rome by August 15![25] In Rome, this alarming news was dismissed as highly improbable. From other intelligence General Kanzler knew that Italian army units were scattered in peacetime cantonments along the frontier and the interior of Umbria, and that an invasion would require that such units first be concentrated into larger operational masses. The pope's commander believed there was no reason to worry so long as Italian units were not concentrating. Within days Kanzler had something to worry about.[26]

Information from papal sources in Florence revealed the decision by the Italian government to combine its army elements along the pontifical frontier into an army corps under General Cadorna. In addition, other sources reported on August 15 that the royal ministry of transport had suspended regular train service between Ancona and Terni for August 15 and 16 to make way for special trains transporting troops and material into Umbria. The intention, according to these well-informed sources was to concentrate ten thousand troops at Passo Corese, near the pontifical border. These were exactly the indicators that Kanzler had feared. The general immediately carried the news to Cardinal Antonelli. The cardinal secretary of state, however, remained unperturbed, speculating that the alleged troop movements were for the purposes of internal security, probably to prevent Garibaldian irregulars from slipping across the border. Despite these assurances, Kanzler remained troubled, but when on August 16 the general revisited the cardinal to press the case for intensified diplomatic efforts to secure European intervention in favor of the papacy, he found the pope's principal adviser no less complacent. Antonelli assured his visitor that there was no cause for alarm; all was in hand, and the general should trust the wisdom and foresight of the Vatican.[27]

The cardinal's complacency rested on misinformation and miscalculation. Antonelli persisted in his belief that the European powers, particularly France and Austria, would never accept the demise of the pope's temporal power and would intervene against any threat to that power. Available information buttressed this belief. Antonelli had received false news that on August 14 the French had defeated the Germans at Metz, and he was confident that the Italians would never be so foolish as to invade the Papal States at the very moment that the French were demonstrating their military superiority. Papal diplomatic representatives in Europe confidently reported that neither Paris nor Vienna would permit the occupation of Rome by Italian armies. Indeed, as late as 3 September, the papal nuncio (ambassador) in Vienna assured the Vatican that Austria would insure the status quo.

Kanzler was not reassured, and the days following his interview with the cardinal secretary of state brought a flurry of intelligence reports that only increased his concern. On August 18, information from Florence revealed that General Cadorna had organized his corps into three divisions. Two days later came word that Cadorna had moved his headquarters to Spoleto, barely 50 kilometers from the papal frontier, and that recent troop movements presaged an invasion. From Viterbo, Colonel de Charette bombarded the Ministry of Arms with a number of increasingly alarming reports. On August 18 the colonel alerted Rome that spies reported that there were fifteen thousand Italian troops along the frontier and that the soldiers were talking openly of marching on Rome. De Charette informed Kanzler that in the face of this threat he was pulling back to Viterbo outposts stationed along the border at Bagnorea, Orte, and San Lorenzo. When Rome assured the commander in Viterbo that other reliable intelligence suggested that the Italians were not moving and that the withdrawal of papal forces from the frontier was premature, de Charette insisted that, in the face of Italian concentrations, he needed to act to avoid (as directed by General Kanzler's operational plans) encirclement and the sacrifice of small outposts to superior numbers. The colonel then reported that the latest intelligence from the gendarmeria's espionage networks on the Italian side of the border indicated that the Italians would invade on the evening of August 20, and he requested instructions as to whether he should defend Viterbo or fall back to another town.[28]

Warnings of an imminent invasion also reached Rome from other field commanders, and Colonel Giuseppe Serra at Civitavecchia asked if he should begin destroying the railway tracks connecting the Papal States with Italian Umbria. General Kanzler worked to calm his commanders. He ordered de Charette not to abandon Viterbo and Serra not to destroy the railway tracks, assuring both that Rome did not consider an invasion imminent.[29] The warnings, however, though certainly premature, could not be entirely ignored. The commanders in the northern provinces were all veterans of the pontifical army, and most had fought with distinction at Castelfidardo and Mentana and in the campaign against the brigands. They were intelligent and steady officers. If they sensed danger, their concerns merited attention. Kanzler decided it was time to go over Cardinal Antonelli's head.

On the morning of August 20 the general obtained an audience with Pope Pius during which he reviewed the recent intelligence and revealed his concern that the Italians might be preparing an attack. He asked the pope to explain developments on the political scene to which he, as a soldier, might not be privy and also requested instructions as to the military posture the army should adopt in the face of the developing threat. If Kanzler expected resolve and direction from the Holy Father, he was disappointed. Nothing in the pontiff's comments suggested that Pius had seriously considered the prospect of an imminent military crisis with Italy. Like his cardinal secretary of state, the pontiff was inclined to dismiss the threat, but whereas Antonelli placed his trust in diplomacy, Pius placed his in God. The pope was inclined to see the hand of divine providence in recent events, such as the victory against Garibaldi in 1867 and the decision in July 1870 by the Vatican Council, an extraordinary assembly in Rome of the world's Catholic bishops, to promulgate the doctrine of papal infallibility. From the perspective of the Vatican Palace, the papacy was triumphant, and it was easy for Pius, always more comfortable with spiritual than political explanations of events, to believe that God would once again steer the boat of Saint Peter through troubled waters. Characterizing the pope's passive response to the crisis of August–September 1870, his leading biographer remarked, "Between realism and mysticism . . . in Pius IX mysticism had the upper hand."[30] Given his attitude, Pius was more likely to listen to his theologians than his generals at times of military crisis. Now he dismissed Kanzler with the instruction that in the unlikely event of an invasion, papal troops should offer no resistance but merely retreat to Rome. As to what would happen then, the pope was unclear. Presumably, God would provide. A frustrated Kanzler summarized the results of his audience in a telegram to de Charette: "The Holy Father, whom I saw this morning, does not believe the rumors concerning the imminent violation of territory by Italian troops."[31]

The failure of the Italians to attack on either the 15th or the 20th of August (as predicted by Colonel de Charette) undoubtedly encouraged Pius, Antonelli, and other papal officials in their conviction that there would be no war. Kanzler, however, was not complacent. Aware that the Italians might stage a provocation in order to justify intervention, he warned his commanders on August 21 that small detachments of Italian troops might violate the border. Papal units were to avoid engaging such intruders and limit their response to notifying the Italians that "by mistake" they had entered papal territory and offering to guide them to the frontier.[32] Over the following days ever more ominous intelligence reached the Ministry of Arms. On August 21 came information that General Cadorna was exercising his forces in regiment-sized units. Internal security and policing missions usually involved smaller detachments, such as companies. Regiment-sized maneuvers suggested preparation for larger field operations. The next day Kanzler learned that additional troops were arriving in Spoleto, the site of Cadorna's headquarters. On August 23 and 24 he received intelligence that the Italians were establishing army field hospitals at Orvieto, Terni, and Rieti, towns near the papal frontier, and warning civilian hospitals in Spoleto, Foligno, and Narni to ready their personnel and facilities to receive battlefield casualties. On August 25 spies reported that Italian cavalry were on the roads heading south. August 26 brought news that Cadorna had ordered all units to survey and report the condition of their equipment and munitions.[33]

The commander-in-chief of the pope's army understood that if this intelligence was accurate (as it was), then there would be serious trouble in the very near future. Kanzler had never shared the complacency of Pius and Antonelli; indeed, at a conference with his staff on August 29 at which he referred to Antonelli's conviction that Italian troop movements were related to internal security and probably indicated nothing more than precautions to prevent cross-border incursions by Garibaldian irregulars, the general commented that no one should be fooled by such assurances. He told his officers that their troops had to be ready to march.[34] Kanzler also realized that if there were to be any effective military countermeasures, he would have to order them on his own authority. From intelligence reports, it was increasingly apparent that the most likely scenario was a straightforward invasion by the Italian army. For such an eventuality, Kanzler's war plans posited a withdrawal of field forces to Rome and an extended defense of the Eternal City. This plan had been compromised by the failure of the papal administration to support the strengthening of the city's defenses. The ancient walls, some of which dated back to the fourth century, were more suited to repelling medieval spearmen than withstanding the fire of siege artillery. The fortifications lacked modern bastions, embrasures for cannons, firing platforms along their summits, and defensive outworks as well as sufficient numbers of cannons to break an assault. Some modest improvements had been set in motion earlier in the summer, and now, in late August, Kanzler accelerated and expanded these preparations without asking anyone's permission. There were too few troops and cannons to defend all of Rome's many gates, so he ordered several closed with masses of dirt. Makeshift barricades and breastworks of sandbags were constructed outside the remaining gates. To facilitate the movement of troops and supplies across the Tiber, he constructed a temporary bridge of boats between Santa Sabina on the left bank and the Ripa Grande on the right. To prevent an enemy from infiltrating the city by sailing upriver or downriver along the Tiber, he arranged for armed launches to patrol the waterway, and he fortified the bridges.[35]

Such warlike preparations could not go unobserved, but if the optimists inside the Vatican noticed, they were deterred from objecting by the arrival, on September 6–7, of news that even they had to admit was troubling. From Naples came word that various Italian army units were being assembled into a division along the southern border of the Papal States. Now there were division-strength units on all of the pontifical frontiers. Then Rome learned that Nino Bixio, a famous Garibaldian, had been appointed to command one of the divisions. To the papal administration Bixio seemed a demonic figure. He was a notorious anticleric and antipapalist, and, as a resolute and ferocious leader of Garibaldi's volunteers, he had relentlessly sought to destroy the pope's temporal power. Elected a deputy to the Italian parliament, he had given a speech demanding the immediate seizure of Rome and calling for the pope and all his cardinals to be thrown into the Tiber. If Nino Bixio, the hammer of the papacy, had been appointed to command Italian troops on the border, then the situation was indeed serious.

On September 7 Kanzler had another audience with the pope to review developments. The latest intelligence indicated that the Italian 11th, 12th, and 13th divisions had recalled various detachments in order to concentrate their strength; that a bridge-building unit of military engineers had moved from Pavia in the north to Terni near the Tiber River frontier of the Papal States; and that medical personnel had been issued special armbands identifying them as noncombatants. Though Pius was still distrustful of the intelligence indicators, he reluctantly authorized his commander to increase precautionary measures. After the meeting Kanzler rushed back to the Ministry of Arms on the Piazza Pilotta and convened a meeting of his staff. He declared general mobilization and issued orders to prepare the troops and the city's defenses for action. Beginning immediately, cavalry would conduct reconnaissance patrols beyond the city walls, and infantry commanders received orders to prepare their troops for field operations. To better cover the gates and approach roads, artillery was repositioned, including a battery that was emplaced in the Vatican Gardens. Observation posts were established in high places around the city, such as the cupola of Saint Peter's Basilica and the bell tower of the Basilica of Santa Maria Maggiore.[36]

With everyone on heightened alert, there were, inevitably, missteps and false alarms. On September 8, for example, several battalions from the Roman garrison were sent into the countryside for a day of tactical maneuvers, a sign that General Kanzler's plans were not limited to sheltering behind Rome's walls in a purely defensive posture. During their absence, the Ministry of Arms received a telegram from the commander of the military detachment at Monterotondo, 25 kilometers north of the city, reporting that Italian cavalry had crossed the frontier without detection and had been observed moving about on papal territory. There was near panic inside the papal ministry. How could enemy troops approach within 25 kilometers of Rome undetected? Were other Italian units now on papal territory? Was this the invasion? Would the battalions on maneuvers, which represented a significant proportion of the garrison, be cut off? Staff officers immediately galloped away to recall the absent units while orders went out to prepare the defenses for an early attack. In the midst of the alarms and confusion, a second telegram arrived from Monterotondo. The local commander now informed headquarters that his earlier report had been unfounded. Apparently, someone had seen a patrol of papal dragoons on the main road to Rome and mistakenly reported them as Italian.[37]

By September 9 General Kanzler believed he had an accurate picture of the size and deployment of the Italian forces gathering on the borders. From intelligence reports, he concluded that General Cadorna had concentrated a large formation of three divisions (approximately 30,000 men) on the left bank of the Tiber in the area bounded by the towns of Narni, Terni, Rieti, and Magliano. Another division (10,000 men), commanded by General Nino Bixio, was concentrated around Orvieto on the right bank of the river. A third formation of one division (10,000 troops) under General Diego Angioletti was on the southern frontier between Arce and Isoletta. The total Italian force significantly outnumbered Kanzler's army by a ratio of six to one. Still, the papal general saw a slim opportunity in the threat. So long as Cadorna's force remained divided into three elements, its numerical superiority was vitiated. Alone and separated from immediate support, neither Bixio's nor

Angioletti's divisions had a significant numerical advantage. A papal force, taking advantage of surprise and interior lines, might expect to engage them on relatively equal terms. In the almost certain event of an Italian invasion, Kanzler saw an opportunity to upset Cadorna's plans and possibly put one of the Italian divisions out of action with a quick strike against either Bixio or Angioletti. An offensive, however, would require approval from higher authority. Kanzler steeled himself for another audience with the Holy Father.[38]

The pope's commander called at the papal apartments in the late morning of September 10, only to find that Pius had another visitor. Count Gustavo Ponza di San Martino, a representative of the Italian government, had arrived in Rome the previous day with the unenviable mission of presenting an ultimatum to a leader who in addition to being Supreme Pontiff, Successor to Saint Peter, and Vicar of Christ on Earth was also an irascible individual of fiery temper and blunt language. Count di San Martino carried a personal letter from King Vittorio Emanuele in which the monarch, assuring the pontiff of his personal devotion and sincere religious faith, announced that he was unfortunately forced to send his army into the papal domains in order to quell popular disturbances and ensure public security and order. The count's presentation was made the more awkward by the complete absence of popular disturbances and disorder in the Papal States, a covert Italian effort to create a pretext for intervention by manufacturing uprisings inside Rome having failed miserably. The pope's response was predictable. Di San Martino's subsequent report to his monarch, describing the pope as "calm and serene but absolutely and inflexibly resolved not to make any accommodation whatsoever," did not quite capture the tenor of the brief conversation. Although Pius angrily rejected the rationale behind the imminent Italian aggression, he was particularly outraged by the mendacity and hypocrisy of Vittorio Emanuele, dismissing the king's assurances of devotion and piety as "nice words, but ugly deeds." Count di San Martino was so unsettled by Pius's response that, upon being dismissed brusquely from the papal presence, he mistook a window for a door and narrowly escaped a dangerous fall.[39]

When General Kanzler and his chief of staff, Major Rivolta, entered the papal apartments immediately after the departure of the Italian envoy, they found an angry pope who was now painfully aware of the seriousness of the situation. If, however, the general expected that this anger would lead to a resolve to resist the imminent aggression and an urgent desire to prepare defenses, he was again disappointed. After reviewing the latest intelligence and the defensive measures already in hand, Kanzler outlined his plan to take the offensive by striking at one of the Italian concentrations, buttressing his arguments with assurances concerning the fierce loyalty and high morale of the papal army. Pius listened without comment, and when his commander had finished he remained silent for a while. "Well," he finally said, "I am going to have to disappoint this army. It will have to surrender."[40]

The pontiff rejected out of hand any idea of offensive operations, and he was deeply ambivalent even about defensive measures. He worried about the irony of the government of the Prince of Peace waging war, particularly a war that could not be won. Furthermore, Pius IX did not want to be known in history as the pope who exposed the Eternal City and its populace to death and destruction merely for the sake of military glory or honor. He explained to his commander that at the first sign of an Italian invasion, he wanted his army to refuse combat and fall back to Rome to await events, although in a few instances it might display "a bit of resistance" in order to demonstrate to the world that the kingdom of Italy was seizing the traditional states of the church by force.

General Kanzler did not attempt to disguise his surprise and displeasure at these instructions. Did His Holiness understand, he asked, that such a response would open the papal domain to Italian occupation and that the enemy would simply walk into Rome "as on a promenade"? Pius remained unperturbed. "There is no question of an Italian entry into Rome," he replied, "They will stay out. They will not be able to enter."[41] The pope did not reveal to his commander the basis for this confident assertion. Perhaps he expected a miracle or, in the absence of divine intervention, a move by less exalted powers, such as a concert of European powers, to safeguard the traditional temporal rights of the papacy. Ever the professional soldier, Kanzler could not accept Christian forbearance as an adequate response to the threat. The general made one last effort. "Holiness," he pleaded, "the entire army from the highest officer to the most humble soldier wants to fight and die." Pius was unmoved. "We choose to surrender," he retorted, "Not to die is sometimes the bigger sacrifice."[42]

After this audience Kanzler called on the cardinal secretary of state, whom he found "explicitly and decisively opposed to any effort at resistance." Thinking perhaps of European opinion, Antonelli insisted that resistance would only worsen the already difficult position of the papacy. He argued that it would be both more dignified and more convenient for the pope's troops to remain passive, stacking their weapons and calmly allowing the Italians to smash open the closed gates of the city. When the pope's commander-in-chief observed that such a response was exactly what the Italians would prefer and that in war one generally tried not to defer to the wishes of one's adversary, the cardinal was unmoved.[43]

A rather shaken Kanzler returned to the Ministry of Arms to make what dispositions he could. Any doubt concerning Italian intentions had been removed once and for all by the mission of Count di San Martino. Invasion was imminent. On the evening of September 10, as the royal emissary returned to Florence and the commander-in-chief of the pontifical armies brooded in his headquarters over the prospect of surrendering his forces without a fight, General Cadorna received from the Italian Ministry of War a secret telegram instructing him to lead his army across the pontifical frontier no earlier than 5:00 P.M. on the afternoon of September 11 and no later than 5:00 A.M. on the morning of September 12. In a remarkable feat of espionage, the invasion date was picked up by the informant networks of papal intelligence and reported to Rome that same evening.[44] The information energized the pontifical military command. After consulting with his staff, Kanzler ordered the immediate closure and blockage of seven previously designated gates, the creation of apertures for cannons at the remaining gates, the deployment of troops at the gates and along the walls, and the recall to Rome of selected units then in the provinces. On September 11 Kanzler sent a war warning to his field commanders. Throughout that day the Ministry of Arms received messages from local commanders reporting Italian movements near the border and rumors of imminent attack. The commander at Civita Castellana, a town on the northern border, informed Rome that intelligence sources were reporting that the Italians would attack by crossing the Tiber at the nearby Ponte Felice and marching directly on Civita Castellana. This was another demonstration of the effectiveness of papal intelligence because only the evening before Cadorna had issued orders for his 12th Division to cross the Ponte Felice on September 12 and assault Civita Castellana.[45]

Initially, General Cadorna had planned to concentrate the 11th, 12th, and 13th divisions at Passo Corese, a town where the border approached the closest (25 kilometers) to Rome, from which point he would cross the frontier and strike swiftly down the left bank of the Tiber to the Eternal City. This path was the shortest and easiest approach to Rome. The Ministry of War in Florence accepted this plan on September 5, and Cadorna began deploying his fighting regiments and support services accordingly. On September 7, however, the Ministry of War canceled the plan and directed the general to transfer his entire force north to Orvieto, launch the invasion from that point, and advance down the right bank of the Tiber. Cadorna was outraged at these new orders, which not only disrupted the deployments already in hand but required him to move his force almost a hundred kilometers farther away from Rome before launching an attack. The commander fired off a blistering response to Florence. In the meantime, the ministry had changed its mind again. It now directed Cadorna to maintain part of his force at Passo Corese to deceive the pontifical army as to the true direction of the attack and prepare the bulk of his command to attack across the Tiber at Orte and the Felice bridge outside Magliano Sabina. This attacking force would then advance down the right bank of the river until it neared Rome, when it would then cross the Tiber again in order to attack the city from the left bank. General Cadorna's plan was to pass the 12th Division across the Tiber at the Felice bridge and capture Civita Castellana. The 11th Division (Major General Enrico Cosenz) would follow across the same bridge on the morning of September 12 and join the 12th. Together the two units would move south down the right bank of the Tiber toward Rome. Farther north, Major General Emilio Ferrero's 13th Division would advance from its assembly point at Narni, cross the Tiber at Orte (where the railway bridge would service the Italian artillery train and supply column), and march west to take Viterbo. Ferrero's force would also provide support for General Nino Bixio's 2nd Division, which was to launch from Orvieto and advance toward the port of Civitavecchia. Major General Angioletti's 9th Division was to invade across the pope's southern border and move north toward Rome.[46]

The invasion began late on the evening of September 11 when elements of the Italian 13th Division crossed the frontier and occupied the border town of Orte to secure the bridge that crossed the Tiber at that location. The local defenses consisted of a papal police post manned by four gendarmes who exchanged fire with the invaders before escaping into the countryside. By the early hours of September 12 Italian cavalry patrols were reconnoitering across the Tiber, and at 4:00 A.M. Major General Gustave Mazè de la Roche's 12th Division began crossing the Felice bridge and moving toward Civita Castellana, 7 kilometers from the river. By dawn the commander at Civita Castellana had reported the river crossing, and this report was soon followed by messages from other locales reporting Italian forces crossing the frontiers.[47]

Civita Castellana, 53 kilometers north of Rome, was the first serious obstacle in the path of the invaders. The town, with its fifteenth-century Rocca (fortress) constructed by the noted Renaissance architect Antonio da Sangallo the Younger, was defended by a company of papal Zouaves, a disciplinary company of disarmed soldiers transferred from other units for indiscipline or minor crimes, and a detachment of gendarmes, about two hundred men in all.

Zouave captain Zénon de Résimont, who had courageously directed the Zouave relief efforts in cholera-stricken Albano in 1867, assumed command of the fighting force. The fortress itself, which had been converted into a civil prison, was under the authority of another officer, Captain Carlo Pappi. At 11:00 P.M. on September 11 a gendarme galloped into the town to report that an Italian attack could be expected at any moment. De Résimont telegraphed the news to Rome and informed the Ministry of Arms that he was preparing to fight. The captain rushed to organize his defenses. After two hours of frantically constructing barricades and distributing rifles and ammunition (including arming the disciplinary company, whose disgraced soldiers begged for the opportunity to prove their loyalty and mettle), the garrison gathered to hear mass celebrated by the chaplain. Captain de Résimont then deployed his small force, sending detachments of riflemen to cover the approaches to the town and establishing an outpost in the convent of the Capuchins situated beyond the walls on the main road from the north.[48]

To take the town, General Mazè de la Roche pushed forward along the main road an advance element under General Angelino composed of an infantry regiment, a bersaglieri battalion, two squadrons of lancers, and an artillery battery. To cut off any chance of escape by the garrison and block potential reinforcements, Angelino sent a battalion along a mule track running to the left of the road. Their task was to cross the deep ravine formed by the Treja River that ran along the town walls and rejoin the main road on the other side of the town. As this unit reached the river it came under fire from papal troops positioned along the top of the ravine. The main force advancing up the road also came under fire from the force de Résimont had positioned inside the Capuchin convent. The papal officer understood that he was heavily outnumbered, and when he learned that the attackers were encircling the town, he quickly concluded that a defense of the walls and gates would be futile. He pulled back his detachments and ordered the troops to withdraw into the Rocca. From the battlements and embrasures of the fortress the papal soldiers continued to fire on the Italians, though with little effect because the attackers could easily find cover in the narrow streets and alleys of the town. General Angelino ordered his artillery battery into action, but the guns could not breach the walls of the old castle. Additional artillery was brought up, and Italian troops soon encircled the redoubt. After forty-five minutes of resistance, the fortress commander, Captain Pappi, convinced Captain Résimont (who had dismissed earlier advice to surrender by announcing that he would die in the ruins of the castle before surrendering) that further resistance was not only futile but would cause casualties among the civilian inmates incarcerated in the penal wing of the castle. A white flag appeared above the walls, and Captain Andrea Ruffini, the commander of the disciplinary company, emerged to offer the surrender of the town. Casualties on both sides were light. The Italians had two dead and seven wounded, and three defenders were wounded.[49] Upon entering the fortress, the Italians, who had been led to believe that the pope's soldiers were a ragtag bunch of miscreants and layabouts, were impressed by the professional appearance and bearing of the disarmed papal Zouaves. For their part, the pope's soldiers were not exactly overawed by their captors. Passing by General Mazè de la Roche, who had hurried forward to savor the first victory of the war, one Zouave was heard to mutter, "Such glory; ten thousand against two hundred."[50]

Aside from Civita Castellana, the Italians encountered very little resistance to their invasion. This avoidance of combat had nothing to do with the pope's desire, expressed in his meeting with General Kanzler on September 10, to avoid bloodshed. In accordance with General Kanzler's prewar plans, which had taken shape as early as 1868, papal units fell back in good order to Rome, preferring to preserve force integrity rather than sacrifice soldiers in hopeless battles against superior numbers.[51] When General Ferrero's 13th Division, after a forced march from the frontier, reached Viterbo in the late afternoon of September 12, it found the town practically undefended, Colonel de Charette having slipped away with the garrison at the approach of the invaders. The only opposition came from the local gendarmeria post, where a sergeant and twelve gendarmes—having failed, apparently, to receive an order to abandon the city—exchanged fire with the invaders for several minutes before surrendering to overwhelming force.[52] As his infantry subdued the feisty papal gendarmes, Ferrero sent his cavalry after the escaping papal soldiers. Italian lancers scoured the roads and villages, but Colonel de Charette kept his small force on farm paths and mule trails, eventually reaching Rome (via Civitavecchia) without the loss of a single man. In the south pontifical forces fell back before the advancing attackers. General Angioletti's 9th Division, which had crossed the southern frontier at dawn on the 12th, captured its first major objective, Frosinone, without opposition. The story was repeated across the line of advance. Cadorna's forces were capturing towns and villages but few papal soldiers; indeed, except for occasional glimpses of papal dragoons shadowing their advance, the Italians didn't even see many of their opponents.

Inevitably, the anticipated drama of war degenerated occasionally into farce. Advancing beyond Civita Castellana, advance elements of General Mazè de la Roche's 12th Division were thrown into panic as they approached the town of Monterosi. Cavalry scouts galloped back to the main body to report that they had seen a unit of uniformed men approaching down the road. The uniforms included red pants. Within seconds the news was racing down the column of Italian infantry. *"Pantaloni rossi!"* Red pants! Even the newest recruit knew that red pants were the uniform of the French infantry. What could this mean? Were French soldiers blocking the road ahead? Could it be that France's support for the papacy remained so strong that in the midst of a war for national survival against Prussia the French had released troops to defend the Holy Father? Now the cry was "The French!" and panic rippled down the columns. As officers struggled to rally and deploy their men, another cavalryman galloped up with the latest intelligence. The advancing men were not crack French infantry but the town band of Monterosi, which had been sent out in gala uniform by the mayor to serenade the Italian army as it passed.[53]

Some encounters were less benign. By September 14 advance elements of the 11th and 12th divisions had moved within a few kilometers of Rome. Scouting ahead along the Via Trionfale, near the village of Sant'Onofrio, a squadron of Italian lancers unexpectedly encountered a company of papal Zouaves. This company, along with a detachment of pontifical dragoons, had been sent out early that morning to set up an outpost in the convent of Sant' Onofrio. While the Zouaves established themselves inside the convent, the dragoons advanced a bit farther to the hamlet of La Giustiniana. The Zouaves pushed out a picket of ten men into the vineyards that separated the convent from La Giustiniana. A heavy fog lay over the countryside, and the picket lost sight of the dragoons, who they thought were patrolling to their front. In fact, just as the sun began to rise, the scouting Italian lancers reached La Giustiniana, and the papal dragoons pulled back, not toward their compatriots at Sant'Onofrio but toward the nearby Ponte Molle, a bridge over the Tiber that was protected by another company of Zouaves. Unfortunately, the dragoons did not communicate their movements to the Sant'Onofrio outpost. When the Zouaves in the vineyards saw horsemen emerging from the fog, they assumed they were friendly, an assumption that was quickly shattered when the Italian lancers charged the papal soldiers, who were quickly overrun. The Zouaves inside the convent opened fire, forcing the lancers to fall back under a hail of bullets. The pope's soldiers, fearing the arrival of enemy reinforcements, then retreated back across the Tiber, carrying with them an Italian cavalry lieutenant who had been unhorsed during the firefight. In this brief but sharp engagement the Italian lancers lost, in addition to their captured lieutenant, one killed and two wounded. They claimed to have killed three Zouaves, although other sources record the Zouaves suffering only four wounded, one of whom later died in hospital.[54]

While the 11th and 12th divisions, with the 13th in support, advanced on Rome, General Bixio's 2nd Division moved on Civitavecchia. The main port of the Papal States was defended by 173 pieces of artillery and some 1,400 men, including gendarmes, customs officers, and the crew of the corvette *Immacolata Concezione*, the last remaining warship of the papal navy. Papal regulars, four companies of Zouaves and two companies of cacciatore, formed the backbone of the defense. Upon learning of the Italian invasion, the garrison commander, Colonel Giuseppe Serra, had immediately declared a state of siege and convened a defense council of his unit commanders. Unlike smaller garrisons, which had standing orders to fall back to Rome at the first signs of attack, Civitavecchia was expected to fight. It wasn't clear, however, that the city wanted to fight. Elements of the population supported the cause of Italian unification; indeed, by September 14 at least one terrorist bomb had exploded in the city and an antipapal manifesto had appeared on the streets. Colonel Serra was concerned that sedition had spread to the native Italian units under his command and that these units would refuse to fight. On September 14 the commander had these units confined to barracks, where they were harangued by officers who spoke about honor and the duty to follow orders. Serra reported his concerns to Rome, but Kanzler dismissed them, reminding the colonel that similar doubts about the loyalty of native Italian soldiers had been raised during the campaign against Garibaldi in 1867, but these troops had remained loyal and effective fighters.

While Serra worried about mutiny, steps were in motion in Rome to ensure that the troops at Civitavecchia would not have to fight. On September 14 Cardinal Antonelli transmitted to General Kanzler a letter from Pope Pius containing final instructions for the defense of Rome. After condemning the "great sacrilege" and "most enormous injustice" of a Catholic monarch threatening the capital of the Catholic world and expressing his appreciation for the loyalty of his soldiers and their willingness to defend the Eternal City, the pontiff directed that the response to the Italian threat should consist only of a protest against the aggression and that negotiations for the surrender of Rome should begin immediately "at the first cannon shots." Referring to the Franco-Prussian War, then reaching its climax, Pius added that at a time when all of Europe deplored the great loss of life, it should not be said that the Vicar of Christ, no matter what the provocation, consented to the spillage of more blood. He concluded, "Our cause is God's, and we place our defense entirely in his hands."[55] To the papal directive Antonelli attached a cover letter, which contained a further order for General Kanzler. "His Holiness," the cardinal wrote, "wishes that in conformity with the orders given you for the defense of Rome you will give corresponding instructions to Civitavecchia in order to save that city from useless destruction."[56]

The papal letter of September 14 represented a victory for Cardinal Antonelli and his policy of nonresistance. Hermann Kanzler knew that if the cardinal secretary of state had his way, the role of the pontifical soldiers would be limited to stacking their rifles at the first sign of the Italians and standing at attention as the troops of Vittorio Emanuele marched into Rome. Kanzler had always resisted that policy, which he considered fatalistic and dishonorable, and he was not yet ready to abandon his opposition. Despite his explicit instructions, the papal commander-in-chief did not order Colonel Serra to surrender Civitavecchia. Instead, on September 14 he telegraphed instructions merely directing the colonel to avoid a defense so tenacious and extended that it would leave the city in total ruin.[57] Serra could fight, but not to the last man, bullet, and brick. This was not exactly what Cardinal Antonelli had in mind. The absence of a surrender order is also evident from the fact that on September 15 Colonel Serra and his senior officer, Major Numa d'Albiousse, both acted as if they still fully expected to fight Bixio's army, which was now ranged outside Civitavecchia's walls. Early that morning Major d'Albiousse assured the Ministry of Arms in Rome, "The city will probably fall, but the honor of the pontifical army will be saved." At 9:00 that same morning Serra informed Kanzler, "Every soldier is at his post. Everyone will do his duty."[58] These are not the words of officers resigned to opening the city gates to the enemy.

On September 15 General Nino Bixio and his 2nd Division were outside Civitavecchia. The general personally inspected the walls, but he had already prepared his plans in consultation with Admiral Del Carretto, the commander of an Italian flotilla cruising off the port. The admiral would sail his warships close to the city and by their intimidating presence add to the psychological pressure on the city's garrison and populace. Bixio would then send an emissary to propose the capitulation of the city. If the proposal was refused, he would signal Admiral Del Carretto to begin bombarding the city in anticipation of an assault by the infantry and artillery of the 2nd Division.[59]

That morning an Italian staff officer, Captain Orero, appeared under flag of truce at the city gates and requested a meeting with the garrison commander. Colonel Serra listened silently as the emissary presented Bixio's demand for the surrender of the city. The colonel then asked the Italian officer to wait in a side room while he consulted his defense council. The papal officers met for almost thirty minutes and, in a certain sign that the council was divided over the appropriate course of action, agreed only to request from the Italians an additional twenty-four hours to reach a decision.[60] Captain Orero departed only to return within two hours, but this time the papal staff insisted that they be present for any discussions. Apparently, some of the officers feared that if left unwatched, their commander might succumb to pressure and surrender the city without a fight. Their fears were justified. Serra was torn between a desire to satisfy military duty and honor by defending Civitavecchia and, mindful of his instructions from Rome, a reluctance to affirm those goals at the cost of destroying the city.

In the presence of General Bixio's emissary, the papal officers debated the merits of defending Civitavecchia. Colonel Serra acknowledged that military honor required a defense, but he asked the Italian officer if the city could be spared a naval bombardment. Captain Orero, perceiving that Serra's will was the weakest point in the city's defenses, asked to speak privately with the pontifical commander, a request that raised a storm in the meeting. Major Numa d'Albiousse, commanding the Zouave companies, declared that a surrender without resistance would be disgraceful, and he told Captain Orero that the Italians already had their answer: The city would resist. Serra, however, asserted his prerogative as commander and took the Italian emissary aside for a private discussion. During this brief exchange, the captain reiterated that General Bixio was fully prepared to attack the city from land and sea with all force necessary to compel submission. The papal commander still could not decide. Without an answer to the ultimatum, Orero returned to his camp, where the 2nd Division was preparing an assault for the next morning. Shortly before midnight, however, these preparations were interrupted by the arrival of two pontifical officers. After several hours of agonizing over his responsibilities, Colonel Serra had decided to surrender the city without a fight. This decision, which was made without consulting Rome and against the majority opinion of his military council, was probably influenced by appeals from municipal authorities, supported by the French and Spanish consuls, who feared that an active defense would result in the destruction of the city.[61]

With the capitulation of Civitavecchia, the Italians controlled all the important towns and most of the territory of the Papal States and were within striking range of Rome. On September 14 General Cadorna had established his headquarters in an old coaching inn, Posta della Storta, on the Via Cassia, barely 15 kilometers from the Eternal City. The next day he dispatched one of his staff officers, Colonel Caccialupi, to Rome under a flag of truce with a letter for General Kanzler. Arriving at the city walls, the colonel was blind-folded; placed in a carriage; and escorted to the Ministry of Arms, where he was introduced to the pope's commander-in-chief, to whom he presented Cadorna's letter. The Italian general, in the name of King Vittorio Emanuele, requested that Italian troops be allowed to occupy Rome for the purpose of maintaining public order. Lacking any further purpose, the pontifical army would be disbanded. The foreign regiments would be discharged and their soldiers repatriated to their homelands, and the pope's native-born soldiers would be welcomed into the royal army at their current ranks. To this request Kanzler, without consulting Pope Pius or Cardinal Antonelli, wrote a brief reply: "I have received the invitation to allow entry to Italian troops under the command of Your Excellency. His Holiness wishes to see Rome occupied only by his own troops, and not by those of other sovereigns. Therefore I have the honor to respond that I am resolved to resist [the occupation] with all means at my disposal as required by honor and duty."[62]

Upon receiving Kanzler's response, Cadorna decided to move the 11th, 12th, and 13th divisions across the Tiber the next day in anticipation of an early attack on Rome. On the morning of September 16, however, before he could begin the advance, the general received a telegram from his govern-ment directing him to make another effort to convince the pontifical govern-ment to allow the royal army to occupy the Eternal City without resistance. Specifically, he was ordered to send a senior officer to inform General Kanz-ler of the capitulation of Civitavecchia, which Cadorna himself had learned of only that same morning, and to suggest to the pope's commander that fur-ther bloodshed would be useless. Dutifully, Cadorna sent off another staff of-ficer, General Orlando Carchidio, with another letter for Kanzler. The papal general sent back a curt reply, stating that the fall of Civitavecchia changed nothing and that although he would do nothing to provoke a "sacrilegious" attack on Rome, he could only trust that General Cadorna would display a similar respect for humanity by refraining from "unjust aggression."[63] After his meeting with General Kanzler, General Carchidio was escorted from the city by Major Rivalta and several other papal officers. The Italian officer took the liberty of suggesting to his escort that they might seize the opportunity to abandon the hopeless cause of the papacy and transfer their loyalties to the kingdom of Italy. The papal officers coolly rejected the suggestion that they defect. One observer dryly noted that such treachery, though perhaps "common in Piedmont, was not the vogue in Rome." Although Carchidio raged against the impertinence of "those monsignors and priests in military uniforms," Cadorna was more measured in his reaction, simply informing Florence that Kanzler's negative reply was "less courteous" than his previous communication. The Italian commander then ordered his army to cross the Tiber.[64]

In Rome, the pontifical army was preparing a reception for the Italians. The pope and his ecclesiastical advisers may have been in denial, but the papal military command was not surprised when the Italians crossed the frontiers.[65] In the days immediately preceding the invasion, work on Rome's defenses had been dramatically accelerated. Kanzler seems to have determined that the crisis was at hand. On Sunday, September 11, for example, the soldiers of the light infantry battalion were just falling in for church parade when orders came to prepare for immediate deployment to an unspecified location. Dress uniforms gave way to field uniforms, and prayer books and rosaries to rifles and rucksacks as noncommissioned officers rushed about shouting orders and cursing the slow. The disappointment was palpable when the men found themselves marching not to the frontier but to the nearby Porta San Giovanni, where they were put to work constructing barricades, a labor that went on day and night.[66] When, on the morning of September 12, the Ministry of Arms had received sufficient information from its provincial commands to conclude that an invasion had begun, Kanzler was ready with a proclamation of a state of siege inside Rome that denounced as "a most horrible crime" the fact that the Holy Father was "without reason threatened by the soldiers of a Catholic king" and enjoined the populace "to remain tranquil inside their homes so that troops might monitor those few malcontents who might seek to disturb public order and threaten public security."[67] Authorities took steps to prevent Italian agents or Garibaldian revolutionaries from infiltrating Rome to spark an uprising or conduct sabotage in support of the Italian army. On September 13 papal gendarmes began visiting homes and apartments in the city to identify foreigners and nonresidents and expel those deemed suspicious. Now only food and wine purveyors were allowed to enter the city, and to better screen and search visitors, additional gendarmes were assigned to the city gates that remained open.[68]

In the first days of war, Rome remained quiet. Kanzler accelerated work on the city's defenses and monitored the movement of his troops as, pursuant to established plans, units fell back to Rome. By September 14 the bulk of the pontifical army was inside Rome, giving the commander-in-chief almost 8,000 first-line infantry, 500 dragoons, and 750 artillerymen to defend the city.[69] Aside from mining the bridges across the Tiber and dispatching cavalry scouts to shadow Cadorna's advance, the papal commander, reluctantly subordinating his aggressive instincts to the express wishes of the Holy Father, avoided offensive operations. The loss of towns and territory to the advancing Italians was neither unexpected nor particularly disturbing because Kanzler realized the issue would be decided not at Civita Castellana or Viterbo or even Civitavecchia but under the walls of the Eternal City. Still, the pope's commander strained at his leash, peppering the Ministry of Arms's war diary with frustrated references to missed opportunities to strike at the divided Italian invasion force. Contrary to the pope's preferences, Kanzler had not entirely abandoned the possibility of a more aggressive military response. On September 15, the day after Pius had explicitly ordered the surrender of Rome "at the first cannon shots," staff officers at the Ministry of Arms were still preparing a preemptive strike to disrupt Cadorna's envelopment of the city. This offensive operation was to include two battalions of Zouaves, squadrons of dragoons, and batteries of mobile field artillery. Although the plan was never implemented, it suggests that, as the Italians neared the Eternal City, Kanzler was keeping open his military options.[70]

The Italians were fast approaching. Cadorna's divisions crossed the Tiber unopposed. Retreating papal units had blown the bridges across the river immediately north of Rome, but Italian army engineers quickly repaired the damage or built floating bridges of boats alongside the collapsed structures.[71] In the meantime, General Bixio's 2nd Division had marched rapidly from Civitavecchia to join the main force outside Rome. Also, General Angioletti's 9th Division had arrived from the south. By the evening of September 18 the Italian army had encircled the Eternal City. That day the royal government in Florence, abandoning finally any hope that it could negotiate an arrangement to occupy the city peacefully, authorized Cadorna to attack at a time of his choosing but urged him to act with prudence and moderation. The only restriction was that he could not attack the so-called Leonine City, the area on the right bank of the Tiber encompassing the Vatican, the Castel Sant'Angelo, and the adjacent neighborhoods. With world opinion in mind, the royal government recoiled at the prospect of artillery shells exploding around the Vatican or musket fire resounding down the streets around the papal palace. In the early days of September the Italian government had received assurances from its ambassadors in Berlin, Bern, London, Madrid, and Vienna that the European powers would not intervene to prevent the occupation of Rome. Reports and photographs of dead priests and cardinals or a bomb-damaged Saint Peter's Basilica could, however, change attitudes overnight.[72]

The Italian commander had decided upon a simple plan of attack. To confuse the papal command about the true focus of the assault and to force General Kanzler to disperse his troops to defend all sectors of the city's walls, Cadorna intended to give the impression of simultaneous attacks at many points. To this end, on the east and south the 9th and 13th divisions would launch strong demonstrations emphasizing artillery bombardments against the Santa Maria Maggiore and San Giovanni in Laterano gates and the Tre Archi, the opening in the wall where trains entered the city. On the west the 2nd Division would launch a similar feint against the San Pancrazio gate and the walls below the Vatican. On the north the main assault would be made by the 11th and 12th divisions against the length of wall between the Pia and Salaria gates. Artillery would create a breach in the wall through which infantry would enter the city. Cadorna set the attack for 5:15 on the morning of September 20.[73]

Despite Cadorna's plan, the first shots in the battle for Rome were fired not on the morning of September 20, but on the evening of the preceding day. Throughout September 19 General Ferrero had been moving infantry elements of his 13th Division nearer to the city walls. Ferrero's infantry occupied a small suburban villa, the Casa Bellardi, from which reconnaissance parties probed papal defenses. One such party pushed close to the Tre Archi and immediately came under fire from papal defenders. The Italians promptly retreated, leaving behind one of their number dead. Apparently General Kanzler had not passed on to his officers along the walls the pope's directive to surrender at the first shots because a squad of papal Zouaves immediately sortied from the walls in hot pursuit of the attackers, only to encounter intense fire from other Italian units that had moved forward to cover their retreating comrades. The Zouaves retired in good order to the safety of the walls, returning fire every step of the way and carrying with them a gravely wounded Italian soldier. The skirmish had been brief but sharp, and upon learning of the encounter, General Kanzler expressed his pleasure at the initiative of the Zouaves and sent a message congratulating them on their offensive spirit.[74] In his earlier directive to his commander-in-chief, Pope Pius had specifically prohibited any provocative or offensive actions. The overture to the battle for Rome suggested that Kanzler intended to interpret that directive very loosely.

Later that evening Kanzler, accompanied by his two senior commanders, Generals Raphael De Courten and Giovanni Battista Zappi, called at the Vatican to discuss the situation with the Holy Father. After the skirmish at Sant'Onofrio on September 14, Pius had ordered all currency and letters of credit in the Bank of the Holy Spirit, the Vatican-controlled banking house in the city, to be brought inside the Vatican for safety. After his injunction against offensive operations and needless bloodshed, however, the pontiff had left military arrangements to his army commander and had limited his involvement in the defense of his territory to visiting important religious sanctuaries in the city and praying for deliverance from the Italians.

With the crisis upon them, Kanzler visited the Vatican to warn Pius that the Italians would attack during the night or, more probably, early the next morning. There was, however, a more important reason for the visit. Freshly returned from the Gianiculum and his meditations on papal Rome and his responsibilities to the city and the papacy, the general was determined to convince the pontiff to fight for the patrimony of the church. Did Pius want to go down in history as the pope who supinely handed Rome to the enemies of the Catholic Church? He pressed the Holy Father to forsake the idea of a purely symbolic defense in favor of a more active and substantial resistance. Thinking, perhaps, as much about his own place in history as the pope's, Kanzler insisted that to surrender without a fight would be dishonorable and infamous. Backed by Generals De Courten and Zappi, he emphasized that this was the opinion of all the pope's military officers.

The appeal had its effect. Though still unwilling to authorize a full-scale battle for the city, Pius agreed that the Italians should be forced to breach the city walls in order to demonstrate to the world that their seizure of Rome was based on violence. The Holy Father retrieved the earlier instruction of September 14, changed the date, and revised the moment of surrender from "at the first cannon shots" to "as soon as a breach has been opened." This decision was not without a certain ambiguity. Did Pius still expect his commanders to avoid bloodshed? Did the pontiff intend for his soldiers to withdraw from the walls before the attack to avoid casualties? Was the breach to be purely symbolic, such as any hole in the walls, or did it have to be a militarily significant breach through which Italian infantry could pour into the city? Could papal soldiers actively resist attacks in order to prevent as long as possible a breach in the walls? Kanzler chose not to raise such questions with the Holy Father. The general would have preferred a more bellicose position, but at least the pope's decision was a step away from the despised policy of abject surrender. When the attack came he could interpret the new policy as events required; in the meantime, he would keep the pontiff's instructions from his field commanders.[75]

From the Vatican, Kanzler returned briefly to his office in the Piazza Pilotta to review the most recent reports and intelligence. Later, seeking some relaxation after the pressures of the day, the general invited a staff officer, Colonel Giacomo Ungarelli, to accompany him to the home of a friend, Count Blome, an Austrian nobleman who had retired to Rome. The count was hosting a whist party. One of the players, Cardinal Gioacchino Pecci, gave up his place at the card table to Colonel Ungarelli and joined Kanzler at the buffet. The cardinal and the general chatted amiably over canapés for several minutes before Kanzler suddenly turned to his subordinate and said, "Enough, Ungarelli. After this round we have to go because in the morning we may wake up to cannon fire." These words so startled Pecci that he dropped the canapé he was holding. "What do you mean?" he stammered. Kanzler calmly replied, "If it doesn't happen tomorrow, Eminence, it will happen the day after, but I'm pretty sure it will be tomorrow."[76]

Thoroughly alarmed, the cardinal excused himself and left immediately for his residence in the Palace of the Consulta, where he lived with several other cardinals. Upon his arrival, he found his fellow prelates gathered around a table playing cards. "Cards!" Pecci shouted, "Tomorrow the Italians will be in the city and you are playing cards!" The players looked at Pecci with disbelief. "What are you talking about?" they scoffed and returned immediately to their game.[77]

The first indications of battle appeared in the small hours of the morning of September 20. At 3:20 A.M. the officer in command at the Porta Pia notified the Ministry of Arms, "Lights are visible in the distance . . . continuous sounds that seem to be getting closer." Ten minutes later the commander at the Porta Salaria reported, "Faint but continuous noises suggesting the enemy to my front is beginning operations." At 3:40 the unit defending the Tre Archi notified headquarters, "Continuous noises towards the San Lorenzo cemetery. . . . Believe the enemy camp has awakened and is preparing for action." All these reports came from the front on the left bank of the Tiber; there was no alarming information from the Vatican side of the river, where all seemed quiet. Still, the papal command was not about to wait on events. At 4:40 the Ministry of Arms issued a general alarm for all sectors and ordered units to their battle positions. Within minutes the observer in the bell tower of the Basilica of Santa Maria Maggiore telegraphed, "Enemy positively closing on the walls."[78] It was beginning.

Ironically, it was the defenders who seized the initiative. General Cadorna had ordered that his artillery commence firing at 5:15. To this end Italian batteries began to move into forward positions as early as 4:00. Three batteries (5th, 6th, and 8th) of the 9th Artillery Regiment in General Mazè de la Roche's 12th Division established themselves around the Villa Albani, about 500 meters from the wall connecting the Pia and Salaria gates, and the Villa Macciolini, opposite the same stretch of wall but 1,000 meters out. These movements had been observed and reported by Zouave lieutenant Ernest Rabé des Ordons, who had been placed as an observer in the north tower of the Porta Pia. At 5:00, as the batteries were awaiting the designated time to commence the bombardment, the bells of the city began to announce the hour. Before the third peal rang out, gunfire erupted from the walls.[79]

A detachment of some thirty papal Zouaves under Lieutenant Paul Van de Kerkhove opened the fight. In another sign that the papal commander planned a more active defense than that envisioned by his pontiff, Kanzler, on September 19, had pushed out beyond the walls several small detachments to establish advance posts for the purpose of impeding the Italian assault. Lieutenant Van de Kerkhove's unit had moved unobserved by the Italians into the Villa Patrizi. A jewel of seventeenth-century residential architecture about a hundred meters beyond the Porta Pia, the villa and its large park had hosted a long list of distinguished guests, including King Carlos III of Spain, Goethe, Stendhal, and Pius IX himself, who early in his pontificate had occasionally visited to play billiards.[80] The Zouaves had turned the elegant residence into a strongpoint within easy range of the Italian batteries setting up in the nearby villas Albani and Macciolini.

The sudden burst of rifle fire from what had seemed an abandoned structure surprised the Italian gunners, and their surprise turned into alarm when that fire was joined by an explosion of musketry and cannonade from the city walls. Within minutes the 5th Battery had two dead and three wounded, and the 6th and 8th, under intense fire, had also taken casualties. To cover the hard-pressed batteries, which had yet to fire a shot, and suppress the rifle fire from the Villa Patrizi (which General Cadorna characterized as "especially brisk"), General Cosenz ordered sharpshooters from the 34th Bersaglieri Battalion forward to harass the papal infantry on the walls while the 35th Bersaglieri Battalion from General Mazè de la Roche's 12th Division attacked the villa.[81] Though seriously outnumbered, the thirty Zouaves inside the villa stood their ground. "At 300 meters, fire," shouted Lieutenant Van de Kerkhove, and almost immediately a volley staggered the advancing bersaglieri. Only when the attackers poured through a hole blown in a wall by Italian army engineers did the Zouaves abandon the villa, Van de Kerkhove leading his men in a fighting retreat to the safety of the city walls. As they sprinted the final meters to the gate, another Zouave officer, Lieutenant Bonvallet, ran out to encourage them forward. "Come on, boys," he yelled as Italian bullets whizzed overhead. "I'll stand here until everyone is inside."[82] Everyone made it. In their stout defense of the Villa Patrizi, the Zouaves suffered not a single casualty.

The capture of the Villa Patrizi relieved some of the pressure on the forward Italian artillery batteries, which now opened fire on the city, focusing their aim on a thirty-meter section of the wall between the Pia and Salaria gates, the point selected by General Cadorna as the focus of his main attack. Additional batteries rushed forward, and by 5:45 thirty-four pieces of artillery were deployed against that section of wall. In the meantime, other Italian units began the feints that were intended to confuse the defenders as to the direction of the main attack. On the north, the 35th Infantry Regiment supported by the 21st Bersaglieri Battalion and two cannons attacked the Porta Pinciana, which was defended by a company of Zouaves and a company of line infantry. At the Tre Archi, on the east, the defenders, a company of papal carabinieri, were soon in action against enemy artillery and rifle fire. To the southeast, Italian cannons had opened up at 5:20 against the San Giovanni gate, with some shells falling beyond the gate to explode in the adjacent piazza and near the large Basilica of San Giovanni in Laterano. Outside the gate, Italian infantry attacked an outpost manned by papal carabinieri who, under heavy fire, retreated into the city carrying several wounded comrades. On the south, the first shells of the bombardment fell amid soldiers of the Legione Romana attending a mass celebrated by their chaplain, Father Luigi Klingenhoffen. No one was hurt, and Father Klingenhoffen hurriedly blessed his congregation as they raced to their posts. On the Vatican side of the Tiber, the pope's soldiers did not wait for the Italians to attack. Cannons positioned at Bastion 10 at the western end of the Vatican Gardens, scarcely a hundred meters from Saint Peter's Basilica, opened fire and wounded several Italian infantrymen of General Bixio's 2nd Division, forming up to face the Gianiculum near the outlying Villa Pamphili and convent of San Pancrazio.[83]

When the papal guns began firing, an Italian battery under Captain Venini had been preparing to bombard the San Pancrazio gate several hundred meters south of the Vatican. Venini immediately turned two of his four pieces toward Bastion 10 and opened counterbattery fire. Since the bastion was in the papal gardens, the Vatican was now under direct bombardment. General Bixio was touring his lines prior to ordering the attack when he realized that some of his artillery was shooting toward the Vatican. General Cadorna had issued explicit orders that, no matter what, the Vatican should not be the object of any military action. Although a rabid anticleric and sworn foe of the papacy, Bixio was horrified at the thought that at its glorious climax, the long effort for Italian unification would be sullied by damage to the Vatican or physical harm to any of its denizens. No one in Florence wanted to see the name of Pius IX on casualty lists. Accompanied by his staff, the general galloped to Venini's position and angrily ordered the cessation of fire and the realignment of all guns toward the Pancrazio gate. His dark mood was not brightened by a sudden rain of shells from Bastion 10 as papal gunners noticed the concentration of horsemen. Bixio was unscathed, but two of his officers were wounded.[84]

The battle for Rome was now well and truly engaged. It became quickly apparent to the defenders that the well-handled Italian artillery posed the most serious threat and that the danger was most immediate at the length of wall between the Pia and Salaria gates. Soon the number of cannons bombarding that short stretch of wall would increase to fifty-two, and the bombardment became so intense that at one point the defenders were driven from their positions along the wall. By 6:30 Lieutenant Rabé des Ordons, observing the fall of Italian shells from his post above the Pia gate, had counted 210 hits on the wall. The defenders were hard-pressed to respond. There were only forty-three papal cannons to protect the 17 kilometers of wall on the left bank of the city, and only four of these were deployed at the critical Pia and Salaria gates. The gunners of the two pieces emplaced at the Pia could hardly work their guns amid the explosions, smoke, and collapsing masonry.[85]

The situation became more serious when, about 6:40, the Italian artillery shifted from firing singly to firing in salvos. Under the concentrated bombardment, the wall began to collapse. Major Ferdinand le Caron de Troussures, commanding the sector, rallied his Zouaves, and the unit chaplain, Monsignor Jean Baptiste Paaps, standing fully exposed amid the fallen masonry, encouraged the troops with cheers of *"Viva Pio Nono!"* The major took advantage of a temporary suspension of the cannonade to order his men to close the developing breach with a makeshift barricade of hay bales, mattresses, carts, boards, and whatever else could be hurriedly rushed to the wall. Concluding that the hiatus in the bombardment heralded an infantry attack, he rushed sharpshooters into the damaged gate towers to cover the broken wall with a crossfire and positioned riflemen on the roof and among the trees of the Villa Bonaparte, a large city mansion whose gardens abutted the wall, to fire on any Italian infantry who tried to climb over the rubble into the city. The major also prepared to ignite the makeshift barricade and create an obstacle of fire when the first enemy soldiers reached the ruined wall.[86]

Linked to his field commanders and observation posts by telegraph and dragoon messengers, General Kanzler closely followed the developing battle from his office in the Ministry of Arms. At 6:45 a false report (soon corrected) that the Pia gate had fallen to the Italians jolted the headquarters briefly, but in the first ninety minutes of the fighting the combat reports were generally positive. Although the defenses were under bombardment at several points, papal troops remained in good spirits, and officers fully expected to hold the walls against the anticipated infantry assault.[87] The commander at the Tre Archi was so confident that he actually proposed a counterattack to capture or at least push back the Italian batteries on his front, a suggestion promptly rejected by headquarters.[88] The one trouble spot was the Pia-Salaria front, which by 7:00 was clearly emerging as the focus of the enemy attack. The lull in the artillery bombardment had not been the prelude to an infantry assault, and when the Italian cannons reopened fire, they did so with increased intensity. At 7:30 Major de Troussures warned headquarters that under the relentless bombardment the wall, crumbling with each explosion, might well be fully breached by midmorning.[89] A papal commander more timid or more punctilious about honoring the spirit of his orders than Kanzler might now have decided that the collapsing wall at Porta Pia represented the point at which His Holiness would conclude that the violent intentions of the Italians had been demonstrated to the world and that capitulation was necessary to avoid needless bloodshed. Kanzler could have run up the white flag. Instead he ordered additional cannons to reinforce the Pia gate.[90]

Inside the Vatican, Pope Pius knew nothing of what was happening to his city. Although he had left orders that he should be awakened at the first sound of gunfire, the instructions proved unnecessary. The pope had spent a restless night; several times the valet stationed outside the papal bedroom had heard his master rise from his bed to pace about the room. When the duty chamberlain entered the papal apartment at 5:00, he found the pontiff already shaved and dressed. Pius went directly to his office. When, fifteen minutes later, the bombardment began, the explosions were clearly audible inside the papal palace. As the minutes passed and the sounds of battle multiplied, Pius asked for a report on developments, but no one had any information. Although General Kanzler was linked to his subordinate commanders around the city by telegraph and mounted courier, his only connection to the Vatican was a staff officer, Lieutenant Colonel Filippo Carpegna, the chief of the First Section (infantry and cavalry) in the Ministry of War, who was temporarily assigned to the papal palace as military liaison. Unfortunately, the minister of war had made no particular provision for passing information to his liaison officer. There was a telegraph post in the cupola of Saint Peter's, but Kanzler did not think of using this link, or did not want to use it, to send news updates to the Vatican. Thus, as the battle opened, Lieutenant Colonel Carpegna was no better informed about developments along the city walls than the pope's butler. An hour into the combat, still having heard nothing from his headquarters, Carpegna (who, though now a desk officer, had fought at the battles of Vicenza, Castelfidardo, and Mentana and knew his way around a battleground) decided to find out for himself what was happening. He grabbed a horse and dashed off for the Piazza Pilotta without informing any senior Vatican officials of his departure. When the pope's secretaries went in search of the liaison officer, he was nowhere to be found.[91]

As Carpegna left the Vatican, he passed a stream of carriages traveling the other way. At this time of supreme crisis, all of papal Rome seemed to be drawn to the pope's side. By 7:00 the corridors and anterooms of the papal palace were filling with a bevy of prelates, monsignors, functionaries, diplomats, and nobility. Princes shared the latest rumors with porters, and priests in simple cassocks mingled with chamberlains in court dress. At 7:15 Pius celebrated mass in his private chapel. Present were several cardinals, including Cardinal Secretary of State Antonelli, and members of the diplomatic corps accredited to the Papal States who had assembled to share the moment of crisis with the Holy Father. The rumble of cannon fire penetrated the marble walls and served as a counterpoint to the Latin phrases of the mass. Under the circumstances, it was understandable that some might be distracted from their prayers. The Prussian ambassador, Count Harry von Arnim, had brought with him a pair of large binoculars, and during the mass he several times popped out of the chapel to see what could be observed from the windows of the papal apartments. To a cardinal scandalized by this affront to protocol and decorum, another diplomat explained, "He acts like that because he is a Protestant."[92]

While Pius celebrated mass, his guards were deploying to defend the Vatican. Though usually dismissed as little more than decorative appendages to papal ceremonies, the Swiss, Noble, and Palatine Guards were just as prepared to do their duty in this time of crisis as the elite Zouaves. Directly subordinate to the Holy Father, the pontifical guard corps was not part of the regular army and, therefore, were ignored by General Kanzler, who assigned them no role in the active defense of the city. In August the commander-in-chief had actually refused a request from the commandant of the Swiss Guard, Colonel Alfred von Sonnenberg, to replace the guard's antique muskets with 120 of the modern Remington breech-loading rifles issued to the papal infantry.[93] Left to their own devices, the commanders of the guard units agreed on a deployment of their forces. Since patrols of gendarmes covered the street approaches to the Vatican, and the main reserve for the defensive sector on the right bank of the Tiber, six companies of line infantry and a squadron of dragoons, was actually stationed in Saint Peter's Square, the guard commanders could focus on protecting the papal palace. Resplendent in their gala dress uniforms, the Noble Guards, the personal bodyguard of the Holy Father, took up posts in the papal apartment, their numbers augmented by retired guardsmen who from fealty to the pope spontaneously showed up to offer their service. On September 12, upon learning of the Italian invasion, Colonel von Sonnenberg had ordered the Swiss Guards to remain in uniform and in their barracks, ready to respond to any emergency. Now, with the Italians under the walls of Rome, the commandant divided his halberdiers into seven detachments. The largest detachment defended the Bronze Door, the portal in the right colonnade of Saint Peter's Square that was the principal entrance to the papal palace. The remaining detachments were assigned to other palace entrances and corridors. Acting as a ready reserve, the Palatine Guard mustered in the courtyards of San Damaso and the Belvedere, the largest courtyards of the palace, from which points they could rush to meet any threat. The commanders of the various guard units had received no orders from the pope, and there was no particular plan to defend the Vatican. The guardsmen simply assumed they would resist any effort by the Italians to enter the papal palace.[94]

Along the walls of the city the battle was reaching its crisis as combat intensified on all sectors. On the northern front, encompassing the Porta Pinciana and the Porta del Popolo, the combatants had been exchanging rifle and artillery fire. About 8:00 Italian infantry launched a determined assault. The defenders, a recruit training company of Zouaves and a company of line infantry, were hard-pressed to hold their positions, even when a squadron of papal dragoons moved forward to reinforce them. At the Popolo gate the attack faltered and the Italians fell back, but fighting continued around the Pincio until 9:20, when the Italian commander decided to shift his troops south to support the main attack against the Salaria gate.[95]

On the opposite side of the city, at the Porta San Giovanni in Laterano, Lieutenant Colonel de Charette, who had been given command of this sector after leading the Viterbo garrison back to the Eternal City, had climbed into the bell tower of the Basilica of San Giovanni to observe Italian troop dispositions. Noticing General Angioletti's 9th Division gathering for an assault, de Charette rushed to ready his men, three companies of foreign carabinieri and two companies of Zouaves. The papal army's sole Claxton gun had been assigned to the San Giovanni gate, and the colonel ordered the weapon hidden in one of the gate towers. From that position it could surprise and mow down any infantry attacking the gate. A battery of field artillery under Captain Daudier, a gunner who had distinguished himself at both Castelfidardo and Mentana, galloped up to reinforce the position, and de Charette deployed the guns to sweep the approaches to the gate. The previous day, in another indication that papal field commanders knew nothing of the pope's instructions to surrender at the first breach in the wall, the colonel had had his men construct barricades of carts, cobbles, lumber, and mattresses on the far side of the Piazza San Giovanni in Laterano to serve as a second line of defense from which to carry on the fight should the Italians break through the gate or wall. Now soldiers had to be deployed behind these barricades to provide covering fire should their comrades have to retreat across the large piazza.

A storm of explosions disrupted these frenzied preparations as the Italian artillery suddenly opened an intense bombardment that unhinged the gates in the wall, smashed the defensive works, ignited the materials in the makeshift barricades in the piazza, and drove the defenders from their positions. The papal soldiers were so shocked and disoriented by the intensity and accuracy of the shelling that an immediate infantry assault might well have taken the gate and entered the city. The Italian commanders, however, perhaps mindful that their assignment was not to capture Rome but to distract the defenders from the main attack on the Pia-Salaria front, hesitated to seize the opportunity. That hesitation allowed de Charette to rally his troops, some of whom rushed to douse the fires and reconstruct the barricades while others returned to their firing positions. Captain Daudier, who had experienced much worse when, ten years earlier, he had commanded a half battery in the ferocious fight for the Upper Farm at Castelfidardo, quickly had his cannons back in action, blasting off sixty rounds in ten minutes.[96]

On other fronts the action developed into artillery duels. At 7:00 the commander at Porta San Sebastiano, Major Count Paul de Saisy, had requested and received artillery reinforcements. An hour later he received six more cannons from the increasingly hard-pressed papal artillery reserves. Almost immediately, the newly emplaced guns silenced an Italian battery. Three battalions of Italian infantry moved to within 700 meters of the walls, but, pursuant to their orders to tie down the defenders, they limited their effort to exchanging rifle fire with the pontifical infantry defending the gate. The defenders were more aggressive. A patrol of Zouaves under Lieutenant Emil Stuchy actually sortied from the walls to reconnoiter and test the Italian lines. Stuchy not only completed this dangerous mission without loss but returned to the safety of the city with an Italian prisoner his men had snatched up along the way.[97]

On the right bank, where Kanzler had concentrated the bulk of his artillery to protect the Leonine City, the cannonades proved particularly intense. By 8:15 thirty papal cannons were in action around the San Pancrazio gate, and these fired so quickly that the sector commander, Colonel Achille Azzanesi, sent urgent appeals for more ammunition to the central arsenal at the Castel Sant'Angelo. By 9:15 Azzanesi's gunners had fired off 830 rounds and were forced to reduce their rate of fire as their supply of shells diminished. At 9:30, however, wagons with additional ammunition had arrived from Castel Sant'Angelo, and the papal cannons reopened fire with renewed intensity. The Italian artillery responded in kind. Inadvertently, some of the Italian shells passed beyond the walls and fell in the Trastevere neighborhood of the city, causing damage along the Via Lungara and around the Convent of San Callisto and the hospital of San Gallicano. Little infantry action took place on this front; indeed, the threat from Italian infantry was deemed so slight that corporals in the cacciatore company defending the wall at San Pancrazio were allowed to send the men of their sections, one by one, to the rear to collect their breakfasts.[98]

Along the Pia-Salaria front the men were too busy for breakfast. The efficient Italian artillery now focused on the gap it had punched into the wall. Rather than widening that breach, the guns worked to pulverize the collapsed masonry in the existing opening in order to reduce the obstacles to an infantry attack. At 8:20 Major de Troussures warned the Ministry of Arms, "The breach is almost complete." Ten minutes later, just as Lieutenant Rabè des Ordons, still clinging to his precarious perch in the battered gate tower, reported enemy infantry formations assembling, the major notified headquarters, "The demolition of the breach at Porta Pia is complete and the opening is suitable for assault."[99]

Upon receiving Major Troussures's ominous news, General Kanzler realized that the time for decision had arrived. With the Pia-Salaria wall in ruins, it was difficult to ignore the fact that the pope's requirement for surrender—a breach in the wall—certainly had been satisfied. Was the pope's commander-in-chief prepared to ignore the express wishes of the Holy Father? Accompanied by Major Rivalta, Kanzler moved from the Ministry of Arms to the Wedekind Palace, the seat of the Committee of Defense in the Piazza Colonna. Composed of senior officers, the committee had been established as an advisory body by Kanzler when it had become apparent that Rome would be besieged. In all matters it deferred to the judgment of the commander-in-chief. Kanzler hurriedly convened a meeting with brigade commander General Raphael De Courten; Colonels Cesare Caimi, commander of the artillery corps, Giorgio Lana, commander of engineers, Filippo Lopez, commander of the city's permanent garrison, and Luigi Evangelisti, commander of the papal gendarmes; and an uninvited guest, Lieutenant Colonel Filippo Carpegna, the Vatican liaison officer. Carpegna had spent the morning galloping from one defense sector to the next, observing the situation and badgering distracted officers for information to deliver to the pope. His reconnaissance eventually brought him to the Wedekind Palace, where he discovered the defense committee in session. Within minutes he had all the news he needed.[100]

General Kanzler opened the meeting by observing that despite the tenacity of the pope's soldiers, it was becoming increasingly difficult to defend all fronts. He quickly reviewed the military situation for the assembled officers, emphasizing that between the Pia and Salaria gates there was now a large breach open to infantry assault. He then read aloud the letter from Pope Pius instructing the army to lay down arms as soon as the Italians had established a breach in the walls. Except for General De Courten, who had been present at the Vatican on the evening of September 19 when Pius had issued the instructions to his commander, the officers were hearing the surrender directive for the first time. Kanzler suggested that the pope's conditions for surrender had been met, and the Committee of Defense unanimously agreed. Rome would capitulate. Carpegna, beside himself with excitement, immediately rushed from the conference to carry the news to the Vatican.[101]

As Lieutenant Colonel Carpegna galloped out of the Piazza Colonna, Major General Zappi galloped in, accompanied by two Zouave officers. A brave though rather excitable officer who had made his reputation by his resolute defense of Pesaro against a superior Piedmontese force in the war of 1860, Zappi rushed into the conference room just as the committee members were affixing their names to a surrender proclamation. Zappi, supported by his Zouave companions, heatedly made the case for continued resistance, arguing that everywhere troop morale remained high, that on all fronts the defense was holding, and that even at the endangered breach the Zouaves were still in control and not a single Italian soldier had reached the breach, let alone entered the city. The general's arguments made a strong impression on the committee, which concluded that its decision to surrender was perhaps premature. The committee decided to send Major Rivalta and Colonel Lana to the Pia-Salaria front to evaluate the situation and report back. In the meantime, another company of Zouaves would be sent from the central reserve to reinforce the breach.[102]

Although General Kanzler and his staff had acknowledged that the pope's conditions for surrender had been satisfied, the papal commanders were clearly still prepared to carry on the fight. The final decision would depend not upon the pope's letter but upon the report of their reconnaissance party. If Major Rivalta returned with a positive appraisal of the tactical situation along the Pia-Salaria front, the defense would continue. In the minutes immediately following the departure of their reconnaissance party, the defense committee actually considered the possibility that things might turn out well after all. Reports from the battle lines fueled their optimism. The troops remained in good spirits and were resisting stoutly, and casualties were light. A situation report from Colonel de Charette at the San Giovanni gate was positively upbeat: "Everything is going well despite the numerical superior-

ity [of the enemy]. If reserves arrive a counterattack might well succeed."
The mood shifted, however, with the return of Major Rivalta and Colonel
Lana. The pair had required little time to assess the threat at the Pia gate.
They considered the situation irretrievable. The breach might be defended,
but only at the cost of heavy casualties, and even then the enemy would
inevitably prevail. The committee absorbed the unwelcome news in silence.
The hush was broken by General Kanzler, who ordered the promulgation
of the surrender proclamation whose preparation had been suspended after
General Zappi's appeal. No one dissented from the commander's decision.
The committee sent out couriers with orders to sector commanders to raise
the white flag. It was 9:35.[103]

It proved easier to proclaim a cease-fire than to actually stop the fighting. When a dragoon galloped up to Major de Troussures at the beleaguered
Pia gate and announced, "General Zappi orders you to cease fire and raise a
white flag," the major simply refused to credit the order. The situation was
certainly serious, but it was not yet desperate; the Zouaves were still holding
the wall. De Troussures was not about to surrender the critical point in the
city's defenses merely on the say-so of an excited cavalry trooper. He dismissed the messenger, shouting, "Go! Go and tell the general that I receive
such an order only in written form or by hand of an officer," and ordering
Lieutenant Van de Kerkhove to accompany the dragoon to headquarters to
confirm the instructions.[104] The courier had caught the commander at a bad
time. The major's Zouaves had moved back up to the wall and into the breach
itself, firing furiously over the rubble at the Italian infantry formed in three
columns beyond the wall, waiting for the order to attack. Amid the crack of
rifles, cries of "Sauniers! Sauniers!" went up from the defenders. From its
intelligence sources the papal army had learned that for several days before
the attack many regiments of the Italian army had failed to receive their issue
of salt because of a breakdown in provisioning arrangements, a failure that
had caused much grumbling in the ranks. Now the pope's soldiers taunted
their opponents by shouting, "Salt merchants! Salt merchants!"[105]

Suddenly, a tricolor flag appeared over the tower of the Villa Patrizi,
which had become the Italian army's forward command post. All firing
stopped on the Italian side. As if in synchrony, the papal guns fell silent too.
For several seconds an eerie quiet descended over the front. The flag was the
signal for the Italian artillery to cease their bombardment and for the infantry to begin their assault. Then, just as the first Italians advanced from their
start line, there occurred one of those unexpected moments that occasionally
lend a rare poignancy and poetry to human combat, moments that live for-
ever in the memory of veterans and the pages of regimental histories. From
the direction of the Salaria gate, down by the section of the wall defended
by Captain Jourbert's 6th Company of the 1st Zouave Battalion, came the
sound of voices raised in song. The melody was picked up by the neighboring

company and then moved quickly along the wall from one company to the next. It was the regimental song of the Zouaves, sung in canteens and along the route of march and now at the regiment's supreme test. Three hundred voices joined in the refrain: "Onward, onward, noble sons of France. Sons of Crusaders, it is God who guides you." Captain Étienne Berger of the 4th Company of the 2nd Battalion rose and stood in the middle of the breach, pistol in one hand, sword held aloft in the other as he sang the words. It was the Zouaves' moment, and every soldier, from the veteran Captain Berger to the greenest recruit clutching a Remington on the wall, knew it as they looked out at the masses of enemy infantry bearing down on them in three columns. They would not let that moment slip away. As the last words of the song faded, total silence fell along the wall. Then came the cry *"Viva Pio Nono!"* followed by a volley of three hundred rifles. The wall was soon aflame with the muzzle flashes of Zouave rifles.[106]

The rain of bullets stopped in its tracks the central Italian column, spear-headed by the 12th Bersaglieri Battalion, which had been moving on the breach. As the bersaglieri rallied and bravely renewed their assault, they became mixed with the unit that had been advancing on their heels, the 2nd Battalion of the 41st Infantry Regiment. The two battalions, now in-termingled, got within 100 meters of the wall before being forced to seek cover behind a natural rise in the terrain. Meanwhile, the column to their left, composed of three battalions of the 39th Infantry Regiment, advanced directly against the Porta Pia, which was defended by two companies of Zou-aves. The Zouaves showered the advancing enemy with rifle fire, but the defenders were distracted by intense fire from the Villa Patrizi, where rifle-men of the 35th Bersaglieri Battalion provided effective cover for the assault column. The outnumbered Zouaves simply did not have enough firepower to stop the attack, and elements of the 39th Regiment reached the wall. On the Italian right flank, the 34th Bersaglieri led the attacking column, followed by the 19th Infantry Regiment. Under papal fire this column veered to its left and was soon intermingled with the center column, causing some confusion in the Italian lines.[107]

With the Italians under the walls and within meters of the breach, Cap-tain François de France, an officer on Kanzler's staff, galloped up to the Porta Pia waving a white flag and shouting, "Cease fire. Cease fire." The noise and action around the gate were so intense that no one noticed him, and while trying to control his agitated horse, he dropped the flag. Lieuten-ant Leon Manduit, commanding the Zouaves in the forecourt of the gate, saw him, picked up the flag, and ran to wave it in the breach. He reached the breach just as the first Italian infantrymen scrambled over the rubble and ran into the city. With rifles blasting, bayonets flashing, and soldiers running and shouting all around him, Manduit, who must have been protected by the an-gel of war, vainly waved his white flag. Finally, an Italian officer noticed him.

"Sta bene" (It's OK), the officer said as he approached the Zouave lieutenant, and with those words the guns gradually fell silent at the breach.[108]

Combat continued on other fronts for some time after the surrender at Porta Pia. At the San Giovanni gate, the Italian artillery bombardment had intensified. Lieutenant Colonel de Charette was rushing from point to point, rallying his troops, when a cavalry messenger rode up with the surrender order. De Charette disdainfully ripped the message into pieces and tossed the fragments on the ground, but ever the professional, he ordered his troops to cease firing and stack their rifles.[109] Lieutenant Colonel Castella, commanding a mixed force of line infantry and foreign carabinieri along the sector immediately south of the Porta Pia, had watched the Italian infantry moving forward and had concluded that the main assault was beginning. At 9:40 he alerted his company commanders on the wall: "The decisive moment has arrived. Do you know how to die at your posts? I am at Tre Archi and will provide an example." Within minutes the company officers had replied: from Captain de Stockalper, commanding the 3rd Company, 2nd Battalion foreign carabinieri at the San Lorenzo gate, "We know how to die"; from Captain Burdo of the 2nd Company, 3rd Battalion foreign carabinieri at the Tre Archi, *"Viva Pio Nono!"*; from Captain Garroni of the 1st Company, 3rd Battalion, also at the Tre Archi, "Yes sir. At my post." At 9:45, as the papal soldiers steeled themselves for the imminent assault, a dragoon carrying a white flag rode up to the sector commander and told him to cease fighting. Castella, however, was not about to accept such an important order from a simple trooper whom he had never seen before. He curtly dismissed the cavalryman and continued fighting. He was still fighting at 10:25 when another dragoon arrived with orders from General Zappi to raise the white flag. Again Castella refused, insisting that he would obey only a written order signed by a hand he recognized. Still, he could not help but notice that rifle fire from the direction of the San Giovanni gate had ceased, as had the sounds of combat from the San Sebastiano gate. The situation clarified when, at 10:55, yet another horseman galloped up. This trooper carried a written order, signed by General Zappi, ordering an end to the fighting. Castella immediately put out white flags and ordered his troops to lower their weapons. The Tre Archi surrendered fully forty-five minutes after combat had stopped at other points along the eastern and southern walls.[110]

Meanwhile, inside the Vatican, the pope was completely unaware of what was happening along the walls of his city. In the first hours of the fighting Pius had received no information from General Kanzler's headquarters and therefore knew nothing about the course of the battle. The first news had arrived at 9:20 when Lieutenant Colonel Carpegna, covered with dust and sweat from his mad dash across the city, stuck his head into the papal library, where Pius was conversing with the foreign diplomats who had assembled in the papal apartment. Motioning Cardinal Antonelli outside, Carpegna told the cardinal secretary of state that he had urgent news for the Holy Father. The cardinal reentered the library to inform the pope that an officer had arrived from military headquarters. Pius immediately sent the diplomats from the room and summoned Carpegna to report. The pontiff listened for several minutes as the officer recounted his personal observations of the fight along the walls and described the meeting at the Wedekind Palace at which the defense committee had decided to capitulate.[111]

Pius was angry and confused. The sound of cannon and rifle fire was clearly audible through the windows of the papal apartment. Why had it taken the Italians so long to effect a breach? If an order to surrender had been issued, then why was the fighting continuing? Carpegna, who had left the Wedekind Palace before the defense committee had temporarily suspended the decision to surrender, had no answers. He knew nothing of the problems involved in transmitting the final capitulation order to the various fronts. The pope had had enough. In the final moments of the Papal States, Pius found an energy, purpose, and resolve that had eluded him in the preceding days of crisis. He curtly announced that the moment for surrender had arrived, and he ordered Lieutenant Colonel Carpegna to raise the white flag over the cupola of Saint Peter's, the highest building in the city. The pope then recalled the diplomats to his library and, visibly moved, announced, "At this moment I have given the order for surrender. Further defense would be impossible without great bloodshed, and that I refuse to accept." Meanwhile, Carpegna had sent a papal guard to carry the pontiff's surrender order to Lieutenant Giulio Cesare Carletti, who manned the observation post in the cupola of the basilica. The lieutenant was distressed to find that, white flags not being among the standard equipment issue and furnishings of army observation posts, he could not fulfill the Holy Father's order. Frantically, the junior officer searched for a substitute, finally grabbing a large, pale tarp that the *sanpietrini*, the laborers responsible for the fabric of the basilica, used in their work. It would have to do. When, at 10:00, Pius opened a window to see if his instructions had been followed, he could see a large rectangular "flag" of surrender displayed over Saint Peter's. The battle for Rome was over. During the attack, 32 Italian soldiers were killed and 145 wounded. The pontifical army suffered 12 dead and 47 wounded.[112]

White flags began appearing around the walls as Italian troops moved deeper into the city. At 10:00 General Kanzler ordered Major Rivalta and two other staff officers, Lieutenant Colonel Carpegna, who had returned to the Ministry of War from the Vatican, and Captain De Maistre, to proceed to General Cadorna's headquarters with a letter for the Italian commander. Escorted through the lines to the Villa Albani, Cadorna's headquarters, the papal delegation was left to cool its heels in a reception hall for some time until the Italian commander agreed to receive only the senior officer. Lieutenant Colonel Carpegna entered Cadorna's room alone and without comment handed Kanzler's letter to the general. In this note the papal commander, perhaps with an eye to history and his professional reputation, made it clear that he could have continued the fight but for the intervention of higher authority. Kanzler wrote,

> Although all defensive measures have not been exhausted, His Holiness recognizes that Rome, though internally perfectly tranquil, must yield to violence, and in a desire to avoid further bloodshed he has ordered me to cease hostilities provided it is possible to secure honorable terms. To this end I am sending you my chief of staff, Major Rivalta, together with Lieutenant Colonel Carpegna, director of the Ministry of War, and Captain De Maistre to discuss terms.[113]

General Cadorna took strong exception to the reference to violence in the letter, pointing out that he had made every effort to avoid bloodshed, including twice sending envoys to propose the peaceful entry of Italian troops into the city—proposals that General Kanzler had refused. The Italian commander made it clear that negotiations could not continue until Kanzler retracted the offending word. Although Lieutenant Colonel Carpegna, on his own authority, provided a verbal retraction, Cadorna declared the meeting over and said he would discuss terms only with the pope's commander himself. The papal delegation returned to the city. Upon hearing their report, Kanzler, accompanied by Rivalta, set out for the Italian headquarters, where his reception was courteous but cool. For an hour the two commanders discussed the terms of surrender. There was little disagreement over the specific terms, but Cadorna remained preoccupied with Kanzler's original letter and its reference to Cadorna's dependence on violence to conquer the Eternal City. This preoccupation was entirely a matter of personal honor because the letter would not be included as part of the official capitulation agreement. The Italian general insisted that the papal general retract the letter. Kanzler refused. In the end, they agreed to disagree. Cadorna stated that he would consider the letter as never having been received. Kanzler did not demur.[114]

The capitulation agreement, signed on the afternoon of September 20, contained six articles. The first stipulated that the city, except that part on the right bank comprising the Leonine City, with all its arms, arsenals, and government properties, was consigned to the army of the kingdom of Italy. The second article granted the defeated pontifical army the honors of war, specifically the right to march from the city with its flags, weapons, and baggage. Outside the city the army would stack its weapons and relinquish its equipment and horses. Officers, however, would be allowed to retain their swords. The third, fourth, and fifth provisions concerned the future status of the pope's soldiers, specifying that all would be removed to Civitavecchia, where the pope's foreign troops would be immediately discharged and repatriated to their homelands at the expense of the Italian government. The indigenous troops would be bivouacked and retain their current ranks until the royal government determined their future status, specifically their ability to transfer into the royal army at their present rank and years of service. The last article created a joint commission of Italian and papal officers to supervise the transfer of weapons.[115]

As news of the surrender spread across the city, pontifical units began to fall back, with their weapons, to the Vatican where most gathered in Saint Peter's Square. This movement was unimpeded by Italian forces that were rather slow to extend their control over the city, limiting their initial movements to occupying important buildings and squares. By command of General Cadorna, no Italian soldiers crossed the Tiber into the Leonine City. Some of the citizens of the Eternal City, however, proved less courteous. Some papal troops moving toward the Vatican were insulted and occasionally assaulted by anticlerical or pro-unification elements who now judged it safe to exhibit their political feelings. Papal gendarmes, symbols of the old political order, were singled out for special vituperation. A detachment of mounted gendarmes, posted in the Piazza Montecitorio during the battle, found itself pressed on all sides by a growing crowd of citizens and had to force its horses at a trot against the crowd in order to break out of the piazza and make its way to the Vatican. Elements of another company of gendarmes, surrounded by vengeful civilians, could not cross the Tiber and had to seek temporary refuge in churches and convents.[116]

By evening, Saint Peter's Square had become a military encampment. General Kanzler had gone directly to the Vatican from his meeting with General Cadorna and had met privately with the Holy Father to report on the events of the day. He spent that night inside the papal palace. At 10:00 on September 21 Kanzler appeared before his assembled troops to read a brief order of the day. "The fatal moment has arrived in which we must abandon the service to His Holiness, which we cherish more than anything," the general announced, "Rome has fallen, but thanks to your valor, your loyalty, and your admirable unity, it has fallen honorably. . . . Good-bye, dear comrades-in-arms, remember your commander who will cherish an indelible and dear memory of you all."[117] When their commander finished, the troops remained standing silently in ranks. They sensed that there would be something more. Then, flanked by two chamberlains, the pope appeared in his window overlooking the square. Pius had come to say good-bye to his army. The soldiers shouted, "Viva Pio Nono," and the cheer was repeated again and again. The roar was deafening. The dragoons added to the tumult by firing their carbines into the air. Pius raised both his arms as if to embrace the crowd. He then blessed the troops and withdrew into his apartments.

It was now 11:00. The papal troops picked up their rifles and fell into line behind their officers. Generals Zappi and De Courten stood at their head.[118]

With drums beating and flags flying, the units marched out, first the Zouaves, then the Legione Romana, the foreign carabinieri, the line regiments, the dragoons, the artillery, the engineers, and the service units. It was the final muster of the pontifical army. From Saint Peter's Square the formation turned south, marching through silent streets to the Porta San Pancrazio, where Generals Cadorna, Mazè de la Roche, and Bixio waited with several Italian units drawn up alongside the road. The pope's soldiers marched past the Italian generals, then halted in the roadway, stacked their rifles, and sat down to await the trains that would carry them to Civitavecchia and demobilization. The pontifical army was no more.

The military details of the invasion of the Papal States and the assault on Rome in 1870—events sometimes characterized as the "Third War of Italian Independence"—have received relatively little attention from historians. With a few exceptions, Italian commentators, and non-Italian historians who have relied on their accounts, have generally downplayed the defense of Rome by the pontifical army, treating the fall of the Eternal City as little more than an armed demonstration during which the pope's soldiers surrendered at the first whiff of gunpowder.[119] This treatment complements the preferred narrative of Italian unification. This narrative requires a description of the war of 1870 that affirms the inevitability of a unification process sustained and welcomed by all right-thinking Italians and resisted only by the representatives of reaction and obscurantism who were so out of touch with national sentiments that they could turn for their defense only to unreliable and ineffective foreign mercenaries. These mercenaries, according to the narrative, could never match an army that embodied the aspirations of a nation, and consequently their defense of Rome could never be more than brief and nominal. There was no room in this script for a scene in which the army of the House of Savoy actually had to fight its way into Rome against active, sustained resistance from highly professional troops, the majority of whom were Italians who were loyal to the Holy Father and committed to the maintenance of his temporal power.

As we have seen, the capture of the Eternal City required more than a few minutes and several cannon shots, and its defense was rather more than a token effort by hopelessly outmatched mercenaries. In September 1870 Pius IX had the best army the papacy had fielded in almost three hundred years. Largely through the efforts of General Hermann Kanzler, the pontifical army was as well led, well trained, and well motivated as the royal Italian army it faced across the walls of Rome. Throughout the brief ten-day war that culminated in the surrender of Rome, Kanzler's troops exhibited a level of discipline, professionalism, and courage that was the equal of its opponent; indeed, the equal of almost any contemporary European army.

The papacy did not lose the war of 1870 because of the deficiencies of its army. The papacy lost its last military conflict because it had neither the imagination to avoid war, the resources to deter war, nor the will to fight a war when it came. Nor could it any longer convince other powers to risk war on its behalf. Refusing to pursue any settlement that compromised or lessened their traditional claims to temporal authority over territory and subjects, the popes of the early nineteenth century could contrive no policy to maintain the status quo. Their temporal power crumbled in the face of political, social, cultural, and economic changes that made such power increasingly anachronistic. As the crisis of September 1870 neared, Pope Pius IX, so confident, purposeful, and directed in his approach to dogma, morals, and spiritual authority, could think of no response to the looming threat beyond prayer and faith that God would see his church through the crisis. His principal collaborator, Cardinal Giacomo Antonelli, chose to place his faith in international law and diplomacy, but in the late summer of 1870 the various European powers were too distracted (France), too weak (Spain), too indifferent (Austria and Britain), or too hostile (Italy) to pursue a diplomatic solution. In this context, diplomacy by itself was no more efficacious than prayer. Military resistance was hardly more promising.

For all of his bravado, General Kanzler did not contrive a strategy that offered a path to military victory. At best his heavily outnumbered soldiers could blunt and bloody the Italian invasion and buy time for Cardinal Antonelli's diplomacy to mobilize the international community to defend the papacy. However, in the absence of any commitment in that community to stand beside the Holy Father, buying time promised little beyond the profligate expenditure of a currency measured in human lives. This was the ultimate paradox of General Kanzler's military reforms. He had created the best army the Papal States had seen in centuries, but this army could do nothing to prevent the demise of those states. Ever the professional soldier, the pope's commander was well aware of the harsh realities. In the end, Hermann Kanzler, like most of his men, preferred to fight not because he thought he could win, nor because of an exaggerated concern for military honor, but because he believed that Rome and the centuries-long tradition of the pope as both spiritual and temporal ruler were worth defending even if defeat was inevitable. The cause was no less honorable because it was lost, and Kanzler's militancy was no less proper than the fatalism of Cardinal Antonelli or the mysticism of Pius IX.

CHAPTER 6

An Army without a State

The capture of Rome marked the end of the pope's temporal power and the unification of Italy under the House of Savoy. Having occupied the Eternal City, the Italian government organized, in early October 1870, a plebiscite to determine whether the pope's former subjects wished to become part of the Kingdom of Italy. The Italian authorities counted 40,785 votes in favor of union and 46 opposed, a rather improbable majority. On October 9 a royal decree announced the incorporation of Rome and the territories of the pope into the kingdom. Pope Pius IX, however, had no intention of quietly acquiescing in the loss of his temporal power. Rejecting the legitimacy of the plebiscite, characterizing the House of Savoy as usurpers, and pronouncing excommunications against those involved in the seizure of the states of the church, Pius sequestered himself in the Vatican and announced that he considered himself a prisoner of King Vittorio Emanuele II. The pontiff insisted on his historical rights as a secular ruler and refused out of hand any suggestion of compromise or accommodation such as the so-called Law of Guarantees, approved by the Italian parliament in 1871 in an effort to calm church-state relations, reconcile the papacy to the new order, and placate Catholics at home and abroad. The law recognized the pope as a monarch with sovereignty over the Vatican and the right to engage in diplomatic relations with foreign powers, guaranteed his complete freedom in matters of religion, and promised a tax-free subsidy in perpetuity to underwrite the expenses of the Vatican. Pius IX contemptuously rejected this offer. The result was a politically awkward situation (known as the "Roman Question") that would continue well into the twentieth century. The Italian government treated the Holy Father and the Vatican according to the provisions of the Law of Guarantees while the obdurate pope, and his immediate successors, dismissed those provisions and the Italian "occupation" of Rome as illegitimate, declined the financial subsidy, refused to set foot outside the Vatican, and sought the diplomatic support of European powers in support of a restoration of the pope's temporal power.[1]

The political entity known as the Papal States no longer appeared on maps of Europe, and for the first time in more than a millennium a pope no longer exercised sovereignty over a territory and a population. The fall of Rome also marked the end of the pontifical army. Under the terms of the capitulation agreement signed by Generals Raffaele Cadorna and Hermann Kanzler, the army's various units were disbanded and the veterans dispersed. General Kanzler retired with his family to an apartment inside the Vatican, where he lived quietly, much esteemed by Pope Pius, emerging occasionally to visit old friends in Rome for an evening of whist. If encouraged to talk about the past, he would recall old army comrades—Durando, de Lamoricière, De Courten—or reminisce about important battles—the defense of Vicenza in 1848, the hair-raising escape from Leotardi's 7th Piedmontese Division at Sant'Angelo in 1860, the assault on Mentana in 1867. He never spoke, however, about the events of September 20, confiding near the end of his life to a friend that he still felt deeply the humiliation of surrendering Rome without a proper defense.[2] The pope's native Italian soldiers were free to return to their homes, and officers were invited to transfer with their commissions into the army of the Kingdom of Italy. A handful of officers, including Fortunato Rivalta, Kanzler's erstwhile chief of staff, accepted the invitation, but the majority refused to serve a monarch whom they considered a usurper.[3] The foreign volunteers were repatriated to their homelands, where most returned to civilian life, although not a few (ninety-nine from the Zouaves alone), exhibiting the same religious fervor that had moved them to enlist in the pope's defense, entered the religious life as priests and monks. Some of the foreign volunteers sought out new battlefields and new lost causes. Many of the French members of the regiment of Zouaves simply transferred from one army to another. With France fighting for its life against Prussia and tens of thousands of French troops in prisoner-of-war stockades, the homeland was desperate for soldiers of any type, let alone battle-tested veterans. Within two weeks of Rome's capitulation, many of the papal Zouaves followed their former lieutenant colonel, Athanase de Charette, into the French army, where they formed a unit known as the Volontaires de l'Ouest (Volunteers of the West) and, still wearing their papal uniforms, fought gallantly in some of the last encounters of the Franco-Prussian War, including the defense of Orleans. Other papal soldiers found their way to Spain and the Carlist civil war, where they fought again for traditionalism and legitimism on behalf of Carlos VII, the Carlist claimant to the Spanish throne, whose brother, Don Alfonso de Bourbon, had been an officer in the papal Zouaves.[4]

The fall of Rome marked the end of the pontifical army, but it did not mark the end of the pontifical armed forces. Just as the Holy Father continued to maintain a formal court with officials, attendants, court costumes, elaborate ceremonies, and strict protocol and continued to exchange diplomats with certain foreign powers, so too did he still have a use for soldiers. The persistence of some armed units under the papal flag supported the claim that the pope remained a temporal ruler with all the accoutrements of sovereignty (except, of course, territory).[5] In addition, armed units were necessary to ensure the security of the pope. Now that the city was in the hands of allegedly anticlerical and radical forces, staunch papists believed that any blasphemy was possible. The sanctity of the Vatican, indeed, the very safety of the Holy Father, could no longer be taken for granted. In the aftermath of September 20 the danger seemed immediate. Both Pope Pius and Cardinal Secretary of State Giacamo Antonelli retained vivid memories of that day in 1848 when a Roman mob had stormed the pope's Quirinal Palace and placed the Holy Father under virtual house arrest. The very evening of the surrender they had decided to draft a request for Italian troops to maintain order in the Leonine City even though such a request was a technical violation of Article 1 of the capitulation agreement signed only hours earlier. As the hours passed and no bloodthirsty mob appeared in Saint Peter's Square, the request for assistance was not dispatched.[6] The threat, however, remained real.

On September 21, 1870, as General Cadorna watched the papal army march out of the Porta San Pancrazio, Count Harry von Arnim, the Prussian ambassador, arrived with information that fights had broken out between papal gendarmes and civilians in the Leonine City. One gendarme had been killed and several wounded. According to the ambassador, Pope Pius, fearing that these encounters were harbingers of larger and more violent disorders around the Vatican, wanted the Italian commander to deploy troops in the neighborhood to preserve order. Cadorna did not welcome the request. His signature was scarcely dry on a capitulation agreement that explicitly closed the Leonine City to Italian troops. The royal government had expected to allow the pope to retain control over the neighborhood around the Vatican and had ordered General Cadorna to avoid any military deployments into that area. Concerns with avoiding further offending Catholic opinion and supporting the official position of the Italian government that the occupation of Rome did not threaten the standing and independence of the pontiff further counseled against sending troops to the doorstep of the Holy Father. How ironic that the pope himself was now demanding that Italian soldiers patrol the Vatican precincts.

Although prepared to hold two battalions in readiness on the left bank of the Tiber at the Sant'Angelo bridge, the general informed the Prussian ambassador that he would not send his men into the Leonine City without a written request signed either by the pope or by one of his collaborators, Cardinal Antonelli or General Kanzler. Count von Arnim departed only to return within the hour with a letter from General Kanzler. "His Holiness has asked me to inform you," the former commander of the pontifical army wrote, "that he wants you to take energetic and effective measures for the protection of the Vatican, for with all his troops now dissolved, he lacks the means to prevent those who would disturb the peace . . . from coming to cause disturbances and disorders under his sovereign residence."[7] With this request in hand, General Cadorna ordered his troops to occupy the Castel Sant'Angelo, establish an outpost in Saint Peter's Square, and secure the perimeter of the papal palace. Within days fixed guard posts were established at the Zecca (the papal mint) behind Saint Peter's, at the outside gate to the Belvedere Courtyard, and at the foot of the steps leading to the Bronze Door, the main entrance to the papal palace. At these posts Italian soldiers mounted guard only a few steps from the pope's Swiss Guards.[8]

Security was a very real concern. In the aftermath of Porta Pia, there were frequent and often violent encounters between clerical and anticlerical factions inside the city. The former refused to accommodate themselves to the loss of the pope's temporal power, and the latter suspected the pope of plotting a return to power. Tempers flared at the slightest provocation—an antigovernment sermon by a priest, a white-and-yellow (the colors of the Vatican) drape over a doorway, an article in a monarchist newspaper—and crowds would rush through the streets shouting, "Long live the king!" or "Long live Pius IX!" Rocks and bottles were thrown, windows smashed, and partisans bruised. One day a crowd gathered at the Bronze Door and shouted abuse at those entering or leaving the papal residence. At one point elements in the crowd yelled, "Pius IX, the assassin" and "We want to shoot him." There were rumors that anticlericals had received a clandestine shipment of weapons from Florence and were preparing a massacre of priests.[9]

Tensions peaked in early December 1870 when clericals held a large demonstration in Saint Peter's Square, ostensibly to honor the feast of the Immaculate Conception on December 8 but also to manifest their loyalty to Pius IX. Anticlericals rushed to the square to mount a counterdemonstration. Among the most pious and credulous loyalists, rumors had circulated that a miracle would occur. On the feast day, the pope's former subjects would awaken to a city from which all Italian soldiers and policemen had miraculously disappeared. On the appointed day, however, Italian uniforms were all too visible in Saint Peter's Square, and a good thing it was because the mix of hostile groups produced the expected results. By late afternoon fights had broken out on the steps of the basilica and under the colonnades. Shots were fired, several people were wounded, and many more were arrested. Three days later the scene was repeated as crowds again gathered in the square and again turned to violence. During the disorders, anticlericals accosted two Swiss Guards, who were leaving the basilica, and amid the taunting and shoving there were shouts of "Kill them! Kill them!" Italian police managed to force their way through the mob and remove the shaken guards to safety.[10]

Passions did not cool with time. In April 1872 a party of off-duty papal gendarmes walking back to the Vatican in civilian clothes was assaulted on the street by a group of citizens, some of whom wore the uniform of the national militia. One gendarme was killed, and two were wounded. In February 1875 the Vatican informed the Italian police that it had received intelligence that Giuseppe Garibaldi, at the age of sixty-eight presumably still fighting his war to the death with the papacy, was secretly preparing a military assault on the Apostolic Palace. Allegedly, arms and men were already gathered in Rome awaiting the signal to attack. Italian authorities correctly believed such a plot extremely unlikely; nevertheless, the story sparked a frenzy of defensive measures around the Vatican: increased police patrols, especially at night; new iron gates across passageways inside the papal palace; and stonemasonry to close the ancient tunnels connecting the palace with buildings in the Borgo and nearby countryside.[11]

The climate of fear continued after the death of Pius IX in February 1878; indeed, on the evening of July 12, 1881, violence attended the transport across town of the pope's remains for permanent burial in the basilica of San Lorenzo. The funeral procession degenerated into a running street battle between rabid supporters of the papacy and their equally rabid opponents.[12] This scandalous affair reminded papal authorities that, more than a decade after Porta Pia, passions remained inflamed, as did the potential for violence. The new pope, Leo XIII (Gioacchino Pecci), though less confrontational than Pius, continued the policy of no accommodations with the Kingdom of Italy, and he maintained the posture of "prisoner of the Vatican" by refusing to set foot beyond the boundaries of his palace, basilica, and gardens. The Vatican Gardens proved an uncertain refuge. One day in June 1882 bullets suddenly struck the garden path along which the pontiff was strolling. Leo's escort of papal gendarmes and Noble Guards hurried him inside the palace, but not before the guards had spotted a man, dressed as a miller, on a nearby road that overlooked the gardens. They reported the incident to the Italian police, who immediately launched an investigation. An attempt on the life of the pope would have been a public relations disaster for the Italian government, which had invested great effort in assuring the Catholic world that the Holy Father could live and work in the capital of Italy without fear for his safety or his independence. Fortunately, the incident proved to be an accident. A young employee of a mill on the Via Scacciadiavoli, from which road some of the paths in the Vatican Gardens were visible, had fired an old double-barreled shotgun at some feral cats without thinking who might be "down range." Missing the intended targets, the shot had fallen near Leo.[13]

Incredibly, events repeated themselves. In September 1882, only months after the first shooting incident, Leo was again walking in his gardens when a gunshot rang out and a bullet whizzed past the pontiff's head. Again papal gendarmes hurried the pope indoors, but not before observing two men with rifles standing in a nearby vineyard. More disturbingly, two uniformed Italian police officers were observing the riflemen from only a short distance away. When Italian police authorities received the report of this incident, there was great consternation. The potential for embarrassment was even greater than that of the June incident, since Italian police agents, who were under standing orders to arrest immediately anyone discharging a firearm near the Vatican, had actually been on the scene and done nothing. This was fodder

for those who wanted to believe that the royal government was complicit
with antipapal troublemakers. Fortunately, an immediate investigation confirmed that the gunfire was entirely accidental. A Roman physician had been
out hunting with a friend and had decided to test his rifle by firing a practice
shot at a distant tree. The bullet had missed the tree and sped toward the
Vatican Gardens and the strolling pontiff. The patrolling Italian police officers had been guilty of ignoring the order to arrest anyone firing a gun near
the Vatican, but they had not been part of an assassination attempt.[14]

Believing itself besieged and threatened on all sides, with the very
safety—let alone the independence—of the Holy Father uncertain, the Vatican required an armed force. A realistic survey of the available resources,
however, would not have inspired confidence. To defend the Vatican and
protect the Holy Father, papal authorities had to rely on a motley and ill-
prepared assemblage of superannuated veterans, bored policemen, and
fancy-dress palace guards.

Despite the abolition of the pontifical army and navy, a few remnants
of General Kanzler's once proud force continued to serve the Vatican long
after the events of 1870. Their presence, often in faded and archaic uniforms, provided a reminder of bygone days. The papal corvette *Immacolata
Concezione* remained at Civitavecchia, unmolested by the Italians and flying
the pontifical flag, until 1872. Then it sailed to the French port of Toulon,
where it anchored, still under the papal flag, until 1878, when Pope Leo XIII
ordered it sold. Inside the Vatican a handful of veterans of the artillery regiment continued to care for a few cannons now stored in the old armory in
the Belvedere Palace. Toward the end of the century, Pope Leo XIII was so
moved by the loyalty (and unkempt appearance) of these old gunners that
he authorized a special stipend to restore their threadbare uniforms. Some
troopers from the regiment of dragoons kept their uniforms and mounts and
served as messengers for the papal court, carrying letters and packets around
the maze of offices, reception rooms, loggias, courtyards, and gardens that
made up the Vatican Palace complex. At the end of the nineteenth century
two former dragoons were still on duty, and a horse was kept saddled in the
Courtyard of Saint Damascus for their admittedly infrequent use.[15] Other
former cavalry mounts were more gainfully employed. When the pope's dragoons were disbanded, the regiment's horses were incorporated into Italian
cavalry units. Some were considered so strong and handsome that they were
assigned to the royal household cavalry, which served as a mounted escort to
the king. For years after the capture of Rome veterans of the papal dragoons
would recognize the horses of their former squadrons trotting alongside the
royal carriage at state occasions.[16]

The only element of the old pontifical army to survive as a unit beyond
1870 was the Pontifical Gendarmeria. Though primarily responsible for police and internal security duties in the Papal States, the gendarmeria had

always been a paramilitary force subject to the pope's commander-in-chief and available for military operations alongside regular units of the pontifical army. From its pre-1870 strength of some two thousand gendarmes organized into foot and mounted companies, the service was now reduced to one hundred officers and men, barracked inside the Vatican, whose functions had diminished to those of a local police force: patrolling the pathways of the pope's gardens, standing at the entrances to Vatican buildings, monitoring the decorum of visitors to the Vatican museums and Saint Peter's Basilica, and enforcing the internal regulations of the Vatican. Battle-hardened veterans who had recruited spies, penetrated clandestine revolutionary cells, repelled Garibaldian bands, chased brigands across the countryside, and fought Italian regulars in campaigns from Ancona to Frosinone now spent their duty shifts directing tourists to the Sistine Chapel or the Raphael Stanze, recording the details of accidents on papal property, investigating petty thefts and larcenies inside the Apostolic Palace, and reminding the coachmen of diplomats and other official visitors that carriages could not be parked just anywhere on the pope's property. When the pontiff moved from his apartments to another part of the palace or the gardens, he was preceded by a pair of gendarmes who cleared the way and provided personal security.[17]

There simply were not enough gendarmes to provide law enforcement, crowd control, and protective services in the entire Vatican complex, especially during important church ceremonies, when thousands of visitors flooded into Saint Peter's square and basilica. To maintain the security of the Vatican, the Pontifical Gendarmeria were forced to arrange a tacit division of labor with the Italian police. Shortly after assuming control of Rome, the Italian authorities established a special police unit under the command of Commissioner Giuseppe Manfroni, an eighteen-year veteran of the royal police service, to maintain surveillance of the Vatican. Ostensibly, the commissioner and his new unit were responsible for maintaining law and order in the city precincts between the Tiber and the Vatican. Manfroni's chief responsibility, however, was to keep an eye on the pope.

In the years after Porta Pia, church-state tensions threatened to complicate seriously Italy's domestic and foreign politics. The self-described prisoner of the Vatican might conspire with foreign powers to pressure Italy to restore at least some of the political prerogatives and territorial possessions of the papacy. Among devout Catholics inside and outside Italy attitudes toward the Italian government could not help but be influenced negatively by the plight of the Holy Father, who had enjoined the faithful to boycott elections and avoid holding offices under the "usurpers." The royal government needed to anticipate any secret diplomatic or political initiatives by the pope (including a sudden flight to a friendlier refuge, such as Spain) that might embarrass the royal government; align one or more Catholic powers behind the papacy and its claims; or spark political outbursts by pious Catholics, particularly in the Eternal City. The government required political intelligence. Accordingly, Commissioner Manfroni set out to establish an agent network that would place informants at all levels of the Vatican, from doorkeepers and cleaners to officials in various departments of the papal administration. By 1873 the police commander had spies in every corner of the papal palace, and these contacts produced a steady stream of information concerning the personalities, diplomacy, finances, and internal politics of the Vatican.[18]

In addition to spying on the Holy Father, Commissioner Manfroni was supposed to protect him. In particular, the commissioner was charged with preventing any outrage by anticlericals against the pope that would embarrass the Kingdom of Italy by challenging official assurances that the pontiff was guaranteed the respect due a monarch and the free and unimpeded exercise of his spiritual responsibilities. Visions of a knife- or gun-wielding assassin rushing the Holy Father during a ceremony in Saint Peter's; fanatical anticlericals dynamiting the papal palace; or rowdy crowds disrupting solemn ceremonies with fisticuffs, catcalls, and rotten vegetables haunted the imaginations of royal officials. It was Manfroni's job to prevent such incidents. To this end, the commissioner assigned uniformed and plainclothes officers to maintain order day and night in Saint Peter's Square (a potential focal point for antipapal demonstrations). From the steps of the basilica, the passageways of the adjacent colonnades, and fixed posts opposite the gates, Italian police monitored visitors as they entered and exited the precincts of the Vatican. Manfroni also deployed foot and mounted police patrols to secure the perimeter of the papal palace complex. Persons engaging in suspicious behavior or individuals pointed out by papal guards were followed and invited to police offices for questioning. Anyone attempting to scale the walls of the Vatican was arrested, as was anyone who fired a gun near the Vatican. The Italian police also blocked any effort to mount a public demonstration or protest near the Vatican.[19]

For their part, the Pontifical Gendarmeria assumed responsibility for order and security inside the basilica and within the precincts of the palace and its gardens. In conjunction with the Swiss Guard, which controlled the external entrances to the Vatican, the papal police were well able to ensure the personal safety of the Holy Father within the palace. Although duty assignments varied over time in response to changes in circumstances or force levels, typically gendarmes, in wide bicorn hats and armed with sabers, would be posted between 5:00 A.M. and midnight at the interior gates of the Vatican; each of the loggias surrounding the Cortile San Damascus, the main courtyard of the papal palace; the Sala Clementina, the main antechamber to the papal apartments; and the Vatican Gardens. Between midnight and 5:00 A.M. most of these stationary posts were closed in favor of roving pairs of gendarmes armed with rifles.[20] Coverage was sufficient to satisfy even the demanding Commissioner Manfroni. When, in 1886, a young man, discovered hiding inside Saint Peter's, explained that he intended to wait for nightfall and then make his way to the papal apartments to discuss "very secret things" with the pope, Manfroni was not unduly alarmed: "I know the internal security of the Apostolic Palace well enough to know that even if he was familiar with the layout of the Vatican, he would have fallen not once but ten times into the hands of the Swiss Guards or the papal gendarmes before he could reach the rooms of Leo XIII."[21] So long as the pope remained within his palace, there was little to fear from assassins. Saint Peter's presented a different situation. The basilica was the scene of public religious ceremonies at which the Holy Father officiated. These ceremonies attracted thousands of visitors to the church and the square outside. The majority of these visitors were pious Catholics or curious tourists, but there was always the potential for troublemakers to join the crowds. Even with the assistance of the pope's palace guards, the Pontifical Gendarmeria, only one hundred men strong, was always hard pressed to guarantee order and security at these events.

The funeral for Pius IX exposed the limitations of the papal armed forces. Pius had died on February 7, 1878, after sitting on the throne of Saint Peter for thirty-one years, the longest pontificate in history. Few pontificates had been more eventful and few popes more controversial. Applauded by many as a principled and resolute defender of the traditional rights of the papacy, Pius was vilified by others as a reactionary obscurantist who had set himself firmly against the unification of Italy. His funeral was sure to attract enormous numbers, not all of whom could be expected to maintain a respectful decorum. The ceremony might have been held in the much smaller Sistine Chapel, where it would have been easier to control access by limiting admission to a few select guests. The cardinals, however, decided that the faithful should be allowed to bid farewell to their beloved pontiff, and they announced that the ceremony would be held in Saint Peter's.

On the evening of February 9 the pope's body was placed on a litter and, amid a procession of cardinals, clergy, aristocrats, and Vatican officials, carried in state to the basilica. Inside, the body was placed behind a grate, but the feet were allowed to protrude so the faithful filing past the papal bier could kiss them. The plan was for the body to remain on display from the morning of February 10 through the evening of February 12. On February 13 the body would be interred in the crypt of the basilica. Planners were concerned, however, that the solemn proceedings would be profaned by anticlerical provocateurs. The evening the body was to be moved into Saint Peter's, a representative of the Vatican requested an immediate and secret meeting with Manfroni. In a dark corner of the basilica, with the hammers and saws of the workers who were building the papal bier cloaking their whispered conversation, the two men discussed security for the funeral.

Papal officials were not at all sure that the armed forces available to the Vatican were up to the task of controlling the tens of thousands of people who were expected to pass through Saint Peter's in the following days. Some, however, were reluctant to acknowledge that fact by accepting assistance from the government of Italy. That government, fearing political embarrassment and an international incident should anticlericals perpetrate some outrage, was as eager as the Vatican to avoid any disturbances. Italian authorities had already decided to ban all demonstrations in the vicinity of Saint Peter's Square, peaceful or not, and prohibit news vendors and street-corner orators from shouting anything that might offend Catholics. Manfroni, professionally convinced that Vatican forces were dangerously inadequate for the demands of the occasion and worried more about physical attacks than vocal offenses, offered to place police and soldiers not only in Saint Peter's Square but also inside the basilica. The Vatican representative balked at deploying Italian soldiers within Saint Peter's. Such a deployment would look too much like an Italian occupation of papal "territory" and suggest that the Vatican was dependent upon the Italian state. The papal spokesman was prepared to acknowledge that, in a pinch, Italian police officers, preferably in plain clothes, would be accepted inside the basilica. Eventually, the two men agreed that Italian soldiers would be stationed in the square to control the crowds waiting to enter the basilica. Inside, plainclothes Italian police would support Vatican gendarmes and guards. The soldiers would enter the basilica only upon a written request from the Vatican. The next morning, within hours of the great doors of the basilica being opened to the mourners, a very worried Manfroni sought out his Vatican contact. The crowd was huge, packing Saint Peter's Square and the surrounding streets and pushing into the basilica to view the body. The commissioner warned his contact that more Italian soldiers were necessary and that they were required inside the church. Reluctantly, Vatican officials agreed, and, with Italian uniforms working beside Vatican uniforms, the funeral proceeded without incident. Vatican authorities, however, were reminded of how much their military had declined if they had to turn to the despised Italian government to ensure the safety of the pope in his own church.[22]

The Pontifical Gendarmeria was only one of the armed units available to the Vatican after 1870. The bulk of the pope's much-reduced armed forces was his palace guards. Although insisting on the abolition of the regular pontifical army, the terms governing the surrender of Rome allowed the pope to retain those household units—the Swiss Guard, Noble Guard, and Palatine Guard—that were in his personal service.[23] During the events of September 20, 1870, these units, deployed inside the Vatican Palace, had not participated in the active defense of the city and had seen no combat. In the days immediately following the Italian occupation, when both the pontiff and his cardinal secretary of state feared mob attacks against the pontifical palace, the guards remained on high alert. Well into October, for example, additional Swiss Guards were assigned to the entrances of the Vatican, and these guardsmen carried rifles instead of their traditional halberds. Off-duty guardsmen were confined to their barracks in order to be immediately available in the event of an attack or emergency.[24]

For all their loyalty and bravado, the papal household guards did not represent a serious military force, and whatever martial qualities they may have possessed before 1870 largely disappeared in the decades after Porta Pia. Together they numbered fewer than six hundred men. After 1870 the Noble Guard and the Palatine Guard, neither of which had ever experienced combat, quickly evolved into purely ceremonial units that were more decorative than martial. Both were composed of part-time volunteers who did not live in barracks inside the Vatican but commuted to duty from their homes in the city. They received little training and no pay beyond an allowance for the upkeep of their uniforms. Their duties were modest, particularly after the loss of the Papal States when public appearances by the Holy Father were curtailed as inappropriate for the self-described prisoner of the Vatican. At religious ceremonies and processionals in Saint Peter's or the Sistine Chapel, files of Palatine Guards presented rifles while a handful of Noble Guards, fulfilling their nominal function of personal bodyguards to the pope, walked alongside the *sedia gestatoria*, the papal armchair that was borne on the shoulders of ushers. These Noble Guards were armed only with sabers. At receptions or audiences, a pair of Noble Guards flanked the papal throne, and during the day another pair stood outside the entrance to the papal apartments. When the pontiff left his apartments to move about the palace or take the air in the gardens, a Noble Guard accompanied him.[25] For their part, the Palatine Guards, reflecting their origin as a militia recruited from the tradesmen and artisans of Rome, as a corps now mustered mainly for ceremonial events.

The main responsibility of the Nobles and Palatines was to provide each day a picket of guardsmen for ceremonial duty in the antechamber of the papal apartments. These pickets, along with detachments from the Swiss Guard and the Pontifical Gendarmeria, provided an honor guard for the reception of important visitors to His Holiness. The various duty detachments, in gala uniform and under the overall command of a Noble Guard officer (the *esente*), the officer of the day, would wait at ease in the pope's antechambers until the approach of a visitor, at which time they would form ranks by unit, and upon a shouted command present arms.[26] Few visitors remained unimpressed by the experience of approaching the papal presence through elegant anterooms and receiving salutes from colorfully uniformed soldiers who seemed to have stepped out of the frescoes that formed the backdrop to their service. It was all part of the theater of the papacy, with the Palatine and Noble Guards playing highly decorative bit parts.

The Noble and Palatine Guards insisted on the fiction that they were serious military units. For years after the loss of the Papal States, for example, each corps would muster its troops inside the Vatican on September 20, the anniversary of the fall of Rome, and October 9, the anniversary of the plebiscite that had endorsed the incorporation of Rome into the Kingdom of Italy, to be available to repulse any attack by anticlerical mobs. In reality, the military capabilities of these two units were extremely modest because they lacked modern equipment and received no training beyond learning how to stand in ranks and salute. They seemed to have been little valued, beyond their ceremonial roles, even inside the Vatican. When, for example, Pope Pius, Cardinal Antonelli, and General Kanzler agreed on the need to obtain troops from General Cadorna to protect the Vatican against anticipated mob action in the days immediately following the Italian occupation of Rome, they clearly did not consider the papal household guards up to the task of defending the Holy Father. In those same days, Cadorna suggested that, in the absence of the now abolished papal army, the Palatine Guard might protect the stores of gunpowder in the Castel Sant'Angelo, thereby obviating the need to put more Italian soldiers into the Leonine City. Major Rivalta, General Kanzler's chief of staff, dismissed the idea out of hand, suggesting that the Palatines were totally unprepared for such a serious assignment.[27]

In addition, the peculiarities of the pope's guards lent a rather comic-opera air to their pretenses and earnestness. The Noble Guards provided a case in point. In a highly competitive field, that unit was arguably the most exotic component of the pope's minuscule military. Though rarely counting more than seventy effective members, the Noble Guard was organized as a regiment under the command of a colonel. To join, an aspirant had to prove a title of nobility extending back at least one hundred years and provide evidence of an independent income (not derived from trade or commerce) sufficient to maintain a lifestyle appropriate to membership in the socially exclusive guard. As befitting individuals of distinguished lineage, all personnel, even the most recent recruit, held the rank of officer. This corps took uniforms very seriously. There were four uniforms, each patterned after the costume of a Napoléonic cavalryman and each appropriate for a particular level of ceremony or function. The "day" uniform, worn for routine duties, consisted of a helmet with a curved crest and gold chin strap; a blue tunic with a high, decorated collar, gold epaulettes, and a double row of gold buttons (eight in each row) extending down to a gold waist belt; a gold "Sam Browne"–style belt extending over the left shoulder and running diagonally across the tunic to connect with the waist belt on the right side; dark blue pants; black boots; white gloves; and a sword. The "high gala" uniform, required for the most solemn celebrations, achieved a level of color and decoration seldom seen outside the stockrooms of a theatrical costumer.[28] Originally the Noble Guard had been established as a dragoon regiment, and its troopers carried carbines, pistols, and sabers, but by 1824 the carbine had been withdrawn from service. Before 1870 the Noble Guard's principal function had been to provide a mounted escort for the pope; for example, when the Holy Father visited a Roman church, ten guardsmen accompanied the papal carriage while another eight went ahead to secure the building. As late as 1901 the corps still issued a manual of cavalry exercises that covered subjects from horsemanship to the maneuvers of large mounted units in the field. By that year, however, the unit was only nominally mounted. Its troopers appeared on horseback only when one or two, now armed only with sabers, rode alongside the papal carriage on the rare occasions that Pius IX or Leo XIII was driven around the Vatican Gardens. In September 1904 mounted duties were abolished entirely, and the remaining accoutrements of cavalry service (horses and tack) were sold and the stable hands dismissed.[29] Even without horses the Noble Guard remained an expensive proposition. Somehow this unit, which represented hardly more than 10 percent of the total personnel in the papal armed forces after 1870, managed to spend each year as much as 40 percent of all funds appropriated for the maintenance of those forces.[30]

The Palatine Guard formed a less grandiose organization, as befitted its middle-class origins. Members were recruited from those elements of Rome's petite bourgeoisie that were interested in serving the Holy Father by dressing in a fancy uniform (plumed shakos, dark blue tunics, gold epaulets, and white gloves) and parading and presenting arms with unloaded antique rifles at ceremonies inside Saint Peter's. Since its foundation in 1850 the Palatine Guard had occasionally performed active military service, escorting supply convoys in the War of 1860, patrolling the piazzas and streets of Rome during the Garibaldian invasion of 1867, and securing the Vatican during the Italian assault on Rome in 1870. After the loss of the temporal power, such military service was no longer needed. In the decades after Porta Pia the strength of the guard would fall as low as three hundred men, but the unit maintained a paper organization appropriate for a larger unit: general staff, four guard companies, a depot company, and a band.[31]

Aside from the Pontifical Gendarmeria, the only unit in the Vatican after 1870 with a claim to professionalism was the Swiss Guard. Tracing its origins back to 1506, when 150 Swiss soldiers under the command of Captain Kaspar von Silenen arrived in Rome to take employment in the service of Pope Julius II, the Swiss Guard was the oldest unit in papal service. By 1870 the corps was the last reminder of a bygone time when Swiss mercenaries provided elite troops and royal guards for most of the courts of Europe. The Swiss were arguably the best known of the pope's household guards because of their colorful uniforms, their trademark halberds, and their visible presence at the gates of the Vatican. Relatively few visitors to Rome saw the Noble or Palatine Guards, but no account of a sojourn in the Eternal City was complete without reference to the pope's halberdiers.[32] The Swiss Guard also possessed an authentic record of military sacrifice, an element conspicuously lacking in the relatively brief regimental histories of the Noble and

Palatine Guards. The Swiss never forgot (and never let anyone else forget) May 6, 1527, when the army of Charles V, king of Spain and Holy Roman Emperor, attacked Rome and invaded the Vatican. Guard commandant Kaspar Roeist and 147 halberdiers died on the steps of Saint Peter's in a heroic rearguard action to buy time for Pope Clement VII to escape to the nearby Castel Sant'Angelo. As their compatriots outside the basilica died to a man, another forty-seven guardsmen covered the pontiff as he hurried along the *passetto*, the elevated, covered passage that to this day connects the Vatican Palace and the Castel Sant'Angelo. At the Battle of Lepanto in 1571, a small detachment of Swiss Guards fought valiantly and captured two enemy flags while serving as bodyguards for Prince Marcantonio Colonna, commander of the papal contingent in the combined Venetian-Genoese-Spanish-papal naval force that defeated the Turkish fleet.[33]

Despite its early glory, time had not been kind to the Swiss Guard, and by the early nineteenth century the proud corps was in noticeable decline. Having evolved as a palace unit, completely separate from the pontifical army and the Swiss mercenary regiments that were a part of that army, the guard no longer participated in campaigns or field operations. Indeed, when a detachment of halberdiers defended the Quirinal Palace against an armed Roman mob in 1848, it was the first time the guard had been under fire since the Battle of Lepanto, 277 years earlier. Not surprisingly, the corps had over the years gradually lost its martial qualities. Threats to the personal security of the Holy Father were few and far between, and when threats did appear, as in 1798 and 1809, the guard was usually ordered by the pope to stand down without resisting. There seemed little reason to maintain fighting skills, and the halberdiers gradually lost their edge. Although the guard armory had always included firearms, the retention of halberds and swords as the standard duty weapons when other military and guard units in Europe had shifted to firearms was an implicit admission that the Swiss Guard was no longer meant to fight—an implication that was not lost on the halberdiers. Apparently firearms were so infrequently deployed that in 1848 the guard, expecting a mob attack against the Quirinal Palace, had to hurriedly put a sufficient number of muskets into working order.[34] Guard duties became pro forma, and often the Swiss seemed to act more as ushers than soldiers as they maintained decorum and controlled crowds at papal ceremonies. Low pay, poor housing, indifferent leadership, and financial irregularities by officers contributed to a decline in morale and discipline. Conditions were so bad that in 1783 there had been a mutiny by halberdiers who complained that officers were withholding for their own profit gratuities and supplies meant for the guards. Twenty-seven halberdiers were dismissed, and Pope Pius VI had to intervene personally to restore order.[35]

The Napoléonic period had been a particularly difficult time for the Swiss Guard, with the corps being disarmed and disbanded after each of the

French occupations of Rome in 1799 and 1809. The unit reached its nadir, however, in the second quarter of the nineteenth century when a morass of corruption and indiscipline brought it to the edge of extinction. By then the guard had become a fiefdom of the Pfyffer von Altishofen family; every commandant since 1712 had been a member of that prominent Lucerne clan.[36] In 1827, when the crisis flared, Colonel Karl Josef Leodegar Pfyffer von Altishofen was in his twenty-fourth year of command. Early in his tenure he had pressed the Vatican to improve pay, and he had enhanced the living conditions of the halberdiers by improving the quality of their food and renovating their barracks. Unfortunately, this reforming impulse had eventually degenerated into a career characterized by opportunism, nepotism, and lassitude. Already in 1819 a group of halberdiers had submitted to Vatican authorities a formal complaint against their officers alleging financial irregularities and abuse of office. The recruiting officer in Switzerland, for example, routinely accepted fees from prospective recruits. Frequently, the recruiter (a relative of the commandant) would accept a young man but then summarily dismiss him in order to make a place for someone who was willing to pay a higher fee. In Rome, the corps received an appropriation for uniforms, but the uniforms actually issued were so shoddy that they fell apart easily. There was suspicion that the commandant was buying cheap materials and pocketing the savings.[37] There was so much grumbling among the halberdiers that Father Erasmus Baumgartner, the chaplain of the guard, lamented to authorities in Switzerland that "the Swiss Guard, once so honorable, will bring shame on the Swiss name if they are not restored to order."[38]

Historically, regulations concerning the composition and administration of the Swiss Guard were set out in a "Capitulation" negotiated between the Vatican and Lucerne, the canton that claimed preeminence among the Catholic regions of the Swiss confederation and that historically had been the principal recruiting ground for the corps. These agreements, usually negotiated by the serving commandant in the name of the Vatican, gave Lucerne the right to intervene in the internal administration and discipline of the guard and to influence the appointment of the commandant and other senior officers by submitting a *terna* of three names from which the pope would select one. The canton also claimed the prerogative of monitoring the activities of the commandant by requiring reports concerning the status of the guard. These arrangements complicated lines of authority and responsibility because the commandant had to report to both the canton council of Lucerne and the master of the Apostolic Palace in the Vatican.[39]

The Capitulation of 1825 specified that the Swiss Guard would number 200 men and that the commandant would exercise control over the finances of the corps. In practice the strength of the unit was usually around 125, and never did it reach the authorized strength of 200, even though funds were appropriated to support the authorized level. The result each year was a balance of unspent moneys, which the commandant could dispense as he saw fit. The expectation was that such funds would be used for bonuses or unexpected expenses. Under the terms of the Capitulation the commandant was supposed to issue an annual financial report, but in practice this requirement was ignored and there was little accounting of how the extra money was spent. Often the funds seemed to be used exclusively for bonuses for officers, while the common halberdiers suffered from low pay.[40]

By the 1820s Colonel Pfyffer von Altishofen had come to treat his post as a sinecure, and he devoted little attention to its affairs. A fanatical huntsman, the commandant spent much of his time away from Rome, happily chasing boars, wolves, and other wildlife across the countryside of the Papal States. While on these frequent hunting trips he entrusted the affairs of the guard to his three sons, all of whom he had made officers in the corps. For the eldest, Ignaz, the commandant had created an entirely new position: quartermaster. Bad-tempered, arrogant, and abusive, Ignaz was roundly detested by the rank-and-file halberdiers. The second son, Martin, was temperamentally the opposite of his brother and the more respected of the brothers. The third son, Ludwig, was a younger version of Ignaz.[41]

On October 12, 1827, several halberdiers called on Quartermaster Ignaz Pfyffer von Altishofen (the senior officer present, the commandant being away on yet another hunting trip) with several complaints. At first the quartermaster refused to receive them, claiming he was sick. When eventually he relented and agreed to hear their grievances, his attitude was defensive and hostile. The visitors expressed their concern about certain rules recently instituted by the commandant for the distribution of the bonuses members of the guard received for extra duties, such as special ceremonies in Saint Peter's Basilica or the Sistine Chapel. Apparently, the complainants suspected that certain officers (they were thinking of the commandant and his sons but were too prudent to say so) were financially benefiting from the new rules. The bonuses, however, were merely an excuse to raise other concerns about the mismanagement of the corps under the Pfyffer von Altishofen dynasty. The implicit criticism of his father infuriated Ignaz, who rejected the complaints and angrily dismissed his callers.[42]

The next day Colonel Pfyffer von Altishofen learned of the encounter between his eldest son and the discontented halberdiers. The commandant could not be bothered to abandon his hunting trip to return to Rome, but he sent word to his sons to arrest the complainants. Ignaz, who was probably not the best man for the mission, went immediately to the barracks, where he was confronted by a group of sullen halberdiers. A heated argument broke out when the quartermaster announced his intention to arrest the malcontents. The confrontation quickly turned violent. One source claims that the quartermaster struck one of the men, whereas another source says that the officer was manhandled by halberdiers intent on defending their colleagues.

When the dust settled, several halberdiers were in custody, and, in the hope of quieting the turmoil, Ignaz distributed money among the remaining soldiers. If he thought the angry men could be bribed into compliance, he was mistaken. Insubordination was now rife in the barracks. When a sergeant entered the halberdiers' quarters to restore discipline by threatening to arrest troublemakers, he was driven from the building. An attempt on October 16 to move the men arrested by Quartermaster Pfyffer von Altishofen to a more secure location was blocked by angry halberdiers who actually seized back their colleagues.[43]

Ignoring the chain of command, a delegation of halberdiers stomped off to the office of the master of the Apostolic Palace to complain about the conduct of their officers. The palace official, who was responsible for the administration of all aspects of the papal household, including the palace guard, agreed to investigate the complaints if the corps returned to discipline and the arrested guardsmen accepted their punishment. Unsatisfied with this response, the unhappy guards wrote directly to the pope to present a list of their grievances. They accused the "bandit commandant" of siphoning money from the account reserved for the provision of uniforms and shoes for the halberdiers and complained about the arbitrary demands and insolent demeanor of the commandant's privileged offspring. Insisting that they were not radicals but merely aggrieved soldiers who were being victimized by the commandant and his sons, the halberdiers requested a new commander and a new Capitulation with Lucerne governing the administration of the corps and the conditions of their service. In the meantime, they would no longer acknowledge the authority of the Pfyffer von Altishofens and would accept orders only from the master of the Apostolic Palace.[44]

On October 18 Commandant Pfyffer von Altishofen, now returned to Rome, discussed the unrest with his son Martin. Realizing that his second son was far more respected by the halberdiers than Ignaz, the commandant directed Martin to resolve the situation. It was a prudent choice. When Martin entered the barracks he was well received by the guardsmen, who listened respectfully as the officer explained that, whatever their grievances, the soldiers were wrong to take matters into their own hands. Discipline and the chain of command were essentials for any military organization. The angry halberdiers who had confronted Ignaz now meekly submitted to the correction of his younger brother. Martin's intervention successfully defused the tense situation, and the guardsmen returned to their duties. Unable to leave well enough alone, Commandant Pfyffer von Altishofen insisted on dismissing from the guard three of the men who had played a prominent role in the unrest.[45]

On the surface, peace and quiet now reigned in the Swiss Guard, but the grievances that had sparked the mutiny remained unaddressed, and indiscipline and poor morale continued to plague the corps. By May 1828 twenty-nine guards had voluntarily resigned from the unit. That same month Pope Leo XII decided to intervene. To avoid scandal and further damage to the reputation of the guard, Leo declined to open a formal investigation and explicitly absolved the commandant of responsibility for the disorders. It is clear, however, that the pontiff suspected that the troubles were the result of mismanagement, if not malfeasance, on the part of the Pfyffer von Altishofen family. The colonel was told that he must command the corps personally and not cede his authority to junior officers. The pope then moved to curtail the authority of the commandant by decreeing that henceforth any new rules governing the administration of the guard had to be approved by the master of the Apostolic Palace. The master also had to approve any officer appointments.[46]

Colonel Karl Pfyffer von Altishofen was told to dismiss his eldest son, Ignaz, from the corps, and the commandant was warned that any further trouble would result in his own removal from command. The chastened commander was then called to order by the canton council of Lucerne, which had learned of the unsettled conditions in the guard and demanded an explanation. Displaying again the professional irresponsibility and political obtuseness that were the cause of his problems, the commandant could not be bothered to appear before the Lucerne authorities and appointed his discredited elder son to report on his behalf. In his report Ignaz distanced himself and his family from any responsibility for the problems in the guard, insisting that the culprits were the halberdiers, whom he described as undisciplined, unprofessional, and disloyal.[47]

Karl Pfyffer von Altishofen survived the disturbances in the guard and remained as commandant until his death in 1834, having served longer in the post than any of his predecessors. As provided in the Capitulation, Lucerne submitted a terna of names for the pope's selection of a replacement. At the top of the list was Martin Pfyffer von Altishofen, the deceased commander's second son, who had evaded the ignominy and censure that had befallen his father and older brother. Apparently, the Holy Father also concluded that Martin bore no responsibility for the unrest in the guard because Leo chose him over the other two candidates. The new commandant began his tenure energetically, moving immediately to renovate the living quarters of the halberdiers, but his positive image among his men was soon besmirched by accusations that he had returned to the shady financial practices and profiteering that had sparked the unrest of 1827. By the 1840s the guard was again rife with complaints and discontent.

In August 1847 the master of the Apostolic Palace, Monsignor Giovanni Rusconi, submitted to the cardinal secretary of state a report concerning the condition of the guard and the behavior of its commander. The report was a bombshell. Rusconi accused Martin Pfyffer von Altishofen of shameless nepotism, abuse of office, and financial mismanagement bordering on criminal corruption. In 1836, for example, the commandant had appointed his thirteen-year-old son an officer in the guard. The monsignor also concluded that the commandant had played fast and loose with official moneys, a judgment complicated by the failure of the commander to submit annual financial reports as required by the Capitulation with Lucerne. A widow of a guard lieutenant had endowed a fund to benefit the families of married halberdiers, but the commandant had never distributed the proceeds of this endowment. Halberdiers suspected that he administered the fund for his own benefit. A similar suspicion resulted from his failure to dispense salaries as required to guards who were on leave. The commandant also kept the names of deceased guards on the pay roster, and it was never clear what happened to the salaries he collected in the names of these dead men. Halberdiers were entitled to a new uniform every year, but those who maintained their old costume and did not require a new one were supposed to receive an equivalent stipend. The commandant failed to pay these stipends.[48]

Monsignor Rusconi's indignation did not fall only on the commandant. The scathing report was an indictment of the entire Swiss Guard, which emerged from the investigation as an organization lacking in discipline, leadership, professionalism, and loyalty. The list of charges was long. First, Rusconi noted, the corps, despite its name and its historical connection with the land beyond the Alps, wasn't entirely Swiss. For generations guardsmen had married local women and settled in Rome, most remaining in the Eternal City even after their retirement or resignation from the corps. These men sought to place their sons in the guard, which gave preference in recruitment to children of serving or veteran halberdiers. These new recruits were first- or second-generation Romans, Swiss by ancestry only and thoroughly Italian in language and culture. When Ignaz Pfyffer von Altishofen, born and raised in Rome, had been sent to Lucerne to explain the disturbances of 1828, he had been incapable of addressing the canton council in German (the language of the canton and, at least in theory, the Swiss Guard). He was reduced to submitting a written report in Italian. When Rusconi conducted his investigation, he found that 28 of the 123 members of the corps had been born in Rome. When some of these scions of the Eternal City were enrolled, they were too young to perform duties, except occasionally as drummer boys, but they still drew salaries. When, therefore, Martin Pfyffer von Altishofen, who himself had entered the guard at the age of sixteen, appointed his thirteen-year-old son to the corps, his action was exceptional only in that he sought to make the boy an officer. As late as 1841 the incorrigible and unrepentant Ignaz Pfyffer von Altishofen tried unsuccessfully to obtain an appointment in the corps for his eight-year-old son, Federico, whose Italianized name emphasized his Roman upbringing. Ignaz also insisted that the corps pay the cost of a replacement to perform Federico's duties until the boy, who would still draw a salary, came of age.[49]

Guard officers treated their positions as sinecures, neglected their duties, and did not supervise their men. Supervision was so lax that officers—who were housed in the Quirinal Palace while most of their men were quartered across town inside the Vatican—were not always sure where their men were. In 1839, for example, two off-duty halberdiers were assaulted by thugs while walking in Rome. One died the next day in the hospital, and the other remained seriously injured. It was days before anyone noticed that two halberdiers were missing. The lackadaisical attitude of the officers infected the enlisted men, who performed their duties in a slipshod way and did not hesitate to challenge the orders of their superiors. They received no training beyond cursory instruction in marching and presenting halberds, and guard service was considered a nominal responsibility.[50] On guard duty halberdiers would openly smoke pipes or cigars, slouch against the walls, and make little effort to control access to the papal palace. On one occasion, two masked men walked past a Swiss sentry post and entered the palace without challenge from the halberdiers on watch.

Many of the guards considered their duties inside the Vatican an unwelcome distraction from other activities. Halberdiers were often absent from their barracks because they supplemented their low salaries with second jobs in the city, working as guides for tourists, guards in the palaces of princely families, or artisans or tradesmen in shops. In order to concentrate on their outside jobs, some guardsmen simply hired substitutes to don the uniform and perform their guard service. One group of enterprising halberdiers entered the local real estate market by renting out rooms in the more distant wings of the Quirinal Palace, the pope's second residence in Rome. Apparently, no one noticed this unauthorized activity or the presence of strangers coming and going from the pope's house. For more than one young man, the guard, in return for nominal duties, provided access to room and board while he pursued studies in art, archaeology, or literature in the schools and institutes of the Eternal City.[51]

Monsignor Rusconi concluded that abuses were so rampant that no amount of reorganization or reform could salvage the corps. He recommended the abolition of the Swiss Guard and its replacement by a new palace guard, two companies strong, recruited from the noncommissioned ranks of the line regiments of the pontifical army. Pope Pius IX, elected in 1846, recoiled from outright abolition of the unit that, after more than 325 years of service, had become a fixture at the Vatican. He may also have wished to avoid discomfiting Swiss Catholics. Though the corps would be saved, there was no question that major changes were required, beginning at the top. Fortunately, Martin Pfyffer von Altishofen, apparently aware of Monsignor Rusconi's investigation and anticipating its results, cooperated to avoid a public scandal. In July 1847, shortly before the monsignor submitted his scathing report, the commandant informed the Holy Father that he was resigning his command and leaving the guard for reasons of health.

Under the terms of the Capitulation of 1825, the pope was expected to select a new commander from a list of three names proposed by the canton of Lucerne. Pius unilaterally decided to dispense with this custom by appointing a commander without waiting for Lucerne's nominations. To affirm further his intention of shaking up the guard, Pius broke the monopoly of the Pfyffer von Altishofen family on the colonelcy by picking a commandant from outside the family whose name had become synonymous with the Swiss Guard. In a third departure from hallowed tradition, the pontiff decided to look for his new commandant outside the guard. His choice, Franz Leopold Meyer von Schauensee, had never served with the pope's halberdiers. A professional soldier and native Swiss, the new commandant had served in Swiss regiments in various foreign armies before joining the 2nd Foreign (Swiss) Regiment of the pontifical army in 1832. During the First War of Italian Independence (1848–1849) the 2nd Foreign Regiment had campaigned against the Austrians as part of the army of General Giovanni Durando and had played a prominent role in the defense of Vicenza. During the battle for that city, then Captain Franz Leopold Meyer von Schauensee had distinguished himself by participating in the capture of an Austrian battery, an experience that marked him as the first guard commandant in centuries who had led men in combat.[52]

The new commandant assumed command of a corps crippled by years of poor morale, lax discipline, indifferent supervision, inadequate resources, and blatant nepotism. Furthermore, he inherited a cadre of officers all of whom were themselves products of the discredited Pfyffer von Altishofen regime and some of whom had harbored hopes of receiving the command. They resented the selection of an outsider as an implicit criticism of their own merits. Such officers were not likely to be eager collaborators in any project to reverse the decline of the corps. Despite these obstacles, Colonel Meyer von Schauensee was determined to reform the guard. Fortunately for the new commander, high authorities inside the Apostolic Palace shared the same goal. As the commandant settled into his apartments in the Quirinal Palace, the Vatican was organizing a special commission to consider the reorganization of the Swiss Guard and the negotiation with Lucerne of a new Capitulation to replace the agreement of 1825.[53] The pope and his advisers were open to change, and their new commandant was ready to give them that.

Colonel Meyer von Schauensee studied the recent, troubled history of the guard and concluded that the disturbances of 1828 and the continuing poor morale were the result of legitimate grievances among the halberdiers concerning the blatant favoritism and financial mismanagement of the

Pfyffer von Altishofen dynasty. He also concluded that other deficiencies, such as the unprofessional and undisciplined comportment of the halberdiers, the indifferent performance of duties, and the frequent recourse to "civilian" employment in Rome, reflected the straitened financial situation of the poorly paid guardsmen and an institutional culture that accepted low standards and militated against the cultivation of unit pride. The men simply had little reason to identify with the corps and care about its performance and reputation.

As a first step toward reforming the guard, the commandant proposed to the pope a series of new regulations. To alleviate the financial distress of the guardsmen and reduce their need for outside employment, Meyer von Schauensee suggested that each halberdier receive full compensation for the costs of purchasing and maintaining uniforms, shoes, and belts. To reduce turnover, encourage reenlistments among worthy personnel, and reward loyal service, he proposed bonuses based on years of service, a policy practiced in the pontifical army but hitherto shunned by the Swiss Guard. He recommended that any surpluses or savings in the budget be deposited in a savings account and reserved for any unanticipated or urgent needs of the corps. Finally, he recommended that the commandant be solely and directly accountable to the Apostolic Palace for his administration of the corps and its funds.[54]

In areas of daily administration, where his own authority was sufficient, Meyer von Schauensee instituted small but telling changes. To alleviate suspicion and distrust, he strove to make the financial affairs of the corps as transparent as possible. Food costs, for example, had always been an irritant. Halberdiers had to pay for their midday meal, and in the past a fixed sum had been deducted from their monthly salary. The men, however, had no way of knowing if that sum corresponded to the costs of purchasing foodstuffs. Given the history of financial malfeasance and the climate of distrust within the corps, it was easy for the guardsmen to imagine that the deductions exceeded the actual costs and that the difference was diverted into someone's pockets. Meyer von Schauensee directed that each day a corporal and a halberdier would accompany the cook to the market to buy that day's foodstuffs. The corporal would record the expenditures in an account book, and the halberdier would countersign the entry. This account book would then be made available to any halberdier who wished to inspect it. The costs of lunch would be shared equally across the entire corps. Everyone would know how much was spent on meat, vegetables, and pasta and how much was deducted from salaries to cover those costs.[55]

Although acknowledging the legitimate financial grievances of the halberdiers, Meyer von Schauensee made it clear to officers and enlisted men that service in the Swiss Guard imposed duties that could not be shirked. He reminded the men that the guard was a military unit and that its members were expected to comport themselves accordingly. He placed a new emphasis on discipline and duty, concerns unremarkable to an officer who had spent his career in line regiments but rather unsettling to men accustomed to the undemanding life of a purely ceremonial unit. The commandant reintroduced the requirement that officers and enlisted men exchange salutes, a practice that had lapsed under the lax administration of the Pfyffer von Altishofens. He also enforced regular inspections of the men and their quarters. The barracks had to be swept and cleaned twice a week; beds made daily; and uniforms, gear, and personal items kept tidy. Although never a martinet and always careful to treat his soldiers with respect, Meyer von Schauensee insisted on discipline and order, and he made it clear that the guard was not a democracy or a debating society. When a group of halberdiers, dissatisfied with the pace of reform, went on strike, the commandant appeared before them and informed them that they would immediately return to their duties or be immediately discharged from the corps. The men meekly returned to work.[56]

Plans to reform the guard were delayed, first by the Roman Revolution of 1848, when the corps was "suspended" by the short-lived Roman Republic, and then, after the restoration of the pope, by the routine lassitude of the papal bureaucracy whose decision-making pace was snail-like even in the most placid of times. The same special commission that reviewed the loyalty of members of the pontifical army turned its attention to the Swiss Guard in response to rumors that even before the pope's flight to Gaeta the corps had been infected with republican sentiments.[57] Fortunately, the guard in general, and Colonel Meyer von Schauensee in particular, had recovered some respect after its spirited defense of the Quirinal Palace under the colonel's command during the Roman revolution of November 1848. Still, the wheels of papal government turned slowly—so slowly that it would be ten years before the long-awaited reforms appeared.

On June 17, 1858, Pope Pius IX approved new regulations that represented a dramatic shift from established customs and practices. The Regolamento per la Guardia Svizzera Pontificia unilaterally terminated the long relationship with the canton of Lucerne, which henceforth would have no role in the administration of the guard or the selection of its officers. The Vatican would now exercise complete and exclusive control over the corps. The size of the guard was lowered from 200 to 133 men, a more realistic figure given problems with recruitment and finances, and admission was limited to native-born Swiss men between the ages of eighteen and twenty-five. For purposes of admission, Roman-born sons of serving halberdiers would be considered Swiss, but such "Swiss-Romans" could not number more than twelve in the entire corps. The pope would have exclusive authority to appoint the commandant, who had to be Swiss, but not necessarily from the canton of Lucerne. Promotions within the guard now had to be approved by the cardinal prefect of the Apostolic Palace, and such promotions had to be based on seniority and merit. The new regulations explicitly prohibited any member of the corps from accepting outside employment or practicing a trade or profession. The often-abused practice of giving the men a stipend to purchase uniforms and equipment was abandoned in favor of simply issuing to each man the necessary items and replacing them at stated intervals. In case of injury or illness, guardsmen would be treated in a hospital at the expense of the Vatican and would continue to receive their salary during their incapacity. A new retirement system allowed guardsmen to retire at full pay after thirty years of service, rather than the previous forty, and at half pay after twenty years. Finally, provisions for death benefits for widows and children were introduced.[58]

By subordinating the commandant to the cardinal prefect and master of the Apostolic Palace, affirming the place of seniority and merit in promotions, improving the financial circumstances of the guardsmen, and prohibiting civilian employment, the Regulation of 1858 was an important step toward reforming and renewing the Swiss Guard. By and large, the new rules were welcomed by the rank and file and enthusiastically embraced by the commander who had worked so hard to ensure their promulgation. Unfortunately, Colonel Franz Leopold Meyer von Schauensee, the first of the great reforming commandants, did not live to see the full fruits of his labors. He died in March 1860. Reflecting on his passing and its impact on the corps, guard chaplain Florin Decurtins wrote, "The Swiss Guard had lost its kind father, its fulcrum, its careful defender, its particular embellishment."[59]

Pope Pius IX hesitated in selecting a new commandant. The Pfyffer von Altishofens, who considered the command of the Swiss Guard part of the family patrimony and the tenure of Leopold Meyer von Schauensee as little more than an unfortunate interregnum, seems to have worked behind the scenes to influence the Holy Father to choose Alexander Pfyffer von Altishofen, a lieutenant in the guard and a son of the disgraced former commandant Martin Pfyffer von Altishofen. Pius agreed to promote the lieutenant to provisional commander but delayed making a permanent appointment. There were, however, influential voices inside the Vatican (the guard chaplain was one) opposed to a restoration of the Pfyffer von Altishofens. These voices, undoubtedly reminding the Holy Father of the rather uneven record of the family's commandants and the beneficial results of his decision in 1847 to entrust the guard to an outsider, suggested that the pope should again seek his commandant outside the guard. The anti–Pfyffer von Altishofen faction prevailed.[60]

Pope Pius selected Alfred Gaston von Sonnenberg as the commandant. A native of Lucerne, von Sonnenberg had followed the career path so common to young Swiss men of his time and social class. At the age of sixteen he joined the Swiss regiment of the army of the Kingdom of Naples. Over the following twenty years, with interruptions for military service in Switzerland, he eventually rose to the rank of general in the Neapolitan army. With the collapse of the Kingdom of Naples in 1860 and its incorporation into the Kingdom of Italy, von Sonnenberg intended to return to Switzerland to take a post in the Swiss military, but his plans were interrupted by the invitation from Pius IX to assume command of the pontifical Swiss Guard.

The new commandant found a corps that was beginning to show the effects of the reforms instituted by his predecessor and codified in the Regulation of 1858. Both morale and discipline had improved. The 1860s proved a turbulent period for the papacy because the decade was marked by wars, internal unrest, and brigandage. Throughout this period the guard was reliable and obedient, qualities that should be unremarkable in a military unit but that as recently as fifteen years earlier could not have been taken for granted when considering the pope's guards. Von Sonnenberg was a diligent commander who was particularly concerned with the welfare of his troops. He established music and choral clubs for the halberdiers and replaced all the old, shabby cots in the barracks with new beds. Unlike many of his predecessors, he did not hold himself aloof from his peers in the regular pontifical army, going so far as to join General Hermann Kanzler's staff when the pope's commander-in-chief attacked and defeated the irregular army of Giuseppe Garibaldi at the Battle of Mentana in 1867.[61] No one could remember a time when the guard had operated so smoothly, and it surprised everyone, particularly the commandant and his superiors in the Apostolic Palace, when in 1878 the Swiss mutinied.

To be fair, the disturbances that year in the *quartier Suisse* were not unprovoked. After the fall of the Papal States and the transformation of Rome into the capital of the Kingdom of Italy, the corps experienced significant stress. Toward the end of the pontificate of Pius IX, the Vatican decreed a 30 percent salary increase for all employees except those in the Swiss Guard and the Pontifical Gendarmeria. The halberdiers considered their explicit exclusion from the pay raise a deliberate insult. Their sense of affront increased when Cardinal Secretary of State Giovanni Simeoni rebuffed Colonel von Sonnenberg's personal appeal to include the guard in the raise. The exclusion was especially provocative because the duties of the halberdiers had increased. New Swiss laws restricting foreign military service combined with the availability of better-paying jobs in the civilian sector to create a recruitment crisis for the guard. The number of halberdiers fluctuated in the years following Porta Pia (falling as low as 76 in 1871), but the corps was never at its authorized strength of 133 men. The burden on the small number of halberdiers grew heavy because guard and ceremonial duties had to be performed no matter how few soldiers were available. The stress on personnel was not ameliorated by the commandant's approach to discipline. Von Sonnenberg had built his career in a regular army, and he insisted on tight discipline and a strict code of personal conduct. There were prohibitions against excessive drinking, cursing, indebtedness, leaving the Vatican without permission, and accepting gratuities from civilians. Barracks, uniforms, and equipment had to be clean and in perfect order. Violations of regulations were punished by confinement to barracks for a month or, in more serious cases, incarceration for up to two weeks. Such restrictions would be popular in no military unit, but in the undermanned and overworked guard of the 1870s they were deeply resented. The resentment needed only a spark to flare into open insubordination.[62]

A joke set off the conflagration.[63] Halberdiers were recruited mainly from the farms and small villages of the largely agricultural Catholic cantons of Switzerland. For most new recruits, the trip to Rome was their first extended journey away from home, and Rome was by far the largest city they had seen. For many Romans, including not a few of the denizens of the Apostolic Palace, the halberdiers seemed little more than rough country bumpkins, and as such they often became the subjects of jokes and stories that portrayed them as slow-witted and gullible. One such story, circulating in Rome at the end of 1877, alleged that the guards had been told to admit to the Vatican anyone announcing himself as "Giorgi" (George). This rudely implied that since the halberdiers lacked the intelligence or the facility with Italian necessary to seriously screen visitors, their superiors simply directed them to admit anyone who spoke the password. Pranksters would approach the halberdiers on duty at the Bronze Door and introduce themselves as "Giorgi" or ask with a straight face if it was true that anyone claiming that name would gain immediate access to the pope. It is likely that such sophomoric humor tried the patience of the guards. Irritation turned to anger when Cardinal Simeoni, passing through the palace's Sala Clementina with a colleague, quipped within earshot of the Swiss Guard picket on duty in that hall, "Look! There are the Giorgis." He allegedly repeated the slur in front of a different set of guards a few days later.

The cardinal secretary of state's public disdain combined with the imbroglio over salaries and the resentment over workload and discipline to convince the halberdiers that they were much abused. In the meantime, Pius IX died on February 7, 1878. The death of one pope and the election of another required the Swiss Guard, and other units of the papal military, to perform extra duties—the vigil over the papal bier, the funeral ceremony, the conclave to elect a successor, the coronation of the new pope. Traditionally, the halberdiers received an extraordinary bonus of three months' salary as recompense for the special services. On this occasion, however, the cardinal *camerlengo*, the prelate responsible for organizing the funeral and the subsequent conclave, declined for alleged reasons of economy to pay the bonuses, a decision endorsed by the new pope, Leo XIII, upon his election. For the halberdiers, this was the final straw.

A wave of anger and frustration swept through the Swiss Guard barracks, and the earlier whispered complaints now turned into loud demands for justice and compensation. Some of the guards made threats and encouraged insubordination. In an effort to contain the unrest, guard major Fridolin Bommer entered the barracks and took into custody several of the loudest agitators. Apparently, these men were simply confined to quarters, for almost immediately two of their number "escaped" into Rome in civilian clothes and sought comfort in a tavern not far from the Vatican. The establishment was well known among the halberdiers, so when a guard officer went in search of the escapees, it was the first place he looked. The officer convinced the men to return to the Vatican, where they were promptly arrested and placed behind bars.

Upon learning of the fate of their two comrades, the guardsmen mutinied. Thirty-four halberdiers refused to muster for duty until all their colleagues in custody were released. Trying somewhat belatedly to defuse the situation, Colonel von Sonnenberg agreed to receive the mutineers and listen to their complaints. The commandant, however, declined to release the detained halberdiers mainly for fear of undermining Major Bommer's authority in the corps, a rather curious rationale in view of the fact that the mutiny was an explicit repudiation of the authority not just of the major but of the entire officer corps. Disappointed with their commandant, the mutineers took matters into their own hands, forcing the doors of the jail to liberate their comrades, smashing furniture in the barracks, and sending frissons of alarm along the corridors of the Apostolic Palace. The Italian police stationed outside the Vatican heard that the mutineers had armed themselves with rifles from the armory and that the officers had barricaded themselves in a storeroom.

The situation was serious. No one could predict what the armed mutineers might do, and papal authorities could not be confident that they had the means to prevent the malcontents from wreaking their will. The majority of halberdiers had not actively joined the rebellion, but would they take up arms against their comrades or remain passively on the sidelines? Doubts also arose concerning the reliability of the Pontifical Gendarmeria, which shared many of the Swiss Guard's grievances over pay and bonuses. Apparently, no one seriously considered using the Noble or Palatine Guards to suppress the disturbance. The Vatican might have to ask the Italian government for assistance in putting its house back in order, but this request would represent a shameful loss of face. In the end, papal authorities decided to buy off the malcontents. In return for their submission and resignation, the mutineers were paid a sum equal to one year's salary. The mutiny ended.

The new pope, Leo XIII, was humiliated and infuriated by the affair, which cast a pall over his accession to the throne of Saint Peter. Within the corridors of the papal palace, talk arose again of abolishing the guard.[64] Leo's wrath, however, fell on Colonel von Sonnenberg, whom he blamed for the embarrassment. According to the ways of the Vatican, the commandant—who, to be sure, had remained curiously passive during the uprising—was discreetly made aware of his pontiff's displeasure. After a decent interval, he announced his resignation on September 20, 1878. His replacement, Marie-Joseph-Martin-Louis, Count de Courten, a career officer in the now defunct pontifical army, inherited an unenviable task. The mutiny demonstrated that the seeds of professionalism, discipline, and loyalty planted by Colonel Meyer von Schauensee and cultivated by Colonel von Sonnenberg may have sprouted, but the delicate growths had not set down deep roots. To return the guard to harmony, Colonel de Courten focused on improving the living standards of the halberdiers on the assumption that contented soldiers were more likely to accept discipline and order. The new commandant had the good fortune to begin his tenure at the same time that new regulations governing the Swiss Guard, the Regolamento of 1878, went into effect, replacing the Regulations of 1858. These rules, first planned under the regime of Colonel von Sonnenberg, improved the troops' access to pensions, death benefits for widows and children, and paid leave. The changes were well received within the corps and assuaged somewhat the bitter memory of the recent dispute over wages and bonuses. Building upon this initial good feeling, de Courten instituted a series of modest though thoughtful improvements in the day-to-day living and working conditions of the guards. In the first winter of his command, he secured a stove to warm the hitherto unheated common room where off-duty halberdiers gathered to talk, smoke, and read newspapers. That same year he purchased flannel undershirts to help duty guards ward off the chill of winter nights. He successfully convinced Vatican authorities to renovate and improve bathroom facilities in the barracks and provide better lighting along the passageways between guard posts. To provide distractions for off-duty guards, de Courten established a library and supported a band and chorus that offered concerts for the men and their guests. In a gesture that won him much affection throughout the corps, he allowed wine and spirits at official celebrations.[65]

As a regular army officer, de Courten understood the importance of professionalism, and he worked quietly to instill professional military standards in the Swiss Guard. Incredibly, eight years after Porta Pia and the demobilization of the pontifical army, which made surplus thousands of serviceable, breech-loading Remington rifles, the guard still had nothing but muzzle-loading muskets in its armory. De Courten promptly acquired 120 Remingtons and instituted rifle practice in the Belvedere Courtyard of the Apostolic Palace. The new commandant also made it clear that he would not tolerate any indiscipline. He weeded out malcontents and malingerers. A halberdier who insulted the pope by word or deed was subject to immediate dismissal. For fighting with a corporal, a halberdier was confined to his room for three days and then confined to his barracks for a month. The corporal was demoted for six months and confined to his room for eight days. On duty, halberdiers had to salute everyone above the rank of corporal, and even when off duty in barracks, they had to give a "military greeting" to everyone in and out of uniform. All soldiers had to stand at attention when addressing an officer.[66]

De Courten became a popular commandant. His popularity extended beyond the *caserma Svizzera* to the corridors of the Apostolic Palace, where his quiet and respectful demeanor did much to assuage the memory of the events of 1878. In 1901, at the age of sixty-six, he resigned his command on grounds of ill health and retired to the town of Nancy in France, the home of his wife, where he lived to the venerable age of 102. To replace the beloved commander, Pope Leo returned to the practice of promoting an officer from the ranks of the guard, a procedure that had not been applied since 1847. The choice fell on Major Xavier Leopold Meyer von Schauensee, the son of Franz Xavier Leopold Meyer von Schauensee, who had commanded the corps in the period 1848–1860. Only eight years old at the time of his father's death, Major Meyer von Schauensee had entered the guard in 1872 as a junior officer at the urging of the then commandant, Colonel von Sonnenberg. Eventually, two of his own sons followed him into the corps. He developed into a popular and respected officer and was de Courten's personal choice for his replacement.

To all appearances, Colonel Meyer von Schauensee's tenure was uneventful. Like his predecessor, the commandant was concerned with improving the living and working conditions of his men. He was especially applauded for securing for sick halberdiers the right to recuperate on the grounds of the papal summer villa at Castel Gandolfo, a cool and pleasant retreat in the hills outside Rome that had fallen into disuse since the popes had adopted the posture of prisoner of the Vatican. When, in July 1903, Pope Leo XIII died, the guard dutifully responded to the special requirements of the funeral; the subsequent conclave; and the enthronement of the new pontiff, Pius X. Above all, tranquillity reigned in the Swiss barracks, a condition of supreme importance for the *monsignori* of the papal palace, who recoiled at the thought of another scandal like the one that had tarnished Leo's ascension to the throne in 1878. There seemed little reason to fear for the guard under Meyer von Schauensee's command, so the consternation was all the greater when, on October 6, 1910, the fifty-eight-year-old commandant was felled by a stroke that left him speechless and paralyzed on his right side. Nine days later he died. His untimely demise would prove the catalyst for a series of events that would rock the Vatican even more than the mutiny of 1878 and change fundamentally the very nature of the Swiss Guard.[67]

The quiet in the Swiss barracks after 1878 had misled observers into believing that, finally, all was well with the guard. Each day the halberdiers were at their posts at the gates of the palace and the antechamber of the pope, as they had been for four hundred years, reinforcing the air of tradition and ceremony that formed the bedrock of life in the papal court. They did not do much, but then, nobody expected much of them. Above all, the guard did not cause embarrassment or scandal. To most papal functionaries, who knew little about military affairs and cared even less, there seemed little reason to give the Swiss any thought so long as they remained peaceful and obedient. A more informed perspective would not have been so complacent. Anyone who looked beyond the colorful uniforms and picturesque weapons to consider the guard as a military organization and not just another decorative fixture in the religious and courtly spectacle of the papacy would have had serious concerns.

For all the well-intentioned efforts of reforming commandants such as Meyer von Schauensee *père*, von Sonnenberg, and de Courten, the Swiss Guard had lost its way. To be sure, the egregious abuses and deficiencies of the early nineteenth century had been eliminated, but there remained a fundamental crisis of identity and character. The tension between the guard's two roles—ceremonial household troops and trained infantry unit—had never been formally resolved. The more conscientious commandants had assumed that the corps could perform both roles, but in the absence of any interest, let alone support, for the military role among Vatican officials, that function had been neglected. Resources were always scarce after 1870, but it was always easier to convince the monsignors who held the papal purse strings to cough up funds for a heater in the barracks common room than to pay for bullets for target practice. Inevitably, the military function became marginalized as commandants found it easier and more productive to focus on bread-and-butter issues concerning the daily living and working conditions of their troops. Not only was the need for improvements in those conditions apparent to all, but such a focus asked little of the officers and the men. Not surprisingly, as their military role was neglected, the officers and men saw themselves less as soldiers and more as performers in a long-running spectacle where the audience and the producers were content so long as everyone appeared in costume and performed the expected motions. The guard had become less a military unit than a resident theater company whose members played at being soldiers. The fact that the practices of saluting and standing at attention before officers, commonplaces in every army in Europe, were considered novel reforms in the Swiss Guard is a measure of how demilitarized the corps had become.

The guard had become morally *louche* as well as militarily lax. Again, so long as appearances were maintained and the strict letter of regulations honored, dubious practices were tolerated. Everyone played the system for financial benefit. In order, for example, to allow halberdiers to retire with the best possible pension—based on a soldier's last rank and salary—officers, without reference to merit or service, routinely promoted halberdiers to sergeant only days before they were due to retire.[68] For their part, some officers seem to have been distracted from strict attention to military duties by the allure of the salons, restaurants, and card rooms of the Eternal City. They routinely abused their access to corps accounts to underwrite a dissolute, expensive lifestyle. Abuses became especially egregious during the command of Colonel Xavier Leopold Meyer von Schauensee, which is perhaps one reason why his unexpected death in 1910 so discomfited his men. He turned a blind eye as Major Baptiste Imsand, corps finance officer, allowed the commandant's sons, Max and Franz, both captains in the guard, to dip into official accounts for never-repaid "loans" to cover serious personal debts. The commandant himself was not above using official accounts to cover his own debts. Lieutenant Colonel Karl Pfyffer von Altishofen borrowed so wildly from his fellow officers without the ability to repay that he seriously compromised his reputation, a telling judgment in an officer corps whose moral and professional standards were not exactly a model for the armies of the world.[69]

Officials in the papal palace were aware of the rot, if only because the cardinal secretary of state received angry letters from note-holders demanding to know who would cover the outstanding debts of the guard officers. Word of the dissolute behavior of the officers reached as far as Switzerland. In March 1910, seven months before the death of Colonel Meyer von Schauensee, the bishop of Coira, writing on behalf of all Swiss bishops, implored the commandant to exert control over his officers and to insist on the strict application of the letter and the spirit of the regulations. He emphasized that immediate attention was necessary to reverse the general decline in the corps, especially the status of the officers. "We have noticed with great sadness," the bishop lamented, "that the body of officers of the Pontifical Swiss Guard are no longer worthy of the high honor . . . of maintaining custody of the Vatican Palace." The bishop ended his admonition by offering the services of the Swiss bishops in recruiting more suitable candidates for the officer corps of the guard.[70]

Vatican authorities were slow to respond to the complaints until the unexpected death of Colonel Meyer von Schauensee. Confronted with the need to find a new commandant but unwilling to promote the deputy commander, the dissolute Karl Pfyffer von Altishofen, the Vatican consulted the Swiss bishops. The bishop of Basle, Jakob Stammler, enthusiastically proposed Jules Repond, a former Swiss army officer, journalist, and lawyer who at the time of his nomination was living the life of a country squire on his farm near Fribourg. A man of high character, robust physique, inexhaustible energy, and strict principles, the fifty-seven-year-old Repond had made his mark in several areas of Swiss life. He had studied law at the universities of Munich and Paris before taking a degree in jurisprudence from the School of Law in Fribourg, where his academic record was so impressive that he was invited to join the faculty. While holding the chair of Roman law at the university, he established a private legal practice and became active in Fribourg politics as a vocal member of the liberal faction. Uncompromising in his political beliefs and direct in his political attacks, Repond made enemies easily. His political activity eventually led to his dismissal from his teaching position and the loss of many private clients. He abandoned the law and took up journalism, writing regularly for the *Gazette de Lausanne* and the *Journal de Genève* and serving as editor of *Bien Public*, the organ of the political movement of the same name, until that paper collapsed. He eventually left the Lausanne and Geneva papers over political and confessional differences.

Like all Swiss adult males, Repond had served in the national army, which was based on a citizen militia. As a citizen-soldier he rose, between 1876 and 1902, from lieutenant to colonel, ending his career as commander of the 5th Infantry Brigade. His departure from the Swiss army seems to have been hastened by his refusal to go along with organizational norms that tolerated lax discipline and low expectations in what was, after all, only a part-time army of clerks, farmers, shopkeepers, and mechanics. Having received complaints from his men concerning their commander's insistence on strict discipline, in particular in matters concerning drinking and drunkenness, the military authorities gently eased Repond out of the service. Retiring to his country property northeast of Fribourg, the irrepressible Repond threw himself energetically into local affairs. He founded the first credit union in the canton, established an association for dairy farmers, and lobbied cantonal authorities for improvements in local roads. In his spare time he served as president of the Swiss Alpine Club and the Swiss abstinence movement.[71]

In terms of education, background, and range of experience, Jules Repond was not a typical Swiss Guard officer and certainly not a typical commandant. He was completely unknown inside the Vatican, so his selection must have raised eyebrows inside the Apostolic Palace. His appointment certainly was unpopular in the Swiss Guard, where the current officers resented being passed over and halberdiers, as well as officers, worried about the intentions of an unknown commander. They were right to worry. Jules Repond would hit the Swiss Guard like a freight train, and the impact would shatter once and for all the complacency, amateurism, lassitude, and petty corruption of the corps. From the pieces Repond would build a new guard, and in the process he would prove the most controversial, and arguably the greatest, commandant in the modern history of the corps.

Within a week of his nomination by papal decree on December 8, 1910, Repond arrived in Rome to assume his new command. Upon entering the barracks compound of the guard, he found the halberdiers mustered in the courtyard in full gala uniform to welcome him. After a hectic round of introductions, troop reviews, audiences, banquets, and fanfares, the new commandant took the measure of his unit.[72] He was shaken by what he found.

Concerning his first impressions, Repond would later recall, "The condition in which I found the Swiss Guard at the end of 1910 was pitiful."[73] Everywhere he looked he found problems, deficiencies, and abuses. Although authorized at a force level of 133 men, the corps mustered only 89, including officers, and this number included many individuals who remained on the payroll even though they were too sick or feeble to perform duties. Colonel Repond was dismayed to discover that his new command was only nominally a military unit. Training was limited to practice in marching in formation and handling halberds for ceremonial purposes. Even these minimal exercises were so indifferently conducted that the men could only poorly execute the required maneuvers. Training was further undercut by the practice of excusing veterans with more than eight years of service from any exercise requirement at all. The most modern weapons in the armory were the single-shot, breech-loading Remingtons manufactured in the 1860s and already outmoded when they had been acquired by Colonel de Courten in 1881. Each guard post had several of these old rifles in racks along with cartridge pouches, but it had been six years since the halberdiers had actually drilled with the rifles and practiced marksmanship.[74]

Repond discovered that the internal administration of the corps was in no better state than its training. The list of deficiencies was long: The commandant had no office; the guard chapel, San Pellegrino, was in ruins; the accounts were in disarray and fiscal controls nonexistent; promotions were made without reference to merit; rations were insufficient in size and poor in quality; hygienic standards were abysmal; the guards had uniforms for guard duty and formal ceremonies but, lacking a "fatigue," or service uniform, were compelled to wear civilian clothes around the barracks and during exercises. More disturbing, at least for Repond, was the "moral disorder" of the corps. Officers lacked the character and respect necessary for authority. The halberdiers lacked discipline. A culture of low expectations pervaded the barracks, and everyone sought to get by with the least amount of effort.[75]

If the guardsmen expected to co-opt their new commander into the pervasive culture of mediocrity, they seriously underestimated his purpose, fortitude, and energy. Within weeks of his arrival, Repond had settled on a program to reform the Swiss Guard. Modest improvements and incremental change formed no part of that program. Repond would accept nothing less than a fundamental and immediate reorientation of the culture and practices of the corps that would redefine the unit by elevating its military identity over its ceremonial functions. For Repond, the Swiss Guard was first and foremost a military formation. Its primary purpose was not to amuse tourists or contribute a decorative element to events in Saint Peter's Basilica but to be ready to defend the Holy Father and the Apostolic Palace against any threat. The new commandant was prepared to crack heads and break halberds to drive that point home. When he revealed his plan to Captain Alois

Hirschbühl, the only officer he considered reliable because the young captain had joined the guard only in 1910 and had not been around long enough to be infected by the poisonous culture, he received a discouraging response. Hirschbühl may have been new, but he had quickly sized up his unit. He frankly told his commander that he was being unrealistic in expecting to change the guard. Significant change was unachievable, if only because it would require the immediate dismissal of three-fourths of the force.[76]

Undismayed, Colonel Repond was determined to pursue reform, and he knew he could rely on Captain Hirschbühl to help. On the other hand, he could not entirely count on his superiors. Of course no one in the higher reaches of the papal palace preferred mismanagement or corruption, but few were sufficiently interested in the pope's *corpi armati* to become active collaborators in reform. By 1911 concerns about the physical security of the Vatican had significantly dissipated, and as the threat of anticlerical assaults receded, so too did the need to maintain defenses. For his part, Pope Pius X could not be relied upon for close and active support. Pius, who was less inclined than his predecessors to define his relations with the Italian state in terms of a vendetta, did not consider the condition of his military forces a pressing matter. He was not at all certain that a modern pontiff should rely on armed guards to ensure the security of his throne, an attitude reinforced early in his pontificate when internal disagreements concerning compensation and expenses disturbed· the Palatine Guard and resulted in the resignations of several guardsmen. Known as the "peasant pope" for his simple origins and modest lifestyle, Pius may also have been skeptical of the expense of maintaining not just an armed force but four armed forces. Shortly after his election in 1903, he considered abolishing the Noble Guard, the most extravagant of his soldiers, and combining the remaining units into a single corps, but resistance from Catholic noble families caused him to abandon the idea.[77] Fortunately for Repond, the pope's powerful secretary of state, Cardinal Raphael Merry del Val, took an interest in the Swiss Guard and would turn out to be the new commandant's greatest ally, diligently defending him in the corridors of power and approving most of his requests for funds and proposals.

Repond intended to mold the Swiss Guard into a highly trained military unit characterized by strict discipline, complete professionalism, and an ethic of service and achievement, and he intended to begin immediately. A perfect storm of change descended upon the guard in 1911. Without their father to protect them, the spendthrift Meyer von Schauensee brothers had already resigned from the service. As the first step toward building a reliable officer corps, Repond now pushed out the door the equally compromised Karl Pfyffer von Altishofen, who was nominally his deputy commander. Next to go were eight invalid halberdiers who were on the muster roll and drew full salaries even though their infirmities kept them from performing any duties. The commandant opened an investigation into the abuse of official accounts, with the result that both Karl Pfyffer von Altishofen and the corps finance officer, Major Imsand, another officer on his way out, had their salaries or pensions docked until they made up the moneys that had disappeared through their abuse of office.

Each of the remaining officers was given responsibility for particular aspects of guard life and service, including training, duty assignments, finance, accommodations, and provisions. Each was accountable for any deficiencies in his area. Eager to broaden the professional education of his officers, Repond detached Captain Peter Glasson for a period of service in a German infantry regiment. To bring the corps to its authorized level, the new commandant took personal responsibility for recruiting and prepared a brochure describing the guard and the conditions of service for distribution by bishops and priests in Switzerland. To improve the quality and military preparation of recruits, he instituted a requirement that all applicants for admission to the guard had to have completed the basic infantry training course of the Swiss army. As for the preparation of serving halberdiers, Repond issued an order requiring daily gymnastic exercises, military drill, and weapons practice for all personnel under the direct supervision of officers, and he convinced Cardinal Merry del Val to designate the esplanade along the Belvedere wing of the papal palace for this purpose. Drills extended beyond the rote performance of the manual of arms to embrace tactical exercises, including practice deployments along the rooftops of the palace and Saint Peter's Basilica. To modernize the firepower of the corps, Repond retired the obsolete Remingtons and purchased 200 magazine-fed Mauser model 98 rifles, standard issue in the German army, with bayonets, bandoliers, and 200,000 rounds of ammunition. He instituted frequent target and bayonet practice.[78] He also acquired 210 hand grenades and considered stockpiling flares to provide illumination in the event of nighttime emergencies.

While focusing on military preparations, Repond did not ignore barracks life. He designed and introduced a light uniform for exercise and barracks wear and new, more practical headgear. Weekly footbaths were now required of all personnel, and sergeants were charged with inspecting the state of the quarters and cleanliness of bed linens each week. The restoration of San Pellegrino, the guard chapel next to the barracks, was set in motion, with donations and subsidies inveigled from various sources by the commandant. To reconnect the corps with its traditions and build unit pride and identity, Repond reinstituted the formal induction of recruits on May 6, the anniversary of the guard's supreme sacrifice during the sack of Rome in 1527, a ceremony that had fallen into disuse under previous commandants.[79]

And this was just the first year.

In his second year Repond maintained the pace of change, implementing a range of initiatives, including the acquisition of Dreyse 7.65-mm semiautomatic pistols (the same pistol issued to officers in the German army) for officers and noncommissioned officers; an increase in food rations (the bread ration was doubled); the introduction of daily Italian lessons for the troops; a directive requiring daily baths or showers; a prohibition against visits to taverns in the Borgo and Trastevere; a ban on discussing the affairs of the corps with outsiders, particularly journalists; and the inauguration of a Sunday lecture series covering a range of topics relevant to the ceremonial and protective missions of the guard, from a description of the papal administration to a review of recent assassination attempts against foreign leaders. The new commander also insisted on strict discipline and made it clear that infractions or insubordination would not be tolerated. A halberdier who disobeyed an order was immediately dismissed, as was another who defamed a colleague. For arriving thirty minutes late for duty muster, a halberdier was restricted to Vatican City for a full year, although he was later allowed to resign from the corps.[80]

In his spare time Repond designed and introduced a new wardrobe for the Swiss Guard. Under his command the corps would not just be different, it would look different. Legend has attributed the design and colors of the guard uniform to Michelangelo (or, alternately, Raphael), but in fact the gaily colored costume so recognizable to tourists and so entrenched in the popular imagination was created by Repond. Over the centuries the uniform of the guard had varied, usually reflecting the military fashion of European armies. Headgear, for instance, evolved through a variety of styles, ranging from a bicorn hat to the Prussian spiked helmet.[81] Repond wanted to create a uniform that connected the corps with its past and complemented the practical requirements of ceremonial and guard service. When not observing drills, writing requests for more funds, or thumbing through the catalogs of small-arms manufacturers, the commandant haunted the reading rooms of the Vatican Library and Archive and paced the corridors and chambers of the palace seeking printed references and visual images of the old guard. The result was a series of uniform designs—each appropriate for specific occasions (gala ceremonies, routine guard service) and functions (recruit training, squad exercises) and each complete from gloves and collars to cloaks and rain capes—that remain in service to this day.[82]

The guard reeled under the new regime. Jules Repond was trying to reverse more than a century of lassitude and demolish a deeply ingrained institutional culture. Resistance was inevitable. Most of the halberdiers were unhappy with their commander's reforms (at least those reforms that required them to work harder), and in the culture of the guard, when halberdiers were unhappy, they mutinied. It happened on July 17, 1913, while Repond was on leave in Switzerland. During the morning muster of the duty detachment in the barracks courtyard, twenty-one halberdiers refused to obey orders or perform duties. Ostensibly, their defiance was directed against the overbearing manner of Captain Peter Glasson, who perhaps had returned from his brief attachment to a German regiment overly impressed with German methods of command. That morning the defiant guardsmen hammered the butts of their rifles on the courtyard cobblestones and chanted, "We don't want Glasson."[83] The captain's behavior, however, was merely an excuse for a revolt against the unpopular regime instituted by the commandant. When, that same day, Major Adolf Glanzmann, the acting commandant, sought to pacify the rebellious halberdiers by sending Glasson from the Vatican on indefinite leave and promising that the cardinal secretary of state would consider their grievances with sympathy, the mutiny did not end. The malcontents sent a letter to Pope Pius detailing their grievances and demanding, among other things, the immediate resignation of Captain Glasson and his replacement from within the guard by one of their own; the selection of officers in the future only from among the noncommissioned officers of the guard; the end to the new exercises and drills; the revocation of the prohibition against visits to local taverns; amnesty for all halberdiers who had disobeyed orders or refused duties on July 17; and an order of the day from Colonel Repond, to be read out to the assembled guards by the commandant, announcing the acceptance of these demands.[84]

In the old guard, malcontents simply mutinied and appealed over the heads of their officers, but by July 1913 the old guard was dead. Colonel Repond had killed it. The demands of the mutineers—indeed, the very strike itself—were an attempt to resuscitate the corpse, but there was to be no resurrection, no return to the old days and ways. When informed by Major Glanzmann of the crisis, Colonel Repond departed immediately for Rome. He was inclined to be less accommodating than his deputy. On July 20, by which time the dissidents had not returned to discipline, Colonel Repond strapped on one of the new automatic pistols and strode purposefully into the courtyard outside the barracks, where the entire corps, including the mutineers, was assembled. The commandant had no intention of compromising his authority by submitting to the rebels, and he had bluntly informed Cardinal Secretary of State Merry del Val that it would be better for the Holy Father to abolish the Swiss Guard than to accept the demands, which were fundamentally incompatible with military discipline.[85] In front of his troops Repond read out an order of the day, which was not exactly the order the mutineers had demanded. For a moment they may have been encouraged because Repond began by announcing that Captain Glasson had resigned from the service. Satisfaction quickly turned to disappointment when the commandant went on to express his total contempt for the conduct of the discontented halberdiers, whom he berated for disobeying orders and violating the chain of command by going over his head to the pope. He asserted the necessity of discipline and his firm intention to punish any infringements of that discipline. Finally, he stated that he would not submit to any of the demands of the protesters. This was not what the mutineers had expected to hear, and there were vocal protests and tumult in the ranks. In response Repond put aside his order of the day, rested his hand on his pistol, and announced that he, not the halberdiers, was in command of the Swiss Guard, and he was prepared to demonstrate it.[86]

The mutiny collapsed. The rebels represented only a minority, and they had not been able to win over a majority of their comrades. The malcontents themselves were not willing to push their grievances further, probably because they suspected that their colonel, who had taken the precaution of locking the guard's weapons in the armory, was perfectly prepared to use that new pistol. Finally, their protest generated neither sympathy nor fear inside the Apostolic Palace. Cardinal Merry del Val, who had supported Repond's reforms, stood behind the commandant. As for the pope, he had no patience with the grievances of guardsmen. His initial response to the mutiny had been anger, and his inclination was to abolish the guard to put an end to these irritations, but prudence eventually won out over impulse. In the end, he replied to the mutineers' demands with a letter expressing his understanding of the problems with Captain Glasson but stating explicitly his displeasure with the insubordination of the guards. The pontiff declined to support any of the rebels' demands.[87]

Repond had been vindicated and his authority reaffirmed. The main figures of the mutiny, thirteen halberdiers, were expelled from the corps; their followers were punished with confinement to barracks; and almost everyone else resigned themselves to the new regime. Calm, if not contentment, returned to the barracks. The pace of change certainly did not slow, Repond considering the mutiny merely a bump on the road to reform. In the months following the mutiny the commandant hired a music master to offer guardsmen lessons in various instruments, ordered duty officers to carry pistols when making their rounds, instituted for the halberdiers visits to cultural and historical monuments in Rome, and purchased more small-caliber rifles for marksmanship practice.[88] Nor did the intensity of training let up. On "free" days (i.e., days on which they were not on guard duty), the halberdiers performed calisthenics; marched; and practiced shooting, fencing, and fighting with a bayonet. Sunday was not a day of rest from exercises. If it rained, the halberdiers simply moved into the lecture room to listen to talks about weapons, service regulations, or the history of the corps.[89]

The biggest problem now facing the commander was not resistance but recruitment. Inattention to recruitment, Repond believed, had contributed to the mutiny of 1913 by allowing the admission of young men unprepared by experience and unsuited by temperament for military duty in the service of His Holiness. The challenge was to find men with the necessary moral and martial qualities and then retain them through financial incentives that rewarded long and meritorious service. The corps had not reached its authorized strength of 133 men for years, and the problem was aggravated after the mutiny as the perpetrators were dismissed and others unhappy with the new guard simply quit. A month after the mutiny, the strength of the corps briefly fell to forty-three halberdiers, the lowest ever.[90] Subsequently, the numbers began to inch upward, but the corps remained far below its authorized force level. By the outbreak of World War I a year later, a serious problem had evolved into a full-blown crisis.

The officers and men of the Swiss Guard retained their Swiss citizenship (which by 1914 was an absolute requirement for admission to the corps), with all duties and obligations, including military service, connected to that citizenship. Since the national army of Switzerland was based on a citizen militia with only a small core of regular soldiers, all Swiss males of military age, no matter their place of residence or their occupation, were subject to mobilization. Though none of the pope's halberdiers had ever been recalled into the national army, the possibility was always present. In the aftermath of the assassination of Archduke Franz Ferdinand and his wife on June 28, 1914, as clouds of war darkened the skies over Europe and governments sought protection from the threatening storm in military preparations, possibility turned into reality.

To protect its neutrality, Switzerland mobilized its army. On August 1, 1914, while Repond was on leave at his home in Switzerland, the acting commandant of the guard, Major Adolf Glanzmann, received a notification from the Swiss legation in Rome. The notice identified more than a dozen Swiss Guards who were required to return immediately to the homeland for military service. The men left that very night. Informed of events by his deputy, who warned of additional recalls, Colonel Repond rushed immediately to Berne, the Swiss capital, to speak with the head of the military department, Camille Decoppet, and the chief of the general staff, Colonel Theophil von Sprecher, an old friend from his years in the Swiss army. Repond asked for an exemption from mobilization for his guards. Decoppet told him that such an exemption required a decision by the Federal Council but that he would submit Repond's request for consideration. Upon returning to his country house to await a decision, Repond found two telegrams from Glanzmann requesting his immediate return to Rome. He left immediately for Italy without receiving a definite response to his request from the Swiss Federal Council.[91]

The commandant arrived in the Eternal City to confront a growing crisis. By now almost fifty guards had returned to Switzerland, and additional departures were anticipated. Then, on August 20, Pius X died. From the perspective of the Swiss Guard, it was a most untimely death. Reduced again to forty-three effective members, the corps simply could not handle the additional guard and ceremonial duties that attended the death of a pope, the conclave summoned to elect a replacement, and the coronation of a new pope. Repond was forced to adopt drastic measures. First, he appealed to retired guards who were still living in Rome and its environs to return to temporary duty. When that appeal failed to produce enough bodies, the commandant sought out any Swiss males living in the Eternal City, presumably assuring them that all they would have to do was put on a uniform and stand at a door with a halberd. For a man who had staked his reputation on professionalizing the Swiss Guard, the humiliation of asking civilians to don a costume and pretend to be a halberdier must have been painful. There still were not enough volunteers, but the rector of the German-Hungarian College, a residence for German and Hungarian priests pursuing studies in Rome, offered the services of his students. Fifteen young priests, substituting striped uniforms for black cassocks and halberds for breviaries, and returning each night to their seminary, served for a month, just long enough for Repond to get past the enthronement of the new pope, Benedict XV.[92]

The Swiss Guard suffered from a lack of personnel throughout World War I. The situation improved slightly after June 1915, when the Swiss general staff agreed that tradition and the honor to the homeland of protecting the Holy Father justified exempting current members of the guard from national mobilization, a decision that allowed mobilized guardsmen to return to Rome. Despite the exemption, staffing remained a problem because there could be no recruitment during the war. Repond worried that without sufficient numbers, the corps would be unable to perform its basic function of ensuring the safety of the pope.

From his first day as commander, Repond had operated on the premise that the primary purpose of the Swiss Guard was not ceremonial service but the protection of the Holy Father and the Vatican. Much of the disappointment and frustration he felt upon assuming command stemmed from the discovery that over the centuries the guard had forsaken its protective role in favor of the less demanding ceremonial role. Most of his reforms were directed at redressing that imbalance. By the early twentieth century, the fears of a physical threat to the pope, so pervasive in the aftermath of Porta Pia, had largely receded among Vatican authorities, few of whom could imagine the pontifical guards having to fight off attackers. For his part, Repond believed that the absence of an immediate threat did not negate the possibility of a future threat and that it would be irresponsible for the pope's guards to be complacent rather than prepared. Countries, after all, did not wait for an invasion to organize an army, and communities did not establish a police force only when a crime was being committed.

Repond's robust program to rearm the Swiss Guard with modern weapons and train the officers and men in military maneuvers suggests that he did not consider the defense of the Vatican or the protection of the Holy Father a purely nominal responsibility. The guard, however, shared this responsibility with the Pontifical Gendarmeria. The relationship between the Swiss Guard and the papal police was complicated and often difficult because the division of responsibilities between the two corps was not always clear. Both were jealous of their status and quick to assert and defend their prerogatives. Although Repond was always watchful for any effort by the gendarmeria to intrude onto the "turf" of the guard, there was much about the police that he admired, such as their concern with encouraging firearms training among the gendarmes. Furthermore, he realized that the mission of protecting the Vatican required cooperation between the two services. Indeed, when the guard acquired two hundred modern Mauser rifles in 1911, the commandant promptly transferred eighty of the rifles to the gendarmeria in order to standardize as much as possible the armament of the two corps. Such cooperation did not extend to the Noble and Palatine Guards, units that Repond never took seriously.[93]

Accompanied by Commander Ceccopieri, chief of the gendarmeria, he made his first security survey of the Apostolic Palace in March 1911, noting the placement of guard posts and roving patrols, the location of doorways and staircases, and the arrangement of rooms. Such surveys would be repeated at regular intervals, and even the pope's personal quarters received his detailed attention. While inspecting the papal bedroom during one such survey, Repond noticed that the pontifical bed was positioned against an interior wall, opposite tall windows that opened onto Saint Peter's Square. Concerned that a marksman on the Gianiculum, the hill that overlooks the square from the south and provides an unobstructed view of the Apostolic Palace, could fire through the window and hit any target on the bed, the guard commander advised the papal chamberlains to move the bed to a less exposed position.[94]

Although rearmament and retraining were the keystones of his effort to improve the defenses of the Vatican, Repond also made changes in the way in which halberdiers were deployed. By tradition, the Swiss Guard was responsible for the entrances to the papal palace and the approaches to the pontifical apartments. Upon assuming command, Repond immediately tightened security by establishing two new guard posts inside the palace, directing that between 9:00 P.M. and 7:00 A.M. sentinels at all posts would carry a rifle and fifty rounds of ammunition, and requiring duty officers to carry a loaded pistol while completing their rounds. In the event of an emergency, the commandant expected to call out off-duty halberdiers from the barracks to reinforce the posts. On December 1, 1912, for example, when anticlericals organized a march through Trastevere and along the right bank of the Tiber near the Vatican, Repond called out the entire corps at 2:00 A.M., hours before the scheduled demonstration; issued rifles and cartridges; and deployed the men to positions at the gates and inside the palace. The threat proved illusory because the demonstrators dispersed before reaching the Vatican, but nobody could say the Swiss Guard had been napping.[95]

The recall to Switzerland of more than half the halberdiers upon the onset of World War I seriously compromised Repond's efforts to ensure the security of the Vatican. Before the war, 36 men were required to cover all the posts during a single watch tour.[96] Even at its authorized strength of 133 men, the corps would have been hard-pressed to maintain such a deployment, and the burden on the halberdiers, who had a regimen of exercises and training when not scheduled for guard duty, would have been heavy. When, after Swiss mobilization, unit strength dropped to 40 halberdiers and 3 officers, the usual deployment proved impossible. Repond was compelled to suppress certain guard posts and reduce the number of men assigned to the remaining posts. The guard was so overburdened in the first year of the war that the picket protecting the papal apartments had to be withdrawn and its duties partially assumed by the Noble Guard. During the morning hours reserved for papal audiences and receptions, the picket of a half-dozen or more halberdiers normally assigned to honor-guard duty in the anterooms of the papal apartment was ("at the request of Colonel Repond") withdrawn, leaving only a single halberdier as sentry at the head of the Scala Nobile, the grand staircase at the entrance to the anterooms. Ceremonial duty in the anterooms was now left to the Noble Guard and the Palatine Guard. In the small but fiercely competitive world of the papal armed forces, this transfer of responsibility represented a serious loss of face for the Swiss, but Colonel Repond insisted that the Swiss Guard, even in its reduced state, retain the responsibility for guarding the pontifical apartment at night with a post of two halberdiers.[97]

The situation improved in the second year of the war, when the men recalled to Switzerland were allowed to return to the Vatican. Repond was able to reopen some of the suppressed posts. Force levels, however, remained low throughout the war, not just for the Swiss Guard but for all the units of the corpi armati, especially when Italy's entry into the war on the side of the Allies in May 1915 called to the national colors many of the personnel of the all-Italian Pontifical Gendarmeria, Palatine Guard, and Noble Guard. The gendarmeria alone faced the loss of fifty-nine of its eighty-two men in the face of a general mobilization in Italy, with the prospect of recruiting suitable replacements very dim. So many Palatines were called up that the corps was reduced to barely seventy men, and these were the oldest in the unit. Two Palatine guardsmen were killed in action while serving with the Italian army. By July 1915 the Noble Guard, which usually maintained during the day a detachment of one officer, one cadet, and six guardsmen in the antechamber of the papal apartments as an honor guard to receive visitors, had to reduce that detachment to one officer and two guards because it no longer had enough personnel for a full picket. Recruits were scarce. Between Italy's entry into the war in May 1915 and the armistice of November 1918 the Noble Guard, for example, added only one person, and he was thirty-nine years old, not a prime age for conscription and national military service.[98]

The weakened state of the pontifical armed forces worried service commanders because the political position of the Vatican during the war was precarious. Despite its formal posture of strict neutrality, the Vatican was seen by many in Italy as favoring the cause of the Central Powers, particularly Austria-Hungary. In some Allied countries, particularly France, Benedict XV was characterized unjustly as *la boche pape*, and German and Austrian sympathizers were thought to fill the offices and apartments of the papal palace. The Vatican, which feared that belligerence would bring financial, political, and social ruin to Italy, worked to prevent Italy's entry into the war in the spring of 1915. This effort convinced many that the pope and his collaborators were committed to protecting Austria even at the expense of the perceived national interests of Italy. Allegations of pro–Central Power and, conversely, anti-Italian sympathies were fueled in 1916 when Monsignor Rudolf Gerlach, a private chamberlain and close associate of the pope, was implicated in a German espionage and sabotage ring. This group allegedly disseminated neutralist propaganda through Catholic newspapers in the period before Italian belligerency and, after Italy's entry into the war in May 1915, organized the destruction in port of two Italian battleships.[99]

Given the climate of suspicion, it was easy for the more easily alarmed denizens of the pontifical palace to imagine the Italian government or some anticlerical mob moving to suppress or punish the allegedly traitorous nest of spies inside the Vatican. Concern deepened when, in August 1916, in retaliation for the bombing of Venice by Austrian aircraft, the Italian authorities seized the Palazzo Venetia, the Austrian embassy to the Holy See. When Italy entered the war, the Austrian and German embassies to the Vatican, both of which were located outside the Vatican in Rome, had relocated to Switzerland, so the palace was empty, but the seizure seemingly violated the Law of Guarantees (admittedly never ratified by the Vatican) that assured the unhindered operation of foreign diplomatic missions to the Holy See. If the Italian authorities were prepared to seize that palace, which was the legal property of the Austrian government and theoretically protected under international law, then what might be in store for the Vatican and its properties? Concerns multiplied when the Italian government tried to confiscate the German College, a residence for German-speaking priests pursuing studies in Rome, which was located in the shadow of Saint Peter's Basilica. This action was blocked, but the affair suggested a more aggressive attitude on the part of royal authorities. Any papal official who tried to discern the intentions of the Italian government by reviewing the 1879 Law of Guarantees that set forth the government's view of the legal status of the Vatican would not have been comforted. The Law of Guarantees stipulated that the Holy Father "enjoyed" the possession of the Apostolic Palace and various other properties in Rome, but it did not actually acknowledge that the pope owned the palace and the properties. Would the Italian government be so bold as to occupy the Vatican as it had occupied the Palazzo Venezia?[100]

Separated by almost a century from these events, one can easily dismiss the fears as unrealistic since the Italian authorities were unlikely to risk a dramatic act that would alienate Catholics in Italy and abroad in the midst of a war that was not always going well for Italy. The commanders of the pope's armed services, however, did not have the benefit of historical hindsight. The commander of the Swiss Guard in particular was inclined by temperament to prepare for the worst. After all, there were still individuals in the Vatican who recalled the late summer of 1870, when many observers confidently assured each other that the Italian government would never risk Catholic opinion by daring to attack Rome.

After Italy entered the war, the Vatican adopted special wartime measures. In anticipation of fires, custodians of the Apostolic Palace augmented the Vatican fire service, prepared emergency cisterns for water, and purchased additional fire extinguishers. Bomb-proof refuges were prepared for personnel. Air-raid observation posts were established to scan the night skies for aircraft approaching the Vatican. In an exceptional action, the Pontifical Gendarmeria arranged for the Italian police commander responsible for the Vatican to receive a special pass that allowed entry into Saint Peter's Basilica and the precincts of the Apostolic Palace any time of the day or night.[101]

For the pontifical armed forces, guard duties increased, and the undermanned units were hard-pressed to meet the new demands. Almost weekly there were new directives from Vatican authorities governing the hours when various gates, passageways, and corridors would be open. Additional directives provided guidance on who would be admitted to what sections of the palace at what particular times. Some individuals were excluded by name, such as a certain Signor Kutruff and his wife, who were to be denied entry when they appeared at the gates, although the directive to the Swiss Guard did not mention the reason for this banishment. Sometimes whole categories of people were excluded. No one wearing an Italian uniform, for example, could be allowed past the gates, although an exception was made for employees of the post and telegraph services who delivered the mail. Later the prohibition was extended to anyone wearing the colors of the Italian flag.

For Jules Repond the war was not an excuse to reduce the operational tempo of the Swiss Guard, although activities were constrained by the lack of personnel. Daily exercises continued, with an increased emphasis on weapons training. In April 1916, for example, pistol practice in the more distant reaches of the Vatican gardens, formerly required only of officers, was extended to the entire corps. The commandant continued his security surveys of the palace and its grounds and juggled guard plans and duty assignments in response to changing force levels and circumstances. When, for example, the gendarmeria concluded that the loss of its men to Italian mobilization would force it to eliminate patrols in the Vatican Gardens, Repond agreed to assign halberdiers to the area. To improve the physical defenses of the Vatican, a subject no one had given a thought to in centuries, the commandant stored sandbags and barbed wire at gates and other locations to be brought out in an emergency. At all their posts, halberdiers, except those on daytime honor-guard service in the reception rooms of the papal apartments, abandoned their halberds in favor of rifles and bayonets. In the spring of 1916, after a disgruntled halberdier, angry over his dismissal for insubordination, fired two rounds from his Mauser from the window of his room at an officer, bullets were no longer allowed in the barracks. Thereafter, ammunition was kept in the armory and at each guard post in locked boxes for which the senior guard at the post had a key.[102]

The end of World War I on November 11, 1918, brought a welcome respite to the pope's military units, which throughout the conflict had struggled to fulfill their ceremonial and protective duties. The extra guard posts and patrols, as well as the double duty shifts, were wound down, and force levels gradually returned to normal with Italian and Swiss demobilization. For Jules Repond, the conclusion of the war represented the vindication of his efforts to reform and renew the Swiss Guard. The shameful abuses and distressing inadequacies that had plagued the corps for more than a century were now just an unpleasant memory. The music-hall soldiers who looked and acted as if they were players in an operetta set in the mythical kingdom of Ruritania were also a thing of the past. The new guard—Repond's guard—was a military unit in practice as well as name. Never had it been better prepared by discipline, training, and equipment to fulfill its responsibility to protect the Holy Father and defend the Vatican. It was an achievement that would have attracted the respect and praise of military professionals in any country, but in the Vatican it was barely acknowledged and less appreciated. In some quarters it was even resented.

Repond was concerned with redressing the balance between the ceremonial and protective roles of the Swiss Guard because he believed that the scale had tipped too far in favor of the ceremonial function. Few inside the Apostolic Palace agreed with him because few believed, despite the temporary alarums and excursions of the war, that the threats facing the papacy in the early twentieth century were of a kind that could be deterred, deflected, or defeated by rifles and bayonets. The dangers were no longer Italian military aggression or fanatical anticlericalism but materialism, secularism, and nationalism. Against such threats the pope's best defense was not his soldiers but his stature as a moral leader and teacher. Repond would not have been unaware of this attitude. Swiss Guards still recount a story that captures the tension between the two visions of how best to defend the Vatican. According to the probably apocryphal story, the commandant asked Pius X to review his plans for the defense of the Vatican in the event of an attack. Looking over the diagrams, the pontiff noticed one sector that was marked as important and inquired about it. "That's where we will place a cannon," the commandant allegedly responded. "Can you actually fire that cannon?" Pius asked. "Of course," Repond replied. "Well, then," Pius said, "our cannons are going to stay in the cellar where they belong because the Vatican will not be defended by cannons."[103]

Jules Repond may have been an effective commander, but he was never a popular one either inside the barracks or inside the Apostolic Palace. His position was strong so long as he retained the confidence of his direct superior, the influential cardinal secretary of state, Merry del Val. This support, however, could not be taken for granted, and even with his best ally, the commandant occasionally crossed the line. A request, for example, to purchase a half-dozen machine guns was denied by Merry del Val, who concluded that there were limits to how well armed the Swiss Guard needed to be.[104] Repond lost his patron in August 1914 upon the election of Benedict XV. Merry del Val resigned, to be replaced as cardinal secretary of state first by Domenico Ferrata and then by Pietro Gasparri, prelates much less interested in the state of the guard. The commandant now had no powerful voice to advance his ideas and confound his critics. After the war, those critics became more numerous and more vocal.

By 1920 rumors began to circulate in the Vatican that the commandant would resign. Rumor became fact in the spring of 1921, when Repond submitted his resignation on grounds of ill health. The commandant was sixty-eight, older than his six immediate predecessors at the time of their resignations, so health may well have been a motivation. On the other hand, he lived until the age of eighty, enjoying good health and pursuing his interest in travel and historical research right up to the end of his life, which came during a return visit to Rome in 1933. There is evidence, moreover, that the colonel was pushed out of command and that he did not go quietly. Apparently, his letter of resignation did not please Pope Benedict, who returned it with the order to submit a different letter that referred to health considerations as the only reason for his departure—an order that leaves one wondering what reasons were given in the first letter and why those reasons were found unacceptable by the Holy Father.[105]

Although Jules Repond walked out of the Swiss Guard barracks for the last time on July 1, 1921, his spirit continued to inhabit the corridors and courtyards long after his departure. No commandant in the modern history of the guard had been more influential in defining and shaping the corps. He was the father of the modern Swiss Guard. The persistence and importance of his legacy would become apparent two decades after his departure when danger again visited the Vatican.

CHAPTER 7

Armed Neutrality

It was a few minutes past 8:00 on the evening of November 5, 1943, and at the Bronze Door, the main entrance to the papal palace and the control post of the Swiss Guards, the duty squad had just changed the guard. The halberdiers were teasing Corporal Hoffstetter, a good-natured comrade who was known for his sense of humor, when they heard a plane flying low over Vatican City. By late 1943 Allied air attacks around Rome were common, but the planes generally focused on railway yards and other military targets on the outskirts of the city. It was rare for a plane actually to fly over the pope's tiny domain, which everyone understood to be neutral territory. Seconds later the first bomb landed near the radio station, demolishing a water tank and knocking Vatican Radio off the air. The second bomb landed immediately behind the Palace of the Governor of Vatican City, blasting out doors and windows, collapsing interior walls, and knocking senseless a papal gendarme who was on guard duty. The mosaic workshop received a direct hit from the third bomb, which launched thousands of tiny pieces of colored tile flying through the night and sent two Palatine Guards on duty outside the nearby train station diving for cover. The last bomb exploded in Saint Martha's Square, right next to Saint Peter's Basilica, blowing out the windows of the most famous church in Christendom and peppering the other buildings on the square with shrapnel, including a large fragment that penetrated the apartment of the Brazilian ambassador to the Vatican and embedded itself in the wall of his sitting room.

The explosions rocked the papal palace on the other side of Saint Peter's from the impact points. At the Bronze Door, the blasts showered glass on the guards and knocked halberds and rifles from their racks. The stunned halberdiers had no idea what had happened; the first guess was that the dome of Saint Peter's had collapsed. Corporal Hof, relieved of duty at the door, had just removed his uniform and climbed into a cot in the guardroom to catch a quick nap when the bombs hit. Annoyed by the noise and commotion, Hof, in his underwear, shuffled to the guardroom door—and, unwittingly, into the lore of the Swiss Guard—yelled, "Tell those guys to knock it off. I'm trying to sleep," and then returned to his slumber. Everyone else was quite awake. The post's telephone had begun ringing almost immediately after the last explosion. An official on night duty in the office of the master of the palace had

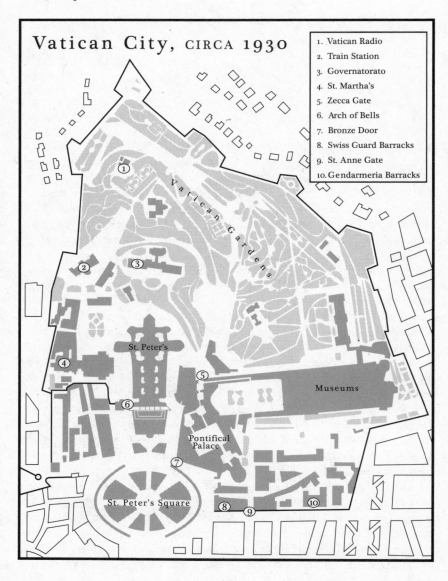

Vatican City, CIRCA 1930

1. Vatican Radio
2. Train Station
3. Governatorato
4. St. Martha's
5. Zecca Gate
6. Arch of Bells
7. Bronze Door
8. Swiss Guard Barracks
9. St. Anne Gate
10. Gendarmeria Barracks

Vatican Gardens

St. Peter's

Museums

Pontifical Palace

St. Peter's Square

heard the blasts and wanted to know what was happening. The guard post at the Zecca, the site of the old papal mint immediately behind the basilica, called to report that the Vatican was under air attack. By this time the duty sergeant had rallied his men and sent out two halberdiers to reconnoiter. Even before the scouts returned, the facts were evident: For the first time in four centuries, the Vatican—residence of the pope, administrative center of the Roman Catholic Church, and religious and cultural icon for hundreds of millions of people around the globe—had been attacked. War had come to the Vatican.[1] It was exactly the situation for which Colonel Jules Repond had worked so hard to prepare the Swiss Guard, but Repond was dead, and it had been almost a quarter century since the hard-driving commandant had tried to reshape the guard into a serious military unit capable of honoring its sworn duty to defend the pope. Now the success of that effort was about to be tested.

In the aftermath of World War I, Italy felt itself more a victim than a victor of the conflict. Disappointed by its failure at the Versailles peace conference to secure its territorial ambitions, weakened by the economic dislocations of the war, racked by increasingly violent class conflict, and directed by a corrupt and discredited political caste that seemingly placed personal advantage over the public good, the country drifted from crisis to crisis. Riding the crest of political instability was Benito Mussolini, a fiery journalist who had led a new political movement, the so-called Fascists, from the distant margins to the very center of Italian politics. Chauvinistic, nationalistic, and contemptuous of traditional politics, the movement preferred clubs to compromise and bullets to ballots, but many in the established political class and the conventional political parties tolerated Fascist violence. In the turmoil of the early 1920s, they courted Mussolini's political support, and they believed they could control him and his armed squads. They were wrong.

As political violence escalated and the political establishment and its institutions proved incapable of guaranteeing social and economic order or articulating a compelling strategy to address the country's ills, conservatives in the royal court, the civil administration, the military, the business sector, and the Catholic Church began to see Mussolini as the only one who could end the disorder. When, in October 1922, Mussolini called on his followers to sweep away the ineffective leaders by marching on Rome and seizing the reins of power, few could find the will or the courage to stand against the Fascists. King Vittorio Emanuele III, typically more concerned with the security of his throne than the well-being of his subjects, meekly acceded to Mussolini's demand that he be appointed prime minister with the power to form a new government.

The Fascists were now in control, and rather quickly they made it clear that they had no intention of sharing power or tolerating opposition. With little objection from other important political institutions, such as the Catholic Church, the monarchy, or the military, Mussolini instituted a series of repressive measures that emasculated the parliament, curbed the press, marginalized the king, elevated violence to a common instrument of politics, and set Italy on an increasingly authoritarian path. Anyone who raised a voice in protest was intimidated into silence or exile or simply murdered. By 1926, the "Duce," Mussolini's preferred title, was effectively the dictator of Italy.

The Vatican made no more protest against the imposition of an authoritarian state than any other organization in Italian life, although it often deplored the "excesses" that were all too often a feature of that state. A fundamentally conservative institution, it viewed with trepidation the social and political disorder that followed World War I and, with the antireligious Bolshevik Revolution in Russia always foremost in its mind, believed that only with a firm hand on the rudder of the ship of state could Italy navigate between the rocks of political anarchy and the shoals of godless social revolution. With the leaders of the traditional parliamentary parties largely discredited, the Vatican concluded that Mussolini was most likely to provide that firm hand.

The view from the Apostolic Palace was also influenced by the fact that the aspiring dictator actively courted the papacy's support. In an earlier, more socially radical phase of his political career, Mussolini had written scurrilous polemics against the Catholic Church, describing priests as "black microbes who are as fatal to mankind as tuberculosis germs."[2] The early manifestos of the Fascist movement were also explicitly anticlerical, calling for the expropriation of church property and the eradication of religious influence from Italian society. These attitudes were conveniently (if only temporarily) abandoned in the early 1920s as Mussolini and his movement sought the favor of the Catholic Church to bolster their political position. Upon assuming power, Mussolini placated the Vatican with several prochurch measures, including the introduction of religious education in state primary schools, the placement of crucifixes in public buildings, and the provision of state funds for the restoration of churches and monasteries. Mussolini's most important change, however, was his clear signal that he was determined to settle once and for all the Roman Question, the contentious issue of the pope's legal and political status in Italy that had poisoned church-state relations since the loss of the Papal States in 1870. By the mid-1920s both sides had wearied of the stalemate, and both were ready for a settlement.

Representatives of the Vatican and the Fascist regime opened preliminary conversations on the subject in the summer of 1926, and these unofficial and highly secret talks continued until the fall of 1928, when sufficient progress had been made that both sides were prepared to announce the opening of "official" negotiations. These negotiations culminated in February 1929 when Cardinal Secretary of State Pietro Gasparri and Benito Mussolini signed the so-called Lateran Agreements, three documents that established an entity, Vatican City, as an independent and perpetually neutral state; regulated church-state relations in Italy by means of a concordat (treaty); and provided the Vatican with financial compensation for the loss of the Papal States in the preceding century.[3]

By recognizing the sovereign independence of Vatican City and defining its borders, the Lateran Agreements resolved the Roman Question and reestablished, though on a much-reduced scale, the temporal power of the

Holy Father. Smaller than most golf courses and college campuses, the new city-state encompassed a mere 110 acres of territory, not counting several basilicas and buildings in Rome and Castel Gandolfo, the papal villa in the Alban Hills outside the city, over which the Lateran Agreements recognized the pope's dominion. Despite its diminutive size, it proudly adopted and self-consciously displayed all the accoutrements of sovereignty. There now were Vatican citizens (the few hundred individuals who actually lived inside the papal city), and they traveled on Vatican passports. The Vatican flag—yellow and white vertical fields with the papal tiara and crossed keys of Saint Peter in the white field—flew over buildings and land. Vatican stamps graced envelopes, postcards, and packages mailed in the Vatican post office, although all items had to be entrusted to the Italian postal service for transport beyond the pope's walls. Vatican coinage purchased items, tax free, in Vatican stores. There were Vatican laws, Vatican courts, and even a Vatican jail. And, of course, the Vatican military, no longer an army without a state, protected the papal frontier, which, counting every angle and salient in the perimeter walls that encompassed the new state, extended only a little farther than 3 kilometers.

Assuming, somewhat unimaginatively, that Italy faced a choice between social chaos and Fascist authoritarianism, the papacy initially bet on the latter as the lesser of two evils. Initially, the general détente in church-state relations in the 1920s, culminating in the Lateran Agreements, suggested that the Vatican had wagered wisely. Events, however, would prove it wrong. For Mussolini, accommodation with the Catholic Church was simply a political expedient to harness the Vatican to Fascism in order to buttress the legitimacy of his regime at home and abroad and disarm a potentially significant political opponent. When the church proved an unreliable or recalcitrant partner in pursuit of his goals, the Duce did not hesitate to abandon accommodation in favor of hostility. For his part, Pope Pius XI did not intend to become the chaplain of Fascism, nor did he believe that the resolution of the Roman Question and improved church-state relations required blanket support for Mussolini and his regime.

The ink was hardly dry on the ceremonial copies of the Lateran Agreements when cooperation turned into conflict. Now that he had his propaganda victory, Mussolini and his fellow Fascists returned to their polemical attacks, criticizing the church for its failure to embrace enthusiastically the social and political revolution that was allegedly cleansing Italy and returning the country to the greatness it deserved. In addition, the fascists launched a political campaign of insult, innuendo, and intimidation against Catholic Action, an umbrella organization for Catholic lay associations such as Catholic Boy Scouts and Catholic university students. Catholic Action had been established to imbue Italian associational and professional life with Christian principles, but with the collapse of traditional political parties and the "fascisization" of youth, student, trade, and professional groups, it remained the only independent organization in Italy. As such it became a magnet for opponents of the regime. In a regime with totalitarian aspirations, no such group with its pretensions to independence of thought and action could be allowed to exist. In response to the Fascist attack against Catholic Action and the broader threat to the independence of the church represented by that attack, Pius XI issued, in June 1931, an encyclical, *Non abbiamo bisogno*, which by criticizing the regime's assault on Catholic associations, rejecting its claim to control all aspects of private life, and condemning the glorifica-tion of the state and the cult of violence sharply challenged the pretensions of Fascism and confirmed that the church would not be a quiet handmaiden of the government.

The conflict over Catholic Action was eventually defused by an agree-ment that the movement would continue as a social and religious association that explicitly eschewed any political program or action, but the "Crisis of 1931" set the pattern for church-state relations throughout the 1930s. The papacy and the Fascist regime coexisted in an uneasy relationship marked as frequently by tension and distrust as by accommodation and collabora-tion. Tensions increased markedly after the German annexation of Austria in March 1938, when Pope Pius, particularly concerned that Italy was following in the wake of Germany, became more vocal in his condemnation of nation-alism, militarism, and racialism.

Pius XI died on February 10, 1939, and on March 1 the conclave of cardi-nals elected as his successor the cardinal secretary of state, Eugenio Pacelli, who took the name Pius XII. In the early months of his pontificate, the new pope hoped to mediate the differences and tensions among the great pow-ers that threatened to push Europe into another war. The German invasion of Poland on September 1, 1939, marked the collapse of those hopes. Over the following nine months Pius worked to prevent the war from spreading, particularly to Italy. In the hope of ending the war by ending the regime that had started it, he secretly agreed, in the fall of 1939, to be a channel of communication between anti-Nazi conspirators in the German army and intelligence service and the British government as the German conspirators sought to determine how London would react to a military coup in Berlin. These clandestine exchanges, the "Roman conversations," extended over several months but came to nothing, foundering on distrust in London and indecisiveness in Berlin.[4] For his part, Pius had dangerously exposed himself by collaborating in a conspiracy to overthrow the Nazi regime. This exposure was magnified in early May 1940, when the pope, having learned from the German conspirators that Hitler was about to invade Belgium, France, and the Netherlands, sent warnings of the impending attack to the intended tar-gets. Despite the warnings, the German offensive on May 10, 1940, caught the targets unprepared. Within weeks German armies would reach the Atlantic, and Hitler would be the master of Europe.

In the spring of 1940 Pius was also preoccupied with keeping Italy out of the war. Bedazzled by German military victories, convinced that Hitler would soon command Europe, and tempted by the rewards that would accrue to any friend who stood by the Führer's side at the moment of final victory, Mussolini had by the late spring of 1940 decided to lead Italy into the war. As the Fascist propaganda machine blew the trumpets of war, discordant notes could not be tolerated. The Vatican, which Mussolini publicly decried, on April 25, 1940, as the "chronic appendicitis of Italy," was especially open to attack because Vatican Radio and the Vatican daily newspaper, the *Osservatore Romano*, were the only sources in Italy of uncensored news and opinion.[5] In the first months of the war the paper in particular was justifiably seen by the Fascist regime as unsympathetic toward Germany and Italian participation in the war, and in May 1940 the regime launched a campaign of intimidation and violence to suppress the paper and, by implication, to warn the Vatican away from any antiwar or antiregime posture. Fascist newspapers warned citizens against purchasing the *Osservatore Romano* ("the servant of the enemies of Italy and the evident mouthpiece of the Jews," according to *Regime Fascista*); police turned away shipments of the paper at railway stations in various Italian cities and arrested vendors; and thugs destroyed news kiosks that sold the paper and manhandled citizens found reading it on the streets.[6]

It was clear, however, that the Vatican was the real target of this campaign of intimidation. In May 1940, while carrying Pius across Rome to say mass at a local church, the papal limousine was held up by stopped traffic. At that moment a mob of Fascist youths surrounded the vehicle, screaming, "Down with the pope" and "Death to the pope." The roadway suddenly cleared, and the limousine sped away with a badly shaken pope, but it had been an ugly scene and one certainly orchestrated by the regime.[7] Around the same time a mob appeared at the Saint Anne gate, the service entrance to Vatican City, demonstrating against the *Osservatore Romano* and shouting for the editor, the anti-Fascist count Giuseppe Dalla Torre, to come out and face them. The Swiss Guards on duty at the gate, which is next to the guard barracks, promptly closed and barred the entry, but this did little to discourage the demonstrators, who intensified their shouts and threats. The Swiss duty officer, who had rushed to the scene, concluded that there could be real trouble. "Load rifles," he shouted, and for a moment the halberdiers were frozen by surprise. Each Swiss post had a rack of Mauser rifles and a supply of ammunition, but the weapons were kept unloaded even when carried by a sentinel. This was the first time in anyone's memory that an order to load rifles had been given except in drills. Recovering from their shock, the guardsmen jumped to the weapons rack. Metal ammunition boxes, which had grown stiff and rusty from lack of use, were broken open, and cartridges were hurriedly pressed into magazines. "We felt like an old plow, rusted from long disuse," recalled a halberdier who was on duty that day, "but shining like new after the first furrow when it has again been set into the hard soil." Before the situation deteriorated into violence, the duty officer received a phone call. The cardinal secretary of state, Luigi Maglione, had learned of the disturbance and now ordered the Swiss Guards to remain behind the closed gates and to refrain from shooting under any circumstances. Anyone climbing the gate or gaining entry into Vatican City was to be taken into custody but not harmed. Fortunately, the mob dispersed without further incident, but to the halberdiers deployed with their loaded rifles behind the gate, it was clear that the business of protecting the Holy Father and Vatican City would no longer be business as usual.[8]

The political currents of the interwar period created waves in church-state relations, and ripples of change reached even the pontifical armed forces. The Lateran Agreements of 1929 and the subsequent papal decrees that delineated the political institutions, processes, and laws of the new Vatican city-state introduced certain changes in the disposition of the corpi armati.[9] Some changes were minor and, at the time, of little practical significance, such as the granting of Vatican citizenship to the Swiss Guards while they were in papal service or the transfer of the Pontifical Gendarmeria from the authority of the cardinal secretary of state to that of the newly established office of governor of Vatican City. Other changes affected the living conditions of the forces. With funds provided by the financial settlement from the Italian government, Pope Pius XI went on a building spree to complete and adorn his tiny kingdom. The papal domain became one large construction site as the pontiff ordered new buildings, roads, walls, and utilities. A train station with less than a hundred yards of track connecting to the Italian rail system was paid for by the Italian government. Some projects, such as new walls to delimit the frontier, were required under the terms of the agreements, but most, particularly a radio station, a governor's palace with lavish reception rooms and apartments, and a power plant in the new "industrial quarter," were intended to improve the papal domain and impress its visitors.[10] Some of the new construction directly benefited the pope's soldiers. The accommodations of both the Pontifical Gendarmeria and the Swiss Guard were expanded and improved, with the guard quarter receiving a whole new barracks wing for living quarters and offices.

Although the Lateran Agreements improved the living conditions of the pope's soldiers, they also increased their work load. The Vatican city-state may have been the smallest country in the world, but its formal sovereignty now extended to more territory (including Castel Gandolfo and the extraterritorial properties around Rome) than that of the pre-1929 Vatican, which had encompassed simply Saint Peter's Basilica, the Apostolic Palace, and the adjacent gardens. Under the pre-Lateran arrangements, Italian territory had at certain points, such as the Zecca Gate behind the basilica, approached so close to the walls of the palace that in the nineteenth century Pope Leo XIII had been compelled to construct a tunnel under the Belvedere wing of the residence so that he could visit his gardens without crossing Italian territory. Now the frontier had been pushed back, if only by a few hundred yards. For the Swiss Guard and the Pontifical Gendarmeria, this additional space meant additional guard posts and patrols, especially after Pius XI's construction program produced more buildings and gateways to guard and more roads and paths to patrol.

The Swiss Guard established new posts at the Scala Regia, the grand staircase inside the palace, and at the Arco delle Campane (Arch of the Bells) at the foot of the clock tower on the left of Saint Peter's, which now became the formal vehicular entrance to Vatican City. The post at the Saint Anne gate, now the service entrance to the city with access to the new shops, warehouses, and offices of the industrial quarter, required additional halberdiers to control the increased foot and truck traffic. In the summer of 1934 Pope Pius XI left the sweltering city for the cooler hillsides of Castel Gandolfo, becoming the first pope since 1870 to visit the papal summer residence. This and subsequent sojourns in the country required the deployment of a squad of halberdiers to the villa. For their part, the Pontifical Gendarmeria faced even heavier demands because they were responsible for patrolling the new buildings, particularly the train terminal, the radio station, and the Governatorato (governor's palace), and they too had to assign personnel to Castel Gandolfo as well as other extraterritorial properties. Even the part-time Noble and Palatine Guards found themselves busier because diplomatic reconciliation between Italy and the papacy meant an increase in ceremonial and *servizio d'onore* duties as the pope cast off the self-imposed seclusion of the prisoner of the Vatican.

The interwar period was also marked by changes in the internal affairs of the various pontifical military units, though most reflected the perpetual concerns over pay, precedence, and personnel. Two weeks after the signing of the Lateran Agreements, the pontifical police, whose complement had fallen over the years far below the level of one hundred gendarmes originally established after Porta Pia, requested an increase in the number of personnel to eighty. The additional numbers were needed to improve protective coverage, especially in view of the expansion of papal territory and a threefold increase in the Italian police presence opposite the gates and along the proposed new frontiers of Vatican City. The commandant, Colonel Arcangelo De Mandato, who was determined to build up his force, also wanted additional personnel in order to set up a special investigative unit inside the gendarmeria. The approved force expansion, however, generated resentment among veteran gendarmes due to the source of the new recruits. Seeking perhaps to improve the competence and experience of the service, Colonel De Mandato filled the new positions, especially among the investigators and midlevel supervisors, with men recruited from the royal carabinieri, the military police of the Italian army, a force in which the commandant had himself served before moving into papal service. By 1933 Colonel De Mandato had secured a further expansion to 156 men, bringing the corps to its largest force level since 1870.[11]

The Swiss Guard remained the core of the pope's minuscule military, and for the guard the interwar years had been a period of calm and consolidation. After the resignation of Jules Repond in 1921, the corps had come under the command of Alois Hirschbühl. The new commander had joined the guard as a simple halberdier in 1902. In the lax environment of the "old" guard, he had found that the service provided a comfortable and undemanding billet amidst the artistic splendors of the Eternal City while he pursued a passion for painting. Upon completing his two-year enlistment, the aspiring painter left the pope's service to continue his art studies in Munich. Subsequently, he returned to Switzerland and entered the Swiss army, eventually becoming an officer. At the invitation of then commandant Xavier Leopold Meyer von Schauensee, Hirschbühl returned to the Swiss Guard in 1910 at the rank of captain. Avoiding the scandals that besmirched the reputations and prematurely ended the careers of several of his fellow officers, he emerged as a respected confidant and collaborator of Commandant Jules Repond, who entrusted him with the financial and logistical affairs of the corps. In 1920 he became deputy commander of the guard. More gregarious, accessible, and sympathetic than his stern commander, Hirschbühl quickly gained the respect and goodwill of the halberdiers, who in private referred to him affectionately as "Luigi."[12]

As the first commandant to rise from the ranks of the halberdiers, Alois Hirschbühl was twice blessed. He followed a commandant who was so unpopular that the halberdiers would have embraced any replacement, and he inherited a corps that as a result of the efforts of that unpopular commandant was well disciplined, well trained, and highly professional. In short, Jules Repond was an easy act to follow, and Hirschbühl took every advantage of that fact. Although he had supported his predecessor's efforts to reform and revitalize the guard, the new commandant believed that in seeking to redress the imbalance between the corps's ceremonial and protective roles, Repond had erred too much in favor of the latter function. The guard now seemed too militarized, especially after World War I and the Lateran Agreements, when, at least initially, the world beyond the walls of the Apostolic Palace seemed much less hostile. Honor and reception duties once again took precedence over protective responsibilities. The guard shouldered the burdens of a veritable blizzard of ceremonial events, from state visits and formal receptions, such as those for the emperor of Ethiopia and the king of

England, to the audiences and public rituals attendant on the Jubilee Year of 1925, which brought more than 600,000 pilgrims to the Vatican. Hirschbühl had to contrive a new relationship between the ceremonial and protective roles of the guard. Given the increased burdens of receptions, audiences, and ceremonies, inevitably the balance tipped toward the ceremonial. Without eliminating military training entirely, Hirschbühl significantly cut back on drills and exercises, except for new recruits. Daily marksmanship and bayonet practice was eliminated, and drills of any sort were canceled on the hottest summer days. The halberdiers, who characterized the relaxed regime as "butter instead of guns," now had more free time, which the commandant encouraged them to fill with artistic and cultural pursuits. Recalling his own experience as a simple halberdier, he was always mindful of his men's living conditions and aware that even small gestures made a difference in morale. In the notoriously scorching Roman summers, for example, he had a large water tank constructed in the barracks courtyard for swimming.[13]

For all his moderation in command, Hirschbühl still insisted that the halberdiers conduct themselves as soldiers, and he would not allow any relaxation or informality in the performance of assigned duties. He was scandalized, for example, to learn that a halberdier on duty in the palace had actually spoken to the pope. From time immemorial the custom had been that only guard officers and the chaplain spoke to the pope, and then only when addressed by the Holy Father.[14] Pius XI seemed completely unaware of this custom. Unlike his predecessors, who hardly deigned to acknowledge the presence of their attendants, let alone converse with them (Leo XIII was said to have never spoken a word to his coachman during the twenty-five years of his pontificate), the more gregarious Pius XI was positively chatty, cheerfully greeting his guards as he passed along the corridors of the palace. On one occasion the pontiff stopped to ask a duty halberdier where he was from and was delighted to learn that the young man had grown up in Zermatt. As a young priest Pius had been an avid hiker and mountaineer, avocations not exactly common among the starched and manicured denizens of the pontifical court who were more familiar with protocol than pitons, and now he insisted on delaying his business in order to converse with the guardsman about mountain climbing around Zermatt. When he learned of this exchange between the pontiff and one of his men, Hirschbühl was mortified. In his mind, the encounter violated every precept of military decorum, although it is hard to see how the poor halberdier could have behaved otherwise. The commandant immediately issued an order forbidding guards to speak to the Holy Father. Of course this directive proved impossible to enforce because the commander could not impose the order on the pope, who cheerfully continued his habit of stopping to have a few words with his protectors.[15]

The relatively relaxed regime continued under the next commandant. Alois Hirschbühl resigned in 1935 and was succeeded by Baron Georges von

Sury d'Aspremont, who would lead the guard into World War II.[16] The new commandant had studied law and classical languages at the universities of Munich and Zurich (he spoke Latin fluently) before joining the Swiss Guard in 1912 as one of the first officers recruited by Jules Repond. Entrusted by Repond with responsibility for training and marksmanship, a sure sign of his commander's regard, von Sury rose quickly through the officer ranks. His selection as commandant surprised no one. Every inch the Catholic aristocrat, Colonel von Sury insisted on the highest standards of personal appearance and behavior, going so far as to install a barber in the barracks to ensure that the halberdiers would never muster for guard duty without a recent trim. He also had an aristocrat's paternal regard for the well-being of his charges. Concerned about the cost of living in Rome and aware that his halberdiers might well earn twice their Vatican salaries by returning to jobs such as police officers in Switzerland, von Sury lobbied strenuously for pay increases. Eventually, he convinced a very reluctant cardinal secretary of state to grant a 10 percent raise.[17]

For all the moderation of Hirschbühl's and von Sury's regimes, the spirit of Jules Repond had not been entirely exorcised from the Swiss barracks. All of the former commander's major reforms, such as the requirement that recruits had to have completed the basic infantry training course of the Swiss army before joining the guard or that weapons drill was a necessary component of guard training, continued in force. Obedience, preparation, and pride, the watchwords of the Repond regime, remained the guiding principles of the corps. The approach was not so much "butter instead of guns" as "butter more than guns." In 1927, for example, Hirschbühl issued new drill regulations that in their attention to duty and training could have come from the pen of the long-departed Repond. After affirming, "There is only one kind of discipline: good discipline," the introductory chapter of the regulations went on to discuss the importance of strict discipline in assuring the reliability of a military unit and awakening pride among the soldiers of that unit. The regulations also stipulated that, in addition to discipline, a military unit also required of its members serious training and good character. Training, which should move from easy to more difficult exercises under the supervision of experienced and attentive officers and sergeants, prepared the unit to perform its duties, and sobriety, personal responsibility, and gentlemanly comportment brought honor to the corps and each of its members.[18] These were not merely conventional pieties or rhetorical flourishes but core values, which officers and men were expected to embrace. Upon their arrival in Vatican City, fresh recruits, all of whom had completed a period of service in the Swiss army, were surprised and more than a little intimidated to discover that the discipline, élan, and professionalism of their new corps far exceeded what they had experienced in the Swiss army.[19] Jules Repond would have expected no less.

With the outbreak of war in September 1939, the pontifical armed forces again had to recalibrate the balance between ceremonial and protective responsibilities. As during World War I, the conflict forced a curtailment of audiences and public ceremonies and an increase in guard and security duties, but the latter were now more extensive and more complicated than in the earlier period. The physical safety of the Holy Father was, as always, the principal responsibility of the corpi armati. The pope's soldiers, however, now also had to protect the territorial integrity and security of the Vatican city-state and its extraterritorial properties in and around Rome against any physical threat. It was no longer a case of guarding just Saint Peter's, the palace, and the gardens. In addition, the papal military had to defend against political threats, particularly efforts by both sides to compromise or exploit the neutrality of the Vatican through propaganda, political provocation, and espionage. Some of these tasks would prove easier to accomplish than others.

The pontifical military had adopted some precautionary measures at the onset of the conflict. The gendarmeria, for example, issued gas masks to its personnel and instructed them on their use. Special protection and control measures, however, went into effect only in early June 1940 as papal authorities anticipated Italy's entry into the war on the side of Germany.[20] As always, the burden of protecting the Holy Father and the Apostolic Palace fell primarily to the Swiss Guard and the Pontifical Gendarmeria, as the Noble Guards and the Palatine Guards still provided only daytime pickets for ceremonial reception service in the antechamber of the papal apartments. Continuing their long-established practice, Swiss Guard detachments were responsible for the gates to Vatican City and the palace: the Bronze Door (ten men), the Arch of the Bells (six men), the Zecca (four men), and the Saint Anne gate (four men). At night these entrances were closed and barred and the guard detachments reduced. Inside the palace, the Swiss manned four posts. During the day, a picket of seven to ten halberdiers served as an honor guard in the Sala Clementina, the reception room through which all visitors walked on their way to an audience with the Holy Father. At night this assignment (Post 1) moved to the nearby Sala Verde, with only a single halberdier on duty. Post 2, with one halberdier day and night, was the landing of the Scala Regia, the grand stairway beyond the Bronze Door that was the formal entry to the palace. This post also controlled the corridor that connected Saint Peter's Basilica with the palace. The landing outside the apartments of the cardinal secretary of state on the second loggia of the Apostolic Palace was Post 3, manned day and night by one halberdier. Post 4 was the doorway to the pope's living quarters on the third floor of the palace, and here too there was always a halberdier on duty. Except for the honor guards on daytime duty in the Sala Clementina, who still carried halberds, all guards now routinely carried Mauser rifles and bayonets. The rifles remained unloaded, but boxes of cartridges were at hand at each guard post. Upon the outbreak of the war, Commandant von Sury ordered additional training, with an emphasis on weapons drill and physical conditioning.[21]

The Pontifical Gendarmeria exercised its surveillance of Vatican City from two control posts (*tenenze*): The first was responsible for the Apostolic Palace and Saint Peter's, and the second covered the grounds and all other structures.[22] Each *tenenza* was divided into zones, which in turn were subdivided into patrol areas, each assigned to a gendarme. The *seconda tenenza*, for example, encompassed the garden zone, the museum zone, and the Saint Anne zone. In the garden zone a gendarme patrolled the area of the train station and the nearby mosaic studio. Another man covered the Governatorato. A third agent guarded the radio station, and a fourth observed the pathways of the Vatican Gardens from the Grotto of Lourdes, a large stone shrine near the highest point of the gardens. Gendarmes also backed up the Swiss Guards at the gates to Vatican City, where they were responsible for determining the identity and purposes of suspicious individuals or those seeking entry without an appointment. They had the authority to search the bags and packages of callers, although they were enjoined to adopt "the most urbane" manner in doing so. At the gates gendarmes held a list of individuals whose entry into Vatican City was to be prohibited for any reason. Except for ceremonial reception duties, when full-dress costume was required, the gendarmes wore functional field uniforms (dark trousers, tunic, leather belt, and kepi) and carried a pistol.[23]

Although most of the gendarmeria staff worked inside Vatican City, there were small detachments at various extraterritorial properties, such as Saint John Lateran and Castel Gandolfo. With the onset of war, the increased demands of guard and patrol stretched the resources of the police service. During the 1930s the gendarmeria had been authorized to increase its strength to 156, including command staff, but the service usually had fewer than that number available for duty. The lack of staff prevented the gendarmeria command from maintaining the protective patrols it considered necessary. Commanders were particularly concerned by thin coverage of the gardens and the museums during the night. A few posts (Saint Peter's Basilica, the Saint Anne gate) were manned around the clock, but most were maintained only between 8:00 A.M. and 8:00 P.M. Some posts were folded into other assignments during the night; for example, after 8:00 P.M. the gendarme on the night watch at the Governatorato was also responsible for the train station and the mosaic studio, areas that had their own gendarme during the day.[24]

Fortunately for the overstretched protectors, the job of guarding the Holy Father during the war was facilitated by the pope's tendency to stay close to home. During the war, Pope Pius XII rarely left Vatican City; indeed, he rarely left the Apostolic Palace except to visit his gardens. These garden strolls, however, required a special deployment of security agents because the pontiff was a creature of strict habit and even stricter preferences. The routine did not vary. Each afternoon Pius, accompanied by one of his aides and the esente of the Noble Guard, would leave the palace at precisely 3:30 and enter his vehicle for the short two-hundred-yard drive to the Grotto of Lourdes. There he would alight and begin his exercise: several circuits of the gardens, returning to the vehicle at 4:30 for the return to the palace. Although the aide and the Noble Guard officer might stroll with Pius for a few minutes, the walks were primarily solitary. The pontiff much preferred to read his breviary or review documents than converse with a companion. To the discomfiture of his guards, the pope had a particular notion of solitude upon which he insisted. Not only did he not want to walk with anybody; he did not want to see anybody as he rode to and from the Lourdes Grotto or paced the graveled garden path—not another car, not another stroller, not even a gardener, and certainly not a guard. He wished to be alone, and he meant alone.[25]

Inside Vatican City, the pope was an absolute monarch, and his wishes were everyone else's commands. Every day, an hour before the pope's appearance, gendarmes under the personal supervision of the officer of the day closed the gardens to visitors and vehicles. Other gendarmes inspected every pathway, fountain, hedge, and tree to ensure that no one, not even a gardener, was loitering in the area. At the approach of the papal limousine, each gendarme had to step behind a bush or tree so as to make himself invisible to Pius but had to do so without compromising the surveillance necessary to maintain the Holy Father's security. Toward the end of Pius's final circuit of the garden, the Noble Guard esente, who would have been watching the pope from a distance, would step onto the path within sight of the Holy Father as a silent signal that it was time to return to the palace. When Pius, his solitude inviolate, departed by car, the police agents could emerge from hiding and resume normal patrols.[26]

Although the Swiss Guard and Pontifical Gendarmeria capably protected the Holy Father against assassins and intruders, they were less effective in protecting the Vatican against a different threat. Foreign governments had always believed that, as the administrative center of an international church with bishops, priests, nuns, and monks in every country and territory in the world, the Vatican had access to excellent information from the four corners of the globe. Although this belief was mistaken, and observers seriously exaggerated the pope's access to political and economic information, foreign governments had long sought to penetrate the alleged secrets of the papacy. The Vatican, in short, was a major target for foreign intelligence organizations.[27]

No nation had been more assiduous in spying on the pope than Italy. During its political and military campaigns to overturn the pope's temporal power and incorporate the Papal States into the Kingdom of Italy, the House of Savoy had sent agents to lurk about the pontifical court and spread subversion among the pope's disaffected subjects. Espionage actually intensified after the Italian conquest of Rome in 1870 as Commissioner Giuseppe Manfroni and his successors in command of the police commissariat for the Borgo established a network of informants inside the Apostolic Palace to spy on the prisoner of the Vatican. Papal authorities were incapable of suppressing this espionage. In the absence of a counterintelligence service, the Pontifical Gendarmeria would have been the agency best suited for the task, if only because in the old Papal States it had conducted both espionage and counterespionage operations on behalf of the pontifical government. This experience could have been applied to protecting the secrets of the Vatican after 1870. There is no evidence, however, that after Porta Pia the papal police worked to uncover foreign spies inside the Apostolic Palace. Counterespionage seems no longer to have been part of the organizational mission of the corps, which saw its tasks as protecting the physical precincts of the Vatican, buildings and grounds, and maintaining order and decorum in those precincts. Catching spies formed no part of the job description of a papal police officer or anyone else in the papal administration in the decades immediately following Porta Pia.

Despite the Lateran Agreements, the Fascist government did not moderate, let alone suspend, intelligence operations against the Vatican. Conscious that the church and its network of religious, educational, charitable, and social organizations posed a potential threat to its authoritarian aspirations; convinced that neither Pius XI nor Pius XII would ever be the religious paladin of Fascism; and concerned that the offices and corridors of the papal palace sheltered enemies of the regime, Mussolini's government, even more than its predecessors, needed to discern the political plans of the Vatican and anticipate its actions. This required intelligence coverage far more comprehensive than previous efforts. Under Fascism the Italian intelligence services, particularly the Political Police Division of the Directorate of Public Security, recruited new informants inside the pontifical palace. Censors and eavesdroppers monitored mail, telegrams, and phone calls to and from Vatican City, surveillance facilitated by the fact that all communications with the world beyond the Vatican's walls had to pass through Italian postal and telegraph channels. Even diplomatic correspondence, nominally immune under international law from search and seizure, was at risk. Lacking the personnel and funds to maintain its own diplomatic couriers, the Vatican usually entrusted its diplomatic mail to the couriers of other governments, most frequently those of the Italian foreign ministry. This trust was seriously misplaced because before delivering the sealed diplomatic pouches, the Italians surreptitiously opened them, examined their contents, and then resealed the bags. Of course, like other governments, the Vatican used codes and ciphers to protect its most sensitive messages from unauthorized eyes, but Italian cryptanalysts cracked at least some of these, an effort made easier when the secret police suborned a layman who worked in the Vatican's cipher office.[28]

Italy was not the only power to spy on the pope. During World War II, several countries, including Britain, France, Germany, the Soviet Union, and the United States, ran intelligence operations against the Vatican, but the Italian threat was the most immediate. Of course papal authorities were not completely naive concerning foreign espionage. They guessed that their phones were tapped and their mail was read. They did not believe that their ciphers were secure ("They read everything," a monsignor in the Secretariat of State scribbled in the margins of a memorandum warning that the Italians were interested in papal ciphers), and they suspected that the papal diplomatic pouch was surreptitiously opened while in the custody of Italian couriers. They also assumed that foreign governments had informants inside Vatican City. In response the authorities did what they could—individuals were careful about what they said on the phone or wrote in letters, new and stronger ciphers were introduced, an agreement was reached with the Swiss foreign ministry to allow its couriers to carry papal diplomatic mail—but it was more difficult to deal with the spies in their midst. The pope's men simply resigned themselves to the situation, concluding that there was little they could do to remedy it.

This fatalism was, perhaps, premature because at the outbreak of the war, the Vatican actually had a means to combat espionage. At some point in the 1930s (the available records are unclear about the particular year) the Pontifical Gendarmeria had established a small unit to conduct criminal investigations and maintain internal security. Because crime inside Vatican City (beyond the "I returned to my desk to find my cigarettes missing" variety) was practically nonexistent, this "Special Section" was able to focus on its security role, but it did so with a particular bias. Colonel De Mandato, the gendarmeria commander, harbored Fascist sympathies, and during the expansion of the papal police after the Lateran Agreements, he made a special effort to recruit personnel from Italian police agencies.[29] His motive may have been to secure experienced personnel, but movement of men from the Italian police into the Pontifical Gendarmeria provided Italian intelligence with an opportunity to penetrate the papal service. The opportunity expanded when Colonel De Mandato appointed his son-in-law, Giovanni Fazio, to head the Special Section. An early adherent of the Fascist party, Fazio had led party squads in attacks on strikers and other political targets, and he had participated in Mussolini's "march on Rome." He did not moderate his political beliefs or abandon his political activism when he entered the pope's service. Giovanni Fazio became a spy for Italian intelligence inside the gendarmeria, a role enhanced by his position as commander of the unit responsible for investigations and security. The chief of the Vatican unit charged with catching spies was himself an Italian spy.[30]

Unsurprisingly, the Special Section did not spend much time uncovering Fascist spies inside Vatican City. In fact, under Fazio's command the unit became little more than a subsidiary of Italian intelligence. Before the war Fazio used the unit to collect information on events and personalities inside Vatican City and to monitor anti-Fascists who lived or worked in the papal enclave, such as Count Dalla Torre, the editor of the Vatican newspaper, *Osservatore Romano*, and Alcide de Gasperi, the secretary of the old Popular Party, who worked in the Vatican Library. Each day the Special Section commander passed a report to his Italian contact.[31] When Italy entered the war on June 10, 1940, the Special Section turned its attention to more important targets.

The Lateran Agreements recognized Vatican City as a sovereign and neutral state with the right to send and receive ambassadors. Given the minuscule size of the city-state, it was impossible for diplomatic missions accredited to the Holy See to establish their offices and residences inside the pope's domain. The embassies of the thirty-five or so countries that maintained diplomatic relations with the Holy See were scattered about the larger city of Rome. When Italy joined Germany in the war, the status of the embassies from the Allied powers (e.g., Britain, France, and Poland) became problematic. The Lateran Agreements seemed to guarantee the immunity and continuance of such diplomatic missions on Italian territory. However, elements in the Italian government, particularly the war ministry, argued that the agreements did not actually compel Italy to accept on its territory diplomatic missions accredited to the Holy See and that the presence of enemy missions inside the capital was simply impossible. They would have to be protected against the ire of Italian citizens and monitored constantly to ensure that they did not become centers for enemy espionage and propaganda. One solution was to transfer the Allied diplomats to another neutral country, such as Switzerland, from which they would exercise their functions. This solution had two advantages. It would remove the enemy diplomats not only from Rome but also from Italy. It also had the advantage of precedent: When Italy had joined the Allies in World War I, the German and Austrian embassies to the Vatican had relocated to Switzerland. Of course the distance and the difficulties of wartime communications had made it hard for the transplanted embassies to perform their functions during that war. The same difficulties would certainly afflict the Allied embassies should they too be forced to relocate to Switzerland during this war, but that was not a concern that unduly troubled the Italian Ministry of War.[32]

The alternative to transferring the Allied missions to Switzerland was to move them into Vatican City. Under international law and the Lateran Agreements, the pope's tiny domain was as much an independent country as Italy. Though the Vatican was rather inconveniently located right in the middle of Rome, even the war ministry's lawyers could not argue that the Fascist regime had the legal authority to determine who could live and work in the Holy Father's territory. For its part, the Vatican preferred an interpretation of the Lateran Agreements that allowed the Allied embassies to remain in the city of Rome, but if pushed (and as a group Fascist authorities tended to be a rather pushy lot), it did not want those embassies transferred to Switzerland and isolated from the Holy Father. Reluctantly, it agreed to accept the diplomats into Vatican City.

Unlike the capitals of other countries, Vatican City was not home to a variety of hotels, apartment blocks, and private residences. With the exception of the Swiss Guards and the gendarmes, who occupied military barracks, very few people—perhaps another hundred or so—actually lived inside the walls of the pope's city. Much of the vast palace was a museum, with its chambers and halls given over to tourists rather than overnight guests. The remaining space was occupied by the personal and ceremonial apartments of the Holy Father, reception rooms, the storage and research facilities of the Vatican Library and the Vatican Archive, and a handful of administrative offices, such as the Secretariat of State and the administration of the Apostolic Palace. Since no one was prepared to turn the Raphael Stanze into apartments or partition the Egyptian Museum into studios, papal authorities were hard-pressed to find accommodations for the Allied diplomats who were left on their doorstep.

The only available facility was a small pilgrim hostel attached to the Convent of Saint Martha in the shadow of Saint Peter's. Into this building papal authorities, on June 11 and 12, 1940, moved the diplomatic representatives of Britain, France, Belgium, and Poland; their families; their staffs; and as much office and residential furniture as they could cram into the four or five cell-like rooms each representative was allotted. Initially, the hostel had neither kitchen nor bathing facilities. There wasn't even hot water. The diplomats took their meals in the refectory of the convent and took cold sponge baths from pans. Conditions improved after Vatican workmen renovated the main building of the convent to create on the higher floors small apartments with bathrooms and kitchens for the use of the diplomats. Though now less sordid, the living conditions inside Saint Martha's remained very cramped, especially after the American, Brazilian, and Yugoslav representatives entered Vatican City when their countries declared war on Italy.[33]

Feelings of claustrophobia were fueled by the strict controls placed by the Vatican on the diplomats' movements and activities. The transfer of the Allied diplomatic missions into Vatican City did not really assuage the concerns of the Italian military and security services, which would have preferred to see those missions at a safer distance—say, several hundred kilometers away in Switzerland. These enemy diplomats, after all, had merely moved from one to another (albeit extraterritorial) part of Rome. Without careful supervision, they might still operate as agents of espionage and subversion inside the capital. To counter this threat, Italian intelligence intensified its surveillance of mail and phone calls in and out of the Vatican and recruited informants among the Italian servants working for the diplomats inside Saint

Martha's. The footman of the British representative, D'Arcy Osborne, for example, was suborned under the threat of being immediately called up for service in the Italian army.[34] The Italian government also expected the Vatican to monitor the diplomats. It repeatedly expressed to papal authorities its concerns over the alleged threat posed by the Allied envoys. Italian authorities, for example, presented "evidence" that one diplomat had been observed late at night meeting unknown parties in a courtyard of the palace and that another had been receiving secret messages harmful to Italian interests. The Italians insisted that papal authorities strictly control these individuals to ensure that they did not abuse the neutral status of Vatican City.

Papal officials faced a dilemma. If they simply dismissed Italian allegations that Allied diplomats were abusing Vatican neutrality and the pope's hospitality, then they risked the anger of a potentially very troublesome if not actually dangerous neighbor. Vatican City was an island in an Italian sea. Like any island, almost everything it needed to function had to cross the water. It was totally dependent on Italy for gas and electricity. Every lump of coal, every liter of gasoline, every cut of meat or kilo of pasta, every aspirin and dose of vaccine, every piece of paper, every bolt and nail consumed inside the city came from beyond the pope's walls. Not a single letter, telegram, or telephone call could leave or enter Vatican City without the cooperation of Italian public services. Without the acquiescence of the Italian police, no one could cross the border to enter or leave the Vatican. It was unlikely that the Italian government would risk alienating Catholics by blockading Vatican City and cutting off essential utilities, resources, and services, but if seriously irritated the Fascists could make life and work inside the papal city very difficult. On the other hand, if papal authorities—most of whom believed Italian concerns about espionage to be exaggerated and the purported evidence spurious—submitted to demands for greater surveillance of the Allied diplomats, would they not be compromising papal neutrality by showing favoritism toward one belligerent side?

In the end, large countries do what they can while small countries do what they must. To avoid any pretext for Italian complaint or intervention, papal authorities imposed controls on their diplomatic guests. The decision was made easier by the fact that the political attitudes of the authorities responsible for policing some of those controls—the cardinal governor of Vatican City, Nicola Canali; the commander of the Pontifical Gendarmeria, Arcangelo De Mandato; and the chief of the gendarmeria's Special Section, Giovanni Fazio—did not incline them to sympathize with the plight of the Allied diplomats. The Italian government submitted a list of restrictions that it expected the Vatican to impose on its guests. The enemy diplomats were not allowed to cross the border into Italian territory except for special reasons, for which exceptions they must secure the permission of the Italian government and accept the company of a plainclothes police officer. Outside the Vatican, they could not use a telephone for any purpose. The diplomats could not communicate with their home countries by coded telegram; all telegrams had to be in plain language. The use of their own diplomatic couriers was prohibited. They could send and receive official and private correspondence through the Italian postal service, where the correspondence would be opened, although naturally the Italians did not admit this practice to the Vatican.[35]

To supplement these restrictions, the Pontifical Gendarmeria issued additional guidelines to its officers at the gates to Vatican City and at the Saint Martha residence. These guidelines actually extended controls beyond the requirements imposed by the Italians. The Allied diplomats could freely visit each other and receive visits from high officials in the papal administration, but any other individuals seeking to visit the diplomats were to be courteously denied access and directed to apply for permission at the offices of the papal Secretariat of State. Should anyone leave at a gate a package or letter for a diplomat, these items were not to be delivered directly but forwarded to the Secretariat of State. Servants employed by the diplomats had to live inside Vatican City. These servants were prohibited from leaving papal territory except in the event of necessity, in which case they would be accompanied into Rome by a plainclothes Vatican police agent. Finally, for telephone calls the diplomats, their families, and their servants were allowed to use only the single phone available inside Saint Martha's, a phone connected only to the internal service of Vatican City, with no access to outside lines.[36]

Confinement to the small world of Vatican City proved exasperating for the Allied diplomats. For professionals accustomed to large and often lavish embassies and official residences, the living and working arrangements were cramped and rather unpleasant. Working conditions, specifically the ability to send reports and receive instructions, were worsened by the difficulty in maintaining confidential communications with the foreign ministries in their home capitals. More frustrating was the constricted social life inside the papal city. Social contacts were limited to colleagues or to papal officials resident inside Vatican City. The latter, however, were all priests, and their social activities were limited by ecclesiastical law and custom. Some, moreover, shunned social contact with the diplomats to avoid any suggestion of favoritism or un-neutral activities. Recreational opportunities were even more limited. There were no playhouses, movie theaters, restaurants, or bookstores in Vatican City. Aside from walking in the gardens or reading in the Vatican Library, there was nothing to do, although the British ambassador, D'Arcy Osborne, convinced Cardinal Canali to allow diplomats to use the Vatican's ill-kept tennis court on the condition that no women played and no spectators watched.[37]

Surveillance proved more tiresome than the limited social and recreational opportunities. To ensure that the pope's guests adhered to the restrictions imposed on their official and personal lives, the Pontifical Gendarmeria instituted around-the-clock observation of the Allied diplomats by plainclothes and uniformed agents. This watch was supervised by Giovanni Fazio's Special Section, which assigned gendarmes to monitor the residents of Saint Martha's Convent. If the diplomats left the residence to walk around Vatican City, they were followed by plainclothes agents or their movements were recorded by the gendarmeria posts they passed. Every day the Special Section prepared a report on the activities of the residents and any visitors they received. The report for April 22, 1942, for example, recorded the activities of the American, British, French, Polish, and Yugoslav diplomats. According to the Special Section agents, that day between 5:00 P.M. and 6:15 P.M. Father Vincent McCormick, an American Jesuit priest who was a senior official at his order's headquarters outside the Vatican and an occasional broadcaster of English-language programs for Vatican Radio, visited the U.S. representative, Harold Tittmann. The report noted that Father McCormick did so with the explicit permission of the papal Secretariat of State. Between 6:16 P.M. and 6:45 P.M. Tittmann received in his apartment another visitor, Father Emmanuel Mistiaen, a Belgian Jesuit who also worked for Vatican Radio and whose anti-Nazi broadcasts early in the war had caused outrage among Fascist authorities. Then, at 6:45 P.M., Tittmann and Mistiaen, joined by Mrs. Tittmann, walked in the Vatican Gardens, returning to Saint Martha's at 8:00 P.M. The surveillance report also noted that at 10:45 in the morning Tittmann's secretary had entered the room used as an office by the U.S. representative and remained there until 1:15 in the afternoon. The secretary had returned to the office at 4:40 that afternoon and worked until 7:45 in the evening.[38]

The Allied diplomats were aware of the surveillance and assumed that the Pontifical Gendarmeria were collaborating with the Italian intelligence services. Describing for his foreign ministry the rigor of the surveillance and suggesting its motive, the French ambassador reported, "Inside the precincts of the Vatican the police of the Holy See maintain a close surveillance in collaboration, evidently, with the Fascist police. Italy has infiltrated the Vatican with the agreement, complicity, and active participation of high papal authorities, who wish to avoid difficulties with a government so close next door."[39] Echoing his French colleague's impressions, the British representative noted, "I believe that daily reports are sent out on our doings. . . . The precise connection between the Italian police outside and the Vatican plain clothes police and gendarmerie inside defies precise definition, but it very definitely exists."[40] That connection, however, was interrupted in 1942 when the surveillance reports from Saint Martha's Convent ceased to appear in the daily intelligence sheet prepared by the Special Section. Monsignor Giovanni Montini, the influential deputy secretary of state (and the future Pope Paul VI), did not share the pro-Fascist sympathies of Cardinal Canali and Giovanni Fazio. Montini was aware of the collaboration between the

Vatican and Italian police forces, and he found that collaboration personally distasteful and politically inappropriate for a neutral state. He directed Anton Call, the gendarmeria officer responsible for surveillance at Saint Martha's, to send the daily logs directly to him in the Secretariat of State, not to the office of the papal police. Call, who shared Montini's political sympathies, agreed to this rather irregular order (the police were under the governor of Vatican City, not the Secretariat of State, which was the Vatican's foreign ministry), and, when questioned by his superiors about his failure to submit the daily reports, merely referred them to Monsignor Montini.

As the Governatorato and the Secretariat of State sorted out the lines of authority in the Call affair, Cardinal Canali suddenly dismissed Giovanni Fazio from the Pontifical Gendarmeria. The Special Section and its chief had been the object of many complaints from the Allied diplomats, who did not hide from the Secretariat of State their conviction that Fazio was concerned more with serving the interests of Italian intelligence than those of the Vatican. Cardinal Secretary of State Maglione, who, like his deputy, Montini, did not appreciate the prostitution of the papal police to the requirements of Italian intelligence, passed these protests to Cardinal Canali. Though a power in his own right, Canali could not or would not stand against the cardinal secretary of state. Without his protector, Fazio was forced from Vatican service.[41]

With the departure of Giovanni Fazio the Italians lost an important contact inside Vatican City, but their connection with the Pontifical Gendarmeria was not entirely broken. They still had enough friends inside the papal police to secure the dismissal from the force of Anton Call, the gendarme who had refused to facilitate Fazio's collaboration. Call exacted his own revenge by sending to Monsignor Montini the names of several employees of the Vatican who secretly worked for Italian intelligence. The Italian police also retained enough influence within the gendarmeria to continue what was probably their most important intelligence operation inside Vatican City. During the war, Italian agents clandestinely entered the apartments of several, if not all, of the Allied diplomats and photographed confidential documents, including ciphers. It is extremely unlikely that such operations could have succeeded without the complicity of the papal police, whose officers maintained around-the-clock surveillance of the gates to Vatican City and the entrances and precincts of Saint Martha's Convent. Italian intelligence, for example, acquired the code book of D'Arcy Osborne by arranging for his footman to pass the book to Italian agents waiting outside Saint Martha's while the British diplomat took his daily walk in the Vatican Gardens. These agents then took the material elsewhere, perhaps outside the Vatican, to be photographed. The code book, however, was so extensive, and the window of opportunity so narrow, since Osborne's walks rarely lasted more than thirty minutes, that the Italian agents had to extend the operation over three consecutive days. It is difficult to believe that strangers lurking around Saint Martha's in the daytime for three days would have escaped the notice of the gendarmes posted around the convent.[42]

Security arrangements changed dramatically in the late summer of 1943 in response to dramatic changes in Italian politics. The war had not gone well for Italy. Mussolini had entered the conflict to demonstrate Italy's military power, expand its empire, and allow the Italian people to reap the benefits of glory and conquest. By the summer of 1943, that military power had collapsed, the empire had been lost, and the people had reaped nothing but the terrors and sufferings of a lost war. In Africa and Russia (where the Duce had sent an expeditionary force to fight alongside the Germans), Italy's armies were smashed and hundreds of thousands of Italian soldiers, sailors, and airmen were dead, wounded, or prisoners of war (POWs). Allied aerial bombardments—while far short of the horrors wreaked on Germany—had ruined parts of Italian cities and dislocated the urban populations. Shortages of food, heating fuel, medicines, and clothing were realities of everyday life. On July 10, 1943, an Anglo-American army invaded Sicily, bringing the land war to the homeland. Nine days later, Allied bombers attacked Rome for the first time. The politics of bombast and threat had given way to recrimination and defeatism.[43]

Already in early 1943 there were voices in the army, the administration, the palace, and the Vatican saying, although privately and only to trusted ears, that Italy had to withdraw from the fighting. Mussolini, physically and mentally exhausted and increasingly detached from the realities of the political and military crisis, refused to seek negotiations with the Allies. It became apparent to the peace faction that Italy's removal from the war had to be preceded by the Duce's removal from power. Elements in the army plotted a coup d'état, but it was the Fascist Grand Council, the political paladins of the regime, including some of Mussolini's closest collaborators, that took the decisive step. On the night of July 24–25, 1943, the council, which had not met since the war had begun, voted to restore supreme military command to the king, an explicit repudiation of Mussolini's conduct of the war. It was an omen, which the Duce did not grasp. The next afternoon, during an audience at the palace, he was summarily dismissed from all offices by the king, who appointed Army marshal Pietro Badoglio, a seventy-two-year-old mediocrity who specialized in political survival, as the new prime minister. As Mussolini left the palace, carabinieri arrested the erstwhile dictator and unceremoniously carted him off to imprisonment.[44]

Although the Badoglio regime publicly affirmed its commitment to continue the war alongside Germany, in August it opened secret negotiations with the Allies in Tangiers and Lisbon to secure a way out. An agreement to announce an armistice on September 8 simultaneously with Allied landings south of Rome and the arrival of a U.S. airborne division at military airports around the capital collapsed when, through incompetence or cowardice, Italian commanders made no preparations to receive the U.S. paratroopers. The announcement of the armistice and landings at Salerno went forward as planned, but the airborne operation had to be canceled at the last minute, leaving the Italians alone to defend Rome against the inevitable reaction from their former ally.[45]

Upon learning of Mussolini's arrest, Hitler, anticipating an Italian collapse, immediately began moving additional troops into Italy. Though his actions made Italy's abandonment of its ally more risky, the hapless Badoglio regime made little effort to delay or impede this deployment, and by the end of August there were seven German divisions in the country. When, on the evening of September 8, Badoglio announced that Italy had signed an armistice with the Allies, German forces moved on Rome. Some Italian army units resisted stoutly, and thousands of Romans, armed with rifles and pistols from army and police armories and from the clandestine weapons caches of the underground Socialist and Communist parties, rushed to defend the gates and streets of the city. The defense of Rome, however, was compromised by the absence of any operational plans, confusion in command and control, and panic and cowardice among senior political and military authorities. On September 9 Badoglio, the royal family, the commanders of the army and navy, and several cabinet ministers abandoned Rome for the safety of Brindisi, a town on the Adriatic coast some distance away from the closest Germans. On September 10, after the German commander in Italy, Field Marshal Albert Kesserling, threatened to carpet bomb the city, Marshal Enrico Caviglia, who had assumed command after all his superiors had run away, surrendered the Eternal City.[46]

The Vatican had been aware of whisperings against Mussolini and had been approached by individuals seeking signs of the pope's attitude toward one conspiracy or another, but Pius maintained his reserve and distance from the plotters. He wanted Italy out of the war as much as anyone. The first Allied air raid on Rome on July 19, 1943, shook him badly, and he had no confidence in Mussolini whatsoever, but his experience with the anti-Hitler conspiracy of 1939–1940 may have left him reluctant to risk involvement in new plots. If the Vatican joined a conspiracy against the Duce and that conspiracy failed, the papacy would be dangerously exposed. The Vatican, therefore, limited its activity to serving as a discreet back channel for rather oblique communications between Washington and plotters in Rome concerning the need for Italy to act now to avoid further devastation. Papal authorities seem to have been surprised by the events of July 24–25, and they had no plan to navigate Italy through the dangerous political waters of a post-Mussolini world. They also played only a marginal role in the secret negotiations over the armistice, although they were aware of the exchanges. Foreign Minister Rafaele Guariglia, a former Italian ambassador to the Vatican and a leader in the effort to remove Italy from the war, often spent the evenings of those tense August weeks with his friend Cardinal Secretary of State Luigi Maglione. Their conversations must surely have turned to the contacts with the Allies. Papal officials also turned a blind eye as the British representative at the Vatican, Osborne, despite his earlier agreement to limit his communications to Vatican business, provided a clandestine link between London and Rome as the Badoglio regime tried to establish contact with the Allies.

The German occupation of Rome created the worst crisis of the war for the Vatican. The hostile Fascist government had been removed, only to be replaced by an even more implacable foe. If Pope Pius and his advisers believed that discretion and passivity during the events of July–September 1943 would shield the Vatican from the wrath of the Nazis, they were sadly mistaken. Since its rise to power the Nazi regime had considered the Catholic Church in general, and the Vatican in particular, an obstacle to its totalitarian, imperialistic, and racist aspirations. Hitler's approach to church-state relations veered between tense hostility and outright persecution. By September 1943 papal authorities knew very well whom they were dealing with, and they knew they had reason to be worried. In May 1941 the Secretariat of State had learned that the German foreign minister, Joachim von Ribbentrop, had pressed his Italian counterpart, Galeazzo Ciano, to remove Pope Pius from Rome because the new Europe envisioned by the Nazis would have no place for the papacy. The Italian foreign minister allegedly had deflected this proposal by assuring von Ribbentrop that it was easier simply to isolate and control the Holy Father behind the walls of Vatican City. When approached by the Vatican for a clarification of this rather alarming information, the Italians, not surprisingly, denied its veracity.[47] Papal authorities were not reassured, especially when they learned from an eyewitness that at a dinner party a German official who had attended the recent Holy Week ceremonies in Saint Peter's Basilica had blandly commented, "The ceremonies were very interesting, but this is the last time for them. Next year they won't be celebrated again." This official had made it clear that he didn't expect the pope to be in the Vatican next year. Cardinal Secretary of State Maglione was sufficiently concerned that, in May 1941, he convened a special commission of cardinals to discuss contingency plans to confer special ecclesiastical powers on papal representatives abroad in the event that the Vatican was cut off and unable to communicate with the world.[48] Rumors that Berlin was preparing plans for German commandos to assault Vatican City, seize the papal archives, and kidnap the Holy Father circulated so freely in political and diplomatic circles in Rome that the German embassy to the Vatican felt compelled to warn Berlin against the negative impressions fostered by such stories.[49]

Now that the Germans controlled Rome, the threat was literally at the pope's doorstep. *Wehrmacht* armored cars prowled the streets of the Borgo just outside the Vatican walls, and German paratroopers, ominously in full combat kit, paced along the granite strip in Saint Peter's Square that marked the border between Italy and Vatican city. The Lateran Agreements recognized the sovereign independence and territorial integrity of Vatican City and affirmed the political neutrality of the papacy in international conflicts, but few in the papal enclave expected the treaty to be a reliable talisman against an unscrupulous regime that had repeatedly demonstrated its contempt for international treaties and disregard for the rights of neutrals. Even fewer believed that world opinion would inhibit Adolf Hitler from lashing out at the papacy. Papal authorities would not have been surprised to learn that Hitler was convinced that the Vatican was behind Mussolini's fall from power. Upon learning of the Duce's arrest, Hitler had raged against the duplicity of Pius XII and ordered an assault on the Vatican and the seizure of the Holy Father. "I'd go straight into the Vatican," the Führer ranted. "Do you think the Vatican disturbs me? We will take it immediately. . . . We'll get that bunch of swine out of there. Later we can make apologies."[50] When his anger cooled, the Führer was convinced by Josef Goebbels, his propaganda minister, that such an attack would give the Allies an important propaganda victory. In the minds of papal officials, however, invasion of the Vatican remained a real possibility; indeed, the seizure of the pope and his forcible removal to Germany was not unthinkable. Recalling the daring airborne rescue by German commandos of Benito Mussolini from his mountaintop place of incarceration, these officials feared a similar "snatch and run" operation against the Holy Father.[51] From the moment the Germans entered Rome, these officials began to prepare for the worst.

On September 9, 1943, as isolated Italian army and police units, assisted by armed civilians, mounted a courageous but futile resistance to German troops entering the city, the few Romans who ventured onto the streets noticed that all the gates to Vatican City were shut. Those hoping to visit the Vatican Library or the Vatican Museums were told that the facilities were no longer open. More ominously, the great doors to Saint Peter's Basilica were closed in the daytime, an event unprecedented in the memory of any citizen. Behind the locked and barred doors and gates, invisible to passersby, the Vatican was frantically preparing for an attack.[52]

In anticipation of a German occupation of Vatican City, papal archivists shifted sensitive documents to obscure recesses of the Vatican Secret Archive or moved them to cabinets and closets in the more distant reaches of the thousand-room pontifical palace. The pope's personal files were hidden under the marble floors of the papal apartments. Whiffs of smoke appeared over Saint Martha's Convent as the resident Allied diplomats burned their ciphers and confidential files. Inside the Apostolic Palace the staff of the Secretariat of State, the Vatican foreign ministry, received instructions to keep packed suitcases at their desks in anticipation of a sudden evacuation. Cardinal Nicola Canali, the curmudgeonly governor of Vatican City, ordered workmen to begin heightening the walls around the papal city by adding sharp-tipped steel railings along their tops, a defensive measure local wags promptly designated the "Canali Line." In the frenzy of activity, few noticed a small party of men, garbed in different uniforms, moving from gate to gate, pacing along the walls, and surveying Saint Peter's Square from the steps of the basilica. The commanders of the pope's armed units—the Swiss Guard, the Noble Guard, the Palatine Guard, and the Pontifical Gendarmeria— were assessing the state of the Vatican's defenses. The pope's minuscule army was taking the field.[53]

As the only professional soldiers in the pope's service, the Swiss Guard would form the core of any military defense of Vatican City. Colonel Georges von Sury d'Aspremont had retired in February 1942, only fifty-five years old but exhausted in mind and body by the rigors of protecting the Holy Father in a hostile environment. He had been replaced as corps commandant by an individual whose family name for centuries had been the very embodiment of the Guard. Baron Heinrich Pfyffer von Altishofen, a doctor of law and a Knight of Malta, had risen to the rank of major in the Swiss Army before enrolling as an officer in the Swiss Guard in 1928.[54] Service in the guard was a tradition in the Altishofen family; nine of the baron's ancestors had commanded the corps, and several others had served as officers. One, Franz Alois Pfyffer von Altishofen, had been commandant in 1798 when French troops had seized Pope Pius VI and carried the pontiff off to house arrest in France. In 1808, another forebear, Karl Josef Leodegar Pfyffer von Altishofen, had commanded the guard when French forces again raided the Apostolic Palace to kidnap yet another pope, Pius VII. In the fall of 1943, Colonel Heinrich Pfyffer von Altishofen might well have wondered if history was about to repeat itself. He certainly was well aware of his position as the first commandant since the nineteenth century who might have to honor the oath sworn by every guardsman to defend the Holy Father with his life, and he was not one to shirk that responsibility. When armed German paratroopers in battle dress appeared in Saint Peter's Square, the commandant, who had been forewarned of the arrival of the Germans by a source in the Italian military, was waiting, in full gala uniform with a sword on his belt, to ensure that the occupiers stayed on their side of the white travertine stripe that marked the boundary between Italian and Vatican territory.[55]

Colonel Pfyffer von Altishofen was not so naive as to expect a dress uniform and an antique sword to deter the Wehrmacht. He immediately placed the Swiss Guard on an emergency footing and deployed his limited resources to defend Vatican City. The protective mission of the guard remained the defense of the gates of the city, the entrances to the papal palace, and the apartments of the Holy Father. The German threat, however, required an expansion of this mission; for example, to better defend against any attempt by German commandos or Fascist diehards to seize the Holy Father, a picket of halberdiers had to be deployed to reinforce the gendarmes in the Vatican Gardens when Pope Pius took his daily afternoon walk. Unfortunately, the guard had too few men to meet the demands of the emergency. Although the military department of the Swiss government had agreed upon the outbreak of war in 1939 not to recall to national service members of the guard, it initially had refused to permit any more military-age Swiss males to enroll in the pope's service.[56] Recruitment, therefore, did not replace all the halberdiers who returned to Switzerland at the end of their term of enlistment. When the Germans entered Rome, the guard could muster only sixty-two men. These soldiers represented the first line of the pope's defense. It was a very small force, even for a very small country.

No matter its numbers, the Swiss Guard mobilized for war. At all posts, except the ceremonial honor guard in the pope's reception hall, which retained halberds and swords, each halberdier carried a loaded model 98 Mauser rifle, a bayonet, and ninety rounds of extra ammunition in a bandolier (called "brassieres" by the guardsmen for their close fit across the upper chest). Each guard post also had ammunition boxes with additional rifle cartridges. On duty, officers and noncommissioned officers carried Dreyse 7.65 semiautomatic pistols. World War I–era gas masks were issued to officers and men. Unfortunately, none of this equipment was up-to-date; the rifles and pistols, for example, had been purchased by Commandant Jules Repond before World War I. Even before the arrival of the German army in Rome, the halberdiers had considered their weapons hopelessly antiquated, and this judgment was only affirmed once they got a glimpse of the combat-ready German paratroopers patrolling the boundary of Saint Peter's Square. New recruits, all of whom joined the guard after completing a period of service in the Swiss Army, were surprised to discover that the guard still used the venerable Mauser 98. When issued his rifle, one recruit earnestly asked his sergeant, "Can you really shoot with this?" As for the antique gas masks, everyone just laughed at them.[57]

Colonel Pfyffer von Altishofen shared his men's concern over the inadequacy of their weapons. Even before the crisis of September 1943 there had been talk of replacing the long-serving Mausers with the Swiss Karabiner model 31, a more modern weapon familiar to most halberdiers because it had been the standard rifle of the Swiss Army since 1933. The Mausers had been retained because the cost of replacing them with Karabiners was deemed prohibitive. Also, some in the Apostolic Palace feared that rearming the pope's guards with more modern weapons would project the wrong image to the world and allow critics to accuse the Vatican of militarism and pretensions to worldly power.[58] With the Germans in Rome, however, concerns for the Vatican's image gave way to concerns for its safety.

Colonel Pfyffer von Altishofen's first priority was to secure more soldiers. In early 1941 the Swiss government had dropped its prohibition on recruitment, and that spring six recruits had joined the guard. Another volunteer appeared in 1942.[59] After the Germans occupied Rome, the commandant used his contacts in Switzerland to recruit an additional thirteen young men who had just completed their basic training and a period of service in the Swiss army. On October 5, 1943, Lieutenant Colonel Ulrich Ruppen, the deputy commandant of the guard, arrived at Rome's train station to catch a train to Switzerland to collect the recruits, only to find the platform packed with travelers seeking places in the few coaches. The lieutenant colonel had a document from the papal Secretariat of State identifying him as a diplomatic courier (his baggage included a pouch of confidential mail for the papal embassy in Berne) and a *laissez passer* signed by General Rainer Stahel, the German military commander in Rome. Most important, he had a precious first-class ticket. Unfortunately, so did many other travelers. Unable to find a seat in the packed first-class carriage, Ruppen reconciled himself to sitting on his suitcases in the passageway all the way to the Swiss border. Luckily, a halberdier who had accompanied his deputy commander to the station had discovered at the front of the train a half-empty carriage reserved for German soldiers. Ruppen certainly wasn't a German soldier; he wasn't even wearing a uniform, but he was not inclined to spend several hours in a cramped passageway. He hurried forward and claimed one of the empty seats in this carriage. He had hardly settled his bags when a voice yelled, "What's a civilian doing in here?" He looked up to find a German military policeman looming over him. The policeman's attitude changed as soon as he heard a reference to General Stahel, and Ruppen was allowed to continue his trip in the relative luxury of the German army railway carriage. Unfortunately, Stahel's name proved no magical charm against the frequent delays due to Allied air activity, damaged tracks, and mechanical problems that extended the time required for the journey many times beyond the norm for peacetime. At one point, south of Bologna, Ruppen and his fellow passengers had to descend from the train and walk several kilometers to the next station because the tracks had been disrupted by air attacks. When Bologna railway officials could not say when the next passenger train for points north would be available, the enterprising Swiss Guard officer talked his way onto a German army freight train carrying military supplies toward Milan. Fortunately, the return trip with the thirteen recruits was less eventful. At the Swiss-Italian border a German army captain met the papal group and announced that Field Marshal Erwin Rommel, the German military commander in northern Italy, who had been informed of Ruppen's mission, had ordered that their progress to Rome was to be facilitated in every way. They were given seats in a car reserved for German army personnel and completed their journey in relative comfort.[60]

Ruppen and his charges reached Rome before dawn and arrived at the Swiss Guard barracks just before the duty squad mustered in the main courtyard. Years later one of the group recalled that they were as excited as schoolboys as they crossed Saint Peter's Square and approached a small iron gate in the battlemented walls.[61] From behind the walls they could hear the sound of marching feet. When the gate was thrown open by a halberdier in a dark blue exercise uniform, starched white collar, and floppy beret—which the group later agreed was much more stylish than any uniform they had worn, or even seen, in the Swiss army—they felt as if they were stepping into history. The new arrivals were shown to "California," the large room in the barracks where, by tradition, recruits were accommodated. It was so named because the quarters, directly under the roof, were stifling in the heat of a Roman summer. The room contained a row of iron bedsteads, each with a rolled-up mattress, a metal footlocker, and a bedside table. A large rifle stand dominated the room. A washroom lay across the hall. Still excited by their new surroundings, the men chattered away as they stashed their bags and tested their beds. Suddenly, they were startled by the appearance in the doorway of a figure in white nightshirt and leather slippers who shouted, "Silence!" and stared angrily for another moment before disappearing down the hall, not to be seen again. "The Angel Gabriel," one of the men joked.

Their laughter was interrupted by the peal of bells from Saint Peter's. It was 6:30 A.M., and almost immediately they heard the sounds of soldiers gathering in the courtyard below their windows. Rushing to the windows, they watched as that day's duty squad mustered for inspection. It was a scene familiar to men who only weeks earlier had worn the uniform of the Swiss army, and they took comfort in the sight, thinking that adjustment to their new service would not, after all, prove that difficult. It would be just like the Swiss army, only smaller and more relaxed. Their attitudes, however, changed as soon as a sergeant shouted, "Form up!" The pope's soldiers responded to the command more quickly than a group of Swiss soldiers would have. At the command "Attention!" the halberdiers adopted a posture more rigid and motionless than what was acceptable in the Swiss army. Some of the "first day of school" joviality dissipated as the recruits realized that the standards of the guard were rather higher than what they were used to, and they would have to work hard to meet them.

As the duty detachment marched from the courtyard, a corporal appeared in California to escort the group, still in civilian clothes, to the mess hall for breakfast. There they met some of their new comrades, all of whom were eager for news from home, communications with Switzerland having become infrequent by the fall of 1943. Accustomed to the dark bread and ersatz coffee of the Swiss army mess, the recruits were surprised to be served white rolls, real butter, and real coffee. They would later discover that there were shortages in Rome too, and that the breakfast items were not normal fare but had been set out for them as a special gesture of welcome. After breakfast there was mass in the guard chapel, then a visit to the command offices, where a sergeant measured each man to ensure that each satisfied the minimum height requirement of 177 centimeters. One was alarmed to learn that he fell a full centimeter below the requirement, but he was quickly reassured by the sergeant, who said they were so desperate for men that no one really cared how tall he was. Next the men were escorted to the commandant's office. Surrounded by flags, portraits of past commandants, and memorabilia of the corps, they stood nervously at attention as Colonel Pfyffer von Altishofen stiffly greeted them, made a brief speech welcoming them to the guard, shook each by the hand, and then curtly dismissed them. Used to the more informal relations and easy camaraderie between citizen-officers and citizen–enlisted men in the Swiss military, the new arrivals found their commander's aloof manner rather curious. It was an introduction to the more formal and hierarchical world of the Swiss Guard, where noncommissioned officers ate at separate tables in the mess and halberdiers usually addressed officers only in the line of duty.

Upon exiting the commander's office, the new men found a noncommissioned officer, Sergeant Luigi Sommerhalders, waiting for them. Sergeant Sommerhalders was the recruit instructor who would guide them through their first weeks in the barracks. As the first order of business he led them to the guard armory, where the armorer had laid out each man's gear. They tried to act nonchalant, but the boyish excitement returned as each man was fitted for his uniforms, each of which—even the unadorned "exercise" uniform—was more colorful and exotic than the dull gray, shapeless uniforms they had worn in the Swiss army. As they staggered back to California under the weight of their gear—uniforms, halberd, rifle, sword, bayonet, ammunition bandolier, and gas mask—they began to feel that they were really in an army. The feeling was confirmed the next morning, their first training day and first full day as halberdiers, when they turned out in the barracks courtyard in exercise uniforms with rifles, bayonets, and bandoliers. Determined to make a good impression and demonstrate that they were not green recruits with no idea of military practice, the men had helped each other with the unfamiliar uniform (buttons in unexpected places) and equipment (an uncomfortable bandolier). In the courtyard, a bemused Sergeant Sommerhalders inspected his eleven charges and began their training by marching them briskly to the Belvedere Courtyard, which served as a drill and parade ground.

Since all entrants had to have completed their required military service in the Swiss army before enlisting in the pope's service, it was assumed that all recruits were familiar with basic military procedures (saluting, marching in step) and practices (firing a rifle, fixing a bayonet). Guard training, consequently, was a relatively brief and focused ten to fifteen days. The brevity was promoted by the need to get men out to the undermanned guard posts as quickly as possible, and the focus was encouraged by the rather narrow and specialized tasks assigned to the guard. Under the guidance of Sergeant Sommerhalders, the recruits learned to manipulate their halberds and rifles according to the elaborate choreography required of ceremonial guards in a protocol-conscious court. One movement, for example, challenged the balance of a halberdier by requiring him upon command to drop to one knee and salute with one hand while holding the unwieldy halberd perfectly vertical with the other hand. Marching received a lot of attention, as did the art of maintaining perfect ranks and formations with every body and weapon in flawless alignment. Presentation was everything in the highly competitive world of the papal military, where units, unable to distinguish themselves by battle ribbons and combat records, vied to excel in turnout, discipline, and elegance. In this military community a tarnished sword pommel, stained glove, or misaligned rank would disgrace the corps. Of course in a world where armed and menacing German soldiers were posted within two hundred yards of the Swiss Guard training ground, more practical military concerns necessarily intruded. The recruits rehearsed marching and dressing ranks, but they also practiced bayonet use and rapid loading of rifles. The lessons were not easy because the commands and maneuvers were not similar to those in the Swiss army, and the standards of performance were higher. Still, instruction was facilitated by the patience and good sense of Sergeant Sommerhalders, whom the recruits unanimously judged to be far superior in motivation and engagement to any instructors they had encountered in the Swiss army.

By December 1943 the eleven precious recruits had completed their training and had been integrated into the duty schedule, their presence alleviating, though not solving, the personnel shortage that afflicted the Swiss Guard. Resigned to the fact that another cohort of recruits was unlikely to appear in the near future, Colonel Pfyffer von Altishofen turned his attention to armament. The absence of modern firearms, particularly automatic weapons, in the guard armory troubled him. Should the guard have to defend Vatican City against a German invasion, his Mausers would be seriously outmatched by the MP40 Schmeisser submachine guns of the attackers, and the difference would be measured in dead halberdiers. Through the good offices of his friend Philipp Etter, the Swiss ambassador to Italy, whom he had known since they were young officers in the Swiss army, the commandant quietly arranged for the purchase of thirty Swiss MKPS submachine guns and several thousand rounds of ammunition from the armaments firm Schweizerische Industrie-Gesellschaft (SIG). Given the exigencies of war, it was impossible to arrange for delivery of the weapons, so in the spring of 1944 Lieutenant Colonel Ruppen went again to Switzerland. Unlike recruits, crates of guns and ammunition could not simply be squeezed onto crowded railway carriages, so this time Ruppen traveled by truck. Since both the British and the German embassies in Berne along with the Swiss government had approved the weapons consignment, he and his driver had no trouble crossing the border. The challenge was the drive south to Rome. The truck with its sealed carrier compartment bore Vatican City license plates, and

Ruppen carried papers identifying him as a Swiss Guard officer and a special courier of the Vatican transporting an approved weapons shipment. There was, however, no guarantee that the German army, let alone partisan bands and outright thieves, would respect neutral rights and property. No amount of impressive seals or stamped documents could protect him against the routine vicissitudes of wartime travel: bombed bridges, flat tires, empty gasoline tanks, and frequent delays caused by the incessant movement of troops, matériel, and citizens along overburdened transportation networks. By the time the truck reached Milan, hardly a fourth of the way into its journey, it was evident to Ruppen that the consignment was too heavy for the underpowered vehicle, which was very likely to give out before reaching its destination. To salvage his mission, Ruppen drove to the palace of the archbishop of Milan, Ildefonso Schuster, and convinced that rather discomfited prelate to take temporary custody of half of the weapons, which were then locked in the palace cellar. With a reduced load, the truck puttered south. At one point, not far from Rome, the vehicle was damaged when the driver could not avoid a large bomb crater in the middle of the road. Luckily, Ruppen was able to find a farmer with oxen to pull the vehicle from the hole. After several days on the road, Ruppen finally drove his dusty and dented vehicle through the Saint Anne gate and into the courtyard of the Swiss Guard barracks, where the precious submachine guns were moved into the safety of the armory.[62] Since Colonel Pfyffer von Altishofen immediately transferred half of the weapons to the Pontifical Gendarmeria, Ruppen's mission represented a modest, but very welcome, addition to the firepower of two of the pope's armed units.[63]

The degree to which Colonel Pfyffer von Altishofen's defensive preparations may have been constrained by an order from Pope Pius restricting his freedom of action remains uncertain.[64] The original order came on September 9, 1943, in a telephone call from Monsignor Giovanni Montini. As German troops fought their way into the Eternal City, the deputy secretary of state informed the commandant that the Holy Father had directed that under no circumstances should the Swiss Guard use firearms to protect the Apostolic Palace. As the commandant listened to Monsignor Montini, he may have heard the echoes of history whispering along the telephone line. In 1798 and 1808 two other Pfyffer von Altishofens, also commandants, had at the direction of their pontiffs offered no resistance to French troops intent on seizing Pius VI and Pius VII. On both occasions the Swiss guardsmen had stood passively as the popes they were sworn to protect at the cost of their lives were carried into foreign exile. It was not a scene easy for any commandant to contemplate. Given the circumstances—gunfire could be heard from across the Tiber—and his enormous responsibility, Pfyffer von Altishofen felt compelled to request the order in writing. Two days later a formal directive, signed by Montini, arrived in the guard barracks.[65]

It is unlikely that a commandant would disobey a direct order from the Holy Father; nevertheless, Colonel Pfyffer von Altishofen seems to have accepted the order with silent reservations, perhaps justifying his hesitation on the grounds that the directive did not actually come directly from the Holy Father, only from a subordinate. Whatever his reasoning, the commandant continued to insist on a high state of readiness, acting as if he were prepared to defend every foot of the pope's tiny domain against all comers. Throughout the emergency, duty halberdiers carried loaded rifles and extra ammunition, a readiness posture that seems excessive if the guards were expected to lay down their weapons at the first sign of an attack. After all, if the defense was intended to be purely symbolic, then a halberd carried as much symbolism as a rifle. Altishofen's purchase of the MKPS submachine guns several months after the order from Montini also suggests that the commandant was keeping his options open. If there was no intention of resisting an attack, then why worry about increasing the guard's firepower? Furthermore, the commandant apparently did not communicate the Holy Father's wishes to his troops, who continued throughout the emergency to assume that they might have to fight. Before marching to their posts, duty squads were reminded by their noncommissioned officers of their obligation to protect the pope with their lives. The guardsmen, well aware of the discrepancy between the combat capabilities of their corps and those of the Germans, fully expected to resist any invasion of the Vatican and make the attack as costly as possible for the aggressor.[66] The parallels with General Hermann Kanzler's decision, contrary to Pope Pius IX's expectations, to defend the walls of Rome against the Italian army in 1870 are striking. Like Kanzler, Colonel Pfyffer von Altishofen seems to have intended to interpret a papal directive of nonresistance as liberally as possible.

In preparing the defense of the Vatican, the Swiss Guard commander could rely on assistance from the Pontifical Gendarmeria. During the emergency, the police service expanded its patrol and surveillance activities. Ten gendarmes at seven posts were now on duty day and night inside the Apostolic Palace. The guard posted at the Lourdes Grotto in the gardens became an air-raid warden responsible for phoning headquarters whenever a plane approached Vatican City. Even before the German occupation of Rome, Vatican authorities had outfitted three air-raid shelters, and in the event of an air raid, gendarmes were assigned to the shelters to maintain calm and order. In some patrol sectors, gendarmes now regularly carried Mauser rifles with bayonets and two pouches of cartridges in addition to their pistols. There were not enough Mausers in the police armory to equip all patrols, so the gendarmes assigned to less crucial buildings or sectors were issued obsolete single-shot Remingtons that had been purchased for the old pontifical army in the late 1860s. Off-duty gendarmes had to remain in uniform in the barracks, ready in the event of an emergency to muster in the courtyard with their ammunition pouches before deploying to the threatened sector.[67]

Even combined, the personnel of the Swiss Guard and the Pontifical Gendarmeria were too few to staff the additional guard and patrol duties required by the emergency. To fill the gaps, the Palatine Guard had to be mobilized. Since the loss of the Papal States and the contraction of the pope's temporal domain to the few acres occupied by Saint Peter's Basilica and the Apostolic Palace and its gardens, that unit had been reduced to a purely ceremonial role.[68] Unlike the professionals in the Swiss Guard and the Pontifical Gendarmeria, the Palatines remained unpaid, part-time amateurs who had volunteered to line up in the uniform of a mid-nineteenth-century French infantry regiment and present unloaded rifles during ecclesiastical celebrations or the reception of important visitors to the papal palace. Aside from minimal instruction in marching and presenting arms, the Palatines received no military training, although many had previously served in the Italian army. The corps was authorized as a battalion of five hundred men and grandly organized into a general staff, a band, four guard companies, and a depot company, but its strength had declined as younger guardsmen were called up for wartime service in the Italian military. When the Germans marched into Rome, the unit could muster only about three hundred men.[69]

With the German occupation of Rome, the Palatine Guard had to rediscover its military origins. The guard loyally rose to the occasion. The morning after the announcement of the Italian armistice, as German troops poured into the Eternal City and gunfire echoed along deserted streets, guardsmen spontaneously reported to the Vatican for duty, assuming the Holy Father would require their services. They assumed correctly. That same day the commander of the corps, Colonel Francesco Cantuti di Castelvetri, received orders from the office of the cardinal secretary of state to collaborate with the gendarmeria to establish additional guard posts and patrols inside Vatican City. For the first time in seventy-three years, the Palatine Guard mobilized for active military service. Guardsmen reporting for duty on the day after the German occupation immediately noticed the change: A sentinel in field uniform with a loaded rifle and bayonet now stood at the entrance to the corps's offices inside the papal palace. Within days Palatine Guards were on sentinel duty at the Vatican radio station; the railway station; the museums; and the "industrial zone" that included the Vatican's post office, pharmacy, publishing house, department store, and workshops. Fearing that the German occupation authorities would seal off the Vatican or impose a state of emergency or curfew that would prevent guardsmen from commuting between their homes and Vatican City, Colonel di Castelvetri decided to quarter 150 of his men, in rotation, inside the papal enclave. In a wing of the Vatican Museum artworks were removed and replaced by folding cots, foot lockers, and rifle racks to form a makeshift barracks. A nearby hall, which before the war had been a venue for concerts, became a mess hall for the pope's citizen-soldiers.[70]

The demands upon the small corps increased further when the superintendents of various buildings owned or protected by the Vatican in and around Rome requested guards for their properties. Some of these buildings had extraterritorial status under the Lateran Agreements and were considered, therefore, Vatican territory. On October 5, 1943, fifteen Palatine Guards were dispatched to Castel Gandolfo, the pope's summer villa and farm in the Alban Hills outside Rome. Six days later a detachment was sent across the city to protect the extraterritorial Basilica of Saint John Lateran and its dependent buildings. Eventually, Palatines would be mounting guard at some fifteen sites around the Eternal City.[71]

Like the Swiss Guard and the gendarmeria, the Palatine Guard had too few men to respond to the demands of the emergency. For the corps to provide day-and-night coverage of its assigned posts, each guardsman had to serve six hours every day. This was a very heavy burden for unpaid volunteers with families and jobs in the city, and commanders realized that the corps could not maintain this operational tempo for long.[72] In late September 1943 Colonel di Castelvetri received from the cardinal secretary of state permission to enroll 110 Roman university students as auxiliaries. Even with these auxiliaries the Palatines struggled to meet their obligations, especially after the unit assumed responsibility for the protection of Vatican properties around Rome. Recognizing that they needed more soldiers, papal authorities decided to open enrollment in the Palatine Guard with a view to increasing the size of the corps to a maximum of two thousand men.

The response was overwhelming. Several thousand young Romans presented themselves at the Vatican to volunteer, many moved by loyalty to the pope but not a few incorrectly believing that enrollment in the Palatine Guard would automatically exempt them from the military and labor drafts that were increasingly common in German-occupied Rome. In fact, the treaty component of the Lateran Agreements provided that only Vatican citizens and those personnel of the papal court appearing on a list mutually agreed to by the Vatican and the Italian government would be exempt from Italian military service. Palatine guardsmen did not hold Vatican citizenship, and apparently they did not appear on any joint list because, before the armistice, some of them had been called into Italian military service. After discussions with the Italian and German authorities in late October and early November concerning the expansion of the Palatine Guard, the Vatican agreed that it would not admit into the guard "political personalities," "high officials," or males under the age of twenty-one.[73]

The Vatican decided to interpret the agreement liberally. From the Apostolic Palace the Palatine Guard command received orders to give preference to applicants who were at special risk of arrest or conscription. One student of the period has asserted that several Jews found refuge from the pogroms of Nazi authorities in Rome by donning the uniform of the Palatine Guard.[74] By December 1,500 auxiliaries had been enrolled, an influx that alleviated the personnel crisis but seriously strained the command and matériel resources of the corps. To fill the need for noncommissioned officers to supervise the new arrivals, aged guardsmen were brought out of retirement. Depot personnel scrambled to outfit the recruits, for many of whom a long military cloak over civilian clothes initially provided the only semblance of a uniform. As for weapons, the Palatine armory contained some Mannlicher-Carcano model 91 rifles, which were standard issue in the Italian army, but not enough to arm the enlarged force. The deficiency was made up with more antique Remingtons; by now the pope's hard-pressed military officers were very grateful that the Vatican had held on to the old guns after 1870.[75] Some guardsmen may have wondered whether the nineteenth-century Remington cartridges would still fire.

For all the strains of emergency service and organizational expansion, the Palatine Guard conscientiously tried to transform itself into a serious military unit. No other unit in the papal armed services underwent such change. Guardsmen accustomed to volunteering a few hours of their time each month adjusted to heavy duty schedules. Armed guardsmen manned fixed posts and mobile patrols around the clock. Plumed shakos, fancy epaulettes, and white gloves gave way to crimson berets, gray coveralls with plain cotton shoulder straps, and black cloaks. Ammunition and bayonets were issued for the rifles, although weapons training remained rudimentary. Religion figured more prominently than rifles in the life of the wartime Palatines; indeed, officers often seemed more concerned with the spiritual life of their men than with their military preparation. Throughout the German occupation, the Palatine Guard cultivated the image of a Christian militia, a community of pious Catholic citizen-soldiers who were distinguished by their devotion to their faith and their loyalty to their pope. This idea of a community united by bonds of religious faith as well as personal service was lived by the guardsmen barracked inside Vatican City and propagated explicitly in the pages of *Vita Palatina* (Palatine life), a weekly newsletter published for the corps during the occupation. The newsletters were replete with articles and essays concerning the life of the Holy Father, the organization of the church, the meaning of religious holidays and exercises, and the spiritual responsibilities of a committed Catholic. One article advised the new auxiliaries to devote the hours between guard shifts to prayer and religious meditation. Surprisingly, the newsletter contained scarcely a reference to military affairs. An uninformed reader might easily have mistaken *Vita Palatina* for a publication of a religious confraternity rather than a military unit. In fact, that was exactly how the Palatines saw themselves.

The Noble Guard completed the order of battle of the papal army. Another highly decorative but not particularly martial organization, the Noble Guard had, like the Palatines, evolved after the loss of the Papal States into a purely ceremonial unit. Nominally the personal bodyguards of the Holy Father, the guardsmen, all of whom were recruited from the Italian nobility, were unpaid except for a liberal uniform allowance. They received no training beyond instruction in the drills and protocol relevant to their honor-guard duties in the papal apartments. In 1943 the unit mustered only thirty-two men, although several additional personnel were recruited after the German occupation. For all its comic-opera appearance, the Noble Guard did not need to be reminded of its duty. When the Germans marched into Rome, the commandant was Prince Francesco Chigi della Rovere, a rigorous commander who, even at the height of a scorching Roman summer, always arrived at his office in a dark gray wool vested suit. The prince immediately ordered his men into the Apostolic Palace, the first time the Nobles had been barracked inside the Vatican since the attack on Rome in 1870. The normal daytime ceremonial service was abandoned in favor of around-the-clock protective coverage of the Holy Father. At night Noble Guards now stood watch in the foyer of the pope's apartment, and a couple of guardsmen shadowed the pontiff from behind hedges and trees during his afternoon walks. Usually, Noble Guards carried only sabers while on service, but with the German occupation of Rome, pistols were issued to duty personnel, the first time the guardsmen had carried firearms since the nineteenth century. Unlike the Swiss Guard, the Noble Guard received no orders prohibiting the use of force in defense of the Holy Father.[76]

For the papal armed services, life under the German occupation was a far cry from prewar routines, when the biggest concerns were the shine on a belt buckle, the drape of a dress tunic, or the proper alignment of an honor guard. Now the pope's defenders had to endure the same wartime shortages and privations that afflicted the population of Rome. Communication beyond the city was intermittent as the war disrupted rail and road lines, and all correspondence was censored by the occupation authorities. Communication problems weighed especially heavily on the Swiss Guards, whose families were in Switzerland. They had received no home leave since 1941. Because of downed lines, phone connections with Switzerland were frequently interrupted, and telegrams were prohibited except for emergencies approved by the commandant. Weeks would pass without mail, and probably nothing had a more deleterious impact on morale than the absence of news from home. The requirement that no Swiss guardsman could leave Vatican City, even to walk about Rome, without specific permission from the German occupation authority only increased the sense of isolation and claustrophobia.[77]

Empty cupboards presented as big a problem as empty mailboxes. Before the armistice the inhabitants of Vatican City were better fed than most of the citizens of wartime Rome; indeed, two Swiss Guards were disciplined for selling in the city foodstuffs they acquired inside the Vatican. The administration of Vatican City actually had to promulgate a law prohibiting the "export" of food and other products to Italy.[78] Conditions changed dramatically with the German occupation. Although there was a small farm at Castel Gandolfo, the pope's summer villa in the Alban Hills, most of the food consumed inside Vatican City came from purveyors in Rome. Many items, such as vegetables and fruit, became scarce, and others, particularly eggs and cocoa, were available only on the black market. Produce and cereals were available in the countryside, but transporting provisions to Rome was difficult. Victuals from the south could not cross the battle lines, and shipments from the German-occupied north had to run a gauntlet of poor roads, interdicted rail lines, and Allied air attacks.

Beginning in January 1944, the Vatican assumed much of the burden of supplying the Eternal City. Fleets of trucks, painted in the papal colors of yellow and white or with the Vatican flag stretched across their roofs, scoured the provinces north of Rome as far as Tuscany and the Marche for food products. In January alone the Vatican convoys carried over 100,000 kilograms of flour into the city.[79] It was dangerous work because the colors of the neutral Vatican City did not always protect the trucks, especially when the Germans abused that neutrality. In March 1944 the Marchese Giulio Patrizi di Ripacandida, a sublieutenant in the Noble Guard who was leaving Vatican City after a night on duty, stopped at the Saint Anne gate to watch a long funeral cortege pass along the Vatican walls. Among the mainly working-class mourners he recognized several men who held positions inside the Vatican. "Who died?" the marchese inquired of the Swiss Guard at the gate. The guard answered that it was one of the drivers from the Vatican convoys that supplied Rome. When the lieutenant asked, "Was it an accident?" the halberdier replied, "You might say so, Marchese; he died from wounds received when Anglo-American planes machine-gunned one of our truck convoys."[80] As the convoy had crossed the countryside, several German army vehicles had placed themselves at the front and back of the column of Vatican trucks, hoping, presumably, that any marauding Allied planes would mistake them for part of the convoy. The ruse did not work, but the Germans were not the only ones who paid the consequences. Allied planes machine-gunned and bombed the entire convoy, destroying not just the German vehicles but also two Vatican trucks, killing their drivers and a priest who had accompanied the convoy.[81] Since the provisions that made it to Rome in Vatican trucks were intended for the people of Rome, not just the inhabitants of Vatican City, papal relief efforts did not significantly improve the food situation in the papal enclave. In fact, the situation gradually worsened. By the spring of 1944, Vatican authorities were drawing on emergency stocks of dried lentils and cod that had been stored in cellars before the war.

The mess halls of the pope's soldiers were not exempt from the shortages that affected the general population. From January 1944 on, for example, the mess of the Swiss Guard had no more butter, cheese, or salami. Several dairy cows had been moved from Castel Gandolfo into Vatican City, and a long corridor in the papal palace was converted into what was probably the only marble-floored dairy barn in Europe. The cows' output had to be shared among the inhabitants of the papal city. The daily ration of milk was eight liters for the entire Swiss corps of sixty-two men. The daily bread ration was reduced to 250 grams per halberdier, and then to 150 grams. Though this allowance was still more than the 100 grams available to people in Rome, the soldiers recalled wistfully the 500 grams that had been the norm during their service in the Swiss Army. By the spring of 1944, the halberdiers were on a steady diet of dried lentils (called "gravel rations" by the men) and dried cod from the emergency stocks, although sometimes there would be only fried onions for lunch. Still, the halberdiers knew that conditions beyond the walls of the Vatican were worse, and they shared their meager rations with the children who loitered at the gates of the papal city hoping for scraps.[82]

Most of the pope's guards bore the privation with stoicism and occasional humor. In the mess of the Palatine Guards the pope's citizen-soldiers, well aware of the shortages beyond the Vatican's walls, were thankful to have regular meals, no matter how modest the fare. Over frugal meals in the quarters of the Noble Guard, older guardsmen wistfully recalled prewar duty at Castel Gandolfo, where tasty snacks and excellent wine had always been available for off-duty personnel. Hungry guardsmen hoped to draw duty when Prince Giulio Pacelli was the esente because the nuns who prepared the meals for the Noble Guard mess always made a special effort when the pope's nephew was watch commander.[83] Inevitably, however, grumbling rose in the ranks. The Swiss were particularly irritable. A Christmas party hosted by Colonel Pfyffer von Altishofen provided a candlelit tree, holiday cookies, and carols to the accompaniment of the guard band, but the mood among the halberdiers remained sour. Dispositions did not improve when the chaplain, Monsignor Paul Krieg, devoted a Sunday sermon in the guard chapel to chastising the men for their lack of forbearance in the face of privation. Some halberdiers preferred laughter to lectures. At one Spartan meal halberdier Fridolin Fetz pulled from his tunic a small volume that looked like a prayer book. One of his compatriots, in a not-so-subtle dig at Chaplain Krieg, promptly opined that Fetz had joined those who preached the moral benefits of fasting. With all the hauteur appropriate to a solemn occasion, Fetz enjoined the heckler to show some respect for the proceedings. Then, like a monk reading from the *Lives of the Saints* as his brothers silently consume a frugal meal in an abbey refectory, Fetz began slowly to read from the small book, which contained not pious biographies but traditional recipes from his homeland, the area around the Swiss town of Chur. That day the Swiss

Guards closed their eyes and thought of meat loaf and roasted potatoes as they forced down another meal of dried lentils and cod.[84]

Some soldiers preferred direct action. The morning following Chaplain Krieg's edifying sermon, Halberdier Moritz Werlen, in contravention of unit custom and the chain of command, walked into Colonel Pfyffer von Altishofen's office with a cup of the ersatz brew that had replaced coffee in the guard mess. Werlen politely asked his commander to taste the beverage so that he would know what the men had to drink. Although some of his predecessors might have considered the uninvited appearance of a halberdier in the command office an impertinence, the commandant accepted this request in good spirit. Upon tasting the liquid, the colonel promptly announced, "This is not coffee; it's dishwater." Believing that the guard kitchen received a ration of coffee beans, the commander could not understand why the product of those beans was not finding its way to the mess tables. He decided to investigate personally. Interrogations of kitchen staff, a review of account books, and an inspection of cupboards revealed that the staff had been diverting to their own use a significant portion of the coffee beans. Presumably, the halberdiers noticed an improvement in their morning hot beverage after the commandant's inquiries.[85]

The pope's military forces did not escape the unit rivalries that characterized the much larger armies of other countries. In fact, the emergency exacerbated some of these rivalries. There had always been keen competition as each corps tried to outdo the others in drill, presentation, and status. In the tiny, hothouse world of the Vatican, trifles of military etiquette, ceremonial position, or court precedence assumed huge importance. In the years after the loss of the Papal States, for instance, an inordinate amount of time, energy, and erudition was expended on the question of whether the Swiss or the Palatine Guards should have precedence in matters of court ceremony and protocol. Before the question was settled in favor of the halberdiers, one Swiss Guard commandant had commented facetiously that his Palatine counterpart spent all his time trying to trace the origins of his unit to the time of the Emperor Constantine. After the German occupation, competition focused on military preparedness and contribution to the defensive effort. The Swiss Guards, for example, expressed dismay when some of the coveted submachine guns delivered in the spring of 1944 were transferred to the Pontifical Gendarmeria. In the minds of the halberdiers, the police were unqualified for such weapons, which should have been reserved for the use of "real" soldiers. They felt particular outrage when they learned that gendarmes were issued the automatic weapons without receiving any training in their use.[86] Whatever their differences, however, halberdiers and gendarmes found common ground as professionals against the amateurs of the Palatine and Noble Guards.

The Palatine Guard, which, perhaps unjustly, developed a reputation for indiscipline and irresponsibility, was a frequent target of criticism. Many of the men who had joined the guard during its expansion after the armistice had enrolled merely to avoid conscription into the army or labor battalions, and these auxiliaries lacked the motivation and commitment of the "old" guard. The Palatine command had neither the time nor the facilities to develop a training program that might have instilled unit pride and confidence in the new arrivals. Not surprisingly, the performance of these auxiliaries was uneven. Most performed their duties conscientiously, but some did not. It was not unknown for guardsmen to leave their posts or fail to control entry into the papal properties they were ostensibly guarding. In January 1944, for example, an administrator at the Pontifical Urban College complained that thrice in a single week he had discovered that the Palatines ostensibly on night duty at the college were not at their guard posts. On one occasion, the guardsmen stationed at the gate of the Urban College fled their post at the approach of a single German army truck that was delivering several boxes of ecclesiastical records as a favor to papal authorities.[87]

Word of such embarrassments inevitably made its way through the barracks and mess halls of the papal army. The Swiss simply dismissed the Palatines, especially the auxiliaries who joined after the armistice, as little more than pretend soldiers and ridiculed their unmilitary bearing, lack of training, obsolete Remingtons, and dowdy field uniforms. At certain posts, such as the Vatican radio station, that were nominally the responsibility of the Palatine Guard, Swiss Guards were often assigned special duty to reinforce the pope's citizen soldiers—a sign that papal authorities were not entirely convinced of the reliability of the Palatines. The Swiss, already overburdened by emergency duties, did not appreciate having to chaperone another unit. One evening at the Vatican Radio post, two halberdiers were so scandalized by the lax and unprofessional behavior of their Palatine fellow guards, who apparently preferred to converse, smoke, and joke than walk their post, that they seriously considered firing their rifles into the air to focus the attention of the amateurs. The halberdiers decided that the pleasure of scaring the callow fellows was not worth the uproar that would follow a report of gunfire at Vatican Radio.[88] In the event of real gunfire, the Swiss expected little support from "soldiers" who, at least in the eyes of the professionals, could hardly affix a bayonet to a rifle. Not surprisingly, the disdain was reciprocated. The Palatines considered the Swiss arrogant, condescending, and privileged, and resented their claim to be the only real soldiers in the Vatican.[89]

For all their criticism of the Palatines, the rank-and-file halberdiers reserved their greatest scorn for the Noble Guards whom they were inclined to disdain as idle fops and arrogant poseurs compared to whom the Palatines seemed a crack infantry unit. The Swiss, who considered themselves by corps seniority and training the real protectors of the pontiff, begrudged the Nobles their claim to be *the* bodyguards of the pope and the premier corps in the pontifical army. They also resented having to salute the young Noble Guards—some of whom were rumored to live rather dissolute lives in exclusive Roman society—simply because every member of the corps held an officer's rank. If the halberdiers expected little from the Palatine Guard in a combat situation, they expected nothing from the Noble Guard.[90] This dismissive attitude was unfortunate and unfair. The Noble Guard was a proud and venerable unit (as a direct descendant of the Lance Spezzate and the Corpi dei Cavalleggeri, it could arguably claim a pedigree older than that of the Swiss Guard), and its response to the crisis of the German occupation was exemplary. Like most of the Palatines, the Nobles performed their duties no less conscientiously and honorably than the Swiss, and they were no less committed to the defense of the Holy Father. Ironically, many of the "amateurs" in the Noble and Palatine Guards, because of their previous service in the Italian army, had actually been in combat, an experience none of the "professionals" in the Swiss Guard could claim.[91]

The German occupation significantly changed daily routines and duties. For some of the pope's protectors, these changes brought new assignments. Swiss Guards, for example, had not served outside Rome in more than a century. Now, with communications to the north increasingly uncertain, halberdiers were occasionally employed as diplomatic couriers, carrying confidential communications or chaperoning shipments between the Vatican and the papal nunciature (embassy) in Switzerland, which served as a transit point for Vatican communications with the world beyond Italy. In April 1944, for example, Colonel Pfyffer von Altishofen personally carried confidential mail to Switzerland and returned to Vatican City with five sealed crates, nine sealed suitcases, six packages, and two sacks. The missions were not without risk. In November 1943 German soldiers at the Italian-Swiss border temporarily detained Halberdier Leopold Tscherrig, who was traveling alone by motorcycle with a consignment of diplomatic mail. Although Tscherrig carried credentials identifying him as a courier for the Vatican and a member of the Swiss Guard, the Germans confiscated his pouch of letters. On his next courier trip Tscherrig was arrested by the Germans and held in a Milanese prison for five months.[92]

Inside Vatican City, the number of papal audiences and receptions declined, and routine ceremonial service gave way to emergency guard and patrol duties. A Swiss or Palatine guard was now more likely to find himself in field uniform, a bayoneted rifle over his shoulder and ammunition bandolier across his chest, standing at an ornately carved door, pacing a frescoed corridor, or patrolling a section of wall or a garden pathway than presenting arms in formal dress to a visiting head of state. For nighttime duty in the papal apartment, the sartorially flamboyant Noble Guards exchanged their high cavalry boots, decorative tunics, and polished helmets for the *uniforme sem-plice di quartiere* (barracks service uniform): unadorned dark blue jacket, light blue pants, plain leather belt and pistol holster, and dark kepi. At gates and building entrances, sentinels stopped all visitors and closely examined identity papers. Callers with appointments inside the papal city could not proceed until their host was telephoned and their appointment confirmed. Daily logs recorded the arrival and departure of visitors. At night, duty be-hind the closed and barred gates was tedious and lonely for the cloaked sen-tinels who patrolled the silent corridors and pathways or paced the dark-ened courtyards. Swiss Guards had it somewhat easier because regulations allowed night-duty halberdiers to sit at a table at their post and write letters or read, so long as they remained awake and kept their rifles within reach. During the night officers visited the posts to ensure that the sentinels were awake and alert, but inevitably there were lapses. On one occasion a pair of Noble Guards, scheduled at midnight to relieve their colleagues on duty at the papal apartment, walked from the Noble Guard quarters in the palace to the apartment and were alarmed to discover no gendarmes at their posts along the way. On another night, three escaped Allied POWs, seeking refuge inside Vatican City, somehow climbed over the walls and wandered around the papal gardens for several hours before encountering a guard.[93]

Fortunately for his protectors, Pius did not complicate their duties by leaving Vatican City. Once Italy entered the war, there were no more visits to Castel Gandolfo, sojourns that required the deployment to the villa of de-tachments from all the pontifical guard units. Only twice, on July 19, 1943, and August 13, 1943, did the Holy Father leave the Vatican, both times to visit Roman neighborhoods devastated by Allied air raids. On the first occa-sion bombs had heavily damaged portions of the working-class San Lorenzo district. Pius was in an audience with a visiting bishop in the late afternoon when he learned that San Lorenzo had been hit. Terminating the audience, the pope phoned Monsignor Montini, telling him to collect as much cash as he could find. When Montini arrived with a satchel of money, Pius led him to a courtyard where the papal limousine was waiting, and together they im-mediately set off for the devastated district without any attendants or escorts. The guard detachments seem to have been completely unaware of the ex-citement. They did not learn of the pope's actions until he was driving away, accompanied only by a chauffeur, an official of the Secretariat of State, and a large sum of money. Colonel Pfyffer von Altishofen, the commandant of the Swiss Guard, was in his office in the Swiss barracks when he received a phone call from frantic attendants in the papal apartments asking if the guard knew that the Holy Father was at that very moment leaving Vatican City for San Lorenzo. Dropping everything and yelling for his deputy, Lieu-tenant Colonel Ruppen, to follow him, the commandant rushed from the barracks to find a vehicle to chase after the pope. Meanwhile, at a desk in the anteroom of the papal suite, the esente, the Noble Guard duty officer who commanded all guard detachments assigned to the apartments and who was personally responsible for the pontiff's safety, anticipated a relatively quiet duty tour. A flustered chamberlain broke the calm by announcing that the Holy Father had decided on the spur of the moment to go to San Lorenzo. In fact, the functionary added, the pope had already left. In the world of the Noble Guard, this was quite simply impossible. The Holy Father never left his rooms without the esente walking a few steps behind. The astonished officer was further staggered to learn that not only had Pius left, but he was traveling with only his chauffeur and Monsignor Montini. "What?" he yelled. "You let the Pope go unescorted!" The esente immediately phoned the Noble Guard offices in another wing of the palace, and within minutes several guardsmen were rushing for a car. Meanwhile, Pius had reached San Lorenzo and freely mingled with the crowd that quickly gathered at the news that the Holy Father had come to them. The pope prayed with the survivors and comforted them while Monsignor Montini distributed all the money. Eventually, Pfyffer von Altishofen and Ruppen arrived and served as an ad hoc security detail, but there were no incidents, and the pope was never in any danger.[94]

Each of the guard corps endured unpleasant assignments. The winter of 1943–1944 was extremely cold, and duty inside the papal palace provided no escape from the damp and the low temperatures. The marble floors and stone walls held the cold like a refrigerator. "It is repetitive and boring to mention every time the cold in the quarters is horrible," a young Noble Guard wrote in his diary, "but unfortunately that is the dominant note of this severe winter." That season the Noble Guards particularly dreaded night duty in the papal apartment. The two duty guardsmen, pistols on their belts and heavy white uniform cloaks around their shoulders, huddled at a small table and tried to warm their hands by the small lamp and its single bulb. To set an example for others in a time of privation and rationing, Pius had ordered the heat turned off, so the post was chilly as well as dark. "We froze in that vestibule," a guardsman would later recall.[95]

The Palatines hated the post at the Loggia delle Dame on the roof above the Bronze Door. It provided an important observation point because it controlled Saint Peter's Square and offered a clear view the length of the Via della Conciliazione, the wide street that ran from the square to the Tiber River. Unfortunately, the position was exposed to the elements, yet the guards were expected to maintain surveillance of the square and the street no matter how cold, windy, or rainy the conditions were.[96]

For the Swiss Guards, the worst assignment was Post 4 on the landing outside the door to the pope's apartment. There was neither a table nor a chair because the landing was too small to accommodate such items and because this sentinel was expected to maintain special vigilance. The guard could either stand in place with his rifle or pace a few steps back and forth in front of the door. The landing was so small that the guard had to be careful that his long bayonet did not scratch the wall as he pivoted to retrace his steps. Lieutenant Colonel Ruppen, when he was officer of the guard, made a point of looking at the walls when he checked Post 4, and he would always throw a tantrum if he noticed a new scratch. Guilty halberdiers would often lick a thumb and try to rub away the scratch mark before Ruppen arrived, but the lieutenant colonel was never fooled.[97]

Working conditions changed with the season. With the arrival of hot and humid summer days, the pope's guards particularly appreciated duty in the Vatican Gardens. They could enjoy the shaded pathways and quiet fountains and, perhaps, visit the eagle that was kept in an enclosure in one corner of the gardens. The bird's death in April 1944 was much lamented among the guards.[98] Despite the attractions of garden duty, the guards were irked by the requirement to remain completely hidden when the pope took his afternoon stroll. On one occasion the garden picket of Swiss Guards, who normally observed the progress of the pontiff by peering around the corners of buildings or the trunks of trees, was distracted by the flight overhead of a large formation of Allied planes on their way to bomb German positions in the Alban Hills outside Rome. As the guards were staring at the sky, they heard a voice behind them ask, "What is happening?" Startled, the halberdiers turned to find Pius standing a few feet away. In accordance with regulations, each guardsman immediately dropped to one knee, rifle perpendicular to the ground and saluting hand touching the rim of his beret. One would later recall that surprise and chagrin at being discovered by the Holy Father, whose insistence upon complete solitude in his gardens was well known among his protectors, caused them to execute the maneuver with less precision than was usually shown at ceremonies in Saint Peter's Basilica. When one halberdier explained that they had been observing the passage of the Allied bombers, Pius asked them to join him in a prayer for the victims of war.[99]

The approaches to the pontiff's apartments were especially closely controlled, and no one was allowed entry without specific authorization. Late one evening a cardinal appeared at the pope's door, demanding immediate access to the Holy Father. As part of their training, Swiss Guards had to memorize the names and faces of all cardinals, so the halberdier on night duty at Post 4 recognized the visitor. Nevertheless, the guard, rifle in hand, barred the way, stating that his orders were that no one could pass. The cardinal, who was after all a prince of the church and accustomed to deference, vociferously insisted on his prerogatives, but the halberdier would not give way. The outraged prelate stomped off to find the duty officer, who returned with him to the papal apartment to assure the sentinel that an exception to the standing orders could be made. As he entered the pope's quarters, the barely mollified cardinal muttered, "These Swiss are rough, but at least you can trust them."[100]

Some encounters proved less benign. On one occasion a squad of German troops took up a station in front of the Bronze Doors and insisted on checking the papers of all those entering the papal palace. The Germans were on Vatican territory, and their attempt to control access to papal buildings was a clear violation of the sovereignty guaranteed by the Lateran Agreements. The Swiss Guards at the entrance ordered them off. There were some tense moments as armed Swiss and Germans faced off, and papal commanders, immediately informed of the provocation, wondered if the incursion presaged a more aggressive move by the occupiers. After thirty minutes the Germans withdrew. On another occasion Vatican gendarmes on duty in Saint Peter's Basilica intervened when German agents tried to kidnap Monsignor Hugh O'Flaherty, an Irish-born papal official whom the Gestapo correctly suspected of running an escape line for Allied POWs from his residence inside the Vatican.

Germans were not the only intruders. Many people wanted to get inside Vatican City. Refugees, believing that the Vatican offered physical safety, food, shelter, and medicine, sometimes gathered in such numbers at the Bronze Door seeking entry that off-duty halberdiers had to be mobilized to control the crowd.[101] Some refugees even camped out in Saint Peter's Square. Allied POWs presented a bigger problem. In the summer of 1943 there were eighty-two POW camps and hospitals in Italy. After the armistice the Italian guards at many of these camps released the prisoners or simply abandoned their posts, leaving the prisoners to walk away. Some of the freed prisoners hid in the countryside; some joined the bands of anti-Nazi partisans that were springing up across German-occupied Italy; and some made their way to Rome, where they were assisted by an escape and evasion network organized by Monsignor Hugh O'Flaherty. The Irish priest had worked for the Vatican since 1921 and occupied an apartment in the shadow of Saint Peter's. Using funds provided by D'Arcy Osborne or contributed by Roman sympathizers, such as Prince Filippo Doria Pamphili, Monsignor O'Flaherty had, by the fall of 1943, developed an elaborate clandestine organization to find, house, and feed escaped POWs and others sought by the Germans. Most of these escapees were hidden in safe houses around the Eternal City, but not a few were sheltered inside Vatican City. Upon their arrival in Rome, many actually made a run for the Vatican in the mistaken belief that the papal enclave offered official sanctuary. Every evening Monsignor O'Flaherty would pace the steps of Saint Peter's, reading his breviary and making himself visible and available to anyone seeking asylum.[102]

Concerned about maintaining their neutrality, provoking the Germans, and encouraging a rush on their gates by asylum seekers, papal authorities adopted an official policy of denying entry to escaped POWs or others seeking refuge. In practice, however, some officials winked at violations of that policy. Papal gendarmes, for example, were ordered to be especially alert for individuals trying to sneak into Vatican City from the steps or portico of Saint Peter's.[103] For the pope's guards, this was a difficult policy to enforce because most sympathized with the plight of the escapees. In general they enforced the strict letter of their directives to bar asylum seekers but were prepared to ignore the spirit of those orders. The Vatican police, who patrolled Saint Peter's Square and the steps to the basilica, tended to be the most scrupulous about enforcement, but even they were not inflexible. On one occasion two escaped British seamen somehow acquired Italian naval uniforms and gained entry into Saint Peter's in this disguise. Inside the basilica, a papal gendarme confronted them and quickly recognized their ploy. When he attempted to expel them, they resisted and were subdued only when additional gendarmes raced to their colleague's assistance. The police officers bodily carried the seamen from the basilica with the intention of depositing them across the frontier in Saint Peter's Square. Before they could return the men to Italian territory, they were intercepted by John May, the valet to Osborne and a member of Monsignor O'Flaherty's escape network. The gendarmes readily agreed to hand the seamen over to May without questioning where he planned to take them. The police probably guessed that the escapees would be given refuge, but they were not likely to protest because the Pontifical Gendarmeria was itself providing refuge to escaped Allied prisoners. Several British soldiers who had managed to gain entry into Vatican City were housed inside the police barracks. The gendarmeria, in fact, was an equal-opportunity refuge. While the British internees took the air every morning on a barracks terrace, two German army deserters who had escaped into the pope's domain took the air on a terrace on the opposite side of the barracks.[104]

The Swiss Guards also honored the strict letter of the "no asylum" policy while undermining its spirit. For several months, for example, two Jews were hidden in the barracks apartment of the deputy commandant, Lieutenant Colonel Ruppen.[105] When intercepting an escaped POW who was trying to sneak through one of the gates, the halberdiers would deny him entry but notify Monsignor O'Flaherty or his collaborator, John May, who would arrive to take charge of the desperate man and lead him to refuge. Not everyone was thankful. One day a British officer on the run appeared at a Vatican gate in the hope of talking his way into the papal enclave. The Swiss at the gate were not impressed and politely but firmly refused to let him pass. When the officer insisted, the halberdiers picked him up and carried him to the frontier. The guards then notified Monsignor O'Flaherty that another British soldier was seeking asylum, and the priest hurried out to collect the man and take him to a safe house. Refusing to leave well enough alone, the officer wrote a letter to the cardinal secretary of state complaining about the ungentlemanly conduct of the Swiss Guards. Monsignor O'Flaherty, who was known for his sense of humor, personally delivered this letter to the Secretariat of State.

The secretariat actually replied, thanking the officer for his concern and suggesting that he might call again at the Vatican at a more convenient time.[106]

Given the many opportunities during the German occupation for provocation, misunderstanding, and accident, violence inevitably occurred. The Palatine Guards on duty at Vatican-owned or Vatican-protected buildings around Rome were especially exposed. Given their poor reputation among their counterparts in the other units of the pontifical armed services, it is ironic that the Palatines were the only one of the pope's units to come under direct fire during the war. The Germans and their Fascist collaborators knew that anti-Fascist political leaders, Jews, young men avoiding labor drafts, and escaped Allied POWs found refuge in churches and monasteries around Rome. The occupation authorities, hunting wanted individuals, considered these ecclesiastical properties easier and less controversial targets for raids than Vatican City itself. Vatican properties also attracted the attention of lawless or desperate individuals seeking money, food, or clothing. Almost daily Palatine Guard detachments reported gunfire near their positions. Several times during the occupation, Palatine Guards (who, apparently, received no prohibition against the use of firearms to defend papal territory) exchanged fire with unidentified parties trying to enter protected premises, including the pope's summer villa at Castel Gandolfo. Places of worship were not immune to attack. On one occasion, for example, assailants threw grenades at Palatines protecting the Basilica of Saint John Lateran, which hid some two hundred anti-Fascists, including Ivanoe Bonomi, the head of the National Liberation Committee, the underground resistance organization.[107] Even small outposts experienced incidents. In December 1943 Palatines on duty at the Urban College were fired upon when they chased an intruder from a college building. The following month the college's Palatines opened fire on a pair of intruders who threw hand grenades at the guardsmen before being driven off. The detachment at the Vatican-owned Palazzo San Calisto in Trastevere successfully resisted an assault by Fascist thugs seeking to seize refugees who had found shelter inside the papal building. By April 1944 violent incidents around the city were so common that all Palatine detachments were issued grenades and additional ammunition.[108]

The worst provocation occurred on the night of February 4, 1944, at the Basilica of Saint Paul Outside the Walls. Earlier that day two men had tried to gain entry to the monastery attached to the basilica but had been turned away by suspicious guards. That evening a Palatine Guard on patrol discovered several men climbing over the wall of the monastery garden. The guardsman got off a shot before being subdued by the intruders. At the same time, two men disguised as monks rang the bell at the main entrance, yelling, "Help, Help, we're priests being chased by the Germans." When the Palatine guardsman on duty opened the gate, several dozen armed men led by Pietro Caruso, the chief of the Fascist police in Rome, rushed the entrance and disarmed the sentinel. The intruders then searched the premises for several hours, arresting sixty-six individuals, including nine Jews. A Palatine guardsman was included among the arrestees and was later executed by the Germans. To justify their violation of the extraterritorial property, the authorities announced that the ecclesiastical building contained weapons, including rifles, pistols, ammunition, and gas masks, thereby insinuating that the basilica was a hideout for the anti-German resistance. They failed to mention that this equipment belonged not to partisans but to the uniformed and authorized Palatine Guard detachment assigned to the property.[109]

The Germans and their Italian friends did not present the only danger. Allied air attacks proved the greater threat. Castel Gandolfo was particularly exposed, due to its location near several German facilities in the Alban Hills south of Rome. To escape the approaching battle lines and the frequent bombing raids, thousands of refugees crowded into the pope's summer villa, believing the property to be safe from attack. A detachment of Palatine Guards protected the property and maintained order among the refugees. On February 2, 1944, the war came to Castel Gandolfo. During an Allied air bombardment of nearby Albano, a bomb fell on a convent on the papal estate, wounding a Palatine Guard and killing several nuns who had been ministering to the refugees. That evening a dozen more bombs fell around the villa. In the following days bombs frequently struck the property, posing a serious threat to the Palatine Guards, who maintained their patrols despite the bombardments. At one position a pair of guardsmen resolutely held their post while bombs destroyed several buildings around them, and when the bombardment lifted, they rushed out to pull wounded from the rubble. On February 10 a bomb collapsed an outlying building where refugees were living. Hundreds of people were killed, and the guards, reinforced by a detachment of papal gendarmes sent out from the Vatican, spent days dragging victims from the ruins.[110]

Of course Rome had been the target of Allied air attacks since the summer of 1943, and the bombing of Vatican City on November 5 demonstrated that no one could assume that the pope's home was automatically immune from the death and destruction that rained from the skies on other parts of the city. Papal authorities instituted a blackout and constructed several bomb shelters inside Vatican City to which employees and residents could repair when the city air-raid sirens sounded. A special shelter was prepared for Pope Pius in the medieval Tower of Nicholas III, but he steadfastly refused to use it. Another bombing incident took place on March 1, 1944. Several bombs fell on Vatican property on the Gianiculum, a hill overlooking Saint Peter's Square, killing a worker, wounding a priest, and damaging buildings. The pope insisted on waiting out every air raid in his apartments on the exposed upper floor of the palace. One night an unidentified plane dropped a flare, which drifted over Vatican City and landed, still burning, on a terrace of the papal palace near the Noble Guard quarters. Two guardsmen rushed to the scene and extinguished the fire with their heavy cloaks.[111]

By the end of May 1944 it was apparent to everyone in Vatican City that the battle for Rome was well engaged. For some time the explosions of bombs and artillery had been audible in the Vatican, and the silence of night-time duty would often be broken by the rattling of palace windows. From their posts on the upper floors of the papal palace, Swiss Guards could watch Allied artillery shells exploding among Wehrmacht positions on Monte Cavo outside the city, while German antiaircraft batteries on Monte Mario, only a few blocks from the Vatican, daily engaged Allied aircraft. On June 3, how-ever, the guns fell silent, and an ominous quiet fell across the city. Among papal officials there was concern that the Allied and German armies might turn the Eternal City into a combat zone that would inevitably include Vati-can City. In the Swiss Guard barracks, halberdiers exchanged the addresses of their families to facilitate notification of loved ones should combat (and casualties) come to the pope's tiny domain.[112]

In the early morning of June 4 the gendarmeria observed that the Ger-man sentries normally posted on the borders of Saint Peter's Square were gone. The Swiss Guard post at the Saint Anne gate reported that large num-bers of German soldiers and troop transports, including horse-drawn wagons, were moving along the adjacent Via di Port'Angelica and past Saint Peter's Square in the direction of the nearby Via Aurelia, one of the main thorough-fares leading from the city. The troop movements continued throughout the day and into the evening. The Wehrmacht was abandoning the Eternal City. Some of the withdrawing Germans approached the Swiss Guards and asked for asylum inside Vatican City. The halberdiers refused the soldiers entry but directed them to a nearby convent of German nuns where they could find refuge. That afternoon the Noble Guard esente sent one of his junior officers into the city to reconnoiter. The lieutenant found most of the bridges over the Tiber blocked by German military police. He managed to cross on the Duca d'Aosta span and proceed hurriedly through some of the main streets and squares of the city on a circular route that brought him back to the Vatican in the early evening. He reported that German offices on the Via Sistina, the Via Veneto, and the Corso d'Italia were vacant, and everywhere he observed Wehrmacht units on the move. There was no panic. In fact, the commander of one German unit moving past Saint Peter's actually stopped his column and for several minutes calmly lectured his men on the site, de-scribing its history and pointing out the presence of the Swiss Guard.[113]

With the withdrawal of the Germans and their Fascist allies from Rome, the beleaguered occupants of Vatican City felt a palpable relief. The threat of attack and occupation was over. Nowhere was the relief more welcome than in the barracks of the pope's small army. Easily dismissed as comic-opera sol-diers, the papal halberdiers, guardsmen, and gendarmes had adapted to an unprecedented emergency and, surrounded by hostile forces, fulfilled their mission of protecting the Holy Father. They had also ensured the neutrality and territorial integrity of Vatican City while guarding some of the most precious artistic and cultural treasures of Christianity and defending thousands of refugees who sought shelter and security in papal properties. Though no one can be sure why Hitler abandoned his intention to invade the Vatican and kidnap the pope, it is certain that German diplomatic, military, and police authorities in Rome opposed the idea, largely because they wanted to avoid the ignominy of fighting their way into one of the world's greatest cultural and religious monuments. The prospect of dead Swiss Guards on the steps of Saint Peter's and in the antechamber of the pope's apartments was enough to give even the most battle-hardened German officer pause. In the end, the pope's small army proved a big deterrent.

At 8:00 P.M. on June 4, as the last German soldiers disappeared down the Via Aurelia, the command office of the Palatine Guard informed Vatican officials that its detachment at the Basilica of Saint Paul Outside the Walls was reporting U.S. infantry patrols around the church. Ninety minutes later word reached the Vatican that Americans were at the Piazza Venezia.[114] The Allies were in Rome, but the future course of events remained uncertain. Gunfire could still be heard in the city. Would die-hard Fascists resist the occupation? Would there be an uprising by anti-Fascists and antimonarchists? The Vatican took no chances. All guard posts were immediately reinforced and all entrances to Vatican City closed and barred. From the windows of the papal palace the next morning, unfamiliar uniforms and vehicles were visible in the Borgo Pio, the neighborhood immediately beyond the walls of the papal city. At 6:00 A.M. the Swiss Guards at the Bronze Door reported that a scout car with a large white star on its side had pulled into Saint Peter's Square. After making a circuit of the square, the vehicle drove up to the steps of the basilica, and an American officer stepped out. From their station at the top of the steps, papal gendarmes moved down to block the officer's progress while the Swiss Guards at the nearby Bronze Door monitored the encounter and prepared to reinforce their police comrades. The gendarmes explained to the Americans that while driving across Saint Peter's Square, they had crossed an international border and, albeit without malice, violated the neutrality of a sovereign state. Ordered to withdraw, the liberators of Rome meekly drove back to "their" side of the white line. The Germans may have left, but the Vatican was still the pope's territory, and his troops were still defending it.[115]

CHAPTER 8

Guardian Angels

With the liberation of Rome, the anxieties concerning the defense of Vatican City and the personal security of the Holy Father gradually lessened, a change that accelerated after the end of the war in Europe on May 8, 1945. Peace ended the need for the special protective measures adopted when the Germans had occupied the Eternal City and maintained even after the liberation: expanded guard force, additional armed patrols and guard posts inside the Vatican, strict entry controls, and deployment of armed detachments to papal properties around Rome. There would be occasional alarms. During the Italian national elections of 1948, for example, Swiss Guard officers distributed rifles and ammunition to the halberdiers and reinforced guard posts in response to rumors that communists planned to attack the transmitter of Vatican Radio in the Vatican Gardens. Mostly, however, the early postwar years witnessed a return to the more relaxed conditions of peacetime.[1] Force levels dropped dramatically as personnel recruited during the emergency left papal service. The Palatine Guard, for example, lost most of the men who had enlisted in November–December 1943, falling from a wartime high of two thousand guardsmen to a level closer to its prewar strength of about five hundred. In the Swiss Guard, thirty-three experienced halberdiers, approximately a third of its personnel, had departed by 1946, although new recruits made up part of that loss.[2] Workloads changed as emergency guard posts and patrols were eliminated and special duties, such as the enhanced protective coverage of the Holy Father during his daily walks in the Vatican Gardens, were curtailed. In the Noble and Palatine Guards, the emphasis shifted from around-the-clock protection and defense duties to daytime ceremonial and guard of honor service in Saint Peter's Basilica and Square and the antechambers of the papal apartment. The Pontifical Gendarmeria reverted to its normal patrol and crowd-control functions now that foreign diplomats, reestablished in their embassies in Rome, no longer required surveillance and escaped POWs and desperate refugees no longer tried to sneak into Vatican City. The Swiss Guard returned its cartridge bandoliers and gas masks to the armory, where halberds and breastplates were now in greater demand than Mauser rifles and MKPS submachine guns as the duty schedules filled up with ceremonial events. The tempo of postwar ceremonial duty is suggested by the fact that in 1950, a Holy Year, Rome received 3.5 million visitors, almost all of whom came to Vatican City. That year Pope Pius XII appeared at two hundred general audiences and received more than six thousand individuals in private audiences. Everyone knew that normalcy had returned to the pope's corpi armati when the Swiss Guard and the Noble Guard began a bureaucratic battle of letters and orders of the day over the finer points of ceremonial etiquette in the pope's reception halls.[3]

The postwar years would prove difficult for the Swiss Guard. Alone among the pontifical units during the war, it had not significantly increased its personnel to match its increased responsibilities, with the result that the halberdiers had carried an especially heavy workload. Also, in contrast to their colleagues in the papal armed services, the halberdiers had been cut off from homes and families and could take no leaves, an isolation that worsened after the German occupation as mail and phone communications with Switzerland became increasingly problematic. The guard, however, had served well and honorably. If anyone thought that the culture of discipline, professionalism, and training instilled by Jules Repond forty years earlier would not long survive that commandant's tenure, they would have been reassured by the guard's performance during the war. Still, for all its wartime commitment to duty and service, the Swiss Guard seems to have drifted off course in the decades immediately following the war. Attracting qualified personnel became a serious problem. In the 1950s Switzerland began a period of economic expansion that had a negative impact on recruitment. As the booming Swiss economy promised good-paying jobs and a comfortable life at home, it was increasingly difficult for the guard to lure suitable young men to Rome with the prospect of low pay, barracks life, tedious duties, and enforced bachelorhood. By 1955 the corps roll had fallen to seventy-three men, barely enough to perform its duties.[4]

Command issues also afflicted the Swiss Guard. In March 1957 Commandant Heinrich Pfyffer von Altishofen died of a heart attack. On the day that the Wehrmacht had occupied Rome and combat-ready German paratroopers had approached Saint Peter's Square, the commandant, in full gala uniform of plumed helmet, breastplate, doublet, knee breeches, and rapier, had marched up to the invaders and bluntly informed them that they would not cross into the pope's territory. After that bold gesture, he had guided his corps through the vicissitudes of the occupation with firmness and purpose. Nine of his ancestors had commanded the guard, not all with distinction, but he had been an excellent war commandant and lived to lead his halberdiers in the celebrations surrounding the 450th anniversary of the Swiss Guard in 1956. His replacement proved more controversial. Most inside and outside the guard expected Pfyffer von Altishofen's deputy, Lieutenant Colonel Ulrich Ruppen, to receive the command. A thirty-year veteran of the corps and much trusted by his commander, Ruppen was respected and well liked by the halberdiers. In the unlikely event that the cardinal secretary of state passed over Ruppen, the consensus opinion was that another guard

officer, Major Dieter von Balthasar, would receive the nod. Surprise, therefore, was pervasive when the Vatican reached outside the corps for the next
commandant. Robert Nünlist, a native of the canton of Lucerne, was only
forty-six years old when he assumed command of the guard. The son of a
railway worker, the new commandant had seemed marked from childhood
for a military career; in primary school his nickname had been "the General." The family was devout: One brother entered the priesthood, another
joined the Swiss Guard as a halberdier, and a sister became a nun. Nünlist
himself pursued his university studies in Rome at the Angelicum, a Catholic
university run by the Dominican friars. There he completed a doctorate in
philosophy. Rather than pursuing an academic career, he joined the Swiss
army, becoming one of the small cadre of full-time professional officers in
a force based on part-time citizen-soldiers. His early assignments included
stints as an instructor at the army's weapons training school and as commander of an infantry battalion. Eventually, he would rise to become chief
of staff of the 2nd Army Corps and then commander of the infantry training school. In 1956, as Colonel Pfyffer von Altishofen's health slipped, papal
representatives approached Nünlist about assuming command of the Swiss
Guard when Pfyffer von Altishofen retired, but he declined the offer. The
next year he accepted the second offer, even though on the same day that he
accepted the Vatican's invitation the Swiss army offered him the command of
all army schools and training programs.[5]

His fifteen years as commandant were not untroubled. Nünlist came
from the mold of Jules Repond, the great early-twentieth-century commander and reformer of the guard. Repond had been an unpopular commandant for his insistence on strict discipline and intensive training, and
Nünlist experienced a similar response for the same reasons. Although after
Repond the guard had never returned to the abuses of power and privilege,
petty corruption, and indiscipline that had afflicted the corps at the beginning of the century, a certain laxness had crept back into the corps. Officers,
for example, turned a blind eye to halberdiers who paid colleagues to serve
their duty assignments so that they could be free to work as paid tour guides
in Rome. Training and discipline had also slipped. Nünlist introduced a new
regime that reflected his high expectations for the conduct and performance
of his corps. He reminded his men that they were not simply costumed employees of Vatican City but soldiers in a military unit, and he expected them
to act as such. Unprofessional practices, such as buying replacements for
guard duty, ended immediately, as did the relaxed approach to discipline.
The new commandant did not hesitate to remand for punishment or even
dismiss from the service halberdiers who did not follow orders.[6]

Nünlist reinvigorated the training program of the Swiss Guard. Weapons training, which had lapsed after the war, received renewed attention.
By 1957 the firearms available to the guard were obsolete. The basic rifle

remained the Mauser, which had entered service in 1911 and was beginning to show its age. Even the few MKPS submachine guns, the only automatic weapons in the armory, dated from 1937. It was extremely unlikely that Vatican officials would fund the purchase of new arms. Since the end of the Papal States, the prelates in the papal Secretariat of State and the administration of the Apostolic Palace had always been reluctant to consider improvements in the weaponry of the pontifical guard force for fear of appearing to critics of the papacy unduly concerned with the trappings of secular power. Any initiative to rearm the Swiss Guard would have to come from outside the Vatican, and the celebration of the guard's 450th anniversary on May 6, 1957, provoked just such an initiative. In 1921 veterans of the corps had organized the Association of Former Swiss Guards to provide fellowship and services to ex-halberdiers and support the current work of the guard. Aware from experience of the deficiencies in the corps's armaments, the association, in March 1957, petitioned the military department of the Swiss federal government to lend the guard 100 Karabiner model 1931s. Commonly known as the K31, this weapon had been the standard rifle of the Swiss army since 1933, so all recruits to the guard were familiar with it. Since it was being replaced in Switzerland, surplus numbers would soon be available. The military department was receptive to the petition and passed the request to the Swiss Federal Council, which decided in May 1957 to make an outright gift to the guard of one hundred K31s plus appropriate ammunition in honor of the unit's 450th anniversary.[7] Although welcomed by the halberdiers, the six-round, bolt-action K31 carbines did not significantly modernize the weaponry of the Swiss Guard because by 1957 most European armies were moving to semiautomatic and automatic rifles.

The K31s immediately replaced the antique Mausers at duty posts. Fifty-two Mausers were rendered inoperable and sold to a movie production company for use as props in a war film. The remaining rifles were held in reserve.[8] Colonel Nünlist, who had in his earlier career with the Swiss army commanded a weapons training school, immediately instituted a marksmanship program under the direction of Major von Balthasar. The course was mandatory, and every halberdier had to qualify with firearms. To encourage further practice, the commandant established a shooting club inside the guard barracks. Membership in the organization was voluntary, but it seems that most, if not all, guardsmen were members. To encourage firearms practice among Swiss expatriates, who remained eligible for mobilization in Switzerland's citizen army, the Swiss government sponsored an annual competition, the Guison Prize, for marksmanship. Nünlist made sure that the guard club competed against other expatriate Swiss gun societies for this prestigious award. For the halberdiers, the biggest problem was the lack of a suitable rifle range. By the 1950s the tiny territory of Vatican City had filled with buildings, squares, and roads, and there was no space for target practice. The commandant began looking for a suitable site outside the Vatican, and in 1960 he secured permission to use an Italian army weapons range that had originally been constructed for that year's Olympics, which were held in Rome. Because it was on an Italian army base and because the Vatican did not want to publicize the fact that its guards were receiving firearms training, the Swiss guardsmen wore civilian clothes when visiting the range.[9]

The halberdiers already resented Nünlist as an outsider, and the renewed emphasis on discipline and training did nothing to endear the commandant to his men. Tensions were inevitable and extended beyond the barracks. The Association of Former Swiss Guards split into a group that supported the new commandant and another that believed the command should have gone to Lieutenant Colonel Ruppen. In 1959 the Nünlist faction split away to form an alternative veterans' association, La Guardia. Though he might have been better advised to ignore the conflict, the commandant intervened by forbidding the "Ruppenists" access to the barracks and its facilities, a courtesy normally extended to former halberdiers. The Swiss press covered the disagreement, and the media attention caused no small scandal inside the Vatican and among Swiss Catholics. Tensions peaked with an attempt on the life of the commandant. On April 8, 1959, a halberdier who had just been dismissed from the corps for concealing his epilepsy during his entrance medical evaluation went to the commandant's apartment in the barracks. Upon knocking and gaining entry, he shot Nünlist twice with a service pistol. Nünlist's son was present and intervened to restrain the shooter until other halberdiers arrived in response to the gunshots. Miraculously, the commandant received only slight wounds. Arrested and taken to an Italian hospital for observation, the assailant was later returned to Switzerland after an investigation by the Italian police concluded that the young man was mentally disturbed.[10] The shooting shocked the Vatican, embarrassed the guard, and generated sympathy for the wounded commander. The dramatic events may have contributed to a general reduction in tension, although it is more likely that the halberdiers simply came to accommodate themselves to the new regime. Although strict and demanding, Nünlist demonstrated his concern for the well-being of his troops, and this concern eventually earned him the respect if not the affection of his men. Nünlist was particularly concerned with fostering the collective identity of the guard and improving the living conditions of the halberdiers. He instituted an annual report to detail for guardsmen, as well as their superiors and paymasters in the Apostolic Palace, the many duties and services performed by the corps. He improved the living quarters of the halberdiers, avidly supported the corps's chorus and band (which at one point in his tenure included one-third of the halberdiers), and encouraged the men to further their education. On occasion he personally led small groups of halberdiers on visits to historical sites in and around Rome.[11]

Although Robert Nünlist made his mark on the Swiss Guard, larger changes were in the offing that would influence the corpi armati of the Vatican more seriously than any event since the loss of the Papal States. At 3:00 in the afternoon of Monday, October 6, 1958, all Noble Guards were summoned urgently to the Vatican. When the guardsmen had mustered in their headquarters, they were informed that Pope Pius XII had suffered a "cerebral disturbance" while at the papal country villa at Castel Gandolfo. Amid general anxiety over the condition of the eighty-year-old pontiff, the men gathered in the guard chapel to recite prayers for his recovery. Later that night the Noble Guard commandant, Prince Mario del Drago, who had rushed to Castel Gandolfo, returned from the villa with the reassuring news that the Holy Father had rallied. The Nobles, however, remained on alert, and guardsmen moved into the dormitory facilities in the unit's quarters inside the Apostolic Palace. The next day passed with conflicting reports about the pope's condition. On Wednesday morning, however, the Vatican was rocked as Rome's newspapers rushed onto the street special editions announcing the pope's death and providing details concerning his last moments and his final words. Inside the Apostolic Palace, Noble commanders had heard no such news from the guard detachment on duty at Castel Gandolfo, but they decided to take no chances. Standing orders provided that in the event of a pope's death, the papal apartment and all its contents, particularly the pontiff's private papers, were to be immediately secured. Count Clemente Pietromarchi, the cadet assistant to the commandant (the deputy commandant and officer responsible for the day-to-day operations of the Noble Guard), ordered Count Ladislao Sterbini, the officer of the day, to secure the papal apartment in anticipation of the arrival of the cardinal camerlengo (a prelate whose office exercised particular responsibilities upon the death of a pope, including placing seals on the doors of the apartment). Sterbini immediately led a detachment of guards to the pope's private rooms. The apartment was empty and quiet as the guardsmen set about checking the rooms and closing the doors, but the silence was broken unexpectedly by the ringing of the telephone. A Noble Guard picked up the receiver to discover at the other end of the line a papal chamberlain calling from Castel Gandolfo. The caller was surprised that a Noble Guard had answered the phone and even more surprised to learn that the guard was exercising its sad duty of securing the apartment of the dead pontiff. "But the Holy Father isn't dead," the chamberlain cried. "He's very much alive!" This news perplexed the guards; on the one hand, the chamberlain was on the scene and should know whether the pope was dead or not, but on the other hand, they had their orders. Their confusion was assuaged when the phone rang again. Apparently the chamberlain, upon ending his conversation with the guardsman, had immediately phoned the Secretariat of State to report that Noble Guards had taken over the papal apartment and to recommend that someone investigate the situation. The secretariat was calling to tell the guardsmen to return to their quarters. They would, however, soon revisit the apartment. That evening the Noble Guard duty officer at Castel Gandolfo phoned the guard headquarters to report that the Holy Father was failing. The next morning the officer reported that at 3:52 A.M. on October 9, the pope had died. The Noble Guards, this time in earnest, immediately secured the pope's rooms to ensure that no one except the camerlengo entered.[12]

As the pontifical guard corps performed their assigned roles in the pageantry of a papal funeral, the more perspicacious sensed that an era was passing. In his embrace of the forms, protocol, and regalia of spiritual and temporal sovereignty, Pius XII had been the last of the "pope kings." He had become increasingly aloof and imperious in his last years, allegedly expecting subordinates to kneel in his presence and leave by walking backward away from him. His successors would abandon such pretenses in favor of a more simple and accessible posture in keeping with the temper of the times. To address the times, his immediate successor, John XXIII (Angelo Roncalli), convened at the Vatican a general council to consider reforming and revitalizing the Catholic Church. Although Pope John would not live to see the end of the council, his openness, his manifest goodwill, and his sincere conviction that the church had nothing to fear from the modern world set a new tone inside the pontifical palace. For his guards, the change was evident from his first day on the Throne of Saint Peter. At the new pope's first audience, the Swiss Guards nearly dropped their halberds when they heard loud laughter coming from his chambers. Jocularity in the papal apartments was unheard of. Pius XII may have had many good qualities, but an infectious sense of humor had not been one of them. John treated his guards as part of his extended family rather than as functionaries in a protocol-conscious court. He made a point of visiting the quarters of his guard units and would often stop to chat with sentinels as he passed along the corridors of his palace. On a visit to the quarters of the Noble Guard, the pope pointed to the unit's flag, which, as was customary, bore the coat of arms of the reigning pontiff and commented that the coat of arms was not legitimately his but that of the family whose land his father, a tenant farmer, had cultivated. The family, coincidentally also named Roncalli, had allowed the pope to adopt their coat of arms.[13] On another occasion he decided to invite all the off-duty Swiss Guards to his apartments for a late-afternoon *aperitivo*. The Holy Father was the perfect host, moving about the room, speaking individually to his soldiers, and checking to see that each had refreshments. When other obligations compelled him to leave the reception, he insisted that the halberdiers remain and enjoy themselves and asked his staff to serve them a meal. Such sociability was unprecedented. Popes traditionally ate alone and never received guests. Pius XII had been so aloof that he only saw his family once a year, at precisely 4:00 on the afternoon of Christmas Day, for a brief session of hot chocolate and cakes. John broke the mold in other ways. Except for occasional summer trips to Castel Gandolfo and visits to Roman churches, even after the Lateran Agreements with Italy the popes had stayed inside the Vatican. When, in 1962, John decided to visit the shrine at Loreto, ten Swiss Guards accompanied the papal entourage to provide an honor guard, the first time a detachment of the guard had deployed beyond the pontifical palace or Castel Gandolfo since 1870.[14]

John died in 1963, but his successor, Paul VI (Giovanni Montini), continued the policy of embracing the modern world. He saw the Second Vatican Council to a successful conclusion and resolutely stripped away the vestiges of monarchical power and pretense that still gilded the apparatus of the papacy. The latter effort had serious consequences for the pontifical armed forces. Paul and his advisers were convinced that the elaborate papal court, with its chamberlains, ushers, gentlemen-in-waiting, and other functionaries, all costumed as if for a play set in the court of Queen Elizabeth I, was an extravagant anachronism that had no place in the simpler, more accessible, less pretentious papacy that was emerging from the deliberations and decisions of the Vatican Council. Paul decided to abolish the court and retire its personnel, and this decision extended to his household guards. Aside from tradition, there seemed little justification for the maintenance of four separate guard units, and in the heady environment of the Second Vatican Council, when change and modernization were the watchwords, tradition was no longer a weighty factor in decisions. Few in the papal palace could imagine a serious threat to the physical security of the Holy Father or Vatican City. Certainly some organization was necessary to supervise tourists, maintain decorum at public ceremonies, and protect the architectural and artistic treasures of Vatican City, but it was no longer apparent that the elaborately costumed guard units were necessary for such services. Indeed, except during World War II, the Noble, Palatine, and Swiss Guards had always served the person of the Holy Father and had little to do with such mundane issues as controlling traffic, herding tourists, or protecting paintings. The personal guards now seemed not only ostentatious relics of an older time and mentality but also barriers that physically and symbolically separated the pontiff from the faithful.

In the late 1960s word began to spread through Rome that Pope Paul was considering the abolition of his armed forces. The rumors were so pervasive and seemed so authoritative that Roman newspapers openly predicted the demise of the famous Swiss Guard, some going so far as to report erroneously that the prospect of dismissal had brought the halberdiers to the verge of mutiny.[15] The ax fell on September 14, 1970, but it missed the Swiss. In a formal letter to his secretary of state, Cardinal Jean Villot, Pope Paul announced the outright abolition of the Noble Guard and the Palatine Guard, asserting that "our Military Corps, even though much esteemed . . . , no longer correspond to the needs for which they have been created."[16] The Pontifical Gendarmeria evolved into a new force, the Central Vigilance Office of Vatican City. The only unit to emerge unscathed was the Swiss Guard.

The corpi armati survived, but in a truncated form. In the end, even critics of the papal military units agreed that some sort of police force was necessary, so the future of the gendarmeria was never in doubt. The only alternative was to turn crowd control and site security over to the Italian police, but even in the afterglow of the council, this seemed an unacceptable compromise of Vatican sovereignty. The Swiss Guard survived because it had a 460-year history and a very strong public image. Because of their colorful uniforms and visible presence at the entrances to Vatican City, the guardsmen were favorites of tourists. No visit to the Vatican was complete without a snapshot of the Swiss Guard at the Bronze Door or at the Arch of the Bells, and souvenir shops sold Swiss Guard dolls and figurines. The halberdiers also had the active support of two influential prelates, Archbishop Giovanni Benelli, the powerful deputy secretary of state, and Archbishop Karl Josef Rauber, the papal nuncio in Switzerland, who spoke for the guard in the discussions concerning the future of the corpi armati.

In contrast, the Noble and Palatine Guards had no influential advocates inside the pontifical palace and lacked the public visibility of the Swiss Guard. Few tourists went home with photos of the Palatine Guard, and there were no romantic stories about the Nobles and Palatines, such as the supreme sacrifice of the Swiss during the sack of Rome or the legend that the great Renaissance painter Raphael had designed the Swiss Guard's gaily colored uniforms. The Noble Guard had the particular burden of an elitist image at a time when inclusion and simplicity, rather than elitism and privilege—alleged faults of the Nobles—had become watchwords inside the Vatican. Considering their long record of loyal service, the two units were demobilized with surprisingly little ceremony and even less sympathy. The Noble Guard, for example, knew by 1970 that there would be changes in the pontifical armed services. Archbishop Benelli told the commandant, Prince Mario del Drago, to anticipate a general reform of the services. The extent and nature of the projected reform remained unspecified. Subsequently, the guard was told that the changes would be only cosmetic; for instance, the formal name of the corps would be changed from "Noble Guard of Honor" to simply "Guard of Honor," a change that mattered little to the guardsmen. Benelli assured Prince del Drago that discussions concerning the armed services were continuing but that no major decisions had been made. These assurances continued until the day when the Nobles were curtly notified of their abolition, September 20, 1970. The date of notification, the centenary of the fall of papal Rome to the forces of the Kingdom of Italy, when the Noble Guards had loyally gathered in the pontifical palace to protect Pius IX, was ill-chosen. When Noble officers pointed this out to Benelli, he agreed to change the date of the abolition announcement to September 14. The corps then requested permission to take formal leave of the Holy Father and present him with their flag as a final token of their esteem. Initially, Benelli, an imperious administrator who was not known for his people skills, dismissed their request, adding that they could just send their flag to the Vatican museum. He eventually relented, but only after receiving assurances from Prince del Drago that the guardsmen would not make a scene at the audience with the Holy Father. In the end, the promised farewell audience with the pope was canceled. The Noble Guards had to remain content with a meeting with Cardinal Secretary of State Villot, who happened to be acquiring the now superfluous guard quarters for his personal apartment. The cardinal thanked the guardsmen for their loyalty and service and told them to take all the time they needed to collect their equipment, records, and materials and vacate their rooms. Taking the cardinal at his word, the guard formed a committee to inventory, pack, and remove the unit's possessions. This committee had hardly begun its work when two functionaries from Villot's office, the Secretariat of State, arrived to demand the keys to the quarters. When the guardsmen pointed out that they had just begun to collect their unit's possessions, they were told that everything there was the property of the pope, and the only action required of them was to turn over the keys and leave.[17] It was a sad end for a proud and venerable corps. After their demobilization, the men of the Noble Guard formed a veterans' organization, the Lance Spezzate (Broken Lances), to perpetuate the fellowship and memory of their corps. Each year the surviving members convene for a mass on January 19 to celebrate the feast day of their patron saint, Saint Sebastian, and on November 30 to commemorate the memory of their deceased comrades. For their part, the veterans of the now defunct Palatine Guard organized the Association of Saints Peter and Paul, a confraternity engaged in cultural, liturgical, and charitable projects.

The reform of 1970 left the Swiss Guard as the sole military unit in Vatican City and the Corpo di Vigilanza (Vigilance Corps) as the police force. For the police, the transition amounted to little more than a change in name, but the reforms caught the Swiss at a bad time. The guard had not recovered from the recruiting crisis of the 1950s, and the unit remained far below its authorized strength. In 1959 Pope John had authorized a significant increase in salaries and one month of annual vacation for all halberdiers, but these improvements had had little effect on recruitment. Traditionally, the modern guard had recruited through personal contacts and word of mouth, but in 1961 it began publicly advertising for men. To increase its visibility in Switzerland, the guard in 1965 permitted a Swiss television company into the barracks to film a documentary and encouraged the veterans' association to open an information center in the town of Wettingen. These expedients did not reverse the decline in numbers. As numbers dropped, the guard was increasingly hard-pressed to perform its duties. In September 1965 it had to transfer control of the Zecca guard post to the Vatican police because it had too few men to cover its assignments. For the handful of recruits that appeared during this time, training was condensed to two weeks in order to rush men onto the duty schedules. Weapons practice suffered particularly from this curtailed training. There were no live-fire exercises, and firearms training was limited to learning how to present arms with the Karabiner 31 rifle. By 1971 the guard roster had fallen to forty-seven men, the lowest number in the unit's history.[18]

It is doubtful that senior officials in the Vatican were much concerned about the personnel crisis in the Swiss Guard. Few could imagine a situation in which the Holy Father might require a strong guard force because few could imagine a threat to his personal safety or to the security of Vatican City. The apparent absence of such threats—combined with the current practice of portraying the Holy Father as a simple pastor rather than a sovereign pontiff—had made it easier after the Vatican Council to justify the abolition of the Noble and Palatine Guards. It also encouraged complacency toward the condition of the armed units that remained. If the only functions of the guard and the Vigilanza were to direct tourists to the museums, keep worshippers behind the ropes inside Saint Peter's, and look decorative at ceremonies and receptions, then how much training and equipment did they require? If all a halberdier needed to do was stand in place and present arms with a halberd, then why not draft in and costume young seminarians as needed? As for weaponry, a few antique swords and halberds that were obviously decorative and unthreatening might be acceptable, but firearms were definitely to be avoided as counter to the new post–Vatican Council atmosphere, as were bodyguards separating the Holy Father from the faithful. Until, that is, people started trying to kill the pope.

Paul VI was the first pope since the Napoléonic Wars to travel willingly beyond Italy. By the end of his pontificate, in 1978, the "pilgrim pope" had visited Africa, Asia, Australia, Europe, the Middle East, and North and South America. On November 27, 1970, as the Holy Father moved through a throng gathered at Manila airport to welcome him to the Philippines, a disturbed Bolivian artist, dressed in a priest's cassock and wielding a long knife, rushed at the pontiff. Only the intervention of Monsignor Pasquale Macchi, the pope's secretary, who was walking at his side, and the security detail of Filipino president Ferdinand Marcos, who was at the airport to greet the pope, prevented a deadly encounter.[19] The Manila incident should have been a wake-up call for papal officials, but most continued to doze through the 1970s. Inside the Apostolic Palace, papal functionaries failed to appreciate that the respect and affection of the people for formerly sacrosanct offices and institutions could no longer be taken for granted. Indeed, ill-intentioned individuals and groups were prepared to attack those offices and institutions

precisely because they were deemed sacrosanct. Despite the Manila incident, papal authorities refused to acknowledge that anyone would want to
harm the Holy Father. Preoccupied with appearances and protocol, these officials interfered in any effort by security professionals to enhance the safety
of the pope by adjusting his movements and accessibility. Archbishop Paul
Marcinkus, an American prelate who worked as the Vatican's advance man,
arranging with local authorities the details of pontifical trips, received complaints from the papal entourage that at public assemblies or motorcades local police officers faced away from the Holy Father. The pope's men considered this a sign of disrespect. Marcinkus could not make these functionaries
understand that the job of the police was not to watch the pope but to scan
the crowds for potential threats, and this responsibility required them to face
away from the pontiff.[20]

The disregard for security continued when John Paul II (Karol Wojtyla)
assumed the throne of Saint Peter in October 1978 after the brief pontificate
of John Paul I (Albino Luciani), who died in his sleep only thirty-three days
after his election. When Francesco Pasanisi, the director of the police unit
from the Italian Directorate of Public Security (PS) responsible for maintaining order in Saint Peter's Square and protecting the pope when he left
Vatican City, proposed to make changes in the papal motorcade, he caused
a furor among the pope's attendants. Typically, the motorcade would have
eight or nine vehicles preceded and followed by Italian police motorcyclists.
The cars deployed in the following order: a car of the Rome traffic police, a
PS car containing Pasanisi; the papal limousine containing the driver and the
pope's personal valet in the front and the Holy Father and one of his secretaries (on a jump seat) in the back; another Vatican car carrying the prefect
of the pontifical household and a priest assistant; a third Vatican car carrying
the pope's physician; a fourth Vatican car containing agents of the Vatican
police service (Corpo di Vigilanza); another Vatican vehicle carrying journalists from Vatican Radio and *Osservatore Romano*, and then one or two
cars carrying Italian police agents. Pasanisi, who had been a senior officer
in the protective detail of the president of Italy before his assignment to the
Vatican, wanted to move the vehicles containing security personnel closer
to the pope's limousine. Believing that in an emergency the pontiff would
require his bodyguards more than the prefect of the pontifical household, he
wanted to place a security car immediately behind the pope, instead of three
cars back, to facilitate the rapid deployment of bodyguards around the papal limousine. To achieve his purpose, Pasanisi had to overcome vociferous
opposition from the pontifical household, which complained loudly about
the police placing a screen between them and the Holy Father. The Italian
police director also waged a running battle with papal officials over whether
the Italian police dog teams that patrolled the perimeter of the papal villa at
Castel Gandolfo should be armed. When he suggested that the Holy Father

might consider using an armored limousine with bulletproof windows, Pope John Paul II reputedly replied, "I want to go among the crowd like a man among brothers. My defense is my cross."[21]

The cross proved an uncertain defense on the afternoon of May 13, 1981, when, during a scheduled public appearance, the Holy Father made two circuits of a crowded Saint Peter's Square in his open "popemobile." When the papal vehicle stopped to allow John Paul to embrace a child, Mehmet Ali Agca, an armed Turkish thug, seized the opportunity. Agca, who seems to have been an instrument of Soviet-bloc intelligence services concerned about the Polish pope's influence on emerging anticommunist popular movements in Eastern Europe, fired several shots at the pontiff from close range. Two bullets struck the pope, the first penetrating his abdomen and the second hitting his right elbow. Italian and Vatican plainclothes agents, who had been walking before and behind the popemobile, immediately surrounded the vehicle. At the first shot, Francesco Pasanisi had jumped into the backseat from his position at the left rear of the vehicle. He yelled at the driver, "Get us out of here! Get us to the aid station! Move!" The driver took the car through the Arch of the Bells to the nearby medical station, where an ambulance was always stationed during papal ceremonies in Saint Peter's Square. Bleeding heavily, John Paul was transferred to the ambulance, which screeched away, circling behind the basilica and leaving Vatican City through the Saint Anne gate on its way to Gemelli Hospital. Following close behind was a car of Vatican functionaries and a police vehicle containing Francesco Pasanisi and two PS agents. Pasanisi radioed the city police to have their traffic police stop traffic along the approaches to the hospital and to alert Gemelli medical personnel to prepare for the arrival of the ambulance. With a trained police driver at the wheel, Pasanisi's car soon passed the Vatican car and caught up with the ambulance. Several times along the way, the speeding motorcade barely escaped serious collisions, but within seven minutes of leaving Vatican City, the ambulance pulled into the emergency entrance to the hospital. Physicians and nurses were already waiting to rush the Holy Father to the trauma surgery, where, after more than five hours of labor, the surgeons saved his life.[22]

The near tragedy of May 13 convinced even the most obstreperous and stubborn Vatican functionaries that the world outside the walls of the Apostolic Palace was perhaps more dangerous than the world inside those walls. The major lesson of that terrible day was that the Holy Father was no longer immune to the threats that other world leaders and their security staffs took as givens. There was no longer anything special about the Holy Father. That hard reality was reaffirmed a year to the day after the attack in Saint Peter's Square. That attempt had occurred on the anniversary of the alleged apparition of the Blessed Virgin Mary to three children in the small Portuguese village of Fatima in 1917. John Paul firmly believed that the intercession of the Blessed Virgin had saved his life that day, and he confidently assured his surgeon, "One hand fired the bullet, but another hand guided it."[23] On May 13, 1982, the anniversary of his brush with death, Pope John Paul visited the shrine at Fatima to thank the Blessed Virgin for her intercession. Five hundred uniformed Portuguese police lined the paths along which the Holy Father walked, and hundreds more in plainclothes mingled with the crowd of several hundred thousand people. As John Paul walked from the main church, a Spanish priest wielding a long bayonet pushed through the crowd and lunged toward him, shouting, "Down with the pope!" Although the fact was suppressed at the time, the deranged priest wounded the Holy Father before security officers tackled the assailant.[24] The would-be assassin was a member of an ultraconservative Catholic faction led by a renegade archbishop named Marcel Lefebvre. The group had broken away from the church in protest of the reforms of the Second Vatican Council. In his pocket the attacker had a letter declaring that John Paul had been condemned to death because he had usurped the Throne of Saint Peter.[25] This close call was followed by others as physical threats appeared wherever the pope traveled. During a papal visit to Toronto, Canada, in 1984, police arrested a man carrying a knife who had stolen his invitation to a papal reception. In Brisbane in 1986, Australian police arrested a man who had five firebombs in his possession as he was looking for the best place to launch them against the visiting pontiff. In 1995 Philippine police foiled a bomb plot by a Muslim terrorist cell, whose members planned to approach the Holy Father disguised as priests. Other plots or threats were foiled by rigorous police measures in Bosnia, India, and Syria.[26]

The attempts upon the lives of Paul VI and John Paul II had a serious effect upon the attitude, organization, training, and deployment of the two remaining elements of the papal armed services: the Swiss Guard and the Vigilance Corps. Once again the balance between ceremonial service and protective duties began to shift in the direction of the latter. The pontifical guards and police now confronted the need for improved executive protection and, after the attacks on the World Trade Center in New York City on September 11, 2001, counterterrorist capabilities, requirements that remain in place today. When the pope travels, for example, the host country still provides the bulk of the security coverage, but the Holy Father is accompanied by a protective unit of two Swiss Guards and a half-dozen or more Vatican police agents who, in plainclothes, form the protective ring closest to the pontiff. During public appearances, such as those in Saint Peter's Basilica, the Holy Father is flanked by plainclothes Swiss and Vatican police (the Swiss always covering the pope's right side and the police the left). For events in Saint Peter's Square, this coverage is supplemented by plainclothes and uniformed members of the Italian police who, by arrangement with the Vatican, provide routine security surveillance of the square up to the steps of the basilica. After the events of May 13, 1981, some popemobiles were enclosed in bulletproof glass, although John Paul II still preferred open vehicles, a preference also exhibited by his successor, Benedict XVI. In 2002 the Vatican acquired from the Daimler-Chrysler motor company an armored limousine for motor trips beyond Vatican City.[27]

For the Vatican police—renamed the Gendarmeria of the Vatican City State in 2002—this shift required revisions in the operational mission of the corps. It has moved from a primarily service mission focused on directing and monitoring the millions of harmless tourists who visit Vatican City each year to a more explicitly protective mission emphasizing the deterrence and, if necessary, suppression of serious threats to the Holy Father and the Vatican. This redefinition of mission involved more than changes in identity. Training needed to change because the skills useful for dealing with hot, impatient tourists in Saint Peter's Square are not necessarily the skills useful for maintaining a correct and impermeable security perimeter around a moving subject. Finally, the new missions required specialized units to deal with the particular challenges of growing responsibilities and emerging threats. To address such challenges, the all-male, all-Catholic Gendarmeria Vaticana has evolved into a highly professional and modern police and security organization of 152 men, with detachments specializing in executive protection, bomb disposal, and counterterrorist operations. All recruits (including those who join from the Italian police services) complete a three-month basic police training course that includes instruction in criminal and legal procedures, languages, weapons, and unarmed combat.

Upon completion of their basic training, recruits must complete a two-year probationary period. Agents subsequently assigned to special units, such as the counterterrorist team, receive additional specialized training. Uniformed and armed agents man fixed posts at the entrances to Vatican City and inside the Apostolic Palace, while others, including some in plainclothes, conduct roving patrols. Gendarmes also provide protective services at the papal summer villa at Castel Gandolfo and at various Vatican properties around Rome. A central command center provides around-the-clock monitoring of the extensive system of electronic sensors and video cameras that covers every part of the pope's tiny domain. To improve access to intelligence concerning potential threats to the Holy Father and Vatican City, the gendarmeria collaborates with transnational police and security organizations, such as Interpol, and maintains contacts with the police services of various countries.[28] Modernization and liaison have been the special concerns of Domenico Giani, who succeeded the long-serving Camillo Cibin as commander of the Gendarmeria Vaticana in the summer of 2006. A former senior officer in the Italian Customs Police, Giani also worked on the protective detail of the Italian prime minister before entering the pope's service in 1999.

Perceptions of increasing threats also stimulated changes in the Swiss Guard. By 1980 the guard had emerged from its personnel crisis as the number of effective members approached the authorized force level of 100 men. In 1980 the guard mustered 85 men, and by 1985 the unit had reached its approved size. Since then the corps has never fallen below 92 men, and some years it has actually exceeded its authorized strength. In 2000 its authorized size was increased to 110 personnel. The years after the 1970 attack on Paul VI at the Manila airport also witnessed an improvement in the equipment and training of the guard. Commandant Robert Nünlist resigned in 1971 because of a worsening heart condition. His replacement was Franz Pfyffer von Altishofen, a Lucerne lawyer and the eleventh in his ancient family to command the Swiss Guard. During his tenure he purchased for the corps twenty-five Hispano-Suiza 9mm submachine guns. When he resigned in 1982, his replacement, Roland Buchs, promoted from his position as deputy commander, added another twenty-five of the submachine guns to the armory. The most significant improvement in the guard's arms, however, occurred in 1990. The commander-in-chief of the Swiss army made a formal visit to the Swiss Guard barracks in Vatican City and presented to Commandant Buchs one hundred SIG Sturmgewehr assault rifles and a dozen SIG P225 semi-automatic pistols, the standard infantry weapons in the Swiss army. This gift thoroughly modernized the weaponry of the guard. The pistols were especially welcome because the service handgun of the guard was still the Dreyse 7.65mm pistol, which Commandant Jules Repond had purchased in 1912. To provide the halberdiers opportunities to practice with their new firearms, Buchs secured permission from the Italian army to use the army's rifle range at Tarquinia, a town 70 kilometers northwest of Rome.[29]

In addition to increased weapons practice, the guard also expanded its training program to include subjects relevant to executive protection. Halberdiers could no longer assume that their duties would be limited to guarding a fixed post at a gate or doorway. Officers and noncommissioned officers now might find themselves deploying from a backup car to surround the pope's vehicle as it slowed in a motorcade, watching hands and faces as they preceded the pope along a reception line, or opening a path for the Holy Father through a throng of admirers. New responsibilities required new skills. Beginning in 1984, the guard invited security professionals from Switzerland to Vatican City to offer lectures and supervise exercises relevant to executive protection. In 1999 it began detailing personnel to a special course taught in Switzerland by the Protective Detachment of the Swiss Federal Council, the police unit responsible for providing personal security for Swiss national officials and visiting dignitaries.[30]

When Roland Buchs retired in early 1998, Alois Estermann, lieutenant colonel of the corps, assumed command, first as acting commandant and then, on May 4, 1998, as full commandant. That same day, Corporal Cédric

Tornay, armed with a service pistol, went to Estermann's apartment in the barracks and shot dead the commandant and his wife before turning the gun on himself. The shooting shocked the Vatican and created a sensation in the world media, where journalists and self-described "Vatican watchers" speculated wildly about the dead corporal's motives. Some claimed that Estermann and Tornay had been lovers and that the murder-suicide was the result of an affair gone sour. Others charged that Estermann had been a spy for East Germany and that his death was part of the secret war of intelligence services. Such claims either remain unsubstantiated or have been thoroughly discredited. The truth behind the shooting is more mundane. From a note he wrote before his final walk to the commandant's apartment, it is apparent that Tornay had accumulated a series of grievances in regard to his commander, and that he considered Estermann to be harsh and unfair. Estermann had disciplined Tornay for infractions of regulations, and because of these infractions the commandant had denied the corporal a medal routinely awarded to halberdiers after three years of service. Unable to bear the frustration and disappointment, Tornay simply struck out at his perceived tormentor.[31]

To help the guard navigate through the ensuing scandal and crisis, the Vatican reached outside the corps for a new team of senior officers. The new commandant, Pius Segmüller, had reached the rank of colonel in the Swiss army and had worked in relief and police agencies before entering the pope's service. His deputy, Elmar Mäder, was also new to the guard, having served as an officer in the Swiss army and run a financial services company. In 2003 Mäder succeeded Segmüller upon the latter's resignation and in turn was succeeded in August 2008 by Daniel Anrig, the current and thirty-fourth commandant. Before his appointment to the guard, Anrig had served as a captain in the Swiss army, professor of civil law at the University of Fribourg, and director of police services in the Swiss canton of Glarus.

These recent commandants have furthered the process of modernization and adaptation that began in the 1970s. In 2010 the Swiss Guard mustered 112 men (including five officers) organized into three squads. In rotation, each squad is responsible for guarding the entrances to the Vatican (where they are observed and photographed by thousands of tourists each day) as well as various locations inside the Apostolic Palace. Depending on their duty assignments, halberdiers wear the gaily colored costume and beret designed by Commandant Jules Repond in 1912 or the navy-blue "exercise" uniform with beret and white collar, also designed by Repond. When forming part of the protective detail around the Holy Father during his public appearances and travels, guardsmen wear civilian suits and ties. In a peculiarity of the corps, officers wear civilian clothes, even when on duty, except for ceremonial occasions and unit exercises. The gala uniform of plumed helmet, white gloves and ruffled collar, breastplate, and shoulder armor is worn only at major ceremonies, such as the annual event on May 6, the anniversary of the guard's supreme sacrifice during the sack of Rome in 1527, when new halberdiers are sworn into the corps. Recruits in training wear a gray overall and the standard beret. Except for the recruit coveralls, uniforms are custom-made by a full-time tailor who works inside the barracks. The armor, some of which dates back to the sixteenth century, is maintained by Austrian specialists. The halberds and swords carried by the guards on daytime duty are purely decorative and not intended for use as defensive weapons. Modern firearms are accessible, but not visible to visitors and tourists, at all guard posts.

The corps remains entirely Swiss, Catholic, and male. Aspiring halberdiers must be unmarried and between the ages of nineteen and thirty. They must also have completed the basic training program of the Swiss army. The Swiss Guard is probably unique among the armies of the world in requiring applicants to submit evidence—usually in the form of a testimonial from a parish priest—of good character and religious practice with their application. Enlistment is for twenty-five months. Once dependent on personal contacts and word of mouth to secure recruits, the guard now maintains a professional recruiting program with well-designed promotional materials and representatives who visit secondary schools and army centers in Switzerland. Potential applicants can also spend a weekend at the Vatican learning about the guard and its duties.

There are usually three recruit schools over the course of a year, each lasting approximately thirty days. The program includes courses on the organization and personalities of the Vatican, intensive Italian, the working language of the Vatican, firearms and unarmed combat, and the theory and practice of ceremonial service and protective surveillance. Once sworn into the corps and assigned to a squad, each halberdier participates in a program of continuing education and training. Some of this training, such as martial arts and periodic firearms practice at Italian police facilities, is mandatory, and some, such as additional language instruction, is optional.[32] At the end of his first year of service, each halberdier must sit for the Saint Anne Exam. This examination tests his knowledge of the geography of Vatican City, the various offices and departments of the papal city, and the principal personalities of the papal administration (halberdiers are expected to recognize by sight all cardinals and important papal officials); his ability to speak, read, and write Italian; and his proficiency in the use of the ceremonial halberd and modern firearms. Those who fail this exam cannot serve at the Saint Anne gate, the heavily trafficked service entrance to Vatican City, or at Castel Gandolfo. Guardsmen may retake the exam once, but if they fail a second time, they cannot reenlist after their two-year term. Once past the Saint Anne Exam, halberdiers prepare for the Chief of Post Exam, which is required of all guards in charge of external posts, such as the Saint Anne gate, the

Bronze Door, and the Arch of the Bells. For sergeants and corporals, there are mandatory courses on leadership. In 2006, for example, the director of military security for the Swiss army, himself a former halberdier, conducted a one-week course for guard noncommissioned officers that covered the theory and practice of small-unit leadership and the problems of deploying and controlling small units in the particular physical environment of Vatican City. Every year or so three or four officers or noncommissioned officers are sent to Switzerland to complete the executive protection course offered by the Protective Detachment of the Swiss Federal Council.[33]

The activities of the Pontifical Swiss Guard and the Vatican Gendarmeria suggest that a military tradition remains alive and vibrant inside the Vatican. That tradition, extending back to the earliest popes, has always been an important element in the history of the papacy. It is a mistake to imagine that military and security concerns have long since ceased to matter in papal affairs and that popes bade farewell to arms and armies sometime after the Renaissance. Even modern pontiffs have faced the prospect of violence against their person, their authority, and their independence and have, often despite their preferences, found the need to employ armed men to confront that prospect. Since the French Revolution the papacy has been militarily threatened or attacked by foreign governments, including their proxies, or domestic armed groups at least thirteen times and has been involved in six wars or significant military campaigns.[34] In that same period armed groups assaulted or invaded the pontifical palace on three occasions. Two popes, Pius VI and Pius VII, were kidnapped; one, Pius IX, was compelled to flee Rome; and one, Pius XII, faced the prospect of kidnapping. Since 1971 there have been three assassination attempts against popes, several known assassination plots, and probably others that remain unknown. Many of the armed conflicts marked critical points in the evolution of the papacy so that it is fair to suggest that the history of that institution since the French Revolution—particularly the period 1796–1870—is as much a military history as an ecclesiastical or a political history.

The military history of the modern papacy is not only an account of battles; it is also the story of an institution, the pontifical armed forces. When recounted at all, that story has been presented either as crude melodrama, with the pope's soldiers appearing as ruthless foreign mercenaries forcing the yoke of tyranny on the papacy's subjects, or as broad farce, with the pope's military units appearing as inconsequential or incompetent soldiers of whom little could be expected and by whom little could be accomplished. Such accounts, however, seriously misrepresent the history of the pontifical armed forces. Although the pope's military has been no stranger to defeat and disgrace, its history is more than a tale of futility and failure. It is also a tale of duty, courage, and sacrifice. The path between the ragtag companies that ran from the Senio River in 1797 and the smartly turned-out squads that protect

the Holy Father and Vatican City today marks a long and often difficult journey toward modernization and professionalism. Progress toward those goals
was uneven, frequently interrupted, and occasionally undercut by a return
to worst practices, but in the more than two centuries since the rout on the
Senio, the papal corpi armati gradually evolved from an ill-disciplined, ill-
trained, and ill-reputed force into the highly competent and confident units
that exist today.

The evolution of the pontifical armed services has reflected the interplay
among three elements: community sensibilities, organizational leadership,
and historical circumstances. At first glance, the first of these elements seems
the most influential. It is reasonable to assume that the status of the papal
army changed as attitudes concerning the nature of the papacy and the role
of the pope changed. The papacy has evolved from a monarchical and temporal model toward a more self-consciously spiritual and pastoral model, a
shift already apparent in the nineteenth century. Particular events, such as
the loss of the Papal States and the Second Vatican Council, accelerated
this change and influenced the views of popes and the Catholic Church toward the utility and propriety of a papal military. As the grandiose Pontifex
Maximus of the fifteenth century gradually evolved into the modest Holy
Father of the twenty-first century, the accoutrements of status and authority deemed necessary and proper by the former were gradually discarded as
irrelevant and unseemly by the latter. Quite simply, the papacy is not about
soldiers and weapons anymore and hasn't been for a long time; indeed, the
very idea of the Holy Father commanding armed forces, even nominally, is
ridiculous if not repugnant to most people today. It is no surprise that changing sensibilities concerning the nature of the Catholic Church and the role
of the man who claims to guide it have had a dramatic impact on the papal
corpi armati. Sometimes, as in the decision in 1970 to abolish the Noble
and Palatine Guards, the influence of new attitudes has been immediate and
explicit. In other cases, such as the decision to demilitarize the image of the
Swiss Guard by avoiding the open display of modern firearms at guard posts,
the changes have been more subtle.

Shifting attitudes toward the use of force, however, have not entirely
determined the role of the military in the modern papacy; in fact, an examination of modern papal military history reveals a paradox. As the papacy
became more demilitarized and pacifist, the papal armed forces actually became stronger. The pontifical army of 1870, for example, was far superior
to its predecessors of 1796 or 1848. The Swiss Guard of 1914 was vastly
improved over the guard of 1860. Today the Swiss Guard and the Vatican
Gendarmeria are probably the best-trained and best-equipped units ever to
serve under the papal flag. Clearly, changing sensibilities concerning the nature of the papacy and apprehensions about image have not been alone in
influencing the history of the pontifical armed forces in the nineteenth and

twentieth centuries, if only because papal authorities did not always share the same sensibilities and concerns.

The history of the modern corpi armati is a story of increasing professionalization and modernization. That progress occurred despite the indifference, if not outright opposition, of ecclesiastical leaders, most of whom considered the pontifical armed forces (when they thought of them at all) to be little more than a shameful necessity or decorative bit players in papal ceremony and protocol. Since the Napoléonic period, few popes have exhibited much systematic interest in their armed forces beyond formal expressions of appreciation and congratulation at ceremonial events or gestures of kindness or courtesy toward individual policemen or soldiers. This attitude of benign neglect has always been pervasive in the papal administration. With the exception of Monsignor Frédéric François Xavier de Mérode and, to a lesser degree Cardinal Raphael Merry del Val, the pope's soldiers never had a powerful advocate or patron inside the pontifical palace. Indeed, they sometimes faced powerful enemies, such as the cardinals Tommaso Bernetti and Giacomo Antonelli, both of whom, it should be emphasized, denigrated the military not for theological or pastoral reasons but on the grounds of political and financial expediency.

The success of military reforms relied primarily on the vision, energy, and dedication of military leaders such as Christophe de Lamoricière, Hermann Kanzler, and Jules Repond, who set out consciously and resolutely to drag their troops into the modern era. The influence of such individuals was so great that the military history of the modern papacy might easily be written as biography. Working always with few resources and often against the indifference of higher authorities, these officers were always more likely to be guided by professional standards and a highly developed sense of personal duty than by debates over the changing image and role of the Holy Father. Today Lamoricière is remembered largely for his role in French political and military history, and Kanzler and Repond have disappeared into obscurity, rarely mentioned in even the most detailed histories of the modern papacy. If they had served a regime more appreciative of military service, they would be honored by biographies and memorials. In relatively small organizations, individuals can have a significant impact. This was particularly the case in the pontifical armed forces, where every advance in organization, discipline, and operational effectiveness reflected the influence of gifted and energetic military leaders who were determined to give the papacy not the army it preferred but the army it needed.

Of course, need varied with time. The evolution of the pontifical armed services and their deployment as protectors of the papacy has often reflected more the particular circumstances of the time than any religious sensibilities or prescriptions from theology or ecclesiastical law. Pius IX did not have a better army in 1870 than he had in 1860 because he was receiving different advice from his theologians concerning the morality of force. Jules Repond did not successfully reform the Swiss Guard in response to the requirements of ecclesiastical law. The creation of an antiterrorism unit in the Vatican Gendarmeria was not a manifestation of the spirit of the Second Vatican Council. Events, such as a mutiny or an assassination attempt, or conditions, such as the "prisoner of the Vatican" period or the rise of international terrorism, often intruded upon the sensibilities and preferences of authorities to compel a particular military posture.

The pontifical armed forces evolved in response to historical developments and changing conditions. In the decades before the French Revolution, for example, the papacy faced no military threats and could rest content with a military force that was little better than a rough town guard and rural constabulary. In the 1860s, in contrast, the blight of brigandage and the constant threat of Red Shirt incursions stimulated the creation of a mobile, professional military force. After Porta Pia and the loss of their temporal power, popes no longer faced military foes but were especially concerned with exhibiting the trappings of sovereignty. In the financially and geographically restricted confines of the Vatican, this concern was most economically satisfied not by a combat-ready force but by a token handful of smartly uniformed retainers whose military skills had no need to extend beyond those required for parade-ground maneuvers and ceremonial display.

By the end of the twentieth century, the preoccupation with the symbols of sovereignty and worldly stature had become passé, but the perceived threat to the physical security of the Holy Father and the Vatican had become more immediate. In these new conditions, the highly picturesque but untrained household guard units were superfluous if not actually dysfunctional. What were required now were professional units with specialized training in executive protection, counterterrorism, and facility security—retainers who could disarm an assailant as smartly as they could dress ranks and fire a pistol as deftly as they could present arms with a halberd.

The pontifical armed forces have survived into the twenty-first century not because they are particularly wanted but because they are needed. Contemporary pontiffs must perform their service to their church and humankind in an age when religious institutions and their leaders are no longer immune to violence and outrage. One might plausibly argue that the dangers surrounding the papacy have never been so grave since the tenth century, when several popes were murdered or imprisoned. It would be irresponsible to consider this situation with complacency. Those who dismiss the need for papal armed units, either by minimizing the threat to the Holy Father and the Vatican or by trusting in the protection of divine providence, might do well to consider the impact not just on the Catholic Church but on the relations between peoples and between states of a politically or religiously motivated assassination of the pope or a devastating terrorist attack on Saint

Peter's or the Vatican. The era of militaristic popes is certainly past, but so should be the era of martyr popes. The time when popes deployed fleets, battalions, and squadrons is distant history, but so long as the world presents an environment of potential physical threat, popes will, however reluctantly, have need of their soldiers.

Notes

Chapter 1. The Worst Army in Europe

1. D. S. Chambers, *Popes, Cardinals and War: The Military Church in Renaissance and Early Modern Europe* (London: Tauris, 2006), 3–5.

2. Ibid., 20.

3. Ciro Paoletti, *A Military History of Italy* (Westport, CT: Praeger, 2008), 23, 32, 36–37.

4. Frank J. Coppa, *The Modern Papacy since 1789* (New York: Addison Wesley Longman, 1998), 21–23; E. E. Y. Hales, *Revolution and Papacy, 1768–1846* (Garden City, NY: Doubleday, 1960), 76–77.

5. An encyclical is a formal, written statement by the pope of the Catholic Church's position on an issue. It takes its title from the opening words in the Latin version of the text.

6. Coppa, *The Modern Papacy since 1789*, 26.

7. Susan Vandiver Nicassio, *Imperial City: Rome, Romans and Napoleon, 1796–1815* (Garden City, NY: Ravenhall Books, 2005), 221.

8. Virgilio Ilari, "L'esercito pontificio nel XVIII secolo fino alle riforme del 1792–93," *Studi Storico-Militari* 6344 (1985): 607.

9. Ibid., 607–608.

10. Ibid., 608, table 16; Flavio Russo, *La difesa costiera dello Stato Pontificio dal XVI al XIX secolo* (Rome: Stato Maggiore dell'Esercito, Ufficio Storico, 1999), 326–327.

11. Ilari, "L'esercito pontificio nel XVIII secolo fino alle riforme del 1792–93," 610; Virgilio Ilari, "I tentativi di riforma dell'esercito pontificio nel 1792–1798," pt. 2, *Studi Storico Militari* 6389 (1987): 154; Russo, *La difesa costiera dello Stato Pontificio dal XVI al XIX secolo*, 327–328.

12. Nicassio, *Imperial City*, 15.

13. Ilari, "L'esercito pontificio nel XVII secolo fino alle riforme del 1792–93," 615–616; Virgilio Ilari, "L'esercito della Repubblica Romana, 1798–1799," *Studi Storico-Militari* 6323 (1984): 184–185. In 1790 the personnel of the pontifical navy numbered 600, significantly below the numbers for the navies of Venice (10,000), Naples (8,600), and Sardinia (700). The pope spent on his navy only 8 percent of what the king of Naples spent on his. Virgilio Ilari, Ciro Paoletti, and Piero Crociani, *Bella Italia militare: Eserciti e marine nell'Italia pre-napoleonica, 1748–1792* (Rome: Stato Maggiore dell'Esercito, Ufficio Storico, 2000), 23.

14. Ilari, "L'esercito pontificio nel XVII secolo fino alle reforme del 1792–93," 616; Ilari et al., *Bella Italia militare*, 248–249.

15. Carla Lodolini Tuppoti, "Esclaves Barbaresques sur les Galères Pontificales," *Revue d'Histoire Maghrebine*, 18, nos. 61–62 (1991): 96.

16. Ilari, "I tentativi della riforma dell'esercito pontificio nel 1792–1798," pt. 1, *Studi Storico Militari* 6372 (1986): 817–818.

17. Hales, *Revolution and Papacy*, 98.

18. Ilari et al., *Bella Italia militare*, 277.

19. Coppa, *The Modern Papacy*, 29.

20. Giuliano Friz, *Burocrati e soldati dello Stato Pontificio, 1800–1870* (Rome: Edindustria Editoriale, 1974), 73–75.

21. Paolo Dalla Torre, "Materiali per una storia dell'esercito pontificio," *Rassegna Storica del Risorgimento* 28 (1941): 51–52.

22. Ilari, "I tentativi della riforma dell'esercito pontificio nel 1792–1798," pt. 1, 745, note 21.

23. Ilari, "I tentativi della riforma dell'esercito pontificio nel 1792–1798," pt. 2, 155.

24. Nicassio, *Imperial City*, 13.

25. Ilari et al., *Bella Italia militare*, 279.

26. Giovanni Mestica, "La battaglia di Faenza e il generale Colli," *Nuova Antologia*, 4th ser., 95 (September–October 1901): 616.

27. In the territories "liberated" by the Army of Italy, Napoléon had organized republics that were little more than satellites of France. Originally territories above the River Po were organized into the Transpadane Republic, whereas those below the Po (including the papal Romagna) were organized into the Cispadane Republic. Eventually these two entities combined into the Cisalpine Republic. These satellite states deployed small military forces, and these all-Italian forces marched and fought with the French Army of Italy.

28. Mestica, "La battaglia di Faenza e il generale Colli," 618.

29. Ibid.

30. Dalla Torre, "Materiali per una storia dell'esercito pontificio," 52, states that Ancajani had 500 cavalrymen on the Senio. Ilari, "I tentativi della riforma dell'esercito pontificio nel 1792–1798," pt. 1, 744, says that the papal commander had only 145 cavalrymen.

31. Dalla Torre, "Materiali per una storia dell'esercito pontificio," 53.

32. Ilari, "I tentativi della riforma dell'esercito pontificio nel 1792–1798," pt. 1, 747–748.

33. Ibid., 748.

34. Quoted in Coppa, *The Modern Papacy*, 30.

35. Ilari, "I tentativi della riforma dell'esercito pontificio nel 1792–1798," pt. 1, 748–749.

36. Mestica, "La Battaglia di Faenza e il generale Colli," 622.

37. Nicassio, *Imperial City*, 20.

38. Andrea Frediani, *Gli assedi di Roma: Razzie, violenze e saccheggi ai danni della città piu assediata nella storia d'Europa* (Rome: Newton & Compton, 1997), 222; Hale, *Revolution and Papacy*, 113.

39. Ilari, "I tentativi di riforma dell'esercito pontificio nel 1792–1798," 748–749.

40. Frediani, *Gli assedi di Roma*, 223–224.

41. Ibid., 226.

42. Paul Krieg and Reto Stampfli, *Die Schweizergarde in Rom* (Zurich: Orell Füssli Verlag, 2006), 178–179.

43. Nicassio, *Imperial City*, 21.

44. Owen Chadwick, *The Popes and European Revolution* (Oxford: Oxford University Press, 1981), 464–465.

45. Ibid., 472–474.

46. Ilari, "L'esercito della Repubblica Romana, 1798–1799," 185–186.

47. Krieg and Stampfli, *Die Schweizergarde in Rom*, 180–181.

48. Ibid., 183. The enlisted men of the Swiss Guard were known as halberdiers because their standard weapon was the halberd, a combination lance and battle-ax that dated back to the Middle Ages.

49. A concordat is an agreement, akin to a treaty, between the Holy See (the institutional personification of the universal Roman Catholic Church that is recognized by international law and diplomatic practice) and a particular state regarding church affairs in that state.

50. Coppa, *The Modern Papacy*, 42–44; Ilario Rinieri, *Napoleone e Pio VII (1804–1813): Relazioni storiche su documenti inediti dell'Archivio Vaticano* (Turin: Unione Tipografico-Editrice, 1906), 360–362.

51. Rinieri, *Napoleone e Pio VII*, 415–416. Rinieri notes that one contemporary account of the French entry into Rome maintains that when the French arrived at the Porta del Popolo they found the gate closed and barred by the guards. According to this account the French fired on the guards, wounding one, and forced the gate.

52. Ibid., 425–426.

53. Quoted in Nicassio, *Imperial City*, 172.

54. Krieg and Stampfli, *Die Schweizergarde in Rom*, 185; Ulrich Nersinger, "Adlige im Dienste Seiner Heiligkeit," *Der Schweizergardist* 3 (2008): 28.

55. Michael Broers, *The Napoleonic Empire in Italy, 1796–1814: Cultural Imperialism in a European Context* (New York: Palgrave Macmillan, 2005), 53–55.

56. Rinieri, *Napoleone e Pio VII*, 472.

57. Nicassio, *Imperial City*, 173–174, quotation on 174.

58. Bartolomeo Pacca, *Historical Memoirs of Cardinal Pacca*, trans. George Head (London: Longman, Brown, Green, & Longmans, 1850), 141–143.

59. Quoted in Nicassio, *Imperial City*, 198.

60. Ibid., 199.

61. Rinieri, *Napoleone e Pio VII*, 548.

62. Pacca, *Historical Memoirs of Cardinal Pacca*, 149–151.

63. Nicassio, *Imperial City*, 181.

64. Krieg and Stampfli, *Die Schweizergarde in Rom*, 186.

65. Ibid., 187.

66. Christian-Roland Marcel Richard, *La Guardia Svizzera Pontificia nel corso dei secoli* (Milan: Leonardo International, 2005), 77; Rinieri, *Napoleone e Pio VII*, 547.

67. The scene in the pontifical apartments and the exchange between the pope and General Radet are recorded in Pacca, *Historical Memoirs of Cardinal Pacca*, 152–153.

68. Ibid., 159.

69. Chadwick, *The Popes and European Revolution*, 512–513; Coppa, *The Modern Papacy since 1789*, 47.

70. Krieg and Stampfli, *Die Schweizergarde in Rom*, 192–193.

71. Ulrich Nersinger, *Soldaten des Papstes* (Ruppichteroth: Kirchliche Umschau, 1999), 61–62; Paoletti, *A Military History of Italy*, 60–61; Broers, *The Napoleonic Empire in Italy*, 127–128.

72. Luigi Rivera, "I fatti del 1831: Il generale pontificio Filippo Resta," *Rassegna storica del Risorgimento* 19 (1932): 209.

73. Alan J. Reinerman, *Austria and the Papacy in the Age of Metternich,* vol. 2: *Revolution and Reaction, 1830–1838* (Washington, DC: Catholic University of American Press, 1989), 81–82.

74. Quoted in ibid., 102.

75. Ibid., 102–103.

76. Narciso Nada, *Metternich e le riforme nello Stato Pontificio: La missione Sebregondi a Roma, 1832–1836* (Turin: Deputazione Subalpina di Storia Patria, 1957), 123–124.

77. Henri Ganter, *Histoire du service militaire des régiments suisses a la solde de l'Angleterre, de Naples et de Rome* (Geneva: Eggimann & Cie, 1902), 457.

78. Quoted in Nada, *Metternich e le riforme nello Stato Pontificio,* 135.

79. Reinerman, *Austria and the Papacy in the Age of Metternich,* 2:201.

80. Ibid., 207–209.

81. Alfonso Ventrone, *L'amministrazione dello Stato Pontificio* (Rome: Edizioni Universitarie, 1942), 196; Giuliano Friz, *Burocrati e soldati dello Stato Pontificio, 1800–1870* (Rome: Edindustria Editoriale, 1974), 196.

Chapter 2. A Cause Worth Fighting For

1. Frank J. Coppa, *Pope Pius IX: Crusader in a Secular Age* (Boston: Twayne Publishers, 1979), 23.

2. Ibid., 45–48.

3. Ibid., 57–59, 61.

4. Ibid., 62–63.

5. Ibid., 79–80.

6. [Pier Giorgio Franzosi], "La Repubblica romana e il suo esercito," *Rivista Militare,* no. 4 (1987): 32. Firm numbers for the force levels of the pontifical army and its respective units in this period are elusive, and various observers, depending on when they count and whom they count, come up with different totals. Because he focuses specifically on the last months of 1847, I have relied on Piero Pieri, *Storia militare del Risorgimento: Guerre e insurrezioni* (Turin: Giulio Einaudi Editore, 1962), 374–375.

7. Camillo Ravioli, *Viaggio della spedizione romana in Egitto fatto nel 1840 e 1841* (Rome: Tipografia delle Belle Arti, 1870), 29–30; Duane Koenig, "The Last Cruise of the Pope's Navy, 1840–1842," *Social Studies* 66, no. 6 (November–December 1975): 270–272.

8. Renato Lefevre, "La marina militare pontificia," *Le marine militari italiane nel 1848,* ed. Ufficio Storico della Marina Militare (Rome: Tipografia Stato Maggiore Marina, 1948), 39–40.

9. Ernesto Ovidi, *Roma e i romani nelle campagne del 1848–49 per l'indipendenza italiana* (Rome: Roux e Viarengo, 1903), 13–14.

10. Demetrio Diamilla-Muller, *Da Roma a Cornuda: Ricordi della spedizione romana nel Veneto, marzo-giugno 1848* (Turin: Tipografia Fodratti, 1886), 6–7.

11. Ibid., 28; Carlo Falconi, *Il Cardinale Antonelli: Vita e carriera del Richelieu italiano nella chiesa di Pio IX* (Milan: Arnoldo Mondadori Editore, 1983), 168.

12. Ovidi, *Roma e i romani nelle campagne del 1848–49,* 26–27; Henri Ganter,

Histoire du service militaire des regiments suisses a la solde de l'Angleterre, de Naples e de Rome (Geneva: Eggimann & Cie, 1902), 460.

13. By a decree issued December 29, 1847, the *presidenza delle armi* was transformed into the *ministero delle armi*.

14. Quoted in Ovidi, *Roma e i romani nelle campagne del 1848–49*, 30–31.

15. Lefevre, "La marina militare pontificia," 43–44.

16. Ovidi, *Roma e i romani nelle campagne del 1848–49*, 32–33. Developed for the British army by Sir William Congreve in 1804, the rockets had been used with mixed results in the Napoléonic Wars and the War of 1812.

17. Diamilla-Muller, *Da Roma a Cornuda*, 13.

18. Camillo Ravioli, *La Campagna nel Veneto del 1848 tenuta da due divisioni e da corpi franchi degli Stati Romani sotto la condotta del Generale Giovanni Durando* (Rome: Tipografia Tiberina, 1883), 25; George M. Trevelyan, *Manin and the Venetian Revolution of 1848* (London: Longmans, Green, 1923), 169.

19. Diamilla-Muller, *Da Roma a Cornuda,* 25.

20. Lefevre, "La marina militare pontificia," 45; Ganter, *Histoire du service militaire des regiments suisses a la solde de l'Angleterre, de Naples e de Rome*, 464; Pieri, *Storia militare del Risorgimento*, 374.

21. Coppa, *Pope Pius IX*, 82.

22. Frank J. Coppa, *Cardinal Giacomo Antonelli and Papal Politics in European Affairs* (Albany: State University of New York Press, 1990), 58; Diamilla-Muller, *Da Roma a Cornuda*, 26.

23. Ovidi, *Roma e i romani nelle campagne del 1848–49*, 58–59.

24. Ibid., 76.

25. Ibid., 80; Pieri, *Storia militare del Risorgimento*, 377–378.

26. Pieri, *Storia militare del Risorgimento*, 378–379.

27. Ibid., 379; Diamilla-Muller, *Da Roma a Cornuda*, 60. Pieri maintains that the Austrians pushed the papal volunteers back into Cornuda that night, but Diamilla-Muller, who was on the scene, reported immediately after the battle that the papal troops halted the Austrians outside the town and that it was the Austrians who fell back that evening.

28. Ravioli, *La campagna nel Veneto del 1848*, 28.

29. Lieutenant Federico Torre would end his military career as a general in the army of the kingdom of Italy and as director general of the Italian ministry of war.

30. Pieri, *Storia militare del Risorgimento*, 379–380; Diamilla-Muller, *Da Roma a Cornuda*, 62.

31. Diamilla-Muller, *Da Roma a Cornuda*, 61.

32. Ibid., 62–63.

33. Trevelyan, *Manin and the Venetian Revolution of 1848*, 174; Vincenzo Bortolotti, *Storia dell'esercito sardo e de' suoi alleati nelle campagne di guerra, 1848–49* (Turin: Fratelli Pozzo, 1889), 135.

34. A later student of the battle concluded that papal casualties (killed and wounded) were closer to two hundred; Trevelyan, *Manin and the Venetian Revolution of 1848*, 172. There are no estimates of Austrian losses.

35. Ibid., 178; Ovidi, *Roma e i romani nelle campagne del 1848–49*, 97.

36. Ovidi, *Roma e i romani nelle campagne del 1848–49*, 111.

37. Ganter, *Histoire du service militaire des Regiments Suisse*, 465.

38. Bortolotti, *Storia dell'esercito sardo e de' suoi alleati nelle campagne di guerra, 1848–49*, 151.

39. Ovidi, *Roma e i romani nelle campagne del 1848–49*, 112; Trevelyan, *Manin and the Venetian Revolution*, 181; Ganter, *Histoire du service militaire des Regiments Suisse*, 464. As always during the papal campaign in the Veneto, casualty figures vary with the source. Ovidi reports that Durando's regulars suffered 10 killed and 33 wounded, whereas casualties among the civic guards and volunteers equaled those numbers. He says Austrian losses were 170, including 50 to 60 soldiers captured by the defenders. Trevelyan says only that the Austrians lost several hundred men, including prisoners. Ganter, relying on a Swiss officer who was present, maintains that papal casualties amounted to 150 dead or wounded, whereas the Austrians suffered 800 casualties. Ganter's numbers seem exaggerated.

40. Trevelyan, *Manin and the Venetian Revolution*, 189.

41. Ibid., 190–191.

42. Ibid., 191–192.

43. Ovidi, *Roma e i romani nelle campagne del 1848–49*, 120–122.

44. Lefevre, "La marina militare pontificia," 46–47.

45. Ovidi, *Roma e i romani nelle campagne del 1848–49*, 178–180.

46. Ibid., 196, 203.

47. Coppa, *Cardinal Giacomo Antonelli*, 59–60.

48. Paul Krieg and Reto Stampfli, *Die Schweizergarde in Rom* (Zurich: Orell Füssli Verlag, 2006), 218–219; letter from Christian-Roland Richard, March 30, 2009.

49. Ulrich Nersinger, "Adlige im Dienste Seiner Heiligkeit," *Der Schweizergardist* 3 (2008): 28, maintains that several Noble Guards were present inside the Quirinal Palace during the events of November 16, 1848, but no other source mentions their presence either that day or the next.

50. Quoted in Coppa, *Cardinal Giacomo Antonelli*, 60.

51. Augusto Rossi, *Pio IX e la distruzione della Repubblica Romana, 1849* (Rome: Serarcangeli, 2001), 48.

52. Krieg and Stampfli, *Die Schweizergarde in Rom*, 219–220; Christian-Roland Richard, *La Guardia Svizzera Pontificia nel corso dei secoli* (Milan: Leonardo International, 2005), 83.

53. Krieg and Stampfli, *Die Schweizergarde in Rom*, 219–220.

54. Quoted in Richard, *La Guardia Svizzera*, 84.

55. Krieg and Stampfli, *Die Schweizergarde in Rom*, 220–221.

56. Coppa, *Cardinal Giacomo Antonelli*, 62. The few brief histories of the Noble Guard that are available make no mention of Antonelli's approach for assistance.

57. Owen Chadwick, *A History of the Popes, 1830–1914* (Oxford: Oxford University Press, 1998), 84.

58. Frank J. Coppa, *The Origins of the Italian Wars of Independence* (New York: Longman, 1992), 53, 55; Giulio Andreotti, *La fuga di Pio IX e l'ospitalità dei Borbone* (Rome: Edizione Benincasa, 2003), 18–20.

59. Camillo Ravioli, *Notizie storiche dei corpi militari regolari che combatterono negli assalti ed assedi di Bologna, Ancona, Roma nell'anno 1849* (Rome: Tipografia Nazionale, 1884), 52.

60. Pier Giorgio Franzosi, ed., *La Repubblica romana e il suo esercito* (Rome: Rivista Militare, 1987), 5.

61. Krieg and Stampfli, *Die Schweizergarde in Rom*, 221–222; Robert Royal, *The Pope's Army: 500 Years of the Papal Swiss Guard* (New York: Crossroad Publishing, 2006), 127.

62. "Espoliazione sofferta dal Corpo della Guardia Nobile durante il Governo del 1849," Vatican City. Archivio Segreto Vaticano, Fondi Speciali: Guardia Nobile, Titolo XIV, parte 1a.

63. Quoted in Franzosi, *La Repubblica romana e il suo esercito*, 6; Rossi, *Pio IX e la distruzione della Repubblica Romana, 1849*, 91, 101.

64. Franzosi, *La Repubblica romana e il suo esercito*, 10.

65. Giuseppe Leti, *La rivoluzione e la Repubblica Romana, 1848–1849* (Milan: Vallardi, 1913), 375–378. Ancona surrendered to the Austrians after a siege of twenty-five days.

66. Ibid., 12.

67. Attilio Vigevano, *La Compagna delle Marche e dell'Umbria* (Rome: Stabilimento Poligrafico per l'amministrazione della guerra, 1923), 72–73.

68. Richard, *La Guardia Svizzera*, 86.

69. Niccolò Del Re, *La Guardia Palatina d'Onore: Una istituzione piana scomparsa* (Rome: n.p., 1997), 17–18, quotation on 18.

70. Vigevano, *La Compagna delle Marche e dell'Umbria*, 76–77.

71. The percentages are based on the figures in Giuliano Friz, *Burocrati e soldati dello Stato Pontificio, 1800–1870* (Rome: Edindustria Editoriale, 1974), 168–169. Precision in determining the percentage of foreign enlistments is difficult because it is possible that the indigenous units contained a few individuals who were not subjects of the pope, although they may have been Italians.

72. Ibid., 79–80, 82; Massimo Brandani, Piero Crociani, and Massimo Fiorentino, *L'esercito pontificio da Castelfidardo a Porta Pia (1860–1870): Uniformi, equipaggiamento, armamento* (Milan: Intergest, 1976), 7–9.

73. Vigevano, *La Compagna delle Marche e dell'Umbria*, 74–75; Brandani et al., *L'esercito pontificio da Castelfidardo a Porta Pia (1860–1870)*, 66, 70.

74. Friz, *Burocrati e soldati dello Stato Pontificio, 1800–1870*, 73.

75. Vigevano, *La Compagna delle Marche e dell'Umbria*, 87–89, 92.

76. Chadwick, *A History of the Popes, 1830–1914*, 141–142; Coppa, *The Origins of the Italian Wars of Independence*, 79–81.

77. Chadwick, *A History of the Popes, 1830–1914*, 143; Coppa, *The Origins of the Italian Wars of Independence*, 94–95.

78. Paul de Vallière and Henri Guisan, *Honneur et Fidélité: Histoire des suisses au service étranger* (Lausanne: Editions d'Art Suisse Ancienne, 1940), 735; Giacomo Martina, S.J., *Pio IX (1851–1866)* (Rome: Editrice Pontificia Università Gregoriana, 1986), 90–91.

Chapter 3. A War Too Soon

1. François Besson, *Frederick Francis Xavier de Mérode: Minister and Almoner to Pius IX, Archbishop of Miletensis: His Life and Works*, trans. Mary Herbert (London: W. H. Allen & Co., 1887), 38.

2. Ibid., 94–96.

3. Carlo Falconi, *Il Cardinale Antonelli: Vita e carriera del Richelieu italiano nella chiesa di Pio IX* (Milan: Arnoldo Mondadori Editore, 1983), 345–346.

4. Besson, *Frederick Francis Xavier de Mérode*, 125–127, quotation on 127.

5. Attilio Vigevano, *La Campagna delle Marche e dell Umbria* (Rome: Stabilimento Poligrafico per l'amministrazione della guerra, 1923), 102; Emile Keller, *Le Général De La Moricière: Sa vie militaire, politique et religieuse* (Paris: Rene Haton, 1891), 2:290–291.

6. Vigevano, *La Campagna delle Marche e dell'Umbria*, 102.

7. Besson, *Frederick Francois Xavier de Mérode*, 140.

8. Massimo Brandani, Piero Crociani, and Massimo Fiorentino, *L'esercito pontificio da Castelfidardo a Porta Pia, 1860–1879: Uniformi, equippagiamento, armamento* (Milan: Intergest, 1976), 87.

9. Keller, *Le Général De La Moricière*, 311–314.

10. Attilio Vigevano, *La fine dell'esercito pontificio* (Rome: Stabilimento Poligrafico per l'amministrazione della guerra, 1920), 10–11, 14.

11. Vigevano, *La Campagna delle Marche e dell'Umbria*, 103.

12. Keller, *Le Général De La Moricière*, 318.

13. When the Bourbon king Charles X abdicated in favor of his ten-year-old grandson after the revolution of July 1830, the National Assembly rejected the Bourbon child and proclaimed Louis-Philippe d'Orléans king. Charles X and his family went into exile in Britain, and the grandson, known as the comte de Chambord, continued to insist that he was the legitimate monarch of France. Those who supported the Bourbon claim to the throne and rejected the claims of the Orleanists and Bonapartists were known as Legitimists.

14. George F. H. Berkeley, *The Irish Battalion in the Papal Army of 1860* (Dublin: Talbot Press, 1929), 19–20.

15. Vigevano, *La Campagna delle Marche e dell'Umbria*, 124. Percentages calculated from Vigevano's numbers.

16. Louis de Becdelièvre, *Souvenirs de l'armée pontificale* (Paris: Lecoffre, 1867), 35.

17. Keller, *Le Général De La Moricière*, 304; Jean Guenel, *La dernière guerre du pape: Les zouaves pontificaux au secours de Saint-Siège, 1860–1870* (Rennes: Presses Universitaires de Rennes, 1998), 30–31.

18. General Vicenzo Longo, "L'esercito pontificio nel 1860," in *Scritti sul 1860 nel centenario*, ed. Stato Maggiore Esercito–Ufficio Storico (Rome: Tipografia Regionale, 1960), 267–268; Besson, *Frederick Francis Xavier de Mérode*, 134–135, 138.

19. Becdelièvre, *Souvenirs de l'armée pontificale*, 24–25.

20. Guenel, *La dernière guerre du pape*, 28; Keller, *Le Général De La Moricière*, 315.

21. Théodore de Quatrebarbes, *Souvenirs d'Ancone* (Paris: Charles Douniol, 1866), 64.

22. Guenel, *La dernière guerre du pape*, 32; Besson, *Frederick Francis Xavier de Mérode*, 137.

23. Longo, "L'esercito pontificio nel 1860," 269.

24. Christopher Hibbert, *Garibaldi: Hero of Italian Unification* (New York: Palgrave Macmillan, 2008), 240.

25. Frank J. Coppa, *The Origins of the Italian Wars of Independence* (Harlow: Longman, 1992), 106–107.

26. Carlo Pellion di Persano, *Compagna navale degli anni 1860 e 1861* (Turin: Roux e Favale, 1880), 194; Vigevano, *La Compagna delle Marche e dell'Umbria*, 187.

27. Vigevano, *La Campagna delle Marche e dell'Umbria*, 147; Piero Pieri, *Storia militare del Risorgimento: Guerre e insurrezioni* (Turin: Giulio Einaudi Editore, 1962), 712. Pieri places General Fanti's total strength at almost 33,000 men.

28. Longo, "L'esercito pontificio nel 1860," 273.

29. Quoted in Mario Montanari, *Politica e strategia in cento anni di guerre italiani*, vol. 1: *Il periodo Risorgimentale* (Rome: Stato Maggiore dell'Esercito, 1996), 477.

30. Vigevano, *La Campagna delle Marche e dell'Umbria*, 147, 201.

31. Christophe de Lamoricière, *Rapporto di S. E. il Generale de Lamoricière a S. E. il Ministro delle Armi intorno alle fazioni guerresche combattute dall'esercito pontificio nel settembre del 1860* (Rome: Tipografia della Civltà Cattolica, 1860), 4.

32. Giuseppe Ioli, "Il battaglione irlandese di San Patrizio," in *Scritti sul 1860 nel centenario*, ed. [Stato Maggiore Esercito–Ufficio Storico] (Rome: Tipografia Regionale, 1960), 211.

33. Giuseppe Amori, *L'esercito pontificio nell'ultimo dodicennio* (Rome: La Fedelta, 1873), 6. Unlike the gendarmeria, the customs police had been heavily influenced by nationalist and antipapal appeals. Many customs officers assisted the antipapal underground by facilitating the movement of arms, propaganda, and individuals across the papal borders. During the events of September 1860, large numbers of customs police defected or refused to fight for the pope. Giuliano Oliva, *La Guardia di Finanza Pontificia* (Rome: Museo Storico della Guardia di Finanza, 1979), 138.

34. Vigevano, *La campagna delle Marche e dell'Umbria*, 176–177.

35. Ibid., 181–182, 185.

36. Ibid., 517–518.

37. Lamoricière, *Rapporto*, 2; Falconi, *Il Cardinale Antonelli*, 351.

38. Longo, "L'esercito pontificio nel 1860," 276.

39. Quoted in Eugenio Barbarich, *Castelfidardo e la campagna delle Marche e dell'Umbria* (Rome: Tipografia dell'Unione Cooperativa, 1904); Lamoricière, *Rapporto*, 6.

40. Carla Meneguzzi Rostagni, *La crisi del potere temporale e la diplomazia europea, 1859–1860* (Padua: Signum Edizioni, 1983), 202.

41. Lamoricière, *Rapporto*, 7–8; Noel Blakiston, ed., *The Roman Question: Extracts from the Despatches of Odo Russell from Rome, 1858–1870* (Wilmington, DE: Michael Glazier, 1980), 124–125; Longo, "L'esercito pontificio nel 1860," 276.

42. Amori, *L'esercito pontificio nell'ultimo dodicennio*, 6.

43. Vigevano, *La campagna delle Marche e dell'Umbria*, 286–287.

44. Ibid., 288–290.

45. Ibid., 292–294.

46. Gabriel de Pimodan, *Vie du Général de Pimodan* (Paris: Champion, 1928), 300. As late as September 15 Pimodan was still anticipating French military support.

47. Lamoricière, *Rapporto*, 12.

48. Vigevano, *La Campagna delle Marche e dell'Umbria*, 179–180, 217.

49. Ibid., 220.

50. Ibid., 222–223.

51. Ibid., 221.

52. Berkeley, *The Irish Battalion in the Papal Army of 1860*, 116–119. After the war against Piedmont, Private Clooney resigned from the pontifical army and immigrated to the United States, which was then embroiled in a civil war. He enlisted in

the Union army, rose to the rank of captain, and was killed leading a company in the fight for the Sunken Road at the Battle of Antietam. A popular lithograph, *Clooney's Charge*, memorialized this action.

53. Although many Perugians welcomed the Piedmontese, there is no evidence to support Henri Ganter's claim that the populace (including women and children) rose up en masse to support the Piedmontese attack by using any available weapon (including chairs and flower vases) to attack the pontifical troops, and that more than four hundred bodies littered the streets when the pontificals barricaded themselves inside the Rocca. See Henri Ganter, *Histoire du service militaire des Regiments Suisses à la solde de l'Angleterre, de Naples et de Rome* (Geneva: Eggimann & Cie, 1902), 488.

54. Vigevano, *La Campagna delle Marche e dell'Umbria*, 226, 228.

55. Berkeley, *The Irish Battalion in the Papal Army of 1860*, 141, 143.

56. Ioli, "Il battaglione irlandese di San Patrizio," 211.

57. Berkeley, *The Irish Battalion in the Papal Army of 1860*, 127.

58. Ibid., 135.

59. Ibid., 142. O'Reilly mistakenly places the lancers' adventure on September 15. General Brignone did not even begin to move toward Spoleto from Foligno until September 16.

60. After the War of 1860, John Coppinger, like several of his compatriots in the Irish Battalion, would immigrate to the United States to fight for the North in the American Civil War. He received a commission in the Union Army; fought at several major battles, including Second Bull Run, Chancellorsville, and Gettysburg; and after the war remained in the U.S. Army, retiring in 1908 as a major general.

61. Berkeley, *The Irish Battalion in the Papal Army of 1860*, 151.

62. Ibid., 161–162. In preparing his account of the bersaglieri attack against the gate, Berkeley benefited from the recollections of two veterans of the Irish Battalion: former lieutenant M. T. Crean, who fought and was wounded at the gate, and former private Edward Dunne, who fought on the wall.

63. Ibid., 166–167; Vigevano, *La Campagna delle Marche e dell'Umbria*, 258.

64. For Piedmontese losses, see Vigevano, *La Campagna delle Marche e dell'Umbria*, 259. In his postwar report, General Lamoricière claimed that at Spoleto the attackers lost one hundred dead and three hundred wounded. This was wild speculation. Vigevano worked from official records and was able to identify each of the Piedmontese casualties by name.

65. Berkeley, *The Irish Battalion in the Papal Army of 1860*, 168.

66. Lamoricière, *Rapporto*, 9–10.

67. [Corpo di Stato Maggiore–Ufficio Storico], *La Battaglia di Castelfidardo (18 settembre 1860)* (Rome: Tipo-litografia del Genio Civile, 1903), 14–16.

68. Vigevano, *La Campagna delle Marche e dell'Umbria*, 320–321.

69. "Rapport du caporal Morlet," document no. 5, [Corpo di Stato Maggiore–Ufficio Storico], *La Battaglia di Castelfidardo*, 92.

70. Pimodan, *Vie du Général de Pimodan*, 311–312.

71. [Corpo di Stato Maggiore–Ufficio Storico], *La Battaglia di Castelfidardo*, 22.

72. Antonine de Segur, *The Martyrs of Castelfidardo* (Dublin: Gill & Son, 1895), 89.

73. [Corpo di Stato Maggiore–Ufficio Storico], *La Battaglia di Castelfidardo*, 24–25; Berkeley, *The Irish Battalion in the Papal Army of 1860*, 179–180.

74. General Lamoricière concluded that when Piedmontese bullets began to fall among the 2nd Cacciatori, the pope's Italians fired toward the enemy, which was to their front, as were the Swiss of the Carabinieri Battalion. Lamoricière, *Rapporto*, 20.

75. Segur, *The Martyrs of Castelfidardo*, 188.

76. [Corpo di Stato Maggiore–Ufficio Storico], *La Battaglia di Castelfidardo*, 26.

77. Segur, *The Martyrs of Castelfidardo*, 189. Private Lanascol survived the battle and from his hospital bed described his experience in a letter to his father. He died a month later from an infection of his wounds.

78. Vigevano, *La Campagna delle Marche e dell'Umbria*, 347.

79. Pimodan, *Vie du Général de Pimodan*, 325.

80. Vigevano, *La Campagna delle Marche e dell'Umbria*, 351.

81. Pimodan, *Vie du Général de Pimodan*, 326.

82. Vigevano, *La Campagna delle Marche e dell'Umbria*, 353–354.

83. Phillipe-Antoine de Tournon, *Les volontaires Pontificaux a cheval* (Paris: Charles Douniol, 1860), 11.

84. Segur, *The Martyrs of Castelfidardo*, 89–90. Daudier was decorated for his bravery at Castelfidardo and promoted to captain.

85. The circumstances surrounding Lamoricière's departure from the battlefield remain unclear. In his postwar report to the minister of arms, Lamoricière said that he transferred command to Goudenhoven with instructions to continue the resistance as long as possible before falling back across the Musone to Loreto. In his after-action account, however, prepared two days after the battle, Goudenhoven reported, "Observing the rout, General Lamoricière left for Ancona without informing any unit commander or senior officer. The colonels asked [me] to assume command." Writing three weeks after the battle, Colonel Blumensthil, who commanded the papal artillery, noted simply, "Colonel Goudenhoven took command of the troops." Colonel Louis de Becdelièvre, who was General Pimodan's senior officer in the attack column, recorded that "Colonel Goudenhoven [was] elected commander-in-chief." It is possible that the witnesses were conflating two events: the transfer of battlefield command and the later selection of an officer to arrange surrender terms with General Cialdini.

86. Tournon, *Les volontaires Pontificaux a cheval*, 11.

87. Vigevano, *La Campagna delle Marche e dell'Umbria*, 358; Oscar de Poli, *Les soldats du pape (1860–1867)* (Paris: Amyot, 1868), 144–145. De Poli was one of the defenders of the Lower Farm.

88. Vigevano, *La Campagna delle Marche e dell'Umbria*, 362. Papal casualty rolls reflected the presence in the pope's service of many scions of Europe's Catholic nobility. Reviewing such a list, a Piedmontese officer allegedly commented, "Why, it looks like the guest list for a ball at Versailles."

89. Tournon, *Les volontaires Pontificaux a cheval*, 12–13.

90. Becdelièvre, *Souvenirs de l'armée pontificale*, 82; Georges Cerbelaud-Salagnac, *Les Zouaves Pontificaux* (Paris: Editions France Empire, 1963), 47.

91. For Chérisey's report of his odyssey, see de Poli, *Les soldats du pape*, 184–190.

92. Quatrebarbes, *Souvenirs d'Ancone*, 161.

93. Ibid., 173–176, quotation on 176.

94. Ibid., 42.

95. Vigevano, *La Campagna delle Marche e dell'Umbria*, 415.

96. In June 1860 an artillery officer sent by General Lamoricière to inspect the city's cannons found twenty-seven of the guns in very poor condition. Ibid., 407.

97. Guenel, *La dernière guerre du pape*, 32; quote in Quatrebarbes, *Souvenirs d'Ancone*, 44.

98. Lamoricière, *Rapporto*, 30.

99. Quatrebarbes, *Souvenirs d'Ancone*, 191–192; Berkeley, *The Irish Battalion in the Papal Army of 1860*, 204.

100. Vigevano, *La campagna delle Marche e dell'Umbria*, 443, 445–446. After fighting his column through the Piedmontese 7th Division and leading it into Ancona in the early days of the war, Colonel Kanzler had been promoted to general.

101. Ibid., 447–448.

102. Berkeley, *The Irish Battalion in the Papal Army of 1860*, 208. After the War of 1860, one of the Irish officers at Ancona, Lieutenant Myles Keogh, resigned from the pontifical army and entered the Union Army in the American Civil War. Upon the conclusion of the Civil War, Keogh remained in the U.S. Army, serving on the frontier with the 7th U.S. Cavalry, and dying with Lieutenant Colonel George Armstrong Custer at the Battle of the Little Big Horn in 1876.

103. Lamoricière, *Rapporto*, 32–33, 35. Although the Piedmontese did not deliberately target civilian areas of the city, nonmilitary buildings were occasionally hit. The archbishop's residence was struck, as was the French consulate.

104. Quatrebarbes, *Souvenirs d'Ancone*, 208, quotation on 215.

105. Vigevano, *La campagna delle Marche e dell'Umbria*, 463.

106. Ibid., 466.

107. Quoted in Quatrebarbes, *Souvenirs d'Ancone*, 229–230.

108. Vigevano, *La campagna delle Marche e dell'Umbria*, 467–468.

109. Ibid., 477–479, 483.

110. See, for example, Giulio Cesare Carletti, *L'esercito pontificio dal 1860 al 1870: Quale era, quanto era, cosa operò* (Viterbo: Agnesotti, 1904), 19–20.

Chapter 4. Red Shirts and Brigands

1. Attilio Vigevano, *La compagna della Marche e dell'Umbria* (Rome: Stabilimento Poligrafico per l'amministrazione della guerra, 1923), 514.

2. Frank J. Coppa, *Cardinal Giacomo Antonelli and Papal Politics in European Affairs* (Albany: State University of New York Press, 1990), 123–124.

3. François Besson, *Frederick Francis Xavier de Mérode: Minister and Almoner to Pius IX, Archbishop of Miletensis: His Life and Works*, trans. Mary Herbert (London: W. H. Allen & Co., 1887), 64.

4. General Vicenzo Longo, "L'esercito pontificio nel 1860," in *Scritti sul 1860 nel centenario*, ed. Stato Maggiore Esercito–Ufficio Storico (Rome: Tipografia Regionale, 1960), 283; Attilio Vigevano, *La fine dell'esercito pontificio* (Rome: Stabilimento Poligrafico per l'amministrazione della guerra, 1920), 29–30.

5. Besson, *Frederick Francis Xavier de Mérode*, 172, 175.

6. Oscar de Poli, *Les soldats du pape (1860–1867)* (Paris: Amyot, 1868), 111–112; Louis de Becdelièvre, *Souvenirs de l'armée pontificale* (Paris: Lecoffre, 1867), 123–125, 131.

7. Coppa, *Cardinal Giacomo Antonelli and Papal Politics in European Affairs*, 129.

8. David Chislain Emile Gustave de Mévius, *Histoire de l'invasion des États Pontificaux en 1867* (Paris: Victor Palmé, 1875), 52.

9. Quoted in Giacomo Martina, S.J., *Pio IX (1867–1878)* (Rome: Editrice Pontificia Università Gregoriana, 1990), 13.

10. Quoted in Besson, *Frederick Francis Xavier de Mérode*, 207–208.

11. Ibid., 226–228; Martina, *Pio IX*, 15.

12. Piero Raggi, *La nona crociata: I volontari di Pio IX in difesa di Roma (1860–1870)* (Ravenna: Libreria Tonini, 2002), 64–65; Vicenzo Vannutelli, *Il Generale Kanzler: Cenni biografici* (Rome: Armanni, 1889), 13, 18.

13. Vigevano, *La fine dell'esercito pontificio*, 32–35. Luigi Cicconetti, *Roma o morte: Gli avvenimenti nello stato pontificio nell'anno 1867* (Milan: Alfieri, 1934), 41–42.

14. Coppa, *Cardinal Giacomo Antonelli*, 132.

15. Ibid., 138.

16. Mévius, *Histoire de l'invasion des États Pontificaux en 1867*, 44–46, 48.

17. Ibid., 115.

18. Joseph Powell, *Two Years in the Pontifical Zouaves* (London: R. Washbourne, 1871), 51–52.

19. Alberto Ghisalberti, "Carlo Canori: Soldato del Papa," *Rassegna storica del Risorgimento* 23 (1936): 433.

20. Christopher Duggan, *The Force of Destiny: A History of Italy since 1796* (Boston: Houghton Mifflin, 2007), 220–221.

21. Ibid., 221–223.

22. Cesare Cesari, *Il brigantaggio e l'opera dell'esercito italiano dal 1860 al 1870* (Bologna: Arnoldo Forni, 2002), 24, 42, 46; Giuseppe Bourelly, *Il brigantaggio dal 1860 al 1865 nelle zone militari di Melfi e Lacedonia* (1865; reprint, Venosa: Edizioni Osanna, 1987), 63–64.

23. Carlo Falconi, *Il Cardinale Antonelli: Vita e carriera del Richelieu italiano nella chiesa di Pio IX* (Milan: Arnoldo Mondadori Editore, 1983), 416–418; Salvatore Lupo, "Il grande brigantaggio: Interpretazione e memoria di una guerra civile," in *Guerra e pace*, ed. Walter Barberis (Turin: Giulio Einaudi, 2002), 489–490.

24. Carlo Bartolini, *Il brigantaggio nello Stato Pontificio: Cenno-storico-aneddotico dal 1860 al 1870* (Rome: Arnoldo Forni Editore, 1897), 14–15; Giuseppe Tosi, "La Gendarmeria Pontificia" (doctoral thesis, University of Rome ["La Sapienza"], 1966), 402, 405–406.

25. Bartolini, *Il brigantaggio nello Stato Pontificio*, 19–21.

26. Cesari, *Il brigantaggio e l'opera dell'esercito italiano dal 1860 al 1870*, 57.

27. Ibid., 34–35; Paolo Dalla Torre, *L'anno di Mentana: Contributo ad una storia dello Stato Pontificio nel 1867* (Milan: Aldo Martello Editore, 1968), 47–48; Tosi, "La Gendarmeria Pontificia," 401.

28. Quoted in Dalla Torre, *L'anno di Mentana*, 50.

29. C. E. Rouleau, *La Papauté et les Zouaves Pontificaux: Quelques pages d'histoire* (Quebec: Le Soleil, 1905), 63.

30. Ibid., 61–62; Powell, *Two Years in the Pontifical Zouaves*, 4.

31. Frank J. Coppa, *The Wars of Italian Independence* (New York: Longman, 1992), 126–128. Shortly before the outbreak of the war, Austria had ceded the Veneto to France in return for a promise by Paris to remain neutral and to urge

neutrality on Italy. After the peace agreement, Emperor Napoléon transferred the Veneto to Italy.

32. Ibid., 132–133.

33. Ibid., 133; Christopher Hibbert, *Garibaldi: Hero of Italian Unification* (New York: Palgrave Macmillan, 2008), 353–354.

34. Dalla Torre, *L'anno di Mentana*, 116.

35. Mévius, *Histoire de l'invasion des États Pontificaux en 1867*, 118–119.

36. Cicconetti, *Roma o morte*, 41.

37. In October 1867 only 35 percent of the pontifical army (43 percent of its combat personnel) was non-Italian. Non-Italians could enlist only in the Zouaves, carabinieri, and Legione Romana. The percentage of non-Italians might, in fact, have been slightly lower because Italians served in the Zouaves (which were a multinational force), but it is impossible to break out the number of Italians in that regiment. Percentages have been calculated from order of battle data in Cicconetti, *Roma o morte*, 40.

38. Mévius, *Histoire de l'invasion des États Pontificaux en 1867*, 113.

39. In his account of the Garibaldian campaign against the Papal States in the fall of 1867, Piero Pieri records the Red Shirt capture of Acquapendente and other papal towns but fails to mention the prompt recapture of these towns by pontifical forces, thus giving the false impression that Garibaldi's irregulars were capturing and holding a lengthening list of papal communities in an unending series of victories. When he does acknowledge the loss of an occupied town by the Red Shirts, Pieri refers to their "withdrawal" from the town, suggesting that the departure was voluntary when in fact in almost every case the Red Shirts were forcibly expelled by pontifical troops. Piero Pieri, *Storia militare del Risorgimento: Guerre e insurrezioni* (Turin: Giulio Einaudi Editore, 1962), 773, 781.

40. Raggi, *La nona crociata*, 14–15; Jean Guenel, *La dernière guerre du pape: Les Zouaves pontificaux au secours du Saint-Siège* (Rennes: Presses Universitaires de Rennes, 1998), 94.

41. Dalla Torre, *L'anno di Mentana*, 120. Sources disagree as to the size of Gentili's force, with references to 70, 95, or "around 100" men.

42. Roberto di Nolli, *Mentana* (Rome: Bardi Editore, 1965), 57.

43. Dalla Torre, *L'anno di Mentana*, 121.

44. Quoted in Antonmaria Bonetti, *Da Bagnorea a Mentana ossia storia della guerra pontificio-garibaldina* (Trento: Tipografia Ed. Artigianelli, 1891), 148.

45. Ibid., 122; Georges Cerbelaud-Salagnac, *Les Zouaves pontificaux* (Paris: Editions France Empire, 1963), 126; de Poli, *Les soldats du pape (1860–1867)*, 318–319.

46. Dalla Torre, *L'anno di Mentana*, 144–145.

47. Di Nolli, *Mentana*, 57–58; Cerbelaud-Salagnac, *Les Zouaves pontificaux*, 127.

48. Di Nolli, *Mentana*, 58; Dalla Torre, *L'anno di Mentana*, 148–149.

49. Di Nolli, *Mentana*, 63.

50. Vannutelli, *Il Generale Kanzler*, 73–74.

51. Falconi, *Il Cardinale Antonelli*, 427–428; Dalla Torre, *L'anno di Mentana*, 214.

52. Dalla Torre, *L'anno di Mentana*, 143.

53. Pieri, *Storia militare del Risorgimento*, 781, mistakenly asserts that the Red Shirts had inflicted "grave losses" on the pontifical army in the first weeks of October 1867. In fact, by the third week in October papal casualties (killed, wounded, and

prisoner) amounted to less than 1 percent of the strength of the pontifical army. Red Shirt losses were far greater than those of their opponents.

54. Guenel, *La dernière guerre du pape*, 95; Charles Coulombe, *The Pope's Legion: The Multinational Fighting Force That Defended the Vatican* (New York: Palgrave Macmillan, 2008), 126.

55. Guenel, *La dernière guerre du pape*, 95–96; Cerbelaud-Salagnac, *Les Zouaves pontificaux*, 130–131.

56. Guenel, *La dernière guerre du pape*, 96. For their actions at Montelibretti, Sergeant Major Bach and Sergeant Bégassière were promoted to lieutenant.

57. Di Nolli, *Mentana*, 61.

58. Dalla Torre, *L'anno di Mentana*, 150–151, 199–201; Denis Mack Smith, *Italy and Its Monarchy* (New Haven, CT: Yale University Press, 1989), 40.

59. From Serra, October 19, 1867, "Riassunto sulle invasioni Garibaldinesche dal 24 sett.e 1867 a tutto il 12 nov.e 1867," Vatican City, Archivio Segreto Vaticano (ASV), Carte Kanzler-Vannutelli, Fondo A33. This "Summary of the Garibaldian Invasion" is a war diary of the pontifical Ministry of Arms consisting of summaries of incoming and outgoing messages.

60. Ibid., minister to Zappi, October 19, 1867; ibid., minister to Serra, October 19, 1867; Gendarmeria Pontificia, "Avvenimenti dal giorno 22 al giorno 23 ottobre," in "Rapporti giornalieri della Gendarmeria dal 27 settembre al 4 novembre 1867," ASV. Carte Kanzler-Vannutelli, Fondo A1.

61. Smith, *Italy and Its Monarchy*, 39–40; Bonetti, *Da Bagnorea a Mentana*, 80, asserts that the Italian government secretly shipped six hundred rifles to the mouth of the Tiber to support a Roman uprising.

62. Dalla Torre, *L'anno di Mentana*, 215; David Alvarez, *Spies in the Vatican: Espionage and Intrigue from Napoleon to the Holocaust* (Lawrence: University Press of Kansas, 2002), 32–33.

63. Paul Krieg and Reto Stampfli, *Die Schweizergarde in Rom* (Zurich: Orell Füssli Verlag, 2006), 234; Niccolò Del Re, *La Guardia Palatina d'Onore* (Rome: n.p., 1997), 24–25, 28.

64. Dalla Torre, *L'anno di Mentana*, 215–216; Powell, *Two Years in the Pontifical Zouaves*, 16.

65. Guenel, *La dernière guerre du pape*, 98–99; Raggi, *La nona crociata*, 16; Ferdinand Gregorovius, *The Roman Journals of Ferdinand Gregorovius, 1852–1874*, ed. Friedrich Althaus (London: George Bell & Sons, 1907), 295.

66. Gendarmeria Pontificia, "Avvenimenti dal giorno 22 al giorno 23 ottobre."

67. Report by Zappi, "Avvenimenti del 22.a Roma," October 23, 1867, "Riassunto sulle invasioni Garibaldinesche dal 24 sett.e 1867 a tutto il 12 nov.e 1867," ASV, Carte Kanzler-Vannutelli, Fondo A33; Guenel, *La dernière guerre du pape*, 98–99; di Nolli, *Mentana*, 78–79.

68. Minister to Azzanesi, De Courten and d'Argy, October 22, 1867, "Riassunto sulle invasioni Garibaldinesche dal 24 sett.e 1867 a tutto il 12 nov.e 1867," ASV, Carte Kanzler-Vannutelli, Fondo A33.

69. Minister to Zappi, October 23, 1867, "Riassunto sulle invasioni Garibaldinesche dal 24 sett.e 1867 a tutto il 12 nov.e 1867," ASV, Carte Kanzler-Vannutelli, Fondo A33.

70. Report by Zappi, October 25, 1867, "Riassunto sulle invasioni Garibaldinesche

dal 24 sett.e 1867 a tutto il 12 nov.e 1867," ASV, Carte Kanzler-Vannutelli, Fondo A33. Di Nolli, *Mentana*, 85, says eleven of the occupants of the house were killed.

71. Di Nolli, *Mentana*, 88; Dalla Torre, *L'anno di Mentana*, 260.

72. Di Nolli, *Mentana*, 88–89; Raggi, *La nona crociata*, 17.

73. Di Nolli, *Mentana*, 94–96.

74. Hibbert, *Garibaldi*, 354–355.

75. Pieri, *Storia militare del Risorgimento*, 776.

76. The size of Red Shirt forces during the campaign of 1867 is difficult to fix with any accuracy. Accounts by papal partisans present higher numbers, whereas those from observers less sympathetic to the papal side offer lower numbers. Estimates must always be "soft" because Red Shirt bands were constantly moving about the countryside, sometimes joining together, sometimes splitting apart, so that the strength of a particular band varied over time. Force levels among the Red Shirts also varied according to the arrival of new volunteers and the desertion of disenchanted men. Antonmaria Bonetti, an extreme papal partisan, claims (*Da Bagnorea a Mentana*, 98) that Garibaldi had 10,000 men at Monterotondo. Pieri, much less sympathetic to the papal cause, maintains (*Storia militare del Risorgimento*, 776) that Garibaldi probably had no more than 8,000 irregulars in all of the Papal States. Luigi Cicconetti, probably the most evenhanded commentator, estimates (*Roma o morte*, 117) that Garibaldi had more than 5,000 men fighting at Monterotondo. A report from the gendarmeria post at Monterotondo on October 24 informed the Ministry of Arms in Rome that the previous night "a thousand" Red Shirts had seized the town's railway station but that 4,000 Garibaldians were in the area. From Poccioni, October 24, 1867, "Riassunto sulle invasioni Garibaldinesche dal 24 sett.e 1867 a tutto il 12 nov.e 1867," ASV, Carte Kanzler-Vannutelli, Fondo A33.

77. From Costes, October 23, 1867, "Riassunto sulle invasioni Garibaldinesche dal 24 sett.e 1867 a tutto il 12 nov.e 1867," ASV, Carte Kanzler-Vannutelli, Fondo A33.

78. Report from Poccioni, October 24, 1867, "Riassunto sulle invasioni Garibaldinesche dal 24 sett.e 1867 a tutto il 12 nov.e 1867," ASV, Carte Kanzler-Vannutelli, Fondo A33; Mévius, *Histoire de l'invasion des États Pontificaux en 1867*, 254, 258.

79. Giuseppe Locatelli, *Monterotondo e Mentana: Ricordi d'un Garibaldino della colonna Mosta e Stallo* (Bergamo: Tipografia Fagnani e Galeazzi, 1895), 22–23.

80. Di Nolli, *Mentana*, 100; Mévius, *Histoire de l'invasion des États Pontificaux en 1867*, 264–265; Eugenio Barbarich, ed., *Ricordi sui combattimenti di Monterotondo e di Mentana, ottobre–novembre 1867* (Rome: Tipografia del Comando del Corpo di Stato Maggiore, 1911), 8.

81. Cicconetti, *Roma o morte*, 113. In the afternoon Garibaldi circulated orders to his commanders indicating that in the event of a retreat, the columns should rejoin at Monticelli.

82. Eugenio Valzania, "Relazione della colonna Valzania," in *Ricordi sui combattimenti di Monterotondo e di Mentana, ottobre–novembre 1867*, ed. Eugenio Barbarich (Rome: Tipografia del Comando del Corp di Stato Maggiore, 1911), 22. Valzania commanded the Red Shirt assaults against the Porta Romana.

83. In Rome, the Ministry of Arms knew that the Garibaldians were concentrating around Monterotondo, but it lacked information about the course of events. At 1:30 A.M. on October 26, Kanzler sent a company of the Legione Romana north from Rome to reconnoiter. By 9:00 it was within a few kilometers of Monterotondo but was roughly

handled in an encounter with a Red Shirt force south of the town and turned back, leaving several prisoners in the hands of the Garibaldians. A much stronger papal column (approximately 1,200 infantry, cavalry, and artillery under Colonel Allet of the Zouaves) marched north from Rome around noon on October 26 and recaptured the Monterotondo train station (where, Garibaldians later claimed, Zouaves ruthlessly bayoneted four already wounded Red Shirts), but late that night Kanzler recalled this column in order to concentrate his troops in Rome. Cicconetti, *Roma o morte*, 116–117.

84. Di Nolli, *Mentana*, 100–101; Raggi, *La nona crociata*, 70; Guenel, *La dernière guerre du pape*, 104; Cicconetti, *Roma o morte*, 117–118. For Red Shirt casualties, see Locatelli, *Monterotondo e Mentana*, 28. Locatelli, a Garibaldian, was present at the battle. For pontifical losses, see Dalla Torre, *L'anno di Mentana*, 283–284.

85. For conflicting claims concerning Red Shirt casualties at Monterotondo, see Locatelli, *Monterotondo e Mentana*, 28; and Cicconetti, *Roma o morte*, 117–118. Cicconetti, one of the most trustworthy students of the battle, believes that Red Shirt losses were closer to Kanzler's estimate.

86. Dalla Torre, *L'anno di Mentana*, 133.

87. Ibid.

88. Azzanesi to Minister, October 24, 1867, "Riassunto sulle invasioni Garibaldinesche dal 24 sett.e 1867 a tutto il 12 nov.e 1867," ASV, Carte Kanzler-Vannutelli, Fondo A33; ibid., Freddi to Minister, October 24, 1867; ibid., Levengiani to Minister, October 24, 1867.

89. Dalla Torre, *L'anno di Mentana*, 134–136; Bonetti, *Da Bagnorea a Mentana*, 61–62.

90. Dalla Torre, *L'anno di Mentana*, 166.

91. From de Charette, October 27, 1867, "Riassunto sulle invasioni Garibaldinesche dal 24 sett.e 1867 a tutto il 12 nov.e 1867," ASV, Carte Kanzler-Vannutelli, Fondo A33; ibid., Minister to Charette, October 27, 1867; ibid., from de Charette, October 27, 1867.

92. Minister to Azzanesi and De Courten, October 27, 1867, "Riassunto sulle invasioni Garibaldinesche dal 24 sett.e 1867 a tutto il 12 nov.e 1867," ASV, Carte Kanzler-Vannutelli, Fondo A33.

93. From Azzanesi, October 27, 1867, "Riassunto sulle invasioni Garibaldinesche dal 24 sett.e 1867 a tutto il 12 nov.e 1867," ASV, Carte Kanzler-Vannutelli, Fondo A33; ibid., from Papi, October 27, 1867.

94. Writing without access to pontifical military records, Giuseppe Branzoli argued that from the start of the campaign, Kanzler had planned an eventual concentration of forces at Rome and Civitavecchia as a preliminary to a joint Franco-papal offensive, and that the troop movements of October 27 were part of a larger plan. Giuseppe Branzoli, "La Spedizione Garibaldina del 1867 control lo Stato Pontificio," *Rivista Militare* 23, no. 10 (1967): 1124. Papal records clearly indicate that the movements of October 27 were not part of a grand plan but a reaction to the presumed invasion by Italian regulars.

95. Di Nolli, *Mentana*, 108. As early as October 24 papal intelligence sources were anticipating the appointment of Menabrea and reporting that the Italian army would block further movements of volunteers across the border. Minister to De Courten and Azzanesi, October 24, 1867, "Riassunto sulle invasioni Garibaldinesche dal 24 sett.e 1867 a tutto il 12 nov.e 1867," ASV, Carte Kanzler-Vannutelli, Fondo A33.

96. Hibbert, *Garibaldi*, 355.

97. Guenel, *La dernière guerre du pape*, 105; Cerbelaud-Salagnac, *Les Zouaves pontificaux*, 150–151.

98. Mazio to Minister, November 1, 1867, "Riassunto sulle invasioni Garibaldinesche dal 24 sett.e 1867 a tutto il 12 nov.e 1867," ASV, Carte Kanzler-Vannutelli, Fondo A33.

99. Di Nolli, *Mentana*, 108–109; Guenel, *La dernière guerre du pape*, 106.

100. Di Nolli, *Mentana*, 114–115.

101. On October 18, 1867, the noted historian and longtime resident of Rome, Ferdinand Gregorovius, a confirmed opponent of the temporal power and critic of the papal administration, reluctantly acknowledged in his diary, "The papal troops are fighting well; Kanzler has taught them discipline. Their attitude upsets the calculations of the Italians who had hoped for a rising." Gregorovius, *The Roman Journals of Ferdinand Gregorovius*, 294.

102. Di Nolli, *Mentana*, 115.

103. Ibid., 124. For units and personnel levels, di Nolli draws upon the final report of General Kanzler. Pieri, *Storia militare del Risorgimento*, 780, asserts that the papal-French force totaled nine thousand men, a gross exaggeration.

104. Mévius, *Histoire de l'invasion des États Pontificaux en 1867*, 330.

105. Branzoli, "La Spedizione Garibaldina del 1867 contro lo Stato Pontificio," 1127.

106. Estimates concerning the number of Garibaldians at Mentana vary from 4,000 to 14,000. For evidence that Kanzler's intelligence indicated that he might well face as many as 10,000 irregulars as he marched on Mentana, see Charette to Minister, October 26, 1867, "Riassunto sulle invasioni Garibaldinesche dal 24 sett.e 1867 a tutto il 12 nov.e 1867," ASV, Carte Kanzler-Vannutelli, Fondo A33. For Menotti's estimate, see Menotti Garibaldi, "Rapporto del Colonnello Menotti Garibaldi al Generale Giuseppe Garibaldi sulla giornata di Mentana," in Barbarich, ed., *Ricordi sui combattimenti di Monterotondo e di Mentana, ottobre–novembre 1867*, 25, 26. At one point in his report Menotti says 4,529 men were available, but at another point he refers to 4,752 fighters.

107. Di Nolli, *Mentana*, 116.

108. Mévius, *Histoire de l'invasion des États Pontificaux en 1867*, 332.

109. Bonetti, *Da Bagnorea a Mentana*, 127.

110. Di Nolli, *Mentana*, 117–118.

111. Ibid.,118–119.

112. Mévius, *Histoire de l'invasion des États Pontificaux en 1867*, 342.

113. Paolo Dalla Torre, "Materiali per una storia dell'esercito pontificio," *Rassegna Storica del Risorgimento* (1941): 76.

114. Mévius, *Histoire de l'invasion des États Pontificaux en 1867*, 346–347.

115. Major de Troussures had marched his small column toward the sound of guns. By 3:30 P.M. he was immediately northwest of Mentana, where his Zouaves threatened Garibaldi's line of retreat toward Monterotondo. He later moved forward to support the French column that attacked Mentana from that direction.

116. Vannutelli, *Il Generale Kanzler*, 78.

117. Mévius, *Histoire de l'invasion des États Pontificaux en 1867*, 355.

118. The words of Chappedelaine and Moeller are recorded in Dalla Torre, *L'anno di Mentana*, 317–318.

119. Di Nolli, *Mentana*,138.

120. Ibid.

121. Duggan, *The Force of Destiny: A History of Italy since 1796*, 256.

122. Pieri, *Storia militare dell Risorgimento*, 774ff.

123. Barbarich, ed., *Ricordi sui combattimenti di Monterotondo e di Mentana, ottobre–novembre 1867*, 6.

124. Alessandro Mancini Barbieri, "Nuove ricerche sulla presenza straniera nell'esercito pontificio, 1850–1870," *Rassegna storica del Risorgimento* 73 (1986): 186.

125. Smith, *Italy and Its Monarchy*, 41.

126. Hibbert, *Garibaldi*, 355.

127. Coppa, *Cardinal Giacomo Antonelli*, 147; Falconi, *Il Cardinale Antonelli*, 428.

128. Branzoli, "La Spedizione Garibaldina del 1867 contro lo Stato Pontificio," 1131.

Chapter 5. The Last Stand of the Papal Army

1. Attilio Vigevano. *La fine dell'esercito pontificio* (Rome: Stabilimento Poligrafico per l'amministrazione della guerra, 1920), 448.

2. Jean Guenel, *La dernière guerre du pape: Les zouaves pontificaux au secours du Saint-Siège, 1860–1870* (Rennes: Presses Universitaires de Rennes, 1998), 116–117; Massimo Brandani, Piero Crociani, and Massimo Fiorentino, *L'esercito pontificio da Castelfidardo a Porta Pia, 1860–1870: Uniformi, equipaggiamento, armamento* (Milan: Intergest, 1976), 34–35.

3. Guenel, *La dernière guerre du pape*, 120; Vincenz Oertle, *Vom Remington zum Sturmgewehr 90: Die Schußwaffen der Päpstlichen Schweizergarde: Geschichte und Bestandesaufnahme* (Zurich: Thesis, 2001), 17.

4. Vigevano, *La fine dell'esercito pontificio*, 39–40.

5. David de Mévius, *Histoire de l'invasion des États Pontificaux* (Paris: Victor Palmé, 1875), 52.

6. Vigevano, *La fine dell'esercito pontificio*, 128; Joseph Powell, *Two Years in the Pontifical Zouaves* (London: R. Washbourne, 1871), 76, 86, 105.

7. The Claxton gun, named for its American designer, F. S. Claxton, dated from the U.S. Civil War. The British preferred the Gatling gun, and the French relied on the De Reffye Mitrailleuse. E-mails on February 8 and 9, 2009, from Roger Cook, president of the Ordnance Society and an authority on nineteenth-century heavy weapons.

8. Vigevano, *La fine dell'esercito pontificio*, 43–47, 101; Brandani et al., *L'esercito pontificio da Castelfidardo a Porta Pia*, 22; Carlo Bartolini, *Il brigantaggio nello Stato Pontificio: Cenno storico-aneddotico dal 1860–1870* (Rome: Arnaldo Forni Editore, 1897), 93–94; Antonmaria Bonetti, *Il volontario di Pio IX* (Lucca: Tipografia Arciv. San Paolino, 1890), 101.

9. The order of battle of the pontifical army is detailed in Vigevano, *La fine dell'esercito pontificio*, 51–68.

10. Ibid., 124.

11. Ibid., 127–128.

12. Piero Raggi, *La nona crociata: I voluntari di Pio IX in difesa di Roma (1860–1870)* (Ravenna: Libreria Tonini, 2002), 88; Paolo Dalla Torre, "Materiali per una storia dell'esercito pontificio," *Rassegna storica del Risorgimento* (1941): 76; Powell, *Two Years in the Pontifical Zouaves*, 54, 103, 156, quotation on 54.

13. Guenel, *La dernière guerre du pape*, 66–67, 71; Powell, *Two Years in the Pontifical Zouaves*, 54.

14. Vigevano, *La fine dell'esercito pontificio*, 137.

15. Ibid., 140.

16. John Pollard, *Money and the Rise of the Modern Papacy: Financing the Vatican, 1850–1950* (Cambridge: Cambridge University Press, 2005), 39.

17. Noel Blakiston, ed., *The Roman Question: Extracts from the Despatches of Odo Russell from Rome, 1858–1870* (Wilmington, DE: Michael Glazier, 1980), 292.

18. Giacomo Martina, S.J., *Pio IX (1867–1878)* (Rome: Editrice Pontificia Università Gregoriana, 1990), 234–235.

19. Frank J. Coppa, *Cardinal Giacomo Antonelli and Papal Politics in European Affairs* (Albany: State University of New York Press, 1990), 155–156.

20. Frank J. Coppa, *The Origins of the Italian Wars of Independence* (London: Longman, 1992), 139.

21. Ibid., 138; Christopher Duggan, *The Force of Destiny: A History of Italy since 1796* (Boston: Houghton Mifflin, 2007), 255–256.

22. Martina, *Pio IX*, 234.

23. Vigevano, *La fine dell'esercito pontificio*, 185. At one point, papal intelligence even acquired the secret passwords and recognition signals used by General Cadorna's army.

24. Ibid., 181–182, 185. For a survey of papal intelligence capabilities in the period, see David Alvarez, *Spies in the Vatican: Espionage and Intrigue from Napoleon to the Holocaust* (Lawrence: University Press of Kansas, 2002), chap. 1.

25. De Charette to Kanzler, August 11, 1870, Vatican City, Archivio Segreto Vaticano (ASV), Carte Kanzler-Vannutelli, Fondo B, busta 17.

26. Antonio Di Pierro, *L'ultimo giorno del papa re: 20 settembre 1870, la breccia di Porta Pia* (Milan: Mondadori, 2007), 29.

27. Vigevano, *La fine dell'esercito pontificio*, 197–198. For reports of Italian troop concentrations, see Serra to Kanzler, August 16, 1870, ASV, Carte Kanzler-Vannutelli, Fondo A40.

28. De Charette to Kanzler, August 18, 1870, ASV, Carte Kanzler-Vannutelli, Fondo B, busta 17; Rivalta to De Courten, August 19, 1870, ASV, Carte Kanzler-Vannutelli, Fondo B, busta 17.

29. Kanzler to Serra, August 18, 1870, ASV, Carte Kanzler-Vannutelli, fascicolo A40; Kanzler to de Charette, August 19, 1870, ASV, Carte Kanzler-Vannutelli, fascicolo A40.

30. Martina, *Pio IX*, 236.

31. Kanzler to de Charette, August 20, 1870, ASV, Carte Kanzler-Vannutelli, Fondo B, busta 17.

32. Rivalta to Zappi, De Courten, and Evangelisti, August 21, 1870, ASV, Carte Kanzler-Vannutelli, Fondo B, busta 17.

33. Vigevano, *La fine dell'esercito pontificio*, 204–206.

34. Memo by Rivalta, August 29, 1870, ASV, Carte Kanzler-Vannutelli, Fondo B, busta 17.

35. Roger Beauffort, *Histoire de l'invasion des États Pontificaux et du siège de Rome par l'armée italienne en septembre 1870* (Paris: Victor Palme, 1874), 192–194.

36. Vigevano, *La fine dell'esercito pontificio*, 221–223; Entries 19 and 30, Septem-

ber 10, 1870, "Giornale del Capo di Stato Maggiore Pontificio, September 1870," ASV, Carte Kanzler-Vannutelli, Fondo B, busta 17.

37. Di Pierro, *L'ultimo giorno del papa re*, 33.

38. Vigevano, *La fine dell'esercito pontificio*, 218.

39. Coppa, *Cardinal Giacomo Antonelli and Papal Politics in European Affairs*, 157–159, quotation on 158.

40. Vigevano, *La fine dell'esercito pontificio*, 242; Hermann Kanzler, "Appunti sull'usurpazione di Roma nel 1870," 2, ASV, Carte Kanzler-Vannutelli, Fondo A1.

41. Vigevano, *La fine dell'esercito pontificio*, 243.

42. Ibid., 244.

43. Kanzler, "Appunti sull'usurpazione di Roma nel 1870."

44. Vigevano, *La fine dell'esercito pontificio*, 250–251; Raffaele Cadorna, *La liberazione di Roma nell'anno 1870 ed il plebiscite* (Turin: L. Roux Editori, 1889), 462.

45. Di Pierro, *L'ultimo giorno del papa re*, 34; Vigevano, *La fine dell'esercito pontificio*, 255–256; Cadorna, *La liberazione di Roma*, 462.

46. Cadorna, *La liberazione di Roma*, 463.

47. Ugo Pesci, *Come siamo entrati in Roma* (Milan: Palazzi Editore, 1970), 44–46. Pesci was a journalist who accompanied the 12th Division throughout the campaign.

48. Entry 35, September 11, 1870, "Giornale del Capo di Stato Maggiore Pontificio, Settembre 1870," ASV, Carte Kanzler-Vannutelli, Fondo B, busta 17; Beauffort, *Histoire de l'invasion des États Pontificaux*, 174–175.

49. Beauffort, *Histoire de l'invasion des Etats Pontificaux*, 178; Vigevano, *La fine dell'esercito pontificio*, 266–267.

50. Vigevano, *La fine dell'esercito pontificio*, 267.

51. Di Pierro, *L'ultimo giorno del papa re*, 34, maintains that the retreat of papal units from the frontiers reflected Kanzler's acquiescence in the pope's directive of September 10, 1870, to avoid bloodshed by withdrawing all troops to Rome. In fact, even before his meeting with Pius on September 10, Kanzler had issued orders to field commanders to withdraw in the event of an invasion. See, for example, the note by Colonel Evangelisti, August 18, 1870, ASV, Carte Kanzler-Vanutelli, Fondo B, busta 17.

52. Beauffort, *Histoire de l'invasion des États Pontificaux*, 172 (footnote 1); C. E. Rouleau, *La Papauté et les Zouaves Pontificaux: Quelques pages d'histoire* (Quebec: Le Soleil, 1905), 141–143.

53. Pesci, *Come siamo entrati in Roma*, 63–64.

54. Cadorna, *La liberazione di Roma*, 142; Coulombe, *The Pope's Legion: The Multinational Fighting Force That Defended the Vatican* (New York: Palgrave Macmillan, 2009), 159–160; Di Pierro, *L'ultimo giorno del papa re*, 19.

55. Carlo Falconi, *Il Cardinale Antonelli: Vita e carriera del Richelieu italiano nella chiesa di Pio IX* (Milan: Arnoldo Mondadori Editore, 1983), 459–460.

56. Ibid., 459.

57. Serra to Kanzler, September 19, 1870, ASV, Carte Kanzler-Vannutelli, fascicolo A40.

58. Major d'Albiousse to minister of arms, September 15, 1870, ASV, Carte Kanzler-Vannutelli, Fondo B, busta 17; Colonel Serra to minister of arms, September 15, 1870, ASV, Carte Kanzler-Vannutelli, Fondo B, busta 17.

59. Vigevano, *La fine dell'esercito pontificio*, 339.

60. The deliberations of the defense committee are yet another indication that Colonel Serra had received no surrender orders from Rome.

61. Vigevano, *La fine dell'esercito pontificio*, 341–343. Colonel Serra was unable to consult Kanzler because telegraphic communications seem to have been cut. The last communication between Rome and Civitavecchia was at 9:00 A.M. on September 15. The reason for the break in telegraphic communications remains unclear. Having surrounded Civitavecchia, Bixio's army may have cut the lines, but the Italian army's official history of the campaign states that nowhere did the Italian army interfere with pontifical telegraph lines. It is unlikely that Kanzler ordered the lines broken. Although on September 17, two days after the fall of Civitavecchia, he ordered all telegraphic communication between Rome and the provinces to be broken, there is no record of a similar directive on September 15. Ibid., 406.

62. G. Ruffoni, *XXV anniversario della Breccia di Porta Pia: Cenni storico-militari sulle operazioni per la liberazione di Roma* (Verona: Vicentini e Ferrari, 1895), 25–26.

63. General Raffaele Cadorna to General Hermann Kanzler, September 16, 1870, ASV, Carte Kanzler-Vannutelli, fascicolo A41, cartella 7.3; General Hermann Kanzler to General Raffaele Cadorna, September 16, 1870, ASV, Carte Kanzler-Vannutelli, fascicolo A41, cartella 7.3.

64. Cadorna, *La liberazione di Roma*, 158–160; Beauffort, *Histoire de l'invasion des États Pontificaux*, 236.

65. Cardinal Antonelli seems to have been practically immobilized by the approach of the Italians. He failed to take even the most elementary precautions to prepare the Vatican for the imminent loss of Rome. For example, he made no provision to secure all the records of the papal government, many of which subsequently fell into the hands of the Italian government. Martina, *Pio IX*, 237.

66. Bonetti, *Il volontario di Pio IX*, 133.

67. Di Pierro, *L'ultimo giorno del papa re*, 35.

68. Memorandum by Colonel Evangelisti, September 13, 1870, ASV, Carte Kanzler-Vannutelli, fascicolo A40.

69. Entry 60, September 14, 1870, "Giornale del Capo di Stato Maggiore Pontificio, Settembre 1870," ASV, Carte Kanzler-Vannutelli, Fondo B, busta 17; Vigevano, *La fine dell'esercito pontificio*, 485. The numbers for the defenders do not include 1,278 gendarmes (assigned to internal security duties) or the more than 1,000 service, support, and auxiliary troops.

70. Entries 46 and 49, September 13, 1870, "Giornale del Capo di Stato Maggiore Pontificio, Settembre 1870," ASV, Carte Kanzler-Vannutelli, Fondo B, busta 17; Vigevano, *La fine dell'esercito pontificio*, 457; Beauffort, *Histoire de l'invasion des États Pontificaux*, 227.

71. Cadorna, *La liberazione di Roma*, 171. On September 17, as General Cadorna was personally supervising the river crossing, he received a visit from Count Harry von Arnim, the Prussian ambassador to the Papal States. Count von Arnim had driven out from Rome to ask the Italian commander to delay his attack on the city for twenty-four hours in order to give the ambassador time to convince Pope Pius to abandon any thought of resistance. Understanding that his government continued to hope for a peaceful resolution of the crisis and knowing that it would take at least twenty-four hours to position his forces around the city, Cadorna granted the request. The next day the general received a note from von Arnim stating that his efforts had not been successful. Ibid.

72. Vigevano, *La fine dell'esercito pontificio*, 501; Di Pierro, *L'ultimo giorno del papa re*, 46.

73. Vigevano, *La fine dell'esercito pontificio*, 503–507.

74. Ibid., 480–481.

75. Kanzler, "Appunti sull'usurpazione di Roma nel 1870," 5; Falconi, *Il Cardinale Antonelli*, 460; Martina, *Pio IX*, 242.

76. Di Pierro, *L'ultimo giorno del papa re*, 40.

77. Ibid., 41.

78. Vigevano, *La fine dell'esercito pontificio*, 497–499.

79. Pesci, *Come siamo entrati in Roma*, 109.

80. Di Pierro, *L'ultimo giorno del papa re*, 27.

81. Vigevano, *La fine dell'esercito pontificio*, 520.

82. Quoted in Di Pierro, *L'ultimo giorno del papa re*, 85.

83. Vigevano, *La fine dell'esercito pontificio*, 523–526, 528.

84. Di Pierro, *L'ultimo giorno del papa re*, 94–95.

85. Ibid., 87.

86. Vigevano, *La fine dell'esercito pontificio*, 540–541.

87. Entry 116, September 20, 1870, "Gironale del Capo di Stato Maggiore Pontificio, 20 September 1870," ASV, Carte Kanzler-Vannutelli, Fondo B, busta 17.

88. Vigevano, *La fine dell'esercito pontificio*, 534.

89. Ibid.

90. Ibid., 543.

91. Di Pierro, *L'ultimo giorno del papa re*, 100.

92. Ibid., 105.

93. Paul M. Krieg and Reto Stampfli, *Die Schweizergarde in Rom* (Zurich: Orell Füssli Verlag AG, 2006), 236.

94. Ulrich Nersinger, *Soldaten des Papstes: Eine kleine Geschichte der päpstlichen Garden* (Ruppichteroth: Canisius-Werk, 1999), 45–46; "Entrata delle truppe italiane il 20 Settembre 1870," Vatican City, Archivio della Guardia Svizzera Pontificia, Funktionenbuch A, 1860–1879.

95. Beauffort, *Histoire de l'invasion des États Pontificaux*, 288, 291.

96. Vigevano, *La fine dell'esercito pontificio*, 526, 555–556; Entries 112 and 114, September 20, 1870, "Giornale del Capo di Stato Maggiore Pontificio, Settembre 1870," ASV, Carte Kanzler-Vannutelli, Fondo B, busta 17.

97. Di Pierro, *L'ultimo giorno del papa re*, 128–129.

98. Vigevano, *La fine dell'esercito pontificio*, 560–561; Bonetti, *Il volontario di Pio IX*, 151–152.

99. Vigevano, *La fine dell'esercito pontificio*, 542.

100. Di Pierro, *L'ultimo giorno del papa re*, 127.

101. Ibid.; Vigevano, *La fine dell'esercito pontificio*, 563.

102. Vigevano, *La fine dell'esercito pontificio*, 564.

103. Ibid., 565.

104. Beauffort, *Histoire de l'invasion des États Pontificaux*, 300.

105. Vigevano, *La fine dell'esercito pontificio*, 570.

106. Ibid., 571.

107. Ibid., 572–575.

108. Ibid., 583–584.

109. Di Pierro, *L'ultimo giorno del papa re*, 134.

110. Vigevano, *La fine dell'esercito pontificio*, 593–595.

111. Di Pierro, *L'ultimo giorno del papa re*, 137.

112. Ibid., 137–138; "Nota dei morti e feriti nell'attaco di Roma del 20 Settembre 1870," ASV, Carte Kanzler-Vannutelli, Fondo B, busta 17.

113. Cadorna, *La Liberazione di Roma*, 200–201.

114. Kanzler, "Appunti sull'usurpazione di Roma nel 1870," 6.

115. Cadorna, *La Liberazione di Roma*, 201–202.

116. Vigevano, *La fine dell'esercito pontificio*, 635–636.

117. Ibid., 692.

118. Whether from shame or some other emotional or physical distress, General Kanzler declined to lead his troops on their last march. His absence made a poor impression on his soldiers.

119. A recent military history of Italy, for example, treats the entire battle for Rome in four sentences suggesting that the event encompassed four simple actions: The Italian army appeared before Rome; the Italian army blew a hole in the wall next to the Porta Pia; the pontifical army promptly surrendered at the order of Pius IX; and the Italian army marched into Rome. Ciro Paoletti, *A Military History of Italy* (Westport, Conn.: Praeger, 2008), 119.

Chapter 6. An Army without a State

1. Frank J. Coppa, *The Modern Papacy since 1789* (New York: Addison Wesley Longman, 1998), 112–113; David Kertzer, *Prisoner of the Vatican: The Pope's Secret Plot to Capture Rome from the New Italian State* (Boston: Houghton Mifflin, 2004), 63–66.

2. Filippo Crispolti, *Politici, guerrieri, poeti: Ricordi personali* (Milan: Fratelli Treves Editori, 1938), 134–135. Hermann Kanzler died on January 6, 1888.

3. Piero Raggi, *La nona crociata: I volontari di Pio IX in difesa di Roma (1860–1870)* (Ravenna: Libreria Tonini, 2002), 111–112, 117–118.

4. Charles A. Coulombe, *The Pope's Legion: The Multinational Fighting Force That Defended the Vatican* (New York: Palgrave Macmillan, 2008), 177ff., 208–209; Jean Guenel, *La dernière guerre du pape: Les Zouaves pontificaux au secours du Saint-Siège, 1860–1870* (Rennes: Presses Universitaires de Rennes, 1998), 167.

5. On the persistence of the papal court as a symbol of sovereignty, see John Pollard, "A Court in Exile: The Vatican, 1870–1929," *Court Historian* 12, no. 1 (June 2007): 35–38.

6. Attilio Vigevano, *La fine dell'esercito pontificio* (Rome: Stabilimento Poligrafico per l'amministrazione della guerra, 1920), 666.

7. Ibid., 667.

8. Giuseppe Manfroni, *Sulla soglia del Vaticano, 1870–1901* (Milan: Longanesi, 1971), 116; Hermann Kanzler, "Appunti sull'usurpazione di Roma nel 1870," Vatican City, Archivio Segreto Vaticano (ASV), Carte Kanzler-Vannutelli, Fondo A1, 5–6. Readers familiar with Vatican City should be reminded that the current boundaries of the territory are a function of the Lateran Agreements of 1929 and that many of the buildings and roads of the present city were constructed after that date. In 1870 the "Vatican" was commonly understood to include only Saint Peter's Basilica and square, the Apostolic Palace, and the attached gardens.

9. Manfroni, *Sulla soglia del Vaticano*, 30, 43; Kertzer, *Prisoner of the Vatican*, 112–113.

10. Manfroni, *Sulla soglia del Vaticano*, 45; Kertzer, *Prisoner of the Vatican*, 113–114.

11. Manfroni, *Sulla soglia del Vaticano*, 127, 253–254.

12. Kertzer, *Prisoner of the Vatican*, 183–186.

13. Manfroni, *Sulla soglia del Vaticano*, 545–546.

14. Ibid., 546–547.

15. Niccolò Del Re, *Mondo Vaticano: Passato e presente* (Vatican City: Libreria Editrice Vaticana, 1995), 395, 455.

16. Ibid., 455.

17. For a glimpse of the gendarmeria's routine activities in the decades after 1870, see ASV, Palazzo Apostolico, Titolo 235, fascicolo 2, Rapporti vari.

18. David Alvarez, *Spies in the Vatican: Espionage and Intrigue from Napoleon to the Holocaust* (Lawrence: University Press of Kansas, 2002), 51–52.

19. Giuseppe Manfroni, August 22, 1886, "Prescrizioni di vigilanza nei pressi del Vaticano," ASV, Palazzo Apostolico, Titolo 235, fascicolo 1, Disposizioni generali.

20. Entry for March 15, 1911, "Diario del Colonello Jules Repond, 1910–1918," E.2.24, Vatican City, Archivio della Guardia Svizzera Pontificia (AGSP) (henceforth referred to as Repond Diary).

21. Manfroni, *Sulla soglia del Vaticano*, 613.

22. Ibid., 384–385; Kertzer, *Prisoner of the Vatican*, 134–135.

23. During the discussion concerning the terms of capitulation, General Kanzler had proposed an article specifically permitting the pope's household guards to continue their service. The final terms did not include this provision, but General Cadorna had verbally acknowledged the pope's right to retain his palace guards.

24. "Entrata delle truppe italiane il 20 Settembre 1870," AGSP, Funktionenbuch A, 1860–1879.

25. Giovanni Amadi, "The Pope at Home," *North American Review* 155, no. 429 (August 1892): 201.

26. The esente was personally responsible for the safety of the Holy Father. From a post in the Anticamera Segreta of the pontifical apartments, he commanded the detachments of Noble, Palatine, and Swiss Guards and Pontifical Gendarmeria on honor-guard duty in the apartments. He was also responsible for keeping a daily log of all visitors to the apartments. If the Holy Father left the apartments for any reason, the esente accompanied him. When the Noble Guard still performed mounted service, the esente rode alongside the right door of the papal carriage. Del Re, *Mondo Vaticano*, 464–465.

27. Vigevano, *La fine dell'esercito pontificio*, 663.

28. Gastone Imbrighi, *I corpi armati pontifici* (Vatican City: Poliglotta Vaticana, 1953), 19.

29. [N.a.], *Manuale per la Guardia Nobile Pontificia* (Rome: Officina Poligrafia Romana, 1901); "Cavallerizza ai prati di Belvedere al Vaticano fino alla soppressione del servizio a cavallo, 1863–1904," ASV, Fondi speciali: Guardia Nobile, Titolo XIV, parte 1a. In 1905 mounted guardsmen made their final appearance when a pair flanked the carriage of Pope Pius X as the pontiff dedicated the Grotto of Lourdes in the Vatican Gardens. Del Re, *Mondo Vaticano*, 465.

30. In 1883, for example, the total budget for the papal household and the administration of the Vatican Palace was 2,064,021 lire, including 492,167 lire for the four units of the pontifical armed forces: Noble Guard, Palatine Guard, Swiss Guard, and Pontifical Gendarmeria. In this budget 187,820 lire were reserved for the maintenance of the Noble Guard. John F. Pollard, *Money and the Rise of the Modern Papacy: Financing the Vatican, 1850–1950* (Cambridge: Cambridge University Press, 2005), 47.

31. [Comando della Guardia Palatina d'Onore di Sua Santità], *Fedeltà Palatina* (Rome: A Belardetti Editore, 1946), 12–13.

32. George Stillman Hillard, *Six Months in Italy* (Boston: Ticknor, Reed, and Fields, 1853), 1:229; James P. Cobbett, *Journal of a Tour in Italy* (London: Mills, Jowett, & Mills, 1830), 185.

33. The most recent history of the Swiss Guard is Christian-Roland Marcel Richard, *La Guardia Svizzera Pontificia nel corso dei secoli* (Milan: Leonardo International, 2005). For the role of Swiss mercenaries in European armies, see John McCormack, *One Million Mercenaries: Swiss Soldiers in the Armies of the World* (London: Leo Cooper, 1993). Each year new recruits are sworn into the Swiss Guard on May 6, the anniversary of the unit's greatest sacrifice.

34. Though early records and accounts contain few references to firearms, it is clear that almost from its inception the Swiss Guard possessed such weapons. After the death of Pope Leo X (1521), for example, the commandant of the guard informed the city council in Zurich that the guard had deployed cannons to protect the gates of the papal palace. A report from the end of the seventeenth century notes that muskets were part of the equipment of the guard detachment assigned to the papal summer villa at Castel Gandolfo. Letter from Christian Richard, March 30, 2009.

35. Paul Krieg and Renato Stampfli, *Die Schweizergarde in Rom* (Zurich: Orell Füssli Verlag, 2006), 173–175. The complaints of the pope's Swiss Guards were not unique. Financial malpractice was common in the Swiss mercenary regiments in service with the Dutch, French, Neapolitan, Sardinian, and Spanish armies. Commanders often skimmed money from payments owed their troops and profited from forcing soldiers to pay for necessities such as food and uniforms. McCormack, *One Million Mercenaries*, 142–143.

36. Antonio Serrano, *Die Schweizergarde der Päpste* (Dachau: Druckerei & Verlagsanstalt Bayerland, 1992), 91.

37. Krieg and Stampfli, *Die Schweizergarde in Rom*, 194. In 1823 the noncommissioned officers formally complained to the master of the Apostolic Palace that the commandant exhibited favoritism and did not respect seniority in making promotions. "Li sargenti e caporali della Guardia Svizzera" to Monsignor Maggiordomo Marazzani, 1823 [no day or month], ASV, Palazzo Apostolico, Titoli 202, "Disposizioni e gli affair diversi." In other European armies it was not uncommon for the colonel commanding a regiment to purchase uniforms with a sum provided by the government. In the British army this practice led to complaints that colonels purchased the cheapest possible uniforms and pocketed the leftover funds. Richard Holmes, *Redcoat: The British Soldier in the Age of Horse and Musket* (New York: W. W. Norton & Co., 2001), 109.

38. Quoted in Robert Royal, *The Pope's Army: 500 Years of the Papal Swiss Guard* (New York: Crossroad Publishing Co., 2006), 129.

39. Alois Jehle, *Il diritto proprio della Guardia Svizzera Pontificia nella capitolazione del 1825 e nei regolamenti, 1858–1959* (Rome: Pontificia Studiorum Universitas a S. Thoma, 2006), 16–18.

40. Royal, *The Pope's Army*, 131.

41. Krieg and Stampfli, *Die Schweizergarde in Rom*, 203.

42. Royal, *The Pope's Army*, 132–133.

43. Ibid.; Krieg and Stampfli, *Die Schweizergarde in Rom*, 203–204.

44. Krieg and Stampfli *Die Schweizergarde in Rom*, 204–205.

45. Ibid., 205.

46. Monsignor Maggiordomo Marazzani to Carlo Pfyffer D'Altishoffen [*sic*], May 7, 1828, ASV, Palazzo Apostolico, Titoli 202, "Disposizioni e gli affair diversi."

47. Krieg and Stampfli, *Die Schweizergarde in Rom*, 207.

48. Ibid., 211–212.

49. Alois Jehle, "La Guardia Svizzera Pontificia sotto i regolamenti del 1858 e del 1959," in *Hirtenstab und Hellebarde: Die Päpstliche Schwiezergarde in Rom, 1506–2006*, ed. Urban Fink, Hervé de Weck, and Christian Schweizer (Zurich: Theologischer Verlag, 2006), 395.

50. Peter Leo Johnson, *Stuffed Saddlebags: The Life of Martin Kundig, Priest, 1805–1879* (Milwaukee: Bruce Publishing Co., 1942), 25. Before entering the priesthood and a life as a missionary in the United States, Martin Kundig served briefly in the Swiss Guard in 1827–1828. His diary suggests that he received no training during his service in the guard.

51. Krieg and Stampfli, *Die Schweizergarde in Rom*, 210–211; Royal, *The Pope's Army*, 135–136.

52. Krieg and Stampfli, *Die Schweizergarde in Rom*, 215–216.

53. "Inviti a Congressi per discutere sulle Riforme della Capitolazione per la Guardia Svizzera," 1847, ASV, Palazzo Apostolico, Titoli 202, "Capitolazioni."

54. Francesco Leopoldo Meyer de Schauensee [*sic*] to Pope Pius IX, n.d., "Progetto di Riforma," ASV, Palazzo Apostolico, Titoli 202, "Capitolazioni."

55. Krieg and Stampfli, *Die Schweizergarde in Rom*, 226.

56. Ibid., 224, 226.

57. The investigations resulted in the dismissal of one halberdier and the suspension of another. Ibid., 221–222.

58. "Regolamento per la Guardia Svizzera Pontificia," June 17, 1858, ASV, Palazzo Apostolico, Titoli 202, "Capitolazioni."

59. Quoted in Richard, *La Guardia Svizzera Pontificia*, 88.

60. Ibid., 88; Krieg and Stampfli, *Die Schweizergarde in Rome*, 230.

61. Serrano, *Die Schweizergarde der Päpste*, 109. Despite the voluntary service of its commander, the Swiss Guard, as a unit, did not participate in the campaign against Garibaldi's irregulars. Throughout the military campaigns of the 1860s the guard never took the field, limiting its activities to the protection of the pontifical palaces.

62. Krieg and Stampfli, *Die Schweizergarde in Rom*, 238–239.

63. This account of the Swiss Guard mutiny of 1878 relies on two sources. The first is an eyewitness report by a guard officer. This report, titled "La Mutineri di 1878 reconti per li Lt. Colonello Kost," is inserted in Repond Diary, AGSP, E.2.24.1. The second is the memoirs of Italian police commissioner Giuseppe Manfroni, who

monitored the affair as it unfolded through his informants inside the Vatican. See Manfroni, *Sulla soglia del Vaticano*, 417–419.

64. Bishop of Basel to the cardinal secretary of state, March 12, 1878, ASV, Segreteria di Stato, Anno 1878, Rubrica 207, fascicolo unico.

65. Krieg and Stampfli, *Die Schweizergarde in Rom*, 243; Royal, *The Pope's Army*, 152.

66. Krieg and Stampfli, *Die Schweizergarde in Rom*, 245.

67. Ibid., 255.

68. Jules Repond, "Memoires du Colonel Repond, commandant de la garde suisse pontificale" (unpublished manuscript), 17, AGSP, E.2.24.22.

69. Colonel Jules Repond to Cardinal Merry del Val, March 16, 1911, ASV, Segreteria di Stato, Anno 1911, Rubrica 207, fascicolo 2; Colonel Jules Repond to Cardinal Merry del Val, March 9, 1912, ASV, Segreteria di Stato, Anno 1912, Rubrica 207, fascicolo 2.

70. Bishop of Coira to Commandant Meyer [*sic*], March 9, 1910, ASV, Segreteria di Stato, Anno 1910, Rubrica 207, fascicolo unico.

71. Dominic Pedrazzini, "Jules Repond: Le dernier condottiere," *Der Schweizergardist* 2 (2007): 16; Reto Stampfli, *Die Päpstliche Schweizergarde, 1870–1970* (Solothurn, Switzerland: Zweite Auglage, 2004), 118.

72. Entry for December 15, 1910, AGSP, Funktionenbuch B, 1901–1923.

73. Repond, "Memoires," 11.

74. Ibid., 11–12; Vincenz Oertle, *Vom Remington zum Sturmgewehr 90: Die Schußwaffen der Päpstlichen Schweizergarde: Geschichte und Bestandesaufnahme* (Zurich: Thesis, 2001), 18.

75. Repond, "Memoires," 14–15, 17–18.

76. Ibid., 18.

77. Royal, *The Pope's Army*, 155; Pollard, "A Court in Exile," 40.

78. The story that the German monarch, Kaiser Wilhelm II, donated the Mausers to the Swiss Guard is without foundation. The records of the guard clearly indicate that Repond ordered the rifles from the manufacturer and that the Vatican paid for the weapons.

79. Repond, "Memoires," 70–78. For details on Repond's rearmament of the Swiss Guard, see Oertle, *Von Remington zum Sturmgewehr*, 21–22.

80. Repond, "Memoires," 78–83; Agostino Schmidt to Cardinal Merry del Val, n.d., ASV, Segreteria di Stato, Anno 1913, Rubrica 207B, fascicolo uno; Jehle, "La Guardia Svizzera Pontificia sotto i regolamenti del 1858 e del 1959," 404.

81. In 1830 a visitor to the Vatican described a Swiss Guard uniform that no modern tourist would recognize: "They have coats and big breeches of yellow and red cloth, alternate stripes of each colour sewed together; a black beaver hat of simple shape, with one side of the rim turned up, and a short black feather; red stockings, and shoes." Cobbett, *Journal of a Tour in Italy*, 185.

82. Richard, *La Guardia Svizzera Pontificia nel corso dei secoli*, 219–221.

83. [George von Sury d'Aspremont], "Meuterei v. 13 July," AGSP. This document, a brief account of the mutiny by an officer eyewitness, is included in the file that contains Repond's "Memoires." The author is not identified, but it is almost certainly George von Sury d'Aspremont, who was a captain at the time of the mutiny.

84. "Dal Quartiere degli Svizzeri," July 21, 1913, ASV, Segreteria di Stato, Anno 1913, Rubrica 207B, fascicolo unico.

85. Colonel Jules Repond to Cardinal Merry del Val, [n.d.], ASV, Segreteria di Stato, Anno 1913, Rubrica 207B, fascicolo unico.

86. Richard, *La Guardia Svizzera Pontificia nel corso dei secoli*, 112.

87. Ibid.; Royal, *The Pope's Army*, 157.

88. Repond, "Memoires," 84–85.

89. Johann Holenstein, "Erinnerungen," *Der Exgardist* [no number] (February 1969): 6. Holenstein joined the guard in August 1913.

90. Entry for July 25, 1913, Repond Diary.

91. Krieg and Stampfli, *Die Schweizergarde in Rom*, 260; Richard, *La Guardia Svizzera Pontificia*, 113.

92. Krieg and Stampfli, *Die Schweizergarde in Rom*, 260–261.

93. Entry for March 15, 1911, Repond Diary; Vincenz Oertle, *Vom Remington zum Sturmgewehr*, 21. The archival files of the Swiss Guard and the pontifical gendarmeria are full of more or less acrimonious exchanges complaining of infringements of responsibilities, denial of prerogatives, or confrontational (and sometimes violent) encounters between halberdiers and gendarmes. See, for example, Roberto Mengucci to Maresciallo di servizio dei Gendarmeria Pontifici, March 5, 1916, Vatican City. Archivio della Gendarmeria Pontificia (AGP), Faldone 1916.

94. "Reconnaissance de l'appartement du pape le 21 septembre 1915," Repond Diary.

95. Entry for December 1, 1912, Repond Diary. The commandant was not overreacting. Italian authorities were also worried about the march turning ugly. These authorities reinforced the police presence in the Borgo, stationed Italian soldiers along the colonnades of Saint Peter's Square, and deployed a cavalry squadron just outside the square.

96. Undated entry [1912], Repond Diary. Not all these men were standing alert and armed at their posts at the same time. Each post would be manned by several men who alternated the guard every couple of hours. At any given post at any given time, only one or two men were actually on guard while the others were resting but on site and available.

97. "Service reduit des le 2 aout 1914," Repond Diary; Prince Camillo Rospigliosi to the cardinal secretary of state, August 7, 1914, ASV, Segreteria di Stato, Anno 1914, Rubrica 206, fascicolo unico.

98. Entry for July 13, 1915, Repond Diary; Niccolò Del Re, *La Guardia Palatina d'Onore: Una istituzione piana scomparsa* (Rome: n.p., 1997), 28; Giulio Patrizi di Ripacandida, *Quell'ultimo glorioso stendardo: Le Guardie Nobili Pontificie dall'11 maggio 1801 al 15 settembre 1970* (Vatican City: n.p., 1994), 69.

99. John Pollard, *The Unknown Pope: Benedict XV (1914–1922) and the Pursuit of Peace* (London: Geoffrey Chapman, 1999), 97–98; David Alvarez, "A German Agent at the Vatican: The Gerlach Affair," *Intelligence and National Security* 11, no. 2 (April 1996): 345–356.

100. Pollard, *The Unknown Pope*, 91.

101. "1915: Il Vaticano e il pericolo aereo," *Gnosis: Rivista Italiana di Intelligence*, no. 2 (2007), http://gnosis.aisi.gov.it/Gnosis/Rivista11.nsf/ServNavig/21.

102. Entry for March 2, 1916, Repond Diary; Report by Salvatore Ciprotti, February 28, 1916, AGP, Faldone 1916.

103. Richard, *La Guardia Svizzera Pontificia nel corso dei secoli*, 227. In another version of the story, Pius speaks with Captain Ruppen, not Colonel Repond. It should be noted that at the end of the nineteenth century, while Leo XIII was still pope, the cannons still stored in the old armory in the Belvedere wing of the palace were sold for scrap, and the Vatican was left with no heavy weapons. There would have been no cannons to defend the Vatican of Pius X. Antonio Martini, "Corpi militari nello Stato Pontificio e nella Città del Vaticano," in *1929–2009: Ottanta anni dello Stato della Città del Vaticano*, ed. Barbara Jatta (Vatican City: Biblioteca Apostolica Vaticana, 2009), 199.

104. Stampfli, *Die Päpstliche Schweizergarde, 1870–1970*, 120.

105. Krieg and Stampfli, *Die Schweizergarde in Rom*, 263.

Chapter 7. Armed Neutrality

1. This account of the bombing of Vatican City is drawn from Alexander Good, "Erinnerungen: Wacht ins Gwehr! [*sic*] Persönliche Gardeerinnerungen aus der Zeit zwischen 1943–1946," *Der Exgardist* 52 (February 1992): 94–97. Halberdier Good was on duty that evening at the Bronze Doors. Under various titles his memoirs appeared serially between 1973 and 1994 in *Der Exgardist*, the magazine of the association of Swiss Guard veterans. His account of the recruit experience appeared over several issues in 1979–1983.

2. Quoted in Peter Kent, *The Pope and the Duce: The International Impact of the Lateran Agreements* (New York: St. Martin's, 1981), 5.

3. Frank Coppa, "Mussolini and the Concordat of 1929," in *Controversial Concordats: The Vatican's Relations with Napoleon, Mussolini, and Hitler*, ed. Frank Coppa (Washington, DC: Catholic University of America Press, 1999), 94–99.

4. Harold Deutsch, *The Conspiracy against Hitler in the Twilight War* (Minneapolis: University of Minnesota Press, 1968), chap. 4.

5. Owen Chadwick, *Britain and the Vatican during the Second World War* (Cambridge: Cambridge University Press, 1986), 107–108, quotation on 107.

6. Ibid., 109, 112, quotation on 109.

7. Ibid., 114. It is extremely unlikely that the attack on the papal limousine was spontaneous. The Italian police would have been informed ahead of time of the pope's travel plans. How likely is it that the papal vehicle would have just happened to be stopped in traffic at precisely the point where a crowd of young Fascists was gathered?

8. Anton Gahlinger, *Der Schweizergardist im Vatikan* (Saint Gallen: Ostschweiz AG, 1949), 16.

9. Reto Stampfli, "Die Geburtsstunde des Vatikanstaats," *Der Schweizergardist* 2 (2009): 30–31.

10. John F. Pollard, *Money and the Rise of the Modern Papacy: Financing the Vatican, 1850–1950* (Cambridge: Cambridge University Press, 2005), 150–151.

11. Commander of the Pontifical Gendarmeria to the Cardinal Secretary of State, February 27, 1929, Vatican City, Archivio Segreto Vaticano (ASV), Segreteria di

Stato, Gendarmi, Anno 1929, Rubrica 274, fascicolo 1; "Regolamento Organico e di Disciplina per il Corpo della Gendarmeria Pontificia," May 8, 1933, ASV, Segreteria di Stato, Busta Separata, 204, Corpi Armati Pontifici: Gendarmeria.

12. Paul Krieg and Reto Stampfli, *Die Schweizergarde in Rom* (Zurich: Orell Füssli Verlag, 2006), 264.

13. Ibid.

14. Reto Stampfli, *Die Päpstliche Schweizergarde, 1870–1970* (Solothurn, Switzerland: Zweite Auglage, 2004), 117.

15. Krieg and Stampfli, *Die Schweizergarde in Rom*, 267.

16. During World War II, Hirschbühl returned to military life, commanding the 12th Mountain Brigade of the Swiss army.

17. Krieg and Stampfli, *Die Schweizergarde in Rom*, 280.

18. [N.a.], *Exerzier-Reglement für die Päpstliche-Schweizergarde* (Vatican City: Tipografia Vaticana, 1927), 7–9, quotation on 7.

19. Alexander Good, "Wacht ins Gwehr! [*sic*] Erinnerungen eines päpstlichen Schweizergardisten," Folge 5, *Der Exgardist* 26 (February 1979): 7.

20. "Disposizione di servizio, No. 28," August 30, 1939, Vatican City, Archivio della Gendarmeria Pontificia (AGP), Faldone: Disposizioni di servizio dal 1939 al 1944.

21. Alexander Good, "Erinnerungen: Wacht ins Gwehr! [*sic*] Persönliche Garde-erinnerungen aus der Zeit zwischen 1943–1946," Folge 2, *Der Exgardist* 53 (September 1992): 38; Krieg and Stampfli, *Die Schweizergarde in Rom*, 285.

22. Dario Delcurato, *Storia della Guardia Svizzera Pontificia e dei corpi militari pontifici disciolti nel 1970* (Varese: Macchione Editore, 2006), 87.

23. "Disposizioni di servizio di carattere permanente," December 19, 1940, AGP, Faldone: Disposizioni di servizio dal 1939 al 1944; ibid., "Disposizione di servizio" [no number], July 12, 1941. For an example of an access control list, see Ufficio controllo del Portone di Bronzo, "Registro delle persone pericolose-indesiderate-sospette," October 18, 1937, AGP.

24. "Servizio di polizia e d'ispezione mediante orologi controllo," June 6, 1940, AGP, Faldone: Disposizioni di servizio dal 1939 al 1944.

25. Chadwick, *Britain and the Vatican*, 130.

26. "Disposizione di servizio, No. 21," June 24, 1939, AGP, Faldone: Disposizioni di servizio dal 1939 al 1944; ibid., "Disposizioni di servizio di carattere permanente," December 19, 1940.

27. The myth of the Vatican as information center and the pope as the best-informed leader in the world is addressed in David Alvarez, *Spies in the Vatican: Espionage and Intrigue from Napoleon to the Holocaust* (Lawrence: University Press of Kansas, 2002).

28. Carlo Fiorentino, *All'ombra di Pietro: La Chiesa Cattolica e lo spionaggio fascista in Vaticano, 1929–1939* (Florence: Casa Editrice Le Lettere, 1999), introduction; Alvarez, *Spies in the Vatican*, 160–161.

29. Owen Chadwick asserts that Colonel De Mandato was not a Fascist, but after an examination of Italian police files, Carlo Fiorentino, the leading student of Fascist espionage against the Vatican, concludes that the Vatican police commander was "a sincere admirer of Mussolini." Chadwick, *Britain and the Vatican*, 169; Fiorentino, *All'ombra di Pietro*, 34n93.

30. Chadwick, *Britain and the Vatican*, 169; Fiorentino, *All'ombra di Pietro*, 34.

31. Chadwick, *Britain and the Vatican*, 169.

32. Ibid., 115–116. Article 12 of the treaty that was part of the Lateran Agreements stipulated, "The Envoys of foreign governments to the Holy See will continue to enjoy throughout the kingdom all the privileges and immunities that are due to international Agents according to international law, and their residences *may* [emphasis added] continue to remain on Italian territory and to enjoy all immunities granted to them according to international law, even if the States have no diplomatic relations with Italy." For the text of the treaty, see John Pollard, *The Vatican and Italian Fascism, 1929–32: A Study in Conflict* (Cambridge: Cambridge University Press, 1985), 197–203, quotation on 200.

33. Chadwick, *Britain and the Vatican*, 124–126.

34. Ibid., 167.

35. Ibid., 152.

36. "Schema di istruzioni," June 25, 1940, AGP, Faldone: Disposizioni di servizio dal 1939 al 1944.

37. Chadwick, *Britain and the Vatican*, 129.

38. "Ospizio di Santa Marta: Novita del giorno 22 Aprile 1942," AGP, Faldone: Disposizioni di servizio dal 1939 al 1944.

39. Quoted in Alvarez, *Spies in the Vatican*, 214.

40. Quoted in Chadwick, *Britain and the Vatican*, 168.

41. Alvarez, *Spies in the Vatican*, 214.

42. Ibid., 217–218; Carlo De Risio, *Generali, servizi segreti e fascismo* (Milan: Mondadori, 1978), 183.

43. Christopher Duggan, *The Force of Destiny: A History of Italy since 1796* (New York: Houghton Mifflin, 2007), 521–522.

44. Denis Mack Smith, *Mussolini: A Biography* (New York: Vintage Books, 1983), 296–298; R. J. B. Bosworth, *Mussolini* (London: Arnold, 2002), 400–402. In September 1943 German commandos rescued Mussolini from the resort hotel in the Apennine mountains where he was confined. He was then set up by the Germans as the head of a rump-Fascist regime in north Italy (the "Republic of Salo"). In April 1945, while attempting to flee into Switzerland, he was caught by anti-Fascist partisans and executed.

45. Richard Lamb, *War in Italy, 1943–1945: A Brutal Story* (New York: St. Martin's Press, 1993), 15–17.

46. Ibid., 21–22.

47. *Actes et Documents du Saint Siège relatifs à la Seconde Guerre Mondiale* 4 (Vatican City: Libreria Editrice Vaticana, 1967), 483.

48. Ibid., 484–485; *Actes et Documents du Saint Siège relatifs à la Seconde Guerre Mondiale* 5 (Vatican City: Libreria Editrice Vaticana, 1969), 214–215, quotation on 215.

49. David Alvarez and Robert A. Graham, S.J., *Nothing Sacred: Nazi Espionage against the Vatican, 1939–1945* (London: Frank Cass, 1997), 83–84.

50. Dan Kurzman, *A Special Mission: Hitler's Secret Plot to Seize the Vatican and Kidnap Pope Pius XII* (Boston: Da Capo Press, 2007), 6. Dan Kurzman asserts that there was a serious plot to kidnap Pius XII after the fall of Mussolini. For contrary evidence, see Alvarez and Graham, *Nothing Sacred*, 85–86.

51. Leo Leder, "Seltene Dienstjahre in der Schweizergarde," Folge 2, *Der Exgardist* 48 (February 1990): 86.

52. "Jane Scrivener," *Inside Rome with the Germans* (New York: Macmillan, 1945), 4.

53. Alvarez and Graham, *Nothing Sacred*, 84, 92.

54. Christian Roland Marcel Richard, *La Guardia Svizzera Pontificia nel corso dei secoli* (Milan: Leonardo International, 2005), 129.

55. Robert Royal, *The Pope's Army: 500 Years of the Papal Swiss Guard* (New York: Crossroad Publishing, 2006), 167.

56. Krieg and Stampfli, *Die Schweizergarde in Rom*, 283.

57. Gahlinger, *Die Schweizergardist im Vatikan*, 32; Vincenz Oertle, *Vom Remington zum Sturmgewehr 90: Die Schußwaffen der Päpstlichen Schweizergarde* (Zurich: Thesis, 2001), 21–22, 30, 97; Alexander Good, "Wacht ins Gwehr!" Folge 7, *Der Exgardist* 29 (August 1980): 4. Carlo Gasbarri, *Quando il Vaticano confinava con il Terzo Reich* (Padua: Edizioni Messaggero, 1984), includes a photograph (no page number) of Swiss Guards loading their Mausers in an assembly room. The halberdiers have gas-mask pouches hanging from their shoulders.

58. Gahlinger, *Die Schweizergardist im Vatikan*, 32.

59. Leo Leder, "Seltene Dienstjahre in der Schweizergarde," Folge 1, *Der Exgardist* 47 (September 1989): 69.

60. Ulrich Ruppen, "Erinnerungen eines Gardeoffiziers," in *Die Schweizergarde in Rom*, ed. Paul Grichting (Brig: Rotten-Verlag, 1975), 52–54.

61. Alexander Good, "Wacht ins Gwehr!" Folge 5, *Der Exgardist* 26 (February 1979): 5–8; Folge 6, *Der Exgardist* 27 (August 1979): 13–17; Folge 7, *Der Exgardist* 29 (August 1980): 3–5; Folge 8, *Der Exgardist* 33 (August 1982): 4–8.

62. Alexander Good, "Wacht ins Gwehr! [*sic*] Persönliche Erinnerungen aus der Zeit zwischen 1943 und 1946," Folge 6, *Der Exgardist* 57 (September 1994): 40–41.

63. Krieg and Stampfli, *Die Schweizergarde in Rom*, 286; Oertle, *Von Remington zum Sturmgewehr 90*, 30, 77.

64. This point may be clarified when the wartime records become available. In the Swiss Guard archive, the author was permitted to examine only records dated before 1939.

65. "Notes de Mgr. Montini," September 9, 1943, *Actes et Documents du Saint Siège Relatifs à la Seconde Guerre Mondiale* 7 (Vatican City, 1973): 611.

66. Alexander Good, "Wacht ins Gwehr!" Folge 9, *Der Exgardist* 35 (August 1983): 26.

67. "Modifiche ai servizi di guardia e di piantone a decorrere dal 16 corr.," [1944], AGP, Faldone: Disposizioni di servizio dal 1939 al 1944; ibid., "Disposizione di servizio, No. 93," October 7, 1943; ibid., "Disposizione di servizio No. 97," [1943]; ibid., "Disposizione di servizio, No. 107," [1943].

68. Nersinger, *Soldaten des Papstes: Eine kleine Geschichte der päpstlichen Garden* (Ruppichteroth: Canisius Werk, 1999), 45–46.

69. [Commando della Guardia Palatina d'Onore di Sua Santità], *Fedeltà Palatina* (Rome: A. Belardetti, 1945), 13.

70. Ibid., 13–14, 22; Carlo Gasbarri, *Quando il Vaticano confinava con il Terzo Reich* (Padua: Edizioni Messaggero, 1984), 122.

71. [Commando della Guardia Palatina], *Fedeltà Palatina*, 15, 24.

72. Antonio Martini, "Guardia Palatina: Accasermamento, 1943–1944," vol. 2 [June 2008]. This memorandum was prepared for the author by Dott. Antonio Martini, a former noncommissioned officer in the Palatine Guard and a student of the guard's history.

73. Gasbarri, *Quando il Vaticano confinava con il Terzo Reich*, 123. Article 10 of the Lateran Agreements stipulated, "Church dignitaries and persons belonging to the Papal Court inscribed in a list *mutually arranged between the two High Contracting Parties* even if not Vatican subjects, are always and in any case, as regards Italy, exempt from military service" [emphasis added].

74. Martini, "Guardia Palatina," 3; Ulrich Nersinger, "Eine Miliz von römischen Bürgen," *Der Schweizergardist* 1 (2009): 27, says that many of the new recruits were Jews. He does not provide any evidence for this claim.

75. Ibid., 18, 20; "Scrivener," *Inside Rome with the Germans*, 37; Martini, "Guardia Palatina," 3–4.

76. Ulrich Nersinger, "Der Vatikanstaat und der Zweite Weltkrieg, 1943–44: Eine Neutral Armee in besetzten Rom," *Militär und Geschichte*, no. 32 (April–May 2007), 21; interviews with the Marchese Giulio Patrizi di Ripacandida, Rome, January 27, 2010, and February 18, 2010. During the German occupation of Rome, the Marchese di Ripacandida was a lieutenant in the Noble Guard.

77. Ruppen, "Erinnerungen eines Gardeoffiziers," 50, 52; Good, "Wacht ins Gwehr!" Folge 2, 38.

78. Krieg and Stampfli, *Die Schweizergarde in Rom*, 283.

79. "Scrivener," *Inside Rome with the Germans*, 91, 99.

80. Giulio Patrizi di Ripacandida, "Dal diario di una Guardia Nobile del Papa," *Rivista Araldica* 87, fascicolo 841 (October–December 1989): 208.

81. "Scrivener," *Inside Rome with the Germans*, 138.

82. Krieg and Stampfli, *Die schweizergarde in Rom*, 285; Alexander Good, "Wacht ins Gwehr!" Folge 3, *Der Exgardist* 54 (March 1993): 41–43.

83. Giulio Patrizi di Ripacandida, "Dal diario di una Guardia Nobile del Papa," *Rivista Araldica* 87, fascicolo 840 (July–September 1989): 155. According to Dott. Antonio Martini, a veteran of the Palatine Guard, "In the period of the German occupation, when the guards and the auxiliaries were on duty, they ate every day. Not all Romans ate every day!" Martini, "Guardia Palatina," 6.

84. Good, "Wacht ins Gwehr!" Folge 3, 47.

85. Ibid., 41–42.

86. Ibid., 41.

87. Giovanni Antonazzi, *Roma città aperta: La cittadella sul Gianicolo: Appunti di diario* (Rome: Edizioni di Storia e Letteratura, 1983), 188, 240.

88. Good, "Wacht ins Gwehr!" Folge 6, 46.

89. Information from Dott. Antonio Martini.

90. Good, "Wacht ins Gwehr!" *Der Exgardist* 36 (February 1984): 42.

91. Many members of the Noble Guard, for example, had been wartime officers in the Italian army before entering papal service. Interview with the Marchese Giulio Patrizi di Ripacandida, Rome, February 8, 2010. Before entering the Noble Guard, the marchese had been a lieutenant in the elite Granatieri di Sardegna division of the Italian army and on September 10, 1943, had fought the Germans in the action

at the Porta San Paolo. When his unit was disbanded after the occupation of Rome, he was invited to join the Noble Guard by the guard commandant, Prince Francesco Chigi della Rovere.

92. Kreig and Stampfli, *Die Schweizergarde in Rom*, 290.

93. Giulio Patrizi di Ripacandida, "Dal diario di una Guardia Nobili del Papa," *Rivista Araldica* 88, fascicolo 842 (January–March 1990): 18–19. For an example of a duty officer visiting guard posts, see Tenente Guglielmo Jacobelli, "Ispezione ai servizi di vigilanza," November 27, 1943, AGP, Faldone: Disposizioni di servizio dal 1939 al 1944. During this nighttime inspection, gendarmeria lieutenant Jacobelli formally admonished a gendarme for not having his rifle at hand.

94. Ruppen, "Erinnerungen eines Gardeoffiziers," 48–49; interview with the Marchese Giulio Patrizi di Ripacandida, January 27, 2010.

95. Ripacandida, "Dal diario di una Guardia Nobili del Papa," fascicolo 840, 156.

96. Martini, "Guardia Palatina," 2.

97. Good, "Wacht ins Gwehr!" Folge 2, 40–42.

98. Ripacandida, "Dal diario di una Guardia Nobile del Papa," fascicolo 841, 211.

99. Leo Leder, "Seltene Dienstjahre in der Schweizergarde," Folge 2, *Der Exgardist* 48 (February 1990): 88.

100. Fridolin Fetz, "Der Dienst im Schatten der Kolonnaden," Folge 3, *Der Exgardist* 44 (February 1988): 60–61. Fetz was a halberdier during World War II.

101. Alexander Good, "Wacht ins Gwehr!" Folge 10, *Der Exgardist* 36 (February 1984): 43.

102. Brian Fleming, *The Vatican Pimpernel: The Wartime Exploits of Monsignor Hugh O'Flaherty* (Wilton, Cork, Ireland: Collins Press, 2008), 44–48.

103. Untitled directive, September 12, 1943, AGP, Faldone: Disposizioni di servizio dal 1943 al 1944.

104. "Disposizione di servizio, No. 80," August 20, 1943, AGP, Faldone: Disposizioni di servizio dal 1943 al 1944. By the fall of 1943 these British soldiers were allowed to walk in the Vatican Gardens with Ambassador Osborne so long as they wore civilian clothes.

When visiting the armory of the Swiss Guard, the author noticed a German helmet on a shelf and a lone German Schmeisser MP40 submachine gun on a rifle rack. When asked about the presence of these items, the guard officer who was escorting the author replied that the helmet and weapon belonged to a German soldier who had found asylum inside Vatican City during the war.

105. Ruppen, "Erinnerungen eines Gardeoffiziers," 51.

106. Fleming, *The Vatican Pimpernel*, 44.

107. [Commando della Guardia Palatina], *Fedeltà Palatina*, 36; Niccolò Del Re, *La Guardia Palatina d'Onore: Una istituzione piana scomparsa* (Rome: n.p., 1997), 44.

108. Antonazzi, *Roma città aperta*, 170–171, 189, 229; Gasbarri, *Quando il Vaticano confinava con il Terzo Reich*, 124. Unlike the Swiss Guard, the Palatine Guard seems to have received no orders prohibiting the use of firearms in the defense of Vatican territory.

109. Gasbarri, *Quando il Vaticano confinava con il Terzo Reich*, 217–218. Besides the Palatine guardsman executed by the Germans, the only other wartime fatality among the pope's soldiers was Sublieutenant the Duke Leopoldo Torlonia, a Noble Guard

who was arrested by the Germans for assisting escaped Allied POWs and who died under circumstances that were never explained. Nersinger, *Soldaten des Papstes*, 14; interview with the Marchese Giulio Patrizi di Ripacandida, Rome, February 8, 2010.

110. V. B., "Le tragiche ore di Castelgandolfo: Il servizio della Guardia," *Vita Palatina* (February 22, 1944): 1.

111. Interview with the Marchese Giulio Patrizi di Ripacandida, January 27, 2010. The marchese was one of the guardsmen involved.

112. Leo Leder, "Seltene Dienstjahre in der Schweizergarde," Folge 3, *Der Exgardist* 49 (September 1990): 34–35.

113. Good, "Wacht ins Gwehr!" Folge 6, 45; Ripacandida, "Dal diario di una Guardia Nobili del Papa," fascicolo 842, 21–22. The chronology of the liberation of Rome in the Ripacandida diary is a bit confused. The Americans entered Rome on June 4, but writing on June 7, the diarist at times suggests that the city was liberated on June 6.

114. Ripacandida, "Dal diario di una Guardia Nobili del Papa," fascicolo 842, 23.

115. One of the first American officers to visit the Vatican was Captain Carlo Fehr, who, before immigrating to the United States in the 1930s, had served more than three years in the Swiss Guard. While stationed in Rome, Captain Fehr spent much of his free time with his former comrades and was a welcome source of scarce food items, such as chocolate.

Chapter 8. Guardian Angels

1. Anton Gahlinger, *I Served the Pope* (Boston: Fandel Press, 1953), 28.

2. Paul Krieg and Reto Stampfli, *Die Schweizergarde in Rom* (Zurich: Orell Füssli Verlag, 2006), 291.

3. Ibid., 292; Ulrich Ruppen, "Erinnerungen eines Gardeoffiziers," in *Die Schweizergarde in Rom*, ed. Paul Grichting (Brig: Rotten-Verlag, 1975), 58.

4. Krieg and Stampfli, *Die Schweizergarde in Rom*, 299.

5. "Zum Tod von alt Gardekommandant Dr. Robert Nünlist," *Der Exgardist* 52 (February 1992): 78–79.

6. Krieg and Stampfli, *Die Schweizergarde in Rom*, 301.

7. Vincenz Oertle, *Von Remington zum Sturmgewehr 90: Die Schußwaffen der Päpstlichen Schweizergarde: Geschichte und Bestandesaufnahme* (Zurich: Thesis, 2001), 31.

8. When the author visited the Swiss Guard armory in the summer of 2009, there were still approximately two dozen Mausers in the weapons racks.

9. Oertle, *Von Remington zum Sturmgewehr 90*, 40–41.

10. Krieg and Stampfli, *Die Schweizergarde in Rom*, 305. The split in the veterans' association was not mended until 1965.

11. Ibid., 302.

12. Giulio Patrizi di Ripacandida, "La morte del pontefice Pio XII nel diario di servizio di una Guardia Nobile," *Rivista Araldica*, fascicolo 860 (2002), 4–7.

13. Interview with the Marchese Giulio Patrizi di Ripacandida, Rome, January 27, 2010.

14. Krieg and Stampfli, *Die Schweizergarde in Rom*, 304, 308.

15. Ibid., 314.

16. Quoted in Robert Royal, *The Pope's Army: 500 Years of the Papal Swiss Guard* (New York: Crossroad Publishing, 2006), 21.

17. Interview with the Marchese Giulio Patrizi di Ripacandida.

18. Jahresbericht, 1965, Vatican City, Archivio della Guardia Svizzera Pontificia (AGSP); e-mail from Major (ret.) Peter Hasler of the Pontifical Swiss Guard, who enlisted in the guard in December 1966.

19. Royal, *The Pope's Army*, 177.

20. John Cornwell, *A Thief in the Night: The Mysterious Death of Pope John Paul I* (New York: Simon & Schuster, 1989), 84.

21. Glauco Benigni, *Gli angeli custodi del Papa* (Turin: UTET Libreria, 2004), 56–57; John Follain, *City of Secrets: The Truth behind the Murders at the Vatican* (New York: HarperCollins, 2003), 152. It is suggestive of the Vatican's approach to security that as late as 2003, the pope's principal bodyguard was the then eighty-year-old commander of the Vigilance Corps, Camillo Cibin.

22. Benigni, *Gli angeli custodi del Papa*, 63–64.

23. Ibid., 67.

24. Official reports maintained that John Paul was uninjured by the assailant at Fatima. In 2008, however, the late pope's personal secretary, Stanislaw Dziwisz, said that the Holy Father received a knife wound, but the fact was kept from the media. http://news.bbc.co.uk/2/hi/europe/7673443.stm.

25. Benigni, *Gli angeli custody del Papa*, 71–72.

26. Royal, *The Pope's Army*, 184–186.

27. Jahresbericht, 1984, AGSP; Benigni, *Gli angeli custodi del Papa*, 24. Swiss Guards first accompanied the Holy Father on a foreign trip in 1979.

28. Ulrich Nersinger, "Die Gendarmen des Papstes," *Der Schweizergardist* 2 (2009): 27; e-mail from Fabio Vagnoni, October 28, 2009; conversations with Domenico Giani and Fabio Vagnoni, Vatican City, June 17, 2009. Fabio Vagnoni is an officer in the Gendarmeria Vaticana and that agency's liaison with Interpol. Domenico Giani is the commander of the Gendarmeria Vaticana.

29. Oertle, *Von Remington zum Sturmgewehr 90*, 33–34, 41. In addition to the old Dreyse pistols, the guard armory held seven Beretta model 1934 semiautomatic pistols, which had been transferred from the Noble Guard when that unit was disbanded in 1970.

30. Jahresbericht, 1984, AGSP; information from a former member of the Swiss Guard.

31. Royal, *The Pope's Army*, 187–189.

32. Beginning in 2003, there has been increased attention to rifle and pistol practice. Recently, the Swiss Guard has been using the firearms training facility of the Italian Guardia di Finanza outside the city of Orvieto or the firearms range of the Italian Polizia di Stato in Rome. "Jahresbericht," 2003, AGSP.

33. Christian-Roland Marcel Richard, *La Guardia Svizzera Pontificia nel corso dei secoli* (Milan: Leonardo International, 2005), 165–166. For a survey of training activities in a recent year, see "Jahresbericht," 2003.

34. The military invasions or threats include the French invasions of 1796, 1797, 1798, and 1807–1808; the insurrections of 1831–1832; the war against Austria of

1848; the Roman Revolution of 1848; the insurrections and Piedmontese intervention of 1859; the war with Piedmont of 1860; the campaign against the brigands in the 1860s; the Garibaldian campaign of 1867; the war with the Kingdom of Italy of 1870; and the German occupation of Rome of 1943–1944. The formal wars and significant military campaigns include the Napoléonic invasions of 1796 and 1797; the Austrian war of 1848; the war against Piedmont of 1860; the campaign against the brigands; the campaign against Garibaldi of 1867; and the war against the Kingdom of Italy of 1870.

Bibliography

Primary Sources: Vatican City

Archivio Segreto Vaticano
    Carte Kanzler-Vannutelli
    Fondi Speciali
        Guardia Nobile
    Palazzo Apostolico
        Guardia Svizzera
        Gendarmeria
    Segreteria di Stato
        Gendarmi
        Guardia Nobile
        Guardia Svizzera
Archivio della Gendarmeria Pontificia
    Faldone: Annuali, 1870–1939
    Faldone: Bombardamenti
    Faldone: Delitti
    Faldone: Disposizioni di Servizio
Archivio della Guardia Svizzera Pontificia
    Corpo della Gendarmeria Pontificia
    Funktionenbuch
    Jahresbericht
    Jules Repond
        Diario
        Memoires

Secondary Sources

Actes et Documents du Saint Siège relatifs à la Seconde Guerre Mondiale. 12 volumes. Vatican City: Libreria Editrice Vaticana, 1965–1981.

Alvarez, David. *Spies in the Vatican: Espionage and Intrigue from Napoleon to the Holocaust.* Lawrence: University Press of Kansas, 2002.

Alvarez, David, and Robert A. Graham, S.J. *Nothing Sacred: Nazi Espionage against the Vatican.* London: Frank Cass, 1997.

Amadi, Giovanni. "The Pope at Home." *North American Review* 155, no. 429 (August 1892): 196–209.

Andreotti, Giulio. *La fuga di Pio IX e l'ospitalità dei Borbone.* Rome: Edizioni Benincasa, 2003.

Antonazzi, Giovani. *Roma città aperta: La cittadella sul Gianicolo: Appunti di diario.* Rome: Edizioni di Storia e Letteratura, 1983.

Barbarich, Eugenio, ed. *Ricordi sui combattimenti di Monterotondo e di Mentana, ottobre–novembre 1867*. Rome: Tipografia del Comando del Corpo di Stato Maggiore, 1911.

Barbieri, Alessandro Mancini. "Nuove ricerche sulla presenza straniera nell'esercito pontificio, 1850–1870." *Rassegna storica del Risorgimento* 73 (1986): 161–186.

Bartolini, Carlo. *Il brigantaggio nello Stato Pontificio: Cenno-storico-aneddotico dal 1860 al 1870*. Rome: Arnaldo Forni Editore, 1897.

Beauffort, Roger. *Histoire de l'invasion des États Pontificaux et du siège de Rome par l'armee italienne en Septembre 1870*. Paris: Victor Palme, 1874.

Becdelièvre, M. L. A. de. *Souvenirs de l'armée pontificale*. Paris: Lecoffre, 1867.

Benigni, Glauco. *Gli angeli custodi del Papa*. Turin: UTET Libreria, 2004.

Berkeley, George F. H. *The Irish Battalion in the Papal Army of 1860*. Dublin: Talbott Press, 1929.

Besson, François. *Frederick Francis Xavier de Mérode: Minister and Almoner to Pius IX, Archbishop of Miletensis: His Life and His Works*. Trans. Mary Herbert. London: W. H. Allen & Co., 1887.

Blakiston, Noel, ed. *The Roman Question: Extracts from the Despatches of Odo Russell from Rome, 1858–1870*. Wilmington, DE: Michael Glazier, 1980.

Bonetti, Antonmaria. *Da Bagnorea a Mentana ossia storia della guerra pontificio-garibaldina del 1867*. Trento: Ed. Artigianelli, 1891.

Bortolotti, Vincenzo. *Storia dell'esercito sardo e de' suoi alleati nelle campagne di guerra, 1848–49*. Turin: Fratelli Pozzo, 1889.

Bosworth, R. J. B. *Mussolini*. London: Arnold, 2002.

Bourelly, Giuseppe. *Il Brigantaggio dal 1860 al 1865 nelle zone militari di Melfi e Lacedonia*. Venosa: Edizioni Osanna, 1987 (reprint of 1865 edition).

Brandani, Massimo, Piero Crociani, and Massimo Fiorentino. *L'esercito pontificio da Castelfidardo a Porta Pia, 1860–1870: Uniformi, equipaggiamento, armamento*. Milan: Intergest, 1976.

Branzoli, Giuseppe. "La Spedizione Garibaldina del 1867 contro lo Stato Pontificio," *Rivista Militare* 23, no. 10 (1967): 1119–1132.

Broers, Michael. *The Napoleonic Empire in Italy, 1796–1814: Cultural Imperialism in a European Context*. New York: Palgrave Macmillan, 2005.

Carletti, Giulio Cesare. *L'esercito pontificio dal 1860 al 1870: Quale era, quanto era, cosa operò*. Viterbo: Agnesotti, 1904.

Cerbelaud-Salagnac, Georges. *Les Zouaves pontificaux*. Paris: Editions France Empire, 1963.

Cesari, Cesare. *Il brigantaggio e l'opera dell'esercito italiano dal 1860 al 1870*. Bologna: Arnoldo Forni, 2002.

Chadwick, Owen. *Britain and the Vatican during the Second World War*. Cambridge: Cambridge University Press, 1986.

———. *A History of the Popes, 1830–1914*. Oxford: Oxford University Press, 1998.

———. *The Popes and European Revolution*. Oxford: Oxford University Press, 1981.

Chambers, D. S. *Popes, Cardinals and War: The Military Church in Renaissance and Early Modern Europe*. London: Tauris, 2006.

Cicconetti, Luigi. *"Roma o Morte": Gli avvenimenti nello Stato pontificio nell'anno 1867*. Milan: Alfieri, 1934.

Coppa, Frank J. *Cardinal Giacomo Antonelli and Papal Politics in European Affairs*. Albany: State University of New York Press, 1990.

———. *The Modern Papacy since 1789*. New York: Addison, Wesley Longman, 1998.

———. "Mussolini and the Concordat of 1929." In Frank J. Coppa, ed., *Controversial Concordats: The Vatican's Relations with Napoleon, Mussolini and Hitler*. Washington, DC: Catholic University of America Press, 1999, 81–119.

———. *The Origins of the Italian Wars of Independence*. Harlow: Longman, 1992.

———. *Pope Pius IX: Crusader in a Secular Age*. Boston: Twayne Publishers, 1979.

Cornwell, John. *A Thief in the Night: The Mysterious Death of Pope John Paul I*. New York: Simon & Schuster, 1989.

[Corpo di Stato Maggiore-Ufficio Storico]. *La Battaglia di Castelfidardo (18 settembre 1860)*. Rome: Tipo-Litografia del Genio Civile, 1903.

Coulombe, Charles. *The Pope's Legion: The Multinational Fighting Force That Defended the Vatican*. New York: Palgrave Macmillan, 2008.

Crispolti, Filippo. *Politici, guerrieri, poeti*. Milan: Fratelli Treves Editori, 1938.

Dalla Torre, Paolo. *L'anno di Mentana: Contributo ad una storia dello Stato Pontificio nel 1867*. Milan: Martello, 1968.

———. "Materiali per una storia dell'esercito pontificio." *Rassegna Storica del Risorgimento* 28 (1941): 45–99.

De Cesare, R. *Roma e lo stato del Papa dal ritorno di Pio IX al XX settembre*. Rome: Forzani e C., 1907.

Delcurato, Dario. *Storia della Guardia Svizzera Pontificia e dei corpi militari pontifici disciolti nel 1970*. Varese: Macchione Editore, 2006.

Del Re, Niccolò. *La Guardia Palatina d'Onore: Una istituzione piana scomparsa*. Rome: n.p., 1997.

———. *Mondo Vaticano: Passatto e presente*. Vatican City: Libreria Editrice Vaticana, 1995.

De Marco, D. *Pio IX e la rivoluzione romana del 1848*. Modena: Tip Modenese, 1947.

De Risio, Carlo. *Generali, servizi segreti e fascismo*. Milan: Mondadori, 1978.

Deutsch, Harold. *The Conspiracy against Hitler in the Twilight War*. Minneapolis: University of Minnesota Press, 1968.

Diamilla-Muller, Demetrio. *Da Roma a Cornuda: Ricordi della spedizione romana nel Veneto, marzo-giugno 1848*. Turin: Tipografia Fodratti, 1886.

Di Nolli, Roberto. *Mentana*. Rome: Bardi Editore, 1965.

Di Pierro, Antonio. *L'ultimo giorno del Papa Re: 20 settembre 1870: La breccia di porta Pia*. Milan: Arnoldo Mondadori Editore, 2007.

Duggan, Christopher. *The Force of Destiny: A History of Italy since 1796*. Boston: Houghton Mifflin, 2007.

Falconi, Carlo. *Il Cardinale Antonelli: Vita e carriera del Richelieu italiano nella chiesa di Pio IX*. Milan: Arnoldo Mondadori Editore, 1983.

Fetz, Fridolin. "Der Dienst im Schatten der Kolonnaden." Folge 3, *Der Exgardist* 44 (February 1988): 59–62.

Fiorentino, Carlo. *All'ombra di Pietro: La Chiesa Cattolica e lo spionaggio fascista in Vaticano, 1929–1939*. Florence: Casa Editrice Le Lettere, 1999.

Fleming, Brian. *The Vatican Pimpernel: The Wartime Exploits of Monsignor Hugh O'Flaherty*. Wilton, Cork, Ireland: Collins Press, 2008.

Follain, John. *City of Secrets: The Truth behind the Murders at the Vatican*. New York: HarperCollins, 2003.

[Franzosi, Pier Giorgio]. *La Repubblica romana e il suo esercito*. Rome: Rivista Militare, 1987.

Frediani, Andrea. *Gli assedi di Roma: Razzie, violenze e saccheggi ai danni della città piu assediata nella storia d'Europa dall'invasione etrusca all'occupazione nazista (Quest'Italia)*. Rome: Newton & Compton, 1997.

Friz, Giuliano. *Burocrati e soldati dello Stato Pontificio, 1800–1870*. Rome: Edindustria Editoriale, 1974.

Gahlinger, Anton. *I Served the Pope*. Boston: Fandel Press, 1953.

———. *Der Schweizergardist im Vatikan*. St. Gallen: Ostschweiz AG, 1949.

Ganter, Henri. *Histoire du service militaire des Regiments Suisse à la solde de l'Angleterre, de Naples et de Rome*. Geneva: Eggimann & Cie, 1902.

Garibaldi, Menotti. "Rapporto del Colonnello Menotti Garibaldi al Generale Giuseppe Garibaldi sulla giornata di Mentana." In Eugenio Barbarich, ed., *Ricordi sui combattimenti di Monterotondo e di Mentana, ottobre–novembre 1867*. Rome: Tipografia del Comando del Corpo di Stato Maggiore, 1911.

Gasbarri, Carlo. *Quando il Vaticano confinava con il Terzo Reich*. Padua: Edizioni Messaggero, 1984.

Ghisalberti, Alberto. "Carlo Canori, Soldato del Papa." *Rassegna storica del Risorgimento* 23 (1936): 431–454.

Good, Alexander. "Erinnerungen: Wacht ins Gwehr! [*sic*] Persönliche Gardeerinnerungen aus der Zeit zwischen 1943–1946." *Der Exgardist* 52–57 (February 1992–September 1994) [memoir appearing serially with varying titles; continuation of below].

———. "Wacht ins Gwehr! [*sic*] Erinnerungen eines päpstlichen Schweizergardisten." *Der Exgardist* 26–36 (February 1979–February 1984) [memoir appearing serially with varying titles].

Guenel, Jean. *La dernière guerre du pape: Les zouaves pontificaux au secours du Saint-Siège, 1860–1870*. Rennes: Presses Universitaires de Rennes, 1998.

Hales, E. E. Y. *Revolution and Papacy, 1769–1846*. Garden City, NY: Doubleday, 1960.

Hibbert, Christopher. *Garibaldi: Hero of Italian Unification*. New York: Palgrave Macmillan, 2008.

Holenstein, Johann. "Erinnerungen." *Der Exgardist* [no number] (February 1969): 5–10.

Ilari, Virgilio. "L'esercito pontificio nell XVIII secolo fino alle riforme del 1792–93." *Studi storico militari* 6344 (1985): 555–664.

———. "I tentativi della riforma dell'esercito pontificio nel 1792–1798," part 1, *Studi storico militari* 6372 (1986): 731–853.

———. "I tentativi della riforma dell'esercito pontificio nel 1792–1798," part 2. *Studi storico militari* 6389 (1987): 137–241.

Ilari, Virgilio, Ciro Paoletti, and Piero Crociani. *Bella Italia military: Eserciti e marine nell'Italia pre-napoleonica, 1748–1792*. Rome: Stato Maggiore dell'Esercito, Ufficio Storico, 2000.

Imbrighi, Gastone. *I corpi armati pontifici*. Vatican City: Poliglotta Vaticana, 1953.

Ioli, Major Giuseppe. "Il battaglione irlandese di San Patrizio." In [Stato Maggiore Esercito–Ufficio Storico], ed., *Scritti sul 1860 nel centenario*. Rome: Tipografia Regionale, 1960, 207–217.

Jatta, Barbara, ed. *1929–2009: Ottanta anni dello Stato della Città del Vaticano*. Vatican City: Biblioteca Apostolica Vaticana, 2009.

Jehle, Alois. *Il diritto proprio della Guardia Svizzera Pontificia nella capitolazione del 1825 e nei regolamenti, 1858–1959*. Rome: Pontificia Studiorum Universitas a S. Thoma, 2006.

———. "La Guardia Svizzera Pontificia sotto i regolamenti del 1858 e del 1959." In Urban Fink, Hervé de Weck, and Christian Schweizer, eds., *Hirtenstab und Hellebarde: Die Päpstliche Schweizergarde in Rom, 1506–2006*. Zurich: Theologischer Verlag, 2006, 393–413.

Keller, Emile. *Le Général De La Moricière: Sa vie militaire, politique et religieuse*. 2 volumes. Paris: René Haton, 1891.

Kent, Peter. *The Pope and the Duce: The International Impact of the Lateran Agreements*. New York: St. Martin's, 1981.

Kertzer, David. *Prisoner of the Vatican: The Pope's Secret Plot to Capture Rome from the New Italian State*. New York: Houghton Mifflin, 2004.

Koenig, Duane. "The Last Cruise of the Pope's Navy. 1840–1841." *Social Studies* 66, no. 6 (November–December 1975): 270–273.

Krieg, Paul, and Reto Stampfli. *Die Schweizergarde in Rom*. Zurich: Orell Füssli Verlag, 2006.

Kurzman, Dan. *A Special Mission: Hitler's Secret Plot to Seize the Vatican and Kidnap Pope Pius XII*. Boston: Da Capo Press, 2007.

Lamb, Richard. *War in Italy, 1943–1945: A Brutal Story*. New York: St. Martin's Press, 1993.

Lamoricière, Christophe de. *Rapporto di S. E. il Generale De Lamoricière a S.E. il Ministro delle Armi*. Rome: Tipografia della Cività Cattolica, 1860.

Leder, Leo. "Seltene Dienstjahre in der Schweizergarde." *Der Exgardist* 47–50 (September 1989–February 1991): 68–72, 84–92, 34–39, 42–45.

Lefevre, Renato. "La marina militare pontificia." In Ufficio Storico della Marina Militare, ed., *Le marine militari italiane nel 1848*. Rome: Tipografia Stato Maggiore Marina, 1948, 37–54.

Leti, Giuseppe. *La rivoluzione e la Repubblica Romana del 1848–49*. Milan: Vallardi, 1913.

Locatelli, Giuseppe. *Monterotondo e Mentana: Ricordi d'un Garibaldino della colonna Mosto e Stallo*. Bergamo: Tipografia Fagnani e Galeazzi, 1885.

Longo, Vincenzo. "L'esercito pontificio nel 1860." In Stato Maggiore Esercito–Ufficio Storico, ed., *Scritti sul 1860 nel centenario*. Rome: Tipografia Regionale, 1960, 251–289.

Lupo, Salvatore. "Il grande brigantaggio: Interpretazione e memoria di una guerra civile." In Walter Barberis, ed., *Guerra e pace*. Turin: Giulio Einaudi, 2002, 465–502.

Manfroni, Giuseppe. *Sulla soglia del Vaticano, 1870–1901*. Milan: Longanesi, 1971.

Martina, Giacomo, S.J. *Pio IX (1851–1866)*. Rome: Editrice Pontificia Università Gregoriana, 1986.

————. *Pio IX (1867–1878)*. Rome: Editrice Pontificia Università Gregoriana, 1990.

Martini, Antonio. "Corpi militari nello Stato Pontificio e nella Città del Vaticano." In Barbara Jatta, ed., *1929–2009: Ottanta anni dello Stato della Città del Vaticano*. Vatican City: Biblioteca Apostolica Vaticana, 2009.

Mathuisieulx, H. Mehier de. *Histoire des zouaves pontificaux*. Tours: Mame, 1913.

McCormack, John. *One Million Mercenaries: Swiss Soldiers in the Armies of the World*. London: Leo Cooper, 1993.

Mestica, Giovanni. "La battaglia di Faenza e il generale Colli." *Nuova Antologia*, 4th ser., 95 (September–October 1901): 613–629.

Mévius, David Chislain Emile Gustave de. *Histoire de l'invasion des États Pontificaux en 1867*. Paris: Victor Palmé, 1875.

Nada, Narciso. *Metternich e le riforme nello Stato Pontificio: La missione Sebregondi a Roma (1832–1836)*. Turin: Deputazione Subalpina di Storia Patria, 1957.

Nersinger, Ulrich. "Adlige im Dienste Seiner Heiligkeit." *Der Schweizergardist* 3 (2008): 28–31.

————. "Die Gendarmen des Papstes." *Der Schweizergardist* 2 (2009): 24–27.

————. "Eine Miliz von römischen Bürgern." *Der Schweizergardist* 1 (2009): 26–29.

————. *Soldaten des Papstes: Eine kleine Geschichte der päpstlichen Garden*. Ruppichteroth: Canisius-Werk, 1999.

————. "Der Vatikanstaat und der Zweite Weltkrieg, 1943–44: Eine Neutral Armee in besetzten Rom." *Militär und Geschichte*, no. 32 (April–May 2007): 20–27.

Nicassio, Susan Vandiver. *Imperial City: Rome, Romans and Napoleon, 1796–1815*. Garden City, NY: Ravenhall Books, 2005.

Oertle, Vincenz. *Vom Remington zum Sturmgewehr 90: Die Schußwaffen der Päpstlichen Schweizergarde: Geschichte und Bestandesaufnahme*. Zurich: Thesis, 2001.

Oliva, Giuliano. *La Guardia di Finanza Pontificia*. Rome: Museo Storico della Guardia di Finanza, 1979.

Ovidi, Ernesto. *Roma e i Romani nelle campagne del 1848–49 per l'indipendenza Italiana*. Rome: Roux e Viarengo, 1903.

Pacca, Bartolomeo. *Historical Memoirs of Cardinal Pacca,* trans. George Head. London: Longman, Brown, Green, & Longmans, 1850.

Paoletti, Ciro. *A Military History of Italy*. Westport, CT: Praeger, 2008.

Patrizi di Ripacandida, Giulio. "Dal diario di una Guardia Nobili del Papa." *Rivista Araldica* 87, fascicolo 840 (July–September 1989): 152–161; 87, fascicolo 841 (October–December 1989): 206–215; 88, fascicolo 842 (January–March, 1990): 12–27.

————. *Quell'ultimo glorioso stendardo: Le Guardie Nobili Pontificie dall'11 maggio 1801 al 15 settembre 1970*. Vatican City: n.p., 1994.

Pedrazzini, Dominic. "Jules Repond: Le dernier condottiere." *Der Schweizergardist* 2 (2007): 16–19.

Persano, Carlo Pellion di. *Compagna navale degli anni 1860–1861*. Turin: Roux e Favale, 1880.

Pesci, Ugo. *Come siamo entrati in Roma*. Milan: Palazzi, 1970.

Pieri, Piero. *Storia militare del Risorgimento: Guerre e insurrezioni*, 2nd ed. Turin: Giulio Einaudi, 1962.

Pimodan, Gabriel de. *Vie du Général de Pimodan*. Paris: Champion, 1928.

Poli, Oscar de. *Les soldats du Pape (1860–1867)*. Paris: Amyot, 1868.

Pollard, John. "A Court in Exile: The Vatican 1870–1929," *Court Historian* 12, no. 1 (June 2007): 35–48.

———. *Money and the Rise of the Modern Papacy: Financing the Vatican, 1850–1950*. Cambridge: Cambridge University Press, 2005.

———. *The Unknown Pope: Benedict XV (1914–1922) and the Pursuit of Peace*. London: Geoffrey Chapman, 1999.

———. *The Vatican and Italian Fascism, 1929–31: A Study in Conflict*. Cambridge: Cambridge University Press, 1985.

Powell, Joseph. *Two Years in the Pontifical Zouaves*. London: R. Washbourne, 1871.

Quatrebarbes, Théodore de. *Souvenirs d'Ancone: Siége de 1860*. Paris: Charles Douniol, 1866.

Raggi, Piero. *La nona crociata: I volontari di Pio IX in difesa di Roma (1860–1870)*. Ravenna: Libreria Tonini, 2002.

Ravioli, Camillo. *La campagna del Veneto del 1848, tenuta da due divisioni e da corpi franchi degli Stati Romani sotto la condotta del Generale Giovanni Durando*. Rome: Tipografia Tiberina, 1883.

———. *Notizie storiche dei corpi militari regolari che combatterono negli assalti ed assedi di Bologna, Ancona, Roma nell'anno 1849*. Rome: Tipografia Nazionale, 1884.

———. *Viaggio della spedizione romana in Egitto fatto nel 1840 e 1841*. Rome: Tipografia delle Belle Arti, 1870.

Reinerman, Alan J. *Austria and the Papacy in the Age of Metternich*, vol. 2: *Revolution and Reaction*. Washington, DC: Catholic University of America Press, 1989.

Richard, Christian-Roland Marcel. *La Guardia Svizzera Pontificia nel corso dei secoli*. Milan: Leonardo International, 2005.

Rinieri, Ilario. *Napoleone e Pio VII (1804–1813): Relazioni storiche su documenti inediti dell'Archivio Vaticano*. Turin: Unione Tipografico Editrice, 1906.

Rivera, Luigi. "I fatti del 1831: Il generale pontificio Filippo Resta." *Rassegna storica del Risorgimento* 19 (1932): 205–220.

Romano, Gaetano Moroni. *Dizionario di erudizione storico-ecclesiastica*. Venice: Tipografia Emiliana, 1845.

Rossi, Augusto. *Pio IX e la distruzione della repubblica Romana, 1849*. Rome: Serarcangeli Editore, 2001.

Rouleau, C. E. *La Papauté et les Zouaves Pontificaux: Quelques Pages d'Histoire*. Quebec: Le Soleil, 1905.

Royal, Robert. *The Pope's Army: 500 Years of the Papal Swiss Guard*. New York: Crossroad Publishing, 2006.

Ruffoni, G. *XXV Anniversario della breccia di Porta Pia: Cenni storico-militari sulle operazioni per la liberazione di Roma*. Verona: Vicentini e Ferrari, 1895.

Ruppen, Ulrich. "Erinnerungen eines Gardeoffiziers." In Paul Grichting, ed., *Die Schweizergarde in Rom* (Brig: Rotten-Verlag, 1975), 41–59.

Russo, Flavio. *La difesa costiera dello Stato Pontificio dal XVI al XIX secolo*. Rome: Stato Maggiore dell'Esercito–Ufficio Storico, 1999.

Segur, Antoine de. *The Martyrs of Castelfidardo*. Dublin: Gill and Son, 1895.

Serrano, Antonio. *Die Schweizergarde der Päpste*. Dachau: Druckerei und Verlagsanstalt Bayerland, 1992.

Smith, Denis Mack. *Italy and Its Monarchy*. New Haven, CT: Yale University Press, 1989.

——. *Mussolini: A Biography*. New York: Vintage Books, 1983.

Stampfli, Reto. "Die Geburtsstunde des Vatikanstaats." *Der Schweizergardist* 2 (2009): 30–31.

——. *Die Päpstliche Schweizergarde, 1870–1970*. Solothurn, Switzerland: Zweite Auglage, 2004.

Tosi, Giuseppe. "La Gendarmeria Pontificia." Thesis, La Sapienza, Rome, 1966.

Tournon, Phillipe-Antoine de. *Les volontaires Pontificaux a cheval*. Paris: Charles Douniol, 1860.

Trevelyan, George M. *Manin and the Venetian Revolution of 1848*. London: Longmans, Green, 1923.

Tuppoti, Carla Lodolini. "Esclaves Barbaresques sur les Galères Pontificales," *Revue d'Histoire Maghrebine* 18, nos. 61–62 (1991): 95–134.

Vallière, Paul de, and Henri Guisan. *Honneur et fidélité: Histoire des suisses au service étranger*. Lausanne: Editions d'Art Suisse Ancien, 1940.

Valzania, Eugenio. "Relazione della colonna Valzania." In Eugenio Barbarich, ed., *Ricordi sui combattimenti di Monterotondo e di Mentana, ottobre-novembre, 1867*. Rome: Tipografia del Comando del Corpo di Stato Maggiore, 1911.

Vannutelli, Vincenzo. *Il generale Kanzler: Cenni biografici*. Rome: Armanni, 1889.

V. B. "Le tragiche ore di Castelgandolfo: Il servizio della Guardia." *Vita Palatina* 22 (February 1944): 1.

Ventrone, Alfonso. *L'amministrazione dello Stato Pontificio dal 1814 al 1870*. Rome: Edizioni Universitarie, 1942.

Vigevano, Attilio. *La Compagna delle Marche e dell'Umbria*. Rome: Stabilimento Poligrafico per l'Amministrazione della Guerra, 1923.

——. *La fine dell'esercito pontificio*. Rome: Stabilimento poligrafico per l'amministrazione della guerra, 1920.

Index